D1562305

Intimate Relationships:

an introduction to Marriage & the Family

Intimate Relationships: an introduction to Marriage & the Family

Dennis K. Orthner
University of North Carolina, Greensboro

ADDISON-WESLEY PUBLISHING COMPANY
Reading, Massachusetts • Menlo Park, California • London • Amsterdam • Don Mills, Ontario • Sydney

Sponsoring Editor: *Ronald R. Hill*
Production Editor: *Barbara H. Pendergast*
Designer: *Robert A. Rose*
Illustrator: *Robert F. Trevor*
Cover photograph: *Richard A. Chase*
Cover design: *Richard Hannus*

Library of Congress Cataloging in Publication Data

Orthner, Dennis K.
Intimate relationships.

Bibliography: p.
Includes index.
1. Marriage. 2. Family. 3. Interpersonal relations. I. Title.
HQ734.0716 306.8 80-21527
ISBN 0-201-05519-8

ISBN-0-201-05519-8
ABCDEFGHIJ-DO-8987654321

Preface

Writing this book has been a genuine challenge. After more than a decade of teaching marriage and family courses at a community college and a major university, I have found my own professional goals of research and teaching excellence being reflected in the writing of *Intimate Relationships*. The ever-present tug to leave no stone unturned, to be careful and precise in my explanations, reflects the research orientation that I have tried to develop over the years. At the same time, I have sought as a dedicated teacher to present this material clearly and simply in a way that engages students and allows them to understand the subject matter in light of their own experiences, observations, and expectations.

Over the years, I have become disillusioned with most introductory marriage and family texts. Some are so oriented toward explaining research studies that they read more like an encyclopedia than a carefully integrated text. Others are so humanistic and simplistic that they ignore most of the knowledge and research in the field as they lead students down a primrose path of questionable assumptions and biased platitudes. Still other texts are so narrow that they only present one theoretical perspective or a very limited number of subjects, often ignoring vital information on sexual intimacy, parenthood, or the later years of marriage and family life.

My philosophy and the philosophy of this book is that it is possible to examine current research, discuss critical issues, and present areas of debate in a straightforward manner without making the material so difficult or simplistic that students are turned off or led astray. I have tried to make this book scholarly without being stuffy. At times, issues are not resolved since not all issues presently can be. Our facts are still coming in. Contrasting views and theories are presented, as are many controversial aspects of intimate relationships today. I believe that students should be exposed to some emerging perspectives, whether they agree with them or not.

This is not an "everything you always wanted to know about intimate relationships, marriage, and family but were afraid to ask" book. The emphasis is on the social psychology and development of intimate relationships among friends, lovers, family members, married couples, parents and children. Some consideration is given to individual development and cross-cultural comparisons but this is not the primary focus of the book. As a family sociologist, I am concerned with the place of the family in society, but here I have chosen to concentrate on the interactional aspects of intimate relationships, how they are formed, maintained, and strained.

To implement my goals for this text, I have tried to review and present theories, findings, and statistics as clearly and concisely as possible. The reader will find many examples that help interpret this information in a way that allows each of us to better understand the world in which we live. Throughout the book are *vignettes*, or excerpts from research reports, magazines, case studies, or other illustrated materials that complement and make more meaningful my writing in the text. These vignettes should make interesting "grist for the mill" in class discussions or issues to be discussed with friends and family.

Intimate Relationships also contains some topics that are unusual for an introductory text. For example, I have included discussions on the nature of pair relationships and interpersonal commitments. These serve as a foundation for understanding some of the differences between personal, intimate relationships and other types of relationships. Consideration is given to the roles of love, sexual intimacy, gender-role expectations, communication, conflict, economic decisions, and parenthood on the development of intimate relationships. Also, the often-neglected areas of marriage and family in the middle and later years of life are included in this book. This should be of particular interest to older students and those who want to better understand life-cycle changes and the future challenges they may face as maturing youth and adults.

Other aids to learning are incorporated in this book as well. Throughout the book, there are marginal *call-outs* that identify key ideas and concepts. Each chapter contains a *summary* of the major points covered in the chapter. *Suggestions for additional reading* are provided to help the reader reach beyond this book to discover some of the wealth of other writings and research that is available. Easy-to-read *charts and tables* are used to illustrate important findings and trends. The study guide, *Understanding Intimate Relationships* by Jay Mancini, is also a most useful supplement that will help students reflect on what the text is saying and apply this knowledge to themselves and their observations of others.

In the final analysis, I hope each person who reads this book, whether a student of human behavior or a person primarily interested in applying this information, will find this study as challenging and rewarding as I have found it. On the surface, intimate relationships sometimes appear to be deceptively simple, but as I have discovered over the years, their intricacies and variations can be as complex as mathematics and as fascinating as art. Enjoy.

Greensboro, North Carolina D.K.O.
September 1980

Acknowledgments

Writing a book of this scope has required thousands of hours in the library and in my office with a Do Not Disturb sign prominently posted. But the effort has not been mine alone. Many others have contributed their ideas, insights, criticism, and help in making this a successful venture.

I especially appreciate my students from whom I believe I have learned as much as I have taught. The information they have wanted, the ideas they have liked, the criticisms they have offered have shaped this book into what it has become. They have been patient with me as I tested new theories, explanations, and frameworks on them. They have opened themselves to me so that I could learn from their experiences and their insights what makes their intimate relationships work. In every sense of the word, this is a class-tested book.

To my faculty colleagues, I owe much gratitude for the guidance and help they offered when I needed it and the quiet hours they let me work uninterrupted when I needed that. I especially appreciate the encouragement and support of Jim Watson, Rebecca Smith, Bud Rallings, Hy Rodman, and John Scanzoni. I also owe much to many of my respected colleagues and friends whose insights and ideas have helped to shape my own. Their work and influence are unseen but a significant part of this book.

I am indebted to several worthy assistants without whose help this book would not have been possible. Nancy Wight and Gary Bowen now know every nook and cranny of this university's library. Patty Herring should now be able to type from anybody's writing since she can decipher mine.

My appreciation is extended to those colleagues who reviewed the manuscript for this book and contributed to its improvement. I am very grateful to those who gave careful review of the chapters during their development.

Special thanks go to Marilyn Ihinger-Talman (Washington State University), Ken Davidson (University of Wisconsin-Eau Claire), Kay Murphey (Oklahoma State University), John Touhey (Florida Atlantic University) and Irwin Kantor (Middlesex Community College) for their thoughtful and careful analysis of the manuscript in the later stages of the review process. Each of these reviewers helped in the development of this book but I hold myself responsible for its content.

To the people at Addison-Wesley, I cannot extend enough appreciation for their efforts. My tireless editors, Ron Hill, George Abbott, and Stan Evans believed in me and kept me going even when the task seemed impossible. The editorial assistance of Linda Bedell and Cheryl Wurzbacker is gratefully acknowledged. The production department, especially Barbara Pendergast, captured my imagination, cleaned up my writing, and turned the hundreds of pages of typed, sterile manuscript into this beautiful work.

Finally, and most important, I need to recognize the contributions of my wife, Barbara, and my children. Their efforts have been more than incidental. Barbara is a talented scholar in her own right and her ideas and criticisms are an integral part of this book. Our children, Jason, Melissa, and Kristen, keep me humble and in touch with the realities of today and my hopes for tomorrow. To my family, I ask forgiveness for the precious hours lost while researching and writing. I hope I can repay this debt through what I have learned in the process.

D. K. O.

Contents

Part I Introduction

Part II The Pairing Process

Part III Factors in Pair Development

Part VI The Middle Years and Beyond

Introduction *Part I*

Chapter I

Understanding Marriage and the Family

The study of marriage and the family should be an interesting adventure. Almost all of us have had family experiences, and we feel that we can relate to the subject matter because of these experiences. But a careful study of the family can sometimes be difficult, even threatening, since many of our ideas about marriage and the family may not be shared by others, and in some cases, our beliefs may be incorrect.

The paradox of family analysis is that while we feel we somehow ought to understand the family, we realize that it is an area of our lives about which we still have important questions. Evidence of this anxiety is easily found in any segment of society. Millions of books, magazines, and pamphlets that give advice on marriage relations and child rearing are sold every year. Advice columnists are deluged by queries from hopeful readers concerning all aspects of marriage and the family. Classes on family life, marital enrichment, and child rearing attract numerous participants. Many people seek guidance from marriage and family counselors, psychologists, psychiatrists, and other interested professionals. Even college students sometimes complain that the course on marriage and the family that they had expected to be "easy" in fact turned out to be more difficult than anticipated.

Since the purpose of this book is to analyze how interpersonal relationships are formed, maintained, expanded, and strained, it is very important that we first examine why family analysis is sometimes difficult and how we can more constructively approach a study of marriage and family relations. In this chapter, we will also establish a context for further family analysis by defining many of the basic terms used in the study of the family, contrasting several different models of family analysis, and examining the variety of responsibilities carried out by families in this society.

DILEMMAS OF MARRIAGE AND FAMILY ANALYSIS

Whether we recognize it or not, our family backgrounds, experiences, and beliefs can severely limit our ability to be objective in our observance of family behavior. As the goal of scientific analysis is to reduce as much as possible the effects of personal biases, we will now look at several factors that commonly influence our ideas about marriage and the family. In this way, we should be better able to recognize and control the influence of these factors on our interpretation of what we read about the family.

Personal bias

Limits of Experience

One of the principal problems we face in family analysis is that most of our experience is limited to only one family network—our own. While some family experience may be better than none at all, it leads to our understanding other families only within the context of the one we already know. There is a strong tendency, therefore, to develop a **familiocentric** stance; that is, a stance in which we accept our own family's life-style as normal while others are variously interpreted as abnormal. William Goode (1971) comments critically, "We are all so emotionally involved in our own observations that we are not good observers. Our comments are all too likely to be self-justifications and rationalizations rather than cool attempts to find out how even our own family has operated" (p. 4).

Conflicting viewpoints

This problem is enhanced by the fact that our personal interests often blind us to conflicting viewpoints that exist within our own family. For example, the child-rearing experiences of boys and girls are frequently different, and this commonly leads men and women to develop quite different perspectives on family life. Jessie Bernard (1972) has gone so far as to suggest that the experiences of husbands and wives may be so different in some areas that we can characterize a "wife's marriage" and a "husband's marriage." Research on family decision making adds a further dimension—not only are there differences in perspective between husbands and wives, but the children in these families frequently hold another view entirely (Larson, 1974).

Limits of observation

If experiences within our own family are often subject to misinterpretation or differing points of view, then our understanding of other families must be even more limited. After all, we rarely see much more of the family life of friends and neighbors than they want us to see. And we rarely get more than a casual glimpse, if that, into the lives of families from other social classes, ethnic backgrounds, racial groups, or even other parts of town. Is it any wonder then that we are frequently surprised to learn that a couple we have known for some time is separating or that many people are quite happy living in family arrangements very different from our own?

One way of overcoming the limits of our own personal experience is to become more aware of the perspectives of others. If, for example, we are interested in knowing how the arrival of the first child influences a marriage, we might ask a large number of new mothers and fathers about their experiences and their feelings. We could develop some kind of scale to help measure their parental adjustment and compare the adjustment of some couples with others. Even better, we might examine how couples expecting a child think they will feel as parents and then, some time after they become parents, question them again to see how their feelings have changed. If the couples we studied represented a broad range of possible parental experiences, and if we were as unbiased as possible in interpreting the information we received, then our conclusions would probably provide much more insight into parental adjustment than we could get from analyzing only our own experiences.

Advantages of research

This, in very simple terms, is what social-science researchers attempt to do. By gathering information from a large number of persons, the researcher is better able to determine the extent to which a particular behavior or attitude exists and perhaps get some idea of its cause and potential implications. Comparisons can also be made between different groups to find out if experiences vary according to characteristics such as sex, race, or social class. The research of social scientists trained in objectivity and using systematic procedures to measure the phenomenon under study will usually lead to results that reflect quite well the experiences of the people examined at the time of the study.

Research problems

As a caution, we should mention that the present state of social-science research is not without problems. All too often, the samples of people that are studied are neither large enough nor truly representative of the variety of perspectives that exist in the population. Nevertheless, limitations such as these are small when compared to the bias that comes from reliance on our own experience alone. For this reason, keep in mind the potential problems, but also realize that there are important benefits to be derived from a careful analysis of available research studies.

Family Myths

A second problem in family analysis is the widespread belief in a number of myths about marriage and the family. William Lederer and Don Jackson (1968) suggest that the institution of marriage in particular exists within a "mirage" of false assumptions and unrealistic expectations. These myths, they reason, limit the ability of individuals to understand their own relationship, let alone to examine objectively the relationships of others. Some of the more commonly held myths about marriage and the family are that successful marriages must be based on love, that inherent differences between men and women cause most relational trouble, that single people are unhappy and feel rejected, that children automatically improve a marriage, and that conflict is an indication of a poor relationship. Each of these may be true in selected circumstances, but as broad generalizations, they are inaccurate.

A factor which further complicates family analysis is a largely mythical concept of the family in the past. The popular images of family life as it supposedly existed a few decades or generations ago contain so many distortions that they little resemble the realities of that time. For example, research on the American family after the colonial period has revealed that the average age of marriage then was considerably higher, not lower, than today; that few families had several generations living together in the same household; that the average family size was not very different from today; that women had considerable influence in decision making; and that most young couples were quite independent of their parents after marriage (Seward, 1978).

Myths of the past

Nevertheless, in spite of the findings of research, the tendency to reconstruct a family of the past that is more idealistic than real continues. Goode (1963) notes that we have accumulated our heritage of myths because "each past generation of people writes of a period *still* more remote, *their* grandparents' generation, when things were much better" (p. 7). This results in a stereotype of the "good old days," which Goode labels "the classical family of Western nostalgia." These images, while unreal, are given further life as they become part of our folklore and even enter our media programming, as in the once popular television series "The Waltons." In turn, they reinforce a perspective of what the family used to be like that distorts our analysis of the family today. Therefore, if we are to undertake a concerted study of the family, we will also have to accept the fact that some of our more cherished beliefs may be seriously questioned and others disproven.

Folklore

Interpretations of Family Change

Controversy over changes

While many of our notions about the history of the family may be incorrect, this should not be interpreted to mean that the family is not changing. It is, and this further complicates family analysis; contemporary changes are often difficult to interpret because their effects are unknown and open to conjecture. Changes that occur within a generation lead to disagreements between parents and children as well as to controversy among the different professionals with interest in the family.

While the fact of family change is becoming more accepted, debates over the *impact* of this change remain. Analyses of the changing family are frequently offered by a growing variety of commentators and social scientists, but often the same set of statistics may be interpreted to mean very different things. For example, the trends shown in Figs. 1.1 and 1.2 are commonly reported. These indicate that the marriage rate has been leveling off while the divorce rate continues to climb, and that the birthrate is declining while the proportions of wives in the labor force and children being reared by one parent are rising. There are also statistics that show that the age of marriage is going up, that more couples are living together outside of marriage, that childless marriages are increasing, and that rates of nonmarital sexual intercourse are also increasing. Trends such as these have been used to support the

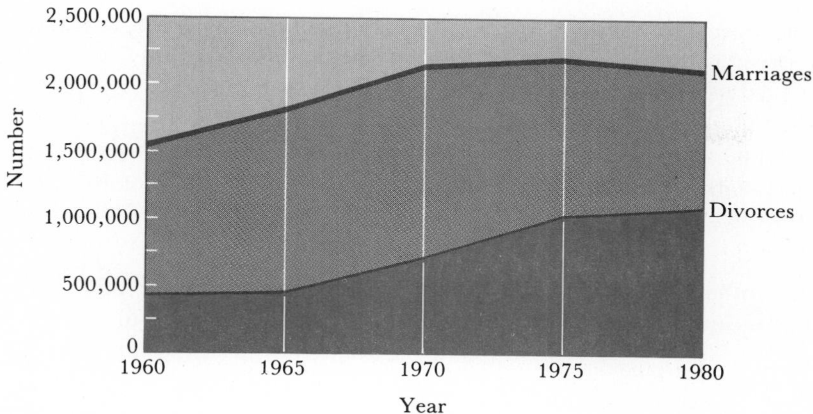

Fig. 1.1
Marriage and Divorce Trends in the United States

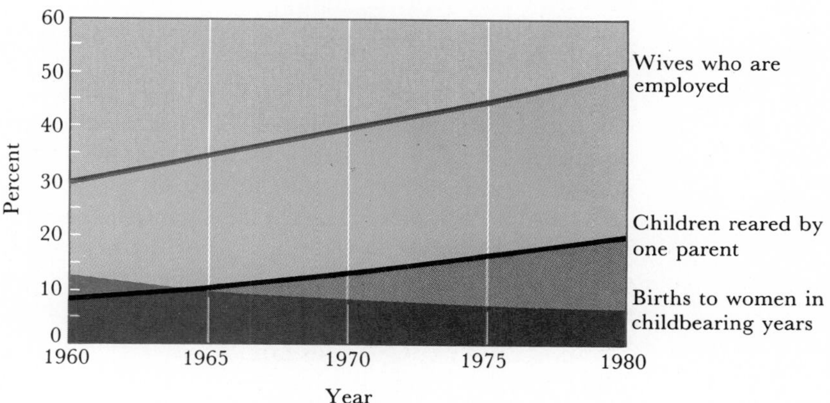

Fig. 1.2
Current Family Trends in the United States

following basic arguments: (1) the family is declining in importance for society and individuals; (2) the family is no longer necessary in a modern society; or, alternatively, (3) families are merely adapting to the changing requirements of society.

Family declining?

The notion that the family is "falling apart" or "breaking down" appears to be one of the more frequently expressed themes in current public discussions of the family. According to a 1980 Gallup survey, 45 percent of Americans believe that family life has deteriorated since the mid-1960s. Some social scientists have argued that families no longer fulfill many of their traditional responsibilities, that parents have become too permissive and are neglecting their child-rearing responsiblities, and that family disorganization is fostering much of the tension and insecurity that are so prevalent in American society. Although written in 1937, Pitirin Sorokin's prediction sounds similar to some of those heard today:

> The family as a sacred institution of husband and wife, of parents and children will continue to disintegrate. . . . The main sociological function of the family will further decrease until the family becomes a mere incidental cohabitation of male and female while the home will become a mere overnight parking place mainly for the sex-relationship. (p. 776)

Family not necessary?

While some argue that the family is declining because of increased individualism, others claim that the family is no longer necessary because it constricts the individual freedom required in a highly mobile, urban, postindustrial society. As early as 1929, Bertrand Russell somewhat sarcastically offered the opinion, "The family in the Western world has become a mere shadow of what it was. . . . In its fullest development, it was never suitable either to urban populations or to seafaring people" (p. 173).

Recent attacks on the family have tended to focus on several perceived weaknesses in its basic framework. First, critics claim that families foster behaviors and values that diminish personal autonomy and lead to "false" dependencies and neuroses. Second, they claim that families provide rigid models which deprive children of their natural creativity and a unique identity. Third, they claim that families limit sexual expression by demanding lifelong sexual bonds (Crosby, 1975). These conclusions are quite forcefully presented by the psychiatrist David Cooper in his book, *The Death of the Family*. Cooper (1970) defines the family as "that system which, as its social obligation, obscurely filters out most of our experience and then deprives our acts of any genuine and general spontaneity" (p. 6).

Family adapting?

Although much of the rhetoric regarding family change might lead us to believe that the family is dying, either through overattention or underattention to individual needs, there remains a third perspective which holds that the family is not breaking down but, rather, is adapting to the new requirements of a modern society. This more optimistic view is widely held by those who have carefully examined the experiences and adjustments being made by most families today. In the introduction to her recent study of American family policies, Mary Jo Bane (1976) candidly admits to her own change in perspective:

> The arguments predicting the imminent decline of the family seem to be supported by a good deal of statistical evidence. . . . Yet, as I delved further into the data that described what Americans do and how they live, I became less sure that the family was in trouble. Surprising stabilities showed up, and surprising evidence of the persistence of commitment to family life. I became convinced that the time had not yet come to write obituaries for the American family or to divide up its estate. (p. xiv)

Positive prognosis for families

A brief examination of some of the trends noted earlier should demonstrate why a more positive prognosis for the family is possible. For example, even though the divorce rate in the United States is currently the highest in the world, the majority of couples in their first marriages do not divorce and those that do tend to remarry rather quickly. The rising age of couples at marriage may indicate that some people are deciding not to marry, but most young adults appear to be simply delaying their marriage plans until they are ready. Childlessness is rising, but longer waiting lists in adoption agencies indicate that the proportion of couples wanting children is still greater than the proportion who are capable of having them. Also, there are more married women employed, but husbands of employed wives are the strongest supporters of women's work roles. Today's youth are obviously not dissillusioned, since "a good marriage and family life" was rated the most-sought-after goal in life by a national sample of 17,000 high-school seniors (see Table 1.1).

Recent studies indicate the American family is changing, not dying.

Table 1.1

Most Important Goals in Life: American High-School Seniors

Goal	College-Bound	Non–College-Bound
A good marriage and family life	79%	76%
Strong friendships	69%	57%
Finding purpose and meaning in my life	66%	62%
Finding steady work	65%	67%
Being successful in my work	63%	52%
Making a contribution to society	23%	10%
Having lots of money	16%	19%
Being a leader in my community	10%	4%

Source: Jerald Bachman and Lloyd Johnson, "The Freshman, 1979." Reprinted from *Psychology Today* magazine, copyright © 1979, Ziff-Davis Publishing Company.

Given this picture of underlying stability, we might understand family change better in terms of evolution rather than decline. Throughout the known history of Western civilization, the family system has been changing. In part, this is because every aspect of society—every institution—is interrelated. Because change in one part creates changes in another, the family has been influenced by such profound developments as the growth of technology, urbanization, secularization, education, and democracy. Even the steady cultural drift toward individual autonomy has not so much destroyed the family as it has made family activities and responsibilities more distinctly separate from those of the village, the clan, the church, and the state.

DEFINING THE FAMILY

Variety of family forms

What exactly do we mean by the term "family"? Up to this point in our discussion, we have assumed considerable agreement regarding what a family is and what it is not. But given the variety of experiences, perspectives, and interpretations of the family we have already examined, it should not be surprising to learn that it is difficult to define the family in a way that satisfies everyone. It is also important to recognize that families can take a variety of forms and acquire different responsibilities depending upon the cultural norms and social situations under which they exist. What seems to be normal to us may not be to someone else, and the range of acceptable family styles found in one society may be much narrower in another. While it is not the purpose of this book to explore all possible family variations, our subsequent analysis of marriage and family processes will require an understanding of the basic family structures and functions found in Western society.

Table 1.2

Distribution of Households in the United States, 1977

Household Type	Distribution (%)
Single-breadwinner nuclear families	13%
Dual-breadwinner nuclear families	16
No-breadwinner nuclear families	1
Single-parent families	16
Child-free or postchildbearing families	23
Extended families	6
"Experimental" families	4
Single, widowed, divorced, or separated adults	21
	100%

Source: United States Bureau of Labor Statistics, 1977.

Family Structures

Nuclear families

The structure of the family refers to its composition: who is included and what roles they play. The most common structural arrangement in North America and throughout the world is the **nuclear family,** consisting of a father, mother, and children. Eventually, most individuals live in two nuclear families, the family of their parents (called the **family of orientation**) and the family they establish through their own marriage and parenthood (the **family of procreation**).

Beyond these basics, exactly defining the parameters of the nuclear family becomes considerably more complex. For example, marriage is often assumed to be necessary to the initiation of a family since it bestows social approval on the sexual relationship. But we find in Latin America and in the lower class in the United States that many nuclear family units begin by "consent" or common law rather than in formal marriage (Voydanoff and Rodman, 1978). Also, one-parent families are not usually defined as nuclear, although today, many women and men are quite capable of rearing children without a coparent, and the label "abnormal" or "deviant" that usually accompanies nonnuclear family status may no longer be warranted.

If we add to our list of nonnuclear family arrangements childless marriages, older couples whose children no longer live at home, and communal or other experimental family units, we find that traditionally defined nuclear families are fewer than we might have expected. In 1977, it was found that only 40 percent of the households in the United States could be defined as traditional nuclear families (Ramey, 1978). And of these, more than half had two employed parents, a departure from the stereotype of the nuclear family containing a breadwinner-father, a housewife-mother, and children (see Table 1.2.)

Extended families

There are several types of family structures that are more complex (but less frequently found) than nuclear families. Of these complex structures, the type considered the most acceptable in North America is the **extended family,** which consists of two or more kinship-linked nuclear units living in the same household. Most often, the link is between two or more generations, and the family includes a married son or daughter, spouse and children living with an older set of parents. While this traditional arrangement is sometimes idealized, it is very rarely preferred, here or elsewhere. Three-generation households have never been common in America (Hess, 1979). In fact, according to one large study of national population statistics, the only nation that has recently had more than 20 percent of its families living in extended-family arrangements is India (Burch, 1967).

Polygamy

Polygamy is a single family unit based on the marriage of one person to two or more mates. If a man has more than one wife, this is termed **polygyny;** if a woman has more than one husband, it is termed **polyandry.** While polyandry is very rare, polygyny was at one time quite common in Africa and Asia. The only formal attempt to institute polygamy in the United States occurred among the Mormons, but this was ruled illegal by the courts in the late nineteenth century.

Multilateral family

Perhaps the most complex family structure is the **multilateral family,** a group of three or more adults and their children in which all of the adults consider themselves married to at least two other adult members of the group (Constantine, 1978; Ramey, 1972). Unlike polygamy, in which only one person maintains multiple pair-bonds, each person in the multilateral relationship holds multiple pair-bonds. Often maintained by what is informally termed a *group marriage,* multilateral relationships have been found in North America, but usually these arrangements only contain three or four adult members. Like polygamy, this type of family structure is illegal in the United States and Canada.

Family Functions

Families can be defined not only by their structure but also by their functions; that is, what they do for their members and for society. George Peter Murdock (1949), in his classic cross-cultural analysis, claimed that the family, particularly the nuclear family, is a relationship that performs four basic functions: (1) it provides opportunities for regular sexual contact; (2) it promotes cooperation in responsibilities; (3) it is the agent of reproduction of new members for society; and (4) it is an agent of socialization of children. These functions are not exclusive to families, since other institutions or arrangements might also share these responsibilities, but Murdock contended that the family holds primary control over these functions in any society.

Disagreement over functions

Not everyone agrees with Murdock's interpretation of the basic functions of the family. The discovery of several societies in which the family does not carry out all these functions has led some sociologists to suggest a smaller number of essential functions. Ira Reiss (1965), for example, defines the family as a small, kinship-structured group whose only principal function is providing nurturance to the newborn. Other functions, he explains, can conceivably be carried out in other relationships.

Past family functions

At the other end of the spectrum, there are observers who believe that families are multifunctioning entities which fulfill many basic needs of individuals and society. Several decades ago, William F. Ogburn (1938) argued that the family established its importance by performing seven basic functions: serving as an economic unit in the production of goods and services; conferring status on its members; educating its youth; and providing protection, recreation, religious instruction, and affection. Unfortunately, this perspective tends to equate what the traditional American family once did with what is ideal and normal. This leads to an impression of family decline when schools, industries, retirement programs, recreation departments, social security, churches, and a host of other agencies and institutions acquire some of the responsibilities previously held by families. Ogburn concluded his analysis with the finding that only the function of providing affection remains; therefore, "Family status has been lost in marked degree along with these other functions in an age of mobility and large cities" (p. 140).

In modern society, responsibility for education of children is shared by family and schools.

Those who argue that families have a particular number of basic functions are usually concerned with universal principles of human behavior. While this is important, it should also be recognized that the actual functions performed by families depend more on personal preferences and the societal conditions surrounding the family than on some ideal set of traditional responsibilities. In rural agricultural settings, families had to be more multifunctioning in order to fulfill member needs. For example, without local schools, churches, or playgrounds, the amount of education, religion, or recreation that could be provided was determined by the family alone. Even today, in some remote areas of the United States and Canada, there are families that are quite independent and that carry out most of the functions Ogburn lists with little outside help. But usually, as societies become more urbanized and mechanized, households are located closer to one another. The heightened demand for services then makes it easier for people to combine resources and create agencies that fulfill those functions that are less central to the basic purposes of the family. As a result, the more complex the society, the fewer the functions prescribed solely for its families.

Settings and functions

It is questionable whether families have "lost" most of the functions they used to perform. For example, although it is true that the economic *producing* role of the family has declined, its economic *consuming* role has certainly increased. Likewise, it is now deemed the family's responsibility to prepare its children for moral and educational instruction, to do things together in their leisure time, and to reinforce the accomplishments of one another. This means that functions that were previously controlled by families are today more frequently shared, but not lost. It would probably be inaccurate to interpret this as a net decline in responsibility.

In effect, families have become more specialized just as our society has become more specialized. Talcott Parsons and Robert Bales (1955) interpret this trend to mean that the family in this society is now asked to fulfill two basic functions: "First, the primary socialization of children so that they can truly become members of the society into which they have been born; second, the stabilization of adult personalities of the population of the society" (p. 16).

Responsibility of the family

Taken together, we can conclude that *the principal responsibility of the family today is to provide nurturance and support for its members*—children and adults. Still, this is not an exclusive function, since other relationships, agencies, and institutions—such as work associates, schools, day-care centers, welfare offices, and medical personnel—also provide help and support to family members. But the contribution of the family to human reproduction, early child rearing, and consistent contact makes the family the principal source of this interpersonal nurturance.

Lifetime support

We should also note that the increased specialization of families in nurturance means that families are now focusing on those responsibilities that will most help individuals cope with the insecurity of a changing world. In Vignette 1.1, Nena and George O'Neill (1972) explain that the family has persisted largely because of its ability to fulfill a basic need for order and structure in our lives. Clark Vincent (1966) adds that a growing responsibility

Vignette I.I

On Structural Needs and the Family

One of the simplest explanations for the persistence of marriage, in spite of the widespread disillusionment with the institution as it stands, lies in man's innate need for structure. Structure and form are the essence of all existence and the molders of all creativity. Structure is also necessary to the convenience of living and to the ordering of our experience out of chaos into meaningful units. Structure is knowing that traffic lights go on and off, that night follows day, that spring follows winter and that the rent is due at the end of the month. Addresses and adding machines, bill and banks, clocks and calendars—the list of structural supports for modern life is endless. And as society becomes more complex, as the population continues to grow, more and more—and different—structural forms become necessary.

Institutions are merely our way of formalizing some of the structures underlying human behavior. The institutions of marriage and the family, no matter how diverse in style and configuration they may be, are fundamental to every society. Each marriage institution operates within a specific cultural context of interlocking, interdependent institutions of other kinds—kinship, social, political, and economic. This close intermeshing of institutions means that as our society is impelled toward change, each institution will tend to readjust or realign itself in conjunction with the others. Marriage, because of its very personal nature, has been slower to adapt itself to change than other institutions; but it, too, must and will change.

The patriarchal marriage system of the Judeo-Christian tradition, based on an agrarian economy, is simply outmoded today. In the old days back on the farm, Ma and Pa literally pulled the yoke together, forming a cooperative unit for survival. The economic and psychological interdependence of this marital unit occurred in a setting where social sanctions and the entire matrix of society encouraged it to perpetuate itself. Marriage structure matched marriage function. But times have changed.

We live today in a high-speed technological world that knows only flux and change, and it is obvious that what served as a marriage format in the past is no longer adequate to the task. New and complex life-styles call for a new marriage format. Conditioned to obsolescence, we may be tempted to pitch marriage out altogether. But patriarchal marriage is just *one* particular format among many alternative formats—or ways of fulfilling an underlying structural impulse.

From Nena O'Neill and George O'Neill, *Open Marriage* (New York: Avon, 1972), pp. 19–20.

of the family is to help each of us adjust to the disorder and confusion that often accompany individual development and social change. According to Vincent, the family, more than any other institution, consistently serves as a buffer between the individual and society. Only families are consistently in a position to prepare and motivate children and adults to meet the changing demands of society. Only the family can provide lifetime support for individuals first through the family of orientation and then through the family of procreation. In essence, the acceleration of social change and the increased need for individual and family adaptation are major factors in expansion of the nurturance-support function of the contemporary family.

On the negative side, Vincent notes that families are sometimes forced to make adjustments, even to adapt to undesirable or potentially disruptive changes. Usually, they lack any formal means by which they can resist change, and all too often it is assumed that the family will somehow adjust. To illustrate, industries uproot and upset millions of families with their policies for moving personnel, yet the problems that result are considered those of the family, not the company. Likewise, mental illness, delinquency, alcoholism, illegitimacy, and other social ills are frequently blamed on the family, even though other influences may be equally or more at fault.

Changing personal needs

Another potential problem lies in the inability of many families to adjust to the changing needs for nurturance of their members. When families were primarily concerned with survival, interpersonal nurturance was understood in terms of surviving together, a shared sense of competence. But now, survival is assured largely by other institutions so feelings of nurturance are based more on individualistic needs for affection, support, communication, sex, or whatever is most on the mind of the person at the moment. Since these needs can change and vary much more than, say, the basic need for food or shelter, the likelihood of personal dissatisfaction increases. The current high rate of divorce is but one indication of the inability of many families to reconcile what may be diverging or conflicting personal interests.

UNDERSTANDING INTERPERSONAL RELATIONSHIPS

A study of marriage and the family can be approached from several different levels of analysis, most notably, from the perspective of the individual, the interpersonal relationship, or the society. If primary interest is in the *individual,* then marriage and the family are usually considered important contexts for personal development and means for meeting individual needs. At the *interpersonal* level of analysis, attention is shifted toward the relationship between individuals and the interpersonal processes that operate on or within that relationship. When the focus is on *society,* the institutional qualities of marriage and the family are examined, especially as they play a major role in ensuring the survival of the society.

In this book, our principal concern is with the interpersonal dimension of marriage and the family. We will examine how relationships normally develop and the many processes that contribute to this development. But this does not mean that we can exclude the influences of society or the respective needs of individuals who make up these relationships. Just as a picture on a jigsaw puzzle might be unrecognizable if we excluded many of its pieces, our analysis of marriage and family must give attention to those aspects of society and of individuals that contribute to our understanding interpersonal relationships.

Family frameworks

Because interpersonal relationships are so complex, however, analysts of family behavior have developed a number of different frameworks to call attention to various components of these relationships. Each of these examines marriage and the family from a somewhat different perspective, and each contributes important concepts and related research that help us better understand the processes involved in relational development. In this book, we will primarily use what is called an "interactional approach" to marriage and family analysis. But we will also utilize the ideas and research behind several other approaches, including the developmental and social-exchange approaches. A brief introduction to each of these will better prepare us for understanding the chapters that follow.

Interactional Approach

In his pioneering effort to explain relationships between family members, Ernest W. Burgess (1926) came to define the family as a "unity of interacting personalities." He went on to suggest:

> By a unity of interacting personalities is meant a living, changing, growing thing. . . . The actual unity of family life has its experience not in any legal conception, nor in any formal contract, but in the interaction of its members. For the family does not depend for its survival on the harmonious relations of its members, nor does it necessarily disintegrate as a result of conflicts between its members. The family lives as long as interaction is taking place and only dies when it ceases. (p. 3)

This conception of the family has been considerably refined over the years, but the interest in how relational bonds are formed and maintained through interaction remains its principal concern (Burr *et al.*, 1979).

Role expectations

A central concept in the interactional approach is **role,** or the behaviors expected of individuals who occupy certain positions in a relationship. In a marriage relationship, for example, the positions of husband and wife usually have a number of roles associated with them. These may include such expected behaviors as breadwinner, parent, gardener, dishwasher, or lover. Individuals acquire these roles through a combination of modeling the behavior of others who were observed in those roles and through a trial-and-error process of behaving in a certain way and then seeing whether the behavior is accepted or not.

In any given situation, a person usually acts out those roles that conform to the expectations of a **reference group** or **reference relationship.** A young husband, for instance, may behave in much the same way as his father did if his role expectations are based on the reference group of his family of orientation. If these behaviors are challenged by his wife, however, he may

Meal preparation is not always the exclusive role of the wife.

develop a new set of role expectations, making his marriage the primary reference relationship for his husband roles. In specific terms, the individual who has the most influence on a particular set of behaviors is called the **significant other.** In the above example, the husband's father may have been the significant other in early definitions of the husband role, but his wife then became the principal referent after marriage. When the roles that we play do not reflect our reaction to the needs of any specific person or group, then we say that these roles are responding to the general expectations of our society, or the **generalized other.**

Role changes

The interactional approach allows for the fact that role expectations may change over time and vary considerably from family to family. But it is important to understand that while each individual relationship is unique in the particular combination of roles that is expected of its members, the task of every relationship is to develop similar ideas of what each member is supposed to do. This means that much of the interaction that occurs in marriage is designed to share feelings or ideas that allow a husband and wife to know what is expected of them and what they can expect of each other. When role expectations differ, conflicts occur that require new role adjustments in the relationship. This process is never-ending, since most individuals acquire and change roles regularly.

Communication

We can see that communication is very important from an interactional perspective. Since communication between individuals is largely the product of commonly shared symbols, both verbal (words) and nonverbal (gestures or expressions), this approach is often called **symbolic interaction.** Therefore, the principal focus of the interactional approach and this book is on how the roles played in marriage and the family are acquired and maintained through communication, how factors internal and external to the relationship influence the communication process, how decision making occurs within the family, and what strains result from conflicts and changes in role expectations. Overall, the interest of the interactional framework is on the creation of interpersonal family bonds and the variety of processes that affect these bonds.

Developmental Approach

Cycles of generations

Relationships in families change over time. Over a period of generations, these changes appear to be *cycles* of expansion and contraction as children come and go. Each generation continues this process with the birth of its own children who eventually leave and form relationships much like those of their parents. This type of family life cycle, called the **lineage family** (Feldman and Feldman, 1975), is primarily centered around the responsibility of child socialization, which accounts for the similarity in family roles and structure from generation to generation.

Within each nuclear or **lifetime family** (Feldman and Feldman, 1975), relational development can be considered in terms of *careers* rather than

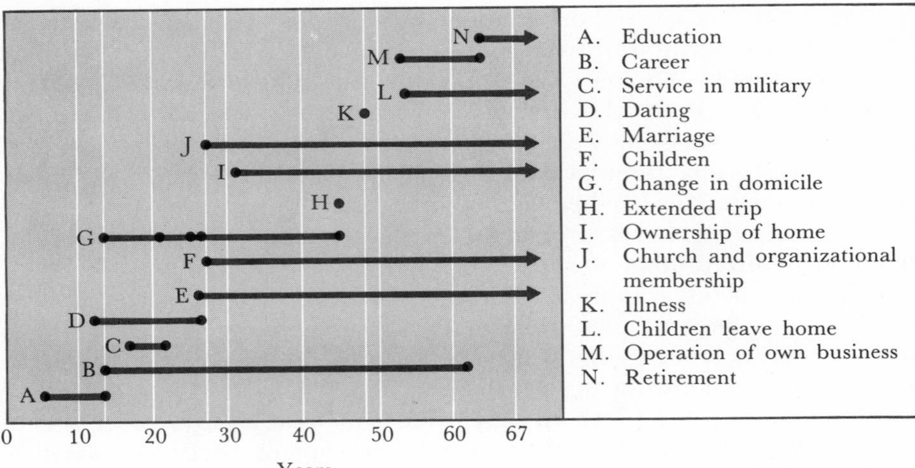

Fig. 1.3

Potential Life Careers for an Individual

Source: M. Koller, *Families: A Multigenerational Approach* (New York: McGraw-Hill, 1974), p. 37. Reprinted with permission.

cycles. We use the term career because it assumes continual forward movement from the inception of the career to its demise rather than a tendency to return to the beginning as in a cycle. Actually, a lifetime family can be considered to have a number of individual and relational careers operating at the same time, each of which influences the other. Figure 1.3 diagrams a hypothetical pattern of careers for one person within the context of that individual's overall family life cycle.

Life-cycle events

Since a lifetime family begins at marriage and lasts as long as both partners remain together, the developmental approach most often bases its analysis on changes in the adult pair relationship. The principal contribution of the approach appears to be in its identification of what Ralph Turner (1970) calls "turning points" or "crucial events" in the time sequence of relational development—in other words, those factors that tend to alter the nature of interpersonal interaction. Usually, the presence of children and the period of the parent-child career is singled out as having the most influence over the marital career. Evelyn Duvall (1957), for example, developed a multistage theory of family development based on the assumption that marital relationships have different "tasks" or responsibilities before children arrive, when children in the home are younger or older, when children are leaving "the nest," and during the postparental years. While this developmental sequence has been very important and has led to a considerable amount of family research, we must also keep in mind that some couples do not have children and all couples are influenced by the interaction of other career patterns as well. For example, changes in occupation, retirement, illness, death of one's parents, or a change of residence can also have dramatic influences on a marriage. The developmental approach, therefore, should encourage us to look for and anticipate the variety of events, decisions, and potential career conflicts that will affect the future course of a relationship.

Social-Exchange Approach

A somewhat more pragmatic approach to social interaction is based on the assumption that humans are benefit-seeking and cost-avoiding creatures. In the realm of personal finances, we can see this quite clearly. When we want to purchase something, say a car, we often shop around until we get the "best deal." This means that we feel we have received the most benefits for the least cost. At the same time, however, salespeople consider the money that is costly to us a benefit to them. Therefore, both parties benefit from the exchange.

Benefits and costs

This exchange principle can be applied to interpersonal relationships. Since each individual comes into contact with a variety of other persons, we can assume that relationships are formed primarily with those persons from whom the expected benefits are equal to or greater than the expected costs. In the case of a marriage, benefits might include such important qualities as affection, support, or companionship, while the costs incurred might include time, money, energy, or inconvenience. But if a relationship is to continue to be profitable for all its members, each person must balance a concern for his or her own benefits with an interest in providing benefits to the other members as well. Quite often, this exchange of benefits takes the form of negotiation—for example, "If you do this, then I will do that." Usually, we do not even recognize that we are negotiating until we feel we are being "used" or giving up more than we think we should at our end of the bargain (Scanzoni, 1979).

Bargaining

This dynamic process of conscious and unconscious bargaining for benefits is quite characteristic of families. Turner suggests, "Bargaining may seem like a cruel word to apply to the deliberations of members in an intimate family relationship. But bargaining is simply a general term for any interaction in which the concessions that one member makes to another are expected to be reciprocated in some manner, so that over the long run the sacrifices of each will balance out" (p. 106).

If, however, a relative balance in benefits does not occur over time, then the exchange approach would predict that the very existence of a relationship is threatened. The person who feels that he or she is not profiting as much will probably argue that the relationship is unfair or one-sided and may even threaten to leave if the situation does not improve. This conflict over needs can force a reordering of roles and responsibilities, providing a more equal distribution of benefits and costs in the relationship. But if this does not occur, we should not be surprised to find that long-term exchange imbalances may ultimately lead to separation and divorce.

RELATIONSHIPS IN PROCESS

It has been said that one of the few things we can count on in this life is change. As we have already seen, this also applies to the family. While most of us look to our own family for personal support and stability, we also recognize that our needs and interests often change, and we expect our parents, spouse, or children to change with them. Over time, therefore, interpersonal relationships are never continually stable; they are *normally in process,* pulled by a variety of factors which encourage the formation, maintenance, and disintegration of their fragile intimate bonds.

As we continue our study of marriage and the family in the following chapters, we will find that a dynamic or **process approach** allows us to balance our examination of relational similarities with an interest in the unique aspects of each individual relationship. In Part II of this book, beginning with the next chapter, we will examine the normal progress of pair development into marriage in this society. The discussion will center on sociocultural and social-psychological pressures for relational development based on the nature of human personalities, interpersonal interaction, and societal systems. These developmental patterns, common to almost all intimate relationships, do change over time and vary somewhat within different subsets of society. Yet it is the fundamental similarity between relationships that makes a disciplined study of marriage and the family possible.

In Parts III and IV of this book we will examine some of the factors that continually shape intimate relationships, including affection, communication, conflict, companionship, sexual intimacy, role expectations, kinship and friendship supports, and parental responsibilities. Each of these factors can vary a great deal, and this results in considerable differences from couple to couple and family to family. For example, we will discover later that in some relationships, individuals easily communicate, in others they do not; some couples develop rigidly defined roles, others are more flexible in their roles; some families spend a great deal of time together, others prefer to be apart. To a large degree, it is this sense of uniqueness that makes marriage and family relationships personally attractive as well as challenging to investigate.

Summary

As we embark upon a study of marriage and the family, we find an interesting paradox: our own personal experiences and values, which make this study somewhat attractive, can actually be a handicap to our understanding how families operate. This should be quite apparent when we consider the fact that in any other field, if someone had twenty or more years of regular apprenticeship, he or she would be considered an "expert" in the area. Yet, when it comes to marriage and family relations, many of us are still anxious about our knowledge and capabilities. And public and private concerns about the family are growing, not lessening, even to the point of doubts concerning whether many families will survive in this day and age.

In our attempts to understand the nature of the family, we must recognize that families can vary considerably in structure and functions. The most common structural arrangement is the nuclear family containing parents and children. Less frequently found but still present are extended, polygamous, and multilateral family structures. Family functions can also vary, especially with simpler, agricultural societies demanding more responsibilities of their families than complex, industrial societies. At the present time, the primary function of the family in Western society is to provide nurturance and support for all its members, adults and children.

While a study of the family can focus on the society, the interpersonal relationship, or the individual, our primary attention will be drawn to marriage and family relationships. Overall, our examination of the family in this book should lead us to understand that families have many similarities, but that each relationship is also unique, the result of diverse processes that influence every family within the context of similar societal and individual pressures.

SUGGESTIONS FOR ADDITIONAL READING

Aldous, Joan. *Family Careers: Developmental Change in Families.* New York: Wiley, 1978.
A good examination of family development as a process which attempts to fulfill the interactional needs of family members and the institutional needs of society.

Bane, Mary Jo. *Here to Stay, American Families in the Twentieth Century.* New York: Basic Books, 1976.
Excellent coverage of the recent changes that have been occurring in the family and the implications these have for family-related policies and legislation.

Kantor, David, and William Lehr. *Inside the Family.* San Francisco: Jossey-Bass, 1975.
A careful analysis of the many internal processes that create, maintain, and strain contemporary families.

Lederer, William J., and Donald D. Jackson. *Mirages of Marriage.* New York: Norton, 1968.
An important attempt to separate myth from reality in interpersonal marriage relationships.

Shorter, Edward. *The Making of the Modern Family.* New York: Basic Books, 1977.
This book provides a most thought-provoking look at the history of the modern family and the factors that have made families what they are today.

The Pairing Process Part II

Chapter 2

Pairing: Commitments and Alternatives

Approximately every six seconds a new child is born in the United States. Each baby has been incubated in a warm nurturing environment while developing its capacity for independence. Then suddenly its mother's uterus transforms itself from a comfortable nest to a crushing muscle, stronger than that of any man, expelling the child into the outside world. The child is immediately cut off from the life-support system it has depended on, gasps for its breath, screams in panic at its helplessness, and begins to grope for the contact, the intimacy, that has been so rudely wrenched from it. If everything has gone as planned, we call this a normal birth and we expect normal development to follow. If the child is a girl, in approximately twenty-two years (at the present rate) she will probably get married. If it is a boy, he will probably marry in about twenty-four years (United States Bureau of the Census, 1980). This also seems to be part of the normal process.

But what transforms these children into adults with desires to establish long-term relationships with other persons, especially those of the opposite sex? The newborn child yearns for someone to grasp, but has very little personal commitment to anyone in particular. In fact, children may be adopted by strangers and come to accept and love them as well as their natural parents. Yet these same children, so naively acceptant of their parents, may promise their allegiance to someone else "till death do us part" some twenty years later.

Explanations as to why pairing is such a predominant pattern vary widely. Yet, in order for us to understand adequately the development of intimate relationships, we must first identify the principal factors that influence pairing and pair commitments today. In this chapter, a variety of alternative pair-commitment patterns will be considered. Also, since not everyone conforms to the pairing mandates, it is important that we examine the characteristics and life-style of single persons. The option to remain single is increasingly being recognized as a viable one for men and women.

THE EXTENT OF PAIRING

Marriage rates

One indication of our present commitment to heterosexual pairing is the marriage rate. However, the reader should note that marriage and pairing are not one and the same. Marriage involves pairing; but pairing does not always involve marriage. Many pair arrangements are never accounted for in formal marriage statistics. This is usually because they occur in courtship or in cohabitation without marriage. Nevertheless, marriage rates do provide some indication of the extent of pairing in a modern society.

In the United States, 93 percent of all men and 96 percent of all women forty-five years of age and older have been married at least once (United States Bureau of the Census, 1980). Historically, the overall trend in the twentieth century has been for a higher proportion of adults to marry. This fact is quite evident in the census data reported in Fig. 2.1. Two things are important to note in this figure. First, the proportion of people marrying has been increasing rather steadily since the 1920s. Second, over the entire period represented (1890–1979), the proportions having been married are relatively high. Evidently, individual motivations to marry have been quite strong throughout the past century in the United States, and recent increases only indicate its continued popularity. Slight changes upward in the average age at marriage in the 1970s might indicate a change in the overall marriage rate for the future, or might simply reflect the fact that young adults are delaying marriage, much as they did during the Depression of the 1930s.

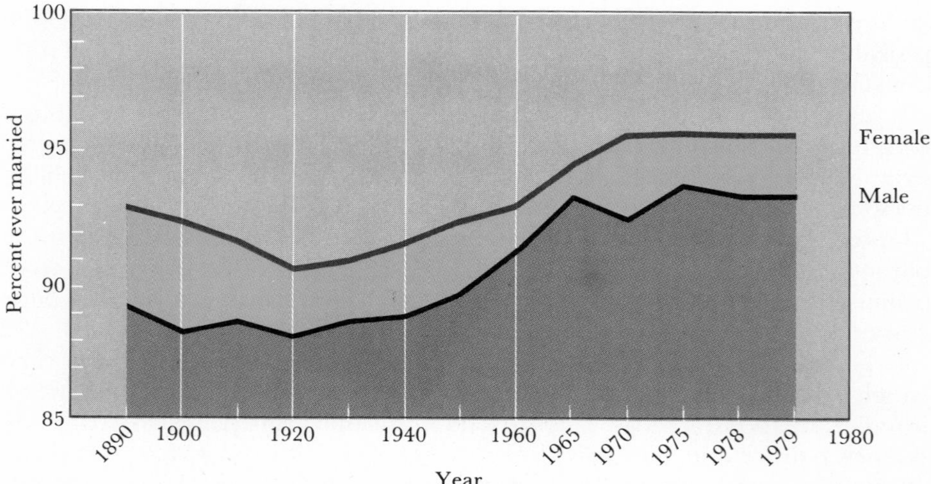

Fig. 2.1

Percent Ever Married by 45–54 Years of Age, 1890–1979

Source: United States Bureau of the Census, 1980.

It is interesting to note that the proportion of men and women marrying has continued to rise in the United States despite an ever-faster rise in the divorce rate. Apparently, divorce has not reduced interest in pairing. Rather, it has enhanced people's opportunities for changing pairing partners. This is quite evident in the remarriage rates of divorced persons; they remarry, on the average, three years after their divorce.

By worldwide standards, American marriage rates are quite high. This is probably because they more closely represent the tie between pairing desires and formal, legal commitment in marriage. Not being financially able to marry is very unusual in our modern credit economy. Marry now and pay later seems to be the current slogan.

Consensual relationships

But in many of the less well developed and Third World countries, marriage statistics do not adequately represent the extent of heterosexual pairing. In some cases, this is because financial problems make it difficult to acquire the property and assets necessary to support a spouse on a permanent basis. This often leads to **consensual unions,** or relationships that are relatively permanent but lack the formal tie of marriage. This is a common practice in much of the world (Voydanoff and Rodman, 1978). In most areas, however, the overwhelming majority of both men and women enter into paired relationships of some type.

Monogamy and Polygamy

Some smaller societies and subcultures have allowed and even encouraged **polygamy,** a marriage of more than two persons. This would seem to indicate that **monogamy,** a marriage of only two persons, is not the only natural form of adult pairing. In fact, the Swiss ethnologist J. J. Bachofen (1861) went so far as to propose that early humans lived in promiscuous bands without any pair commitments at all. Subsequent anthropological studies of primitive tribes, however, have refuted this idea, although a number of polygamous cultures have been examined.

Polygamy restrictions

George P. Murdock (1949), in his study of over 250 societies, found that 80 percent allowed polygamy at some time. Nevertheless, the normal practice in all of the societies was monogamy; polygamous relationships were restricted to selected circumstances or particular groups, usually the wealthy. But even the practice of polygamy does not weaken the fundamental nature of the paired relation. The anthropologist Malinowski reported that plural marriages can best be understood as a series of one-to-one individual paired relationships (Briffault and Malinowski, 1956). More importantly, those societies that permit polygamous unions now make up only a very small part of the world's population and gradually they too are becoming exclusively monogamous. A major factor influencing this change is the rise in the status of women, since polygamy usually exists in societies in which women are strongly dominated by men. The costs involved in maintaining the large family system and the need for mobility in an industrial economy are also

Demise of polygamy

factors in the demise of polgamy. It should be interesting to examine some of the developments in modern-day communes and group marriages in light of this trend (see Chapter 5).

PRESSURES TOWARD PAIRING

There seems to be an almost universal tendency toward paired marital relations. Even when other patterns are allowed or encouraged, this pairing unit emerges as the dominant theme. This should not be taken to mean that pair members do or should pay exclusive attention to a particular relationship. On the contrary, it would be highly unusual for any one relationship to meet all of a person's needs. We live out our lives in numerous groups, and each contributes something to our personality and well-being. The emphasis here is on the heterosexual couple because this is the basic unit of a marriage. The interpersonal networks in which this pair develops and is nurtured should always be kept in mind.

But why is the paired unit the dominant theme? Why not a three-person group, or each person for him or herself? Why is the tendency toward pairing so universal? The answer to these questions lies in the nature of the paired relation itself and the biological tendencies, interpersonal needs, and cultural mandates that influence our development. Each of these factors will be discussed in turn.

The Nature of the Pair Relation

Types of relationships

People develop different kinds of relations with others to meet different types of needs. When we buy a toothbrush in the drugstore, we expect a friendly, courteous manner in the clerk. But we might be offended if he or she became too friendly or too interested in us. Sociologists call this a **secondary relationship.** Among friends, colleagues, roommates, or our family, on the other hand, we expect more attention and close, personal communication. The sharing of even our most private thoughts may be permitted. It is in this latter type of **primary relationship** that we find the seeds of intimacy.

Intimate groups may vary from two persons to whatever number can be managed and still retain close contact. But most of us can rarely provide individual attention to more than a few people at any one time. The sharing of very personal feelings may be reserved for the ears of only one special person. As a result of these tendencies, it is quite common to find that a party, a group date, or a family gathering often breaks down into small groups and pairs. Research studies point out that when people are observed in settings such as parks, playgrounds, and shopping malls, two-person groups are consistently found to be the most common of all (Wilmot, 1975).

Pairing off within group settings is a common pattern.

Characteristics of dyads

Georg Simmel (1902), a German sociologist, was one of the first researchers to demonstrate the importance of the pair, or **dyad,** a two-person group. His initial attention was directed toward male-male dyads, but his studies soon led him to explore the male-female pair as well. What he found was that the paired relationship is quite different from any other size group. First of all, it has a unique *fragility:* the loss of either member destroys the relationship. In a larger group, the loss of a member, even an important one, may cause some disruption, but it rarely destroys the group. What this means in the intimate pair is that there are usually more commitments expected of one another and greater feelings of loss if the partner should leave.

Simmel (1950) also found that a pair has *no built-in majority.* This means there is more freedom for each person to have a voice. More importantly, it means that all pair actions require coresponsibility. Lindsey (1972) notes that even when decisions are dominated by one member, the acceptance of the other is necessary for any action to be taken. Thus it is always possible for either person to have a voice or to threaten the relationship itself. From this, we get the ultimatum: "If you don't listen to what I say, then I will leave!"

As a result of these dyadic characteristics, the pair relationship may take on a special role. The power of each person, and yet the perceived danger that results from the fragile nature of the pair, leads to a feeling that this relationship is special, irreplaceable, and intimate. Also, since it is characteristic of a good thing to want to share it, others, like friends or children, may be added or attracted to the pair.

Coalitions

For short periods of time, small intimate groups of more than two persons can be quite stimulating. They can heighten creativity, and the excitement of giving and receiving personal support from several different people at the same time may be quite rewarding, as members of encounter groups often discover. But maintaining these multiple relationships for a long time is also exhausting, and there is a tendency for coalitions of pairs to form, eventually reducing the group in size (Caplow, 1968).

Triads

It is little wonder that the three-person group, the **triad,** sometimes breaks down into a pair with an isolated or somewhat isolated member. This is common in many families when the first child develops an attachment to one parent and the other parent begins to feel left out. The four-person group often breaks down into two pairs after a time. In general, the cliché "two's company, three's a crowd" deserves more credit than we give it.

Biological Factors in Pairing

The social nature of the paired relation provides only a partial explanation as to why this type of group is so fundamental. There are a number of characteristics in our biological heritage that also are important.

Childhood dependency

First of all, it is readily apparent that the newborn child cannot be independent at birth, or for some time thereafter. Humans experience a longer period of physical dependency than any other animal. This means that simply to survive the child must have someone to meet its dependency needs immediately after birth (Rossi, 1978).

The human child's physiological capacity for complex language allows the reinforcement of early biologically required relationships through learning and the accumulation of teachings by parents and others. Foote and Cottrel (1955) viewed this ability to use language symbols as the most significant factor in developing "interpersonal competence." Only in this form of communication can we abstract feelings and transmit messages over distance and time. It is through language that we are conditioned by our culture.

Innate capacities

Another factor that makes long-term attachment important is the lack of genetically transmitted **instincts.** Most lower animals can be independent of their parents immediately or shortly after birth. Without language, they have to know innately what to do, where to feed, how to nest, and so on. While humans do have many simple **reflexes,** such as eye blinking, and **drives,** which are the biologically impelled actions evident in hunger and thirst, there is little evidence that we have any complex behaviors predetermined at birth.

Sexual balance

One other biological factor in human heterosexual pairing is the **sex ratio** of males to females. Demographers usually analyze this in terms of the number of males per 100 females in a population. At conception, this ratio is balanced in favor of males with an estimated 120 to 150 males conceived for every 100 females conceived. A large number of these potential males, however, are spontaneously aborted, resulting in a sex ratio at birth of approximately 105. During the period when most pairing occurs, the numbers of men and women are about equal. This balanced sex ratio would appear to favor paired relations as being most able to meet the needs of the greatest number of people.

To summarize, in general, our biological nature seems to impel us toward making early attachments and gives us the capacity to continue to form attachments as we mature. The sexual complementarity of men and women encourages heterosexual pairing as a dominant form for long-term commitments. But any perspective that suggests that our biology *determines* a particular pattern of paired behavior should be considered only with caution.

Interpersonal Needs

Personality needs

It is obvious that interpersonal relationships represent more than a meeting of physiological demands. The psychologist Stanley Schachter (1959), in studying grouping behavior in laboratory situations, reports: "People, in and of themselves, represent goals for one another; that is, people do have needs which can be satisfied only in interpersonal relations" (p. 2). Clinebell and Clinebell (1970) call this the "will to relate," which they feel results from a push-pull phenomenon: the need to move away from anxiety and loneliness, and the need to move toward interpersonal sources of personality needs. Schachter lists some of these personality needs as approval, support, friendship, and esteem. Taken together, these represent our basic need for nurturance and intimacy (see Vignette 2.1).

The foundations for adult nurturance and pairing begin in childhood. In the beginning, children will accept care and affection from almost anyone, but after a time, only a specific person or persons will be able to satisfy their nurturance needs (Rossi. 1978). Because of children's immature abilities to handle many different stimuli and their need for a relationship they can depend on, children attach to the person providing the most care, usually their mother in Western society. At this point, children have shifted from general to particular sources of need fulfillment. In time, they will add other particular persons to their list of acceptable "reference others," but initially that list is quite short.

Vignette *2.1* The Pursuit of Intimacy

Intimacy is an issue of great concern to citizens of our time. The steady popularity of "intimate" themes in the various media, the "pop intimacy" of encounter groups, and, for some, the restless moving in and out of alternate life-styles and marriages suggest the need of modern individuals for encounter, for understanding, for self-discovery, and for intimate union. The stresses of modern living—those that bring ulcers, heart attacks, and suicides—are thought to be soluble in the medium of the intimate experience. For many individuals, intimacy has become the new religion.

The age-old attempt of human beings to resolve the separateness of individual existence has for many modern individuals become the frantic *pursuit* of intimacy. Millions of desperate individuals are "pursuing" intimacy in ways that bring rewards that are certainly less than optimal. There are, of course, the sordid aspects of the search for intimacy: prostitution, rape, and other manifestations of this type exist today and perhaps always will. Beyond this negative aspect, however, is the more common situation of the pursuit of an *ersatz intimacy* that provides few rewards and little or none of the growth potential that genuine intimacy offers to individuals. Many persons have sought this ersatz or false intimacy in alcohol or in drugs. Many others have resorted to "intimacy surrogates" or nonhuman substitutes for interpersonal closeness; the adult who must always have a radio or television playing when s/he is alone and the teen who keeps a blaring transistor radio strapped to his/her belt are examples of the modern dependence upon intimacy surrogates. Other contemporary individuals find ersatz intimacy in "scavenger" forms of pursuit. The person who frequently visits the prostitute, the male or female who derives all or nearly all of his/her interpersonal closeness from "pick-ups" or "one-night-stands," and the "social leech" who attempts to derive intimacy from others while giving little in return are examples of this not-infrequent phenomenon.

Parental importance

This means that parents have a tremendous responsibility in setting the tone for how their children will meet their interpersonal needs (Baumrind, 1978). While in the past too much attention has been given to the idea that our personalities are fixed in the first years of life, it is clear that these early years are important. After a study of several hundred persons over a period of twenty-five years, a team of Harvard psychologists were forced to conclude that specific early child-rearing techniques were less crucial than had frequently been supposed in determining how children developed. "But," they added, "this hardly means that the way parents *feel* about their children cannot have a substantial impact. We found that when parents—particularly mothers—really loved their children, the sons and daughters were likely to achieve the highest levels of social and moral maturity" (McClelland *et al.*, 1978, p. 45).

For many modern individuals, the *pursuit* of intimacy amounts to little more than an attempt to resolve personality problems of dependency. Unfortunately, for many of us the need to "have someone to call our own" represents a very basic problem of needing to depend upon and cling to another person. The individual who comes to an intimate relationship with the need to "find" him- or herself in another person has very little to offer or to gain in the relationship. Once again, we must realize that the ability to be alone is one of the most important characteristics in a potential intimate. As Fromm has stated, "If I am attached to another person because I cannot stand on my own feet, he or she may be a lifesaver, but the relationship is not one of love."

Mature intimate relationships are not the proper home for dependent people! On the other hand, one of the first steps in the development of the ability to be intimate is the realization that none of us is independent. We must be able to be alone, and yet none of us can survive very well in isolation.

It is then, in our *interdependence* as human beings that the greatest rewards and the greatest potential for individual development are to be found. The realization of our basic *inter*dependence is one of the basic insights that comes with maturity. The individual who has made great progress in learning to be alone and in learning to be intimate is a person to be admired. Of all of our personal and nonbiological human needs, it would seem that the need for intimacy and the complementary need for self-hood and autonomy comprise our most basic and most unheralded of needs. The need to be alone and the ability to be intimate are two challenges facing modern individuals and modern societies. Each person must have satisfying experiences with each if s/he is to realize his/her potential as a human being.

Levels of interaction

Harry Stack Sullivan (1953) notes that supportive family interaction develops at three levels: sensory, emotional, and intellectual. Especially critical to the newborn is sensory interaction. Physical contact is the first representation of an intimate relationship that it can understand. Touching, patting, embracing, and rocking are all means by which the child first experiences affection with another. Later, we communicate and reinforce these impressions through the sharing of excitement, smiles, and supportive sounds. Eventually, our language integrates and further expresses these and other concerns.

Once they are all established, each level continually reinforces the other. Usually, if someone stimulates us intellectually, our initial reaction is a desire to reach out and shake this person's hand, or excitedly express our feelings in words. When a touchdown is scored on the football field, this is followed by

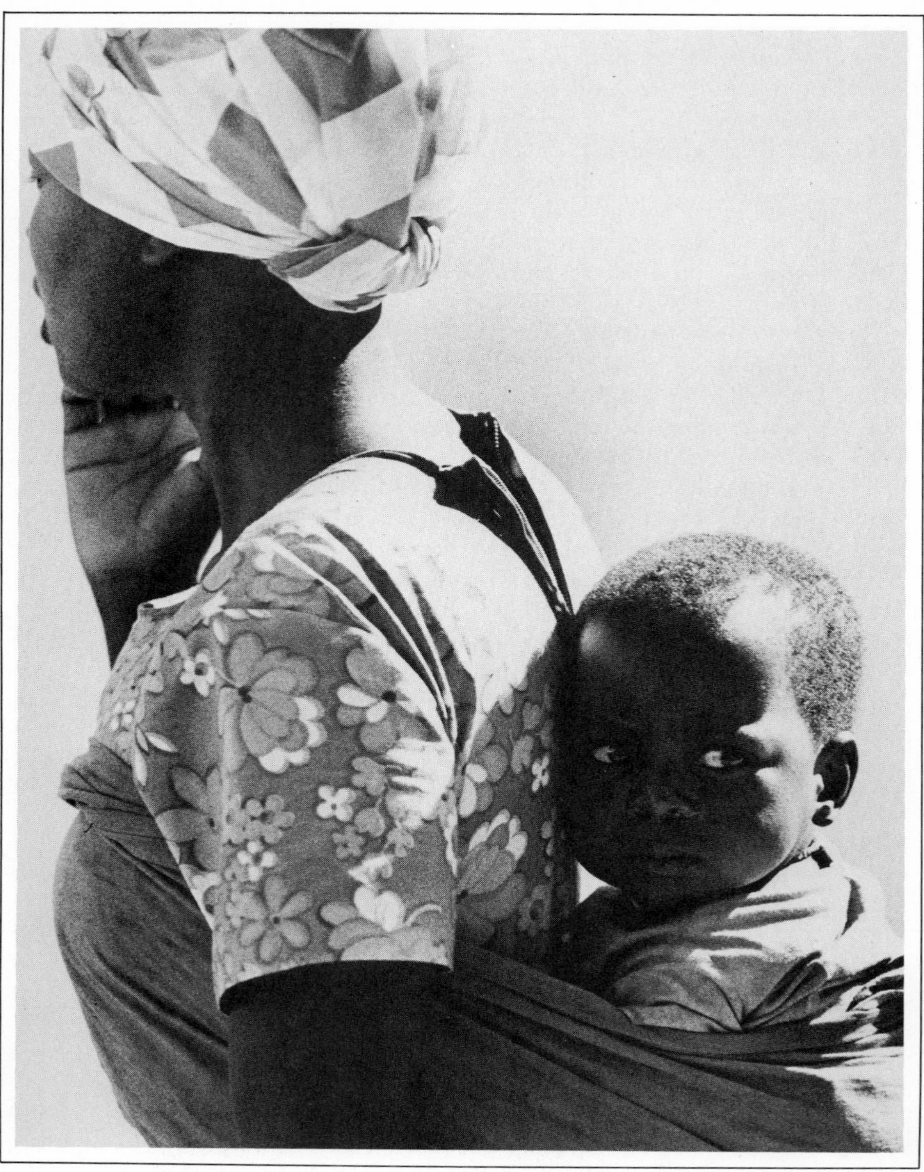

The importance of physical contact to infants is recognized in nearly all cultures.

slaps, shouts, and "piling-on" of the players. Likewise, between lovers, if there is an emotional bond coupled with understanding, there follows an almost natural desire for touching and embracing. The initial desire for basic nurturance in the child has now become the foundation for establishing new intimate relationships as well.

Nurturance deprivation

What happens when children are deprived of a nurturing environment, when their interpersonal needs are not met? Will this harm their ability to form attachments later? There is some controversy about the amount of attention infants require, but little argument that their needs are considerable. Harlow and Harlow's (1966) studies of body contact in baby monkeys demonstrated that feelings of security and a reduction in fear came simply from contact with a soft, pleasant object. Monkeys without this source of security had no way to dispel their fear, and they cowered in isolation. Later, the Harlows found that the deprived monkeys were also less able to provide comfort to other monkeys in fear situations, indicating that nurturing behavior is both basic and learned.

Some caution should be exercised in applying animal studies to humans, but similar results have been found in children as well. Investigations of infants who have been deprived of early emotional support compared to those who have received adequate nurturing have consistently found higher death rates, more illness, and greater emotional and intellectual retardation in the deprived group (Bowlby, 1980; Sroufe, 1978).

Children who received from their parents the gift of an intimate, nurturing environment have the tools to move out and diversify their relationships with others. Individuals able to accept their own selves are better equipped to accept the needs of others with whom they come into contact (Safilios-Rothschild, 1977). This means they can be nurtured and accept the approval, support, friendship, and esteem that may be offered by an intimate friend. Even more important, they can also meet these needs for another, thereby generating the kind of give and take that should characterize an intimate relationship. Because the pair relation is the simplest form in which this process can occur, and because providing for the needs of many additional persons is quite exhausting, it is not surprising that pairing becomes dominant in courtship and marriage.

Socialization toward Pairing

Cultural pressures

Our biological nature and interpersonal needs create certain propensities toward pairing, but pairing rates vary considerably from one society to another and even within a given society over time. Cultural influences, therefore, must be considered in order to account for the extent of male-female paired behavior that we find today, especially in the United States.

There seems to be little question that American society goes to great lengths to promote pairing. Religious authorities are much more likely to preach that "It is not good that man (or woman) should be alone" (Genesis 2:18) than ". . . it is better to marry than to burn" (I Cor. 7:9). The popular song from the musical *Funny Girl* exclaims that people who need one another "are the luckiest people in the world." Books and magazines try to outdo one another in telling us how to attract a date, a mate, or even a casual pick-up. Even some "authorities" use terms like "winners" and "losers" in remarks on the pairing process: "*Winners* successfully make the transition from total helplessness to independence to interdependence. *Losers* do not" (James and Jongeward, 1971).

Bach and Deutsch (1970) in their book, *Pairing,* complain that these coupling forces are often so strong that they short-circuit the natural development of a relationship and prejudice those who are not paired.

> Ours is a family-oriented culture. And it so values family life that it treats unmarried adults at best as undeveloped, immature, and incomplete—and at worst as failures and willful renegades who cannot or will not take up a respectable and responsible family role. . . . Singleness immediately raises questions about one's sense of responsibility and about one's desirability as a tenant, a neighbor, a customer, even a friend. The unattached man or woman, after all, may be cagily waiting for a chance to steal one's husband or wife. (p. ix)

Modeling

Socialization toward pairing begins very early in America's marriage-oriented culture. To some extent, it begins even before we are born because our parents have accepted the dictum of leaving their parents' home, dating, selecting a mate, and marrying. They, in turn, view this model as normal and somewhat unconsciously reinforce the idea that this is "*the* way."

Parents are particularly successful in socializing their children to accept certain behavior patterns as appropriate. This is because they are the primary agents of socialization during the time when children are forming their basic personalities, values, and role expectations. While other influences are also important and may even alter family wishes, parents initiate and reinforce a **style of life** that is most often followed by their children. This style of life is an unconscious as well as a conscious script for life that may even require rejection of the parents to change.

Pair supports

Part of the script that we get from our parents is the example that they provide of a paired relationship. If their marriage is viewed as "successful," then there is a greater inclination to follow their example. If their marriage is not successful, then one has to find a model of success from some other relationship. Parents and friends also play an important role in the **labeling** of pairs, that is, supporting the identity of the relationship. Because of their role as "significant others," parents may treat their son or daughter and a potential partner as a couple by inviting them as a pair, thinking of them as a pair, and even arranging opportunities for them to be together. Friends may encourage a particular relationship by initiating meetings between persons they think are "perfect" for one another and supporting the relationship (Ryder *et al.*, 1971). One study found that the survival of a pair relation over time was positively associated with these supportive reflections and the labeling of friends and relatives. Interestingly, family support was found to be of more importance than peer support (Lewis, 1973).

It should be noted that cultural mandates for pairing influence girls earlier than boys. The toys, dolls, and games girls receive, usually from their parents, orient them more toward marriage and parenthood than the trucks, baseballs, and "G.I. Joe" figurines that boys are given (Kacerguis and Adams, 1979). In general, peer groups during childhood and adolescence are more likely to reinforce the interpersonal aspects of male-female relations in girls and the sexual aspects of these relations in boys. While this differential socialization is currently changing, its legacy creates certain problems in pairing that we will return to later.

PAIR COMMITMENT

Search for security

As we noted in our discussion of the work of Georg Simmel, it is the nature of a pair relationship to develop commitments. People search for security in relationships, so they try to fulfill one another's needs and thus resolve their contrasting emotional, intellectual, and physical desires. It is this desire for security that translates itself into commitment, an assurance that the investment one is making will have long-term dividends. According to Murray Davis (1973), "intimates, like college professors, want tenure" (p. 192).

Pair commitment, in the present day and age, may be an especially important commodity. We live in a world that is characterized by impermanence, what Toffler (1970) called a "throw-away" society. There is little security to be found in the "planned obsolescence" of many industries, the cog-in-a-wheel feeling of most jobs, and the increasing escalation of "defense" armaments. In his studies of student dissidents of the 1960s, Kenneth Kenniston (1968) found a common malaise among the students which led to their being what he called "The Uncommitted." With the events that have occurred since then, including Watergate, factory recalls, antitrust suits, and voter apathy, we may have reached the point where most people feel that any commitment is difficult to make. These feelings are reflected well in Hobart's statement regarding commitment and value conflicts (see Vignette 2.2).

Freedom vs. security

In John Edwards' (1967) thoughtful critique of Hobart's study of commitment, he raises the point that personal freedom has become more important today than long-term commitments. In every individual, there is an abiding conflict between the desire for individual freedom and the desire for relational security. Western society seems to value both, but they are somewhat incompatible. In the past, the need for security was emphasized at the expense of freedom. This was symbolized in the marriage pledge, "in sickness and in health, for better or for worse, for richer or for poorer, till death do you part." But the nature of the security that was found in the traditional society existed more in the community or in kin relations than in pairing. The pair existed only as part of an overall security network.

Today, the security function of the kinship network has been considerably reduced, and pair relations have now become the primary source of security for individuals. This is a more focused type of relational commitment than was found earlier, and it permits more individual freedom than was possible in a traditional marriage. The O'Neills, in their book *Open Marriage* (1972), made the point that this new type of pair relation makes possible the creation of a new balance between individual and relational needs that was not

Vignette 2.2

Commitment and Value Conflict

The crucial significance of values depends upon the fact that man is a being who must live his life since it is not lived for him by imperious drives or instincts, as Fromm says. Man, thus emancipated from the security of nature's control, needs human community to humanize him and to structure his choice between the alternatives which confront him. The basis for choice is a set of values, generated in society, in terms of which choice priorities may be assigned.

One linkage between values and the family lies in the fact that the original unit of human community and the universal humanizing unit of all societies is the family. It is in the family that many of the most important values, bases for choice, are learned. The family not only transmits values; it is predicated on, and in fact symbolizes some of the distinctively "human" values: tenderness, love, concern, loyalty.

Man's capacity for consistent and responsible action depends on his being able to orient himself and to act on the basis of commitment to values; thus a certain level of value consistency is important. But a prominent feature of American society today is a pervasive value conflict. The family depends upon and symbolizes "inefficient values" of being, knowing, caring, loving, unconditionally committing oneself. These values are incompatible with the urban industrial values of production, achievement, exchange, quantification, efficiency, success. Simultaneous unlimited commitment to people—in love and concern—and to achievement, success, prosperity, is impossible. The resultant tension in a society which pays uncritical lip-service to both sets of values, is disruptive and potentially incapacitating. It tends toward resolution, in favor of the "inhuman" urban values. Fromm has noted that as a society we tend to *love things,* and *use people,* rather than the reverse. And Whyte has remarked that the "organization men" he interviewed seemed to prefer to sacrifice success in marriage to career success, if forced to choose between them.

This value confusion is, of course, a source of instability within the American family. A family presumes unlimited commitment between family members: "til death do you part" between husband and wife, "all we can do for the kids" on the part of parents toward children. But the priority of these love and concern values is directly challenged by success and achievement values which may imply that status symbols are more important than babies; that what a child *achieves* is more important than what he *is;* that what we *own* is more important than what we *are.* Thus the stage is set for conflict between a success-oriented husband and a child-people welfare-oriented wife, or for a rather inhuman family which values things over people, and which may raise children who have difficulty living down this experience of worthlessness.

possible before. Nevertheless, this balance depends upon our recognizing the importance of commitment, and unless this recognition occurs, shifts toward individual freedom and rationality may make marriage in the future more unstable than we know it today.

Levels of Interpersonal Commitment

Commitment as process

There is a tendency to view commitment as an all-or-nothing phenomenon; one is either committed or not committed to a relationship. However, it is probably better to examine commitment as a *process* which begins with little more than mutual attraction and extends to a bond that is exceptionally difficult to break. Because of the obligations to another that commitment implies, few people will commit themselves to anyone or anything without first receiving some assurance that it will be worth it. For this reason, interpersonal relationships only gradually develop the security that we often demand from them.

Davis describes three levels in the process of developing couple commitment. First, there is an **exclusion period** when other potential pairing partners are temporarily removed from consideration. Primary attention is given to one person in an attempt to intensify and test this relationship. This usually involves "steady" dating and the initial "labeling" of the pair that was discussed earlier.

Increasing obligations

A second stage in pair commitment is the creation of a **common space,** maximizing the opportunity for pair identity. Joint activities and experiences are increased even more at this time. The "life-spaces" of the individuals begin to converge, and discussions often center around "our" friends, family, school, and so on. The obligations to the relationship now involve the pooling of some resources, responsibilities to one another's friends and family, and perhaps the sharing of sexual intimacy with the other.

The third level of commitment occurs when the couple creates a **common future.** This implies not only a spatial commitment, but a time commitment as well. Each person figures in the future plans of the other, so the relationship itself now engenders a sense of permanence. Davis indicates that this last stage is what marital commitment, in the broadest sense, is all about.

De-commitment

Not all paired relationships can be expected to advance in level of commitment. The greater the commitment, the more that is learned of the other, the more that is learned about oneself, and the greater the obligation to the relationship. If what we learn makes us very uncomfortable or if we feel that obligating ourselves to some other relationship would make us more comfortable, then we are likely to retreat in level of commitment. A long-term future commitment at Davis's third level, however, is likely to develop a set of reciprocal obligations not only between the pair, but also with children, parents, friends, and others. The greater the number of these commitments, the more difficult it is to de-commit without considerable pain. Usually in

During the "exclusion" period of couple commitment, primary attention is given to one person.

divorce, there is a gradual drop in commitment, beginning with a fall-off in pair communication, followed by separations, and finally a loss of exclusive attention. Often, the exact order is muddled because one or both partners actually makes a commitment to someone else prior to the separation.

Commitment differences

It is also possible in the development of a pair relationship for one person to be more committed than the other. Women, for example, have traditionally been more socialized to seek interpersonal commitments, and it is more likely that they will advance faster in these commitments than their male partners (Reiss, 1976). One recent study found that young women more often use their close relationships as a basis for their developing identity. Young men, however, were more likely to seek their identity through work and other measures of personal competence (Hodgson and Fischer, 1979). This means that women may respond more quickly to intimate relationships, especially to the commitments that foster these relationships.

Different people look for different things in relationships. Obviously, we enter into secondary relations for different reasons than primary relations. But even persons in primary relationships may vary in their reasons for making a commitment. One way of examining this issue is to explore two fundamental types of commitment: instrumental and intrinsic commitments.

Exchange oriented

Instrumental commitments are made because they are useful to us: they produce an outcome that we desire. When a relationship is characterized by instrumental commitments, there is an underlying concern for what each person can *do* for the other. The pair bond is viewed as an exchange: she cooks, he mows the lawn; she raises the children, he "brings home the bacon." Interestingly, most dating relationships begin with an instrumental "commitment." Each person is primarily looking for a good time, sex, or just someone to look good with. They evaluate one another and their relationship in terms of what it offers them personally.

Trust

Intrinsic commitments, however, are different from instrumental commitments in that the relationship is valued for its own sake without always considering the trade-offs and ultimate consequences. The emphasis in this type of commitment is on what a person *is* rather than on what he or she *does*. Sidney Jourard (1968) deals with this concept in terms of what he calls being "transcendental." He says this involves dropping our defenses, maintaining a continuing sense of genuine trust in the other, and allowing ourselves to focus on the whole nature of the other person. Hobart (1963) hints at intrinsic commitments when he indicates that the family represents the "inefficient values" of being, knowing, caring, loving, and *unconditional* commitment.

It is not always possible to tell from a particular activity what kind of commitment characterizes the relationship. For example, sexual intercourse may be for some persons a duty, a responsibility, a personal thrill, or even a way to get a new washer or boat. The behavior is part of their role, and they instrumentally commit themselves to the activity in order to gain certain benefits that it provides. Sexual intercourse for another couple may be a form of communication, a way of mutually giving and demonstrating their concern and love for one another. The act may appear the same (often it will not) but the consequences for the relationship are quite different.

Variations in commitment

When all of these acts and the feelings behind them are examined, we find that pair relations exist on a continuum from highly instrumental to highly intrinsic commitments. The highly instrumental pairs are typically represented by an exchange of favors; almost a businesslike arrangement. He does his "thing," she does hers. When we talk of "intimates," however, we are usually referring to persons having high intrinsic commitments. This type of relationship is based more on shared experiences, companionship, and mutual giving rather than receiving (Ammons and Stinnett, 1980).

Most paired relations that have reached an advanced level of commitment are probably composed of a combination of both instrumental and intrinsic commitments. This results in some compartmentalization, delegating certain times and activities to meet instrumental needs and other times and activities to intrinsic needs. As an example, a husband may commit himself to mow the lawn while his wife feeds the children so that they can go out for dinner together in the evening.

Commitment expectations

It should be remembered, however, that these two forms of commitment often result from basic approaches to male-female relations rather than from accumulated circumstances. The man who views his wife *primarily* as a good cook, effective mother, responsible sex partner, and efficient housekeeper will have a difficult time making intrinsic commitment primary in the relationship. Yet the marriage may be exactly what each person expects, and it may meet the needs they have for one another. There is a tendency today for some people to regard intrinsic pair commitments as a panacea without recognizing the value instrumental commitments have traditionally had for many couples. Over the history of human marriage, it has been these instrumental commitments that have held most couples together. Only recently have demands for "pair togetherness" replaced the cries for businesslike partnerships.

Alternative Patterns of Relational Commitment

Multiplicity of commitments

The focus to this point has been on pairing and commitments in pair relations. However, it is important that we emphasize again the relationship between pair commitments and commitments made to others. Pairing does *not* occur in a vacuum; it usually represents the fulfillment of some of our needs and the fruition of considerable social pressure. For most people, the pair relation represents only a part of their total commitment to others—in some cases, only a minor part. By analyzing the way men and women interrelate instrumental and intrinsic commitments to the pair and to others, we can better understand the variety of ways pairing meets personal needs.

Figure 2.2 demonstrates four different patterns of paired relations that depend on the type of commitment to the pair relation and to other significant persons such as friends or family. This is a hypothetical format which assumes that relationships tend toward being instrumental or intrinsic and that both persons in a relationship look to one another for the same general kind of commitments.

Manipulators

Couples or persons of the **Type I** commitment pattern can be called *social manipulators*. They not only avoid intrinsic commitments with each other, they do not establish them with anyone else either. They interpret personal relationships in general strictly in terms of what they personally can "get out of it." To some extent, this represents a pure "exchange" approach with all the harshness and manipulation that reward-seeking implies. Fortunately, this is a comparatively rare pattern because most children are socialized to want to offer nurturance to others. Persons with the social-manipulator type of personality are probably less likely to pair and, if they do, more prone to early separation.

		Pair commitment: Instrumental	Pair commitment: Intrinsic
Commitment to others (Friends, kin, etc.)	Instrumental	I (Social manipulator)	III (Exclusively intimate)
	Intrinsic	II (Traditional)	IV (Open intimate)

Fig. 2.2
Patterns of Relational Commitment

The **Type II** commitment pattern approximates the *traditional* model. Worldwide, more marriages exist of this type than any other. The usual arrangement is for intrinsic commitments to be maintained with parents, kin, or same-sex peers, while the pair relation fulfills primarily day-to-day useful purposes. William Stephens (1963) summarized his cross-cultural findings this way:

> Traditional barriers frequently stand between husband and wife, curtailing their intimacy, sharing, and togetherness. They usually observe avoidance customs while in public; they may sleep in separate beds, live in separate homes, own separate property, eat separately, go separately to community gatherings, and . . . usually work at separate tasks. In most societies, spouses appear to follow the advice of Kahlil Gibran, to: "Fill each other's cup but drink not from the same cup. Give one another of your bread but eat not from the same loaf. . . . And stand together yet not too near together. . . ." (p. 278)

Outside support system

For these traditional relationships, "togetherness" would more likely refer to friends or parental family than to the spouse. Elizabeth Bott (1971) found that lower- and working-class husbands and wives in England depended much more on their separate closely-knit friendship networks for emotional support than on each other. Mirra Komarovsky's (1964) study of blue-collar families in America reported a similar finding. The men tended to have "buddies" as companions, confidents, and coworkers. The women tended to confide in their mothers and sisters, often sharing things that they would "never tell" their husbands. Until recently, intrinsic commitments were almost exclusively reserved for these "other" relationships. People looked to their parents for security, not to their spouses; men had their world, women had theirs, and "never the twain shall meet."

Accent on togetherness

The **Type III** commitment pattern represents a markedly different life-style from the ones just discussed. The *exclusively intimate* couple gives its intrinsic commitment to the pair relation and only maintains relationships with others that are useful to the couple. The house becomes the "castle"; life revolves around the spouse and family. In some cases, even children may threaten this type of pair relation.

Intrinsic commitments with same-sex peers are characteristic of "traditional" marriage.

The Type III pattern is probably best represented by some newlyweds. In their attempt to learn rapidly as much as possible about each other, sharing and togetherness reach their epitome. The extent to which a couple can maintain this type of relationship depends on the degree of variety they can introduce into it. If they have the independent resources necessary to continue the intrigue (which few couples do), they might be able to make it. Otherwise, the *exclusively intimate* couple usually shifts to one of the other commitment patterns.

Intimate friendships

The **Type IV** commitment pattern represents the couple who maintains intrinsic commitments to one another and to others as well. This *open-intimate* relationship provides the ongoing emotional security of the pair and the variety and support of intimate friendships as well. Like persons in the traditional commitment pattern, there is a recognized need among open intimates for enlarging their repertoire of experiences beyond that which any one relationship can provide. Unlike the traditional model, couples with an open-intimate bond return these experiences to their own relationship, thereby encouraging further sharing. Bach and Deutsch tend to support this pattern and comment that "the overlapping of two social circles provides stimulating grist for the conversational mill" (p. 106).

One variation of the open-intimate commitment pattern has been called "patchwork intimacy" (Kieffer, 1977). This rather common pattern involves the couple in multiple relationships, each meeting different needs for intimacy. Kieffer explains:

> The need for intimacy is met by a *combination* of intimate relationships rather than by one individual. This is not to deny the importance of a central relationship in one's life; however, for an increasing number of individuals a combination of intimate relationships is the mechanism that enables them to meet or to approximate the meeting of their needs for close human contact and for intimate involvement. (p. 277)

In general, the Type II and Type IV forms of commitment which are open to outside influences appear to be the most stable. Type I and Type III commitments, because of their extreme exclusiveness or absence of intimacy, may be difficult to maintain for any length of time, especially since variety and intimacy are so strongly reinforced today. The open-intimate style of commitment has also been somewhat unstable in the past because attachments to family, old friends, work associates, or others continued or developed into stronger obligations than the obligation to the pair. This often resulted in the pair relationship becoming more and more traditional. The future of the open-intimate relationship will depend on the extent to which couples can actively and continually commit themselves intrinsically to one another.

While the pair relationship tends to develop naturally, this does not mean that any couple relationship naturally maintains the momentum of the commitment that initiated it. Couples often learn that it takes some effort for intimacy to be maintained over the long run.

HOMOSEXUAL PAIRING: A RELATIONAL ALTERNATIVE

For the overwhelming majority of men and women in American society, heterosexual relationships and commitments are clearly preferred. There remains, however, a minority who prefer intimate partners of their same sex. Until recently, these homosexual men and women were rarely visible. Fearing that their jobs and friendships might be jeopardized, they avoided public disclosure of their relational preferences. Today, with the Gay Rights Movement providing a forum, more homosexuals are coming "out of the closet" to reveal their needs and experiences.

Homosexuality is not new. Reports of men and women with homosexual preferences go back over 4000 years (Bullough, 1978). Ancient Greece is an often-noted example of a culture that permitted homosexuality, but the existence of these relationships has been recognized in nearly all parts of the world. Still, the values of nearly all societies throughout history have rarely supported the public acceptance of homosexual life-styles. Punishments for homosexuality have often been swift and severe.

Attitudes toward homosexuality

There is a move today to relax some of our official restrictions against homosexual behavior, but public attitudes are changing very slowly. The majority of states in the United States still legally forbid sexual contacts between persons of the same sex, yet a few states do permit couples the freedom to engage privately in whatever intimate behavior they wish, even homosexual behavior. Recent national polls still find, however, that most adults consider homosexual relationships "wrong." By the late 1970s, 78 percent indicated that they felt this way. Nevertheless, changes in public acceptance do appear to be occurring among youth; only half of the men and women under thirty now hold very restrictive attitudes toward homosexuality (Glenn and Weaver, 1979).

The proportion of men and women who prefer homosexual to heterosexual relationships is rather small. During the 1940s, the Kinsey reports estimated that about 2 percent of the women and 4 percent of the men in the United States were exclusively homosexual (Kinsey *et al.*, 1953). Recent studies have found similar percentages in the 1970s (Bell and Weinberg, 1979). This similarity in the proportion of homosexuals in our society over the past few decades suggests that the factors producing homosexual preferences have remained rather stable, despite more open opportunities to opt for this life-style. We still are uncertain whether homosexuality is more biologically or socially based, but from the evidence to date, it appears that both biological and social factors are involved in the development of heterosexuality and homosexuality (West, 1977). It is also important to understand that not all persons who enjoy homosexual intimacy are exclusively homosexual. One recent study found that only about 75 percent of the homosexual men and 50 percent of homosexual women restricted their relationships to homosexual partners (Bell and Weinberg).

Homosexual preferences

Contrary to the view that homosexuals are quite different in their personality or behavior, nearly all studies now suggest that there are more similarities than differences between homosexuals and heterosexuals. Comparison studies have not found major differences in personality traits or sexual development between those who do and do not have a homosexual preference (Weis and Dain, 1979). Homosexuals have been found to respond to sexual intimacy in much the same way as heterosexuals (Masters and Johnson, 1979). Most homosexuals report that they are more comfortable with other homosexual friends, but they have few difficulties maintaining their jobs and acquaintances in their heterosexual world (Albro and Tully, 1979). Over half of the men and women in a major recent study expressed no regret whatsoever about being homosexual (Bell and Weinberg).

Homosexual relationships

In their search for intimate relationships, homosexual couples sometime find it difficult to establish long-term commitments, but this is not always the case. Nearly all the homosexuals interviewed in a large San Francisco Bay Area study had been involved in at least one exclusive relationship that had lasted for a year or more (Bell and Weinberg). Most of these men and women preferred long-term partner commitments, although the men tended to want some sexual encounters with others outside the partnership as well. In general, homosexual women are more likely to be exclusive in their relational commitments, and their intimate relationships often last longer. The fact that two women living together does not raise the public curiosity of two men living together (the "odd couple") may contribute to the greater stability of female homosexual relationships (Chafetz *et al.*, 1974).

When the relational characteristics of homosexual couples are compared to heterosexual couples, again, very few differences usually appear. In one study, it was found that the traits homosexuals look for in a partner are very similar to those heterosexuals look for in a partner (Lee, 1976). In another study, it was found that homosexual couples had only slightly lower scores than the heterosexual married couples on a measure of relational adjustment;

their "caring" for one another, measured on a separate test, was just as great as the married couples' (Dailey, 1979).

Overall, it appears that homosexual pairs have a great deal of potential prejudice to overcome before they can be accepted by society or even by one another. Threats of disclosure keep many of these men and women from being able to develop publicly and privately their relationships with one another. Relational commitments are usually stronger when supported by friends and family, but this is often denied homosexual couples. Without support and without public acceptance, it is not surprising that many of the homosexual relationships succumb to the "self-fulfilling prophesy" that they cannot survive in a heterosexual society.

Prejudice

NONPAIRING: THE SINGLE ALTERNATIVE

But what of those persons who make a deliberate choice not to commit themselves to a pair relationship for the rest of their days, or even on a continuous basis for a period of time? Is pairing really necessary in this day of individual freedom and alternatives? The answer to this question is no. While pairing is almost universal in Western society, singlehood does represent an alternative to conventional pairing for many people.

"Swinging singles"

Usually, when we think of singles, we think of "swinging singles," special bars, clubs, apartments, and even magazines. But it should be remembered that most of this life-style is oriented *toward* pairing, not parallel to or away from it (Libby, 1977). In reality, there are two sides to being single. There are those who are not married (some have been) for whom singleness is merely a stage in the pairing process. For them, it is a temporary condition that will change when they find someone they think is the "right" person. At the present time, one-third of the American men and women over eighteen years of age are single, but the majority of them will most likely marry within a few years (Stein, 1978). These "singles" will not be dealt with here because they are the subject of subsequent chapters.

Voluntary singles

The remaining ones either voluntarily opt for single status or fall into it because they do not find an appropriate partner. Some of these men and women have never married and genuinely prefer the single life, a preference which is growing, particularly among college women (Libby). Other singles have been married but now are widowed or are among the one out of five divorced persons who do not remarry (Glick and Norton, 1977). Still others do not marry because of religious vows, because of homosexual preferences, or because they have not been able to succeed in the marriage market. In general, it is these voluntary singles who have been the most maligned because they have rejected their cultural mandates to pair (see Vignette 2.3).

Even the so-called "swinging-single" life-style is usually oriented toward pairing.

Vignette 2.3

The Experience of Being Single

Excerpts from taped conversations among a group of single women in Boston

Deborah

In college, groups were usually made up of couples. Any activity for couples excluded me, so I felt bad. It seemed like you had to have a boyfriend to go places. It also affected my relationship with women in the couples, since they shared and talked about their relationships with their boyfriends.

Judith

I found that it was hard to just date. Also, women with serious boyfriends often implied that if you weren't with one man consistently you were promiscuous.

I would talk with many of my women friends about careers, but by the time of my senior year I was the only one in my group who wasn't getting married. When I thought about going to graduate school, a male professor told me not to go—that I would become too much like a man and never get married.

Elaine

As a child I was often told it was impossible for a woman to take care of herself alone in the world, that she needed a man to manage things for her. No one took a woman seriously. I knew a repairman would come immediately if my father called, but it would take my mother many phone calls before he'd finally come around.

Kathy

I think there has been a growing respect for women who are more aggressive. A woman who is single is now given a certain amount of respect for having the strength to go out on her own. I always liked doing things that were thought of as boy's things, and in the women's movement these have become acceptable for women for the first time. Learning auto mechanics and feeling that people respected me for it has been very important to me.

Deborah

In high school I decided it was silly that boys should pay for girls. So I remember saying to my family that I should pay for myself, and my father started ranting and screaming at me, "If you have that attitude, Deborah, boys will never like you and no one will ever take you out and you'll never get married!"

In giving up the idea of getting married I gave up one sense of the future. Now it feels as though I'll be making certain decisions for a few years at a time, but I don't have any sense of where my future is headed. Some of that's really good. It allows me to live from day to day and to express my needs for the present. On the other hand, I do need a greater sense of continuity.

I still want some kind of permanent relationship, to feel security and love. I want to have children of my own or share ongoing responsibility for friends' children. Now both those possibilities seem so hard to achieve; I have no models for what I want.

From the Boston Women's Health Book Collective, *Our Bodies, Ourselves* (New York: Simon & Schuster, 1973), pp. 49–51.

Traditionally, there has been discrimination against singlehood because agrarian societies needed manpower and large families to survive. Today, public attitudes toward singlehood are changing. In 1957, 80 percent of American adults reported that they felt single people were either sick, immoral, selfish, or neurotic. In 1976, only 25 percent felt this way (Veroff, 1979).

Pushes and Pulls toward Singlehood

Attractions of singlehood

In Peter Stein's (1978) analysis of the single life-style, he points out that there are certain identifiable factors that determine a person's attraction to singlehood. He calls these pull and push factors (see Table 2.1). **Pull factors** are the drawing cards to the single life, the conditions or beliefs that cause some people to wish they were single and others to remain single. These usually include the promise of self-sufficiency, career opportunities, sexual variety, and personal development. **Push factors** are those that encourage people to leave a pair relationship because of restrictions on their personal development, boredom with a mate, unhappiness, or sexual frustration. The more men and women believe that these pull and push factors are real, the stronger will be their attraction to singlehood.

Personal independence

It is not difficult to document the fact that push factors are involved in dissolving relationships. The current divorce rate attests to this. However, it is more difficult to document whether the attractions of singlehood are as real as they sometimes appear to be. Certainly, career mobility is enhanced by independence, particularly for women, and that goal is commonly shared by single

Table 2.1

Pushes and Pulls toward Singlehood

Singlehood	
Pushes (to leave permanent relationships)	Pulls (to remain single or return to singlehood)
Lack of friends, isolation, loneliness	Career opportunities and development
Restricted availability of new experiences	Availability of sexual experiences
Suffocating one-to-one relationship, feeling trapped	Exciting life-style, variety of experiences, freedom to change
Obstacles to self-development	Psychological and social autonomy, self-sufficiency
Boredom, unhappiness, and anger	Support structures: sustaining friendships, women's and men's groups, political groups, therapeutic groups, collegial groups
Role playing and conformity to expectations	
Poor communication with mate	
Sexual frustration	

Source: Information from Peter Stein, The Lifestyles and Life-Chances of the Never-Married, *Marriage and Family Review* 1 (July 1978):4.

persons. When a national sample of single and married adults in the United States were asked to identify their most important goal in life, the single ones indicated a much higher preference for personal independence (Stein, 1976). Many of these singles still valued family life (and will probably marry), but many more single than married persons preferred to focus on personal and career goals.

While leading a career-oriented life appears to a realistic goal, the likelihood of having an exciting, flexible life-style with many new, sustaining friendships appears to be less. A recent study of over 2300 adults found that singles tend to be socially isolated, much more so than married persons (Pearlin and Johnson, 1977). They experience more difficulty in forming continuous friendships, and the more independent they are, the more likely they are to suffer from psychological depression.

Still, not all singles experience this social isolation, and many who do prefer to spend their time alone or in occupational pursuits. According to recent evidence, many singles are able to live quite contented lives as long as their pulls toward independence and abilities to withstand the pairing mandates of society remain strong (Libby). However, during periods of personal doubt and insecurity, when careers change, friendships break up, or family relationships become more important, there is a tendency for the attractiveness of being independent to wane and marriage to be more eagerly considered (Darling, 1976). This periodic cycle of reevaluating the attractiveness of singlehood, especially during periods of personal-life transitions, is common among singles.

Characteristics of Singles

Childhood experiences

As we have already indicated, people who remain single differ somewhat from those who pair. There is reason to think that these differences have several bases. First of all, the childhood experiences of both single men and single women tend to be less nurturant, a factor which may reduce their ability to form long-term attachments. This is by no means universal, but it does encourage more social isolation, or the development of what we have called the "social-manipulator" (Type I) commitment pattern. This factor of isolation was noted as long ago as the previous century by the French sociologist Emile Durkheim. In his studies of suicide, Durkheim (1897) found that the isolation of single people encouraged many more of them to take their own lives, a fact that remains true even today.

Single men and women

Among men, this isolation is sometimes accentuated by social and personal characteristics that make them somewhat less than a "good catch." Spreitzer and Riley (1974) report that single men are more likely to come from authoritarian, stressful homes and to have had poor parent-child relations, particularly with their mothers. Scores on intelligence tests and evidence of occupational achievement are also lower among men who have never married compared to those who have married.

In contrast to single men, women who do not marry tend to be more educated and career-oriented than married women. Among scientists, engineers, and college instructors, the singlehood percentages for women are far higher than for men in these fields (Bernard, 1972). Women who graduate from college actually increase their chances of never being married (Eisenberger, 1978). But like men, women are influenced by their family background in deciding to be single. Never-married women are more likely to be from homes with only one parent, and they also report poor relations with their mothers (Spreitzer and Riley). Again, this provides an incomplete model of adult pair relations and, when coupled with a high achievement motivation, is likely to create less desire for a permanent paired relationship. The higher abilities that these women commonly display might also represent a threat to most men, so rather than "marrying down," many of these women remain single. John Scanzoni (1972) predicts that:

> . . . there will be more highly educated women in the future, and . . . many of them will be aware of the potential basic conflict that the presence of two achievers introduces into marriage. Consequently, many of them may not marry at all until they can find a male with whom they could achieve consensus over geographic mobility in particular, and the whole dual-achiever pattern in general, and since it is likely that for some years there will be relatively few such males, these women will either marry late or else remain single. (p. 139)

Personal happiness

Individuals who opt for singlehood are not always unhappy about their decision, just as those who marry are not always happy with their decision either. There are many secure and ambitious people who prefer the independence of not being permanently committed to another. The results of national surveys taken in 1972, 1973, and 1974 indicate that 19.7 percent of the men and 24.7 percent of the women who had never married were "very happy" with their life (Glenn, 1975[b]). The figures for the married were higher—36.0 percent for the men and 46.2 percent for the women—indicating that pairing is the preferred system for most people. Nevertheless, the findings do suggest that many men and women can be secure and confident while remaining single.

Summary

Adult pairing has reached almost universal proportions in America. The percentage of men and women who marry has been climbing, and those who leave marriage through divorce seem to reenter at exceptionally high rates.

The reasons for the drive toward pairing are both basic to our biological nature and culturally mandated. Pair relations are a fundamental unit of all human groupings, especially primary groups. The biological make-up of children encourages early dependencies on others, and these are reinforced by ongoing needs for interpersonal support. Adults are not immune from these nurturance needs; adult personalities continue to demand the nourishment of significant relationships.

Pair commitments, the glue that holds a relationship together, differ from couple to couple. Most people, however, must reconcile their contrasting demands for security and freedom in such a way that a pair relation allows their personal needs to be met without stifling their individual growth. Relationships are also characterized by different types of commitment. Instrumental commitments are made to meet utilitarian needs, and intrinsic commitments meet more personal, inner needs.

Finally, heterosexual pair relationships do not appear to be the choice of everyone, but the proportion of men and women in America who choose homosexual pairing or singlehood remains small. Traditionally, there has been severe discrimination against these pairing alternatives, but with increasing demands for individual freedom, more men and women may opt for these life-styles in the future. There is little chance, however, that the pairing mandate will be withdrawn or reduced for some time to come.

SUGGESTIONS FOR ADDITIONAL READING

Bach, George R., and Ronald M. Deutsch. *Pairing.* New York: Wyden, 1970.
A best-selling book that examines the motives for and "art" of establishing pair relations.

Bell, Alan P., and Martin W. Weinberg. *Homosexualities.* Bloomington, Ind.: Institute for Sex Research, 1979.
This study reports on the many dimensions of homosexuality as a life-style. Based on interviews with over 1000 homosexuals.

Davis, Murray S. *Intimate Relations.* New York: The Free Press, 1973.
A philosophical and sociological study of why and how people form commitments.

Jourard, Sidney. *Disclosing Man to Himself.* New York: Van Nostrand, 1968.
A classic investigation into building capacities for personal understanding as a foundation for intrinsic relationships with others.

Srouffe, L. Alan. "Attachment and the roots of competence," *Human Nature* 1 (October 1978): 50–57.
A sound, yet easy-to-understand research report on how early attachments between mother and child help in developing traits that support later adult competence in family relationships.

Stein, Peter. "The lifestyles and life chances of the never married," *Marriage and Family Review* 1 (October 1978): 1–11.
An excellent survey of the recent research on single persons, including the author's own studies of different single life-styles.

Chapter 3

Pair Development: Courtship and Mate Selection

The jump from being single to being married is a big one. While mandates to pair become increasingly obvious during adolescence, it takes personal maturity and time for pair commitments to develop adequately. During this development, potential partners are evaluated, added, and replaced, usually over and over again, until a relationship develops enough momentum to carry it forward toward marriage.

This is not a game of luck. Men and women typically find themselves playing and sometimes inventing new rules that govern their courtship. Indeed, every culture establishes some rather orderly means for carrying out its pairing mandates. Courtship customs as well as criteria and opportunities for selecting suitable mates may vary in flexibility, but they exist everywhere nonetheless. From the perspective of society, these customs ensure some sense of order and continuity from generation to generation. For the individuals involved, courtship and mate selection provide a chance to test their independence, an opportunity to wean themselves away from their parents.

In Chapter 2 we examined some of the reasons behind heterosexual pair relations. Now we turn our attention toward the way in which these relationships develop, the factors involved in making initial pair commitments, and some of the changes that are occurring in premarital relationships between men and women today.

TRADITIONAL PATTERNS OF COURTSHIP

It may be a surprise to some young people to learn that the freedom they expect in courtship is not available to most youth worldwide. In fact, while

Americans tend to separate early courtship from serious mate selection, the usual pattern in non-Western societies is for *any* male-female relations to be viewed as "serious." This often results in young boys and girls being separated in work and play and having very little chance to interact on their own with one another prior to marriage.

Chaperonage

Chaperonage is one way in which courting is controlled in some countries. A young man may go out with the lady of his choice only if he takes along her mother, and perhaps her brothers and sisters as well. The chaperone is there to make sure that the relationship is properly moving toward marriage and that the reputation of the girl is protected from possible interpretations of sexual misconduct. This type of courting is common in the middle and upper classes of Latin America and Spain.

Even more restrictive are those societies that clearly segregate young men and women. In much of the world, boys and girls attend different schools, if the girls go at all; they play different games; they learn different roles; and they may eat at different times, even in the same home. In some more rural areas of the Middle East, for example, there are only particular times of the day when a young woman may appear in public and then she must cover her face.

Parental approval

In these very traditional societies, contacts between a young man and woman must be properly endorsed. No boy can even call on a girl unless her parents have first approved of his visit. In some cases, a **matchmaker** might be contracted by the boy or his parents to act as a go-between with the parents of the girl. This allows the family of the boy to save face in the event that the girl's parents refuse his advances. These kinds of contacts, it should be understood, are clearly expected to lead to marriage. They are not arranged for the couple's personal enjoyment, but are serious indications of an interest in a future commitment.

Courtships in these traditional societies are actually centered more around the respective families and kin than the couple. In some cases, the young woman or the young man *may* have the right to veto the intended marriage, but the parents *always* have that right. The courting takes place between the families with the couple serving as the focus of the parents' arrangements. This is most obvious in the child marriages that were practiced in India for centuries. There was no premarital courtship between the couple at all in these cases. The courting that did occur in child marriages really involved a negotiation of the bride price and other arrangements between the respective fathers. There was little concern over the expected intrinsic satisfaction of the couple.

Parental negotiation

How do the young people in these societies feel about their parents controlling their courtship? David and Vera Mace (1960) interviewed a group of girls in India and found that they preferred their parents' participation to the youthful competitiveness they saw in Western courtship (see Vignette 3.1). Evidently, they were quite comfortable with the customs they had been taught to respect and with which they were familiar. Today, urban youth in India and many other parts of the world are beginning to have more control over their own courtship and mate selection. Parental involvement is still evident,

Vignette 3.1

Let Your Parents Select Your Mate?

"Wouldn't you like to be free to choose your own marriage partners, like the young people do in the West?"

"Oh no!" several voices replied in chorus.

Taken aback, we searched their faces.

"Why not?"

"For one thing," said one of them, "doesn't it put the girl in a very humiliating position?"

"Humiliating? In what way?"

"Well, doesn't it mean that she has to try to look pretty, and call attention to herself, and attract a boy, to be sure she'll get married?"

"Well, perhaps so."

"And if she doesn't want to do that, or if she feels it's undignified, wouldn't that mean she mightn't get a husband?"

"Yes, that's possible."

"So a girl who is shy and doesn't push herself forward might not be able to get married. Does that happen?"

"Sometimes it does."

"Well, surely that's humiliating. It makes getting married a sort of competition in which the girls are fighting each other for the boys. And it encourages a girl to pretend she's better than she really is. She can't relax and be herself. She has to make a good impression to get a boy, and then she has to go on making a good impression to get him to marry her."

Before we could think of an answer to this unexpected line of argument, another girl broke in.

"In our system, you see," she explained, "we girls don't have to worry at all. We *know* we'll get married. When we are old enough, our parents will find a suitable boy, and everything will be arranged. We don't have to go into competition with each other."

"Besides," said a third girl, "how would we be able to judge the character of a boy we met and got friendly with? We are young and inexperienced. Our parents are older and wiser, and they aren't as easily deceived as we would be. I'd far rather have my parents choose for me. It's so important that the man I marry should be the right one. I could so easily make a mistake if I had to find him for myself."

Another girl had her hand stretched out eagerly.

"But *does* the girl really have any choice in the West?" she said. "From what I've read, it seems that the boy does all the choosing. All the girl can do is to say yes or no. She can't go up to a boy and say 'I like you. Will you marry me?' can she?"

We admitted that this was not usually done.

"So," she went on eagerly, "when you talk about men and women being equal in the West, it isn't true. When our parents are looking for a husband for us, they don't have to wait until some boy takes it into his head to ask for us. They just find out what families are looking for wives for their sons, and see whether one of the boys would be suitable. Then, if his family agrees that it would be a good match, they arrange it together."

From David and Vera Mace, *Marriage East and West* (Garden City, N.J.: Doubleday, 1960), pp. 144–146.

but it appears that there is a general cultural drift toward young people having more influence and parents having less influence over the selection of friends and partners in both casual and serious relationships.

Courtship in Early America

New freedoms

Observers of the social history of America have witnessed a recurring pull between the traditions of the European continent and the new freedom and independence sought by the colonists and immigrants. The people who settled America were enticed by fresh opportunities; many had all but cut off ties to their distant kin-relations, and as migrants, they were the individuals least committed to the traditions of their native countries. The New World provided a degree of freedom for experimenting in religion, law, and government—and in interpersonal relations as well. The ideas and customs that emerged were a curious mixture of European yet American thinking. Nowhere is this better seen than in the courtship patterns that began to develop.

In the colonial period, the traditional European custom of parental control over courtship was largely retained. Sons did have the option of moving farther West to gain freedom from their parents, but this was usually done only as a last resort. A study of the public records of seventeenth-century Andover, Massachusetts, led one researcher to conclude that "more often than not, a son's marriage depended upon the willingness of his father to allow it and the ability of his father to provide the means for the couple's economic independence" (Greven, 1973, p. 85). A young man at that time needed land to support a wife, and this land usually came from his father during the negotiations between the parents of a couple proposing marriage. The degree of control that parents exercised over their children at that time is evident in the fact that only 16 percent of the sons left Andover to strike out on their own.

Bundling

Youth in colonial America did have some freedoms that might cause considerable astonishment, even today. One of the most interesting courtship customs of New England and Pennsylvania was **bundling.** This practice allowed a young man and woman to court each other at night in bed under the protective warmth of the covers. While this may seem *avant-garde,* there were legitimate reasons for the custom. Winter days in the North are quite short, and most homes in rural areas were quite far apart. After a young man had received permission to visit his intended lady friend, he had to finish the day's chores and then walk or ride the distance in the late afternoon to her parents' home. This left little time for the couple to talk together before the sun set so the young man would usually have to stay the night. Firewood was too scarce to burn only for the pleasure of the courting couple so the fire was allowed to die down in the evening. Since the family stayed warm by retiring under their quilts and the couple needed a chance to chat to get to know one another, the young man and woman were allowed to spend the night in the same bed. Outer garments such as shoes and coats were shed, but generally, both were fully clothed. After the night of conversation and sleep, the visitor returned to his family in the morning.

Actually, bundling was not as daring as it might appear. What the strict moral code of the day did not prevent, the usual presence of parents or younger siblings in the same room did. Later, a "bundling board" was introduced and placed between the couple to prevent physical contact. But the ultimate demise of this custom was a consequence of efficient heating and urbanization, which made possible the return of the young man to his own home at night. Courting then shifted from the bedroom to the parlor.

Decline in parental control

During the nineteenth century, particularly in urban America, a major change in parental control over courtship began to occur. According to an analysis of the marriage records of Hingham, Massachusetts, parents retained considerable influence over mate selection from 1647 to about 1810. But the records from 1810 to 1880 indicate much more freedom for youth. Courtship by the nineteenth century had become more an arrangement between individuals than families (Smith, 1973).

This new-found freedom, while limited primarily to urban youth, existed only within the context of rather "serious" intentions to marry. While the earlier requirement of asking the girl's parents for permission to call began to drop off, calling on a girl was still viewed as an interest in marriage. Casual boy-girl relationships were frowned upon and severely criticized. Thus, the underlying tension created by greater personal freedom in combination with considerable moral and social restraint probably was a major factor in the whirlwind courtships that characterized this period.

THE DATING SYSTEM

By the turn of the twentieth century, a new dimension to courtship had begun to develop—dating. This represented a revolutionary change in the way young men and women established relationships with one another. Unlike earlier courtship patterns, a "date" does not assume marriage, nor does it even assume a serious interest in marriage. Dating allows and encourages a period of dalliance, of freedom to explore the field of eligibles before settling down into one exclusive pair relationship.

The commitment on a date is for only a short period of time, usually an evening, not a lifetime. And this commitment is contracted by the couple themselves, not their parents, although the latter are often able to influence the dating relationship. Considerable independence is also allowed the dating couple: they can go off alone or with other youths, and direct parental supervision is not required and may even be regarded as interference.

The Emergence of Dating

The practice of dating first became popular among college students in the years after World War I (Gordon, 1978). During the 1920s, the practice

Dating provides a period of dalliance before settling into an exclusive pair relationship.

spread to couples in the high schools. By the 1940s, dating had become the accepted means for initiating pair relations throughout the United States—even junior-high-school youth were asking their parents for permission to date.

Factors encouraging dating

There are several factors that we can identify that probably encouraged the development and acceptance of dating. The first one is industrialization, which radically changed the interdependence of family members. Fathers, who were away from home much of the day, could not easily control the lives of their children. Women joined the labor force, especially during World War I, and generally began to demand more independence from the traditional domination of men. A consequence of this was that individual values began to take precedence over familial values; individual desires for personal happiness and success tended to diminish dedication to the family as a unit.

The urbanization of American society brought larger numbers of young men and women into close proximity with one another and enlarged the immediate availability of potential mates. There was a sense of anonymity experienced by young people in the cities that was not found in the close-knit communities of the rural hinterland. A boy and girl could easily arrange to meet at some predetermined place without their parents knowing. The growth of coeducation in colleges and secondary schools also encouraged informal meetings of young people outside the control of parents. This accented the growth of individual values that accompanied industrialization.

Dating was also encouraged by an increase in the amount of free time available to youth. Family responsibilities, farm work, and household chores no longer absorbed most of the waking hours of young people. The enactment of child-labor laws served to limit the employment of adolescents, and educational opportunities extended further the years of youthful freedom. The increase in potential leisure was accompanied by a decline in family-centered activities and increased dependence on commercial recreation. The cinema, soda fountains, dance halls, speakeasies, and amusements of all descriptions emerged to fill the idle moments of the young. They became places where young people would congregate and meet others, and they structured their leisure-time activities around them. This was the beginning of what we now call the "youth culture": a set of institutions specifically designed to maximize the freedom and expression of young men and women.

Youth culture

Nothing symbolized this new freedom better than the automobile. Like the courting parlor or the bundling bed of earlier times, the automobile became part of the background for developing heterosexual pair relationships. With the turn of an ignition key, the small steel structure with wheels could be transformed into a roving parlor providing more opportunities for intimacy than most couples had ever known before. And now, the youth were away from the watchful eyes of concerned parents.

Initiation into Dating

Dating preparation

As we noted in Chapter 2, preparation for heterosexual pairing begins very early. Broderick and Rowe (1968) discovered a series of stages that preadolescent boys and girls pass through that gradually prepare them for dating and eventually marriage. The first stage occurs in the preschool years, when young children begin to recognize that marriage is a heterosexual relationship. Next, the children come to realize that most people eventually marry and that marriage is an important and attractive part of their future. Broderick and Rowe stress that this is a critical point in relational development because until this personalization of the pairing process occurs, social relations with the opposite sex are very inhibited and most activities are restricted to the same sex. Boys, it appears, take longer to move toward this positive evaluation of marriage and its place in their own future than girls (Broderick, 1965).

Once preadolescents do take this step toward viewing marriage as desirable, however, they then single out one person of the opposite sex as particularly attractive and this person becomes an object of special affection. This "boyfriend" or "girlfriend" is sometimes imaginary, is often someone considerably older, such as a teacher or movie star, and is usually unaware of the secret admirer. Nevertheless, the feeling of being "in love" leads to a desire to be with someone of the opposite sex. This desire prepares the young person for actually going out on his or her first date.

Adolescent identity crisis

Getting into the dating routine is not easy for all young men and women. There are new roles to play, new pressures to handle, and new experiences to negotiate. Adolescence is one of those "in-between" periods of life—in this case, in between childhood and adulthood. This means that the cues regarding expected behavior are not always clear and sometimes are conflicting. The adolescents are frequently confused by being told, on the one hand, "You're too old to do that!" and, on the other, "You're too young to do that!"

Erik Erikson (1968), a psychologist who views human development as the resolution of a series of crises, says that the adolescent crisis is one of establishing a secure identity. The adolescent experiences role confusion, which comes from both parents and peers. Adolescents usually resolve this by placing a great deal of importance on the expectations of the peer group. Since dating is an important expectation of adolescent peers, success in dating is a key to establishing a secure self-concept and personal identity. But peer approval is not automatic: it has to be earned. Some of the anxiety that may accompany this process of acquiring peer approval through dating is well illustrated in Vignette 3.2.

Factors in Date Selection

Interpersonal attraction

Some advertisers would have us believe that by using a particular toothpaste, wearing the right shirt, or taking a series of dance lessons, we can directly manipulate the pairing process. Frankly, it does not hurt to appear clean,

Vignette 3.2

Do I Have to Date?

Through no fault of my own I reached adolescence. While the pressure to prove myself on the athletic field lessened, the overall situation got worse—because now I had to prove myself with girls. Just how I was supposed to go about doing this was beyond me, especially because, at the age of fourteen, I was four foot nine and weighed seventy-eight pounds. (I think there may have been one ten-year-old girl in the neighborhood smaller than I.) Nonetheless, duty called, and off I went.

To get a girlfriend, though, a boy had to have some asset beyond the fact that he was alive. I wasn't handsome like Bill McCord, who had girls after him like a cop-killer has policemen. I wasn't ugly like Romeo Jones, but at least the girls noticed him: "That ol' ugly boy better stay 'way from me!" I was just there, like a vase your grandmother gives you at Christmas that you don't like or dislike, can't get rid of, and don't know what to do with. More than ever I wished I were a girl. Boys were the ones who had to take the initiative and all the responsibility. (I hate responsibility so much that if my heart didn't beat of itself, I would now be a dim memory.)

It was the boy who had to ask the girl for a date, a frightening enough prospect until it occurred to me that she might say No! That meant risking my ego, which was about as substantial as a toilet-paper raincoat in the African stylish, or sophisticated (in some circles), but the fundamentals of interpersonal attraction are somewhat more complicated than that—especially in a society that gives considerable freedom to the participants in deciding whom they want to date. Three general factors that appear to be important in selecting or attracting a good partner include prestige considerations, physical attractiveness, and personality characteristics.

Peer considerations

Prestige. Almost all of us have some **reference group** that at least partially determines what we come to value the most. If we seek out those things that are highly valued by our peers, then we gain status and personal prestige; if not, we lose prestige in their eyes. Selecting a date also works this way. If we choose someone who has the characteristics that are valued by our peers, then this reflects favorably on us as well.

What kinds of factors are more likely to increase prestige in date selection? In some places, prestige may be gained by dating someone with a valued skill, such as surfing, tennis, skiing, swimming, or dancing. Going out with the football-team quarterback, head cheerleader, or student-body president could be considered important. Sometimes, prestige is tied to the date's focus of study. For example, a girl will probably gain more prestige for dating a student in medical school than one in forestry. Likewise, it may be more prestigious to date a lawyer than a bartender. It is not clear whether these occupational or future occupational prestige considerations apply equally to men and women. Because men tend to marry women who are lower in

---

rainy season. But I had to thrust that ego forward to be judged, accepted, or rejected by some girl. It wasn't fair! Who was she to sit back like a queen with the power to create joy by her consent or destruction by her denial? It wasn't fair—but that's the way it was.

But if (God forbid!) she should say Yes, then my problem would begin in earnest, because I was the one who said where we would go (and waited in terror for her approval of my choice). I was the one who picked her up at her house where I was inspected by her parents as if I were a possible carrier of syphilis. Once we were on our way, it was I who had to pay the bus fare, the price of the movie tickets, and whatever she decided to stuff her stomach with afterward. (And the smallest girls are all stomach.) Finally, the girl was taken home where once again I was inspected. The evening was over and the girl had done nothing except honor me with her presence. All the work had been mine.

Imagining this procedure over and over was more than enough: I was a sophomore in college before I had my first date.

The prestige of a football player may make him a preferred date.

occupational status than themselves, the female medical student may not yield as much prestige to the man who is looking for a future homemaker. These and other prestige considerations often differ for men and women, for various age groups, and for regions of the country. And they apply primarily in the initial attraction and selection of a partner.

Physical Attractiveness. The research on pair selection among strangers suggests that personal physical characteristics, such as facial attractiveness, physique, grooming, and dress are also related to an individual's popularity as a partner. In one study, college students at the University of Minnesota were randomly paired at a "computer dance." They were asked how they liked their "date" and later asked if they had gone out again. It was found that the degree of perceived physical attractiveness was the most influential factor in determining whether the men or women liked their partners and whether they had further dates. This factor was much more important to this group of students than personality and intellectual considerations (Walster *et al.*, 1966).

Sex stereotypes

Researchers have also found that the physical attractiveness of a partner tends to be more important to men than to women (Herold, 1979), but that it continues to be an important factor for both sexes over the initial series of encounters (Mathes, 1975). Interestingly, the importance of physical attractiveness in a date has some relationship to an individual's acceptance of sexual stereotypes. When college students were asked to rate the attractiveness of other men and women based on their photographs and a brief biography, those students who were themselves rated the most "macho" or "feminine" considered the pictured physical attractiveness of the individual most important in their evaluation of overall attractiveness. Meanwhile, the men and women who held fewer sexual stereotypes for themselves were less impressed by the pictures and more likely to use the biographies as the basis for their judgments of attractiveness (Touhey, 1979). Apparently, the eyes of highly masculine or feminine persons are more discriminating than others.

Personality Characteristics. When adolescents are asked to list qualities they are looking for in a date, their responses yield a set of valued personality characteristics. As an example, at a California college in 1976, a random sample of 341 men and 372 women were asked to list the three qualities they most valued in a date. The qualities they selected are listed in rank order in Table 3.1.

The fact that "looks" was the characteristic most frequently mentioned by both men and women supports the research on physical attraction. The importance of "sex appeal" to men also supports the contention that physical attractiveness may be more important to men than to women. After this, however, the students then indicated that a series of personality characteristics were important to them. The lists of the men and women are not really very different, although the men valued intelligence and companionship more important than the women did, while the women valued thoughtfulness, consideration, and honesty more than the men did.

Stages in date selection

Edward Herold (1974) has suggested that there are several stages to date selection, and the studies we have examined seem to support his contention. First, a potential date is evaluated in terms of his or her *physical appearance*. If

Table 3.1

Qualities of a Date Most Valued by College Men and Women

Rank	Women Desired in Men:	Men Desired in Women:
1	Looks	Looks
2	Personality	Personality
3	Thoughtfulness, consideration	Sex appeal
4	Sense of humor	Intelligence
5	Honesty	Fun, good companionship
6	Respect	Sense of humor
7	Good conversation	Good conversation
8	Intelligence	Honesty

Source: From *The Individual, Marriage and the Family,* Third Edition, by Lloyd Saxton. © 1977 by Wadsworth Publishing Company, Inc. Belmont, California 94002. Reprinted by permission of the publisher.

this is judged to be desirable or acceptable, then the dating partners evaluate one another's *social sophistication*. This is determined by their ability to get along well with others and by the impression they give of being outgoing and having personal confidence and savoir faire. These are the traits that students commonly refer to when they speak of "personality," the second factor listed in Table 3.1.

Relational commitments

According to Herold, peer-group assessments of the date choice are very important in the first two stages. An individual's prestige in a group may hinge on whether the group thinks he or she has made a "good" choice. The emphasis at this point is on an *instrumental* commitment to a dating partner that serves to enhance one's status among peers and others who are considered important. The *intrinsic* worth of the dating experience is measured primarily in terms of how interesting, stimulating, or exciting the experience is, characteristics which may move the relationship on to a higher level but can easily be outweighed by instrumental concerns. Of course, if an individual is highly independent of peer-group influences, then prestige considerations will not be very important in the dating evaluation.

If a relationship survives the first two criteria, then the couple will evaluate other personality traits such as honesty, reliability, stability, and intelligence. If these are judged to be satisfactory, then the relationship has some chance of continuing and developing the *intrinsic* commitments that ensure its maturity.

Herold concludes that this stage approach explains why students who rank personality traits high still base their initial date selection on more observable criteria. He comments somewhat dryly that:

> We have a dating system whereby . . . the dishonest person who has good looks and social sophistication is likely to date frequently, whereas the person who is honest and dependable but lacks in good looks and charm is less likely to date. Indeed, many students would not date at all rather than date someone who is considered to be physically unattractive and/or socially unsophisticated. (p. 119)

Breakups

Personal growth

Unpairing appears to be almost as normal a process as pairing. It is the rare person who marries his or her childhood sweetheart without ever dating someone else. A century ago, this would have been a typical experience, but today it is unlikely and probably unwise. In a complex society, the experience of "dating around" teaches us a lot about ourselves as well as others, thereby enhancing our personality growth and sharpening our definitions of what is desired in a mate. From this perspective, breakups, as painful as they sometimes are, may be more a sign of personal maturity and relational incompatibility than a consequence of the rather idiosyncratic factors upon which they are usually blamed.

Some years ago, Burgess and Wallin (1953) reported that many of the couples they studied eventually married when it would have been better if they had terminated their relationship. The signs of imminent separation were there and the couples often recognized that they had problems, but they were carried along to marriage by the simple existence of their pair identity. In these cases, the pain of breaking up earlier would have spared them the frustration of conflict and divorce later. Admittedly, many reasons for marital distress emerge only later, often after years of marriage, but in most cases, with careful analysis of the relationship during dating and courtship, people can identify many of the potential problems that can occur (Olson, 1980). The currently high divorce rate, especially in the early years of marriage, suggests that a large proportion of couples should have considered breaking up even earlier.

Factors in breakups

It is difficult to determine the incidence of relational breakups at the lower levels of interpersonal commitment. At one time or another, almost everyone has experienced the breakup of a casual or steady dating relationship. In a study that examined 231 college couples who were "going together," nearly half—103 of the couples—had already broken up after two years (Hill *et al.*, 1976). At the start of the study, the couples who eventually remained together and those who eventually separated differed little in their sexual intimacy, social-class backgrounds, or religiosity. The couples who eventually broke up, however, were found to have been less likely to see the probability of their marriage, less likely to be "in love" or dating exclusively, and tended to have been dating for a shorter period of time. Another important predictor of breakup was "unequal involvement" in the relationship. When one person was more involved than the other, the relationship was less likely to survive.

In this same study, the couples who broke up were asked to list some of the factors they felt contributed to the ending of their relationship. Overall, their major reason for courtship breakups can be described as simply a gradual loss of interest in the partner. In another study (Landis and Landis, 1973, p. 192), this was also the reason most likely to be given by persons who had broken their engagements. However, loss of interest, along with the recognition of differences and desires for independence, does not always mean just waning attraction for the partner; it may also mean a *relative* loss of interest because someone else has become more attractive.

Importance of contact

The fact that one-third of the couples broke up because of separation illustrates the importance of continued interaction and reinforcement of pair commitments. While the old adage, "absence makes the heart grow fonder" may be true in some cases, it is more likely that "absence makes the heart *wander*." This saying is supported by the finding that breakups in college relationships are most likely to occur during the months associated with semester breaks, new classes, and graduation (see Fig. 3.1). Apparently, to expect a couple to remain a couple without regular contact is to deny the very nature of what we call a relationship.

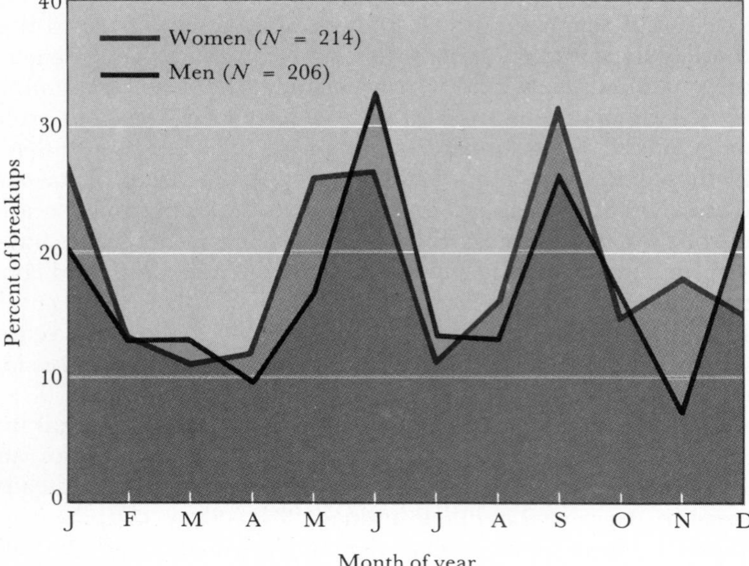

Fig. 3.1

Monthly Variations in Relational Breakups

Source: Hill *et al.*, *Journal of Social Issues* 32 (1976), p. 157. Used with permission of the Society for the Psychological Study of Social Issues.

CHANGING PATTERNS OF COURTSHIP

The process of initiating and developing pair relationships is continuing to undergo change. While many young people adhere to the conventional norms of the traditional dating system, others, particularly those who are college bound, are openly rejecting the structure and formality that characterized courtship in the 1950s and early 1960s. As an example, take a man and woman who room next to one another in a coed college dorm. After studying together for a math exam, they decide to go out for pizza to unwind a little. They split the tab, go for a short stroll around the campus, and return to the dorm. Have they had a "date"? More than likely they might tell a friend that they had "gone out" together, but it is doubtful that they would say that they had dated each other.

New courtship process

The stages of courtship are now much less clearly defined than they used to be. Not long ago, we might have described pairing as normally moving from a period of casual or random dating to going steady, engagement, and marriage. Each step carried clear signals of pair exclusiveness and increasing commitment to permanence. Today, the developmental process appears to be a continuum of growing commitment rather than a series of critical commitment decisions. Relationships between men and women are more casual and not always dependent on pairing. A mixed-sex group may simply go out together for an evening of talking, game playing, watching TV, or whatever. Pairing may not occur until later in the evening, sometimes not at all. This dalliance is followed by dating around, an informal period of going steady, a more serious steady relationship, perhaps pinning, an unannounced engagement, formal engagement, and, eventually, marriage.

This change in the structure of courtship has been accompanied by a delay in relational conmitments to permanency. Going steady, for example, used to be a prelude to formal engagement—a sign of marriage intentions. But today, a teenage girl or boy may have a numerous sequence of "steady" partners with little more than a commitment to "like" one another and to go out on Friday nights. Likewise, several decades ago, an engagement was considered a promise to marry. If this commitment was broken, the girl might have filed a "breach of promise" suit in the courts to force either the marriage or a financial settlement for the embarrassment and potential losses she incurred. But today, these court actions are very rare. We have come to assume that an engagement is still part of the testing period for pair commitment, not an irrevocable decision.

Permanent availability

Bernard Farber (1964) feels that a norm of "permanent availability" has come to pervade the entire process of courtship. That is, men and women today are more likely to maintain the option of considering alternative partners at any time. While this has been normal in early dating for some time, Farber suggests that it now includes engaged couples and even those who are married. In effect, for some people, the entire process of pairing may be characterized as a search for a more satisfactory relationship. Should this norm become generally accepted, there will be even more consideration given to individual values in courtship and there will be a greater decline in those family- and peer-reinforced commitments to permanency that used to characterize pairing.

Individual freedoms

One benefit of the increased individual freedom that we are experiencing can be seen in the relationships between men and women. It is the rare girl who is found huddled next to the hallway phone desperately waiting for some boy, any boy, to call. She also does not have to turn down "last minute" invitations out of a fear that she will be labeled "easy" or unpopular. There is less pressure on the boy to follow a rigorous "one-upsmanship" code of trying to outspend and outimpress all other potential suitors. Social gatherings are arranged much more informally, may result from a girl calling a boy she knows out of some direct or indirect pretense for meeting together, and often occur when a group of girls are introduced to a group of boys at some local meeting spot. Even the question of who pays the expenses is open to negotiation with fewer assumptions that it is the man who always foots the entire bill.

A primary reason for the change in these formal heterosexual relations is a continued decline in direct parental control over dating. By the time most youth are in high school, parents are more likely to be informed of a date than asked for permission to date. Parental concern remains, and controls can be and often are introduced if their wishes are not considered, but dating has become much more a **participant-controlled** as opposed to a **parent-controlled** system.

This is also true in college. The rule of *in loco parentis,* whereby colleges took it upon themselves to act as campus parents, has been considerably relaxed. On most campuses, the curfews, rules about off-campus visits, dress codes, sign-out sheets, and limits on dormitory visitors that used to be common are gone. Many colleges today have coed dorms in which men and women live on alternate floors or even in adjacent rooms. This has made relaxed meetings between men and women the rule more than the exception.

Dorm changes

These changes in courtship structure, formality, and commitment appear to be attracting a great deal of attention, although they may apply more to some regional areas and age groups than others. But it is also important to note that dating reflects personal and group-defined needs, and any city or campus may have several different dating-courtship patterns operating at any one time.

COHABITATION, OR LIVING TOGETHER

Among many youth, a relatively new dimension has been added to the pairing process. Instead of parting at midnight to return to their separate residences, many couples are living together in a life-style that resembles that of married couples. This is not really a new phenomenon, but the extent to which it has increased and the degree to which it has received public acceptance *are* new.

Consensual unions and common-law marriages have existed in practically all cultures. They are found in most of the world today, and they have received a degree of acceptance among the lower class in America. Middle-class America, however, has had a tradition of dealing harshly with those who propose any form of cohabitation without the benefit of marriage. During the 1920s Judge Ben Lindsey (1926) and Bertrand Russell (1929) published proposals for trial marriage and were severely criticized for their efforts. Russell even lost his teaching position at the City College of New York because of the publicity.

Two-step marriage

In the mid-1960s Margaret Mead (1966) wrote an article for *Redbook* magazine suggesting that a two-step marriage system might be workable. The first, an **individual marriage,** would limit obligations and commitments, allow no children, and be easy to end. Those who felt that the relationship was working well could go on to a **parental marriage,** which would be similar to what we expect of a more permanent union. Mead was roundly criticized in the press for this proposal and retracted it only a couple of years later (Mead, 1968).

Frequency of living together

Today, living together has reached such proportions that it can no longer be considered merely the misadventure of a few radical individuals. By 1979, over 1,500,000 adult couples were living together unmarried in the United States, nearly triple the figure for 1970 (see Fig. 3.2). One out of five of these couples lived with one or more children present. In one-fourth of the relationships, the man was under twenty-five years of age. In another

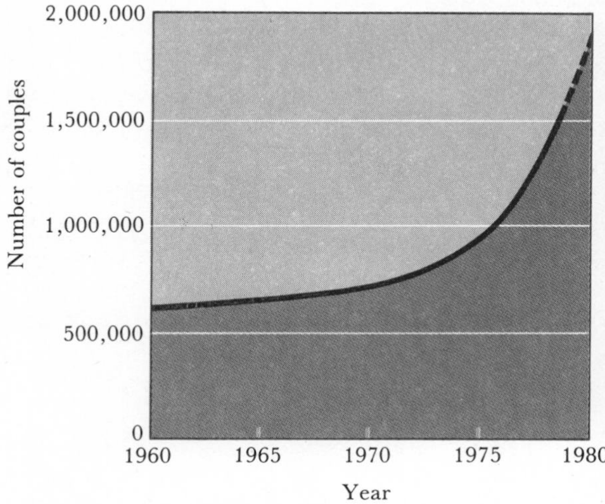

Fig. 3.2

Changes in Unmarried Couples Living Together in the United States

Source: Data from Paul Glick and Graham Spanier (1980), Married and Unmarried Cohabitation in the United States, *Journal of Marriage and the Family* 42: 19–30.

tenth of the couples, the man was over sixty-five years of age (Glick and Spanier, 1980). Many of these couples are from the lower social classes—one out of five cohabitants live below the poverty level—but others are financially successful, students, divorced, or retirees afraid of losing their social security benefits if they marry.

Cohabitation on college campuses has received the greatest attention from social scientists, and most of our discussion will focus on these student arrangements. While a number of studies have attempted to estimate the frequency of living together on campuses, this has not been easy since differences in the definition of cohabitation have varied from study to study and inadequate methods of sampling students' behavior have often been used (Cole, 1977). Nevertheless, it appears that the practice is now represented across the country on most campuses. The estimates of the percentage of students who have *ever* lived with someone of the opposite sex while unmarried range from near 0 percent at single-sex colleges or colleges that require all students to live on campus to about one-third of the students at some larger state universities (Macklin, 1978). Nationally, it has been estimated that about one-quarter of all undergraduate students have already experienced a period of cohabitation at some point in their lives (Bower and Christopherson, 1977).

Characteristics of Cohabitants

It may be surprising to some that researchers have not found many clear-cut differences between those who decide to cohabit and those who do not. Macklin (1978) reports that there is no evidence that cohabitants are more likely to come from broken homes; nor is there any difference in parents' education or income level. Parents who are concerned that cohabitation will

Nearly one-third of students at large state universities have engaged in cohabitation at some time.

result in lower academic performance should note that the grade-point averages are not significantly different between cohabitants and non-cohabitants.

Liberal values

The religion of parents is not an important factor in determining cohabitation experience, but those who cohabit are less likely to indicate a current religious affiliation and they have lower rates of church attendance (Peterman *et al.*, 1974). Couples who live together are also likely to hold more liberal attitudes and to label themselves as liberal compared to those who do not. Their sexual experiences tend to be greater, and they are more likely to have had a variety of sexual partners (Markowski *et al.*, 1978).

Cohabitation attitudes

Overall, most researchers have found more similarities than differences between cohabitants and non-cohabitants. According to a noted researcher in this area, "As people, cohabiting students seem to be representative of the general undergraduate population, with their cohabitation more a consequence of the opportunity for such a relationship" (Macklin, 1978, p. 5). This is evident among the non-cohabiting at sixteen universities surveyed by Bower and Christopherson (1977). When they were asked, "Would you want to cohabit?" over 50 percent indicated they would consider it. At Cornell (Macklin, 1974), the non-cohabitants were asked why they were not living with someone. Only 7 percent felt it was "morally wrong," while most responded that their partner lived too far away or that they had not yet met the right person. It is not clear whether these students were attempting to appear socially respectable or whether they were actually candidates for cohabiting arrangements. But the evidence does suggest that nonmarital cohabitation is likely to increase if opportunities are available.

While the amount of time and resources shared varies considerably, there are some consistent patterns that have been observed. Couples usually eat the majority of their meals together and do some of the chores together, although there is a tendency for the woman to assume responsibility for the cooking and cleaning. They tend to have more mutual than separate friends and to spend much of their time together with others as opposed to spending time only with one another. Very few couples ever totally pool their resources. Cohabitants usually speak of "his car" or "her dishes" rather than "our car" or "our dishes." Nevertheless, most living-together couples do share in the normal expenses for food and entertainment.

Styles of Living Arrangements

Five different styles

There are wide varieties of arrangements that may be included in the term cohabitation. Based on differences in the amount of time the couple spends together, the nature of the living arrangement, and their degree of commitment to one another, five basic types of cohabitation can be identified: (1) **temporary casual convenience,** where the couple shares living quarters because it is expedient; (2) **affectionate dating-going together,** in which the couple enjoys each other's company and will continue the arrangement as long as it is mutually desired; (3) **trial marriage,** which includes those who are consciously testing their relationship before deciding to marry; (4) **temporary alternative to marriage,** in which the couple is committed to staying together but finds marriage currently inconvenient; and (5) **permanent alternative to marriage,** which includes individuals who have long-term stable commitment to their relationship but who do not want traditional legal sanctions (Macklin, 1978).

It is difficult to determine the relative frequency of these types of cohabitation, but most researchers agree that the college cohabitation most approximates the Type 2 pattern, which is a extension of the courtship process (Newcomb, 1979). The majority of cohabitants themselves indicate that their experience is really different from marriage, or at least they want it that way. Most indicate that they are not yet ready for a marital commitment. Nevertheless, couples who are living together usually view their relationship as "intimate" and "loving." About 70 percent of the Cornell cohabitants checked "emotional attachment to the other" as their primary reason for living together (Macklin, 1974). At Penn State, 83 percent of the men and 86 percent of the women indicated that they experienced a "love" as opposed to a "friendship" or other relationship with their partner (Peterman *et al.*). Among Arizona State cohabitants, 6 percent were engaged, 14 percent tentatively engaged, and an additional 49 percent checked "strong affectionate tie—not dating others" to describe their relationship (Henze and Hudson, 1974). These are obviously not casual relationships. Most of the participants share deep emotional ties to one another.

Relational and marital commitments

A study at the University of Georgia compared matched samples of cohabiting, engaged, and married couples to see how they differed in relational and marital commitments (Lewis *et al.*, 1977). There were 61 individuals interviewed in each of the three groups. As expected, the married persons in the study were found to be the most personally committed to their partners. But the researchers were surprised to find that the unmarried cohabitants were equally as committed to their partners as the engaged ones were to theirs. The primary difference between the engaged couples and the cohabitants was their commitment to marriage. Many of the cohabitants did not feel that they could stretch immediate commitment into a long-term obligation. Perhaps this difference in commitment is why one study found that cohabiting couples were just as likely to break up as dating couples (Hill *et al.*).

Options kept open

The dominant attitude of the living-together couples in these studies seems to be one of trying to make their present relationship personally meaningful but keeping their options open for the future. To the extent that this occurs, living together might best be viewed as another dimension in the contemporary courtship process—a means for learning more about oneself and another—not an alternative or "trial" marriage. Whether living together is a better means of determining relational compatibility is still open to question, however. The evidence we have to date does not indicate that married couples who have cohabited experience better or worse marital-adjustment problems than those who have not had this experience (Jacques and Chason, 1979).

Reasons for Living Together

One cannot help being impressed by the very strong, positive attitudes toward cohabitation held by many of those who have experienced it. In every study, the participants have expressed feelings of increased emotional maturity, more self-confidence, better awareness of what they want in marriage, and increased capacities for understanding and meeting the needs of another.

Personality growth

This desire to escape the superficiality that sometimes accompanies courtship is a common theme among youth who are living together. They voice a genuine concern that a person cannot *really know* what another is like as long as their contacts are limited to those times when each can be on his or her best behavior. Living together forces couples to drop these false messages, to let their real selves begin to interact with one another, yet they can still retain the option of terminating the arrangement if it does not appear to be working or growing.

Living together can also be a response to the impersonality of many large campuses (or large cities). The student in a dorm, attending classes with 25,000 strangers, standing in line at the cafeteria, smiling through "mixers" and taking computer-marked exams, often ends up feeling utterly alone. A living-together arrangement, in contrast, offers a sense of intimacy and belonging.

Practical reasons

A practical reason for living together cited by many couples is the time and money it can save. Housekeeping is consolidated, and there are fewer trips back and forth between residences. Undoubtedly, the continued cost of maintaining two "official" residences does limit the actual financial saving for most couples. But a real concern of many of these couples is the loss of their parents' financial support if they were to marry.

Some might consider regular sexual relations the primary motivation for living together. But this appears to place emphasis in the wrong place. Eleanor Macklin (1974) concludes from her investigation:

> The pattern which is evolving is primarily concerned with total relationships, and only incidentally with the sexual aspects, which are assumed to grow as the relationship grows. Cohabitation seems to grow out of a desire to know another as a whole person, and to be with and to share as openly and completely as possible with that person. To focus exclusively on the sexual involvement leads to a very narrow interpretation of the situation. (p. 57)

Problems with Living Arrangements

Overdependence

As might be expected, there are a number of problems that cohabitants often encounter. One of the major emotional problems mentioned by these couples is a tendency to become overinvolved, to feel a subsequent loss of identity and overdependence on the relationship. These feelings were expressed by two-thirds of those living together in two studies (Macklin, 1974; Shuttlesworth and Thorman, 1973). Interestingly, this suggests that the quasi-independence they seem to want may be rather elusive once emotional commitments begin to expand.

Sexual problems are common but not serious, and sound very much like those problems encountered by young married couples. Differing degrees of sexual interest, fear of pregnancy, and occasional failures to reach orgasm are most frequently mentioned by cohabitants. Still, 96 percent of the couples in one study rated their relationship as sexually satisfying (Macklin, 1974).

Parental objections

By far the most difficult and painful problems encountered are those presented by parents—especially parental objections to the partner and fear of parental disapproval of the arrangement. Because of this fear of parental interference, nearly three out of four cohabitants in most studies indicate that they have tried, at some point, to conceal the relationship from their parents and that they do not feel comfortable discussing their relationship with their parents (Macklin, 1974; Peterman *et al.*; Henze and Hudson). The elaborate schemes used by many to conceal the truth from their parents could almost serve as training for the CIA. In fact, local phone company installers claim it is now common practice to install two phones on separate lines in many of these apartments. *She* never answers the red phone and *he* never answers the blue one.

Whether or not the parents know what is going on is often difficult to determine. Parents may be experiencing some of the same anxieties and concerns that the students themselves hold. About half of the women in one study felt that they had successfully concealed their relationship from their parents, while the parents of the other half either knew or were thought to have known about it (Macklin, 1974). The parents of the men were more likely to know and were considered to be less of a problem. Nevertheless, feeling this need to hide the cohabitation experience appears to bring considerable disappointment and conflict into the relationship of the couple because they are unable to communicate or share an important part of their lives with other persons they care for.

MATE SELECTION: DETERMINING THE FIELD OF ELIGIBLES

Throughout the process of dating and courtship, individuals are fine-tuning their expectations for a marital partner. For this reason, it is difficult to make a realistic separation between dating and mate selection. In fact, the entire system of pairing is oriented toward developing competence in making interpersonal commitments, and these eventually lead most people to marriage.

More than luck

It sometimes appears that two people who marry "just happen" to meet, fall in love, and eventually commit themselves to one another. After all, how else can you explain the circumstances that lead a young man and woman from different cities or towns to go to the same college, enroll in the same class, sit next to one another, and so on. At first glance, this all sounds like a matter of luck, fate, or destiny. Nevertheless, a closer examination reveals that luck is actually a minor factor in pairing, and it only operates after considerable preselection has already taken place. We have already identified several factors such as physical characteristics, personality, and prestige characteristics that make initial attraction more than just a matter of luck. But even more than this, there are a number of other controls operating informally and formally to limit the **field of eligibles** to a select group of potential candidates.

Mate-selection rules

The two most restrictive limits on mate selection come from rules of exogamy and endogamy. **Exogamy** refers to those requirements for marrying someone *outside* a particular social group or category. The most common exogamous rules forbid marriages within certain sex and kinship boundaries. In contrast, **endogamy** requires mate selection *between* persons of a particular social group. In American society, racial endogamy is most easily noticed, but elsewhere these rules may also apply to religion, social class, or ethnic background. These in-group and out-group restrictions on mate selection are usually so clear that we rarely give them much thought. But they also carry strong social and often legal sanctions against persons who ignore them.

Another major consideration in mate selection is **homogamy,** or the tendency for persons to marry others who are similar to themselves in characteristics such as age, religion, education, or intelligence. The penalties for not conforming to homogamy are weaker than those for exogamy and endogamy, but there are definite pressures to follow culturally defined homogamous criteria.

Kinship Restrictions

Incest taboos

Practically every society known prohibits marriage, and sex relations in general, between members of the same family. These **incest taboos** vary in the extent of the kin network that is included in the taboo, but Murdock's (1949) survey of 250 societies found evidence of restrictions on incest in every culture he studied. In most societies sex relations are strictly forbidden between siblings and between parents and their offspring. Marriages between these persons are illegal throughout the United States.

Although kinship restrictions in mate selection exist everywhere, the degree of restriction varies considerably. In some parts of the world, a mate cannot be selected from anyone in the entire clan, tribe, or village. Most states in the United States do not permit marriage to uncles and aunts or even between first cousins, although some states do permit first-cousin marriages. In much of the Middle East, on the other hand, first-cousin marriages are legal and often the preferred arrangement.

Sex Restrictions

Certainly, one of the strongest restrictions on the field of eligibles in mate selection is the sex of the individuals. Marriages between persons of the same sex have not been given general support in the public or the legal system. Indeed, homosexuals themselves are not usually accorded a favorable community image, despite the protests of the Gay Liberationists. At present, the legality of homosexual relationships between consenting adults varies from state to state, but no state yet recognizes a marriage between two persons of the same sex.

Age

Age differences

In most heterosexual pair relationships, the age difference between the man and woman is relatively small. While our courtship norms encourage relationships in which the man is older than the woman, they also suggest that he should not be too much older. These norms result in an age difference of less than five years for two-thirds of all marriages.

Pair relationships between younger men and older women are still the exception.

The difference in age between men and women at marriage has been narrowing over the last century. In 1890, women tended to marry men four years older than themselves; this has declined to a two-year differential today. For those who go on to college, the average age at marriage is higher than the national average, but the age difference between partners remains. Also, as the age of the men and women increases, the age differential becomes less important in selecting a mate.

Race

Restrictions on racial intermarriage, while informal, are almost as firm as the legal controls on kinship and sex exogamy. In 1967, the United States Supreme Court erased the statutes of the sixteen states that still prohibited intermarriage by race. Nevertheless, the proportion of individuals who select a mate from another race remains very small. Fewer than 1 percent of all black and white men and women in the United States marry someone of another race. Persons of races other than black or white are somewhat more likely to marry outside their own group, but this is because they make up a smaller percentage of the population and they may have a more difficult time finding a suitable mate from their own race. When there are concentrations of racial or ethnic minorities in particular communities, such as Chinatown in San Francisco, then the opportunities for selecting a mate of the same race are good and the degree of racial endogamy is high.

Racial intermarriages

Even though American society seems to have become increasingly liberal in its attitudes, and even though interracial contact has become more frequent, there has been very little change in the degree of acceptance of cross-racial mate selection. From 1970 to 1978, there was a 92 percent increase in black-white marriages, but this still accounted for fewer than 1 percent of all marriages (United States Bureau of the Census, 1979). Parents and peers are rarely supportive of mate selection across race, and according to one study, "For those who violate this convention, the tuition is high" (Petroni, 1973, p. 145). One high school girl who was dating interracially expressed her feelings this way:

> At school there was a lot of talking behind my back and snickering when I walked down the hallway. I tried to tell myself it didn't matter what people thought, but it still hurt. It hurt an awful lot. My parents made me feel so guilty. They made me feel so cheap. They were worried about what people would say. They made me feel like two pieces of dirt. (Petroni, p. 145)

When interracial mate selections are made, they tend to occur among people from larger cities, who are religiously less devout, and who have been reared in more stressful family situations (Heer, 1966). Clearly, men and women who have these characteristics are more independent and less subject to pressures from parents and peers.

The most common arrangement in black-white marriage is the black husband and the white wife. This pattern is also increasing proportionately faster than marriages of white husbands and black wives. During the 1960s, there was a 62-percent increase in black husband–white wife marriages compared to an 8-percent increase in white husband–black wife marriages (Heer, 1974). The fact remains, however, that the actual frequency of interracial marriages remains quite small, and there is little evidence to suggest that this is changing.

Religion

Religious intermarriage

Attitudes toward religious intermarriage have traditionally been almost as negative as those toward racial intermarriage. Practically all religious groups—Protestant, Catholic, and Jewish—have encouraged or demanded religious homogamy. Many Protestant ministers have been enjoined from participating in weddings of mixed religious couples. Until 1970, Roman

Catholics required the non-Catholic party to sign a "prenuptial agreement" promising to study to learn Catholic doctrine, not to hinder the faith of the Catholic member, and to rear the children of the marriage in the Catholic faith. Jewish leaders have been almost as adamant, even to the point of threatening the loss of family membership among some Orthodox Jewish groups.

How effective have these "encouragements" been in producing religious homogamy? Actually, they have been very effective. Carter and Glick (1970) estimate that if couples completely disregarded religion as a factor in mate selection, 44 percent would marry someone of another faith. But according to the data analyzed by Monahan (1971), only about 10 percent of all couples marry outside their faith. Both of these estimates, however, assume that inter-Protestant marriages are not mixed marriages, which is probably questionable. While specific rates of intermarriage vary, according to most studies, Catholics are more likely to marry outside their faith than Protestants or Jews (Alston *et al.,* 1976).

Social Class

Level of education

Most women and men rather carefully select partners from within their own social class. This is true even today when class lines are considered less rigid than earlier. Among college students at one university, researchers found that there was a clear tendency to date and marry people whose fathers had a similar level of occupational status (Eshleman and Hunt, 1965). Another indicator of social class is level of education, and studies have consistently found that husbands and wives tend to be very similar in their completed years of education. In 1970, for example, the United States Census Bureau (1972) reported that 76 percent of the persons who had married in the previous decade were at the same or adjacent levels of education (each level defined in terms of years of education completed: 0–4, 5–7, 8, 9–11, 12, 13–15, 16, and 17 years or more).

These tendencies toward social-class homogamy may be changing, but, if they are, it is ever so slightly. As long as level of education, income, and occupational prestige influence our life-style, our day-to-day behavior, where we live, who we feel comfortable with, and how we establish and develop our future goals, similarity in social-class background will be found in couples who are courting. If society becomes more homogeneous—that is, if the life-style of the union truck driver begins to resemble that of the corporate accountant—then perhaps this factor will decline in importance. No doubt, we are moving toward a more socially and economically homogeneous society, but it will be a long time before social class becomes an insignificant factor in mate selection.

THEORIES OF MATE SELECTION

We have examined some of the factors that influence who is eligible to be selected as a mate as well as the conditions that lead to initial attraction. This leaves us with still another question: what are the principal factors within the individuals in a pair relationship propelling them toward commitment, even marriage? This question has long interested sociologists and psychologists, and the theories included in this section point to the wide spectrum of opinion that presently exists in this area.

Complementary-Needs Theory

"Opposites attract"?

While homogamy principles are based on considerable evidence that "likes attract," the complementary-needs theory assumes that in certain personality areas "opposites attract." Robert Winch (1963), who initiated this controversial theory, states that "within the field of eligibles, persons whose need patterns provide mutual gratification will tend to choose each other as marriage partners" (p. 607). Furthermore, according to Winch, the needs that most people find mutually gratifying are those that are contrasting or dissimilar to their own rather than those that are similar. For example, his theory would predict that someone who has high achievement motivation would select a mate who has low achievement motivation, and someone who wants to be dominant would select someone who wants to be submissive.

While the theory appears to be logical, the majority of research on married couples has found that the norm in personality needs is similarity—not dissimilarity. Winch's (1958) attempt to demonstrate the theory has been severely criticized for its limited sample size and its dependence upon rather subjective measures of "need." Most studies that have used larger samples with more reliable measures have refuted the theory (Nias, 1977).

Parent-Image Theory

Freudian theory

One of the basic assumptions of Freudian psychology has been that the first love attachment of the child is to its opposite-sex parent (Freud, 1927). This attachment is supposedly repressed after the Oedipal or Electral conflict, but during mate selection the early love manifests itself in a search for a person who is physically and temperamentally similar to that parent. Following this line of reasoning, a man seeks a wife who is like his mother and a woman seeks a husband like her father.

Although this sort of analysis has played a large role in courtship folklore, it is of doubtful importance in the reality of mate selection. When a parent image is important, it is more likely to be mother's image, and it influences both sons and daughters (Aron *et al.*, 1974). The idea that daughters select husbands that are like their fathers, the classical Freudian hypothesis, has received very little support in research.

Exchange Theory

Exchange theory is a general economic or maximum-profit theory of human relationships. It is not a mate-selection theory *per se,* but it has increasingly been examined in these terms. According to exchange theory, individuals are motivated to maximize their own personal gain in relationships with others. Therefore, we are likely to be attracted to those who can give us the greatest rewards with the least personal cost. The problem is that other people are usually doing the same thing, so pairs with fairly equal resource demands tend to pair because they are best able to maximize the rewards each is seeking (Scanzoni, 1979). This kind of equal-exchange process is one explanation of why homogamy is so often found in social and personal resource areas such as education, social class, intelligence, physical attractiveness.

Comparison levels

To a degree, this theory tends to equate interpersonal relations with a market-type economy—each person is assumed to be selfishly trying to get the

Vignette 3.3 The Interpersonal Marketplace

You look up from your menu in an exclusive restaurant to see an unlikely couple enter. The woman is a strikingly attractive blonde in her late twenties. She has bright eyes, a flawless complexion, an outstanding figure. She is smiling down at her escort, who is a short, balding man some fifteen years her elder, with small, beady eyes and protruding ears. If you are the sort who puzzles over such mysteries, you will quickly reduce the situation to several possibilities. He might be a visiting cousin from Kansas City, but that doesn't seem too likely. You notice that both of them are wearing wedding rings. They seem, in fact, to be married to each other. This inference is soon confirmed when the headwaiter greets them deferentially as Mr. and Mrs. Pennypacker. You entertain the possibility that he might be an internationally known poet or philosopher who swept her off her feet when she was in his class at Sarah Lawrence. But much more likely in your mind is the remaining possibility that he is extremely rich—the heir of the Pennypacker Department Stores or the Pennypacker Copper Mines or both.

The chances are good that you would be right. Both the beautiful woman and the wealthy man have something of value to offer one another. She can please him aesthetically, and, perhaps more importantly, she can enhance his esteem in the eyes of others. As Thorsten Veblen put it in *The Theory of the Leisure Class,* attractive women "enable successful men to put their prowess in evidence by exhibiting some durable result of their exploits." He, in turn, can provide her with a standard of living that she would not otherwise be able to attain. The result, following the trading rules of the interpersonal "best deal" he or she can. Actually, however, the market is not that open, as most people come to realize quite early. We can usually hope to establish a meaningful relationship only with someone at or below a certain resource level. This has been called the **comparison level of exchange** (Thibaut and Kelley, 1959). For each individual, this level is a sort of balance between his or her fear of being rejected by someone with more assets and his or her fear of being "used" by someone with fewer assets.

The comparison level, therefore, is an average level of desirability that most people feel they can reasonably achieve without a net loss or risk of failure. For example, exchange theory suggests that a less attractive male may wish a date with a very attractive female, but he will probably not risk a request unless he has other attractive resources such as intelligence, nice clothes, fancy car, or upper-class family background. Likewise, a female lawyer may be chided by her friends if she were to marry a local plumber, but if he is a successful plumbing contractor, prominent in city politics, this would be a different story. Of course, the comparison level varies according to each person's estimate of his or her own attractiveness, which may change over time. But the more serious the potential relationship, the more critical the screening process will be (see Vignette 3.3).

---

marketplace, is that attractive women and successful men are likely to become paired with one another—and that, moreover, the more attractive the woman, the more successful the man is likely to be. North Carolina sociologist Glen H. Elder, Jr., recently documented this principle statistically. Elder analyzed data on the marriages of a group of women whose physical attractiveness had been rated many years earlier, when they were still in high school. He found that the girls rated as better looking were more likely than their less attractive classmates to end up marrying higher-status men.

A woman's beauty and a man's wealth are by no means the only relevant commodities in the interpersonal marketplace. In many contexts, in fact, these commodities are much less important than other characterisitcs. In the small towns of eastern Europe, wealthy Jewish merchants would try—often with the help of the local matchmaker—to marry their daughters off to poor but talented scholars from the local yeshiva. In such a case the woman's economic status was being exchanged for the man's intellectual and spiritual distinction. Other exchanges involve the social status of one partner and the economic status of another. As part of the marriage settlement between Consuelo Vanderbilt and His Grace the Ninth Duke of Marlborough, the Duke was reportedly guaranteed for life the income from $2,500,000 of Beech Creek Railway stock.

From Zick Rubin, *Liking and Loving: An Invitation to Social Psychology* (New York: Holt, 1973), pp. 67–69.

Exchange theory, as an explanation of mate-selection principles, is admittedly somewhat harsh and perhaps overly rational. Also, serious question can be raised over whether exchange theory explains relationships based on intrinsic commitments as well as those based on instrumental commitments. True, love is not blind to status or other social differences, but it may represent more than an efficient bargain over rewards between two people. The sociologist Peter Blau (1964), one of the formulators of exchange theory, noted very carefully the fact that the exchange process differs in these two types of relationships. According to Blau, while people making instrumental commitments are primarily motivated to maximize their own interests, this kind of motivation also leads to exploitation, which is incompatible with intrinsic commitments. Perhaps this is why some studies of engaged and married couples have not supported exchange theory as the primary determinant of advanced relational commitment (Centers, 1975; Murstein *et al.*, 1977).

Exploitation

Developmental Theory

One of the major problems with most mate-selection theories is that they try to predict who will marry whom based on a very limited number of characteristics. Pairing, as complex a process as it is, can rarely be explained so simply. A developmental approach is different in that it attempts to consider the fact that criteria for selection may vary according to the level of pair commitment. The more relational commitment a couple experiences, the more factors each person takes into account in deciding whether to go even further in commitment.

Developmental theorists view evaluation of value compatibility as an important stage in pair commitment.

Murstein (1970) uses a filter model combined with exchange theory to build a multistage theory of mate selection (see Fig. 3.3). He calls his approach **S-V-R theory,** after its principal filter components: *stimulus, values,* and *role.* Murstein says that we evaluate potential partners according to certain criteria, and these criteria change over time. But within each stage of the relationship, an exchange evaluation of relative assets and liabilities takes place.

Mate-selection stages

According to S-V-R theory, initial pair selections are made from a relatively "open field" of eligible partners. In this first, or stimulus stage, attraction is usually based on physical attributes, but social, mental, and reputational factors are also considered. A relationship is established, however, only if "premarital bargaining," in the exchange-theory sense, establishes a balance between the assets and liabilities of each person.

Assuming that an effective stimulus bargain is made, the couple then evaluates their compatibility in values. As they talk to one another, they begin to explore each other's attitudes toward sex, religion, marriage, and work. If their values in most areas are perceived to be similar, then they advance to the role stage. During this final period, the actual and expected behavior of the partners is considered to determine whether their wants and needs are compatible. Murstein explains that these role expectations for the future, for marriage, and for the dating relationship must "fit" together if the pair is to advance further toward marriage. Couples who do not meet each of the filter criteria are more likely to break up and return to being eligible for new relationships.

S-V-R theory appears to provide a good synthesis of most of what we have learned about mate selection. The importance of physical attraction, value similarity, and common role definitions has been noted often in family research. One of the theory's principal advantages may be in mellowing and

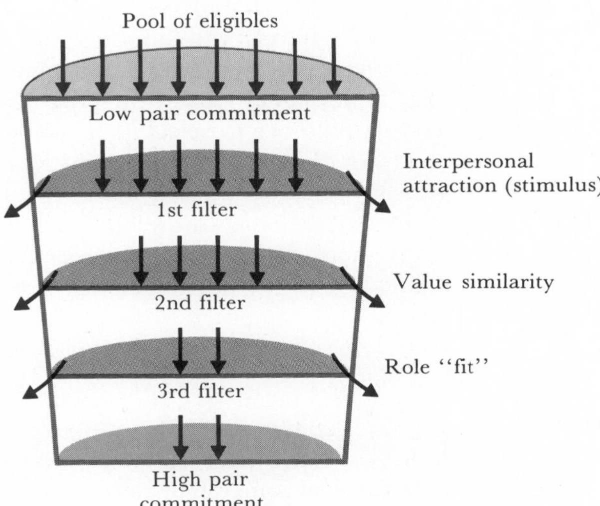

Fig. 3.3
A Developmental Theory of Mate Selection
Source: Adapted from Murstein, 1970.

humanizing exchange theory and demonstrating how it can be effectively used in a developmental model.

Nevertheless, the jury is still out in determining whether S-V-R theory best describes the reality of selecting a mate. Murstein's own study of ninety-nine student couples confirms each of his hypotheses, and a related study by Lewis (1973) also found a similar pattern of relational development. Another study, however, found that the "filtering" of values occurs very early in relationships and that stimulus factors continue to be important throughout courtship (Hill *et al.*). The factors appear to be important, but perhaps the stages are not as clear-cut as Murstein proposes. In any case, this theory represents one of the most carefully considered descriptions of contemporary mate selection that has been offered to date.

Summary

The process of premarital pairing has undergone considerable change. Traditionally, pair relationships were based on more instrumental commitments and parents held more control over courtship than the couple. With dating, intrinsic couple commitments began to take precedence over instrumental concerns.

There appear to be several important characteristics that are evaluated when selecting a pair partner. These include the person's physical attractiveness, ability to provide some prestige with peers, and personality characteristics. The structure of premarital pairing has continued to undergo change, and several new patterns have developed as well. Courtship has become less formal, less dependent upon clearly defined stages, and less committed to pair permanency.

Nonmarital cohabitation has become more accepted as a legitimate experience for determining pair compatibility. Studies have found few differences between cohabiting and noncohabiting students and some indication that this type of relationship may be more common in the future.

When it comes to selecting a pair partner, especially a mate, culturally defined rules of exogamy, endogamy, and homogamy come into play. Several theories have been proposed to explain how our choices are eventually narrowed to one person. Complementary-needs theory, parent-image theory, exchange theory, and developmental theory suggest how partner selections are made, but as yet no theory has received unqualified support.

SUGGESTIONS FOR ADDITIONAL READING

Erikson, Erik. *Identity, Youth, and Crisis.* New York: Norton, 1968.
An analysis by a noted psychologist of the developmental crises faced by youth. An excellent source for understanding the social and psychological strains of adolescence.

Hill, Charles, Zick Rubin, and Letitia Peplau."Breakups before marriage: the end of 103 affairs," *Journal of Social Issues* 32 (1976): 147–168.

Not only is this a unique study of the reasons couples who are seriously dating break up, but the authors also examine some of the factors that explain why other couples stay together.

Huston, Ted L. (ed.). *Foundations of Interpersonal Attraction.* New York: Academic Press, 1974.

A well-rounded source book on a variety of approaches to interpersonal attraction. The chapters are written by respected authorities in the field.

Newcomb, Paul R. "Cohabitation in America: an assessment of consequences," *Journal of Marriage and the Family* 41 (1979): 497–603.

An excellent summary of the research on nonmarital cohabitation in America.

Stephens, William N. *The Family in Cross-Cultural Perspective.* New York: Holt, 1963.

The author discusses courtship and mate-selection in a variety of cultures. A generous use of examples from many of these cultures makes the material particularly interesting.

Chapter 4

Marriage: Contracts and Commitments

There are few events in our lives as significant as marriage. At the time of marriage, we frequently find the rituals of sacred holidays, birthdays, and the New Year all wrapped up together. Gifts are presented, spiritual guidance is evoked, family support is encouraged, parties are given, resolutions for the future are made, and the date is remembered for future anniversaries. All these elements are designed to provide community, family, and interpersonal support for those couples who are creating a more permanent pair identity. This need to support formal pair commitments is so universal that every known human society provides some means for identifying and approving its newly marrying members.

But marriage is more than a ceremony, an event to be fondly recalled in the pictures of a wedding book. It is also an institution, a status, and a contract; it is a multifaceted arrangement designed to meet the needs of individuals and of society. For society, marriage fulfills many of its basic requirements for order and survival. Marriage provides an outlet for sexual intimacy and a stable relationship for socializing children. It provides kinship bonds to link the generations, and it establishes formal channels for economic support and the inheritance of property. The Supreme Court of the United States recognized this in 1888 (*Maynard* v. *Hill*) when it ruled:

> Marriage . . . is an institution, the maintenance of which in its purity the public is deeply interested; for it is the foundation of the family and of society, without which there would be neither civilization nor progress.

For individuals, marriage is a personal status. It represents the culmination of courtship and a new stage in the process of pair development. It symbolizes a higher level of relational commitment, and it is a signal to others that this couple intends to find a common future together. Achieving the status of being married also gives us society's stamp of approval, providing a type of personal **self-validation.** According to Ralph Turner (1970):

> Marriage is one of the key devices, along with becoming financially self-sufficient, for validating personal adequacy, heterosexual normality, and personal maturity. Learning this connection explicitly or implicitly, most individuals expect to become married on reaching maturity. (p. 51)

Another very important dimension of marriage is its contractual nature. There are privileges and rights that accompany marital status, but it also carries social obligations. Some obligations are legally spelled out and bear the full weight of the law. For example, married people are usually aware that by legal contract they cannot marry anyone else. But there are other contractual obligations also included in marriage: those implied by social conventions and interpersonal agreements. Marriage is as much a personal pledge as it is a legal agreement. And some of the implied contracts in marriage, such as not dating anyone else or providing happiness and companionship to one's partner, can be just as demanding and personally restricting as those commitments defined by law.

In the present chapter, we will focus our attention on the contractual obligations of marriage and how they are changing. The legal framework of marriage will serve as a foundation for this discussion since we must understand the variety of rules and regulations that bind the individual to society through marriage even today. The interpersonal contract implied in marriage will then be examined, particularly as it defines the conditions necessary for personal adjustment and marital success. Next, we will explore the ways in which some couples are now redesigning marriage by writing their own contracts in an effort to meet the special needs they feel are important.

MARRIAGE: THE LEGAL CONTRACT

Civil obligations

When we say that marriage is a legal contract, we mean that it involves civil obligations to the state. These obligations reflect the heritage of the marriage institution, which traditionally placed the responsibility for ensuring the marital bond on influences *outside* of the marrying pair, such as the family, community, church, or state. Interpersonal preferences did not play a major role in marital bonding until quite recently. Over the known history of marriage, Jessie Bernard (1972) concludes:

> Estate, income, family connections were important considerations; the nature of the relationship between the spouses was secondary. . . . It was always considered desirable if the partners also found one another congenial; but, in any event, they had to learn to come to terms with each other no matter what happened. The institution was far more important than the individuals themselves. (p. 104)

The earliest conceptions of marriage placed the major responsibility for creating and maintaining a marriage on the social system of the family and community. Little more than a verbal agreement was necessary from the couple since the obligations that were being assumed carried the weight of intense community pressure. The influence of parents on mate selection and marital stability was considerable at that time.

Community responsibility

Church authority

With the growth of the church, particularly the state church during the Middle Ages, marriage came increasingly under sacred authority (see Fig. 4.1). Marital regulations informally controlled by the customs of the community gave way to formally instituted sacraments and divine responsibilities. The concept of "holy matrimony" meant that the couple was tied together in a bond made not by the family, but by God. The community obligation of procreation did not change, but the development of broader, churchwide marital standards gave couples slightly more freedom within the context of what were considered to be divine laws of marriage.

Civil contract

By the nineteenth century, these sacred concepts of marriage had also become the foundation for our civil concepts of marriage. "Because family law matters were originally within the exclusive jurisdiction of the church," says Lewis (1977), "our secular laws have been shaped almost entirely by ecclesiastical precepts" (p. 1). Thus, the civil contract of marriage retained many of the earlier obligations required by community and sacred authorities, including the expectance of procreation, more responsibility to institutional than to personal interests, and the recognition that the obligations of marriage are fixed by God (or the courts), not by the couple.

We can readily see the influence of these traditional marriage interests in the legal requirements for divorce. Not long ago, when marriages were broken it had to be proved that community and religious standards had been abridged, not just that the individuals were unhappy with one another. Grounds for divorce, such as adultery, cruelty, nonsupport, or desertion, placed a strain on the community, and this made them serious indictments against the persons so charged.

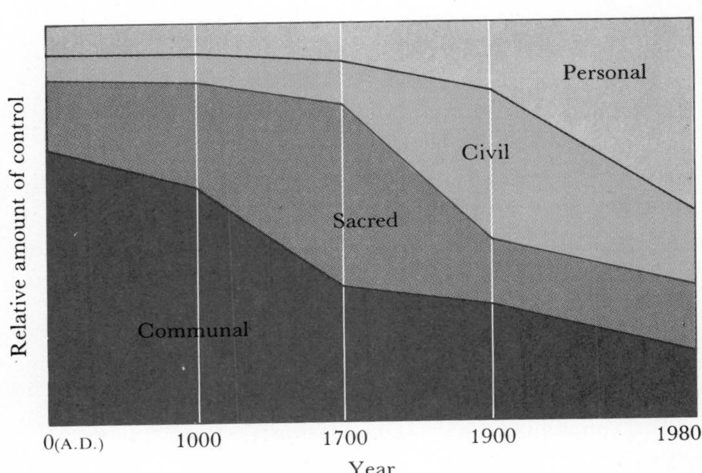

Fig. 4.1

Changing Influences on the Control of Marriage

Personal contract

Today, the situation is again changing. There is growing acceptance of the concept that marital bonds are created and maintained as much by the preferences of the couple as by outside influences. The family, community, and church still play a part in marriage decisions, but their importance has clearly diminished with the rise of personal freedom. Parents are frequently informed of an impending marriage instead of consulted as to whether or not the marriage should occur. Divorces are also explained more in terms of personal failures than as failures of the communal or sacred bond.

But before we examine further the interpersonal commitments implied in marriage, it is important for us to understand the legal conditions of the marriage contract itself. The responsibility for regulating the legal marriage contract lies with the state, and each state defines for its own citizens the qualifications they must meet to create a legally constituted marriage. Even broader than the state marital regulations, however, are the basic legal assumptions of marriage since these represent fundamental civil concerns for the rights of individuals and the interests of the state.

Legal Assumptions of Marriage

Marriage contract differences

Marriage is a unique legal agreement. Essentially, it is a contract between two persons. But the marriage contract differs from other legal contracts in several important ways: (1) the terms of the agreement are not drawn up by the parties involved, (2) the provisions of the agreement are rarely divulged to the parties affected by them, (3) the alteration or termination of the agreement may not be made without approval of the state, and (4) individuals may enter into this agreement even though they are ineligible by age to sign any other legal contract. In the case of *Maynard* v. *Hill* (1888), the United States Supreme Court noted the uniqueness of marriage under the law. It said:

> Marriage . . . is something more than a mere contract. The consent of the parties is of course essential to its existence, but when the contract to marry is executed by the marriage, a relation between the parties is created which they cannot change. Other contracts may be modified, restricted or enlarged, or entirely released upon the consent of the parties. Not so with marriage. The relation once formed, the law steps in and holds the parties to various obligations and liabilities.

It is safe to say that most individuals who marry know little about the laws implied in the contract they sign. Existing social norms usually serve as adequate guidelines for appropriate conduct. Nevertheless, the law remains, and it is only slowly changing, even though societal norms are changing rapidly. Given this, Weitzman (1975) cautions:

> Although private practices within marriage may not always conform to the traditional marriage contract, it is clear that the present marriage contract—the legal contract embodied in both statutory and case law—continues to enforce the common-law obligations of husbands and wives. (p. 532)

What are these "obligations" implied in the marriage contract? Weitzman summarizes them under four categories, depending upon whether the husband or the wife is assumed to have the principal legal responsibility: (1) the husband is the head of the family; (2) the husband is responsible for support; (3) the wife is responsible for domestic services; and (4) the wife is responsible for child care. We can also add another contractual provision: (5) the husband and wife have exclusive sexual rights to one another.

Marriage obligations

With regard to the first provision, the "headship" of the husband in the household is certainly being challenged in many families, but under the law, his position remains quite clear. It is the wife, not the husband, who significantly loses her independent identity after marriage: she is encouraged to change her name, adopt his residence, and assume his social and economic status in the community. In most states, she may retain her own name if she chooses to contend with the administrative pressures to do otherwise, but the Supreme Court has upheld the right of a state (Alabama) to require women to use their husband's surname for certain documents, such as driver's licenses (*Forbush* v. *Wallace*, 1972). The rules concerning residence are more serious. A woman who refuses her husband's choice of domicile can be considered to have deserted him, even if such a move causes her to lose her job, her voting privileges, her in-state college-tuition rights, or her tax advantages. Consumer-credit restrictions for women have been relaxed under the Equal Credit Opportunity Act of 1975, yet pressures remain for credit to be extended in the name of the husband.

Financial responsibilities

The leadership of the husband in the family is reinforced by financial-support responsibilities accorded to him in the marriage contract. All states, even those that assume property to be equally divided between husband and wife, yield to the husband the primary obligation for family support. Even if the wife is employed and capable of sharing this financial responsibility, she is obligated to support the family only if her husband is unwilling or unable to do so. As a result of this situation, the husband has the legal right to control and distribute the family finances. In a divorce, this means that he is more likely to be required to support his separated wife financially than she is to support him. But if they are not separated, he can determine the level of support that she is to receive.

Household responsibilities

In exchange for these support services of the husband, the wife is legally obligated to provide domestic duties and child care. Her contracted responsibility to do household work has been particularly encouraged since "the Supreme Court decisions over the past century which have dealt with women's roles show a remarkably consistent pattern of insisting on the woman's domestic obligations above all else" (Weitzman, 1975, p. 536). Certainly, there is nothing illegal about a wife working outside the home or a husband preparing dinner, but when the courts have ruled on matters related to family responsibilities, the traditional division of labor is usually reinforced. This inequality under the law is particularly a problem for women if they should divorce. Since husbands cannot legally pay their wives for household services (Weitzman, 1974), and since wives do not share equally in their husband's social security benefits nor in property distribution after separation in most states, the effect of the law is to deny women the right to accumulate benefits from the labor they contribute to the family. Thus, the legal structure of marriage encourages women to remain in their domestic roles but punishes them for doing this if their marriages dissolve.

The fourth provision implicit in the marriage contract places the responsibility for child care with the wife. Legally, there has been little change in this assumption since the United States Supreme Court gave the opinion in *Bradwell* v. *Illinois* (1873) that "The paramount destiny and mission of women is to fulfill the noble and benign offices of wife and mother." This interpretation and those that have followed continue to place the child-rearing role at the very center of the lawful place of women in society. Nowhere is this more evident than in child-custody settlements in which we find a "presumption" that the mother is the appropriate custodian for the children, regardless of the relative capabilities and interests of the two parents (Orthner and Lewis, 1979).

Sexual rights

A fifth provision of the marriage contract includes exclusive sexual rights to one's spouse. This follows from the expectation that marriage is a lifelong commitment to a monogamous relationship. These rights to exclusive sexual access are protected from two sides. Laws of adultery and fornication prohibit married persons from having sexual contacts with anyone but their spouses. And the failure to permit sexual access or nonconsummation may be grounds for annulment or divorce.

Reactions against some or all of these provisions in the traditional marriage contract have been mounting, but such concerns are not new. During the nineteenth century the husband's legal right to his wife's property was severely restricted by the Married Women's Property Act. Marriage pledges, such as the one between Henry Blackwell and Lucy Stone in 1855 (see Vignette 4.1), also revealed a growing interest in sexual equality and registered a modest protest against the laws of that day.

Clearly, the major changes over the last century have not been in the laws that govern marriage but in the willingness of the law to isolate itself from social reality. The legal provisions of marriage described above remain largely intact, but they are exercised only when severely questioned. Adultery and fornication laws are rarely enforced, except as grounds for divorce. The duties and responsibilities of the household are determined by each married couple with little interference by the courts. The rights of mothers to be employed and of fathers to receive custody of children have been expanded. And the result of this is that "the law on the books is widely divergent from the law in action. . . . The law in action is a patchwork attempt to stretch the old law to deal with modern realities" (Weitzman, 1974, p. 1277).

Equal Rights Amendment

One attempt proposed to bring the "law on the books" closer to social reality has taken place in the Equal Rights Amendment. The amendment simply states: "Equality of rights under the law shall not be denied or abridged by the United States or by any state on account of sex." The thrust of this law is to equalize the societal and family responsibilities of men and women and to remove many of the sex-linked restrictions implied in previous laws. Opponents of the amendment have argued that these restrictions pro-

Vignette 4.1 The Marriage Pledge of Henry Blackwell and Lucy Stone, 1855

While acknowledging our mutual affection by publicly assuming the relationship of husband and wife, yet in justice to ourselves and a great principle, we deem it a duty to declare that this act on our part implies no sanction of, nor promise of voluntary obedience to such of the present laws of marriage, as refuse to recognize the wife as an independent, rational being, while they confer upon the husband an injurious, and unnatural superiority, investing him with legal powers which no honorable man would exercise, and which no man should possess. We protest especially against the laws which give to the husband:

1. The custody of the wife's person.
2. The exclusive control and guardianship of their children.
3. The sole ownership of her personal property, and use of her real estate, unless previously settled upon her, or placed in the hands of trustees, as in the case of minors, lunatics, and idiots.
4. The absolute right to the product of her industry.
5. Also against laws which give to the widower so much larger and more permanent an interest in the property of his deceased wife, than they give to the widow in that of the deceased husband.
6. Finally, against the whole system by which "the legal existence of the wife is suspended during marriage," so that in most States, she neither has a legal part in the choice of her residence, nor can she make a will, nor sue or be sued in her own name, nor inherit property.

We believe that personal independence and equal human rights can never be forfeited, except for crime; that marriage should be an equal and permanent partnership, and so recognized by law; that until it is so recognized, married partners should provide against the radical injustice of present laws, by every means in their power.

We believe that where domestic difficulties arise, no appeal should be made to legal tribunals under existing laws, but that all difficulties should be submitted to the equitable adjustment of arbitrators mutually chosen.

Thus reverencing law, we enter our protest against rules and customs which are unworthy of the name, since they violate justice, the essence of law.

From Jessie Bernard, *The Future of Marriage* (New York: Bantam, 1972), pp. 96–97.

vide important privileges and protections that would be denied if the laws were changed and reinterpreted. However, the fundamental issue under consideration is whether to make legal many of the changes that have already occurred. If the gap between the law and social reality is allowed to continue, this may result in a meaningless set of laws that fail to provide either direction or protection, thereby ensuring confusion and family instability. Only time will tell if the legal assumptions of the family will be markedly changed by the issues sparked in the ERA debate.

The traditional role of wife as child-rearer has been reinforced by the United States judicial system.

Legal Qualifications for Marriage

While the legal assumptions of marriage may be interpreted differently and sometimes ignored completely, the legal qualifications for marriage are more rigidly reinforced. In each state there are clearly stated requirements that must be met before a person can be legally recognized as married. A **valid marriage,** one that is legally contracted in any state, will be recognized by all other states. This makes it possible for a couple to relocate after marriage and be considered legally married in any state even though they did not meet its regulations at the time of their marriage.

Multiple marriages

Marital Status. One of the qualifications for marriage that all states recognize is the provision that neither person can be currently married to anyone else. No state will knowingly permit a multiple marriage or polygamy. For example, if a man were to desert his wife and some years later marry again, his second marriage would be considered legally *void*—from the perspective of the state, it never happened! There would be no need to divorce or annul the second marriage. The second wife would have no rights to the man's property, social security benefits, or financial support, and any children born to them would be considered illegitimate.

Age. A minimum age for marriage is established in every state. At one time (and in many countries still today) this age centered around the time of puberty, but as the competencies required for adult responsibilities have increased, so have the minimum ages required by law for marriage. Most states now classify four marriage ages, including separate minimum ages for men and women with or without parental consent (see Table 4.1).

Underage marriage

What is the legal status of a marriage that occurs when an underage couple lies about their age? Perhaps surprisingly, in the eyes of the law, the marriage is valid. In some cases, however, such a marriage might be voidable; that is, it may be annulled by a court if one of the individuals is under the minimum legal age for marriage or if fraud can be demonstrated. For example, if a couple travels to another state because its age laws are less strict or if they knowingly claim that their ages are above the requirement for parental consent in their own state, their marriage will rarely be considered void or voidable. But if the woman thought she was marrying a nineteen-year-old man when actually he was only sixteen, then this fraud may be grounds for voiding the marriage, although they will remain married until the court decides whether there is sufficient grounds for an annulment.

Health. Most states maintain certain health qualifications for people who are to marry. These are usually designed to protect an "innocent" party from potential harm. The most common restriction is applied to persons who carry a venereal disease, which is determined by a blood or serology test. Usually, a medical certificate stating that neither the man nor the woman is an active carrier of syphilis must be presented in order to get a marriage license (see Table 4.1).

Table 4.1
State Marriage Regulations

State or Other Jurisdiction	Age at which Marriage Can Be Contracted without Parental Consent		Age at which Marriage Can Be Contracted with Parental Consent		Blood Tests and Other Medical Requirements: Maximum Period between Examination and Issuance of License (Days)	Blood Tests and Other Medical Requirements: Scope of Medical Inquiry	Waiting Period	
	Male	Female	Male	Female			Before Issuance of License	After Issuance of License
Alabama	18	18	17(a)	14(a)	30	(b)	...	...
Alaska	18	18	16(c)	16(c)	30	(b)	3 da.	...
Arizona	18	18	16(c)	16(c)	30	(b)	(d)	...
Arkansas	18	18	17(c)	16(c)	30	(b)	3 da.	...
California	18	18	18(a,c)	16(a,c)	30	(b,e,f,g)	...	...
Colorado	18	18	16(c)	16(c)	30	(b,f,h)	...	...
Connecticut	18	18	16(c)	16(c)	35	(b)	4 da.	...
Delaware	18	18	18(c)	16(c)	30	(b)	...	(i)
Florida	18	18	16(a,c)	16(a,c)	30	(b)	3 da.	...
Georgia	18(j)	18(j)	16(c,j)	16(c,j)	30	(b,e)	3 da.(k)	...
Hawaii	18	18	16	16(c)	30	(b,f)	...	...
Idaho	18	18	16(c)	16(c)	...	(f)	(m)	...
Illinois	18	18	16(c)	16(c)	15	(b,e)	3 da.	...
Indiana	18	18	17(c)	17(c)	30	(b,e)	3 da.	...
Iowa	18	18	16	16	20	(b)	3 da.	...
Kansas	18	18	18(c)	18(c)	30	(b)	3 da.	...
Kentucky	18	18	(a,o)	(a,o)	15	(b,e)	3 da.	...
Louisiana	18	18	18(c)	16(c)	10	(b)	...	72 hrs.
Maine	18	18	16(c)	16(c)	60	(b)	5 da.	...
Maryland	18	18	16(c)	16(c)	...	...	48 hrs.	...
Massachusetts	18	18	18(c)	18(c)	30	(b,f)	3 da.	...
Michigan	18	18	(r)	16	33	(b)	3 da.	...
Minnesota	18	18	18	16(q)	...	...	5 da.	...
Mississippi	21	21	17(c)	15(c)	30	(b)	3 da.	...
Missouri	18	18	15(c)	15(c)	15	(b)	3 da.	...
Montana	18	18	18(c)	18(c)	20	(b)	5 da.	3 da.
Nebraska	19	19	17	17	30	(b,f)	2 da.	...
Nevada	18	18	16(a,c)	16(a,c)	...	...	...	...
New Hampshire	18	18	14(q)	13(q)	30(r)	(b)	3 da.	...
New Jersey	18	18	16(c)	16(c)	30	(b)	72 hrs.	...
New Mexico	18	18	16(c)	16(c)	30	(b)	72 hrs.	...
New York	18	18	16	14(s)	30	(b,e)	...	24 da.(t)
North Carolina	18	18	16	16(c)	30	(b,f,u,v)	...	...
North Dakota	18	18	16	16	30	(b,w)	...	...
Ohio	18	18	18(c)	16(c)	30	(b)	5 da.	...
Oklahoma	18	18	16(c)	16(c)	30	(b)	(m)	...
Oregon	18	18	17	17	30	(b)	...	(a,b)
Pennsylvania	18	18	16(c)	16(c)	30	(b,y)	3 da.	...
Rhode Island	18	18	18(c)	16(c)	40	(b,f,v)	...	...
South Carolina	18	18	16(c)	14(c)	...	...	24 hrs.	...
South Dakota	18	18	16(c)	16(c)	20	(b)	...	...
Tennessee	18	18	16(c)	16(c)	30	(b)	3 da.(ab)	...
Texas	18	18	14(c)	14(c)	21	(b)	...	...
Utah	18	18	16(a)	14(a)	30	(b)	...	...
Vermont	18	18	16(c)	16(c)	30	(b)	...	5 da.
Virginia	18	18	16(a,c)	16(a,c)	30	(b)	...	...
Washington	18	18	17(c)	17(c)	...	(b,r,aa)	3 da.	...
West Virginia	18	18	(q)	(o)	30	(b)	3 da.	...
Wisconsin	18	18	16	16	20	(b)	5 da.	...
Wyoming	19	19	17(c)	16(c)	30	(b)	...	...
Dist. of Col.	18	18	16(a)	16(a)	30	(b)	3 da.	...
Puerto Rico	21	21	18(c)	16(c)	10(ab)	(b,aa)	...	...

(a) Parental consent not required if previously married.
(b) Venereal diseases.
(c) Legal procedure for younger persons to obtain license.
(d) Blood test must be on record at least 48 hours before issuance of license.
(e) Sickle cell anemia.
(f) Rubella immunity.
(g) Tay-Sachs disease.
(h) Rh factor.
(i) Residents, 24 hours; nonresidents, 96 hours.
(j) Parental consent is not needed regardless of age in cases of pregnancy or when couple has a living child born out of wedlock.
(k) Unless parties are 18 years of age or over, or woman is pregnant, or applicants are the parents of a living child born out of wedlock.
(l) Generally no, but may be recognized for limited purposes, e.g., legitimacy of children, workers' compensation benefits, etc.
(m) Three days if parties are under 18 years of age.
(n) However, contracting such a marriage is a misdemeanor.
(o) No minimum age.
(p) No provision in the law for parental consent for males.
(q) Permission of judge also required.
(r) Maximum period between blood test and date of intended marriage.
(s) If under 16 years of age, consent of family court judge also required.
(t) However, marriage may not be solemnized within 3 days of date on which specimen for blood test was taken.
(u) Mental competence.
(v) Tuberculosis.
(w) Some marriages prohibited if a party is severely retarded.
(x) License valid 3 days after application signed and valid for 30 days thereafter.
(y) Court order needed if party is weakminded, insane, or of unsound mind.
(z) May be waived if certain conditions are met.
(aa) Affidavit of mental competence required. Also, no epilepsy in Puerto Rico.
(ab) Maximum time from blood test to expiration of license.

Source: Reprinted from *The Book of the States*, 1980–1981, published by the Council of State Governments, Lexington, Kentucky.

Legal restrictions against marriage may also be based on other health reasons. All states forbit the "insane" or the mentally retarded from marrying, although this is usually limited to voiding those marriages in which one of the parties was incapable of "understanding" what they were doing. Some states restrict alcoholics from marrying for this same reason. There are also provisions in the laws of some states to prohibit the marriages of people who are epileptics or who carry certain communicable diseases, such as tuberculosis.

Kinship Relations. Marriage between particular blood relatives is limited by **laws of consanguinity**. These laws strictly prohibit marriages among immediate family members, such as between mother and son, father and daughter, brother and sister, or any person and his or her grandparents, aunts, or uncles. In thirty states, the law also forbids marriages between first cousins, and in the Virgin Islands, even second cousins are forbidden to marry. These restrictions against consanguinity are extended in about half of the states by **laws of marital affinity.** In states which have this restriction, a marriage can be legally forbidden between nonblood relatives such as a father and daughter-in-law, or a woman and her brother-in-law by a previous marriage.

Last chance to reconsider

Waiting Periods. Even though all of the above qualifications have been met, most states place another barrier before those who wish to marry: a waiting period. The purpose of this delay is to allow couples one last chance to reconsider their decision before they enter into the marriage contract. Legally, marriage is much easier to get into than to get out of, and the waiting period is the state's provision for "cooling off" a hasty or ill-conceived decision to marry. The most common waiting period is three days, and usually, this occurs between the time of application for the marriage license and the time it can be picked up. Some states have this delay only when one of the marrying parties is under a particular age, such as eighteen or twenty-one.

The Wedding Ceremony. At some point, people who want to marry are required to affirm their commitment to one another before some legally recognized official. This official attests to the fact that the requirements of the state have been met. Ordained clergy are delegated this function in all states, and certain civil officials may perform the ceremony in every state except Delaware. Usually, judges, magistrates, justices of the peace, and mayors are accorded this civil responsibility, but some states even allow notaries to officiate at weddings. Approximately four out of five marriages in the United States are still presided over by clergy, reflecting the traditional religious heritage of marriage in North America.

State requirements

Legally, there is no prescribed wedding ceremony. The states do not require a promise to "obey," to pledge a "troth" (fidelity), to provide a ring, or even to love one another. What they do require is that the parties *verbally, mutually,* and *voluntarily* affirm their marriage to one another. As long as this expression is made before and recognized by a designated official and the required number of witnesses, the marriage ceremony is considered legally valid.

Usually, marriage ceremonies go far beyond what is legally required. Elaborate settings are provided, flowers and plants are purchased, invitations to friends and kin are sent, rehearsals are scheduled, gifts are received, songs are sung, special clothing is acquired, seating arrangements are made, food may be served, and solemn promises are offered by the bride and groom to one another. In a nation with comparatively few rituals, the importance placed on this marriage ceremony is evidence of the high regard still given to marriage in American society.

Purposes of weddings

What purposes do wedding ceremonies serve beyond sealing the legal marriage contract? For the bride and groom, the wedding symbolizes a change in their personal status. The ceremony and announcements in the newspapers remind others of the new relationship and the responsibilities

Vignette 4.2 Two Weddings: Traditional and Contemporary

Traditional

Clergyman: We are gathered here in the presence of these witnesses for the purpose of uniting in matrimony Carol and Steven.

The contract of marriage is most solemn and is not to be entered into lightly, but thoughtfully and seriously and with a deep realization of its obligations and responsibilities.

Steven, do you take this woman, Carol, to be your lawful wedded wife?

Steven: I do.

Clergyman: Carol, do you take this man, Steven, to be your lawful wedded husband?

Carol: I do.

Clergyman: Do you promise to love and comfort one another, to honor and keep one another, in sickness and in health, in prosperity and adversity, and forsaking all others, be faithful to each other as long as you both shall live?

Carol and Steven: We do.

Clergyman (if ring ceremony): Steven, place the ring on the ring finger of Carol's left hand and repeat after me, to her: Carol, with this ring I thee wed.

Steven: Carol, with this ring I thee wed.

Clergyman: Carol, place the ring on the ring finger of Steven's left hand and repeat after me, to him: Steven, with this ring I thee wed.

Carol: Steven, with this ring I thee wed.

Clergyman: By virtue of the authority vested in me, I now pronounce you husband and wife.

Contemporary

Steve: We do not know what the future holds for us; whether tomorrow will find us materially secure or impoverished; spiritually sound or morally each has acquired. The wedding also identifies some of the marital obligations that go along with this change in status (Chesser, 1980). Traditionally, the vows have defined some general expectations of the couple, including the obligation to exclusively love, honor, comfort, and cherish one another as long as they both are alive (see Vignette 4.2). Some ceremonies have also added more specific responsibilities for husbands and wives, often with particular emphasis on the husband's obligations. When commitments such as these are made in public, they contain a strong obligation to fulfill them since they are backed by personal reputation and the support of others. Perhaps this is one reason—although it is surely not the only one—why church weddings attended by friends and kin are more likely to survive (Edmonds, 1967).

---

bankrupt; physically well or infirm. But we have chosen to challenge the unknown together, as woman and man, as husband and wife, as two separate people with distinctly different heritages, often, with singular desires.

Carol: We have been linked together by something which defies traditions, yet is itself the oldest tradition of all: something which impudently laughs at man's established institutions because long before they came into being, it was.

Both: The formal recognition of our love for each other which we share with our friends and family today, is an affirmation of life. We love, therefore we live.

Clergyman: (He recited a homily on marriage, parts of which are found in other services.)

Steve: It is not always fun to make a journey alone. There are too many things which get better when they are shared. And when I can share something with someone who demonstrates pleasure at being a part of my life, I like that too. Carol, I wish to share my life with you because of what and who you are, and because you add to my enjoyment of life.
(Gives ring.)

Carol: And I offer you my love and life to share, not only because love generates love in return, but because I like the people we have become together. I ask you to join me in celebrating and enhancing this becoming, so that we may continue to grow and love, both each other and ourselves.
(Gives ring.)

Clergyman: Having declared your intentions, you are now husband and wife.

From Arthur Dobrin and Kenneth Briggs, *Getting Married the Way You Want* (Englewood Cliffs, N.J.: Prentice-Hall, 1974), pp. 99–101.

Whether a small outdoor wedding or an elaborate cathedral ceremony, the marriage ritual is still held in special regard.

For the family as well, weddings symbolize a change in status. Two families are joined together, in-laws are created, and parents are asked to release some of their parental responsibilities. The wedding also provides a chance to congregate and celebrate with the extended family and friends. Some families become quite extravagant in this regard. There is a tendency to spend more than can really be afforded in order to elevate the family in the eyes of the community and kin. Some anthropologists have likened weddings to the "potlatch" rituals held among certain Northwest Indian tribes during which the more wealth one could destroy or give away, the higher one's status would be. In somewhat the same way, the more lavish the ceremony and related rituals, the higher the status assumed by the family and guests who are attending.

Wedding criticisms

The traditional wedding ceremony has not been without its critics. The commercialism, pageantry, and potential for outright submersion of the couple have turned off many youth. The status seeking and high costs have made others very angry. Some complain that the language of the wedding liturgy does not reflect the meaning of their commitments to one another. A growing number of women also reject much of the symbolism that retains the notion that women are property to be shifted from hand to hand.

New wedding styles

For these and other reasons, many weddings are taking a different form. Settings may include places that are important to the couple alone, a park, boat, garden, beach, even a garage. The words spoken are more likely to be chosen by the bride and groom and often conversational in format (see Vignette 4.2). The statements by the official or clergy are likely to be minimized. The guests are close friends and family, less likely to be business and other associates of the parents. The mood is relaxed, not stiff; the music tends to be modern, not traditional; and the parents and guests play a more personal role in the validation of the new marital relationship. Marcia Seligson (1974) comments on these changes:

> The bedrock of society shifts slowly, imperceptibly. But, it does shift. What the New Wedding expresses is the budding claim for Self, for dignity and autonomy, for alternatives and change. The one constant in all of this is our undying hunger for the wedding ritual with all of its apparently crucial qualities and ingredients. (p. 288)

Common-law requirements

Common-Law Marriage. It is possible in some states to assume legal marital status while skirting the licensing qualifications for marriage. This occurs in a common-law marriage in which a man and woman establish a common residence and mutually consent to live together as husband and wife. As long as they are considered old enough to make this decision and recognized in the community as being husband and wife, they can be defined as legally married. The following states and territories permit this type of marriage:

Alabama	Kansas	Rhode Island
Colorado	Montana	South Carolina
Georgia	Ohio	Texas
Idaho	Oklahoma	Washington, D. C.
Iowa	Pennsylvania	Virgin Islands

The history of common-law marriage has been buffeted by controversy. In simpler societies and in times past, marriages were usually arranged by families and bound by a simple matrimonial pledge.

On the American frontier, common-law marriage fulfilled a practical need. Because ministers, judges, and marriage-license bureaus were often some distance away, community and legal acceptance was given to self-proclaimed marriage. The couple might later go through with a marriage ceremony—often they did not—but in the meantime, their relationship was legitimate and they were not considered to be "living in sin." But as cities and townships grew up and the frontier vanished, common-law marriage began to be viewed more as a means of escaping legal responsibilities than of fulfilling personal and community obligations. Common-law marriage was resorted to primarily by the lower classes; those who had the least commitment to the community and the fewest resources to channel into marriage. As a result, these arrangements became synonymous with instability and the reputation of common-law marriage declined. With this decline went its legal support.

Frontier marriage

Criticisms of common-law marriage

Today, there is a strong movement to abolish the common-law marriage alternative for the following reasons: (1) common-law marriages make it possible legally to evade the regulations prescribed under the marital statutes of the state; (2) common-law marriages are not recorded, so they lead to confusion over property and inheritance rights when they are dissolved by death or separation; and (3) common-law marriages hamper governmental and private agencies that attempt to record marriage statistics and provide family services (Kephart, 1977).

Some might argue that marriage is a personal decision and sincerely question why the state should apply a legal contract to their private living arrangements. But consider the 1972 *Thornton* case in the state of Washington: an unmarried couple had lived together for seventeen years when the man died. Over that period, the couple had reared four children and acquired considerable property in a cattle ranch. When he died, however, much of the property was in his name and legally could not be transferred to the woman with whom he had lived and worked. Since they had never married and Washington state does not recognize common-law marriage, his family and his children could inherit his property, but she could not. The investment she had made might have been legally voided by inheritance laws (Weisberg, 1975).

Marvin v. *Marvin*

In this case, however, the Washington Supreme Court ruled that the surviving member was able to prove an *implied* partnership agreement. She was therefore entitled to a share of the property because of a long-term, stable relationship "in which the partners appear to hold themselves out as husband and wife." A similar judgment was made in the celebrated 1976 California case of *Marvin* v. *Marvin*. This time the court held that the couple who had separated must share part of the property they had accumulated while living together unmarried (Myricks, 1980). Cases such as these, in states that do not recognize common-law marriage, indicate that some legal rights to joint property may be retained under current laws. Nevertheless, the courts are not always consistent in granting these rights, and rarely are they extended to retirement or social security benefits.

This legal quagmire should reinforce the legal desirability at this time for couples bonded by strong commitments to marry formally. The number of persons living together outside of marriage is growing today, but it is unlikely that the courts will markedly increase their sympathies for these arrangements. The tendency of the law is to benefit those who conform to the marriage statutes and to recognize only after considerable argument (and financial investment in lawyers) the comparable rights of unmarried cohabitants.

MARRIAGE: THE INTERPERSONAL CONTRACT

While the legal assumptions and regulations that bind a marriage are certainly important, there is another dimension to the marriage contract. This is what we might call the **interpersonal marriage contract**; the set of informal, need-fulfilling agreements that bind two persons into a marital relationship. This contract, unlike the legal one, is tailored by the couple, not the courts. It represents the mutual obligations implied in the many personal pledges and plans made by a couple over the course of their courtship. The obligations can be as broad as the promise to love one another or as specific as the promise to allow each person to continue his or her education.

Marriage as a trust

Marriage, as we have seen, has become a very personal affair, an extension of the cultural drift toward individual growth and personal fulfillment. The concept of an interpersonal contract represents that fact well. To most people, marriage cannot be adequately understood in terms of legal conditions and obligations. To them it is a "trust," a very personal contract based on an assumption that their partner has met and will continue to meet their particular needs.

States only recognize marriage

We should note that the legal contract to marry does recognize the implicit existence of an interpersonal marriage agreement. The reason for this is that a state *cannot create* a marriage, it can only *recognize* the existence of a marriage. The requirement of the law is that a man and woman "take one another" as husband and wife and express this relationship "freely, seriously, and plainly" in the presence of one another and an official witness or witnesses of the state. In states recognizing common-law marriage, the presence of the official witness may not even be necessary for marriage recognition. But in every state, the legal marriage contract is applied only *after* a marital relationship is already indicated. The marital pact or contract is actually made by the man and woman; the state merely places its legal obligations on top of that personal agreement. This does not mean, however, that the state has to recognize the various promises that are part of the interpersonal marriage contract; only those that conform to the statutes of the law receive legal protection. But interestingly, this situation means that *no one*, minister or other official, can legally marry a couple; the man and woman can only marry themselves. Any pronouncement of marriage is after the fact, not an act of creating the marriage.

The timing of marriage

Of course, this question of timing causes some problems in defining when a marriage begins and when it ends. If marriage is defined legally, then it begins at the time when it is solemnized under the regulations of the state and ends when one of the parties dies or when a legal divorce is granted. If marriage is defined interpersonally, it begins when the man and woman are sufficiently committed to one another that they consider themselves husband and wife and ends when this commitment is no longer shared.

Usually, these two marital definitions go hand in hand—mutual commitment leads to solemnizing the union, and loss of commitment leads to divorce. But conceivably, there can be a wide difference in the timing of these two types of marriage. For example, in a two-step marital arrangement, a couple might live together for some time and consider themselves "like" married (which they would be in common-law states) but not become formally married until after a child was born. In this case, the legal marriage would occur considerably after the interpersonal marriage. The opposite of this, however, is not permissible in the United States or Canada, since legal recognition of the marriage can take place only *after* the couple voluntarily and of their own accord express their marital commitment. A "shotgun" or forced marriage is usually voidable on the grounds that both parties were not seriously committed to one another at the time of the wedding.

Dimensions of the Interpersonal Marriage Contract

What are the principal components of the interpersonal marriage contract? From the evidence we have about what men and women expect from marriage, it is apparent that the qualities most frequently desired are quite different from those specified legally—in some cases, they are even opposite. Interpersonally, marriage is considered in terms of commitment instead of legal compliance, companionship instead of duties, personal growth instead of community responsibility, and individual happiness instead of civil rights. Each of these components—commitment, companionship, personal growth, and happiness—has become increasingly important to marriage today.

Exclusivity and permanence

Commitment. Perhaps no word is more consistently linked with marriage than commitment. This is because our concept of marriage is based on two fundamental principles, *exclusivity* and *permanence*, both of which are dimensions of commitment. True, not all marriages remain exclusive and not all are permanent, but these qualities are still hoped for and considered the basic substance of marriage. When neither is present, the interpersonal marriage contract is considered null and void.

In a study of marital commitment by Dean and Spanier (1974), the researchers examined the question of whether the desire to hold a marriage together is related to overall marital adjustment. What they found is not

Companionship has become a central element in marital satisfaction today.

surprising. Among the 280 married college men and women they studied, the greater the commitment to marriage, the higher the score on a scale of marital adjustment. Similar results were found in a study of middle-aged marriages. Ammon and Stinnett (1980) reported that "determination and commitment in the marriage were key predictors of marital satisfaction." Both studies concluded that commitment may be one of the most important yet overlooked variables in marital success.

Early in marriage, this new sense of interpersonal commitment is often described as the most noticeable "turn around" in the relationship. As we described in Chapter 2, premarital commitments are largely existential—based on present circumstances. But marital commitments encompass a "common future" in which each person is included in the desired goals of the other. This contributes to a sense of permanence and enhances the chances for exclusivity since no other relationship usually shares this same set of common ambitions.

Shared experiences

Companionship. A second dimension of the interpersonal marriage contract is companionship—the sharing of time and experiences. Most people who marry today expect their spouse to be a companion during much of their available leisure time. This expectation does not come from mistrust of what the other person is doing, but from a desire to be with the one who provides the most satisfaction. Indeed, several studies have pointed out that companionship is now a central element in marital satisfaction. Blood and Wolfe (1960) found that husbands and wives consider companionship their most important source of gratification. Bradburn (1969) noted that the "quality" of a marriage was markedly affected by the amount of companionship. And Orthner (1975a) reported that time shared in joint activities was a good predictor of marital satisfaction, particularly in the early years of marriage.

New demands for sharing

So important has this quality become in marriage that the contemporary family has been described as "the companionship family." Burgess and Locke (1945), in their now classical treatise on the family, used as the title of their book *The Family: From Institution to Companionship.* Miller and Swanson (1958) have used the term "colleagues" to connote this new relationship between husbands and wives. In these and other writings, the message that comes through is this: marriages today are built on communication, an ability to talk to and understand one another. Since this ability requires shared experiences and opportunities to keep the channels of communication open, companionship has become the new basis for marital integration.

Companionship has not always been part of the interpersonal marriage contract. Traditionally, husbands and wives were integrated into marriage through the roles they contributed to one another rather than the times they shared together. Being a good cook or a good farmer was considered far more valuable than being good company for one another. And for some families even today, marital stability still depends upon defined roles and reduced communication, variables that might be altered in companionship. But for many marriages today, the call to "do things together" has become the motto for marital success. The very practical requirements for survival, so important to the family earlier, have been replaced by an obligation to fulfill the very personal needs of our spouse as well as ourself.

Self-actualization

Personal Growth. Both commitment and companionship necessarily create some obligation of marriage to provide for personal growth as well. There are different terms given for this new dimension of the interpersonal marriage contract—individuation, autonomy, and self-actualization, to name a few—but the basic premise is that marriage should be a facilitator of personal development as well as a source of personal security.

Virginia Satir (1970) expresses this theme of personal growth when she speaks of marriage today as often including a "self-actualizing contract"—a commitment to allow each person to fulfill what psychologist Abraham Maslow (1943) called "the tendency for one to be actualized in what he is potentially. This tendency might be phrased as the desire to become more and more what one is, to become everything that one is capable of becoming" (p. 50). A similar emphasis on personal growth is stressed by Nena and George O'Neill (1972) in their writings on "open marriage." This type of marriage, they propose, is built upon a "growth contract" in which "the partners are committed to their own and to each other's growth. . . . It is a relationship which is flexible enough to allow for change, which is constantly being renegotiated in the light of changing needs . . ." (p. 403).

To a large degree, this current emphasis on personal growth represents a fundamental change in what people have traditionally expected from marriage. Earlier generations allowed little personal freedom within marriage. Rigidly defined marital roles and community-reinforced dependencies emphasized the importance of sacrificing personal needs for family responsibilities. But the situation today is different. And we now find ourselves in a world that beckons us to change our needs as we confront new challenges and experiences. This also means our relationships must be more flexible in reacting to changing personal needs. Often this is not easy, but in their book *Shifting Gears* (1974), the O'Neills point out that:

Relationship flexibility

> . . . in our contemporary world of crisis and change we need something more from relationships than an all-supportive context with built-in dependency. We need relationships that can help us to grow and become *self*-supportive at the same time that they provide a feeling of belongingness. . . . Our relationships today can only be vital and sustained to the extent that they give us the courage and strength to grow: each of us receiving from others the support necessary to our growth and giving back to others the support they need for their growth. (p. 209)

Happiness as a goal

Happiness. Coupled with a new emphasis on personal growth is the current obligation of marriage to provide us with happiness. Marriage has become not only a springboard for personal interests, but a basic source of personal fulfillment. You may be thinking that this seems quite obvious, but this type of interpersonal obligation has not always been part of the traditional marriage contract. In the film *Lovers and Other Strangers* we can see this when a young man trys to explain to his Italian father that he and his wife are divorcing largely because they are no longer happy. To this the father replies: "So what's happiness got to do with marriage?"

In recent surveys, we find that happiness is now a very important part of marriage. A study by the Institute of Life Insurance in 1975, found that 87 percent of the respondents over twenty-nine years of age chose a "happy family life" as their most important goal in life. Angus Campbell (1975) examined the question of personal happiness in a random sample of 2164 adults. In his findings, he remarks:

> "The world has grown suspicious of anything that looks like a happily married life," wrote Oscar Wilde, but if marriages aren't happy today, at least married people are. All of the married groups—men and women, over 30 and under, with children and without—reported higher feelings of satisfaction and general good feelings about their lives than all of the unmarried groups. . . . The link between marriage and satisfaction is striking and consistent; whichever the cause or effect: marriage may make people happy, or perhaps happy people are more likely to marry. (p. 38)

While happiness is eagerly sought in marriage, it is not necessarily unaccompanied by stress. Over a decade ago, Orden and Bradburn (1969)

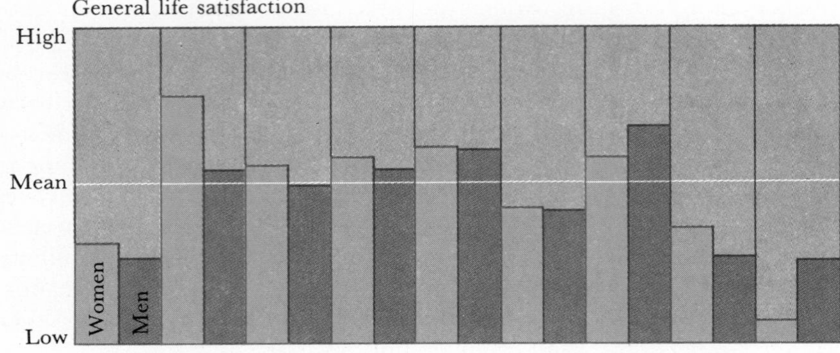

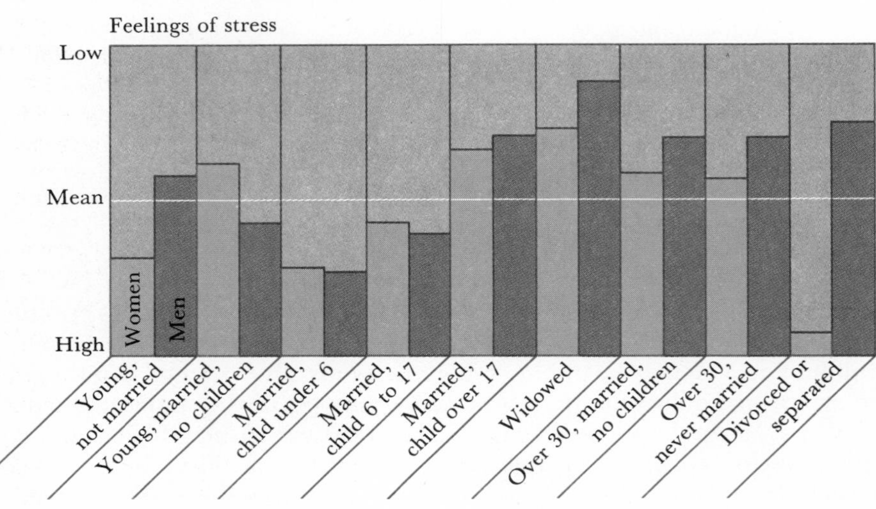

Fig. 4.2

Satisfaction and Stress Over the Family Life Cycle

Source: Angus Campbell, "The American Way of Mating." Reprinted from *Psychology Today* magazine, copyright © 1975, Ziff-Davis Publishing Company.

found that while marital happiness and marital tension were somewhat negatively related, they could be considered rather distinct in their effects on a relationship. Thus, most couples experience some decline in happiness with increased tension, but many others remain happy even though they recognize that tension exists.

Satisfaction and stress

This finding was also discovered by Campbell and examined according to life-cycle variations (see Fig. 4.2). Especially interesting in Campbell's study is the revelation that feelings of satisfaction remain consistently high in marriage despite wide fluctuations over time in the amount of stress that is felt. Parents, in particular, report decreasing amounts of stress as their children mature, and they report increases in satisfaction over this period as well. Overall, happiness or satisfaction in marriage may be as much a response to having successfully dealt with stress as it is an indication of low levels of interpersonal stress.

SUPPLEMENTARY MARRIAGE CONTRACTS

SUPPLEMENTARY MARRIAGE CONTRACTS

Marriage means different things to different people. Not everyone has the same idea of what a husband or wife is supposed to do or even how marriage should fulfill his or her own personal needs. For many couples today, the implications of the legal marriage contract, with its rigidly prescribed roles, are inconsistent with their egalitarian expectations of sharing marital roles and decision making. Courtship is supposed to provide an opportunity to select someone with compatible ideas about marriage, but the currently high divorce rate suggests that it often fails to do this—or we are so caught up in the idealization of courting that we neglect to examine our real marital expectations carefully.

Personal decision making

Some couples are remedying this situation by writing their own marriage contract—a document which reflects what they genuinely expect from one another. In this process of specifying their respective and joint rights, responsibilities, and obligations, they force themselves to look carefully at exactly what they want from their relationship. In a way, contracts such as these are an attempt to unshackle the couple from generalized assumptions that often lead to marital conflict. Furthermore, they provide a means for anticipating future problems and working out solutions beforehand.

Antenuptial Contracts

Historically, one type of marital agreement, the **antenuptial** or premarital contract, has been used frequently. Typically, this is an agreement made between two people about to be married, and it identifies the property rights of the husband and wife. Older individuals or those contemplating a second marriage may use this type of contract to withhold part of their property from joint control so that their children from a previous marriage or other relatives will not lose the rights to inherit from their personal estate. The courts recognize this privilege.

Antenuptial contracts will sometimes include provisions for alimony, in the event the marriage should fail. But the courts have been more reluctant to enforce this type of prearrangement. Several states, including California, Nevada, Illinois, Florida, Oregon, Oklahoma, and Indiana, have upheld alimony provisions in antenuptial contracts, but not without the right to modify the amount of alimony in the agreement if it is subsequently deemed unfair by the court (Lewis, 1977).

Contract limitations

Agreements made before marriage that are contrary to state laws regarding marriage cannot be supported under the law. For example, the courts will not support a contract that relieves the husband of his obligations to support the family, nor will they accept an agreement made by the couple to live in separate residences. In the same manner, any provisions that en-

Premarital agreements identifying property rights of husband and wife have long been popular among the wealthy.

courage or allow separation or divorce, such as the right to leave the marriage at any time or after a particular time period has passed, cannot legally be made.

Even less likely to have any legal weight at all are those antenuptial contracts that specify particular marital responsibilities. Agreements over the number of children, if any, child-care duties, career matters, and division of housework have traditionally been refused a hearing in the courts. However, this should not be taken to mean that these agreements are meaningless. The decision to sit down and carefully consider the many obligations implied in marriage may be very useful to the couple indeed.

Postnuptial Contracts

Often termed "personal contracts," **postnuptial** agreements usually result from an awareness after marriage that certain rights, privileges, and obligations are unevenly distributed. It is the wife, in most marriages, who suggests a personal contract, largely because she feels that the traditional guidelines for marriage place an unfair burden on her. Sometimes this is anticipated before marriage, resulting in some type of antenuptial agreement. But more often, it is not.

Breaking down tradition

The marriage of Alix Kates Shulman and her husband is a case in point. Before their first child was born, the Shulmans were both involved in their respective professions and they shared in household tasks. After parenthood, they found themselves locked into the traditional pattern in which he continued his employment and she remained home with the children. Six years later, and quite frustrated with her life, Alix suggested and her husband agreed to write a contract that more equally divided their household duties and child care (see Vignette 4.3). Remarking on the Shulmans' personal contract, Susan Edmiston (1972) concludes: "Sitting down and writing out a contract may seem a cold and formal way of working out an intimate relationship, but often it is the only way of coping with the ghosts of 2000 years of tradition lurking in our definitions of marriage" (p. 32).

Value of negotiation

Critics of marital-role contracts like the Shulmans' argue that there is little legal justification for the contract. And realistically, this is true. Postnuptial agreements are subject to all the legal limitations of antenuptial agreements plus another: the sanction placed on husbands and wives limiting their ability to contract with one another. Thus, the basic tenets of the implied marriage contract cannot be altered in the eyes of the law.

But as the Shulmans and many others have discovered, a contract does not have to be legally binding to be effective. Marvin Sussman, a sociologist who has studied over 1000 personal contracts, found that these contracts were often the incidental product of a much more fundamental process of negotiation between individuals who were seriously identifying and working on their interpersonal problems. One couple reported to him: "Part of the reason for thinking out a contract is to find out what your problems are; it forces you to take charge of your life. Once you have a contract, you don't have to refer to it. The process is what's important" (Sussman, 1975, p. 7).

If the process of thinking out our respective responsibilities is more important than the piece of paper, one might question the final step of writing down formal intentions. In this regard, J. Gipson Wells (1976) cautions that written documents are too inflexible, they cannot take into account the continuous process of change in marriage, nor can couples anticipate all their potential areas of conflict. Nevertheless, Wells concludes that a document "in black and white" does serve as a valuable reminder of previous mutual agreements. Even better, he suggests, a couple might wish to set up a very tentative and flexible contract, clarifying their basic feelings and intentions,

Vignette 4.3

The Shulmans' Marriage Agreement

I. Principles

We reject the notion that the work which brings in more money is more valuable. The ability to earn money is a privilege which must not be compounded by enabling the larger earner to buy out of his/her duties and put the burden on the partner who earns less or on another person hired from outside.

We believe that each partner has an equal right to his/her own time, work, values, choices. As long as all duties are performed, each of us may use his/her extra time any way he/she chooses. If he/she wants to use it making money, fine. If he/she wants to spend it with spouse, fine.

As parents we believe we must share all responsibility for taking care of our children and home—and not only the work but also the responsibility. At least during the first year of this agreement, *sharing responsibility* shall mean dividing the *jobs* and dividing the *time.*

II. Breakdown and Schedule

(A) *Children*

1. Mornings: Waking children; getting their clothes out; making their lunches; seeing that they have notes, homework, money, bus passes, books; brushing their hair; giving them breakfast (making coffee for us). Every other week each partner does all.
2. Transportation: Getting children to and from lessons, doctors, dentists (including making appointments), friends' houses, etc. Parts occurring between 3 and 6 P.M. fall to wife. She must be compensated by extra work from husband. Husband does weekend transportation and pickups after 6.
3. Help: Helping with homework, personal questions; explaining things. Parts occurring between 3 and 6 P.M. fall to wife. After 6 P.M. husband does Tuesday, Thursday, and Sunday; wife does Monday, Wednesday, and Saturday. Friday is free for whoever has done extra work during the week.

---

but also calling for periodic renegotiation of its terms as new concerns are raised and as the marriage progresses. "Thus," he concludes, "the couple would not be bound to an iron-clad contract, but rather a commitment to communicate continuously with one another on matters which concern them" (p. 36).

Considerations

What considerations are commonly included in personal marriage contracts? The provisions of the Shulmans' contract reported in Vignette 4.3 are one example, but Sussman's study found considerable variation from agree-

4. Nighttime (after 6 P.M.): Getting children to take baths, brush their teeth, put away their toys and clothes, go to bed; reading with them; tucking them in and having nighttime talks; handling if they awake at night. Husband does Tuesday, Thursday, and Sunday. Wife does Monday, Wednesday and Saturday. Friday split according to who has done extra work.
5. Baby sitters: Baby sitters must be called by the parent the sitter is to replace. If no sitter turns up, that parent must stay home.
6. Sick care: Calling doctors; checking symptoms; getting prescriptions filled; remembering to give medicine; taking days off to stay home with sick child, providing special activities. This must still be worked out equally, since now wife seems to do it all. In any case, wife must be compensated (see 10 below).
7. Weekends: All usual child care, plus special activities (beach, park, zoo). Split equally. Husband is free all Saturday, wife is free all Sunday.

(B) *Housework*

8. Cooking: Breakfasts during the week are divided equally; husband does all weekend breakfasts (including shopping for them and dishes). Wife does all dinners except Sunday nights. Husband does Sunday dinner and any other dinners on his nights of responsibility if wife isn't home. Whoever invites guests does shopping, cooking, and dishes; if both invite them, split work.
9. Shopping: Food for all meals, housewares, clothing, and supplies for children. Divide by convenience. Generally, wife does daily food shopping; husband does special shopping.
10. Cleaning: Husband does dishes Tuesday, Thursday, and Sunday. Wife does Monday, Wednesday, and Saturday. Friday is split according to who has done extra work during the week. Husband does all the housecleaning in exchange for wife's extra child care (3 to 6 daily) and sick care.
11. Laundry: Home laundry, making beds, dry cleaning (take and pick up). Wife does home laundry. Husband does dry-cleaning delivery and pick-up.

ment to agreement, depending upon the specific needs and problems of the marital partners. The following types of considerations were most frequently included:

1. *Financial:* Some decision was made in 95 percent of the contracts to combine or separate some or all of the economic assets (such as income and property) of the partners, including those assets brought into the marriage as well as those acquired afterwards.

2. *Career and domicile:* These provisions identify the career objectives of husband and wife. This may include a statement regarding the joint headship of the family and limits on the rights of the husband to determine the couple's domicile.
3. *Children:* Provisions of the contract may specify whether and when to have children, the use of birth control, and responsibilities for parenting. This may also include decisions regarding the custody of children in the event of divorce or death.
4. *Relationships with others:* Agreements sometimes include expectations regarding contacts and relationships with friends, kin, and in some cases, the spouse and children from a former marriage. Desires for sexual fidelity or openness can be specified as well.
5. *Household responsibilities:* Decisions regarding tasks that are to be shared or delegated are often made and sometimes combined with declarations of sexual equality in household responsibilities. Agreements regarding the reallocation of jobs over a period of time are also common.
6. *Duration and review:* Contracts can be indefinite or can include a specific review after a period of one, five, or ten years. The wedding anniversary is the commonly identified time for discussion and renegotiation.
7. *Termination:* Agreements may be made regarding the grounds for terminating the marriage based on mutual or individual desires. This will usually include decisions over how assets are to be divided, support is to be provided, and compensation is to be given for prior relational investments, such as to a wife or husband for financially supporting their spouse through school.

Can such an agreement be enforced? Certainly not in the courts at this time. Nevertheless, while enforcement of a personal contract might be practically impossible, the process of arbitration can help the couple rationally discuss their problems and perhaps aid them in drafting a new agreement that more precisely resolves their areas of conflict.

Summary

Marriage represents a significant step on the ladder of pair commitment. But with this step come contractual obligations as well. Traditionally, marital obligations depended upon commitments created outside the couple from the family and community. These were later replaced by sacred commitments reinforced by the church, which were finally codified in civil law and controlled by the courts. Even though marriage is now based more on personal commitments, the legacy of marriage as a contract remains.

As a legal contract, marriage differs from other contracts, but it does contain implicit legal assumptions. The qualifications for a legally valid marriage vary from state to state. In a minority of states, common-law relationships permit people to self-marry and avoid the legal qualifications that normally would apply to them.

As an interpersonal contract, marriage represents a set of informal, need-fulfilling agreements. Legally, the interpersonal agreement to marry must precede the legal marriage since a state can only recognize, not create, a marriage. Usually, the interpersonal marriage contract assumes relational commitment, companionship, and the promise of personal growth and happiness.

For those persons who do not want the assumptions of their marriage to be implied or unwritten, there is now a growing movement to write supplementary marriage contracts that more carefully specify their expectations. While the legality of many personal contracts is questionable, the process of carefully considering the expectations of each person has been found to be quite helpful in many marriages.

SUGGESTIONS FOR ADDITIONAL READING

Bernard, Jessie. *The Future of Marriage.* New York: Bantam, 1972.

Chronicles the changes in marriage that have been occurring, particularly the growing concept of marriage as a personal venture based on interpersonal commitments.

Henley, Lynda. The Family and the Law. Special Issue of *The Family Coordinator,* October 1977.

A collection of articles dealing with the legal rights of family members, nontraditional family life-styles, divorce, and court-related counseling. Contains an excellent bibliography on marriage and family law.

James, Muriel. *Marriage Is for Loving.* Reading, Mass.: Addison-Wesley, 1979.

A sensitively written book that explores the interpersonal dynamics of marital commitments.

Seligson, Marcia. *The Eternal Bliss Machine: America's Way of Wedding.* New York: Bantam, 1974.

A critical examination of wedding ceremonies, historically and in the present day. The author includes "facts" about weddings as well as the meaning of weddings to participants.

Sheresky, Norman, and Marya Mannes. "A radical guide to wedlock," *Saturday Review/World,* July 29, 1972.

The authors present a very detailed personal marriage contract that may serve as a guide to the kinds of considerations a couple might include in such a contract.

Weitzman, Lenore. "Legal regulation of marriage: tradition and change," *California Law Review* 62(1974): 1169–1288.

A careful look at marriage as a legal contract, its assumptions, and the cases that support the legal structure of marriage.

Chapter 5

Alternative Life-Styles in Marriage

We live today in a culture of alternatives. In the 1920s, Henry Ford could say, "Give them any color car they want as long as it's black," and sell all the black Model T's his company could build. But that approach would not work today—in cars or practically anything else. Few things make us more irritated than not having choices. We shop around for the car, clothes, food, even the college that reflects our own personal needs and preferences. We rarely buy the first thing we see without checking other brands or stores. And if something new comes along, we are often eager to try it out, to see if it is an improvement.

So it is becoming with marriage. Increasingly, we find marriages reflecting the diversity of personalities and life-styles present in our culture. In some marriages, husbands and wives spend much of their time together; in others, they do not. In some marriages, household responsibilities are shared; in others, they are not. Marriages can also vary according to such things as the number of relatives or nonrelatives living in the household, the degree of sexual freedom permitted by the spouse, and the amount of the family's resources that is shared with others.

It would be a mistake, however, to conclude that people shop for a marriage like they shop for a car. Not all the alternatives available are considered by everyone. Some marital life-styles practiced today would be rejected out of hand by many couples. For example, not everyone wants to join a commune or is willing to accept a sexually open relationship. But we must keep in mind that a large number of conventional monogamous couples do not want to imitate the marriages of their parents or their work associates either. What they want is a marriage that fits the particular blend of needs and interests they have developed. When those needs change for whatever reason, a new, supportive life-style is often sought.

Life-styles

Thus, the term **life-style** reflects the growing flexibility that we find in the marital patterns of today. Life-styles involve shared tastes and preferences that are more narrow than those linked to social class, ethnic background, or other subcultural groupings (Zablocki and Kanter, 1976). Rather, they cut across society and categorize people according to similarities in their consumption patterns, moral beliefs, political attitudes, or social networks. People with similar life-styles have more in common, and friendships as well as marital choices evolve more frequently out of life-style preferences than anything else.

In this chapter, we will explore some of the diverse life-styles that are found in contemporary marriages. Our discussion will not be limited to the nontraditional alternatives attracting some couples today, but will also include several of the conventional life-styles typical of most present-day marriages. Our perspective is to be analytical, not judgmental, since most people find life-styles other than their own difficult to appreciate. But if we are truly to understand the nature of marriage today, we must also understand its diversity. Only then can we comprehend the way the institution of marriage meets the needs of a variety of people in a heterogeneous culture.

CONVENTIONAL MARRIAGE LIFE-STYLES

Conventional marriage styles are those that are generally acceptable to most members of a society. In a relatively simple society, such as a tribe or a small, isolated community, the range of acceptable marital life-styles is usually very limited. Although the pattern of marriage that is preferred can vary considerably from one such society to another, within each simple society there are strong pressures placed on everyone to conform to the marital patterns of their parents and peers.

Alternatives in complex societies

In a complex society such as the United States, however, there are more likely to be several alternative marriage styles that are considered legitimate. Certainly, personal and reference-group preferences will orient a couple toward considering a particular marital pattern "better" than another. But there is still likely to be more than one model of marriage which can be followed without undue social or legal penalty.

Out of the numerous attempts to identify the dominant marital life-styles in America today, the most useful results to date have come from a study conducted by sociologists John Cuber and Peggy Harroff (1966). These researchers intensively interviewed husbands and wives from over 400 upper-middle-class marriages for the expressed purpose of identifying normal variations in successful American families. After the interviews were completed, Cuber and Harroff isolated only those couples who had been married for ten years or longer and who said they had never seriously considered divorce or separation. The 211 couples that remained often represented quite different conceptions of marriage, yet each of these husbands and wives considered their marriage adjusted and meaningful.

Since marriages contain distinct personality and relational differences, not all marriages can be easily linked to one marital life-style or another. Nevertheless, Cuber and Harroff were able to identify two basic life-styles into which nearly all their adjusted couples fell: **intrinsic marriage** and **utilitarian marriage.** In the discussion that follows, we will briefly examine each of these marital life-styles as well as a new conventional life-style, **cluster marriage,** which has a growing number of adherents today.

Intrinsic Marriages

Importance of intimacy

Among couples in intrinsic marriages, the husband-wife relationship receives the highest priority in their lives. Cuber and Harroff found that these couples often have extensive career, child-rearing, community, and other obligations, yet they somehow meet these diverse demands without threatening the integrity of their marriage. Intrinsic commitments bind the couple into a highly intimate union in which the greatest source of pleasure comes from being together and sharing in almost every aspect of one another's lives. This marital life-style is well illustrated by the husband in one of the couples Cuber and Harroff studied:

> From the time I was a child I never thought of it any other way. The first and central thing even in my adolescent fantasies was a close couple. I don't know how I came to see it this way because my parents certainly weren't especially close and I can't recall any particular pair who have set the model for me. It seems to come from inside. . .
>
> Now that does not mean that we haven't differences—sometimes sharp ones—or that I haven't inhibited some desires because she doesn't want to share them. All I mean is that I just don't have or want to have any separate existence that amounts to anything. I do my work as well as I can—but—and I'm a little ashamed when I realize it—it doesn't have the importance to me that people think it does. As far as I'm concerned the whole corporation can go to hell any time if it infringes unduly on her, and especially on *us,* and the things that are precious to us. (p. 134)

Not all married couples experience or prefer this intrinsic marital life-style. Cuber and Harroff could place only about one out of six of the couples married for ten years or more in this category (Broderick, 1971). Lois Pratt (1976), in a study of a random sample of northeastern families, found a similar minority of what she called "energized families." Pratt identified 10 percent of the families she studied as fitting this intrinsic model, with another 20 to 30 percent reporting to have some characteristics of this marital life-style.

Preferences

Young couples appear to be more likely to prefer an intrinsic marriage than the more mature couples in the above studies. In a recent examination of college students in Connecticut, Leslie Strong (1978) asked each of the men and women to rate his or her willingness to participate in a variety of alternative marital styles. The option of "egalitarian marriage," a principal component of intrinsic marriage, was by considerable margin the most frequently preferred type of marriage for both men and women. Lest we conclude that the times are changing, however, we should note that Cuber and Harroff estimate that approximately two-thirds of the marriages they studied *started out* as intrinsic (Broderick, 1971). Half of these couples dropped this marital life-style during the first decade of their marriage.

Decline over time

The decline over time in intrinsic marriages points out the difficulty most couples have in maintaining the intense personal commitments that are required. From the outside, the pull of other obligations gradually increases, wearing away at the time and energy needed to maintain this life-style. Social disapproval is also experienced, as represented in the statement from a psychologist interviewed by Cuber and Harroff: "Sooner or later you've got to act your age. People who stay to themselves so much must have some psychological problems—if they don't, they'll soon develop them" (p. 138).

From the inside of the relationship, it takes a sincere effort to continue an intrinsic marriage (Ammons and Stinnett, 1980). Periodic, half-hearted attempts to share experiences are not enough to make this marital life-style work. Other responsibilities can continue, but only to the extent that they do not take away from the marriage. This requires a dedication to one another that few couples can maintain, and many others would disdain. To couples who prefer this life-style, the effort is personally and relationally fulfilling. To others, the demands seem restrictive and stifling.

Utilitarian Marriages

Instrumental commitments

A second major style of conventional marriage identified by Cuber and Harroff is what they termed the utilitarian marriage. Again, these marriages are considered satisfying to the husbands and wives involved, but the relationship itself is considered more rational and purposive than exciting and personal. Instrumental commitments play a much more important role in holding the relationship together. The researchers explain, "By the term Utilitarian Marriage we mean any marriage which is established or maintained for purposes other than to express an intimate, highly important *personal* relationship between a man and a woman. The absence of continuous and deep empathic feeling and the existence of an atmosphere of limited companionship are natural outcomes, since the purposes for its establishment or maintenance are not primarily sexual or emotional ones" (p. 109).

Separate interests

Utilitarian marriages often contain some intrinsic qualities. For example, a husband and wife may claim to feel genuine love and concern for one another. Yet the most apparent quality in these marriages is independence. The marriage serves more as a home base for the separate interests of the husband and wife than as the focus of either of their life interests. Neither person really expects to share in much of the life of the other. This observation that marriages differ in the extent to which couples share or separate their lives was characterized uniquely by a woman in one of Cuber and Harroff's interviews:

> Well, we've got a marriage-type marriage. Do you know what I mean? So many people—and me in my first marriage—just sort of touch on the edges of existence—don't *really* marry. It's funny, but my cookbook distinguishes between marinating and marrying of flavors. You know—the marinated flavors retain their identity—just mix a little—or the one predominates strongly over the other. But the married ones blend into something really new and the separate identities are lost. Well, a lot of people that I know aren't married at all—just marinated! (p. 133)

The transition to utilitarian marriage

While the majority of couples interviewed by Cuber and Harroff fell into the category of utilitarian (or "marinated") marriage, most did not begin their marriage with this intent. Rather, this life-style simply developed over time as their interests grew more and more disparate. Likewise, most of the college men and women studied by Strong report that they do not want a traditional, nonegalitarian marriage. But this preference is much stronger among young women than young men, and without a strong commitment to intrinsic marriage from husbands as well as wives, the likelihood of a utilitarian marriage in the future is also high for them.

Among those couples who experienced a transition from intrinsic to utilitarian marriage, most did so with a note of solemn resignation remembering the earlier times. As one woman put it:

> Judging by the way it was when we were first married—say the first five years or so—things are pretty matter-of-fact now—even dull. They're dull between us, I mean. The children are a lot of fun, keep us pretty busy, and there are lots of outside things—you know, like little league and the P.T.A. and the Swim Club, and even the company parties aren't always so bad. But I mean where Bob and I are concerned—if you followed us around, you'd wonder why we ever got married.
>
> Now I don't say this to complain, not in the least. There's a cycle to life. . . . You have to adjust to these things and we both try to gracefully. (pp. 47–48)

Expectations

Some couples in utilitarian marriages do not need to make this transition; they begin their marriage with the understanding that their lives and roles are moving in separate directions. There is no need for children, jobs, friends, and social life to pull them apart; each respects the other's independent interests from the start of their relationship. Lower-class and blue-collar marriages are most often like this (Komarovsky, 1964), and Cuber and Harroff found that this life-style was not uncommon in the middle class either. There appears to be little disillusionment among these couples since their personal interests have always been focused away from the marriage. They consider their marriage useful to them, try not to distract one another too much, and avoid communication and conflicts with one another as much as possible. This type of relationship is illustrated in the comments of a physician:

> I don't know why everyone seems to make so much about men and women and marriage. Of course, I'm married and if anything happened to my wife, I'd get married again. I think it's the proper way to live. It's convenient, orderly, and solves a lot of problems. But there are other things in life. I spent nearly ten years preparing for the practice of my profession. The biggest thing to me is the practice of my profession. . . . And I'll bet if you talked with my wife, you wouldn't get any of that "trapped housewife" stuff from her either. Now that the children are grown, she finds a lot of useful and necessary work to do in this community. She works as hard as I do. (p. 53)

Cluster Marriages

Characteristics of clusters

In contrast to intrinsic and utilitarian marriages, cluster marriages are not yet very commonly found in North America. Nevertheless, the principles of cluster marriages are beginning to gain national attention, and because they are generally acceptable to most members of American society, we include them in the category of conventional marriage-styles. Basically, cluster marriages include a group of individual families within a community who agree to meet together regularly and provide mutual support for one another (Sawin, 1977). Each family retains its own economic and social identity, but they influence one another through frequent sharing of their problems, needs, satisfactions, and experiences. A cluster will most often contain four or five family units, including perhaps childless couples, couples with children, single persons, or older couples (Pringle, 1974). The variety of backgrounds represented enhances the ability of individuals to learn from one another and to support the unique needs of each family that is represented.

In our impersonal society, the cluster marriage represents an attempt to establish a kinshiplike bond that broadens the intimate support base for its members. But unlike kinship bonds, cluster bonds are more likely to be local, based on commonly felt needs, flexible in the sense that they can expand or contract, and available for frequent, face-to-face reinforcement. Often, kin relations and friends are not immediately available nor are they sought out to provide the variety of personal and family supports necessary to cope today.

Problems in clusters

Cluster arrangements seem to provide a balance between needs for marital independence and needs for a more extended network of friends and family. In the cluster, the marital unit is offered the opportunity for further intimacy and caring without the necessity for comarital sexuality. But still, not all relationships are adequately prepared for the group commitments implied in marital clusters. Some people are too private and others too controlling to be comfortable in this arrangement. Meeting regularly may be a problem. Sustaining the cluster requires planning, coordination, and genuine caring for one another on a continuing basis. There also have to be provisions for replacing members who leave for whatever reason. Not many marriages are capable of making these extended commitments, so the likelihood of attracting many adherents to this life-style is not very great at this time (Wasserman *et al.*, 1979).

NONCONVENTIONAL MARRIAGE STYLES

The search for alternative life-styles

Not all couples marrying or married today feel comfortable in the conventional marriage styles we have just described. There are now, and there always have been, people who "march to a different drummer." They want to go their own way, irrespective of anyone else. Sometimes they are idealists; sometimes they are disillusioned; and sometimes they are prophets who point the way for others to follow. Every generation has had its share of men and women who feel compelled to form living arrangements different from others. But never before has nonconformity reached the proportions it has today. Now, more than ever before, people feel free to choose for a time, or for a lifetime, to leave the mainstream of conventional marriage and enter into sexually open marriages, communes, group marriages, or emerging styles of contractual cohabitation. The legality and morality of these arrangements have been seriously questioned, but for a growing number of people, these life-styles offer an alternative way of living.

Not many decades ago, people were very unlikely to think seriously of adopting nontraditional, nonconventional life-styles. At the turn of this century, our strong national commitment to **ethnocentrism** caused us to view traditional marriage as right not only for members of our own society, but for everyone else as well. Later, as anthropological studies began to discover the stability of a variety of marital arrangements, social values shifted toward an attitude of **cultural relativism.** This meant that the public was increasingly willing to accept the fact that other people could live differently, as long as they lived in some far-off land and did not influence the way we live.

New acceptability of alternatives

By the 1960s and 1970s, a new value system, **intracultural pluralism,** gradually began to spread through society. There was increasing freedom granted to people to consider life-styles that prior to this time would have been strictly forbidden. What previously had been considered *unacceptable* then became merely *nonconventional.* This is not the same as approval, but for the first time society recognized the right of people to search for a different way of life that is more personally meaningful to them. Comments like "Do your own thing, as long as it doesn't affect me" or "Different strokes for different folks" reflected this emerging acceptance of a pluralistic value system.

The reasons behind this revolutionary change in personal and family values are many and varied. The rapid mobility of American society has helped, since frequent moves separate friends and kin and isolate people

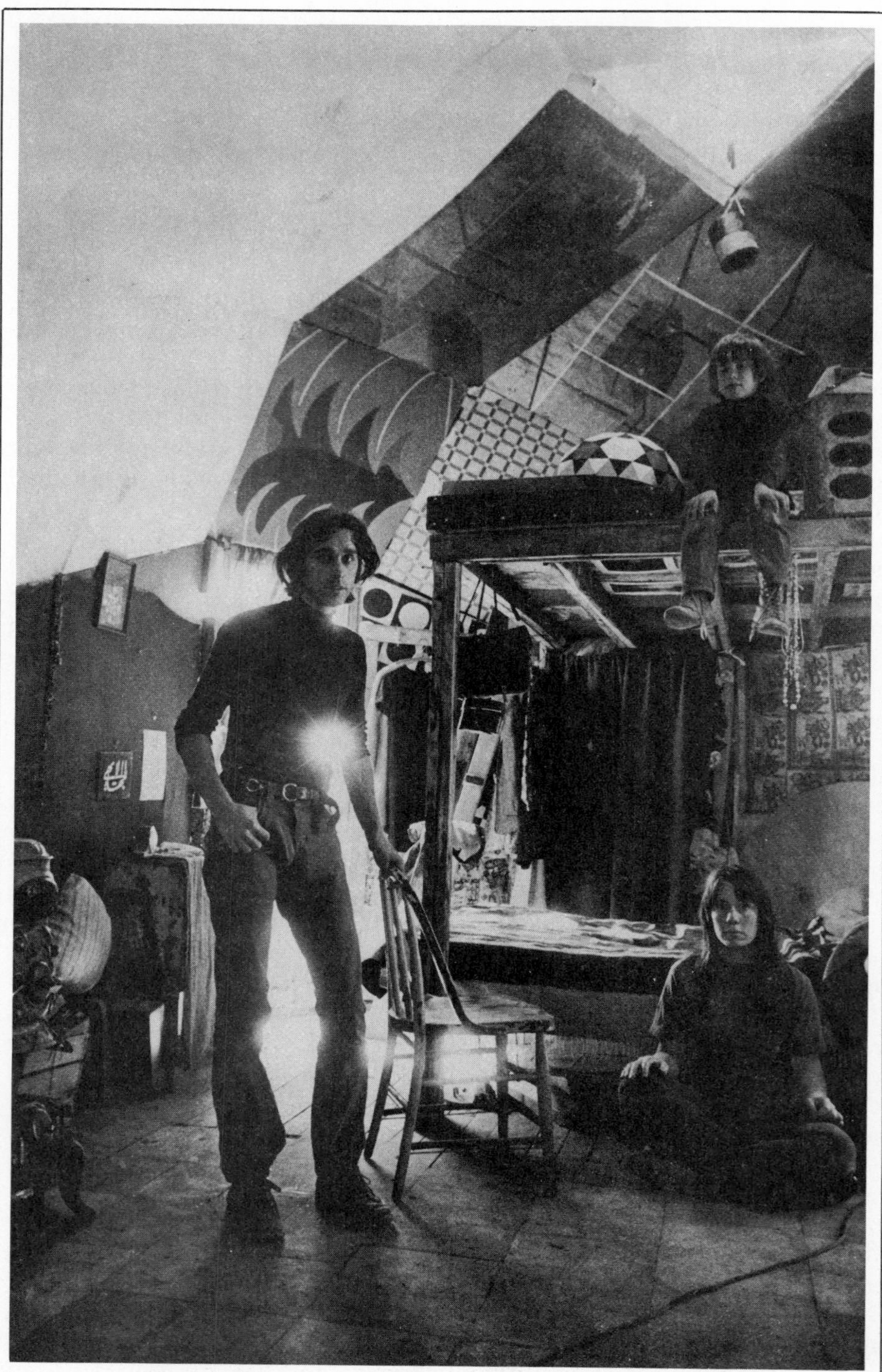

Life-styles once found "unacceptable" are now merely "nonconventional."

from the identity of their roots. Husbands, wives, and children often go in different directions during the day, making each more independent of the other, loosening their common values and intimacy. The rising divorce rate has disillusioned many youth about their prospects in a traditional marriage. And for a growing number of women, conventional marriage is seen as a threat to their personal and vocational flexibility.

Attitudes toward nonconventionality

Still, we must keep in mind that most members of our society, old and young, women and men, do *not* prefer to participate in nonconventional marital life-styles. This point was aptly demonstrated by sociologist Leslie Strong (1978) in his study of Connecticut college students' attitudes toward alternative marriage and family forms. The majority of the women in his study considered intrinsic-egalitarian marriages to be the only option in which they were willing to participate. Most of the women did not favorably consider any of the nonconventional marriage styles for themselves (see Fig. 5.1). The men in the study were somewhat more favorable toward nonconventional marriage styles, but even their willingness to participate indicated quite conservative marital expectations (see Fig. 5.1). Results similar to these were found in a study that included noncollege youth as well (Jurich and Jurich, 1975).

Nevertheless, just as intrinsic-egalitarian marriages were once considered nonconventional and were preferred by only a few couples, perhaps the marital alternatives practiced by a few people today point toward possible directions of marriages of the future. Some of today's nonconventional alternatives are no doubt little more than social experiments of little future

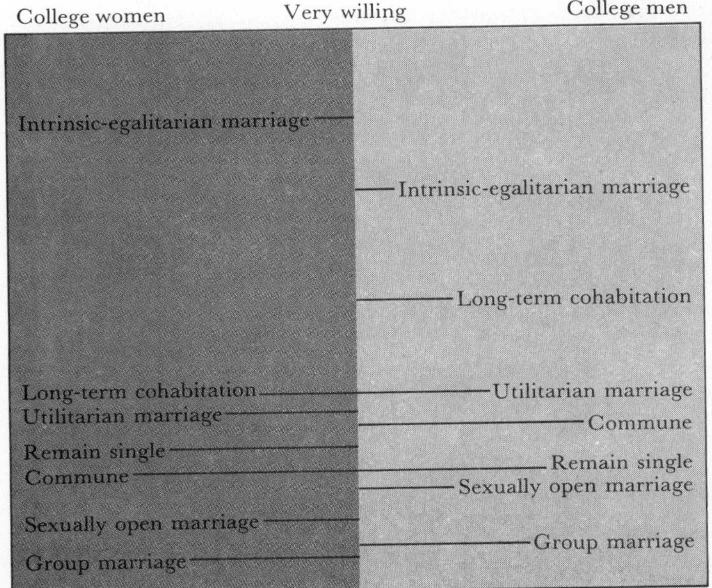

Fig. 5.1

Willingness to Participate in Alternative Marital Life-Styles

Source: Adapted from Strong (1978), p. 495.

importance. But others may offer a different perspective on marriage that will catch on or, at the very least, provide a glimpse of some of the ways in which present strains in conventional marriages are being resolved.

Sexually Open Marriages

Unlike conventional marriages, in which sexual exclusiveness between husbands and wives is the ideal, sexually open marriages permit each spouse to develop intimate relationships with others. Deception is not necessary, since the potential for sexual intimacy is openly recognized. However, relationships

Vignette 5.1 Our Open Marriage

According to the O'Neills in their book *Open Marriage*, an open marriage has the following qualities: living for now, realistic expectations, privacy, open and honest communication, flexibility in roles, open companionship, equality, identity, and trust. We feel that our marriage has all of these qualities so we consider it an open marriage.

The O'Neills believe that couples with open marriages should decide whether or not to be open to outside relationships. . . . But we want to emphasize at the beginning that our interest is in *relationships* with others, rather than just *sex* with others. Our search is for intimacy, caring, and love—all of which can, but don't necessarily, involve sex. In this we differentiate our open marriage from old-fashioned swinging, where the focus was on sex devoid of deep emotions. . . .

Because there are no generally accepted ethical standards for nonmonogamous relationships, each couple must develop their own. Our own personal guidelines have evolved through our experiences, and are always subject to revision. About a year ago we attempted to put our moral standards into words. These four principles are ideals which we try to live up to, but don't always succeed:

1. *Autonomy.* Neither of us has the right to put demands on the other. Where we disagree, we go off separately in our individual ways. Or we try to compromise in ways that don't leave one of us resentful. If neither of these ways will work on an important issue, an ultimate resolution would be ending the marriage. That would be preferable to one of us giving up too much autonomy. Thus, we each have the right to have whatever relationships with others we want.
2. *The primacy of our own relationship.* We feel a deep commitment to each other, and do not want outside relationships to harm our own beautiful relationship. So far, it has only been deepened as we grow through intimate involvements with others. Others must accept that our own relationship is of primary importance.

are not entered into only for sexual gratification but for the fulfillment of a variety of personal needs. According to Francoeur and Francoeur (1973):

> An open marriage is an honest relationship between two people who accept each other as equals, friends, and partners. It is a nonmanipulative, nonexploitive relationship with equal freedom and identity for both partners, allowing and encouraging each to enrich themselves and their primary relationship with a variety of relationships that complement and reinforce the marriage. (p. 30)

Characteristics

A sexually open marriage should not be confused with an extramarital affair, nor would it include what is sometimes referred to as **swinging** (see Vignette 5.1). Affairs involve relationships which are secretly kept from the

---

3. *Honesty.* Open communication is essential to us. This means first that we try to be totally open with each other—even when it hurts. It also means that we will not keep a confidence from each other. If someone wants to tell one of us a "secret," we warn that person that the secret will not be kept from our spouse.

   There is one exception to the principle of honesty for us. We *will* keep each other's confidences from others. So, although Wendy will not keep her lover's confidences from Burt, she will keep Burt's confidences from her lover. This is, admittedly, a double standard of honesty, but there are many times that we want to tell each other something that we are not ready to tell a third person. It would inhibit the openness between the two of us to operate in any other way.
4. *Speaking for ourselves.* We try to avoid getting caught in the middle between our spouse and a lover. If Burt is having problems with his lover, Wendy does not have the right to call up the lover and tell her what is on Burt's mind. To do so would probably only make things worse. Direct communication is likely to be much more effective and accurate than indirect communication through a third party. Thus, unless Wendy were asked by both Burt and his lover to operate as a kind of mutual facilitator, she would just encourage the two of them to work the problem out. Too often in the past, we have each resented the other for trying to interpret our feelings to others. Now if someone asks Burt how Wendy feels about something, he tries to respond, "Ask Wendy."

These standards are highly personal, hammered out through many hours of thought and discussion. We would never propose them as universal standards for everyone, any more than we would recommend open marriage to everyone. These principles may change in the future. But they reflect where we are now.

From Wendy and Burt, reprinted from Bernard I. Murstein, ed., *Exploring Intimate Life Styles.*

partner, usually short-lived, and because of hurried encounters, often sexually motivated. The characteristics of relationships in open marriage are just the opposite. Swinging, which is a comarital activity—both husband and wife participate—involves couples switching partners for a very short time, strictly for sexual, not emotional, gratification. Again, this is the reverse of the emphasis on extended friendships in open marriage. James Ramey (1975) found that during 80 percent of the contacts between nonmarried intimates no sexual activity was involved. Most of their time together was devoted to social and recreational activities.

Younger couples tend to be the most likely to enter into sexually open marriages. In a study of *Psychology Today* readers, it was reported that about 5 percent of the couples under thirty years of age had already experienced comarital sexual activity, while many others indicated some interest if the opportunity arose (Athanasiou, *et al.*, 1970). Most studies have also found that the majority of these couples are from upper-educated, upper-middle class, professional, and semiprofessional backgrounds (Knapp and Whitehurst, 1978). Another tendency is for these couples to have very low religious involvement, little close contact with their parents or other kin, and to report relatively unhappy childhood experiences. They typically report that their spouse and friends are the most important influences in their lives (Pitsiou, 1977).

Attractions of this life-style

After studying over one hundred persons in sexually open marriages, Knapp and Whitehurst conclude that *two polar types of couples* are attracted to this marital life-style. The first type, a minority, includes couples whose marriages are deteriorating and who see this arrangement as an alternative to divorce. These couples agree to support the philosophy of sexually open marriage since, in theory, it provides the emotional and physical support they are not getting from one another. Nevertheless, these marriages continued to deteriorate, often aggravated by the demands of the outside relationships and the hidden resentments that come from seeing one another satisfied by someone else.

The second type of sexually open marriage is motivated by a quite different rationale. These couples maintain "strong, stable, primary relationships in which there is a high degree of mutual affection, respect, understanding, and agreement regarding the choice of life-style" (Knapp and Whitehurst, p. 47). The couple described in Vignette 5.1 would fall into this category, and the ground rules they set for their open marriage appear to be implicit in this type of relationship. In terms of their personalities, couples in stable, open marriages do not appear to be more personally maladjusted than those from the general population. However, Knapp (1976) found that the personality test scores of these men and women indicated much higher individualistic, independent, high achievement, creative, and nonconforming values and behavior than are normally found.

Marriage commitments

From the perspective of the couples involved, sexually open marriage depends upon an ability to integrate outside relationships with the marriage so that each relationship openly benefits the others. This requires a mutual and exceptional commitment to marriage in which new friendships are seen as *additions, not alternatives,* to the primary marital bond. Sexual exclusiveness also has to be explained away as immature or restrictive and replaced with a new attitude of sexual intimacy as normal within any close, affectionate friendship. While some couples may be capable of the trust and openness necessary for this marital life-style, it is doubtful that most marriages can successfully handle the jealousy or guilt that often follows.

Potential problems

There are also moral and social problems with which most people would have to deal. Sexual fidelity is a core principle of the Judeo-Christian concept of marriage, and it is written into the adultery laws of every state. Still, if breaking these traditional mores does not produce guilt, then the pragmatic concerns of hiding intimate friendships from children, kin, work associates, and other friends may induce at least a concern about being caught that is foreign to the personal feeling of openness that justifies these relationships. Are they really that "open" or not? And if not, the insecurity associated with entering into relationships that might affect one's job, child rearing, and ultimately one's marriage can be a heavy burden for some to bear.

Communes

Group concerns primary

Perhaps the most complex alternative to conventional marriage is the commune. Communes involve social and economic ties that bind a group of people into a common residential, cooperative unit. Legal and blood ties are not the primary bonding agents in communes, although many communes do contain married couples and their children. Other common characteristics of communes include an emphasis upon group concerns instead of individual concerns, the sharing of common values, the ownership of common property, the sharing of common space to interact, the sharing of work, and the idealization of intrinsic commitment bonds in which people interact with one another as "wholes" rather than in terms of specific roles (Kanter, 1973).

Communes are not new

Communes are by no means new on the world scene. History has recorded numerous attempts in many societies to form successful communal groups. Even some early Christians practiced communal living according to the book of Acts 2:44-45: "All believers continued together in close fellowship and shared their belongings with one another. They would sell their property and possessions and distribute the money among them according to what they need" (*Good News for Modern Man*). Perhaps the most successful large-scale communal movement resulted in the *kibbutzim* of Israel, now in existence for more than sixty years.

In the United States, according to Murstein (1978), "Communes are as American as apple pie." By 1843, some thirty-four communes were established and attracting members to this alternative life-style. The most successful of these was the Oneida Community in New York, which lasted for over

Sharing is central to communal living.

thirty years. While ultimately none of these communes survived, other attempts followed and a major revival of communal interest occurred again in the late 1960s.

By the early 1970s, over 3000 communal groups could be identified in the United States. Some of these communes were little more than shelters for people evading the Vietnam war and its attendant social frustrations. But the majority were founded as sincere attempts to discover more economically and emotionally meaningful life-styles. The support of youth for this life-style was confirmed in 1972 when over one-third of the young adults nationally sampled by the Institute of Life Insurance felt that communes would become a common alternative to traditional family life. More significantly, over half said they would encourage their children to join a commune if that was what they wanted (Danziger and Greenwald, 1977).

Waning interest

Nevertheless, this initial enthusiam has begun to wane. The number of recognized communes today is perhaps one-third to one-half of what it was in the early 1970s. Yet, while the growth of communes has slowed, so has the decline of those communes still in existence (David, 1978). Networks of communes that mutually support one another have been formed, quietly, confidently, and without the fanfare common a decade ago. The dissident youth drawn into the communal movement earlier have been replaced by more mature, economically self-sufficient men and women and even older people who are trying to live meaningfully in their later years (Hochschild, 1973).

Communal attractions

While the term "commune" refers to a special type of relationship, there are a variety of different life-styles represented by these arrangements. Some communes are as small as three or four people; others may include as many as 1000 members. Some communes are rural; most are urban. Some communes are self-sufficient; others are dependent on the outside labor of their members. Some communes permit sexual freedom; others require sexual exclusivity. As real as these differences are, however, we can identify several distinct **visions**, or ideals toward which communes are drawn, even though these visions are sometimes blurred and changeable, and even though, quite often, several different visions operate at the same time (David).

The first major communal vision is that of a community based on **economic sharing.** Members work together to meet one another's needs with the rewards being distributed equally to everyone in the community. This emphasis on noncompetitiveness is illustrated by one communard: "We are holists—in the sense that each of us sees himself or herself as a functioning part of a whole that is much greater and more valuable than the sum of its parts. We each make an equal contribution. We are totally interdependent" (Sprague, 1972, p. 125).

The second communal vision emphasizes a **pioneer spirit.** For many communes, this means going back to the land to derive some, if not all, of their subsistence. Ecological consciousness is the foundation of many rural communes, and in urban communes, this is expressed through the use of natural foods and participation in various ecological movements. Most important to the pioneer spirit appears to be a feeling of having left a former way of life behind in favor of a new relational frontier.

A third vision is that of an **extended family,** with members sharing a common house and caring for one another's emotional needs. In a sense, this communal vision is a reaction against the individualistic, fragmentary family life many experience today. Kinship ties are involuntary, but communal ties are seen as voluntary and based on a mutual desire to assume responsibility for one another.

A fourth important vision for communes is the sharing of a **common ideology.** For some communal groups, the dominant ideology is political, such as those organized around Maoist revolutionary principles or Gandhian nonviolence. Others are held together by a common spiritual bond. Sometimes, these latter groups are pulled together under the guidance of a guru-type leader. Often, the ideology they share is fundamental Christian or a combination of Eastern religion and Christian principles.

Communal survival

In general, the communal groups that embrace all of these visions have been the ones most likely to survive. From her extensive research, Kanter concludes the communes that succeed are those "that develop common purpose, and an integrating philosophy, a structure for leadership and decision making, criteria for membership and entrance procedures, organize work and property communally, affirm their bonds through ritual, and work out interpersonal difficulties through regular open confrontation" (p. 407).

The majority of communes, however, have not succeeded, and most fail because their commitment to the communal ideals is limited. Some dissolve because their guru leaves and no one can fill the ideological void. Many rural communes have the pioneer spirit but little knowledge of how to work the land or work together. Those who believe in economic sharing sometimes neglect the familylike intimacy that is necessary to maintain long-term commitments to group rather than individual goals. Some religious communes place so much emphasis on personal growth that the individuals involved lose their ability to cooperate with one another.

Children

Children are another source of potential strain in communes (see Vignette 5.2). In some communes, parents are responsible for their children, while in others, children are the responsibility of everyone. The broader the assumed responsibility, the greater the chance that adult disagreements will arise over discipline and appropriate child rearing. While children do benefit from the extended contacts and role models available to them, they are also confused at times by the different expectations to which they are subject (Weisberg, 1977). At Twin Oaks, a successful commune in Virginia, the anticipation of these and other problems led to the rule of "no children" for a number of years. Only recently has this rule been selectively rescinded.

Partner commitments

Coupling also represents a potential problem of sorts for communes. Most communes permit pairing, and couples are often attracted to communal life. Yet communes require group commitments that sometimes supersede couple commitments. According to one study, this frequently led to loss of control over the partner and an overall loss of commitment to the pair relationship (Kanter *et al.*, 1975). This study also found that nearly 50 percent of the couples separated during their first few months in a commune, often because their relationship was already unsatisfactory. However, on the positive side, the remaining couples and the couples that formed later are often strengthened by the group support and their common resolve to make this life-style work.

Contrary to the image of communes as sexually promiscuous, most communes exercise strict controls over sexual behavior. Some communes may permit a variety of sexual partners, but this is the exception, not the norm. In general, the most stable communes practice sexual monogamy and reflect a high degree of commitment in these relationships (Stinnett and Birdsong, 1978).

Group Marriage

Sexual polygamy

A marriage alternative that combines some of the features of sexually open marriage with communal living is group marriage. Group marriages consist of three or more persons who consider themselves interpersonally married to

Vignette 5.2 The Cinderella Children

Once upon a time there was a beautiful little girl who lived in a house with her stepmother and three stepsisters. All day long the stepmother and stepsisters told the girl what to do. "Sweep the floor!" "No, dust the furniture!" "Do the dishes!" The young girl worked from dawn to dusk, but the more she worked, the more her stepmother and stepsisters yelled at her. Cinderella? No, Alice. Alice is five years old and lives in an urban commune.

Small children's experiences in urban communes resemble Cinderella's in many ways, since these children grow up in households with people unrelated to them. Urban communes typically consist of five or more adults who share a kitchen, household chores, and expenses, and a definition of themselves as a group, commune, or family . . .

In nuclear families only one or two adults make and enforce rules at home. In urban communes many adults run the house, own a share of the household property, and therefore have a legitimate claim to what happens around them. The result? The Cinderella effect, in which young children face many authority figures at home.

One five-year-old girl described this phenomenon, "Sometimes it's not so much fun to live here because there's a lot of people that chase you around and tell what to do. Like they tell me sometimes when I'm sneaking food . . . 'Stop eating all the food, it's almost dinnertime.' And sometimes they say, 'Don't stand on the chair; it's very weak!' or 'Don't run around the dining table when we're eating because it spills all the coffee and milk and water.'"

Like Cinderella, communal children often face the double jeopardy of being reprimanded more than once for the same offense. An adult may enter a room and scold a child for not picking up his clothes a few moments after another adult has cited the child for the same offense.

The Cinderella effect—"Do this!" "You didn't do this!"—also produces frustration. As one mother explains, "What really drives Ethan crazy is if someone says to him, 'Ethan, do this,' and he's in the process of doing it when someone says, 'Ethan, do that.' It really flips him out. It must be one of the most difficult experiences for him here.". . .

Do communal children enjoy living with so many adults? Although they don't like having so many bosses, the children agree unequivocally that it is fun to live with many grownups. For communal children, more adults mean more playmates and playthings; "more TVs, more games, and stuff like that"; more people to read bedtime stories, "stories every night, three stories, or ten stories, or forty stories"; and more presents on birthdays, Christmas, and holidays.

More grownups also mean companionship, more people with whom to enjoy favorite activities such as jogging, softball, going to Ping-Pong tournaments or to football games (especially if one's parent hates football). It means learning to cook, to sing, and play guitar, to play adults' games such as Scrabble. It means more people to ask for rides to do an errand or go to a friend's house; more people to help with homework and to talk to after school if parents are not around.

at least two other members of the group. This means they have **multiple pair-bonds,** which in Chapter 1 we identified as a *multilateral relationship.* The members of the group marriage live together, share in the responsibilities of their household, raise their children together, and voluntarily permit sexual access to one another. Thus, they are sexually polygamous, emotionally bonded, and have obligations to maintain a communal household.

The most common group marriage is a **triad** with two women and a man (Constantine and Constantine, 1973). This usually begins with a couple marriage to which another woman is added. Sometimes two couples become sexually and emotionally intimate and a four-person group marriage is formed. Theoretically, any number can join, but group marriages larger than six people are very rare. Sexual relations between opposite-sex members are usually expected in this type of arrangement, and sexual relations between same-sex members are not uncommon, particularly in triads. From a legal standpoint, these groups are *not* "marriages," and their acceptance of the term marriage is derived from their mutual commitment to one another.

Attitudes toward group marriage

Group marriages are not a new family form, but they are culturally unusual. In no known culture has this type of marriage predominated (Murdock, 1949), but the practice is by no means unknown. For example, among the Kaingang, a tribe in Brazil, this style of marriage was entered into quite frequently (Henry, 1964). In the United States, however, group marriages have never been supported, and not until the 1960s were they even widely recognized as a potential marital option. Still, attitudes toward group marriage remain generally hostile; even current college youth rank this alternative most unfavorably (see Fig. 5.1). According to the Constantines' extensive study, "Pressed for an estimate, we would guess there may be fewer than a hundred, almost certainly less than a thousand group marriages in the United States" (1972, p. 206).

While the total number of existing group marriages is small, many others experiment with this life-style at some time. Some were attracted to group marriage after reading one of the popular novels of the 1960s that proposed this life-style. They went out seeking this type of arrangement, but few of these *intentional* group marriages could survive the emotional shock more than a few weeks (Constantine, 1978). Somewhat more stable are those group marriages that evolve in a more natural way, out of a genuine desire to extend their love to others, avoid the sexual restriction of monogamy, restore a sense of community for their children, and gain the economic advantages of cooperative living. This involves a process of multiple courtship and time to develop a feeling of comfort with the network of relationships.

Fragility

Most group marriages, despite their ideals, do not last very long. Some groups have survived for a decade or longer, but most dissolve in twelve to sixteen months (Constantine, 1978). In part, this fragility derives from the people attracted to the life-style. Compared to people in conventional marriages, those in group marriages tend to have exceptionally high sex interests, more extramarital sexual experiences, poorer relationships with their parents, more nonreligious backgrounds, and on personality tests, they rank higher in needs for change and autonomy and lower in needs for endurance and order (Murstein, 1978). This type of person is usually more capable of expanding his or her intimacy, but less likely to maintain long-term interpersonal commitments, even with one other person let alone several others.

The problems associated with maintaining multiple-pair partners in group living are sometimes insurmountable. If communication breakdowns, value or personality conflicts, jealousy over the time spent with others, and provisions for sexual arrangements complicate two-person marriages, imagine the potential for strain in multilateral marriages.

Contract Cohabitation

Emerging out of the legal turmoil of the 1970s is a relatively new relational alternative, **contract cohabitation.** Sometimes labeled "nonnuptial contract agreements," or "contract consortium," these arrangements attempt to fulfill the affectional and support functions of monogamous marriage without the legal commitments implied in the state-defined marriage contract. The conditions of the relationship are negotiated by the couple themselves and specified in terms that reflect their own needs and life-style.

Contract in lieu of marriage

Unlike antenuptial and postnuptial personal contracts (Chapter 4), which assume a relationship based on a legal marriage contract, contract

As Lee Marvin discovered, relational contracts can sometimes be applied to unmarried couples.

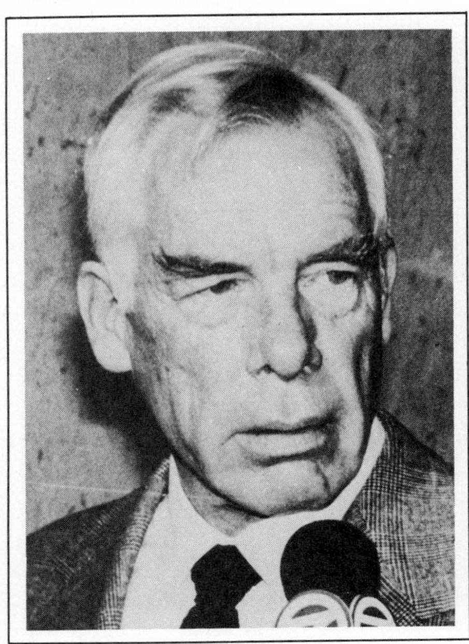

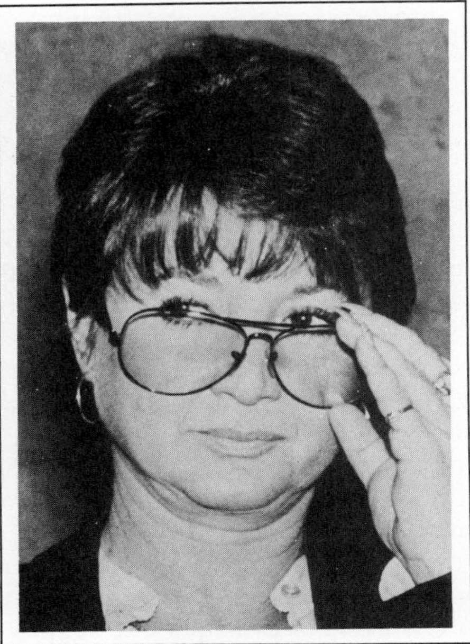

cohabitation involves living together under an alternative contract. Legally, these agreements fall under the classification of a *contract in lieu of marriage.* Such contracts have traditionally been considered null and void by the courts, but this changed in 1976. In December of that year, the California Supreme Court ruled that actor Lee Marvin's oral agreement to share community property with the woman who lived with him was legally enforceable. This judgment does not apply to all states, but it establishes a precedent for recognizing written and unwritten agreements that may bind a couple living together unmarried (Myricks, 1980).

Business-type arrangements

The most radical form of contract cohabitation considers the parties involved to be employer and employee (Van Deuson, 1975). The employer, either a man or a woman, hires the employee for designated services in exchange for certain benefits, such as salary, room, and board. Hours during which services are to be provided can be specified as well as days off and vacation benefits.

A somewhat more personal, still businesslike approach to contract cohabitation is suggested by Lenore Weitzman (1974). Her model for contracts in lieu of marriage is founded on the principles of a business partnership under the Uniform Partnership Act. This act provides rules that can be applied to all partnerships, but leaves the specific terms of each contract flexible. Equality of management, an equal share of the profits and losses, fair distribution of property, and standards for record keeping would be assumed in such a relationship. Termination of the contract could be prearranged or subject to the wishes of either partner at any time.

Consortium contract

Even more flexible is the "consortium" alternative offered by lawyer Barbara Hirsch (1976). This is an arrangement for the "exchange of sex, services, and society" based on the commitment of persons to a relationship. In this case, there are no assumptions that the commitment is based on the payment for services or a partnership arrangement. The consortium contract is negotiated by the parties involved, with terms reflecting their own needs and wishes.

We should remember that at this time none of these alternatives for contract cohabitation can be assumed to carry legal weight. But whether legal or not, the option of contract cohabitation represents a significant change in the way we have traditionally created intimate relationships. The idea that love and companionship can be instrumentally exchanged for property rights and money is somewhat disquieting to many, yet it appears to have worked for some who have tried it. Stuart Walzer (1977), an attorney, asks, "Isn't it better to confront (the issues) now than in a lawsuit three to six years down the road? It does throw cold water on romance, but people have learned that romance has to be tempered with realism" (p. 10). "Of course," comments Marvin Mitchelson (1977), the coordinator of a workshop on cohabitation and the law, "if you do all that, you may end up not living together at all. . . . Personally, I think it's a terrible way to start a relationship" (p. 10). Terrible or not, this alternative life-style appears to be on its way toward achieving a measure of acceptability. Perhaps in the future we may hear the question being asked, "Do you want to live with me? Sign on the dotted line."

Summary

As our culture increasingly accepts diversity in values, it is not surprising that marriage styles are beginning to reflect the different needs that people have. Although most marriages still fall within traditional boundaries of acceptability, these boundaries have expanded, and we now find several alternatives within the conventional marriage model: intrinsic marriage, utilitarian marriage, and a new type of marital arrangement, cluster marriage.

For some men and women, these conventional marriage styles do not make possible the sort of life they want to lead. Every generation has had its nonconformists, but today we find a variety of nonconventional marital life-styles that are more openly practiced among some groups. While the number of people willing to accept these life-styles is small, this does not deter people from experimenting with sexually open marriage, communal living, group marriage, and contract cohabitation.

SUGGESTIONS FOR ADDITIONAL READING

Cuber, John, and Peggy Harroff. *Sex and the Significant Americans.* New York: Appleton-Century, 1966.

This report on the marital life-styles of successful Americans is a modern classic. The discussion of intrinsic and instrumental marriages is well worth reading and understanding.

Murstein, Bernard (ed.). *Exploring Intimate Life Styles.* New York: Springer, 1978.

The chapters in this book are written by noted researchers and participants in nonconventional life-styles. Each chapter contains an up-to-date statement on the status of these life-styles.

Pratt, Lois. *Family Structure and Effective Health Behavior: The Energized Family.* Boston: Houghton Mifflin, 1976.

This book explores the way in which a family's life-style affects its ability to cope personally, sociably, and medically in contemporary society.

Stinnet, Nick, and Craig W. Birdsong. *The Family and Alternative Lifestyles.* Chicago: Nelson-Hall, 1978.

The authors present and discuss a variety of marital alternatives from a fair but somewhat conservative position. Their treatment of why these alternatives have come about is very good.

Strong, Leslie. "Alternative marital and family forms: their relative attractiveness to college students and correlates of willingness to participate," *Journal of Marriage and the Family* 40 (August 1978): 493–504.

This research study on Connecticut university students gives us an idea of how youth today view the marital alternatives open to them.

Factors in Pair Development Part III

Chapter 6

Loving and Liking

There are few words that carry the emotional impact of the word **love**. And when it is placed in the phrase, "I love you," it conveys as no other the special qualities and uniqueness of that relationship. To love or to be loved represents, in a sense, the highest compliment we can give to or receive from someone else. Loving involves a creative *synthesis* of our feelings, our impressions, and our knowledge of another, and it smooths out the rough edges, the ups and downs, that jostle any relationship. When love is mutual, it forms the basis for **intimacy**, that interpersonal dimension which fosters self-acceptance and helps to erase the effects of living in an impersonal, insecure world.

In a recent study of factors that contribute to personal happiness among Americans, no factor was found to be more important than the experience of love. It helped if a person had money, prestige, or a good sex life, but being loved and loving someone else was more crucial to the happiness of more men and women than any of these things (Freedman, 1979).

Still, as important as love apparently is for most of us, it is not a feeling that we always understand very well. And some people, it appears, do not want to understand it either. In the mid-1970s, Senator William Proxmire fired off a press release condemning government support for a psychological study of love. He said:

> I object to this because no one—not even the National Science Foundation—can argue that falling in love is a science. . . . I'm also against it because I don't want the answer. I believe that 200 million other Americans want to leave some things in life a mystery.

Reactions to this salvo by Senator Proxmire were mixed. However, in the *New York Times*, James Reston put this and other such studies into perspective. He agreed that love is and always will be a mystery. "But if the sociologists and psychologists can get even a suggestion," Reston concluded, "of the answer to our pattern of romantic love, marriage, disillusion, divorce—and the children left behind—it would be the best investment of federal money since Jefferson made the Louisiana Purchase" (Walster and Walster, 1978).

Until recently, the reaction of most social scientists has been similar to that of Senator Proxmire—to ignore or belittle the significance of love in marriage and the family. Into the 1920s, parents were advised against giving too much coddling and affection to their children on the grounds that this would lead to unhealthy dependencies (Wolfenstein, 1957). And as recently as the 1950s, textbook writers advised couples that love was a poor basis on which to make lifetime commitments. One particularly strong critic was Denis de Rougemont (1949), who stated, "We are in the act of trying out—and failing miserably at it—one of the most pathological experiments that a civilized society has ever imagined, namely, the basing of marriage, which is lasting, upon romance, which is a passing fancy."

Pronouncements such as these have been based more on philosophy and traditional values than on the careful consideration of love. For while the study of interpersonal attraction has been making rapid strides in the last few decades, the study of love is still in its infancy. Psychologist Zick Rubin (1973) interprets the problem this way:

> Setting out to devise measures of love is like setting out to prepare a gourmet dish with a thousand different recipes but no pots and pans. The recipes for love abound. . . . But whereas the nature of love has long been a prime topic of discourse and debate, the number of behavioral scientists who have conducted empirical research on love can be counted on one's fingers. And, until recently, the tools with which such research might have been conducted have not existed. (p. 211)

DIMENSIONS OF LOVE

Variety of loves

When it comes to defining love, the English language is of little help. A quick glance at any modern dictionary will affirm our general impression that the word love is used in a variety of different circumstances. We find that we can love our boyfriend, girlfriend, husband, or wife, but we can also love fishing, milk, the theater, our country, dogs, and children. Obviously, there are differences between patriotism, humanitarianism, and romanticism, but the claim can be made that each of these is based on love. So to understand love, we must first specify the object of affection. In the discussions that follow, our interest will focus on the love expressed by a man and woman toward one another.

Liking and Loving

Intense love

When attempting to understand the meaning of love, it can be helpful to place it first in the context of its companion concept, **liking**. All of us have personal likes and dislikes, and we usually like some people more than others. Therefore, liking is a matter of degree, and one way of defining love is as an extension of liking. Many definitions of love assume this dimension by using words such as "strong," "vital," or "intense" to precede the particular component of the feeling described as love. For example, according to Burr (1976), "love is a more intense positive affective experience than just liking another person, and there is no other word in the English language to describe that experience other than love" (p. 215). From this perspective, love begins at that somewhat undefined point when liking is no longer adequate to describe one's attraction toward another, as on the continuum below:

No feelings toward another	Liking	Love toward another

Unique love

Rubin (1973), on the other hand, describes liking and loving as having different meanings and different relational consequences. He offers the view that "while liking and loving are surely close relatives, they are by no means identical" (p. 211). Of course, this perspective is in agreement with the legions of sonnets, novels, and other writings which over the centuries have defined love as a "special" experience quite distinct from liking. But Rubin's own research on liking and loving has given considerable support to this point of view (1970).

According to Rubin (1973), liking consists of two fundamental dimensions: *affection* and *respect*. He defines them as follows:

> **Affection** is liking that is based on the way another person relates to you personally, and it is experienced as an emotional warmth and closeness. **Respect** is liking that is based on another person's admirable characteristics or actions in spheres other than personal relations. (p. 27)

Sometimes our liking for someone includes both affection *and* respect, while for another person our liking may result from predominantly affection *or* respect. Once again, this is a matter of degree, and it varies over time and from one person to another.

What then is love? The Greeks, with characteristic precision, identified two types of love: **eros**—sensual, passionate, and possessive love; and **agape**—yielding, other-centered, and compassionate love. In the multitude of definitions that have been offered since, these two components, more broadly defined as **needing** and **giving**, have been reaffirmed as important to love. Rubin defines these two factors more precisely as **attachment,** a bond based on need for the other, and **caring,** the giving which is epitomized in Sullivan's (1953) definition: "When the satisfaction or the security of another person becomes as significant to one as is one's own satisfaction or security, then the state of love exists" (p. 42).

Measure of love

How do these descriptions of loving and liking compare? To answer this, Rubin devised two separate scales to measure his components of love and liking and asked dating and engaged couples to complete them.

The results of this study indicated that scores on the liking scale were not related to scores on the love scale, thus supporting the hypothesis that loving and liking are different. Rubin also found that high love scores but not high liking scores were related to marriage desires. Also, best friends received liking scores almost as high as the dating partner but the love scores were markedly higher for the partner. From results such as these, we can modify our image of liking and loving and create a pair of continuums which look something like this:

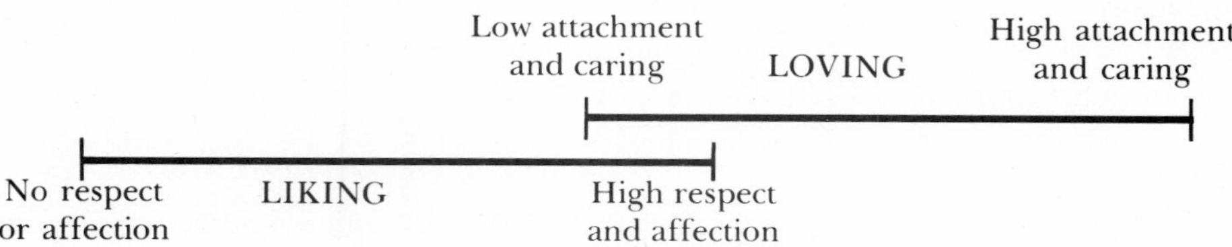

Reciprocity

We can see from our discussion to this point that liking forms a basis for love but that the interpersonal attachments and genuine caring in love are more than just extensions of affection and respect. Also, it is easier to like from afar than to love from afar since loving assumes that the other person will respond to these feelings. Unreturned love, a **crush,** is likely to be quite short-lived. Thus, we have a *reciprocity principle* in love which means that to continue, love must be returned to the satisfaction of the giver. Attachment and caring are basically emotions of an individual, what Rubin (1973) calls "inclinations within one person's mind or heart" (p. 214). But when love is mutually felt and expressed, then we have the third component of the love relationship, **intimacy.** Only through intimacy can we create the link between two people that will foster and maintain long-term attachments and caring.

Romantic and Companionate Love

Throughout the literature on love, a distinction is made between those love experiences that are more emotional and possessive and those experiences that are more stable and relaxed. Some couples portray themselves as being "head over heels" in love while others appear to be entirely calm and sensible in their love for one another. Often, these differences are attributed to the degree of "true" love that exists or, as Fromm (1956) suggests, the degree of maturity of love. But it is probably more accurate to say that these different love experiences result from different needs and orientations toward expressing love than from the degree of love that is felt.

Expressions of love

One way of characterizing these different styles of loving is to distinguish between romantic and companionate conceptions of love. **Romantic love** has its roots in spontaneity, emotionality, and sexual expression. **Companionate love,** which is sometimes called mature love or conjugal (marital) love, is founded on rationality, stability, and long-term adaptability. In both types of love, the central love elements of attachment, caring, and reciprocity (intimacy) are present, but they are expressed quite differently. We can see these differences in several important areas: (1) the amount of time required for impressions of love to develop; (2) the degree of partner trust and independence; (3) the extent to which idealization of the partner occurs; and (4) the emphasis placed on the expression of sexual and emotional intimacy.

Contrasting expectations

Before we proceed to discuss these differences, it should be noted that romantic and companionate love are rarely found in their ideal forms in this society. More frequently, relationships are based on some combination of these two types of love, and often they change in orientation over time. Also, individuals sometimes will vary in the type of love they seek. Thus, relationships can fail due to contrasting love expectations. John Lee (1974), a Canadian sociologist who has studied love extensively, points out that "too often people are speaking different languages when they speak of love. The problem is not *how much* love they feel, but *which kind*" (p. 44).

Time. Oriental matchmakers are fond of characterizing what they consider to be Eastern and Western concepts of loving. According to their popular analogy, Western romantic love is like a kettle which starts boiling soon after a couple meet but gradually it cools down over time. Eastern couples, however, begin with a kettle that starts cold but gradually warms up. Thus, according to their theory, the Eastern couple receives greater satisfaction over the years while the Western couple experiences eventual disappointment. Although the bias toward their own relational-love style is evident, the point they make is valid: romantic impressions of love emerge rather quickly, while in companionate love, these impressions develop only after some time has passed.

Friendship

John Lee (1973) associates companionate love with the Greek concept **Storge** (pronounced stor-gay), or lifelong friendship. In storgic love, intimacy is developed through close association and a basic assumption that the relationship will endure. People grow into this type of love rather than fall into it. According to Lee (1974), "It is the kind of love that sneaks up unnoticed; storgic lovers remember no special point when they fell in love" (p. 48). In contrast, Lee notes that romantic, or what he calls **erotic love,** springs from an immediate, strong attraction based on the physical appearance of the other person. Romantic lovers frequently believe in "love-at-first-sight." Or, if they fail to experience this, they reconstruct the history of their relationship to conform to the belief that their love really could have been recognized early in the relationship.

Trust

Dependencies. A second distinction between romantic and companionate love can be seen in the extent to which the lovers accept one another's independence. In companionate love, some activities are shared together, but each person is allowed to develop his or her own independent interests as well. In both types of love, mutual commitment to the relationship is required, but in companionate love, the implicit trust that each person has in the other permits

The role of love in marriage varies greatly between Eastern and Western cultures.

the development of a separate as well as a mutual identity. Personal hobbies and friendships do not have to be given up, but can be retained and mutually valued. Shared activities, therefore, gain from the insight of individuals who are developing personally as well as mutually. Lee makes the point that this relative independence allows these lovers to withstand separation with less distress, and if they should break up, they often remain good friends. This type of attachment in love is well expressed by Erich Fromm (1956):

> Love is union under the condition of preserving one's integrity, one's individuality. Love is an active power in man; . . . love makes him overcome the sense of isolation and separateness, yet it permits him to be himself, to retain his integrity. In love the paradox occurs that two beings become one and yet remain two. (p. 17)

Dependency and fear

In the minds of romantic lovers, however, separate interests and activities may pose a threat to the future of the relationship. Everything that can be done together is done together. They become so devoted to one another that their own personal needs become wrapped up in fulfilling the needs of the other. To the casual observer, this self-sacrificing dependency might appear to be a beautiful example of mature commitment. But there is another side to this type of romantic attachment—*fear*. Curtin (1973) points out that the claim "I can't live without you" is really an expression of mistrust and real fear that the loved one will find someone else. Social-psychologists Berscheid and Walster (1974) have conducted research studies which confirm that couples frequently develop and maintain attachments out of their fear and frustration.

Some outcomes of this fear-based romantic love are periodic jealousy and an urge to make regular checks on the behavior of the beloved. Comments like, "Where were you last night when I tried to call?" are frequently voiced. This occurs because each lover has come to depend on the other for his or her own self-enhancement. "Security-checks" and demands for exclusive attention ensure that these important personal needs will continue to be satisfied. Miller (1977) likens this dark side of romantic love to "courtship by intimidation" (see Vignette 6.1) in which both partners continually try to change the other into their own concept of the ideal. Some therapists call this process "confluence," a term which refers to two streams that run together, ultimately destroying their separate identities. In companionate love, the pronouns "I" and "you" remain important parts of the pronoun "we." But in romantic love, only the "we" receives emphasis and support.

Idealization. Another important difference between romantic and companionate love is the extent to which the partner is idealized. When we idealize someone, we attribute qualities to that person that we *wish* he or she had, whether or not they exist in reality. In both types of love, some idealization occurs, but in romantic love idealization is maximized, and in companionate love it is minimized.

"Rose-colored glasses"

The phrase "love is blind" specifically refers to romantic idealization and the tendency for romantics to overlook those traits in the loved one that they do not want to see. This results in a **halo effect** which, on the positive side, can be very helpful in smoothing over initial adjustments, thus making the sometimes rocky road to reality more palatable. But this tendency to "look through rose-colored glasses" can also discourage a couple from facing potential conflicts and understanding important differences that might come between them later. For example, she might ignore her impression that he drinks too much, and he might ignore his aversion to her smoking. Or worse, both might succumb to the wishful thought that, since "love conquers all," after awhile the partner will change to conform to their wishes. Eventually, romantics find out that it is difficult to live on love in the real world, but idealization may hide this fact for some time.

Knowledge

Companionate lovers also idealize one another to a degree, but not to the point of being unaware of one another's strengths and weaknesses. Highly valued qualities in the loved one are somewhat exaggerated to compensate for those qualities considered less desirable, but this leads to an impression that the other is special, not perfect. Bell (1975) calls this "idealization within

Vignette 6.1
Love and Terrorism

Our culture has become increasingly aware that intimacy is as much about power as it is about love. The power struggle is rarely explicit at first, because infatuation and courtship are so satisfying, but it begins to surface when the relationship becomes a matter of daily living.

If two people don't make each other feel powerful, they soon seek power at the other's expense, creating a situation I call *intimate terrorism.* Greg and Sarah are a good example. . . . They talk of housekeeping and finances, of moods and lovemaking, but all these topics have been contaminated by the power struggle that compels them both. Each is trying to control the other in a different way: she by pressing claims for intimacy; he by demanding freedom. Every intimate relationship must deal with the needs of each member for both closeness and autonomy. But how inefficiently Greg and Sarah flail away to achieve these ends. They paint each other into separate corners from which neither can escape to reach the other in a fulfilling way. He interprets her demands for more sharing as attempts to destroy his spontaneity and independence. She interprets his pleas for freedom as a denial of love for her and of responsibility for their marriage. Blame has replaced desire, and the role of lover has been exchanged for that of victim.

The tactics Greg and Sarah use against each other are examples of intimate terrorism. Terrorism is usually associated with political struggles for power, but it applies just as well to marriage and other intimate relationships. In its quest for power, terrorism, whether in politics or love, preys on vulnerability. Intimate terrorism feeds on the anxieties we all carry with us from our childhood: fears of being abandoned or overwhelmed by our parents.

---

rational limits" (p. 113). This means that in companionate love, caring or giving springs more from realistic *knowledge* of the other's needs than from idealistic impressions based on fantasy. Knowledge of the partner facilitates taking his or her point of view, which is necessary in developing empathy and helpful in problem solving. Thus, companionate love provides the opportunity for making realistic adjustments based on mutual respect and understanding.

Expressiveness. To an observer, perhaps the most obvious difference between romantic and companionate love is evident in the way feelings of love are expressed. Companionate lovers are not likely to be seen strolling arm and arm together down the boardwalk, quietly sharing their intimate thoughts, and stopping periodically to embrace and kiss. But to the romantic, all the world loves a lover and being in love permits one to display emotion as if no one else were around. The intensity of these psycho-physical feelings, such as excitement, awe, sexual attraction, and palpitations of the heart, has led some to call romantic love "cardiac-respiratory love" (Knox and Sporakowski, 1968).

Sex and love

Although many emotional needs seem to be involved, sexual arousal is definitely a central source of expressiveness in romantic love. Nevertheless,

Love and anxiety are closely allied, and when love fails to bind us to another person, anxiety can fill the same function. Kierkegaard must have recognized this when he compared erotic passion to anxiety and concluded that "anxiety has another element in it that makes it cling even more strongly to its object, for it both loves and fears it."

Social psychologist Elaine Walster has shown in a study that almost any sufficiently stirring emotion, including fear or frustration, can serve as the basis for becoming attached to someone of the opposite sex. Intimate terrorism is the dark underside of love, a form of negative love. It consists of two people clinging to one another in an atmosphere of mutual intimidation.

Couples such as Greg and Sarah stay together because the hungers that united them in the first place—the desire for commitment, for security, for meaning—are so strong that if love fails to provide them, they prefer the heat of intimate terrorism to the coldness of separation. Lovers touch one another in tender places, but so do intimate terrorists; lovers for the sake of pleasure, terrorists for the sake of power. The experience in both cases involves excitement and a sense of intense relatedness.

Those who fall in love speak of not being able to help themselves. Intimate terrorism generally involves a similar suspension of will. In many cases, partners who are actively promoting each other's misery no longer feel certain whether they are choosing to stick together, but feel they are stuck. Each claims to be a prisoner.

there has been considerable debate over the relationship between sex and love. Freud (1922) and others have suggested that when sexual desires are blocked or inhibited, this causes one to develop a more general attraction to the other which is love. But other scholars have found that feelings of love continue after sexual gratification, that love is not necessarily diminished because sexual desires have been rewarded (Malinowski, 1929; Lee, 1974). Based on the research to date, Berscheid and Walster (1974) conclude that while "sexual experience and the anticipation of such experiences are generally arousing . . . sexual gratification has probably incited as much passionate love as sexual frustration has" (p. 370).

To the companionate lover, intimacy springs more from a common desire for a stable marriage, home, and children than from intense sexual desires or emotional expressiveness (Lee, 1974). While sexual intercourse and erotic conceptions of the partner do develop, they occur later in the relationship. Passion is rarely expected, but sex comes to be accepted as a comfortable and important form of self-disclosure. More emphasis is placed on reason than emotionality in companionate love. To be intimate may mean simply to share time with one another, to talk together, or to arrive at a decision jointly, out of mutual concern for the relationship and the development of one another.

Sexual arousal is a major source of expression in romantic love.

Couple differences

Incidence. While the ideal characteristics of romantic and companionate love can be distinguished, most relationships contain a particular blend of characteristics that satisfies the individuals involved. One couple may be romantically idealistic but allow considerable partner independence. Another couple may develop their feelings of love only after some time has passed but then become emotionally expressive and dependent on one another. Overall, however, romantic concepts of love tend to be stronger among individuals who are less traditional and from urban rather than rural areas (Lee, 1974) and among those who are more traditional in their sex-role preferences (Critelli, 1977).

Sex differences

Men and women differ somewhat in their orientations toward love. Some of our popular notions of love might lead us to believe that women are more emotional and therefore more romantic than men. But evidence is mounting that in most relationships men are attracted and aware of love feelings earlier than women. One study concluded: "Regardless of the measure utilized, males consistently appear to develop love feelings earlier in the relationship than females" (Kanin, Davidson, and Scheck, 1970, p. 66). These differences were already apparent by the fourth date when 27 percent of the males but only 15 percent of the females said they felt love for their partner. Even after twenty dates, almost half of the women failed to describe their relationship as based on love, while 70 percent of the men described themselves as being in love.

The finding that women are more "careful" in defining their relationships as being based on love is supported by evidence that they are more rational in their general orientation toward love. Zick Rubin (1973) studied some 200 dating couples and found that men received higher scores on romantic idealism than women. Men were more likely to agree with romantic statements like "A person should marry whomever he loves regardless of social position," and "As long as they at least love one another, two people should have no difficulty getting along in marriage." Women, in contrast, were more likely to agree with unromantic statements like "Economic security should be carefully considered before selecting a marriage partner," and "One should *not* marry against serious advice of one's parents." Hatkoff and Lasswell (1976) explain this difference in romantic idealism in terms of a difference in styles of loving between men and women. In their research, they found that women scored higher on the more companionate or storgic type of love, and men scored higher on more erotic and romantic types of love. Thus, women may feel love just as early as men, but they are more likely to maintain a pragmatic orientation toward the experience.

Love orientations

Why do we find these differences in romanticism between men and women? More than likely it is because boys and girls are socialized to expect different things from long-term relationships. In particular, girls are more clearly oriented in their youth toward marriage. According to Kephart (1973):

> Her romanticism seems to be more adaptive and directive than that of the male. Apparently she is able to exercise a greater measure of control over her romantic inclinations, adapting them to the exigencies of marital selection. (p. 100)

Traditionally women have had more control over love relationships, and they are supposed to weigh the relative advantages and disadvantages of their suitors. This means that while qualities such as rationality and emotional control are important for both men and women in evaluating the potential of their partner, Western culture has given to women more responsibility for ensuring that this takes place. The evidence we have to date indicates that as relationships become more serious, both men and women become more cautious and pragmatic in evaluating the qualities of their partner and the romanticism in their relationship (Knox and Sporakowski).

THE DEVELOPMENT OF INTERPERSONAL LOVE

Learning to love

Love is commonly believed to be something that "just happens," the result of fate or the result of our becoming caught up in the momentum of one another's dreams and emotions. Often, we hear that love itself is an **emotion,** something that is rooted in basic physiology of the human organism, like anger or sexual arousal. But it is more accurate to say that love is a **sentiment,** a complex of feelings incorporating emotion but subject to social definitions and oriented toward those behaviors that are socially appropriate (Turner, 1970). In a manner of speaking, love is a feeling we *learn* to develop and a behavior we *learn* to express. This is why people often express their love in different ways and why our capacities for experiencing love will vary according to how well our lessons of love have been taught and how well we have learned them.

Childhood Foundations of Love

Self-love

The learning of love begins at birth. In the earliest contacts between a parent and child, the roots of interpersonal love are being formed. From this primary attachment, children create their first definitions of themselves, their self-worth and self-acceptance. Children who receive love from their parents come to accept themselves as being lovable, important objects of affection to someone else. When these children mature, this "self-love" translates into their acceptance of their own personal needs as being important. Likewise, fulfilling the needs of others can also be considered important. Thus, the giving of parental love leads to the child's being capable of receiving and giving love in return.

On the surface, this emphasis on the development of self-love may appear to be contradictory. After all, we often think of love as being directed toward others rather than oriented toward the self. But for a person to be able to express love for someone else, he or she must first be able to accept the fact that it is possible to *be loved* as well. Remember, love involves both needing and giving. It requires affirming the value of one's own needs as well as affirming the needs of the other. Erich Fromm (1956) stresses the importance of this linkage:

> An attitude of love toward themselves will be found in all those who are capable of loving others. Love, in principle, is indivisible as far as the connection between "objects" and one's own self is concerned. . . . It is not an "affect" in the sense of being affected by somebody, but an active striving for the growth and happiness of the loved person, rooted in one's own capacity to love. (p. 50)

Capacity to love

All people have the capacity to learn to love. But if this is not nurtured—or worse, if children are taught that they are not capable of being loved—then their ability to love others may be handicapped, perhaps severely (Dinnage, 1980). Sometimes, the low self-esteem created in childhood can be elevated by later experiences (see Vignette 6.2). All too often, however, early self-images

Vignette 6.2

The Love of Johnny Lingo

Johnny Lingo was a handsome eligible bachelor living and trading on a tropical island. Many women of his village hoped he would choose them as his wife. As was the custom, when a man sought a wife he bartered for her. Most girls were purchased for the price of one, two, maybe even three cows. Gradually the status, even the quality of a wife had come to be measured by the number of cows her husband paid for her.

In a hut on the outskirts of the village lived a poor man with his daughter Mahona. His poverty had embittered him and he was a critical, pessimistic man. Much of his frustration was taken out on this daughter. "Come here, you ugly," he would say. "Why couldn't I have a beautiful daughter so I can be rich?" So critical had he been of her that it was widely known she was not only ugly, but lazy and worthless as well.

One day, Johnny arrived in the village and announced he had come for a wife. To people's surprise he wanted to bargain for Mahona, his childhood sweetheart. This news traveled fast and as Mahona's father, Mokey, reflected on this positive turn of events he remembered Johnny's wealth and determined to strike a hard bargain. As two mats were laid on the ground the people of the village gathered around buzzing with excitement. They were thinking Mahona would sell for less than any woman in the history of the village. The two men sat facing each other. Johnny announced, "I have come to seek Mahona. What do you ask for her?"

Johnny sat quietly until the laughter died. Then in a steady and firm voice he said, "I will give eight cows." Stunned silence was the response. Shocked, the townspeople drifted to their homes, failing to see Mahona who had witnessed the proceedings from the nearby forest. On his way to his home Johnny stopped at the traders and ordered a lovely mirror in exchange for a rare and valuable sea shell. The trader, having heard of the eight cow purchase, thought vanity to be the reason Johnny paid so much. "He is so self-centered," he thought, "he wants the status of having paid more than any other man."

Almost a month passed until the fine gilt-edged mirror arrived. Having heard that Johnny and Mahona had returned from their honeymoon trip, the trader determined to deliver the mirror. Arriving at their home, he found a happy and appreciative Johnny, who seeing the mirror wished Mahona to receive it. As she parted the curtain separating the two rooms, the trader saw a slender, confident, and beautiful girl. Taken back, he asked incredulously, "How did this happen?" Johnny answered, "I have loved Mahona since she was a child. I saw how the names she was called made her feel and act ugly. I paid eight cows for her so that she and all who know her would remember that she is an eight-cow wife. I knew what she was like, but she had to discover for herself."

From A. Lynn Scoresby, *The Marriage Dialogue* (Reading, Mass.: Addison-Wesley, 1977), pp. 175–176.

linger and result in the differences in ability to express love that we frequently observe in adults. These observations are confirmed by research studies which indicate that positive self-esteem is related to the ease with which we are able to develop love-oriented attractions (Walster and Walster).

The Socialization of Love

The teaching of love

Love sentiments are developed not only through childhood experiences of parental love but also by direct teaching of love expectations. Udry (1974) points out that when children ask, "Mommy, why did you marry Daddy?" the answer which is commonly given goes something like, "Because we fell in love." Then, to reassure us, we are told that someday we too will meet someone special and fall in love. This theme of love being the foundation for adult male-female relationships is further reinforced in children's literature. Implicit in fairy tales like *Sleeping Beauty* and *Cinderella* are the classic components of romance, which include such ideas as the following:

- people not in love are miserable and unhappy;
- love overcomes all barriers, even those of social class;
- love appears suddenly, almost mystically;
- love inevitably leads to marriage; and
- the notion that "true love never falters" and "they lived happily ever after."

If somehow this message is not ingrained in the nursery, then television series, advertising, movies, magazines, and comic books pick up the gauntlet. The hidden agenda in much of this is surprisingly the same: girl and boy meet, fall in love, overcome their differences, and ride off together into the proverbial sunset.

Love pressures

In adolescence, the pressure to experience love increases. Parents and peers wait expectantly for signs of a budding attraction. The question, "Do you have a boyfriend (or girlfriend)?" is replaced with, "*Who* is your boyfriend (or girlfriend)?" Songs about love, activities that foster boy-girl meetings, the encouragement to exchange class rings or "friendship" rings, and the peer-group status accorded to lovers all serve to push adolescents into realizing their childhood fantasies. The cues which have been memorized from infancy now become legitimate patterns to follow in the "winning" of another. The lines learned earlier help smooth out the first awkward attempts to express these inner feelings. It would be difficult to guess how many youthful lovers have repeated or rephrased the words of Elizabeth Barrett Browning: "How do I love thee, let me count the ways. . . ."

Love propaganda has become so intense that we are frequently reminded that our efforts to experience love can even be enhanced. If somehow we feel unsuccessful in love, then we can read one of the many books and magazine articles on how to be loving and intimate. Prescriptions for love

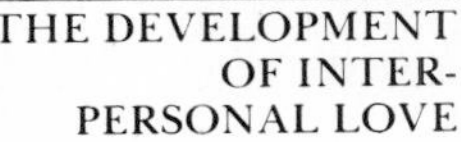

Being "in love" is particularly important to adolescents.

abound, but unfortunately most are simply a sophisticated rephrasing of conventional wisdom and romantic ideology. And when all else fails, we are assured that by using the appropriate cologne, toothpaste, or skin lotion, love will eventually come our way. In his critique of current love practices, Casler (1973) comments:

> It is not surprising that we eventually stop thinking and simply internalize society's pro-love orientation. Most of us can no longer "choose" to love. Loving became something inevitable, like dying or getting married. (p. 7)

LOVE, COMMITMENT, AND MARRIAGE

Love as reason for marriage

If there is one message about love that we hear regularly, it is that love and marriage go hand in hand. From childhood fairy tales to the romantic novels of adolescence and adulthood, there are few ideas so clearly taught as this one. Evidence of our acceptance of this comes from a nationwide survey of marriage attitudes in which 77 percent of the men and 83 percent of the women questioned considered love to be the primary reason people marry today (Roper Organization, 1974). Marriage, it would appear, has become the ultimate indicator of satisfaction and success in love.

But why are love and marriage so intimately linked? The connection stems largely from the assumption that both love and marriage involve relational commitments. Love, by definition, requires interpersonal attachment (or commitment) and marriage, to be successful, must also contain relational commitments. The commitments implied in love are very personal. They are *intrinsic commitments* based on what are considered to be the unique characteristics and contributions of the loved one. If these love-based commitments are strongly felt and culturally reinforced, there's every reason to believe they can and will serve as a foundation for marriage.

Controls on love

But is it necessary to link marital commitment to love? The simple answer is no. While love may be a prerequisite to intrinsic marital commitment, it is quite possible for marriage to be based on *instrumental commitments* that emerge from traditional rules of mate selection, parental pressures, or very practical considerations quite apart from love. In fact, in most cultures throughout history marriage has been considered far too important to the very fabric of society to be left to the somewhat whimsical effects of romance. William Goode (1959) has argued that until quite recently most societies placed strict control on youth before marriage to lessen the chance that love might precede marital commitment. Such controls on love have included child marriage, chaperonage, restrictions on the companions permitted to young people, separation of adolescent males and females, as well as informal parental and peer controls on the selection of mates.

Changes in Love and Marital Commitment

When we examine the relationship between love and marriage historically and in other cultures, we find that many changes have occurred. The most common practice over the centuries and in many societies still today has been to separate love from marital commitment. Most often this is closely linked to direct parental control over the selection of mates (Rosenblatt, 1974). In Eastern societies, such as India, China, or Japan, particularly before World War II, traditional family values clearly restricted love interactions between youth.

Love and marriage separated

When we look toward the roots of love in Western cultures, we find a similar emphasis on separating love from marriage. To Plato, the Ancient Greek philosopher, love was an important element of society, but its preferred form was homosexual. Heterosexual, sensual love also had a place among the Greeks, but not within the confines of marriage. Ovid, the first-century Roman, clearly elevated the importance of heterosexual love in *The Art of Love*. Nevertheless, he held that this love can exist only in adulterous relationships.

The belief that love can be included in marriage did not take root in Europe until the fourteenth and fifteenth centuries (Safilios-Rothschild, 1977). At this time, a merchant middle class was emerging in which the wife played an important role in the economic success of the family. Her friendship and cooperation were valued, and love between husband and wife became more common. Outside of this class, however, the traditional separation of love from marriage continued. Most families were immersed in agricultural production and were united by commitments other than love. Still, the yet small middle class provided the seeds of marital love which would germinate in future generations.

Love before marriage

From these early beginnings to the present there has been a gradual shift toward acceptance of the concept that a marriage can be based on love. This shift probably resulted from a dilemma increasingly facing married people; a growing curiosity and desire to experience love coupled with a fear that love will draw their spouse into an extramarital relationship (Reiss, 1976). To resolve this, love was allowed to develop *before* marriage and to serve, in part, as a basis for marital commitment. Nevertheless, as long as parents controlled the courtship process, love could not be the principal reason for marriage. It was not until youth gained more influence over courtship decisions (as they began to do in colonial America) that it became truly possible to link love and marriage.

Today, North Americans not only allow loved-based marriages, they encourage and expect them. William Goode (1959) declares that the modern courtship system thrives on a "romantic love complex" which prescribes love and intrinsic commitment as the principal reason for marriage. Not only do Americans believe that "love and marriage go together like a horse and carriage," but we also believe that love (like the horse) pulls the marriage along.

Love and Marital Adjustment

Some writers have suggested that a romantic system for marital decision making is basically irrational. They ask, "How can youth make commitments for a lifetime based on little experience and what are essentially their intrinsic preferences for the moment?" Lederer and Jackson (1968) refer to romance as the "quicksilver" foundation for marriage. Fullerton (1972) goes on to suggest that marriage "requires an awareness of who we are and a roughly accurate perception of our partner. A marriage based on romantic love is unlikely to be such a relationship" (p. 354). Are charges such as these valid?

Negative influence

The rising divorce rate has been cited as evidence of the negative influence of romance on marriage, but this explanation is weak when we consider the fact that romantic love influenced marriage long before the divorce statistics rose so high. To date, research does not support the contention that marital adjustment is harmed by romantic love. In one study, couples who had been married for twenty years or more were found to have still retained many of their romantic beliefs, apparently not to their detriment (Munro and Adams, 1978). In another study, romanticism was found to have a slightly positive effect on marital adjustment, but overall its effects were quite negligible. This researcher went on to conclude:

> Romanticism is functional and would change our family institution greatly if eliminated. It probably plays an important part in the mate-selection process, but on the basis of our findings, we cannot conclude that it is harmful to the stability of marriage in particular or the family institution in general. (Spanier, 1972, p. 486)

Love is not blind

We should not be too surprised to find that romantic love does not harm marital adjustment. From the research on mate selection we examined earlier (Chapter 3), it is apparent that most youth are *not* irrational in courtship. Love is rarely entered into lightly and is usually expressed toward people who already conform to parent- and peer-reinforced criteria. From the evidence we have, it seems that love is not nearly as "blind" as people might at first think.

As relationships progress, however, it is the task of any couple to distinguish gradually between romantic dreams and realistic expectations. This does not mean entirely dropping the excitement of romance in favor of boring realism, but making a mature attempt to separate what is necessary to make the relationship work and what can serve to make it more enriching. Research studies indicate that most couples make this adjustment quite well and that they usually begin to do this before marriage. Romance, it would appear, does not fade away over the years as much as it is held in reserve for those times when its vitality can renew earlier commitments. If an appropriate balance between romance and reality can be routinely achieved, a couple will usually be satisfied with their relationship. The words of Amy Lowell (1972) reflect the transition so common in marriage today:

> When you came you were like red wine and honey,
> And the taste of you burnt my mouth with sweetness.
> Now you are like morning bread,
> Smooth and pleasant.
> I hardly taste you at all, for I know your savor;
> But I am completely nourished.*

Summary

Attempts to define and understand love have occupied the thoughts and writings of men and women for centuries. Throughout these many attempts, however, three components of interpersonal love are most frequently mentioned: *attachment,* or need for the other; *caring,* or desire to give to the other; and *intimacy,* the mutual expression of love for one another.

Two forms of loving which have been identified are romantic and companionate love. Romantic love is a more emotional type of love; it develops quickly and rests on rather high partner idealization and interpersonal dependence. Companionate love, in contrast, is slower to realize, is more realistic in its idealization, involves more personal independence, and discourages emotionality. Overall, men tend to be more romantic in their orientation toward love. But both sexes become more pragmatic and companionate in love as they approach marriage.

The foundations for adult love are laid in childhood. The direct socialization of how this love should be expressed also begins quite early, for example, in fairy tales read to children. In adolescence, these messages about love become stronger and acquire new significance. Still, the notion that love can be a reasonable premarital basis for marital commitments is quite recent and limited to only a few cultures, including our own. Concerns over whether romantic love is a satisfactory basis for marriage appear to be unfounded, however, since most people temper their romanticism with realism in making and maintaining their marital commitments.

SUGGESTIONS FOR ADDITIONAL READING

Fromm, Erich. *The Art of Loving.* New York: Bantam, 1956.

A now classic work on the nature of love and loving. The author offers a unique perspective on the importance of love for humanity.

Goode, William J. "The theoretical importance of love," *American Sociological Review* 24 (1959): 38–47.

A significant cross-cultural examination of love and the controls that are often placed on it by society.

Lee, John A. *The Colours of Love.* Toronto, Canada: New Press, 1973.

In this book a multidimensional typology of love is developed. Consideration is given to problems lovers face when they maintain different orientations toward love.

Rubin, Zick. *Liking and Loving.* New York: Holt, Rinehart, and Winston, 1973.

A critical examination of the role love plays in interpersonal attraction. The author's own research is relied upon heavily.

Safilios-Rothschild, Constantina. *Love, Sex, and Sex Roles.* Englewood Cliffs, N. J.: Prentice-Hall, 1977.

A careful look at love within the context of changing definitions of sexuality and male-female sex roles.

Walster, Elaine, and G. William Walster. *A New Look at Love.* Reading, Mass.: Addison-Wesley, 1978.

This is one of the best overviews of research on love available to date. In an easy-to-read format, the answers from science are linked to the questions most often asked about love.

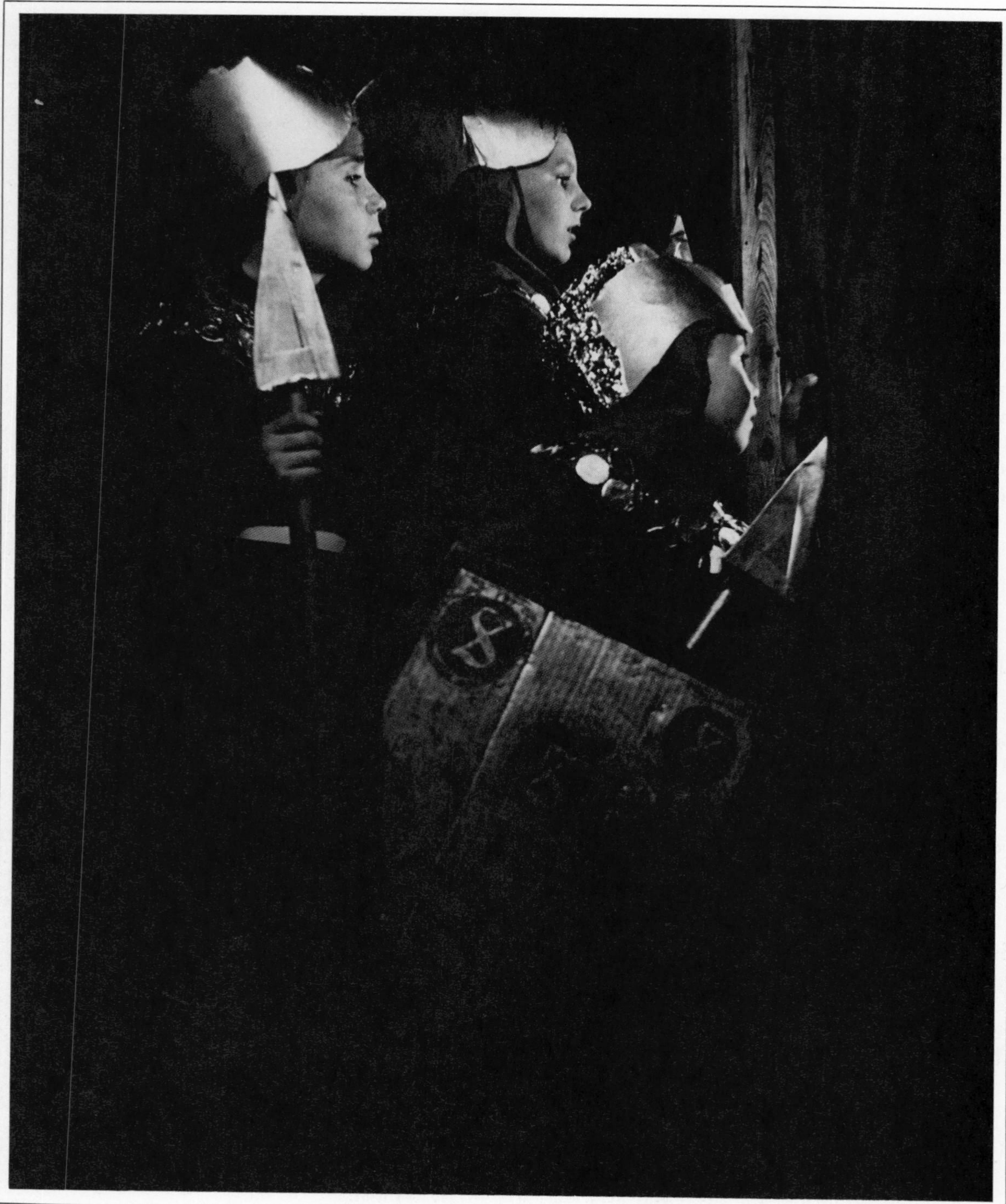

Chapter 7

The Roles of Men and Women

All the world is a stage,
And all the men and women merely players . . .

These lines from Shakespeare's *As You Like It* describe life as a script; the "playing" of a set of roles that have been prescribed for us. Shakespeare could have said that the "*people*" are merely players, but he recognized that the most clearly defined differences between actors result from their sexual identification. While both men and women play numerous roles, it is difficult to avoid being "type-cast" and given a script that is deemed appropriate to one's sex.

Consider, for example, the following situation: A man and his son were returning from a camping trip when they had a serious car accident. They were rushed to a hospital. The boy was sent immediately to surgery while the father, who was all right, sat anxiously in the waiting room. The surgeon took one look at the unconscious patient and said, "I can't operate on this boy. He's my son!" How can the doctor say this? In class discussions, answers to this question often range widely. Some students suggest that the surgeon is the child's stepfather. Others suggest that the child is adopted and the surgeon is his long-lost real father. But the logical answer is really quite simple: the surgeon is the boy's *mother;* an answer that few automatically discover.

This story reveals the common assumptions that most of us make about the roles of men and women. Since most people assume that the surgeon is a man, the story appears to be a riddle. If the story had been about a parent and child, we might have assumed the parent to be the mother. Likewise, other social roles such as the family cook, breadwinner, and housekeeper are stereotypically assigned to one sex or the other.

Nevertheless, many of the assumptions that we have had regarding the roles of men and women are not as likely to be true now as they once were. There are now female surgeons just as there are housekeeping men. There are more girls participating in intercollegiate sports and more boys taking courses in home economics. Over half of all wives are now employed. Some husbands and wives work at different jobs in separate cities during the week with the family getting together only on weekends. Some women get offended if a man opens a car door for them, and some men get offended if it is assumed that their wife cooked the evening meal. With changes like these occurring all about us, it is little wonder that many men and women are often confused about what is expected of them and that harmonizing roles can be one of the most difficult obstacles to relational adjustment today.

THE NATURE AND NURTURE OF ROLES

Status and role

In a play, confusion over behavior is minimized since each actor is assigned a part and a role. Their part is the character they are to become, and their role defines the way in which they are to act out their part. In real life, individuals may claim a number of parts, or **social statuses** such as student, clerk, husband, or wife. Each status also carries **social roles**, or behaviors that are expected of persons who hold that status. Students are expected to study for class; clerks are expected to wait on customers; and husbands and wives are expected to interact with one another in ways that each can usually predict.

One status that none of us can readily change is our **sex**. We refer to this as an **ascribed status,** which means that we are assigned one sex or the other at birth. Our sex is tied to our biology, anatomy, chromosomes, and hormones. **Gender** refers to the social and psychological attributes of maleness or femaleness that we learn to develop. We refer to this as an **achieved status**, which means that people acquire their gender identity—"I am a male" or "I am a female"—only after interacting with others.

Role changes

In the area of male and female roles, the extent to which biology and social learning—sex and gender—influence role behaviors is a major issue. Opponents of change in the traditional roles of men and women typically argue that these roles are "natural," that men and women are born to play different roles, and, usually, that the roles of women are to be dominated by the roles of men. For example, in a study of attitudes toward the Equal Rights Amendment in the state of Washington, the reason most commonly given for voting against ERA was the fear that it would upset "the natural order of things" (Gecas *et al.*, 1977).

On the other hand, proponents of change in male and female roles argue that these roles have little natural basis; they are mostly learned (Stockard and Johnson, 1980). In contrast to the traditional view that the sexes are opposite, the emerging view is that the sexes are somewhat different, but that neither is inherently superior or inferior to the other. It is upon this premise that those who support the opening up of new opportunities for women, particularly in employment and marriage, base their arguments.

The stakes in this new debate are high, especially if relational adjustment is to be achieved in an intimate relationship. A couple who do not share similar role expectations can expect considerable conflicts to develop over their respective rights and duties. Perhaps by examining the sources of male and female role behavior we can better understand the legitimacy of the role changes occurring today.

Sex: The Biological Basis for Role Behavior

Dimensions of sex

There are several bases for the biological concept of sex: (1) **genetic sex** is determined by the chromosomes the individual inherits, either XX for a female or XY for a male; (2) **hormonal sex** is determined by the relative levels of estrogen and androgen produced in the body; (3) **gonadal sex** is defined by the presence of ovaries or testes; and (4) **genital sex** is defined by the presence of a penis or clitoris and vagina. Normally, all of these aspects of male or female sex are interrelated since genetic factors influence the hormones produced, which in turn affect development of the gonads and genitals (Parsons and Ruble, 1978). It is possible for these sexual components to be improperly synchronized, but this is very rare.

Reproductive differences

The links that have been established between biological sex and the roles of men and women are few. The only clear difference lies in the reproductive capacities of the sexes. Only women can give birth and nurse a baby, so they have unique roles related to pregnancy, childbirth, and the physical nurturance of infants. Only men can inseminate during sexual intercourse, so they also have a unique role in the reproductive process.

Reliable methods of birth control are only a recent innovation. Throughout much of history, women have been either pregnant or nursing for most of their adult lives. This partially explains why in most cultures the child-rearing responsibilities were allocated to them (Friedd, 1978). In a modern society, however, the fact that women *may* bear children is less important in determining their family roles than in a less developed society. Efficient contraceptives, bottle feeding, and child-care centers mean that women can control their fertility and their parental roles almost completely. Therefore, we have to look beyond the reproductive factor to find the reason for contemporary role differences between men and women today.

Hormone differences

Hormone differences between males and females may also play a part in behavior, yet their influences are not fully understood. Both males and females produce androgen and estrogen hormones, but it is the initial presence of androgen during the development of the fetus that encourages male organs and structure to develop. Without the presence of a Y chromosome, there would be no signal for androgen to be released and the child would normally develop into a female. It seems, according to Stoll (1973), that "Nature's scheme is to make a female, with males being special elaborations of them" (p. 3).

The presence of androgen influences more than the development of the genitals. The secondary sex characteristics—depth of voice, facial and body hair, skeletal growth, muscle development—are influenced by its presence. There is also some evidence that behavior is affected. For instance, general body activity levels are higher among males, even as newborn infants (McGuiness, 1979).

In a unique study that examined hormonal influences on behavior, Money and Ehrhardt (1972) examined twenty-five genetic girls who had accidentally received excess androgen before they were born. Their results indicate that these girls are more masculine, have more physical energy, and play in more rough games than a carefully matched sample of normal girls. The researchers do not conclude that this demonstrates a biological difference in later roles, but the study does suggest that hormones may influence the initial development of behavior. Altering the sex hormones later, especially after puberty, does not appear to have as dramatic an effect.

Genetic similarity

It should not be too surprising that biological factors provide an incomplete explanation of adult roles. Both sexes share forty-five of the forty-six

Vignette 7.1 Learning Gender: The Case of "Agnes"

The case history of "Agnes," described by Garfinkel, vividly underscores the nature of achieving one's gender learning (Garfinkel: 1967). When Agnes at age nineteen first appeared at the UCLA sex-change clinic, she appeared to be a very attractive, well-endowed young woman. Medical inspection revealed she possessed normal-sized male genitalia, no female genitalia, and only feminine secondary sexual characteristics (developed breasts and subcutaneous fat, pelvic girdle, lack of facial and body hair, etc.). A long series of interviews with her ensued, during which it was learned that she had been identified as a boy at birth and raised as such until she was seventeen. At that age, she decided to "pass" as female. She had come now to the sex-change clinic to have her "tumor" removed and a vagina constructed so that she could have what nature had intended all along. She insisted it was both moral and correct for her to be a female.

Her presentation of her biography underscored her insistence that she really was a female, misunderstood, and mislabeled. Any questions concerning her past identification as a boy were rejected. According to her account, she never had to line up with the boys in school, never had to undergo a physical examination with boys, etc. That is, she had taken the stance of any normal adult in this culture. For her, there were only two sexes and she was female and was always meant to be female.

Once she had decided to pass as a woman (although in her terms once she had decided to *be* the sex she was always intended to be), she had to *learn* how women *are* and at the same time avoid being found out. . . . But she also had to learn how to reveal that she was a woman. Much of her learning about the practices of womanhood was developed in the context of the claim that chromosomes that determine our genetic heritage. Both sexes produce androgen ("masculine") and estrogen ("feminine") hormones in their bodies. There is so much variation from person to person that some women can outrun or outswim many men while some men are much more quiet and passive than most women. According to Rosenberg and Sutton-Smith (1972), "although there are biological differences between the sexes at birth, the overlap in behavior is so extensive and human malleability so great that both sexes are capable of exhibiting most forms of human behavior. At this time there are few behaviors that may be viewed as solely within the province of one sex" (p. 88).

Gender: The Social Basis for Role Behavior

Gender identity

Our gender is a social rather than biological product. We may be born either male or female in sex, but we do not come to accept ourselves as male or female until we are taught this by others (see Vignette 7.1). Adults begin to

---

she already knew what they were. For example, her fiance's mother, while teaching her how to cook Dutch-Indonesian style, was in actuality teaching her how to cook. Agnes was ostensibly learning a style of cooking, concealing the fact she lacked culinary skills, while presenting herself as someone who just didn't know the Dutch-Indonesian way. Her future mother-in-law, a seamstress, taught her how to sew and in the process taught her what styles were becoming to her figure, what colors went with her complexion, and how clothing can be used to present the desired image. Much of the learning of appropriate gender-role behavior, according to her own account, came from the lectures and behaviors of her fiance. For example, when he arrived home and found her sunbathing in front of the apartment, he lectured to her that "nice girls" don't show off that way. She was learning that she was attractive to other men but her boyfriend wanted her pure.

The case of Agnes, although extreme, illustrates the manner in which each of us demonstrates that we have achieved a particular gender, that we are naturally what we claim to be. Women in our culture frequently report feeling undressed without mascara or lipstick. Although they are literally dressed in their clothing, they feel undressed as women. That is, the process of "putting-on" one's face is a behavior through which some women *achieve* their gender identity. Similarly, the baggy-eyed middle-aged man can stand in rumpled pajamas and say to the mirror, "You are the chairman of the board of trustees. Be patient. I'll have you looking the part in half an hour."

"program" children into their appropriate gender right after birth. The first question anyone asks about a new baby is its sex. The initial answer, "It's a boy" or "It's a girl," comes from a rather cursory look at its genitals. Based on that glance, the child is then assigned a gender-appropriate name and wrapped in blue or pink bunting. From then on, reinforcements for gender identity continue to mount. By three years of age, nearly all children are able to classify their gender correctly (Westoff, 1979).

There are a variety of means by which gender identification is encouraged. For one thing, clothing styles are different for boys and girls. Either sex may wear jeans, but only girls wear dresses. There are also gender-appropriate colors, hair styles, mannerisms, and toys. Even the furnishings of children's rooms are usually differentiated by gender. One study found "the rooms of boys contained more animal furnishings, more educational art materials, more spatial-temporal toys, more sports equipment, and more toy animals. The rooms of girls contained more dolls, more floral furnishings, and more 'ruffles'" (Rheingold and Cook, 1975, p. 461).

Gender socialization

These obvious gender signals also cue parents and others to act differently toward boys and girls. If a baby is a boy, the parents—particularly the father—will tend to play rougher with him. It has also been found that mothers give male infants up to six months of age considerably more physical contact than female infants, after which males are more discouraged from contact (Lewis, 1972). If the baby is a girl, the mother will tend to speak to her more frequently (Westoff, 1979). Garai and Scheinfeld (1968) reported that parents are more likely to view girls as fragile and to be more protective and anxious regarding their activities.

While children of both sexes are expected to conform to certain gender-typed practices, girls are permitted much more flexibility in their gender identification than boys. In dress, for example, girls can wear either blue or pink clothes, but boys are not usually permitted to wear pink. Girls are allowed more latitude in toy selection than boys. They are more likely to play with trucks than boys are to play with dolls. Girls can also be labeled "tomboys" with fewer sanctions than boys who are called "sissies." These differences in gender typing have even been found in the homes of parents who claim to believe in "nonsexist" child rearing. It is the girls who usually receive the nonsexist unbringing while their brothers experience a more traditional gender-typed upbringing (Weitz, 1977).

Gender-Role Learning

Gender expectations

By itself, gender does not dictate role behavior. There is nothing inherent in being a male or female that tells a person what he or she should or should not do. Sandra Bem (1977), for example, argues that "a healthy sense of maleness or femaleness involves little more than being able to look into the mirror and to be perfectly comfortable with the body one sees there" (p. 219). All too often, however, the messages of gender identity quickly become mixed with

Little girls are often taught to be "little ladies."

definitions of appropriate role behaviors for each gender. These social expectations can permit a great deal of freedom to one or both genders or they can be very specific, allowing little opportunity for a man or woman to act in any way other than what is deemed to be gender appropriate. The more attention that is given to gender differences in a family or society, the more likely that this will result in gender-role differences.

Parental influences

Parents teach their children gender roles in both obvious and not-so-obvious ways. Overtly, they may direct their child's behavior through statements like: "Little boys don't play house!" or "Little girls don't climb trees!" Other directives come more subtly from the kinds of toys or playthings that they provide and support. A daughter receives her "Barbie" doll with some dresses, perhaps even a doll house, pots, pans, and other homemaking implements for her to practice with. Meanwhile, a son receives a toy gun and the usual store of trucks and balls. A popular child's "medical kit" is sold in two versions: a white one for nurses with a girl on the box and a black one for doctors—a boy is on the box.

Less obvious, but perhaps as effective, is the indirect socialization that adults provide. The physical dependency of the young child means parents are very important, and this gives them the power to reinforce those things in the child that they prefer (Luepton, 1980). Children want support and praise and they learn very early which behaviors get rewarded and which do not. This is why it is very difficult to tell how much male aggressiveness is caused by hormonal influences and how much by social learning. Since mothers and fathers tend to support and tolerate more activity in boys, this could be a major factor in higher aggressiveness.

Role modeling

The specific role models that parents offer are another contribution they make to the child's gender-role identity. The little boy who tries to shave his face with his father's unbladed razor is greeted with smiles but any efforts to dress like his mother are soundly discouraged. Children also learn from their parents how men and women are supposed to relate to one another. Playing "mother" or "father" is quite common. But sometimes this causes problems for the boy who does not have much contact with a male role model. His idea of what men are supposed to do is often ambiguous, as in the following situation:

> A colleague noticed a boy and girl playing house in a front yard. The little girl was very busy sweeping up the play area, rearranging furniture, moving dishes about, and caring for baby dolls. The boy, on the other hand, would leave the play area on his bicycle, disappear to the back of the (real) house, remain for a brief while, reappear in the play area, and lie down in a feigned sleep. (Stone, 1965, p. 30)

The girl in this case was quite familiar with the mother's role. But the boy only knew his father as one who left in the morning, came home and slept, an all-too-common image.

Literature

The books that are read to children or that they read themselves further tend to encourage differences in role perceptions. A National Organization of Women Task Force (1972) examined 2760 stories in 134 children's books and concluded that women were most often presented as passive and home-centered. This stereotyping in literature continues as education advances. Janet Chafetz (1974) reports on a study of high-school history books in which women were found to be typically portrayed as passive and domestic while men were active and working. In one text that was examined, 98 percent of the people discussed were male, and even Madame Curie was relegated to a context in which Monsieur Curie was said to have been "assisted by his wife."

Teachers and peers also play an important role in the learning of gender roles. A study conducted by the United States Educational Testing Service found that teachers and guidance counselors still often direct students into courses that prepare them for traditionally male and female roles and occupations (Casserly, 1978). Peers as well typically reinforce these traditional gender roles. During the school years, pressure to conform to peer values increases and stereotypical gender-role mannerisms, sports, and activities become a visible part of the youth culture. Adolescent women are permitted somewhat more freedom in their gender-role behavior than men, but even young women still hold rather traditional images of the female role (Hansen and Putnam, 1978).

Concepts of Masculinity, Femininity, and Androgeny

Sex-Role Inventory

Although gender roles in American society are changing, this is not happening easily. The traditional images of masculinity and femininity are still widely held today, and nearly all studies report that some traits are respectively associated with being a man and others with being a woman. For example, in the Bem Sex-Role Inventory (Bem, 1977), which measures the strength of masculine and feminine trait preferences, there are three sets of characteristics identified: traditionally masculine, traditionally feminine, and neutral characteristics (see Table 7.1). The neutral characteristics are used as filler items on the scale, but the other items repeatedly have been found to differentiate the gender-role preferences of most men and women.

Femininity

The feminine items on the Bem scale indicate that the highly feminine person is one who is passive, dependent, and affectionate. Femininity is associated with allowing others to lead, taking a supportive role, and being sensitive to the personal needs of others. In a study of mental-health professionals, it was found that clinicians considered "healthy" women to be those who were submissive, noncompetitive, dependent, and somewhat excitable in minor crises (Broverman *et al.*, 1970). Commenting on these findings, Shirley Weitz concludes, "the constellation of traits seen as constituting healthy femininity seems to be quite childlike and not consistent with adult responsibilities" (p. 94).

Masculinity

Masculine traits, on the other hand, are considered to be quite different from feminine traits. Masculinity is consistently linked to personal activity, independence, assertiveness, and control. Men who exhibited these character-

Table 7.1

Sample Characteristics from the Bem Sex-Role Inventory: Masculine, Feminine, and Neutral Adjectives

Masculine Adjectives	Feminine Adjectives	Neutral Adjectives
Aggressive	Affectionate	Adaptable
Analytical	Compassionate	Friendly
Competitive	Gentle	Jealous
Independent	Soft spoken	Reliable
Self-reliant	Tender	Solemn
Willing to take risks	Understanding	Truthful

Note: Each subject indicates how well each item describes himself or herself.

Source: Reproduced by special permission from the Bem Sex-Role Inventory by Sandra Bem, Ph.D. Copyright © 1979. Published by Consulting Psychologists Press, Inc., Palo Alto, CA 94306.

istics were considered "healthy" by the mental-health professionals in the above study. Men are also more likely to be evaluated by their peers on the basis of these same characteristics. In this culture, boys learn very early what Robert Brannon (1978) has identified as some of the unwritten "rules" of masculinity:

1. *No sissy stuff:* characteristics traditionally thought of as feminine, like gentleness, nurturance, and vulnerability have to be hidden.
2. *Be a big wheel:* competing with and beating others is more important than enjoying a task.
3. *Be a sturdy oak:* always cope, be brave, stay cool, and don't express your hurt and sadness.
4. *Be rough and tough:* when you have inner doubts, act tough and aggressive and the world will think you're in charge.

Despite the widespread impression that these traditional masculine and feminine traits are normal and healthy for men and women, research studies are finding quite the opposite. In summarizing much of the current research, Sandra Bem (1975) concludes:

Cross-sex typing

> There is already considerable evidence that traditional sex typing is unhealthy. For example, high femininity in females consistently correlates with high anxiety, low self-esteem, and low self-acceptance. And although high masculinity in males has been related to better adjustment during adolescence, it is often accompanied during adulthood by high anxiety, high neuroticism, and low self-acceptance. Further, greater intellectual development has quite consistently correlated with cross-sex typing (masculinity in girls, femininity in boys). Boys who are strongly masculine and girls who are strongly feminine tend to have lower overall intelligence, lower spatial ability, and show lower creativity. (p. 59)

Findings such as these cast doubt on the current worth of separating traditionally masculine and feminine traits by sex. In a modern, complex society such as ours, women who fail to be assertive and men who fail to be sensitive to the needs of others can be handicapped in their personal and relational development. For this reason, an increasing number of men and women are moving toward **androgeny**—a blending of masculine and feminine traits.

Androgeny

Androgeny, according to Bem (1975), "allows an individual to be both independent and tender, assertive and yielding, masculine and feminine" (p. 62). On her scale of gender preferences (see Table 7.1), androgynous persons are those who report that both feminine and masculine traits equally apply to them. In her studies of students at Stanford University, Bem (1977) found that about one-third of the men and women were androgynous.

Research attempts to discover the differences in behavior between masculine, feminine, and androgenous persons have turned up some interesting results. Traditionally masculine men perform quite well in situations that

Parents can also serve as androgynous role models in performing functions culturally deemed inappropriate for their sex.

require aggressiveness but not in those that demand warmth and playfulness. Traditionally feminine women are good in situations calling for warmth and playfulness but not in those that call for aggressiveness. Androgynous people, however, can handle a variety of situations quite well. Androgynous women and men willingly perform roles that our culture labels as unsuitable for their sex and function effectively in aggressive and nurturing situations. For example, regarding androgynous men, Bem (1977) notes from her research, "He shuns no behavior just because our culture happens to label it as female, . . . he stands firm in his opinions, he cuddles kittens, and bounces babies, and he has a sympathetic ear for someone in distress" (p. 216).

GENDER ROLES IN PAIRING

These changes in gender-role learning are beginning to influence the ways in which men and women relate to one another in adolescence and young adulthood. But the dominant script in early dating and courtship still remains rather traditional, particularly among those from families with parents who are not highly educated (Scanzoni, 1975). Youth in the preadolescent period are still largely controlled by same-sex peers and strong gender identities, so it is difficult for many of them to break out from the traditional male and female patterns of behavior.

Traditional Courtship Roles

Female dependency

Most girls in Western society enter into dating prepared to accept the traditional feminine role in pair relationships. They have been effectively socialized to be dependent, first on their parents, then on their teachers and boyfriends. Lockheed (1978) found that by the fifth grade in school, girls are more likely than boys to score high on measures of dependency. Girls are also more likely to be encouraged by parents and peers to seek success vicariously through a man, to lower their own occupational goals and replace them with desires for a husband and family. A young woman's attention is often directed toward making herself look appealing to men, even reading books and magazines that help her to manipulate her physical attractiveness.

Male inexpressiveness

The childhood socialization of the adolescent boy, however, has more often taught him to be independent and inexpressive with girls. He is pushed toward an occupation, not marriage. He usually acquires a rather ideal concept of manliness, which Balswick and Peek (1971) label the "cowboy" and "playboy" roles of the male—images that come from the media to which many boys are exposed.

> As the cowboy equally loved his girlfriend and his horse, so the present-day American male loves his car or motorcycle and his girlfriend. Basic to both these descriptions is the notion that the cowboy does have feelings toward women but does not express them, since ironically such expression would conflict with his image of what a male is . . . . The playboy departs from the cowboy, however, in that he is also "nonfeeling." He rejects women as women, treating them as consumer commodities. (p. 364)

Contacts between young men and women who have accepted these traditional self-images often appear posed and gamelike. In order to be considered attractive, a young woman can feel pressured to "play dumb" in order to make her date feel superior. One recent study found that men will sometimes do this also, but women are more likely to do so, especially those who are marriage-oriented (Dean *et al.*, 1975). For young men, there is the obligation to "play smart," to act as if they know more than they really do.

When this is combined with the goal of being "in charge" and capable in any competition that they encounter, young men are often forced into trying to appear more dominant and more aggressive than they really are capable of being (Farrell, 1975). The higher automobile-accident rates of young men attest to the problems that they sometimes face in trying to live up to the masculine images they hold of themselves.

Communication problems

Communication is difficult between men and women who have traditional images of their gender roles. In a study of college men and women who had traditional masculine and feminine role traits, it was found that initial interactions were usually quite stilted and uncomfortable. Highly traditional men and women found it difficult to talk with one another, look at one another, or smile and gesture to one another (Ickes and Barnes, 1978).

Emerging Courtship Roles

Changing preferences

In contrast to those who conform to these traditional ways of relating, there are a growing number of women and men who prefer not to be restricted to stereotyped masculine and feminine ways of interacting. They expect to be aggressive as well as sensitive with others, and they want their partners to feel the same. Among both men and women, the traits that are considered "desirable" for a partner are increasingly being redefined along androgynous lines (Gilbert and Holahan, 1978). The traditional man or woman is still seen as "typical," but, given a choice, more women and men say they want a relationship with someone who has some of the traits traditionally assigned to the other sex. For example, in a recent large survey, Tavris (1977) found that women no longer indicate a preference for strong masculine men but are more likely to be looking for sensitivity and responsiveness in the men with whom they relate.

The advantages of androgynous relationships have recently been demonstrated in a study of interpersonal communication. When androgynous couples were compared with traditional couples, the results indicated that the androgynous people talked, gestured, smiled, and looked at each other much more often. They were also more likely to indicate that they felt comfortable with one another. The researchers concluded, "The interactions in which one or both of the participants were androgynous were *consistently* better than the interactions of traditionally sex-typed males and females" (Ickes and Barnes, p. 44).

Nontraditional roles

This shift toward more nontraditional roles is also enhancing the independence and role flexibility of unmarried men and women. Couple relationships can be more egalitarian and companionate when demands for dominance and submissiveness are relaxed. This reduces much of the game playing and artificiality so often found in traditional relationships. Along with this comes a greater commitment to an egalitarian future with women more likely to want careers and men more likely to want to share in parenthood

(Forisha, 1978). This does not mean that men and women are switching roles. Rather, they are *adding* these roles to the ones already linked to their gender.

Gender-role paradoxes

Pressures to form more nontraditional relationships are coming not only from more accepting societal norms but also from pressures that both men and women experience as their relationships become more serious. Jessie Bernard (1975) suggests that advanced relational commitments often create *paradoxes* that make traditional roles increasingly uncomfortable. For example, a woman's early training in dependency may have prepared her to attract a man, but this dependency can also lead to sexual exploitation as the relationship develops. It often becomes obvious that her submissiveness is a one-way street that can cost her time, emotional strain, or even an unwanted pregnancy. This is further impressed on the woman when she realizes that her adult responsibilities today require an independence and assertiveness for which she must be prepared. In the end, a woman often learns that excessive dependency may be more of a liability than an asset (Macke *et al.*, 1979).

A man also experiences some pressure to change his role expectations during pair development. A paradox, the reverse of the woman's, operates on him. The display of strength, independence, and dominance, which may have been considered attractive initially, is difficult to maintain over time. He finds that he cannot effectively make all the decisions or control those areas of the relationship he knows little about. Nor can he expect to have his expressive needs met if he does not provide them to his partner. Intimacy requires a measure of mutual submissiveness, and if that is the goal of the relationship, he must somewhat relax the eternal trappings of dominance.

Professed liberalism

The net result of these trends is a tendency for traditional premarital roles to decline as relationships develop but not to be erased completely. In part, we find that the failure of most single persons to let go of their traditional roles stems from a greater *belief* in egalitarian relationships than personal *commitment* to them. The overwhelming majority of middle-class youth say they favor more sex-role equality, but nearly all men and most women, when pressed, still prefer rather traditional roles for themselves and their partners (Komarovsky, 1976; Patterson *et al.*, 1975). Commenting on this situation, Barbara Forisha concludes, "We should not take people's professed liberation from sex roles too seriously unless there is evidence that belief has been integrated into action" (p. 104).

We can see this pull between traditional and equalitarian attitudes when we look at the roles single men and women expect to play in marriage. In a study of engaged persons who had filed for marriage licenses, it was found that nearly all these couples expected to share many of their marital roles, particularly recreation, child-care, finance, and decision-making roles. But when queried about future household responsibilities, these engaged persons still expected to participate in the roles we traditionally associate with husbands and wives—for example, men mowing the grass and women preparing the meals. Apparently, this emerging sense of equality does not yet extend itself to all areas of the relationship, at least for most couples (Neely and Orthner, 1978).

ROLE RELATIONS IN MARRIAGE

Throughout the later stages of courtship, couples often talk about how they will set up a household. Gradually, the images of their parents' roles and the plans they have developed with one another begin to coalesce into a rather idealized set of roles for one another. Indeed, newlyweds often do share many responsibilities. But as the marriage progresses, obligations and roles increase, and it becomes more and more difficult to share everything together. Requirements for efficiency begin to erode the dreams of romantically washing and drying dishes together by candlelight.

The Traditional Division of Responsibilities

Role specialization

Is a division of responsibilities inevitable in marriage? No, but there are several factors which strongly encourage it. For one thing, in order for us to handle our obligations satisfactorily and still have time for ourselves as persons and partners, we usually find it convenient to develop a **division-of-labor**. Sociologists have long known that the more complex a group becomes and the more tasks it has to fulfill, the less sharing there will be in the system (Durkheim, 1933). This happens as marital responsibilities increase over time, especially with the addition of children. But children are not the only cause for separating tasks between husbands and wives; even marriages that are childless experience role specialization (Neely and Orthner).

Cultural pressure

Another factor influencing the separation of tasks is cultural pressure to conform to traditional responsibilities. Nena and George O'Neill (1972) call this the hidden or "closed contract" for marriage. This is the contract most couples comply with despite their best intentions or verbal agreements. The O'Neills caution that "this psychological contract has been determined for us, to a very considerable extent, long before we began our first day of married life. It is in many ways an unconscious contract, agreed to by default in that it is unwitting. But that does not make it any less binding upon our interaction with our chosen mate, upon our public behavior as a couple, or upon our attitude toward the meaning of marriage" (p. 51).

For many couples, the "contract" of who will do what is quite explicit: he will be the principal provider and she will be the principal homemaker. From the perspective of traditional womanhood, "The American ideal was to catch a man before you were too old, say twenty-two, and to take a deep breath, disappear into a suburban ranch house and not come up for air until your children ('a boy for you and a girl for me') were safely married." The corollary for the man has been the vision of "the successful businessman dashing out the door to catch the 8:18 commuter train, on his way to spend the day in economic pursuits, secure in the knowledge of his domestic nest as a relief from such pressures" (Weitz, p. 131).

Traditional expectations

The reality of these visions for many Americans is questionable, but as John Scanzoni (1975) found in his study of over 3000 adults in five states, a majority of men and women still expect one another to play rather traditional roles in marriage. Men report slightly more modern views on the husband's role, and women are somewhat more acceptant of newer roles for themselves. But if women are to change their roles, primarily through employment, then apparently these new responsibilities are to be *added* to their other roles since both men and women seem to agree on rather traditional roles for wives. Younger women and men with at least some college education are slightly less likely to expect traditional marital roles, and perhaps this indicates that we can expect further changes in marital roles in the future.

At present, when a husband does participate in traditionally female household tasks, there is an overriding tendency for the *responsibility* of the role to remain in its traditional form. This is the "hidden" contract. For example, the young husband says: "Here, let me clear the table *for you*!" He is participating in the role, but the responsibility is clearly hers. Likewise, many women in the labor force still view their work as supplementary to that of their husband. It is clearly understood that he is the principal "breadwinner"

While many husbands are participating in traditionally female tasks, such as child care, the responsibility *for these roles usually remains with the wife.*

and if he is forced to relocate, she will follow. (Recent changes in these assumptions will be discussed later in the chapter.)

Household Responsibilities

Nye (1976) studied a randomly selected group of husbands and wives in the state of Washington to learn how roles are commonly shared or divided in marriage. The results indicate that many of these couples share their household roles, including child-rearing, child-care, and housekeeper roles. In very few of the marriages are the wives solely responsible for these family roles, even though they usually dominate them. In half of the marriages, husbands participate in routine housekeeping tasks, and even more of the husbands help in the socialization of their sons. In the rearing of daughters, in child care, and in housekeeping, however, the women clearly have the major responsibility.

Role sharing

What this and other similar studies suggest is that husbands and wives are sharing more and more of their household roles. In very few marriages today does either the husband or the wife assume sole responsibility for the household. Still, the proportion of responsibility for these roles is heavily weighted toward the wife. Even in the Soviet Union and Sweden, where women have made rapid strides toward occupational equality, wives remain principally responsible for household tasks (Hacker, 1975).

Given the technology that has invaded the household during the twentieth century, it may be surprising to some that many women still spend as much time in homemaking as they did in the 1920s. After analyzing a series of time surveys which began in 1926, Joan Vanek (1974) found that although the time given to homemaking tasks has been rearranged, the total amount of time has remained the same: about 52–55 hours per week among wives who are not employed.

Limits on change

Why have there been so few changes? Part of the reason is that men have not participated very much in household tasks. Higher educated husbands are more likely to participate in housework than lower educated ones (Erickson *et al.*, 1979), but a national survey found that husbands on the average give only a few hours a week to these tasks (Robinson, 1977). Another factor is that our standards have risen. New gadgetry is called on more frequently, not less. For example, the time given to the care of clothing and linen has increased despite innovations in washing, drying, and clothing itself. We simply wash things more frequently than before; we wear a shirt or blouse one evening and throw it in the laundry. Standards for child care have also risen and now take more time. Vanek adds that the time itself may hold value to nonemployed women since the value of the tasks themselves is so often questioned and unclear. "Time spent in work, rather than the results of the work, serves to express to the homemaker and others that an equal contribution is being made" (p. 120).

Changing Wife Roles

Traditional wives

Many women remain satisfied with their traditional roles in marriage. They prefer their homemaking responsibilities and feel threatened by new role definitions that bombard them from magazines, TV, and local consciousness-raising groups. These women flocked to "Total Woman" courses in the mid-1970s that taught them how to be more dependent on their husbands and sought security in the tasks they remembered their mothers doing so well (see Vignette 7.2). John Scanzoni (1975) found that these traditional wives put the interests of their husbands and children first; find their major satisfaction in their family; and if they are employed, see the income earned from their jobs as supplementary in nature—that is, their work does not affect the husband's primary responsibility as provider for the family. A recent Gallup survey found that this description fits the preferences of over half of the adult women in America today (Gallup, 1980).

Vignette 7.2 Wives and Their Husbands: Two Points of View

Marabel: A "Total" Woman

Having lived on both sides of the fence, I can tell you where the greener pastures are. During my early years of married life, I led a one-woman crusade to make my man into my mold. One particular irritation was that Charlie was constantly on the phone with his stockbroker. A dozen times a day they conspired, and each time I became more and more upset. First of all, I was jealous of the time Charlie spent on the phone. Secondly, I was worried sick that he'd gamble away all our savings.

One day the broker, who also happened to be a family friend, called me on the phone. He knew that Charlie was at work and he gave me some advice: "Let your husband do what he wants in the market. Don't ever tell him what to do with his money. You stay out of it and take care of the kitchen."

Oh, boy, did that burn me up! I was furious at both of them! But the wise, old gentleman had sensed my animosity. He had seen that I wasn't accepting Charlie's role as provider, nor was I submitting to his family leadership.

Today my attitudes have changed, and we're both much happier because of it. I have determined to support my husband's plan, and if that seems impossible, at least I'll support the *man!*

I have been asked if this process of adapting places a woman on a slave-master basis with her husband. A Total Woman is not a slave. She graciously chooses to adapt to her husband's way, even though at times she desperately may not want to. He in turn will gratefully respond by trying to make it up to her and grant her desires. He may even want to spoil her with goodies.

From: Marabel Morgan, *The Total Woman* (Old Tappan, N.J.: Revell, 1973), pp. 55–56, 71.

A growing number of women, however, are not satisfied with these traditional roles. Only one out of six American women under twenty-six years of age "strongly agrees" that the statement "A woman's place is in the home" still makes sense. Half of these young women opted for "an opportunity to develop as an individual," when asked about their life goals (American Council of Life Insurance, 1978). These women want new alternatives that take advantage of the skills and training they have had. They agitate for legal reform, seek equality in job opportunities, and demand a marital relationship that recognizes the importance of their contribution.

Increasing employment of wives

The increasing employment of wives outside the home is strong evidence of a major change in women's roles. Attitudes regarding the appropriateness of this occupational role for wives vary widely, but the existence of the trend cannot be questioned. While the proportion of single women employed rose from 48 to 60 percent between 1940 and 1980, the proportion of married women in the labor force increased from 15 to 50 percent over the

Eileen: An Egalitarian Woman

You might wonder what a career-oriented, so-called independent girl like myself is doing getting married. My answer can only be that I found a person with whom I can be a very close friend, lover, and companion, whom I also love very dearly. I have had the best time of my life with him, for he can make me happy and sad, laugh and cry, and feels I am the most important person in the world. He is wonderful, nutty, funny, brilliant, unpredictable, loving, caring, responsible, charming, romantic, honest, and trustworthy. We get along fantastically! He is everything and even more than I wanted in a man.

Our marriage is not geared along traditional lines. If I am to succeed in marriage, my husband has to understand and accept without reservation my need for individuality and expression outside the home. Derek understands, accepts, and welcomes this need because he does not want to get trapped into the male syndrome of being the sole supporter of a family.

I feel freedom within a marriage is a very essential aspect. . . . I had gotten into the habit of doing a lot of traveling before we got married and was afraid I would have to give it up. However, I go on more trips now than I had ever done before. . . . Derek has never so much as expressed resentment or hostility or tried to talk me out of going on my trips.

From Barbara Forisha, *Sex Roles and Personal Awareness* (Morristown, N.J.: General Learning Press, 1978), pp. 128–129.

same period (United States Department of Labor, 1980). The available evidence we have suggests that the percentages will continue to rise, at least for a time.

The roles of women in caring for children are also changing. This is partially in response to the increasing employment of mothers outside the home, but even many parents who are not employed enroll their children in preschool programs to broaden their social and intellectual experiences. Increasingly, the parental role is being shared with schoolteachers, baby-sitters, camp counselors, Little League coaches and many other service personnel and agencies. In Chapter 13 we will consider in depth these changing responsibilities of parenthood.

In the area of household responsibilities, Vanek found that employed women take much more advantage of labor-saving devices and other replacement services (such as restaurants and commercial cleaners) that are available to the family. While nonemployed women still spend about fifty-five hours per week in housework, employed women allocate only twenty-six hours per week to these same tasks. Apparently, they have become much more efficient in performing their household tasks and more likely to enlist their families' support for some relaxation of household standards (Portner, 1978).

Women's employment and marriage

How have these changes in women's roles, principally in occupational roles, influenced the marital relationship? This depends, of course, on the

As women increasingly enter the job market, day care is assuming a new, more important role in the socialization of the next generation.

amount of support a woman receives from the other family members, her reasons for working, and the amount of time she puts into her occupation. Among husbands whose wives are employed, nine out of ten are in favor of it (Hoffman and Nye, 1974). Studies of husbands of nonemployed wives, however, find that these men are somewhat anxious concerning the possible consequences of their wives' employment. These husbands often fear that their wives will become less companionate, unable to fulfill their traditional roles, too independent, neglectful of their family, and likely to cause the overall marital relationship to suffer.

The husband's attitude has a significant influence on how the wife feels about her employment and her marriage. Orden and Bradburn (1969) found that if the wife works because her husband's income is insufficient or if she does not work because of her husband's insistence, then she is less likely to be happily married. The wives who work by their own choice and receive support from their husbands for working are most likely to be happy. In this study, the women who voluntarily worked part-time reported the greatest satisfaction.

Another factor influencing how the wife's employment affects marital adjustment is the total number of role obligations that she has accumulated. Early in marriage, when household responsibilities are minimal, the employed wife is less likely to be frustrated by difficulty in completing her tasks. Contributing to the financial security of the marriage and using the skills that she has developed in school or in her previous career also makes her feel more important in the relationship. There is little evidence of role strain; most men and women support this pattern; and marital happiness and companionship are higher among wives who are working at this time (Orthner and Axelson, 1980).

Children and expanding roles

As the marriage progresses, and especially if children arrive, role obligations expand and the situation may become quite different. Although most children do not seem to suffer socially or intellectually because their mothers are employed (Portner, 1978), the marital relationship does appear to change. Since husbands commonly fail to help very much at home, whether the wife works or not, and children's dependency needs are primarily the responsibility of the wife, working or not, the marital relationship often suffers. Robinson *et al.* found that husband-wife companionship is significantly lower during the parenting years in marriages when the wife is employed than when she is nonemployed. After the children are launched, however, the employed wives once again report more companionate experiences than the housewives.

Mental conflict

On balance, it appears that women who want to expand and change their roles may have to be much more careful in mate selection. These new roles require adjustments and support from the husband if they are to be satisfactorily integrated into the marriage. The fact that studies confirm higher levels of conflict in marriages with a working wife suggest that some strain is accompanying these changes in roles (Bahr and Day, 1978). It is not clear, however, whether this conflict is necessarily harmful. David Heer (1963) says that women who work develop more dominant personalities and are more likely to stand up for what they believe. Wives who are financially dependent on their husbands, on the other hand, often cannot argue from as strong a base. Both wives may feel the same on an issue, but the more independent, employed wife is more likely to challenge her husband's control. In a sense, these new roles for women provide more opportunity for open, equal, two-way communication in marriage. Yet, any time this is possible, it is also possible for differences of opinion to be revealed. The extent to which these differences lead to relational dissatisfaction depends on the amount of give and take each is willing to accept.

Changing Husband Roles

During the 1940s and 1950s, it was not uncommon to find cartoons in national magazines making fun of men doing housework, trying to diaper a baby, chauffeuring children to music lessons, or burning a canned dinner. Today, we rarely see these sorts of cartoons. Has our humor changed, or are men taking on new responsibilities in the home?

Reconsiderations

The evidence we have suggests that many men are reconsidering traditional male roles. Numerous popular and professional books have been written setting forth new definitions of masculinity and fatherhood. Some couples have even reversed conventional roles with the man acting as "househusband" and the wife as breadwinner (see Vignette 7.3). Psychologist Joseph Pleck remarks, "It's becoming clear to many of us that many of our most important inner needs cannot be met by acting in the ways we have been expected to act as men" (Katz, 1976, p. 293).

Reasons for limited change

How significant a movement is this? Among young, college-educated men, the initial stirrings are beginning to be heard, but it would be unrealistic to expect rapid changes even in this segment of the population. New definitions of men's roles have emerged largely in response to changes in women's roles, and if men appear to be dragging their feet in accepting these changes, there are probably several reasons for this. First of all, traditional male roles have been just as rigid and stereotyped as traditional female roles. In fact, society has permitted men even less freedom to depart from traditional male responsibilities than it has permitted women to depart from traditional female responsibilities. Second, men are being asked to give up or share those roles that have given them dominance, and this is perceived as threatening their privileged position in the family and society. Third, it is unclear just what is expected of men in their new roles, and this "fear of the unknown" creates anxiety. Fourth, since the changes in men's roles are largely in reaction to changes in women's roles, and women are not consistent in the expectations they have for themselves, men are not forced to alter their traditional views during mate selection. Thus, even in marriage, men may see their wives as the problem and believe that changing partners will remedy the situation. Finally, because most men retain the role of principal provider, even if they assume new roles, any additional roles may be viewed as threatening their capacity to meet the needs of the family and themselves.

Vignette 7·3

Confessions of a Househusband

Two years ago, my wife Jan and I tried to change (at least within our own lives) society's imposed pattern of dependent servant and responsible master by deciding to share equally the responsibility of housework. We made no specific arrangement (a mistake from which I was to learn a great deal); it was simply understood that I was going to take on roughly half of the domestic chores so that she could do the other work she needed to do.

There was something of a shock for me in discovering the sheer quantity of the housework, and my standards of acceptable cleanliness fell rapidly. It became much easier to see my insistence on neatness as an inherited middle-class hang-up now that I had to do so much of the work myself. One of the long-standing sources of tension between Jan and me was almost immediately understood and resolved. What's more, I enjoyed it, at first. When not interrupted by the children I could, on a good day, do the kitchen and a bedroom, a load of laundry, and a meal in a little over two hours. Then I'd clean up after the meal and relax for a while with considerable satisfaction. So I approached the work with some enthusiasm, looking forward to seeing it all put right by my own hand, and for a while I wondered what all the fuss was about.

But within a few weeks that satisfaction and that enthusiasm began to erode a little more each time I woke up or walked into the house, only to find that it all needed to be done again. Finally, the image of the finished job, the image that encouraged me to start, was crowded out of my head by the image of the job to do all over again. I became lethargic, with the result that I worked less efficiently, so that even when I did "finish," it took longer and was done less well, rendering still less satisfaction. At first I had intellectual energy to spare, thinking about my teaching while washing dishes; pausing in the middle of a load of laundry to jot down a note. But those pauses soon became passive daydreams, fantasies from which I would have to snap myself back to the grind, until finally it was all I could do to keep going at all. I became more and more irritable and resentful.

I can pinpoint the place in time when we saw the necessity for a more careful adjustment of responsibilities, defining duties and scheduling hours more precisely and adhering to them more faithfully. It was at a moment when it became clear that Jan's work was beginning to pay off and her group scored a definite and apparently unqualified success. I went around the house for a full day feeling very self-satisfied, proud of her achievement, *as if it were my own,* which was fine until I realized, somewhere near the end of the day, that much of that sense of achievement resulted from the fact that I had no achievement of my own. I was getting my sense of fulfillment, of self-esteem, *through her,* while she was getting it *through her work.* It had happened: I was a full-fledged househusband.

From Joel Roache, *Ms.*, 1972, © Ms. Foundation for Education and Communication, Inc., 1973.

Whether or not these and other reasons are legitimate, it is evident that many men feel threatened by changing role definitions. Just like the college men who verbalized liberal attitudes toward women's roles but were actually traditional (Komarovsky, 1976), Veroff and Feld (1970) found that many husbands who say they accept egalitarian marital roles actually consider these new roles incompatible with their drives to achieve success and family security. Interestingly, it is the higher educated men who profess these egalitarian sentiments, but they are also the professionals and executives who commonly dedicate themselves to fifty- and sixty-hour workweeks. Therefore, according to a recent Gallup survey, the same men who say they believe in more role freedom are often unavailable to share in the responsibilities of the household (Hunt and Hunt, 1980). Perhaps this explains why studies do not find most husbands significantly involved in housework, even if the wife is employed (Erickson *et al.*, 1979).

Male competition

When men are not pushing themselves, they are being pushed by others. According to Joseph Pleck (1976), "the dominant theme in men's relationships with other men in our society can be termed 'patriarchal competition.' This patriarchal competition is not tied to any particular areas of activity, like sports or the military, but, in fact, pervades nearly every context of encounter among men. Some areas may reveal this competition more explicitly than others, but no area provides a refuge from it" (p. 263).

Women also apply pressure to men in their provider roles. When housewives were queried as to whether they viewed their husbands primarily as husbands, fathers, or breadwinners, most of them stated that his most important role was breadwinner (Lopata, 1971). Nearly two-thirds of the women in Scanzoni's (1975) study agreed that "the man's chief responsibility should be his job" and that he should be "the head of the family." The youngest and most educated wives gave the least support to this view.

Reactions against role strains

A growing number of men, however, are reacting against the strains that they have sensed in their own and their spouse's roles. Some are electing not to take jobs that require them to be separated from their families for inordinately long periods of time. There is a developing awareness, confirmed by researchers such as Portner, that occupations that require very long hours or a great deal of travel are more likely to lead to stress on families. Robert Seidenburg (1973) has documented the plight of numerous marriages in which the husband is really married to "the organization," and his wife must cope with personal and family problems alone. Even at the blue-collar level, stress caused by work commitments is being recognized. The United Auto Workers and several other major unions have insisted on the right of workers to refuse to work overtime, which is a step in the direction of leaving more time for families.

New options for men

Perhaps we can best understand changing husband roles in terms of two new options. The *first option* is for the man to decide whether to commit himself wholly to the provider role or whether some balance should be worked out between family and provider roles. In the past, a man was evaluated according to just one criterion: how much he achieved in his occupation (Gross, 1978). He may have completely neglected his family roles, but if he was professionally successful, then the life-style of the family was taken as evidence that he had fulfilled his responsibility. Even recently, researchers have found that the wives of successful men are less likely to expect their husbands to participate in most other marital and family roles (Clark *et al.*, 1978).

Nevertheless, a desire for an intrinsically satisfying marriage is causing some husbands to consider a balance in roles that gives them more time for their families. This usually costs them in terms of the financial success they might have "enjoyed," but it can be outweighed by personal satisfaction. One man said that reallocating his priorities meant being able to view his wife "more as an equal partner, a whole person, a friend. Before, I saw her primarily as a mother and housekeeper, and I was always playing the big protector, the big man around the house. That's really a pretty crummy role, and besides, you can't have a really open relationship with a servant. It's been a lot nicer lately" (Katz, p. 295).

The *second option* that is developing for men relates to the extent of their participation in child-care and housekeeping roles. In the past, men were taught not to do "woman's work," and to do so led to ridicule. Only if a wife were sick could her husband legitimately take over her tasks, and even then his awkward attempts were treated in a joking manner by others.

Work and family role balance

But flexibility has crept into these roles as well. Those husbands who choose to balance their work and family roles are now more comfortable in the household. The responsibility for household tasks often remains with the wife, but if she is incapacitated or if she is the principal breadwinner, as in many student marriages, he may be *expected* to take a major role in child care and housekeeping. Even for the most "liberated" men, however, the strain of electing to be a "househusband" can be more than he anticipates, as we noted in Vignette 7.3.

Nevertheless, it may take more time for most men to ease into housekeeping than into child-care roles. Today men are more concerned about neglecting their parental responsibilities than their marital or household responsibilities (Nye, 1976). The data we examined earlier indicate that men are more likely to share tasks related to the children than other household tasks. It is too early to tell whether this means that husbands are moving toward wider participation in all family responsibilities or whether it simply means that they are experiencing a greater concern over their parental roles.

DUAL-CAREER MARRIAGES

Over half of all wives are now employed. Most of these women work in what we might call **jobs,** positions that are not a primary life interest but are secondary to family responsibilities and a supplement to their husband's earnings. This is not only the result of occupational discrimination, it is also the preference of most women (Scanzoni, 1975). There is developing a minority of women, however, who are establishing themselves in **careers,** positions that require a high degree of commitment, are personally rewarding, and demand long-term obligations. In the past, women who had careers did not marry; it was believed that women who fulfilled the traditional obligations of marriage could not also be established on the ladder of success (Gilbert and Holahan, 1978). Today, some women want careers but they also want marriage. Can the two interests be reconciled?

Difficulties

From the limited evidence at hand, it appears that marriages in which both husband and wife have careers can be successful, but there are several hurdles they must face. An immediate problem for the wife is that of advancement in her career. Managers and others who control promotions often doubt the commitment that women can make to their careers and are more likely to discriminate against them in advancement and even in hiring (Rosen *et al.*, 1975). While legally unjustifiable, this prejudicial decision making is difficult to control. Career advancement sometimes requires relocation, which forces husbands and wives to choose whose career is most important. The evidence to date indicates that when this issue arises most women usually follow their husbands. Poloma and Garland (1971) argue that professional women rarely seek equality but actually "tolerate domestication." They found that only one of the dual-career couples in their study was truly egalitarian. However, most of the women reported that their situation was satisfactory as long as they could have both their career and family.

Other problems dual-career couples may face include excessive demands on each individual's time, energy, and leisure; conflicts over family and job demands; feelings of competition and resentment over career successes and failures; and tensions that result from each person bringing work problems home. Each of these problems usually takes a greater toll upon wives than husbands (Heckman *et al.*, 1977).

Anticipating potential problems

How do dual-career couples handle their problems? They start by dedicating themselves to their careers early. The professional couples interviewed by Lynda Holstrum (1972) tended to marry later than traditional couples, and because they had completed more years of schooling before marriage, they had more time to develop commitments to their professions. One professional woman said: "I always thought that I would get married, but it wasn't the goal" (Holstrum, p. 15).

Career women have fewer children than noncareer women (United States Department of Labor, 1979), but successfully meeting their children's needs is a very complex commitment. Usually, it is accomplished in one of the following ways: the husband shares more of the child-rearing responsibilities with the wife; they modify one or both of their work schedules, usually the wife's, to enable one of them to be with the children; or they hire outside help (Hall and Hall, 1979).

Economic advantages

Although the intrinsic satisfaction of mutual careers is often cited as the reason for this type of marriage, the financial advantages of two professional careers are considerable. While lack of shared time or energy may be a

Chapter 8

Communication and Conflict

Communication is a basic element in human interaction. Through communication we transmit to one another our wishes, concerns, likes, dislikes, demands, replies, feelings about others, and feelings about ourselves. A popular song some years ago asserted that "fish gotta swim" and "birds gotta fly." If the song had tried to describe people, it might have said "people gotta talk."

For humans, communication is almost as natural as breathing. In fact, it is impossible for us not to communicate. Whatever we say or do is interpreted by others. To say nothing to someone, to snub them, can deliver just as strong a message as a verbal argument. Agreement can be confirmed orally or with a gesture. Also, conflicts can be quiet or loud. Two people "staring one another down" can be saying the same thing as another couple who are ranting and raving.

But while communication may be natural, that does not mean it is always easy. **Miscommunication** is a frequent problem in all intimate relationships. According to one careful estimate, nearly 85 percent of the time in a family or marriage, the message a sender sends is not the exact message that a receiver receives (Watzlawick *et al.*, 1967). Some misinterpretation occurs. The reason for this failure may be in the sender, the receiver, or the method of transmission, but the result is the same—confusion. Each of us is frequently frustrated when we find that we are misunderstood or when we feel we do not know what the other person "really" means.

Concerns about communication ability are becoming widespread. More and more marital failures are being blamed on the inability of couples to communicate effectively. Yet in any intimate relationship, disagreements emerge and conflicts must be resolved. Differences must be negotiated in order to bring about personal satisfaction and relational growth. In this chapter, we will examine some of the ways that couple-communication patterns contribute to the stability and instability of relationships. We will also consider conflict and conflict management as a normal process in marital communication which, if avoided, may lead to more problems for a relationship.

COMMUNICATION IN RELATIONSHIPS

In any relationship or social organization, communication is necessary for success and growth. Businesses have recognized this for some time: "Executives know that communications are the lifeline of business; when the line becomes clogged or breaks down, two things occur: either (1) whatever shouldn't or (2) nothing" (Bach and Wyden, 1969).

Communication and changing roles

While the same thing is true for intimate relationships, the importance of communication here has only recently been emphasized. In business organizations, people often change roles or have to deal with many persons in different roles. This makes communication necessary for the organization to adjust and to work effectively. But in relationships like marriage, we must remember that up until the last few decades, male and female roles have been rigidly distinct and the partners have mutually accepted this. Therefore, opportunities for men and women or husbands and wives to influence one another have traditionally been minimized.

Today, however, this situation has changed considerably. As we have relaxed some of our rigid gender and marital roles, we have been forced to discover new means for understanding one another in couple relationships. This has elevated communication to new importance. Each couple must now organize their own relationship out of the needs and interests of both partners, rather than out of the time-honored traditions of their respective forebears. Instead of couples just *taking* the roles that have been created for them, couples must now *make* and *remake* many of their own roles to fit their particular relationship. This has become an ongoing process that requires frequent adjustments as needs of the individuals involved change over time.

Communication Messages

The basic purpose of communication is to achieve understanding. No one can know what is on our mind unless we communicate it to them. We send messages in order to inform and shape the impressions of another, and we receive messages in order to know and anticipate their needs as well. If both parties are receiving as well as sending messages, then the exchange should encourage understanding, although agreement does not necessarily follow. We can understand people without agreeing with them.

Three types of messages that are commonly transmitted in interpersonal communication have been identified by Kantor and Lehr (1975). These are **affect, power,** and **meaning** messages. Kantor and Lehr call these **target dimensions** since communications tend to be oriented toward each of these foci.

Types of messages

Expressing feelings

Affect Messages. The first of these dimensions is affect—the sharing of feelings and emotions. Affect messages are "exchanges of the heart" in which people disclose to one another their needs for intimacy and nurturance. Usually, these messages convey positive, supportive feelings that encourage mutual, *intrinsic commitments* to the relationship. Sometimes, however, messages of negative affect are transmitted, such as criticism, sarcasm, ridicule, boredom, or indifference. These too are expressions of emotion and may be used to create psychological distance, or they may be a backhanded way for some persons to seek closeness when they have not learned or do not want to send positive affect messages (Scoresby, 1977). The husband who feigns sickness or the wife who uses sarcasm may actually be sending signals that they feel emotionally isolated. Perhaps, they see no other way to get the attention they want.

Expressing control

Power Messages. Some messages are directed toward controlling or influencing the behavior of others. These are power messages, and they express what the person wants to have done in such a way that others are allowed few options of their own. These can be directive messages—such as telling a spouse how to walk or eat—or they may be interpretive messages which tell the other person how to react—for example, to be more responsive or patient. Usually, these are "you" messages, since they are concerned with the other person, not with the feelings or behavior of the sender. "You should do that" is a typical power message.

In most relationships, there is a structure of authority over matters of concern. This is necessary to reduce the anarchy and confusion that would result if people did not know what was expected of them. This is particularly important for the rearing of children, but adults also need to be informed at times of appropriate or inappropriate behavior. Still, power messages tend to be *instrumentally oriented.* The more often they are used, the more often they are directed only one way, and the more often they are used without affect and meaning messages, the more likely that relational commitments will become primarily instrumental.

Meaning Messages. Sometimes the purpose of the communication is for people to exchange information and interpret the meanings this has for one another. Understanding in this sense comes from becoming familiar with the other person, discovering what he or she values and considers important. Meaning messages are designed to reveal ideas, beliefs, values, and concepts of what is good or bad. Kantor and Lehr call these messages the "mind of family experience" (p. 51).

Seeking understanding

For individuals, meaning messages reveal their **identity**—their perception of themselves as reflected in their personalities. For the relationship, meaning messages provide insights into one another—what they have in common and where they are different. Common meanings are usually reflected in "we" statements, like "We love each other." Sometimes when we want to exchange information, solve a problem, or simply verify our feelings about something, we move communication deliberately toward the meaning level (and perhaps away from heavy power and affect messages). To do this, we will often ask a question, such as "Why do you feel that way?" In responding, the other person then has to examine his or her self-perceptions and answer with a meaning message. The conversation can then be more mutually beneficial. Of course, if the person responds with a power message like "It's none of your business!" then further communication is unlikely to be fruitful.

Communication Styles

Communication messages are rarely transmitted without some other person or persons in mind. They are designed to have a purpose—affect, power, or meaning—which causes the receiver to interpret and respond in some manner. The response message, in turn, is interpreted and yields its own reactions. These message exchanges soon develop a sequence of communication which is the basis of **dialogue**. Over time, these dialogues often become predictable and patterned. Lynn Scoresby, author of *The Marriage Dialogue*, comments:

Interaction styles or dialogues

> . . . although the marital relationship is a dynamic, evolving, and ongoing dialogue, there is not an infinite number of ways husbands and wives communicate. Two people talk, act, listen, and interpret in some fairly definite patterns. Collectively, these patterns form an *interaction style* that tends to be regular, in the same situations, over time. Once formed, it is this style of interaction that shapes how one person perceives the other. (p. 16)

Basing his observations on the earlier studies of anthropologist Gregory Bateson (1972), Scoresby concludes that three basic communication styles usually appear in intimate relationships. These are called *complementary, symmetrical,* and *parallel* communication. All of these will occur in most relationships at one time or another, but there is a tendency for relationships to stabilize around a particular style that best fits the communication purposes of the members.

The **complementary communication** style develops when individuals take very different communication stances. One person may be dominant, talkative, and aggressive, while the other is submissive, quiet, and passive—at least on the issue under discussion. In another situation, their communication roles may be reversed. In this type of exchange, power messages are sent primarily from one person and responses from the other person are limited, or perhaps affect-oriented.

Symmetrical communication involves competitive interaction. Each partner tries to maximize his or her own influence. Typically, arguments and fights are symmetrical since both people are trying to send power messages and neither is willing to accept the influence of the other. The result is an escalation of aggression. Often, this type of communication is marked by a mutual fear of losing influence and the belief on the part of both persons that only their position is right (Lederer and Jackson, 1968). Neither person really seeks meaning messages from the other and affect messages are used only when they increase personal power.

A third style, **parallel communication,** offers more flexibility in interaction. Responses are not necessarily opposite or identical but determined in a more independent manner. Meaning messages are used more frequently to clarify positions and affect messages are sent to lend support to one another. Power statements are not automatically challenged nor are they dutifully respected either. Instead, parallel communication emphasizes evaluation and adjustive responses.

But whether evaluation is carefully considered or not, each of these communication styles includes messages that are interpreted by the sender and receiver. Sometimes our interpretations are incorrect, ignored, or chal-

Sometimes our efforts to communicate are misinterpreted or challenged.

lenged, but interpretation occurs nonetheless. As each subsequent message is sent, these interpretations and responses eventually develop the style of communication that is to be used at that time. As an example of how this works, a husband may indicate to his wife that he is very discouraged with his job (affect message). If she responds, "You are nothing but a lazy bum!" (power message) then she has begun a complementary exchange which will continue if he accepts her interpretation. However, should she respond with the question, "Why do you feel that way?" (meaning message), then a parallel dialogue may begin, with very different consequences for the relationship.

Gender differences in communication

Even though communication styles in a relationship may take a variety of forms, there are gender-role and social-class factors that affect the selection of a communication style among many couples. For one thing, men are more likely to dominate conversations with women. This is true despite the myth that women talk more (see Vignette 8.1). Men talk more frequently and they interrupt more often than women do (Henly and Thorne, 1977). One study found that in natural conversations, 98 percent of the interruptions and 100 percent of the overlap in conversations were by male speakers (Zimmerman and West, 1975). Due to this dominance orientation, men are much more likely to initiate power messages and force conversations toward a complementary or symmetrical style. Women, in contrast, are more likely to question, apologize, and elaborate in their communication, which makes them more vulnerable to complementary interaction or helpful in creating parallel interaction (Hirschman, 1974).

Communication and Relational Adjustment

The ability of a relationship to adjust, to take into account the changing needs of its members, hinges on communication. Communication abilities can be minimal as long as *nothing* interrupts the ongoing nature of a relationship, no joint decisions have to be made, and no problems have to be mutually solved. Simple role playing can be sufficient to maintain the facade of a close relationship, but the thin veneer of cordiality that some couples consider communication is rarely sufficient to cope with the stresses that impinge on most intimate relationships at some time.

We should not be surprised, therefore, to find that poor communication is the number-one problem with which family counselors have to deal (see Fig. 8.1). When the case loads of 266 marriage- and family-counseling agencies in the United States were examined, nine out of ten couples with marital problems were described as having communication difficulties (Beck and Jones, 1973). Husbands or wives complained, "We can't talk to each other"; "I can't reach him"; or "She doesn't understand me." Even secondary concerns like children, sex, or money often became serious problems only after communication channels broke down.

Communication and marriage satisfaction

Several studies have found that overall marital satisfaction is higher among couples who rate their communication as good (Rollins and Feldman, 1970). Companionship is also more frequent among husbands and wives who

Vignette 8.1 Womanspeak and Manspeak: Myths of Communication

The first myth is that women speak more and longer than men. This is simply not so. In study after study, men have been found to speak more often and at greater length than women, and to interrupt other speakers more than women do. This finding applies to people in all kinds of social situations—alone, in single-sex or mixed-sex pairs, and in groups. In a laboratory study of married couples, for example, in 52 percent of the cases, the husband did more of the talking; for the rest of the couples, the time was either equally divided or the wives did more talking. Hilpert, Kramer, and Clark (1975) report a study of male-female dyads in which males spoke more than 59 percent of the time. Another study that set up husband-wife discussions found that the husbands talked more in nineteen cases, and the wives more in fifteen cases. In an investigation that used mock jury deliberations, men constituted two-thirds of the jurors but they contributed almost four-fifths of the talk. In a similar study of mock juries, it was found that in all occupational levels, males talked more than females.

The second myth attributes the high pitch of women's speech to anatomical differences alone. While it is true that there are anatomical differences between males and females that produce a slightly higher pitch in females' voices, the difference is nowhere near so great as to produce the variance that is heard. Recent investigators have concluded that at least some of these differences are learned and constitute a linguistic convention. There is such a universal expectation that male voices should be low and female voices high that any deviation from this expectation produces a powerful effect on other people's impressions of one's personality. Men with high-pitched voices may be taken for women in phone conversations (and treated accordingly), disregarded in group conversations, and ridiculed behind their backs. But female newscasters with lower pitch are preferred and are hired; since lower pitch is associated with males, who have more authority in our society, it carries more authority in a female also.

There are other sex differences in speech sounds. For boys in our culture, masculinity and toughness are projected by a slightly nasal speech; girls and "gentlemanly" boys have nonnasal, or oral, speech. Males also speak with greater intensity than females. There are differences in the intonation patterns used by each sex; women have more variable intonations, or more contrastive levels, than men do. Women are said to have more extremes of high and low intonation, and one linguist has proposed that while most men have three contrasting levels of intonation, many women have four such levels. This variability in women's speech sounds is said to produce unsure intonation patterns, ones of whining, questioning, and helplessness. It may also indicate greater emotional expressiveness of a more positive sort.

From Nancy Henly and Barrie Thorne, Womanspeak and Manspeak: Sex Differences and Sexism in Communication. In Alice Sargent (ed.), *Beyond Sex Roles* (St. Paul, Minn.: West, 1977), pp. 205–207.

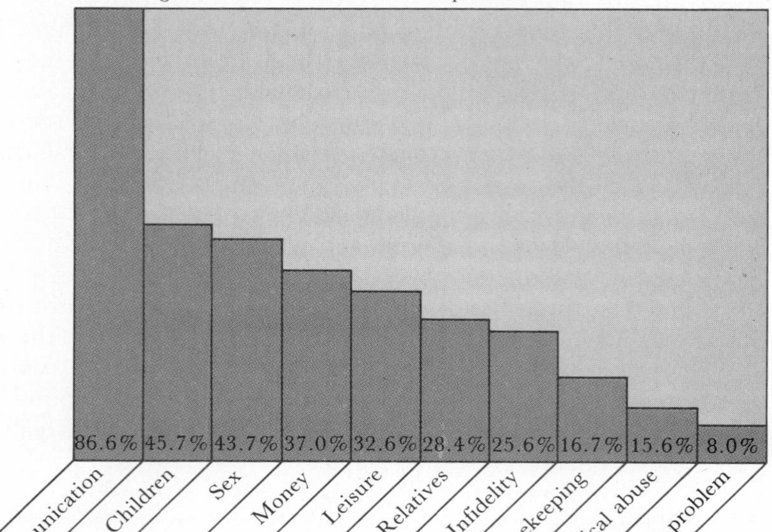

Fig. 8.1

Marital Problems Observed by Counselors

Source: Reproduced from *Progress on Family Problems* (1973), by Dorothy Fahs Beck and Mary Ann Jones, with permission from the publisher, Family Service Association of America.

report that they are more open to communicating with one another (Orthner, 1976). What these and other studies seem to be saying is that good communication does not just involve periodic problem solving, it is a *condition* of the relationship that is continuously reinforced. This is what social psychologist Leslie Navron (1967) found when he compared the answers given on a communications test by happily and unhappily married couples. The happily married, he reports, differ from the unhappily married in that they:

1. Are much more likely to talk over pleasant things that happen during the day.
2. More frequently feel understood by their spouses; that is, their messages are getting across.
3. Discuss things which are shared interests.
4. Are less likely to break off communication or inhibit it by pouting.
5. More often will talk with each other about personal problems.
6. Make more frequent use of words that have private meaning for them.
7. Generally talk most things over together.
8. Are more sensitive to each other's feelings and make adjustments to take these feelings into account when they speak.
9. Are more able to discuss intimate issues without restraint or embarrassment.

10. Are more able to tell what kind of day their spouses have had without asking.
11. Communicate nonverbally to a greater degree.

We should not conclude from these studies that couples with open communication avoid all problems. No relationship can be completely shielded from problems, miscommunications, or communication games. Also, couples who communicate well at one time may not communicate so well at a later period in their relationship. For example, many couples find that their marital communication drops off somewhat during the child-rearing years (Orthner, 1976).

Communication expectations

Furthermore, satisfaction with a relationship is not inseparably linked to good communication. We experience dissatisfaction only when our expectations are not fulfilled. Therefore, a person who does not expect to communicate very much with his or her partner will not experience disappointment if there is little communication. When Komarovsky (1964) interviewed less-educated, blue-collar husbands and wives, this is what she found; the couples did not communicate very much, but they did not expect to, either. The responsibilities of the husband and wife were mutually understood to be distinctly different.

Nevertheless, in most relationships today, communication is not only hoped for, it is expected. This is why a lack of communication more typically causes frustration and dissatisfaction in contemporary marriages. As our expectations for intimacy and sharing rise, the chances that we will not experience the intensity of intimacy we desire also rise. Thus, we find in marriage both the greatest hope for intimacy and the greatest chance of not achieving it. Only by continual reinforcement of their communication network can a couple who wants to be intimate maintain this kind of bond.

ELEMENTS OF INTERPERSONAL COMMUNICATION

There is a children's game called "Telephone" or "Rumor" in which a word or phrase is whispered to one child and passed on from child to child down the line. Inevitably, the message the last child reveals is different from the one the first child heard. Everyone laughs at this and then wonders where the distortion occurred. It may have come from the inability of a child to hear very well, a child may deliberately distort part of the message, or perhaps a child was not paying attention to the rules of the game. Any one of these factors could account for the miscommunication.

Message distortions

In adult communication, where the messages are often more complex, it is little wonder that distortions also occur. Communication ability or success, therefore, is not just a matter of frequency—the number of messages or the amount of talking that goes on—but also a function of how *able* and *willing* the individuals are to communicate. This is not a simple process, as Millard Bienvenu (1970) discovered when he looked for some of the ways in which couples who communicate well differ from those who do not. What he as well as others have found is that there are a variety of elements in communication that fit together like a puzzle. The more elements that are left out, the more distortion occurs in the communication picture. Some of the elements that are most important are: self-awareness, empathy, nonverbal language, self-disclosure, and listening.

Self-Awareness

Communication, by its very nature, involves message interpretation. Our own feelings are interpreted and reflected in the messages we send. The messages we receive are also interpreted before we respond. Ideally, this process means that each person's communication is based on his or her own self-examination and careful consideration of the dialogue. Unfortunately, this does not always occur.

Incomplete message problems

Researchers and marriage counselors who have observed couples trying to communicate find they frequently follow role patterns or make conditioned responses without carefully considering the messages they receive or send (Parlee, 1979). Lack of self-awareness can also result in the communication of incomplete messages—messages that do not contain enough content or information about the sender to be effectively acted upon by the receiver. For example, when we respond to the question "How do you feel today?" with an automatic "OK," the person may not interpret this to mean "everything is all right." Instead, he or she will probably see this as a cordial response that is hiding genuine feelings. Likewise, the husband who is reading the newspaper may periodically respond "Uh-huh" to his wife's talking but with little awareness of what she is saying. It is unlikely that his response has much meaning to her—other than to encourage anger.

In the program they have developed to improve couple communication, Sherod Miller and his colleagues at the University of Minnesota consider self-awareness to be a most important key to communicating. "The first order of business," they conclude, "is to find out how we can maintain awareness of ourselves. When we are in contact with our own awareness, then we can communicate our own thoughts, feelings, intentions, and actions more effectively. From here we can expand our awareness of our partner and our relationship" (1975, p. 30).

Empathy

The other side of awareness in interpersonal communication is empathy. This trait describes the ability to understand, to identify with other people to such an extent that we can put ourselves in their place. With empathy, a speaker is so aware of the other person that the response of the listener can be predicted even before it is uttered. The empathic person genuinely feels what the other person feels and takes those feelings into account in communication.

Predicting responses

The importance of empathy for marital communication has been reported in several research studies. These studies have found that husbands and wives who are able to predict more accurately the responses of their spouses feel happier about their marriages (Scheff, 1967). Empathy has also been found to be an important ingredient for problem solving and for developing more realistic attitudes toward the relationship (Schulman, 1974). Good communication, it appears, comes from being open to negative as well as to positive responses from the partner. Being able to see only the good or the bad side of someone leads to either idealism or pessimism, not the realism that is necessary for honest communication.

Nonverbal Language

While we usually think of communication in terms of spoken or written language, nonverbal language can be an even more important part of the communication process. Researchers have discovered that we obtain only about one-third of the meaning of verbal messages from what we hear or read; two-thirds of the meaning comes from the nonverbal cues we receive (Applebaum *et al.*, 1974). In a laboratory study, it was discovered that nonverbal messages carry over four times the weight of verbal messages in affecting our behavior (Argyle *et al.*, 1970). This means that communication involves not only what we say but also how we look and act toward someone.

Body language

People transmit nonverbal language in a variety of ways. Stony silence, hand gestures, smiles, and embracing are but a few of the means by which we enlarge our communication repertoire. Three basic types of nonverbal messages include: (1) **body language**—shifts of the body, facial expressions, eye movements, and posture; (2) **paralanguage**—voice qualities such as laughing, smiling, or yawning; and (3) **proxemics**—the spatial positioning of the people who are communicating.

Each of these types of nonverbal language is employed when we communicate. When we want to emphasize a point we move our hands and arms, raise the level of our voice, and move closer toward the listener. The more intimate the communication, the more likely that voices will be hushed, eye contact prolonged, and spatial closeness arranged. Anger is evident in silence, piercing stares, folded arms, and movement away from the other person. Emotions, feelings, control, direction, and deference are all communicated more effectively with the addition of nonverbal language.

Message congruency

The ability to read nonverbal language is an important part of interpersonal communication. People may verbally respond one way to a request while their eyes are saying something really different. This **incongruent message** begs for a response. To proceed without asking for clarification and resolving the incongruence is to risk further miscommunication and conflict. When

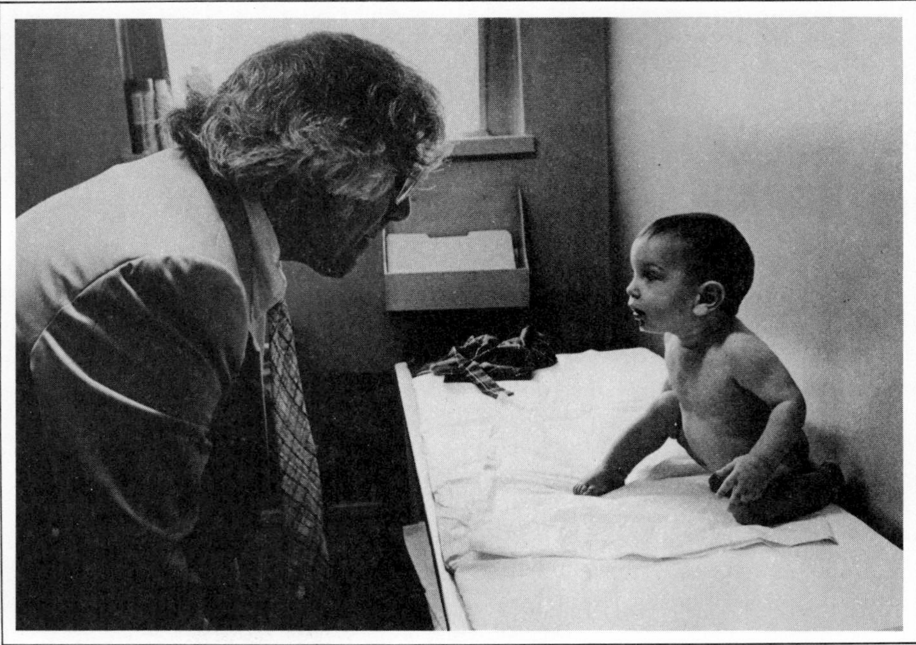

Body language can be an effective method of communication.

nonverbal cues are **congruent** with verbal language, however, the messages are more easily read, communication is enhanced, and the likelihood of conflict is reduced.

Self-Disclosure

While nonverbal language can significantly improve the accuracy of communication, mutual understanding still depends upon the ability of people to reveal their inner thoughts and emotions verbally to one another. Only through **self-disclosure** can we confirm the nonverbal messages that we transmit and allow congruence in interpersonal communication. Colbert (1968) calls self-disclosure a process which allows "two to see one." This does not mean that self-disclosure always promotes agreement, but it does open the channels of communication to mutual understanding, a prerequisite to dialogue and the seeking of agreement.

For some people, self-disclosure is not easy. Marriage counselors frequently hear complaints like "She won't tell me what is bothering her," or "He never tells me anything." Many of these couples can talk about the weather, their children, the neighbors, or whether to buy a new car—things that can be discussed informationally—but they rarely, if ever, let their guard down to reveal their emotions and needs.

Difficulties in self-disclosure

There are two major factors that frequently act to block self-disclosure in communication. One of the most important is **childhood socialization.** Children are frequently taught not to express their feelings. They learn that it is a weakness to show emotion or to tell others how they really feel. Boys, particularly, are showered with this message, and the result is the inexpressiveness frequently noticed in men. Research studies clearly indicate that men do not disclose their feelings as easily to others as women do (Gilbert, 1976).

A second major cause of difficulties in self-disclosure is the fear of **personal risk**. There is always the danger that the feelings one reveals might be rejected out of hand, laughed at, or ridiculed. These fears can cause people to keep their ideas to themselves and thereby limit relational growth (see Vignette 8.2). Jourard (1971) advances the thesis that self-disclosure is a symptom of a healthy personality. His own research, as well as that of others, demonstrates that people who are able to reveal their feelings to others—negative as well as positive feelings—are more likely to consider themselves personally and relationally secure.

Advantages of self-disclosure

There appear to be several advantages to self-disclosure for relationships (Scoresby, 1977). First, the more information and feelings that are shared, the more useful and relevant things there are to stimulate further discussion. Second, self-disclosure improves each individual's perception of the other. This encourages empathy and further understanding. Third, the disclosure of feelings is a statement of trust in the other, an indication of commitment to the relationship.

Self-disclosure in marriage

But the question remains: how much should be revealed to one's partner? Should one disclose everything? Studies of married couples have generally indicated that self-disclosure is good—to a point. Married people who feel less apprehensive about discussing their feelings with their spouses do tend to report higher levels of marital satisfaction (Powers and Hutchinson, 1979). However, satisfied spouses are less likely to report their negative feelings toward one another (Dies and Cohen, 1973). It seems, therefore, that most couples find discretion is the better part of valor. They prefer selective disclosure because they fear that some feelings and behaviors are better left unreported.

These findings suggest that in most marriages there is a curvilinear relationship between self-disclosure and relational adjustment (see Fig. 8.2a)—that is, adjustment is poorer among couples with too little or too much disclosure. Apparently, most couples have too much invested in security, safety, and the status quo to risk a great deal of self-disclosure in their marriage (Cozby, 1973). However, there is an alternative model of self-disclosure. Gilbert (1976) proposes that in highly intimate, committed relationships, a *direct* relationship between self-disclosure and adjustment can be established (see Fig. 8.2b). She suggests, "The issue in disclosure for optimal husband-wife relations may be in learning how to deal with information, disappointments, and conflicts at the far end of the disclosure continuum, where risk is high" (p. 229). While this open style of self-disclosure is certainly

Vignette 8.2 Bug Spray #5

Our wedding was on October 14, 1966. But our marriage began three weeks later.

We were dressed up and on our way to the swankiest restaurant in town. We had saved all week for the big splurge.

One problem—my bride was wearing the most horrible perfume ever manufactured. Smelled like a mixture of mustard gas, black pepper, and vaporized maple syrup. I still get queasy thinking about it.

We had stopped at a railroad crossing. It was cold outside. The windows were up and the heater was on. My nose and lungs silently begged for mercy. But I didn't want to upset my bride with a comment about her perfume.

I had decided the one perfect marriage in history would be ours. No conflicts . . . no harsh words . . . no hurt feelings . . . no tears . . . nothing negative. My wife had made a similar resolution. For three weeks we had walked on eggshells, protecting each other from the slightest unpleasantness.

Dare I break the spell? Dare I be honest and open? She had soaked in that blasted stuff every day of our marriage. I knew I couldn't hold out forever. So I said, in my sweetest, softest voice, "Honey, that perfume smells like bug spray."

Silence! Like the silence that must have followed President Roosevelt's announcement that the Japanese had bombed Pearl Harbor. I stared straight ahead trying to concentrate on the steady, metallic rhythm of the train cars rolling by.

I glanced at my bride out of the corner of my eye. Her lower lip was quivering slightly. The way it still does when she's fighting a good cry.

We drove on. After an eternity, she mumbled softly, "I won't use that brand again."

Any married person can finish the story. We choked down our gourmet dinner. Pouted. Went through the "it's all my fault, Honey" routine. Shed tears. And were finally reconciled, promising never to be cross with each other again.

The whole episode is now part of our family lore. Our repertory of delightful "young and dumb" stories.

But I still think our marriage began with my observation about the perfume. At that point we began to grow. We discovered marriage is a union stronger than emotions. We began to drop the foolishness about unruffled bliss. We took our first steps toward learning that one all-important lesson, a lesson no one ever outgrows—love is a death-resurrection relationship.

As for the perfume . . . I sprayed the rest on roaches. It worked!

From Wes Seelinger, *Encounter with Family Relations,* 1977, p. 177. Reprinted by permission from *Faith At Work,* 11065 Little Patuxent Pkwy, Columbia, MD 21044.

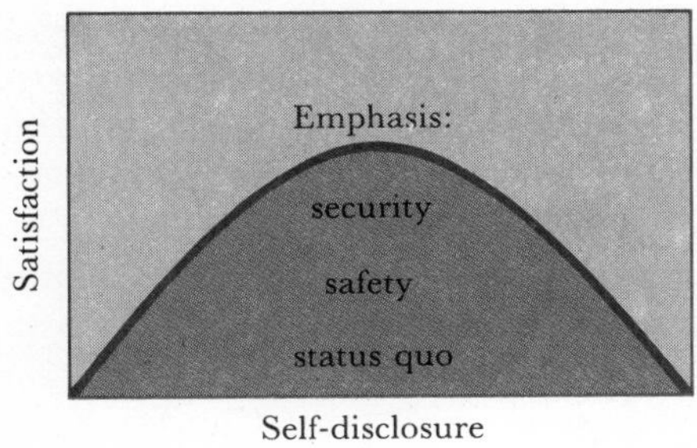

a) Lower intimacy-instrumental relationship

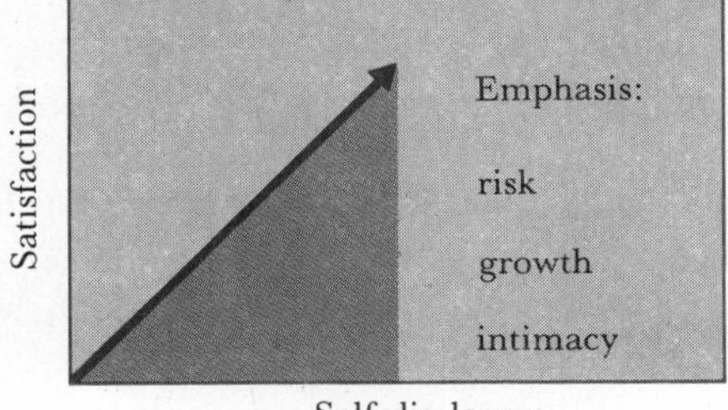

b) Higher intimacy-intrinsic relationship

Fig. 8.2

Two Models of Self-Disclosure and Relational Satisfaction

Source: Shirley Gilbert, *The Family Coordinator*. Copyrighted 1976 by the National Council on Family Relations. Reprinted by permission.

more risky, the potential benefits in intimacy can also be greater. Psychotherapist Carl Rogers adds this caution:

> One rule of thumb which I have found helpful for myself is that in any continuing relationship, any persistent feeling had better be expressed. Suppressing it can only damage the relationship. The first sentence is not stated casually. Only if it is a significant continuing relationship, and only if it is a recurring or persistent feeling, is it necessary to bring the feeling into the open in the relationship. If this is not done, what is unexpressed gradually poisons the relationship. (Derlega and Chaiken, 1975, p. 71)

Listening

Misunderstandings

Listening has been called a lost art of communication. As we have noted, other elements of communication can also be lost, but all too often communication is frustrated by a lack of attention or poor listening. Dialogues that contain little listening typically sound like two monologues or like debates, with each person stating his or her own interests and neither willing to consider the position of the other. In a study of videotape recordings of conversations between married couples who were having communication problems, it was found that "the communication breakdown on most of the tapes occurred because both spouses were sending messages (or speaking) but neither was receiving these messages (or listening)" (Schauble and Hill, 1976, p. 279). This led each spouse to interpret the messages according to his or her own preconceptions rather than according to what the other person was really saying.

Listening failures have a direct effect on the level of couple understanding and an indirect effect on the self-esteem of the speaker. Since understanding is enhanced only when each person is aware of the needs and attitudes of the other, an inability to listen carefully interferes with the development of empathy and mutual understanding. Also, when what someone says is ignored or demeaned, the speaker will probably take this as a personal rejection, not just a rejection of his or her ideas, particularly if this occurs quite often (Satir, 1972). Constant interruptions, disclaimers like "Yes, but . . ." and statements that completely ignore what the other person has just said indicate little genuine listening ability and little respect for the self-worth of the partner.

Types of listening

While the amount of listening going on is important, Charles Kelly (1977) notes that the type of listening being used also affects communication in relationships. **Deliberate listening** is the kind of listening that we use in critical analysis. We deliberately listen in order to find fault, to judge, or to glean all the truths from the statements we are hearing. Deliberate listening is useful in many contexts, especially school, but it tends to be instrumentally motivated by concern for personal gain and only secondarily by concern for understanding the speaker.

Empathetic listening stems from an interest in understanding the speaker.

Empathic listening, according to Kelly, is much more useful in interpersonal relationships. This type of listening is motivated by a sincere interest in understanding the other. It is concerned with relational development more than personal gain. The empathic listener pays attention to the speaker and verbally reflects on what is being said (Scoresby). Comments like, "You seem to be saying . . ." indicate interest and help to clarify what is being heard. The need for reflective "hearing" within empathic listening is stressed by Hugh Prather (1977):

> I can listen to someone without hearing him. Listening is fixing my attention only on the other person. Hearing requires that I listen inside me as I listen to him . . . . And hearing also includes attending to my reactions, such as the "sinking feeling" I get when the other person has stopped hearing me. (p. 235)

INTERPERSONAL CONFLICT

At first glance, it may seem a bit unusual to discuss communication and conflict in the same chapter. Very often, we think of conflict as the opposite of communication—people either talk things over or they fight. But in contrast to this line of thinking, we can understand conflict better if we see it as a *type of communication,* not the absence of communication. Sometimes poor communication can lead to conflict, but when this happens, it may mean that for the first time the couple is really facing the issue at hand and trying to communicate to one another their different feelings about it. The opposite of communication, then, is not conflict, it is *silence,* the failure to talk to one another at all.

Conflict is a process

Conflict, therefore, is a process which is oriented toward resolving differences. It occurs whenever disagreements are mutually realized and brought out into the open. Conflicts can be dealt with in a civil and cooperative manner, as in everyday decision making. Or, conflicts can be intensive and violent if the differences are great and interests are entrenched. Since differences of opinion or interest occur in any relationship, some conflict is unavoidable, but conflicts can be managed if couples are willing to examine their differences carefully.

Constructive Conflicts

While conflicts are often thought of as destructive to relationships, it is becoming more and more apparent that they can actually be good for relationships. Today there is developing a respect for the ability of couples to realize and resolve their differences rather than stubbornly enduring them. As the O'Neills have put it:

> Couples who do not fight may be among those rare few who have reached the promised land of complete understanding and synchronization. But it is more likely that they just don't care enough anymore, that they have given up the struggle. (1972, p. 125)

Conflict benefits

Conflict can have many important benefits for a relationship. It provides an opportunity to share problems, to vent personal tensions and hostilities, to suggest potential solutions, and to develop a new sense of mutual understanding. No relationship can avoid differences, and whether the issues are "big" or "small," they eventually accumulate in personal frustration and tension. A wife may be bitter because she does not feel her husband helps out enough with the children. She feels "used," yet the only way she can expect to get a realignment of the roles in the marriage is to impress him with the strain she feels. Still other conflicts can start from what an outsider might call "trifles"—petty irritants like leaving clothes on the floor, leaving the cap off the toothpaste tube, dropping cigarette ashes on the table, or slurping coffee. These too can cause resentments if they are not brought out into the open and discussed.

Conflict, according to social-psychologist Morton Deutsch (1973), "is the root of personal and social *change*" (p. 9). Through conflict, feelings of injustice and rival claims can be expressed, examined, and negotiated into a new sense of order for the relationship. Conflicts break the inertia that simply permits things to remain the same, despite the fact that the situation may be growing intolerable for one or both persons. If serious problems are repressed, needed changes will be avoided and, even more serious, the tension is likely to be displaced into other unrelated areas of the relationship such as sexual intimacy or companionship. This cycle of rising tensions finally completes itself in a blowup—"I can't take it anymore"—and perhaps in the decision to leave when the relationship is no longer worth the strain.

Conflict can be an important factor in maintaining interpersonal commitments (Scanzoni, 1979). If differences are successfully resolved, there is a rejuvenated sense of interest in the relationship. The pain of the conflict is eased by the good feelings that accompany "making up." There is a sense of mutual accomplishment that comes from having solved a serious problem together. A renewed feeling of camaraderie and trust follows the successful resolution of differences. Once again, it feels good to be part of that relationship.

Mutuality in conflict

These positive elements of conflict—tension reduction, change, and renewed commitment—are important for intimate relationships. For conflicts to be constructive, however, the focus has to be on the relationship and compromises that best meet the needs of all concerned. According to Morton Deutsch, "a conflict has productive consequences if the participants all are satisfied with their outcomes and feel they have gained as a result of the conflict . . . a conflict in which outcomes are satisfying to all the participants will be more constructive than one that is satisfying to some and dissatisfying to others" (p. 17). Constructive conflicts take time and require personal and relational flexibility. Some of the more important "rules" for constructive conflicts are exemplified by George Bach and Ronald Deutsch in Vignette 8.3.

Vignette 8.3

Rules for a Fair Fight

1. Be specific when you introduce a gripe.
2. Don't just complain, no matter how specifically; ask for a reasonable change that will relieve the gripe.
3. Ask for and give feedback of the major points, to make sure you are heard, to assure your partner that you understand what he wants.
4. Confine yourself to one issue at a time. Otherwise, without professional guidance, you may skip back and forth, evading the hard ones.
5. Do not be glib or intolerant. Be open to your own feelings, and equally open to your partner's.
6. Always consider compromise. Remember, your partner's view of reality may be just as real as yours, even though you may differ. There are not many totally objective realities.
7. Do not allow counter-demands to enter the picture until the original demands are clearly understood, and there has been clear-cut response to them.
8. Never assume that you know what your partner is thinking until you have checked out the assumption in plain language; nor assume or predict how he will react, what he will accept or reject. Crystal-gazing is not for pairing.
9. Don't mind-rape. Ask. Do not correct a partner's statement of his own feelings. Do not tell a partner what he should know or do or feel.
10. Never put labels on a partner. Call him neither a coward, nor a neurotic, nor a child. If you really believed that he was incompetent or suffered from some hopeless basic flaw, you probably would not be with him. Do not make sweeping, labeling judgments about his feelings, especially about whether or not they are real or important.
11. Sarcasm is dirty fighting.
12. Forget the past and stay with the here-and-now. What either of you did last year or last month or that morning is not as important as what you are doing and feeling now. And the changes you ask cannot possibly be retroactive. Hurts, grievances, and irritations should be brought up at the very earliest moment, or the partner has the right to suspect that they may have been saved carefully as weapons.
13. Do not overload your partner with grievances. To do so makes him feel hopeless and suggests that you have either been hoarding conplaints or have not thought through what really troubles you.
14. Meditate. Take time to consult your real thoughts and feelings before speaking. Your surface reactions may make something deeper and more important. Don't be afraid to close your eyes and think.
15. Remember that there is never a single winner in an honest intimate fight. Both either win more intimacy, or lose it.

From George R. Bach and Ronald M. Deutsch, *Pairing* (New York: Avon, 1970), pp. 202–204.

Destructive Conflicts and Violence

Spouse abuse

To anyone who reads a newspaper, it is obvious that not all family conflicts are constructive. Reports of abuse and violence between husbands and wives, parents and children, are increasingly prevalent today. According to recent national surveys, one out of six American couples have experienced a violent conflict in the previous year (Straus *et al.*, 1980). Of the 47 million married couples in the United States, 3.3 million wives and over a quarter million husbands reported being severely beaten by their spouse (Steinmetz, 1978). Over 1.7 million of these people were threatened with an exposed knife or gun forced upon them by their husband or wife.

Child abuse

For many men, women, and children, their home is now the most dangerous place they frequent. Three-fourths or more of all "aggravated assaults" occur between husbands and wives. Over 15 percent of all homicides are committed by spouses, half of the time by husbands and half of the time by wives (Steinmetz). Homicides by relatives or former spouses are now more frequent than homicides by nonrelatives. Wife battering has received so much attention that many communities are creating shelters for abused women. Children are often the victims of violent episodes as well. In a representative United States survey, it was found that 20 percent of the parents had hit their children aged three to seventeen with an object during the previous year, 4.2 percent had "beat-up" a child, 2.8 percent had threatened their child with a knife or gun, and 2.9 percent had used a knife or gun on their child (Gelles, 1979). These statistics do not include violence on infants and toddlers, who are the targets of most parental child abuse (Steel and Pollack, 1968).

As shocking as these statistics may be, they represent only a small proportion of the destructive conflicts that occur in interpersonal relationships. Many other conflicts are also destructive, but they do not reach the point of violence, or at least they do not come to the attention of the police and press. In general, Morton Deutsch suggests, *any* conflict is destructive if any of the participants are "dissatisfied with the outcomes and feel they have lost as a result of the conflict" (p. 17). With this standard, it is apparent that many conflicts in intimate relationships can be considered destructive.

Factors encouraging destructive conflicts

One of the major factors in destructive conflicts is the tendency for issues to expand and tensions to escalate. Conflicts often begin the destructive cycle when everything from personalities to past sins and parental weaknesses becomes part of the debate. The issue that started the conflict is often long forgotten, and without it, there is little for the conflict to focus upon. As a result, each new negative disclosure is followed by another negative disclosure until a completely unmanageable set of issues is out "on the table" and realistically unsolvable. In contrast to the idea that it is always good to "ventilate," to "level," with the other person, there is evidence that the more negative verbal disclosures that occur, the more likely that conflict will escalate destructively (Straus, 1974).

Another factor in destructive conflict is poor communication. For conflict to be handled constructively, good communication patterns need to be

Poor communication often leads to destructive conflict and violence.

established. Couples who do not communicate well are much more likely to move toward destructive conflict and violence (Steinmetz, 1977). Not only does good communication help couples anticipate problems, it also shields them somewhat from the misjudgments and misperceptions that are common in destructive conflicts.

Power and Conflict

In any relationship between a man and a woman, there are decisions to be made and issues to be resolved. These range from the frequent "What are we going to do tonight?" to the perplexing "How are we going to meet each of our needs on this limited budget?" With the variety of issues couples often face, it is not surprising that most people seek ways of influencing the decision-making process so that conflicts can be minimized or resolved in their own best interests. Conflicts, therefore, often center around the issue of

power, the potential or actual ability of individuals to influence or change the behavior of others (Cromwell and Olson, 1975). Power, however, can take a variety of forms and some of these are more likely to resist or produce conflict than others.

Types of power

Raven, Centers, and Rodrigues (1975) feel that five types of power can be identified in husband-wife relations. First, there is **legitimate power**. This refers to the "right" to control decisions because of cultural or social norms. Much of the broad authority men have assumed in marriage is based on this type of power (Scanzoni, 1978). Wives can also gain legitimate power in areas such as childrearing where their roles are primary. In general, this type of power is more likely to be experienced in traditional working-class marriages and among the less educated (Raven *et al.*).

Education and power

Expert power is less likely to depend on tradition and more likely to stem from the belief that decision-making authority should belong to the person with special knowledge or ability on the subject. The husband may be the "expert" on the car, the lawn, wall-papering, or backpacking, while the wife is the "expert" in cooking, selecting furniture, gardening, or history. Because expert power is based on knowledge, it is highly influenced by factors that can increase the impression that one person "knows" what is best. Education seems to do this, for individuals with higher levels of education are considered to have greater expert power (Raven *et al.*). Also, men more often than women are viewed as "experts" by their spouses (see Table 8.1).

What about the person who says, "We do it my way or we don't do it at all!" This is exercising **coercive power**, and it too can be an effective way of gaining control, especially for those who lack the knowledge or respect to get it any other way. Coercive power is based on the belief that threats and punishment can be used to gain compliance. Komarovsky (1964), in her study of blue-collar marriages, reported that this kind of power is often exercised by husbands who have little education.

Manipulative power

Reward power is a common companion to coercive power, but it is based on the belief that compliance to another's needs or demands will bring rewards. Both types of power are highly instrumental and self-serving, but reward power is subtle and covert while coercive power is domineering and

Table 8.1

The Type of Power Most Often Used by Husbands and Wives—From the Perspective of the Spouse

	Predominant Type of Power				
Spouse	Legitimate	Expert	Coercive	Reward	Referent
Wives	22%	21%	3%	6%	48%
Husbands	18%	37%	4%	4%	36%

Source: Data from Raven *et al.*, Bases of Conjugal Power. In R. Cromwell and D. Olson (eds.), *Power in Families* (New York: Wiley, 1975).

overt. Reward power can be just as effective, however, as testimonies included in Morgan's *The Total Woman* (1973) indicate. Morgan describes quite vividly how a wife can "reward" her husband with sexual favors to get everything from a vacation trip to new furniture. The idea that one can gain power through manipulating rewards is not unique to women, however.

Reward and coercive power are used more often *situationally* than the data in Table 8.1 may suggest. The same study found that 55 percent of the husbands and wives interviewed considered themselves "somewhat" or "very" likely to be influenced by reward power and 45 percent were "somewhat" or "very" likely to be influenced by coercive power. Apparently, most people do not find it helpful to use these types of power exclusively, but when all else fails, they may call upon them to gain control of the situation.

The last dimension of power examined by Raven *et al.* is **referent power.** This develops from a close identification with another person and the satisfaction of behaving, feeling, or believing like that person. Referent power centers on the relationship, not the individual. Mutual compliance is sought as the couple believes they should be in agreement with one another. In terms of commitment, this type of power is more likely to emerge from an intrinsic rather than instrumental relationship.

Power and relationships

Overall, marriages that depend upon referent power report the greatest relational satisfaction (Raven *et al.*). Shared power has also been found to be more effective when outside stresses require constructive decision making and cooperation (Sprenkle and Olson, 1978). Legitimate and expert power can be constructive and satisfying to couples as well, if they prefer delegated decision making. Since separate domains of authority are clearly established, reliance on legitimate and expert power reduces conflict largely by shrinking the number of areas potentially available to mutual influence. Reward power is used infrequently but can be a useful bargaining technique in conflict situations. Its general impact upon marital satisfaction is small, however.

Relationships dominated by coercive power tend to be the most unsatisfactory (Raven *et al.*). Coercive power may lead to conflict resolution, but it is accomplished destructively, against the partner's will. Usually, this type of power is used only when other means of gaining influence are unavailable. Thus, coercive power is the prototype of competitive, unbalanced power, a situation which might also occur if a husband considers himself to have legitimate authority over an issue while his wife expects to share this authority. In this unbalanced situation, a couple cannot agree to share power nor can they agree to let one person control. This "no-win" dilemma leads to an escalation of conflict, the use of more self-serving methods of gaining power, and, typically, increasingly poor morale in the relationship.

Strategies of Conflict Management

All couples in continuing relationships experience conflict but few relationships are dominated by ongoing hostilities. Cuber and Harroff (1966) discovered that there are some marriages which are "conflict habituated" but that couples who love to fight are comparatively rare. Indeed, most of us prefer to avoid conflict as much as possible, and most couples develop strategies that help them constructively manage conflicts, whether current or anticipated.

Premarital counseling

Prevention Strategies. It is possible to minimize some conflicts by preventing the development of potential confrontations. One way this is done is by keeping apart people who are likely to come into conflict with one another. Premarital counseling, courses on marriage and family relations, and the monitoring of relationships by parents and peers all serve to restrict the development of those couples who are most vulnerable to conflict. The state of California has taken a particularly noteworthy step in this direction. Knowing that the chances of conflict and marital failure are highest in teen marriages, the state legislature passed a Family Law Act in 1970 that requires premarital counseling if either of the parties is under eighteen years of age. Many young people who otherwise would have been incompatibly married have been deterred by this counseling (Elkin, 1977). A new premarital inventory test is also said to discourage from marrying almost one out of ten couples who take it (Olson, 1980).

Another strategy for preventing conflicts is to distribute authority over matters that might lead to conflict. When expert or legitimate power in an area such as child rearing is mutually understood to be held by one person, disagreements in that area are minimized. Joint decision making may be preferred in many marriages, but the stress-reducing effect of delegated decision making is probably a major reason for the finding that couples who divide their responsibilities report being just as happily married as couples who share in most decisions (Centers *et al.*, 1971).

Relational enrichment

Among couples who want to share in most decisions, however, it is possible to prevent some conflicts by maintaining a high level of mutual understanding. Conflicts can then be avoided if differences are anticipated and mutually resolved before they become issues for debate. This means that all the elements of interpersonal communication—self-awareness, empathy, nonverbal language, self-disclosure, and listening—have to be operating in the relationship. Training in these communication skills is now part of what is called *marriage and family enrichment.* These are programs that positively reinforce good relationships and provide couples with the tools they need to reduce strain. At the present time, enrichment programs have been found to be successful in building communication and conflict awareness. It is not known yet whether couples will put these ideas into practice over the long term (Mace, 1979).

Negotiation Strategies. Not all conflicts can be prevented, despite our best intentions. There are times when differences of opinion or differing expectations have to be confronted and resolved. For instance, a husband wants to

Roger and Evonne Goolagong Cawley are one of a growing number of couples for whom shared decision making is an important aspect of marriage.

play golf on Saturday but his wife wants to go on a picnic. Or, a wife may not approve of her husband's drinking habits. If these differences are important to either or both of the individuals involved, some type of negotiated settlement is necessary. Not every personal need and interest can be met, given the limited time, money, and energy of most relationships.

Steps in negotiation

Negotiation is the verbal process of settling differences. Through negotiation, an attempt is made to modify the respective needs and interests of group members so that a new sense of order can be established in the relationship. Successful negotiations usually involve (1) an **identification period,** when the different needs and interests of the parties are tentatively presented; (2) a **deliberation period,** when various alternatives are proposed and weighed; and (3) a **decision-making period,** when some outcome is accepted by the negotiating parties. The outcome of the negotiation may be mutually agreeable or it may be a decision forced by one person on another.

Cooperative negotiations are oriented toward joint conflict resolutions. The interests of the parties are presented and some equitable solution is sought. The outcome of the negotiation may be a **compromise** somewhere between the initial positions of the parties (golf in the morning, picnic in the afternoon), a **trade** in which one person's position is accepted now in favor of the other's later (picnic this week and golf next week), or **compliance** to the wishes of the more convincing partner (both agree that the picnic is preferable). The steps commonly used in cooperative negotiations are:

1. Agreeing to work together on a problem.
2. Selecting one specific part of the problem to work on.
3. Generating possible solutions without judgment or evaluation.
4. Selecting a solution (or solutions) for implementation.
5. Deciding on action (i.e., who will do what, when, and how).
6. Taking the specified action.
7. Evaluating the action. (Thomas, 1977, p. 116)

Mediation Strategies. Sometimes couples cannot resolve their conflicts themselves. When this happens, a third party may be able to assist them in making decisions and developing the skills they need to manage future conflicts. A successful mediator must be objective, impartial, and disinterested. Since relatives and friends are usually aligned more with one partner than the other, they rarely qualify as mediators (Blood, 1974). Hence, professional guidance tends to be more effective in mediating conflicts.

Marriage and family therapy

The ability of marital and family therapists to help distressed relationships has been improving rapidly. No longer is it assumed that the ills of the relationship lie only in personal psychopathology. Rather, we now recognize that relational problems more often arise out of the interaction between members and that healing these relationships requires different skills than healing individual personalities. The techniques of marital and family therapy vary with the therapist and the problems encountered, but most often the therapist-mediator does not tell the couple how they should solve their problems. Instead, therapeutic mediation helps direct couples or families toward negotiating their own solutions and thereby gaining the skills for preventing or negotiating conflicts in the future.

The success of marital or family therapy in mediating conflict-ridden relationships has been quite good, considering the difficulties. When Gurman and Kniskern (1978) examined studies on over 1500 people they found that 61 percent of these people improved their relationships through therapy. The best results, however, were among those couples or families who sought and received therapy together—70 percent of them reported improvement. When only one person in the relationship received help, the improvement rate was only 48 percent. While individual therapy may seem to have a rather poor rate of improvement, it does indicate that outside mediation can sometimes help even if it is not jointly sought.

The shock of separation

Separation Strategies. When conflicts cannot be managed through prevention, negotiation, or mediation, then the likely alternative is separation. By itself, separation does not really resolve any conflicts, but it may be used as a means to bring about conflict resolution (McCubbin, 1979). For example, a separation can shock a couple into realizing their desire to continue the relationship and force them to seek means to reduce the strain. Over one-fourth of all couples who file for divorce reconcile before the divorce can be granted (Gunter, 1977). For many of these couples, the separation gave them time to consider more carefully ways of mediating or negotiating their differences.

Sometimes, separation can be a temporary ploy to gain power in a conflicted relationship. A coercive husband may only recognize the rights of his wife if she threatens to leave or actually does leave him. This could be her only strong suit in negotiation.

Finally, in some relationships separation may be the only effective way out of conflict. When differences cannot be resolved and stress continues to haunt the relationship, many people today consider separation. Since some four out of ten married people in America eventually come to this conclusion, separation is not unusual any longer. According to marital therapist Robert Blood (1974): "Separation is the most drastic way out of family conflict, yet those who have tried it often say that peaceful loneliness is an improvement over perpetual conflict" (p. 312).

Summary

Communication and conflict are normal parts of any continuous relationship. No relationship can be maintained without communication, nor can we communicate very long without experiencing some conflict. Since the basic purpose of communication is to achieve understanding, messages of affect, power, and meaning are sent and received in order to provide a clearer picture of our interests and feelings. Over time, these message exchanges develop into predictable dialogue patterns which reflect the communication style of the relationship.

The importance of communication for intimate relationships has been supported in numerous research studies. Still, effective communication is not just based on the amount of talking that goes on; it includes several interrelated elements. Self-awareness, empathy, nonverbal language, and listening abilities enhance the process of communication by making us continually aware of messages from others and the impact of our own messages as well.

Sometimes, when communications involve disagreements, conflicts occur which attempt to resolve these differences. Constructive conflicts are those that benefit the relationship because the outcomes increase mutual understanding and commitments and ease relational changes. Destructive conflicts are those that do not benefit the relationship and often they expand to the point of violence. Since conflicts involve differing interests, the power arrangements in the relationship have considerable influence on the way conflicts are handled. Most couples try to develop strategies to manage their conflicts more effectively. These strategies can include prevention, negotiation, mediation, and separation.

SUGGESTIONS FOR ADDITIONAL READING

Derlega, Valerian J., and Alan L. Chaiken. *Sharing Intimacy: What We Reveal to Others and Why.* Englewood Cliffs, N.J.: Prentice-Hall, 1975.

Explores the dynamics of self-disclosure in communication. The authors explain the connection between self-disclosure and adjustments in friendships and marriage.

Deutsch, Morton. *The Resolution of Conflict.* New Haven, Conn.: Yale University Press, 1973, Chapters 1, 2, and 13.

This noted authority on interpersonal conflict carefully describes the nature of competitive and cooperative conflicts and many of the factors that make conflicts destructive or constructive.

Miller, Sherod, Elam Nunnally, and Daniel Wackman. *Alive and Aware: Improving Communications in Relationships.* Minneapolis, Minn.: Interpersonal Communication Programs, 1975.

This book is used as a text in marital communication programs and is designed to teach and illustrate communication skills. Many examples of communication styles are included.

Parlee, Mary Brown. "Conversational politics," *Psychology Today* (May 1979): 48–56.

This article discusses the way in which settings and social roles affect our verbal and nonverbal communication messages.

Scoresby, A. Lynn. *The Marriage Dialogue.* Reading, Mass.: Addison-Wesley, 1977.

Examines the variety of elements that are part of effective dialogues in marriage.

The topics that are covered range from interpreting marital messages to managing marital conflicts.

Straus, Murray, Richard Gelles, and Suzanne Steinmetz. *Behind Closed Doors: Violence in the American Family*. New York: Doubleday, 1980.

Reviews the recent research on husband-wife, parent-child, and sibling violence in the United States. Also examines causes of violence and prevention measures.

Chapter 9

Sexual Intimacy

In the late 1920s, James Thurber and E. B. White wrote a humorous spoof on human sexuality. In it, they chided behavioral researchers and the American public for beginning to take sex too seriously, for elevating it to a position in intimate relationships beyond what it might be capable of providing. "Sex," they cautioned, "is by no means everything. It varies, as a matter of fact from only as high as 78 percent of everything to a low of 3.1 percent of everything. The norm in a sane, healthy person, should be between 18 and 24 percent" (1929).

Little did Thurber and White know then how prophetic their words would be. At the time they were writing, information on human sexuality was just barely becoming available. Most people's sexual attitudes erred on the side of silence. So little importance was being given to personal and interpersonal sexuality that most men and women typically felt uncomfortable with their own, let alone their partner's, sexual needs.

Today, the pendulum seems to have swung in the opposite direction. So much emphasis is given to sexual needs and performance that few of us can compete with the sexual images portrayed daily in advertising, books, movies, and television shows. Possibilities for sexual intimacy have certainly grown. Men and women now feel freer to experiment with techniques for sexual arousal and we are more aware of and comfortable with one another's sexual needs. Yet at the same time, sexual expectations have risen to the point that many people have become sexually anxious. This is evident in the number of persons who seek sex therapy, buy books to improve their sexual skills, write letters to columnists about their sexual problems, and seek gratification from the variety of sexual outlets that have become available.

Still, within this mad rush to find sexual fulfillment there remain vestiges of the apprehension and silence of yesteryear. Sexual messages permeate our lives to such an extent that while men and women now find it easier to watch, read, and listen to the sexual experiences of others, most people still find it difficult to reveal their own sexual feelings honestly, even to their partner (Gagnon, 1977). It is as if many in our society have been moved to the point of sexual voyeurism. We now idealize sexual intimacy as the ultimate expression of love and affection, yet for many couples, the union of their personal sexuality and relational intimacy is a rare experience.

How important is sexual intimacy for couples today? Most studies do confirm Thurber and White's suggestion that sex is not "everything" but, clearly, to committed relationships it is very important. When husbands and wives were queried nationally in the mid-1970s, four out of five of those who reported very pleasurable marital sexual activity also rated their marriages as "very close." Practically none of those who were sexually dissatisfied claimed that their marriages were emotionally close. Of course, the frequency and kinds of sexual experiences that were considered pleasurable varied widely, but it is apparent that compared to studies conducted earlier, men and women today are more likely to seek sexual intimacy and to be concerned if they do not find sexual satisfaction (Hunt, 1974).

In this chapter, we will explore some of the roots of sexual intimacy. We will look at the way our society, our relationships, and our physiology affect the development of sexual needs and practices. We will also examine some of the problems that individuals and couples sometimes face in their attempt to find sexual intimacy. Birth control and pregnancy, the preventative and generative aspects of sexual intimacy, will be discussed in Chapter 12, Family Planning.

THE LEARNING OF SEXUAL INTIMACY

Lack of sexual instincts

It is sometimes said that sexual intimacy is doing "what comes naturally." But how much of our sexual behavior is really "natural" or biologically determined? Unlike animals of other species, humans do not have genetically programmed courtship rituals; humans do not instinctively know how to copulate; humans do not emit clear biological signals that readily indicate their sexual interest to everyone around. Indeed, the uneasiness, jitters, and fumbling that often accompany initial sexual courting or intercourse suggest that among men and women, biology offers little guidance. Some young couples may even envy the sexual instincts of other animals when their own lack of programming leaves them unsure of how to respond sexually or what to do next.

Since human sexual behavior is not genetically programmed, it is obviously learned. According to sociologist John Gagnon, "In any given society, at any given moment in history, people become sexual in the same way they become everything else. Without much reflection, they pick up the directions from their social environment. They acquire and assemble meanings, skills, and values from the people around them" (p. 2).

This emphasis on the learning of sexual behavior does not deny the fact that sexual desires and feelings can have some physiological basis too. But the physical sex drive and the behaviors that reflect this drive are still largely stimulated and directed by what we are taught. For example, if we see a nude person and have learned that nudity is supposed to be sexually arousing, then our physical response follows accordingly. But if nudity is treated casually in the family and culture in which we live, it may not be sexually stimulating at all.

Sexual cues

Thus, we learn the cues that trigger our physical sexual responses just as we learn from our parents, religious authorities, teachers, peers, and partners *how* we should feel about our sexuality, *which* sexual outlets are legitimate, *who* can be our sexual partner, and *when* and *where* sexual behavior is appropriate. The extent of our ability to be sexually intimate with another is very much a product of the culture in which we are reared, the childhood experiences we have had, and the relationships we have developed and maintained.

A Century of Change

Inaccurate information

In the United States a century ago, sexual mores were clearer and much more restrictive than they are today. The values of that day supported sexual intimacy only in marriage and then only for the pleasure of the husband and the procreation of the family. Still, a sexual revolution of some sort made its way into nineteenth-century America as a variety of "marriage manuals" began to be published. Unfortunately, these guides to marital sexuality were little more than collections of medical opinion, ethical standards, and religious dogma (see Vignette 9.1). They were horribly inaccurate, even considering the medical knowledge that was available, yet their popularity indicated that there was a growing interest in the populace for information about sexual intimacy.

Sexual attitudes

While these restrictive attitudes certainly limited sexual knowledge and raised sexual anxieties for both men and women, we should not conclude that all sexual behavior conformed to these standards. From the confession records of churches (Smith and Hindus, 1975) and from data collected from elderly women and men in the Kinsey studies (1948), we can estimate that about *one-fourth* of all brides up until 1900 were nonvirgins. The prevailing attitudes of the day were beginning to support the sexual needs of men, but a "good" woman was still not supposed to be interested in sexual pleasure. Women who liked their sexual feelings were considered "bad" women, so a woman was caught between her own feelings and the social labels that she had been taught to apply to those feelings.

During and just prior to the 1920s, a major change in sexual attitudes and behavior occurred. The "Roaring 20s" roared in with a new ethic approving sexual intimacy in marriage. Not everyone approved of this, and attitudes remained conservative by today's standards, but the seeds were sown for the idea that sexuality could be a valuable part of intimate relationships. Even some marriage manuals began to present sex as means of mutual fulfillment.

Vignette 9.1 Sexual Advice in Nineteenth-Century America

A man with great vital force is united to a woman of evenly balanced organization. The husband, in the exercise of what he is pleased to term his "marital rights," places his wife, in a very short time, on the nervous, delicate, sickly list. In the blindness and ignorance of his animal nature he requires prompt obedience to his desires, and, ignorant of the law of right in this direction, his wife, thinking that it is her duty to accede to his wishes, though perhaps fulfilling them with a sore and troubled heart, allows him passively, *never lovingly,* to exercise daily and weekly, month in and month out, the low and beastly side of his nature, and eventually, slowly but surely, to kill her. And this man, who has as surely committed murder as has the convicted *assassin,* lures to his net and takes unto him another wife, to repeat the same programme of legalized prostitution on his part, and sickness and premature death on her part.

There are women—strongly passionate and often diseased—who, like such men, are endowed with strong animal natures, who, when they marry, in the intense exercise of their lustful natures, soon reduce the husband to a standard that physically and mentally places him below the brute, and long before the fulfillment of his just allotment of time on earth, he too dies. The number of such women is very much smaller than is the number of men with like tendencies; but when women are diseased in this direction, they go much further than is possible with men. It is for this reason I advised, in a former chapter, in the choice of a husband or wife, the avoidance of widows or widowers, the death of whose partners was caused by other than accident or well-understood disease; for when such cases, at the last day, come before the bar of judgment, it will be found that these premature deaths were murders, and that these sensualists were murderers.

The exercise of abnormal amativeness is known in all its positive intensity by those newly married. The honeymoon is one nightly repetition of legalized prostitution, sinking the pure, high, and holy into the low, debasing, and animal. Think you, oh! new-made husband and wife, that in this you do right? that in this you elevate your better natures? that in this you find peace, strength, and happiness? that in this you grow into that pure and holy passion akin to God in its exercise—the passion of love? Do not, I pray you, deceive yourselves; for in this exercise of the sexual part of your nature you lower your standard of body and soul; and, as for love, *no man or women can possibly love to be loved who lives other than a life of strict continence.*

From John Cowan, *The Science of a New Life* (New York: Cowan and Company, 1880), p. 103–104.

Premarital sex

The effects of these new attitudes were reflected quickly in sexual behavior. The proportion of men experiencing premarital sexual intercourse rose slightly, but the proportion of women sexually experienced before marriage doubled to 50 percent (Reiss, 1973). The orgasmic responsiveness of women in marriage rapidly increased during this period as did the percentage

The popularity of Rudolph Valentino's seductive "Sheik" reflected a changing mood toward sexuality in the 1920s.

of men and women reporting extramarital sexual intercourse (Kinsey, 1953). Nevertheless, these behavioral changes were not reflected in the values that were culturally supported in early- to mid-twentieth-century America. Many books and novels that openly discussed sexuality were banned. Laws that restricted sex education in the schools remained in force.

The Sexual Climate Today

New freedoms

In the 1960s, Bob Dylan was singing "The Times They Are A-Changing," and his words symbolized the emergence of new ethics in politics, economics, and sexuality. Youth had become estranged from their parents by a war and by leaders they mistrusted. The Kinsey studies had taught them that the sexual activity of their parents did not fit the sexual messages they were being taught. Laws that restricted sexual behavior to certain relationships, certain places, and even certain positions seemed out of place with the civil and personal freedoms being explored.

Even more important, perhaps, were the changes occurring in women's roles and women's sexuality. Educational and occupational opportunities were beginning to open new doors of independence for women. The birth-control pill gave women greater control over their own fertility and freed many women to be sexual without the haunting fear of pregnancy. The decline of parental restrictions and the approval of peers removed some of the sexual inhibitions that had boxed women in. Women learned they could be sexually assertive instead of passively dependent on their male partner for their own sexual needs.

Emerging sexual attitudes

The attitudes that have been emerging from this new sexual climate are beginning to change significantly the role of sexual intimacy in relationships. Virginity before marriage, so important to earlier generations, is no longer regarded as the ideal standard among many youths today. A Gallup Youth Survey taken in 1978 reported that 59 percent of American teenagers now feel that premarital sex is acceptable to them; only 30 percent disapprove. This survey did find, however, that personal sexual preferences remain somewhat more conservative than the standards youth may apply to others. While 41 percent of these teenagers feel it is "not very important" for them to marry a virgin, 27 percent still feel it is "fairly important," and 23 percent "very important" (Gallup, 1978a).

The sexual climate of the college environment is somewhat more liberal than that of youth in general, and this is reflected in the sexual attitudes of college men and women. A national sample of college students in 1969 found that 34 percent agreed with the statement "casual premarital sexual relations are morally wrong." In 1973, only 12 percent agreed with this (Komarovsky, 1976). Two-thirds of the college men and women queried in another survey felt that sexual relations without affection were acceptable (Perlman, 1974). This does not mean, however, that most college students search for sexual satisfaction for its own sake. Rather, sexual intimacy that flows from mutual affection remains the preferred standard. What has changed is the level of affection that is required. Now, a stable, dating relationship—"going together"—appears to be the necessary level of emotional involvement for most youth rather than the standard of engagement which was applied a few decades ago (McCary, 1978).

Extramarital sex attitudes

Adult sexual attitudes also have changed over the years. Single and married adults are reporting more sexually permissive attitudes today. Less than half of all adults in America now feel that premarital sex is wrong (Singh, 1980). And while attitudes toward extramarital intercourse are somewhat more conservative, according to a recent national survey, only half of all adults under thirty years of age consider extramarital sex "always wrong" (Gallup, 1978b).

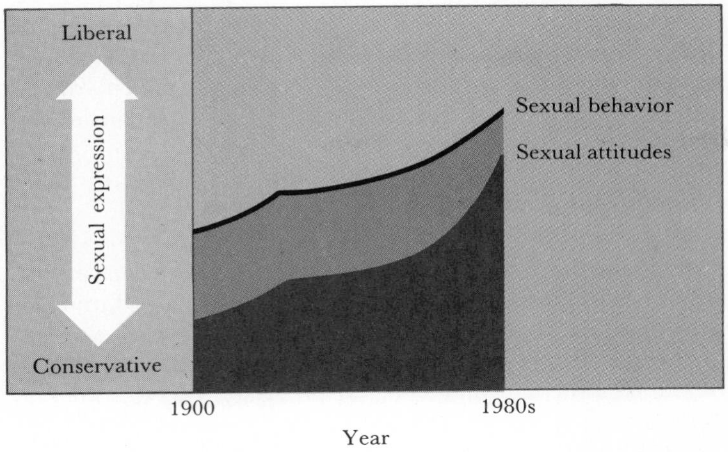

Fig. 9.1

Trends in Sexual Intimacy: Behavior and Attitudes

Attitude-behavior convergence

This liberalization of sexual attitudes is sometimes considered part of a "sexual revolution." But it would be more accurate to say that we are witnessing a convergence of sexual attitudes and behavior (see Fig. 9.1); that is, sexual behaviors that have been rather widely practiced for some time are beginning to be considered more legitimately acceptable. This does not mean that American society has reached the point where anything is acceptable, but it does mean that some of the guilt associated with many sexual behaviors, even different positions of intercourse, has been lessened.

Conservative views

Not everyone, however, feels comfortable with the new sexual attitudes that are emerging. Many youth and adults remain unconvinced that sexually liberal behavior is good for them or for others. Among youth with conservative religious backgrounds or close parental ties, sexual intercourse before marriage is less likely to occur and is often considered morally wrong (Libby *et al.*, 1978). Also, the sexual attitudes of young women are still more conservative than those of young men, given their reluctance to jeopardize their personal reputations or risk the possibilities of an unwanted pregnancy.

Even in marriage, it is not easy for some husbands and wives to free themselves from their traditional attitudes. The new ethics which define sex as a pleasure are sometimes not strong enough to dislodge old ideas of sexual rights and duties. As one young working-class husband complained to a researcher:

> I think sex should be that you enjoy each other's bodies. Judy doesn't care for touching and feeling each other, though. She thinks there's just one right position and one right way—in the dark, with her eyes closed tight. Anything that varies from that makes her upset. (Rubin, 1976, p. 44)

The feelings of this wife are still shared by many. In general, however, sexual attitudes in American society have become more liberal, although this trend has not been uniform for all groups. What has remained fairly uniform across age, race, and economic groups, however, is the belief that "sex cannot be very satisfying without some emotional involvement between the partners." In a national survey, this belief was supported by a very large majority of the men and women interviewed, even in the youngest age groups considered (Hunt, 1974).

Childhood Foundations of Sexual Intimacy

Family context

Children develop their ideas about sexual intimacy not only within the context of the society in which they live but also more directly from the family in which they are reared. For the first few years, the family censors the sexual values of society for the child, interprets the awakening sexual feelings of the child, and sets the scene for how the child will later relate sexually to someone else. Today, children's learning is not restricted to the sexual values of their families; they also pick up sexual cues from television, peers, teachers, and others. Nevertheless, the legacy of early family teachings about sexuality lingers for a long time, and recent research studies indicate that adolescent sexual attitudes are influenced just as much by parents as by peers (Libby *et al.*).

Parents teach their children sexual lessons from the very beginning. The earliest body contacts between infant and parent begin the process of awakening in the child an awareness of the need for physical intimacy. This is not

Vignette 9.2
Sex Education Begins at Home

Everyone agrees that parents should be "open and frank" when they talk to their children about sex, but who is willing to tell parents *how*? After centuries of silence and secrecy, parents today are suddenly asked to "liberate" themselves. How can this transformation be started? How can it be carried out?

First, parents should recognize that before they can communicate freely with their children they must be able to talk freely about sexuality with *each other* and to develop sensitivity to their own feelings.

Husbands and wives can start by asking themselves such questions as "Am I satisfied with our sexual relations?" "Are we able to express the affection we feel for each other?" "How has our sex life changed since we were married?" Often, husbands and wives are "out of touch" with their own feelings. Such talks can make them aware of their own "selves" and more open to their partner's needs. By discovering what is pleasing to themselves—never mind what the books say!—they can understand, and eventually become more comfortable with, their own sexuality. They can come to recognize that orgasm and frequency of intercourse are not as important as a continuing, loving friendship between two people.

At times, too, parents have simply forgotten that before they were parents they were lovers. Taking on the responsibility of parenthood shouldn't lessen one's sexuality or love for each other. Through these open sexually stimulating *per se,* but the child who is warmly and affectionately given physical contact becomes more comfortable with this type of expression and more likely to seek it from others than the child who is deprived of body contacts (Delora and Warren, 1977). Furthermore, when parents themselves feel comfortable embracing and touching one another, this reinforces the child's acceptance of physical intimacy.

Genital play

Parents also prepare their children for sexual intimacy by the way they react to a child's genital play and interest. Infants and young children normally find pleasure in touching their genitals but this behavior can easily be given a strong negative connotation with statements like "Don't touch that" or "That's dirty." At one time, parents were advised to tie their children's hands behind their backs so they could not stimulate themselves. While Americans have given up that practice, repressive sexual attitudes do remain, encouraging many children and adults to feel guilty about their normal sexual feelings and forcing sex play into a closet of secrecy.

Sex education

The difficulty many parents experience with the developing sexuality of their children is illustrated by their lack of participation in sex education (see Vignette 9.2). Libby and Nass (1971) interviewed a broad sample of Connecticut parents and found that nearly nine out of ten did not openly discuss sexual issues with their children. When pressed by their children, these parents issued statements or orders regarding what they considered to be appropriate sexual behavior but little discussion was permitted.

---

talks, as each partner becomes aware of and confident about his or her own sexual needs and desires, he or she will become not only better adjusted sexually but also better prepared to deal with the child's developing sexuality.

In addition to increasing their own sensitivity to sexual feelings, parents often need to brush up on some basic facts. For openers, accurate knowledge about masturbation, intercourse, birth control, and venereal disease is essential for parents who want to develop guidelines for children.

Parents must be willing to *talk* about sex. Those who are uncomfortable hearing or speaking sexual words can practice them—alone, with their spouse, or in conversations with a friend. This step is important because children are sensitive to the emotional value parents give to certain words and can pick up what their parents feel rather than what their parents say.

In effect, sex education begins when children are born, not when they start kindergarten, not when they reach puberty. Developing a healthy attitude toward one's sexuality should mean creating a climate of openness about physical expression, about one's body, and about displays of affection, as well as about more specific sexual matters.

In a more recent study of Ohio parents, similar results were found. Elizabeth Roberts (1979) and her colleagues at Harvard interviewed over 1400 parents of prepubertal children and discovered that less than half of them had discussed menstruation with their daughters; less than 15 percent had mentioned intercourse or masturbation; and less than 6 percent had talked about contraception. While 75 percent had talked about pregnancy and birth, most had done so only in very abstract terms. Commenting on results like these, Ellen Goodman (1978) writes: "It seems that when it comes to talking about sexuality, the average family resonates with silence" (p. 6).

Why are these parents so silent about sexuality? Roberts concludes that it is not because of latent Victorian prudishness; rather, parents are trapped into silence by confusion over long-term and short-term goals for their children. In the long term, she says, "Parents want their children to live personally satisfying and socially responsible sexual lives." But at the same time they are afraid that the girl who accepts her sexuality, who views her sexual feelings as pleasurable, will run a short-term risk of pregnancy. Parents also say that they want their sons to be open and affectionate, but they are afraid that this might make them "sissies" or homosexual. To reconcile these anxieties, most parents remain silent about sexuality, yet unfortunately, their discomfort about sexual intimacy is transmitted to their children loud and clear (Fox, 1980).

Sex-information sources

If children do not get sexual "facts" from their parents, where do they get them? The major source of sexual information—or misinformation—is friends (see Table 9.1). Both men and women depend more upon slightly older friends than anyone else for their knowledge about sex. This reliance on friends is often a poor choice, given findings that indicate the weak sexual knowledge of youth in general (Walters *et al.*, 1979), but friends still remain significantly more influential than reading material, the second most frequent

Table 9.1

Main Source of Sexual Information*

Sources	Men (%)	Women (%)
Friends	59	46
Reading	20	22
Mother	3	16
Father	6	1
School program	3	5
Adults outside home	6	4
Brothers, sisters	4	6
Other or no answer	7	7

* Figures add to more than 100 percent because some persons checked more than one answer.
Source: Reprinted with permission of Playboy Press from *Sexual Behavior in the 1970's*. Copyright © 1974 by Morton Hunt.

Many parents decry school-run sex-education programs, but few actually discuss sexuality with their children.

source of sexual information. Sex-education programs in schools and other adults and family members also rank low as sources of sex information. Nevertheless, when school sex-education programs present complete, comprehensible information about contraception, it has been found that youth rely more on the information they receive (Gallup, 1979a).

Interestingly, one byproduct of this system of sexual learning is greater sexual permissiveness. A study conducted by Spanier (1977) found that youth who depend on friends for sex information are more sexually active than youth whose parents provided them with this information. So parents who abdicate their responsibility for sex education in the vain hopes that their children will not become sexually interested are, in effect, forcing their sons and daughters to rely more on poorer information and peers who are more likely to encourage sexual permissiveness.

SEXUAL AROUSAL

While childhood experiences and cultural conditioning set the scene for sexual behavior, there are also physiological responses that are part of sexual feelings and interaction. For most people, a day does not pass without at least a short period of sexual arousal, however mildly or strongly felt. It may be caused by an obvious sexual advance from one's partner, or it may be stimulated by the sight of an unusually attractive man or woman, the scent of perfume, a fantasy, a song fondly remembered, or the touch of someone in a crowd. But whatever the specific stimulus, there follows a sensual awakening which may be accompanied by an elevation of the heart rate and perhaps a slight hardening of the penis or dampening of the vagina (Gagnon).

It used to be believed that men were sexually aroused easily but that women normally responded only to extensive sexual stimulation. Recent evidence does not support this belief. Women, we now find, can be sexually aroused just as easily as men *if* they have come to believe that it is all right for them to feel sexually aroused.

Sexual excitability

Both women and men can vary a great deal in their sexual excitability. Some members of either sex are quite easily aroused; others are not. Each of us is unique in terms of our learned sexual preferences and the physiological cues that become part of our sexual awareness. But these differences in sexual excitability do not obscure the fact that certain types of stimulation tend to be sexually arousing to most people and that there are patterns of sexual response that nearly everyone follows.

Sexual Stimulation

Conditioned stimulus

Sexual arousal can be initiated through any or all of the senses—touch, sight, hearing, and smell—as long as the stimulation is considered erotic. Unlike some reflexes such as eye-blinking, in which a stimulus automatically results in a physical response, most sexual responses require that the situation be consciously defined as sexually stimulating as well. For example, during a physical examination men or women may have their genitals touched and not be sexually aroused at all. But if their lover were to do the touching, their physical response would be quite different.

Tactile stimulation, or touching, is the most basic means for stimulating sexual arousal. Even infant boys and girls are quite capable of sexual arousal when their penis or clitoris is stroked. In some cultures, this is routinely done in order to quiet children for the night. Among adults, rhythmic pressure on the glans penis or clitoris is almost a prerequisite to orgasmic response, although the stimulation of other parts of the body helps to encourage this response as well.

Areas of the body that are particularly sensitive to tactile stimulation are called **erogenous zones.** Any part of the skin can be erogenous if it contains enough nerve receptors and is believed to be the source of sexual stimulation.

Besides the genitals, the areas most likely to be considered erogenous include the breasts, lips and interior of the mouth, thighs, and ears, but as the data in Table 9.2 indicate, preferences can vary a great deal from person to person.

Erotic dress

Visual stimulation is perhaps the most common means of sexual arousal. All around us are sexual cues which range from revealing dress styles to erotic literature and films. Magazines which portray nude women and men are widely circulated and even prime-time television shows are adding the erotic element to boost their ratings. When women were asked in a recent national survey if they liked to dress to be sexually erotic, one-half of them said they did (Bell, 1976).

Until recently, it was commonly believed that women are not as sexually stimulated by things they see or read as men. The Kinsey (1948, 1953) studies, for example, found that fewer women than men reported being aroused by pornography, stag films, stripteasers, or the like. However, more recent studies have found that both women and men are similarly aroused by films or erotic literature if extended sexual activity is portrayed (Osborne and Pollack, 1977). While pictures of naked people are still not as arousing to women as they are to men, the differences between the sexes in visual stimulation of sexual arousal appear to be declining as women are more exposed to sexual materials.

Sexual conversations

Sounds and talking can also be important sources of sexual stimulation, although they are not nearly as likely to generate arousal as visual and tactile stimulation. Music, particularly rhythmic music, is sometimes considered arousing, especially when it is combined with pelvic movements in contemporary dancing. The sounds of the music then carry over the visual memory as well and serve to stimulate sexual arousal even when the dancing has stopped. Talking about sexual fantasies or sexual experiences can also be arousing and is a common source of sexual excitement among youth. Adults are rarely aroused by direct sexual statements, but indirect statements like "You're beautiful" or "You turn me on" are often stimulating (Gagnon, p. 127).

Table 9.2

Primary Erotic Zone Excluding Genitals

Zone	Men (%)	Women (%)
Back	4.9	4.3
Breasts	4.9	36.5
Chest	4.6	0.24
Ears	7.0	8.1
Lips	10.0	6.0
Neck	4.6	6.5
Stomach	5.2	6.7
Thighs	31.5	14.2
Other	6.1	3.4

Source: Reprinted with permission from Bernard Goldstein, *Human Sexuality* (New York: McGraw-Hill Book Company, 1976), p. 130.

Smell and taste are very important sexual stimulants in other animals but play a minor role in human sexual arousal. While a particular cologne may come to signal sexual availability to someone, most people do not use deodorants, mouthwash, vaginal sprays, aftershave lotions, and other odorous lotions as sexual stimulants *per se.* Rather, these potions are designed to cover up the natural scents that we have been taught are repulsive. For some people, however, the natural odors and tastes of their partner, particularly the genitals, are considered highly arousing. To others, quite the opposite is true.

Importance of beliefs

Attempts to stimulate sexual arousal artifically through the use of **aphrodisiacs** have not been successful. For centuries, people have tried everything from eating oysters or the testes of lambs to putting powdered deer horn or the irritant Spanish fly in their drinks in order to enhance sexual arousal. None of these has been demonstrated to affect sexual stimulation, although Spanish fly can easily kill a person in trying. Recent evidence, however, does suggest that if people *believe* that an aphrodisiac will arouse them, it might do so. This is often the case with people who use marijuana as a sexual stimulant (Gawin, 1978).

Sexual Fantasy

A sexual stimulant that ties together many of the sensory images we receive is **fantasy.** Through fantasy, men and women recall and develop erotic, dreamlike images which often represent some of their ideal or hidden fears and desires. Sexual fantasies are common during masturbation. They can also occur during sexual intercourse when the sexual partner is mentally replaced by someone else (Delora and Warren). Practically any time when the mind is relaxed and mental imagery is permitted can be an occasion for sexual fantasy.

Male fantasies

Through the ages, the fantasies of men have been recorded in art and literature. Male sexual fantasies have been encouraged and condoned to a much greater degree than female fantasies. The fantasies of a man, research studies point out, are quite likely to involve him in a situation in which he sees himself as powerful and aggressive in a relatively impersonal sexual encounter (Biblarz and Biblarz, 1976). But not all sexual fantasies of men are this impersonal and "macho." Often, their fantasies incorporate sensitivity, fond remembrances of loving experiences, and imaginary attempts to cultivate the sexual responses of their partner (Shanor, 1978).

Female fantasies

The sexual fantasies of women have only recently received much attention, but now we find that they have been an especially well-kept secret. Traditionally, women could not as readily communicate their fantasies even to one another since, if they admitted them, they risked losing their "good girl" image. With the lifting of this burden, women have felt more free to admit their fantasies, as 99 percent of them did in a recent Utah study (Brown and Hart, 1978). In this study, the researchers found that most of these women fantasized at least once or twice a week with the most common fantasies including being overpowered, seducing a man, or petting with a woman. The importance of experience for sexual fantasy is pointed out in the finding that older, more sexually liberated women were most apt to fantasize while younger, more traditional women fantasized less often.

Phases of Sexual Response

Predictable patterns

Sexual arousal, whether created by sensory stimulation or fantasy, involves some form of physical sexual response. The research of William Masters and Virginia Johnson has been particularly useful in helping us to understand these responses. From their laboratory observations of 312 men and 382 women volunteers, Masters and Johnson found that there are very predictable patterns of sexual response that both men and women follow. Whether the stimulation comes from intercourse, masturbation, fantasy, or breast stimulation (in some women), a **sexual-response cycle** is initiated which usually passes through *four phases*: excitement, plateau, orgasm, and resolution.

Each of these response phases is associated with observable physiological changes in the individual (see Figs. 9.2 and 9.3). During a sexual experience, however, these phases seem to blend into one another in a way that is uniquely felt by each person. The duration of these phases can be shortened or prolonged and may not always culminate in orgasm. It is also possible for partners to be in different phases at the same time, a factor which sometimes creates sexual frustration (Masters and Johnson, 1970).

Physical response

The Excitement Phase. For both men and women, initial sexual stimulation is followed by slight muscular tension, an increase in the heart rate, and a rise in blood pressure which results in a concentration of blood in the spongy tissues of the genital area. Men experience this almost immediately as an erection of the penis and a tightening of the scrotum as the testicles are drawn closer to the body. In women, the engorgement of blood causes the labia to swell and flare away from the vagina, the clitoris to become erect, and the vaginal tissues to sweat, lubricating the area for easy penile penetration. Both sexes are also subject to a slight **sex flush** in the breasts, abdomen, and shoulders as well as erection of their nipples.

Muscular tension

The Plateau Phase. There is no distinct beginning to the plateau phase. Sexual arousal simply reaches a point in which a balance is reached between intense erotic sensations and the release of orgasm. The genital tissues of both men and women continue to enlarge; the heart rate and blood pressure continue to go up. Muscular tension is more obvious in the face, hands, and feet, and if penile penetration occurs, the outer vaginal muscles involuntarily contract around the penis. Meanwhile, the inner two-thirds of the vagina balloons in size. The clitoris also becomes very sensitive at this time and withdraws

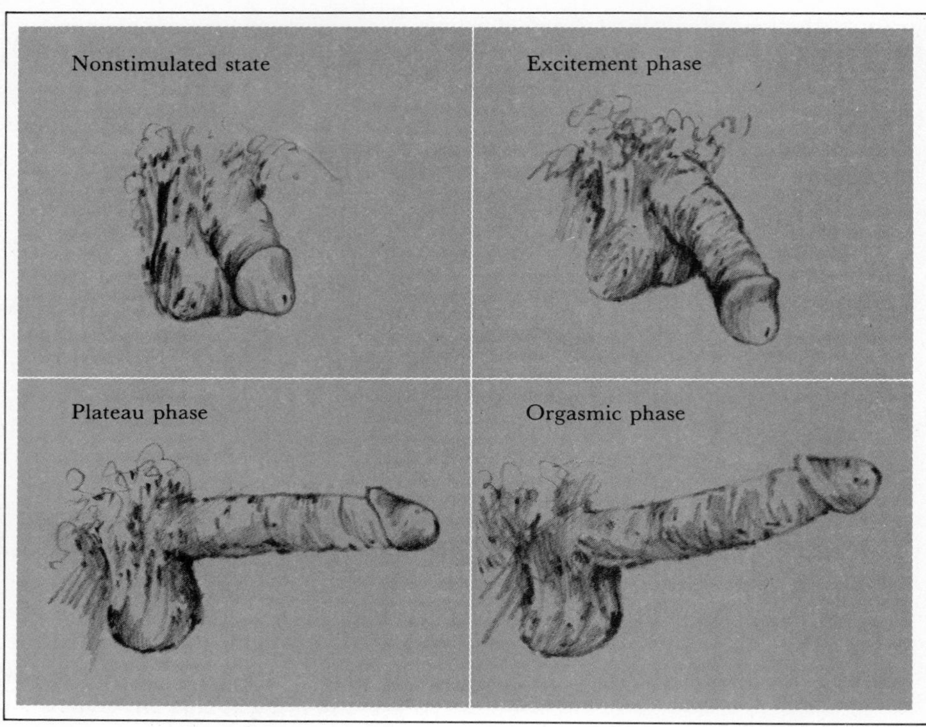

Fig. 9.2
Male Genitals during Sexual Response

beneath the clitoral hood where it can be very pleasurably stimulated indirectly by stroking the flushed labia minora below it or the mons above it.

Contractions

The Orgasmic Phase. For both men and women, orgasm involves the highly pleasurable culmination and release of all the muscular tension and engorgement that has been building. In men, strong rhythmic contractions at the base of the penis ejaculate seminal fluid with an involuntary, pleasurable sense of release. The first two or three expulsions occur at 0.8-second intervals then taper off into weaker contractions. In women, orgasms involve rhythmic pleasurable contractions of the clitoris, uterus, and outer third of the vaginal area. For some women, these contractions are very mild while for others they are very intense and, usually, their orgasms last longer than those of men, often including four to eight rhythmic contractions at 0.8-second intervals followed by a series of weaker contractions. It is also possible for some women under high stimulation to experience multiple orgasms in which waves of contractions rush over them, later orgasms being stronger than the earlier ones. Very few men are capable of this.

The seizurelike response of orgasm transforms most men and women into a quite different psychological state. It is not uncommon for either sex to

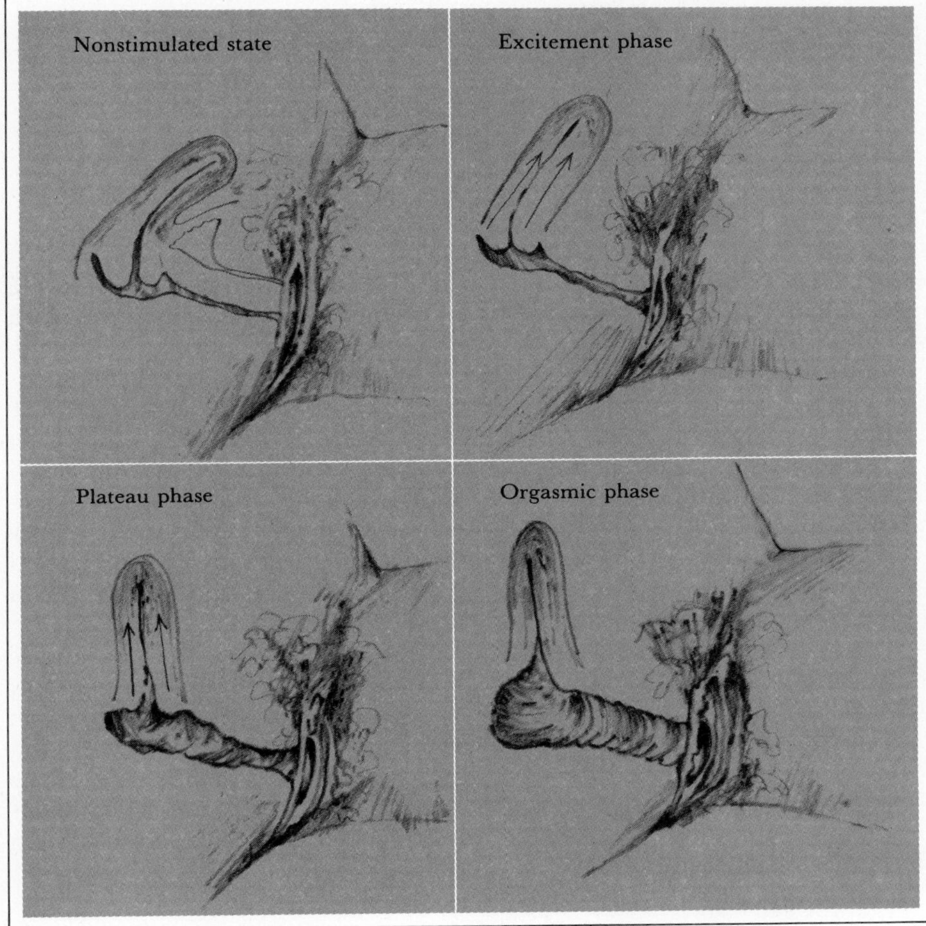

Fig. 9.3
Female Genitals during Sexual Response

lapse into almost uncontrollable thrusting, moaning, laughing, crying, or gibberish. Some women, in contrast, become very quiet, almost serene. Each individual differs in his or her response to orgasmic feelings, but the following are some candid, personal descriptions of sensations to orgasm.

From a woman:

> At a certain point, I know I'm on my way, but it is hard to put into words. Physically my breathing is faster, my body tenses and strains to make my clitoris as open and vulnerable as possible. My vaginal and clitoral area gets absolutely hot and I seem to switch into a pelvic rhythm over which I have no conscious control; every contact with my clitoris at this point is a miniature orgasm which becomes more frequent until it is one huge muscle spasm. (Hite, 1976, p. 160)

From a man:

> Just before it starts there is a kind of welling up urgency in the groin that almost feels like the whole area is enlarged. This welling up feeling is when it all becomes involuntary and the house could burn down and I wouldn't know it because it's a totally consuming sensation and I'm not aware of anything else. . . . Once it starts, there is a combination feeling of contraction and of something coming out of the penis. This combination is just exquisite in sensation. (Delora and Warren, p. 42)

The Resolution Phase. Following orgasm, both men and women experience a relaxation of muscular tension, a drop in blood pressure and pulse rate, and a subsiding of the engorgement of genital tissues. This return to a normal, unstimulated sexual state will take longer if the excitement and plateau phases were longer. If no orgasm occurs at all, then the resolution phase may require an hour or more before all tensions are relieved.

For men, orgasms are followed by a **refractory period** during which further sexual stimulation is uncomfortable and an erection almost impossible. The time period before a new excitement phase can begin again may vary from a few minutes to a few days, with less time required of younger and sexually active men. Women have no refractory period and may be again stimulated to orgasm over and over many times.

Orgasm frequency

Not everyone, however, always completes the full sexual-response cycle when sexually aroused. Approximately half of all married women and nearly all married men experience orgasms regularly during sexual intercourse; only about one out of ten women never experience an orgasm at all (Hunt, 1974). Yet these figures do not take into account the numerous occasions during which sex play at the excitement and plateau phases is enjoyed for its own sake. These encounters are no less valuable to relational intimacy than those that include an orgasm.

Masturbation

Guilt

For most men and women, their first orgasmic experience and most consistent orgasmic response is derived from self-stimulation of their genitals, or **masturbation**. A national survey indicates that over nine out of ten men and six out of ten women masturbate at some time during their lives (Hunt, 1974). These frequencies appear to be rising, especially as negative attitudes toward this form of sexual arousal decline (Diepold and Young, 1979). We now know that there are no physical maladies that descend on those who masturbate but guilt feelings are still common. While women who masturbate are less likely to feel guilty about it, Masters and Johnson (1970) report that every man they interviewed expressed concern about "excessive levels" of masturbation. Usually, however, these imaginary levels were higher than the levels at which the individual was practicing.

Masturbation importance

Contrary to popular belief, masturbation is a very important experience for learning sexual arousal. Both men and women learn through masturbation how to feel comfortable with their sexual selves, how different strokes or touches affect them, how to breathe and move their bodies, and, in general, how to be more aware of their sexual sensations. Sex therapists recommend masturbation as a reliever of sexual tension, especially when the partner is unavailable or when there is not the time or energy to engage in sex play. For women, masturbation can be particularly important as a technique for learning how to be aroused to orgasm. The Kinsey (1953) studies found that three times as many women were able to experience orgasm in their first year if they had previously masturbated to orgasm. And sex therapists now generally agree that for women who are not orgasmic, "learning to masturbate successfully is probably the most important step . . . in learning to come to orgasm" (McCary, p. 154).

EXPRESSIONS OF SEXUAL INTIMACY

Sexual behavior can take a variety of forms, depending upon an individual's needs and relational commitments. At its most basic level, sexuality can be expressed as little more than an unemotional, physical appetite. Sexual intercourse with a stranger, a prostitute, or masturbation usually fits this description. At its most complex level, however, sexuality can be an expression of mutual intimacy, the total sharing of one another's emotional, psychological, and physical selves. Intimacy, as we noted earlier in our discussion of love (Chapter 6), implies **reciprocity**—a desire for mutual more than personal gratification.

Sexuality and intimacy

Sexuality and intimacy do not necessarily have to be linked. Sexuality is personal; intimacy is relational. Scoresby (1977) points out that neither self-motivating physical appetite nor the feeling that the other person's sexual needs are much more important is likely to encourage sexual intimacy. Both women and men can come to see sex as a "duty," and feel so responsible for their partner's sexual satisfaction that they themselves are unfulfilled. After having observed these tendencies in couples they have treated, Masters and Johnson (1975) wrote:

> Effective sexual functioning is something that transpires between two people. To be effective it must be done together. It is something that sexually functional couples do *with* each other. (pp. 7–8)

Sexual Communication

Levels of communication

One important way of understanding sexual intimacy is as an expression of interpersonal communication. As relationships develop, there are demands for expanding the bases of communication. For infants, support and affection are initially communicated in *sensory* terms, by touching, holding, caressing. Later, parent-infant communication is enlarged to include nonverbal, *emo-*

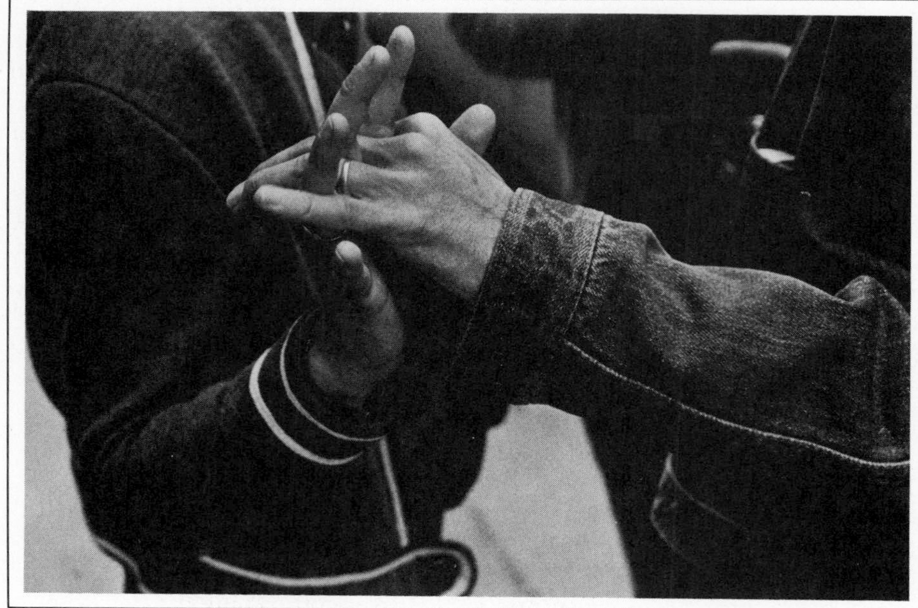

Touching is a fundamental means of expressing one's need for another.

tional support and this is finally reinforced through verbal, *intellectual*-level messages (Sullivan, 1953). Adult communication and intimacy, however, almost seem to develop in reverse fashion. Initial encounters are very superficial, verbal, and intellectual. We talk about the weather, our work or classes, and our backgrounds and interests. Later, if the relationship is satisfying, nonverbal, *emotional* expressions of affection occur more frequently. Finally, the communication cycle is completed when the couple also feels comfortable at the *sensory* level, touching and holding one another.

Touching

The importance of touching as a means of communication cannot be overemphasized. It is a fundamental process through which individuals express their need for one another, whether as infants or as adults. In our culture, however, men and women are not similarly taught to communicate by touching. Young girls are touched more than boys, and adult women are more encouraged to be affectionate through touching and being touched. Men, meanwhile, are not usually taught to be comfortable touching someone and often appear rigid or clumsy when they attempt to do so (Wilson *et al.*, 1978). It is little wonder then that women frequently complain that men do not know how to show tenderness in their sexual approaches and that sexual therapy usually includes some form of training in how to touch one another sensitively (Masters and Johnson, 1970).

In the development of a relationship, these differences in comfort with tactile communication are eased when sexual communication is seen as a multifaceted phenomenon. All too often, we equate sexual communication only with physical touching when that is but one part of it. The verbal communication of sexual feelings, the light touches that might suggest sexual interest, and the nonverbal promptings that direct a partner toward a pleasurable response are all expressions of sexual intimacy, not mere foreplay that precedes intercourse—the "real thing."

Mutual arousal

Sometimes, words of love or a simple kiss may communicate sexual intimacy in their own right without necessarily leading to other sexual behaviors. At other times, when all of the means of verbal, emotional, and physical communication are employed in sexual arousal, it is more likely that this arousal will build mutually and that both partners will be able to stimulate and satisfy each other meaningfully. The assumptions that somehow genital stimulation alone is enough and that one person naturally knows how the other person feels, without other cues to verify, are important sources of failure in sexual intimacy (Bell, 1979).

Petting

As relationships develop and physical expression becomes the next logical step in communicating intimacy, **petting** behaviors normally emerge. Petting, although a somewhat dated term, collectively refers to all forms of erotic contact between couples prior to **coitus,** the penetration of the vagina by the penis. Petting can be part of the sex play that precedes coitus or it can be the alternative when coitus is not desired. In either case, the behavior is oriented toward progressive sexual arousal, ultimately preparing the couple for coitus and orgasmic responsiveness.

Progression of arousal

Petting typically proceeds in a fairly uniform pattern in Western society. Hugging and kissing begin the process, and this is followed usually by tongue kissing, stimulation of the woman's breasts, stimulation of her genitals, and then perhaps to stimulation of the man's genitals. This may be followed by the rubbing together of their genitals in simulated intercourse and sometimes by oral-genital contacts, either as a prelude or an alternative to coitus.

This progression is normal, but it is not inevitable (Kinsey, 1953). Some couples may stop at the kissing stage and go no further. Others may prefer to be aroused in a quite different sequence. But whatever pattern of petting is followed, subsequent sexual encounters usually proceed more quickly to the level previously achieved. Yet the level they progress to is still largely determined by the woman. In our culture, she has been given the restrictive "gate-keeper" role which gives her the right to determine how much sexual intimacy will occur (Gagnon).

Oral stimulation

During adolescence, petting is a fairly common sexual behavior. Nearly all youth today experience petting of some type, and by twenty years of age, about one-half of the girls and two-thirds of the boys have used petting to reach orgasm (Diepold and Young). Marital petting is more likely now to include oral-genital sex than was true a generation ago. At the time of the Kinsey study (1938–1949), very few couples with no college experience had tried either oral stimulation of the man (fellatio) or of the woman (cunnilingus). Only four out of ten couples with college experience had tried either form of oral sex. By the 1970s, however, one study found that fellatio and cunnilingus were being practiced in over one-half of the marriages of noncollege couples and in two-thirds of the marriages in which college backgrounds were represented (Hunt, 1974).

Sexual Intercourse

Sex and love

For most men and women, sexual intercourse represents the most complete expression of their sexual intimacy. Sexual intercourse is not synonymous with coitus or with orgasm but encompasses the full sequence of sexual arousal and petting which includes coitus and subsequent sex play. Sexual intercourse, in its very essence, is a form of communication. Between two people who love each other, it can communicate the total acceptance and desire each uniquely feels for the other. But love does not necessarily have to be the basis for sexual intercourse. In many cases:

> Sex can be used to keep a person interested in you, to relieve loneliness, to dominate another, to make yourself or another feel guilty, to relieve physical tension, to express liking or love. These meanings vary and are infinite. An individual can make love one day to show affection, the next to gain revenge, the next to pretend love. No two occasions are necessarily the same. (Strong *et al.*, 1978, p 172)

Premarital intercourse

Among single people, rates of sexual intercourse have risen significantly in the past few decades. Studies vary in the exact percentages they find, but up until the 1960s, about one-half of the women who married had experienced premarital sexual intercourse compared to the two-thirds to three-fourths of all women who marry today (Gagnon). The percentage of single men who experience sexual intercourse has risen some, but it has been fairly high for several decades. Most studies indicate that about eight out of ten men who marry today are coitally experienced (Hunt, 1974).

The likelihood of premarital intercourse increases with commitment to the relationship. In a study of college youth by Lewis and Burr (1975), both men and women were much more likely to be currently having intercourse if they were engaged than if they were just casually dating (see Table 9.3). The data also indicate that women more than men need greater assurance that the relationship is emotionally bonded before they will have intercourse. Women are much less likely to report having intercourse in very uncommitted relationships. This reflects the more sexually conservative standard that both men and women apply to women in Western society (Hunt, 1974).

Sexual fears

The relatively high frequencies of sexual intercourse among singles today should not suggest that all youth easily incorporate this into their relationships. Tension and anxiety often accompany early intercourse experiences, and many youth feel that they were pressured into intercourse by peers or partners before they were ready. Fears, often justifiable, of pregnancy,

Table 9.3

Frequency of Current Premarital Intercourse According to Level of Commitment—College Students*

Level of Commitment	Men (%)	Women (%)
On first date	21	2
Infrequent dating	27	3
Going steady	42	23
Engaged	56	36

* These percentages do not reflect the total sexual experience of these youth. Many not currently having intercourse have done so in the past or will probably do so before they marry.

Source: Wesley Burr and Robert Lewis, *Archives of Sexual Behavior* 4(1975), p. 76. Used with permission of Plenum Publishing Company.

venereal disease, moral transgressions, and relational readiness sometimes linger to cloud the experience. In one national survey, over one-third of the young unmarried men and almost two-thirds of the women experienced feelings of regret and worry after their first experience of sexual intercourse (Hunt, 1974). These haunting feelings soon subside for most people, and in the long run, sexual intercourse does not appear to have a negative effect on marital adjustment. But most men and women need time and a relaxed atmosphere to feel comfortable in sexual intercourse, and these conditions are sometimes more difficult to ensure before marriage.

Intercourse in marriage

In marriage, sexual intercourse is normal and expected. There are no "normal" frequencies, however, since the need for sexual intimacy may vary considerably from couple to couple. But most studies are fairly consistent in finding that, on the average, young married couples have intercourse about three times per week. Over time, this rate declines so that married couples in their forties tend to experience intercourse about twice per week, and after age fifty, once a week or less is the usual pattern. This decline in frequency of intercourse is also accompanied by a decline in preferences for sexual intimacy by both husbands and wives. One recent study found that the priority given to sexual needs, as opposed to other personal and relational needs, is high in early marriage but steadily drops over the years of the marriage (Mancini and Orthner, 1978).

Intercourse frustrations

Despite these prevalent changes in frequency of intercourse, an overwhelming majority of couples consider their coital activity "pleasurable," whatever their age. This was true of nearly all the men and nine out of ten of the women in the Hunt (1974) survey. Still, not all of these people were completely satisfied. When asked if they would prefer more or less coitus than they were having, a few wanted less, but over a third wanted more. These results are similar to those found in other studies, and most often, it is the men and women with unsatisfactory marital relationships who want more sexual intercourse (Tavres and Sadd, 1977). For women, this is quite a switch from the common plea of thirty years ago that intercourse occurred too frequently (Burgess and Wallin, 1953). Now, women's expectations for sexual intercourse are more similar to those of men, but unfortunately, their frustrations with insufficient intercourse are now also equal to those of men.

Sometimes, frustration with sexual intercourse results from boredom with techniques and positions that have become patterned and routine. Much of the excitement of sexual intimacy is lost when every move and feeling can be expected and no new sensations are explored. The variety of means used by men and women to stimulate each other, however, has increased, and it is now much more likely that precoital sex play will result in greater sexual arousal for both partners. This may partially account for the higher frequencies of female orgasm from intercourse reported today as compared to earlier (Diamond and Karlen, 1980).

Coital positions

Coital positions are also more varied today. Not long ago, it was commonly believed that the only "natural" coital position was the face-to-face, man-above position. Some states even legislated this as the only legal position for sexual intercourse. In most non-Western cultures, however, this position is unusual, and it came to be called the "missionary position" (McCary). While the man-above position is still the most common among Americans, the woman-above, side-to-side, rear-entry, and sitting intercourse positions are much more frequently used, especially by young married couples (see Table 9.4).

Sexual performance

Experimentation with sexual techniques is apparently very satisfying to most couples (Tavras and Sadd). But for some other couples, concern over sexual technique soon causes sex to lose its playful, intimate expressiveness. While the new freedom to talk and write about sex has made many women and men more aware of the possibilities for sexual pleasure, it has also raised sexual expectations. Sociologists Lewis and Brissett (1967) warn that when experiences like multiple orgasms and mutual orgasms become criteria for measuring sexual intimacy, then performance becomes more important than sexual communication and interaction. At this point, sex for a couple is something to be achieved, a goal rather than a process, and *work* rather than *play*.

Table 9.4

Use of Variant Coital Positions among Married Persons

Position	Age: 18 to 24 (%)	35 to 44 (%)	55 and Over (%)
Woman-above	37	29	17
On-the-side	21	15	15
Rear-entry (vaginal)	20	8	1
Sitting	4	2	1

Source: Reprinted with permission of Playboy Press from *Sexual Behavior in the 1970's* by Morton Hunt. Copyright © 1974 by Morton Hunt.

EXTRAMARITAL SEXUAL INTERACTION

Not all married people restrict sexual interaction to their spouse. Approximately one-half of the married men and one-fourth of the married women in the United States have experienced at least one occasion of extramarital sexual intercourse (Hunt, 1974). This proportion is very similar to that found by Kinsey (1953) several decades ago. Among men and women under age twenty-five, however, there has been a considerable increase in extramarital sexual activity, which may indicate that more of these sexual liaisons will occur in the future. This possibility is also raised by married people themselves. In a national study of over 2000 married women, one-third of the wives who had never been involved in an extramarital venture said it "might happen" in the future (Bell and Lobsenz, 1977).

Extramarital sex frequency

Despite these frequencies of extramarital sex, the attitudes of most Americans remain quite opposed to these relationships. In a 1978 Gallup survey, 65 percent of the adults polled felt that sexual relations with someone other than the marriage partner are "always wrong." Younger adults and the college educated are somewhat more liberal in their attitudes on this, but even half of this group categorically opposes extramarital intercourse. Apparently, Americans, like people in most cultures, are more willing to accept or look the other way when considering sexual relations before marriage. But once a couple is married, there are strong legal and social pressures to observe sexual exclusiveness.

Clandestine Extramarital Sex

In the most prevalent type of extramarital sexual arrangement, the parties keep their relationship secret from their spouses. It is assumed, probably correctly, that a spouse will disapprove if he or she finds out about it. Most of these extramarital sex experiences are not long-term "affairs" but rather brief, noncommitted, "one- or two-night stands" which are over before any great emotional involvement develops.

"Affairs"

A clandestine "affair," in contrast, takes much more effort, costs more money, creates conflicting commitments, and makes necessary the invention of regular excuses to be given to the spouse and family. In effect, two different sets of obligations have to be maintained and, if the relationship is to remain secret, the marital obligations have to be given priority, which can frustrate the extramarital partner.

Because of the threat to the marital relationship, clandestine extramarital sex tends to be entered into most frequently by those whose marital satisfaction is low. These individuals have the least to lose if discovered. The more emotionally and sexually deprived a man or woman feels in a marriage, the more likely he or she will be to seek or fall into an extramarital sexual involvement (Walster *et al.*, 1978).

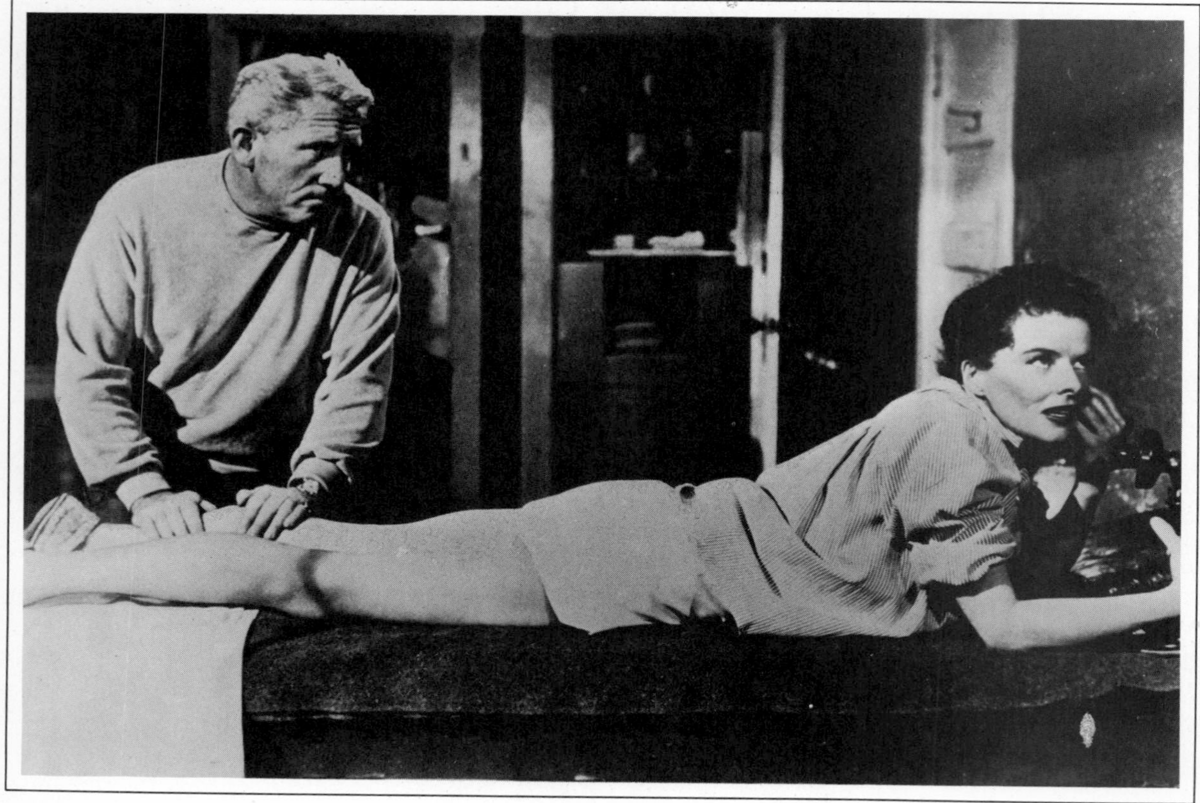

While many extramarital liaisons are brief "one-night stands," others, such as the famous Spencer Tracy–Katharine Hepburn romance, are enduring and deeply committed relationships.

Marital impacts

Sometimes, however, marital satisfaction is not low among those having extramarital sex. Either men or women can be attracted by what they see as an opportunity for sexual gratification that has no emotional "strings" attached. This can happen at conventions, among work associates, and frequently occurs in occupations that require a good deal of travel away from home (Johnson, 1970). Other men and women may find their marriage gratifying but not stimulating to the degree that they would like. This is common in husbands and wives after a few years of marriage, and for some of these people "such affairs, reportedly decrease marital boredom, decrease marital tension, and increase emotional closeness and sexual satisfaction in the marriage" (Glass and Wright, 1977, p. 699).

Nevertheless, whether they expect it or not, some marriages considered satisfactory can be shaken by extramarital sex. Not all marriages are threatened, but divorce probabilities have been found to be higher among men and women with clandestine extramarital-sex experience, even when their marriages had been thought to be satisfactory (Glass and Wright).

Consensual Extramarital Sex

In a minority of marriages, the husband and wife know about and approve of the extramarital relationships of their spouse. In **sexually open marriages** (discussed in Chapter 5), each spouse has the consent of the other to develop his or her own sexually intimate friendships, as long as these do not threaten the marriage. Another form of consensual adultery is actually **comarital** in the sense that the husband and wife participate together in extramarital sex with others. This is usually called **mate-swapping** or **swinging.**

Swingers

It is difficult to know how many people have actually practiced swinging in their marriages, but the proportion is conservatively estimated to be about 2 percent of the marriages in the United States (Hunt, 1974). Contrary to the image that these people are usually young, radical, oversexed and wild-eyed, research studies have found that swinging couples are often older, usually upper-educated, and otherwise fairly conventional suburbanites (Smith and Smith, 1975). Swingers tend to have come from families in which their parents left them emotionally starved, and they have thus learned to seek emotional gratification from a variety of people, friends more than family (Gilmartin, 1977).

The idea of swinging is usually initiated by a husband who has read something about it (Gilmartin). His wife often agrees only after considerable persuasion. Couples who are close friends may talk about it and exchange partners, but it is more common for a couple to be introduced to other couples they have not met before through personal advertisements in swinging magazines, or underground newspapers, or contacts at swinging bars.

Interest in swinging

Once a married couple has become comfortable with swinging, it is interesting that it is the wife who is more likely to want to continue it (Palson and Palson, 1972). Commenting on this, Delora and Warren write: "A woman may enjoy being sought after by a number of men and women whether or not she consistently experiences orgasm. On the other hand, her husband may find that he does not live up to his fantasies of being a great lover romping gleefully, penis erect, through a roomful of nude women. Instead, his inability to respond sexually to every woman can become quite apparent and can be a real threat to his image of himself" (p. 259). While it is too early to tell if this holds true for most couples, recent studies do support this if *both* the husband and wife honestly and wholeheartedly support the activity (Gilmartin). But if interest in swinging is unequal, as it often tends to be, then jealousy and anger soon follow. When this happens, the couple must either mutually decide to drop out of swinging, accept a situation which is not equally to their liking, or separate. How many ultimately separate we do not yet know.

SEXUAL COMPLICATIONS

Sexual intimacy does not come easily for some people or without a price in personal health for some others. Masters and Johnson (1970) have suggested that as many as one-half of all married couples have some sexual dysfunction, although an estimate that may be more reasonable is that one-quarter to one-third of all couples experience serious sexual problems. Of course, one of the difficulties in defining sex and its problems lies in our inability to define adequate sexual health. Until much of the cultural baggage that limits our learning of sexual intimacy is lifted, it will be difficult for many couples to develop healthy practices of sexual behavior.

Venereal Disease

A major health problem that can result from sexual intimacy is the contraction of a venereal disease. These diseases are transmitted by sexual contact (oral, genital, and anal) and, if untreated, will have serious effects on a person's health. There are a variety of different venereal diseases, but **gonorrhea** is the most prevalent in North America and can cause irreparable physical damage, including sterility. **Syphilis,** once the scourge of Europe and America, is now less common than gonorrhea but more likely to be debilitating and fatal. **Herpes Type II** is now a very common skin disorder and particularly painful in women. Each of these venereal diseases can also be harmful to any child conceived by a woman carrying the disease.

Incidence of V.D.

The incidence of venereal disease is increasing rapidly, particularly among youth in their teens and twenties. About 10 percent of all young people in the United States have had one of these diseases by age twenty-five (Gagnon). The rise in premarital sexual intercourse with multiple partners is partly to blame since this creates long chains of infection that can spread rapidly through a community of sexually active persons. Homosexual contacts can also pass these diseases, and it is estimated that as many as one-fourth of these individuals have had a venereal disease (Darrow, 1976).

Prevention of V.D.

There are a variety of ways by which men and women can prevent or control the spread of a venereal disease. One way is to use a condom. A condom prevents skin contact with a genital venereal infection and can be effective if it is put on before *any* sexual contact is made. Antiseptic compounds, including soap and water and douches, can also be used to cleanse areas that may have touched an infected person. Unfortunately, this cleansing needs to be done immediately after a contact to be of value. Antibiotics are the most effective treatment for venereal diseases but they must be taken in sufficient dosages under the care of a physician to control the disease.

Venereal diseases can be prevented almost entirely if sexual contacts are restricted to persons who are uninfected. If neither sexual partner has any history of sexual contact, which is unlikely since even kissing is a sexual contact, then a venereal disease will not intrude into the relationship. The more sexual partners each person has had in the past, the greater the risk of contracting and passing on the disease. Usually, however, people who develop long-term exclusive sexual relationships with partners who are relatively inexperienced sexually have a low risk of acquiring venereal infections (Darrow).

For many men and women, their sexual difficulties are caused not as much by their physical health as by their emotional inability to respond sexually to their partner. The problem may be temporary or it may be persistent, but it represents nonetheless a frustration to both people in the relationship. In a recent study of "happily married" middle-class marriages, 80 percent of the couples said that their sexual relations were usually satisfying. Still, 40 percent of the husbands reported that they had experienced problems with erection or ejaculation in the past. Among the wives, 63 percent reported having experienced problems with sexual arousal or having an orgasm (Frank *et al.*, 1978).

Sex problems

Sexual dysfunctions like these are not simply the result of differing levels of sexual interest. They represent serious problems to these couples that are often embarrassing or guilt producing to the dysfunctioning party as well as frustrating to the partner. Most of the sexual problems that send couples to sex therapists fall within one of six basic forms of sexual dysfunction. Three of these can potentially affect each sex and all are now treatable through *competent* sex therapy.

Fear of failure

In men, **erectile dysfunction,** or impotence, occurs when a man is unable to attain or maintain an erection of his penis. He cannot, therefore, perform coitus. In about 15 percent of these cases, there is some physical reason for the problem. In the remainder, the cause lies in emotional inhibitions or anxieties which block the erectile reflex (Kaplan, 1975). Most of the treatments for erectile dysfunction center around removing the fear of sexual failure the man feels and orienting him to genuine acceptance of his sexual feelings as good (Zilbergeld, 1978). This takes time and guidance, but nearly three-fourths of the treatments are successful.

Learning to control arousal

Premature ejaculation is a common condition which is not always easy to define as a dysfunction. Most men at some time ejaculate during intercourse prior to their partner's orgasm, but some men regularly cannot hold back their ejaculation for any sufficient length of time. These men usually have not learned to control their sexual arousal or they do not even know that it is necessary for them to delay their orgasm in order to satisfy their partner's sexual needs. Fortunately, premature ejaculation is one of the most treatable of the sexual dysfunctions since nearly all men are capable of controlling the development of their sexual arousal once they know it is important to do so and have learned how to desensitize themselves.

A third sexual dysfunction in men, **retarded ejaculation,** is the direct opposite of premature ejaculation. Men with this condition can have an erection but they have difficulty ejaculating during sexual intercourse. Orgasm through masturbation may be possible for these men, but anxiety, fears of pregnancy, or unconscious rejection of women can retard their coital orgasmic ability. In the treatment for this problem, the partner is encouraged to stimulate the man to orgasm lovingly by manual techniques, even if it requires a long time. This allows him to associate her positively with his own pleasure.

In women, one of the most all-inclusive sexual dysfunctions is **female sexual unresponsiveness.** The sexually unresponsive woman may be capable of orgasm and may even experience orgasm periodically, but she is almost completely devoid of any desire for sexual intercourse. Usually, these women find no pleasure in sex play, receive little or no vaginal lubrication, and are often disgusted by the very thought of coitus. For some of these women, their present circumstances are to blame for their inability to become aroused. Others learned to be sexually inhibited in childhood, only to find later that they cannot let go of these inhibitions.

Releasing anxieties

Releasing all of these pent-up anxieties requires time and patience. Unresponsiveness is usually dealt with by teaching the woman to relax and accept erotic stimulation from her partner in a nondemanding, sensuous atmosphere (Kaplan). Self-exploration through masturbation has also been shown to be helpful (Heiman *et al.*, 1976). The woman is encouraged to seek her own pleasure "selfishly" at this point and to communicate to her partner the stimulation she likes and does not like. As a result:

> Both the woman and her lover become more perceptive of the other's needs and responses. She sees that he enjoys making her happy and does not reject her when she seeks sexual pleasure, as she might have feared. (McCary, p. 319)

Orgasmic difficulty in women is the most common sexual complaint of both women and men. Physical causes are rarely the problem. Usually, like impotence in men, the problem is rooted in psychological anxiety, fear, guilt, or hostility toward the partner (Fink, 1974). Inadequate stimulation from an unskilled partner can also be a problem as well as ignorance concerning what is necessary for sexual arousal on the part of the woman.

Orgasmic capability

Contrary to the belief that many women are just not orgasmic, it is estimated that over nine out of ten women are quite capable of orgasms if they are sufficiently stimulated (McCary). It is necessary, however, to free the woman from her sexual inhibitions and maximize the stimulation she receives. This usually involves having a woman first learn to experience an orgasm regularly by masturbation, then by clitoral stimulation from her partner, and when she feels she is ready, by coital stimulation. Often, a vibrator is recommended for initial stimulation since, if properly used, it will almost always cause an orgasm.

Once a woman learns to feel comfortable with her complete sexual arousal, it is easier to transfer these feelings into intercourse. But no matter what her orgasmic history, a woman usually must have focused clitoral stimulation as well, by herself or her partner, in order to orgasm; vaginal stimulation is rarely enough. Only 30 percent of the wives in the Hite (1976) study could orgasm through only thrusting of the penis in their vagina. The rest of the orgasmic women required clitoral contact for their orgasm. According to Shere Hite:

> Most researchers and sex therapists agree that thrusting is less efficient in causing female orgasm than clitoral area stimulation. Pulling your ear

> slightly back and forth can also pull the skin on your cheek. Just so, it is possible for thrusting to pull the skin near your clitoris in just the right way to stimulate you to orgasm, and it may happen regularly for a small percentage of women—but not for most women most of the time. (p. 274)

Vaginismus is a sexual dysfunction that is rare but often quite painful. In this disorder, the muscles surrounding the vagina constrict strongly whenever something starts to penetrate the vagina. Intercourse is almost impossible, and a subconscious fear of intercourse due to a previous bad experience or strong anxiety is usually the cause (Masters and Johnson, 1970). Treatment for vaginismus is usually successful and involves relaxation exercises and then the gradual insertion of a finger or dilator, first by the woman, then by her partner. After a time, insertion of the penis is tried but with no attempt at orgasm. Only later is full coital sex play introduced.

Fear

Each of these sexual dysfunctions represents a different sexual problem, but the underlying condition is usually the same—fear. Whether the fear comes from past or present circumstances, or anxiety over the future, it cripples the individual's ability to interact sexually. Fear keeps the individual on guard and unable to relax enough to enjoy his or her own sensations, let alone to give pleasure lovingly to another.

Overcoming fear and anxiety can be achieved by affectionate and cooperative interaction between the partners and by competent therapists who guide the couple to a mutual understanding of one another's sexual needs. Unfortunately, most so-called "sex therapists" are not sufficiently trained to be of much use to most couples and they frequently raise more anxieties than they cure (Koch and Koch, 1976). But the major problem for any couple, whether currently dysfunctioning or not, is to continue to develop their relationship. Sexual boredom, as one recent writer put it, is a constant threat to relational satisfaction (Murray, 1977). How a couple continues to inject new excitement is up to them, but the variety of sexual techniques and stimulants available is almost endless. Whatever is selected and accepted by both partners is without doubt being practiced by many other couples as well. McCary puts it this way: "Some people prefer vanilla ice cream; others prefer chocolate: the rationale is the same" (p. 323).

Summary

Until quite recently, a general lack of knowledge has prevailed in the area of sexual intimacy. Men and women often did not realize their own personal needs, let alone those of their partners. Although the opposite appears to be true today, it is still difficult for many people to communicate sexually with one another.

Although some of our sexual behavior has a physiological basis, most of our sexual actions and desires are influenced by learning. Our sexual identity begins to develop even when we are infants. As children, the physical contact we experience, the feelings we develop about our bodies, and the ability to communicate our emotions to others all affect our ability to form intimate relationships later in life. Cultural definitions of appropriate and inappropriate behavior play a major role in defining our attitudes about sexual expression.

Various responses may result from sexual arousal but the cycle of sexual response usually passes through four stages: excitement, plateau, orgasm, and resolution. Each of these is associated with physiological changes, yet all blend together in a natural but not necessary progression.

While sexual intimacy is often associated with heterosexual sexual intercourse, there are many ways to express sexuality, including sexual communication, petting, and a variety of ways of performing sexual intercourse. Extramarital sexual interaction is not uncommon and usually occurs in clandestine relationships.

Although sex is generally seen as a highly pleasurable activity, there are several areas of growing concern. The first of these is venereal disease, which in spite of available protective measures, is increasing in incidence. Sexual dysfunctions are also a problem for many individuals and couples. These are often caused by an emotional problem which results in an inability to respond to the sexual partner.

SUGGESTIONS FOR ADDITIONAL READING

Diamond, Milton, and Arno Karlen. *Sexual Decisions.* Boston: Little, Brown, 1980.
This is an excellent basic text on human sexuality. For those who want more detailed sexual information, this is a good, up-to-date source.

Gagnon, John H. *Human Sexualities.* Glenview, Ill.: Scott, Foresman, 1977.
This book provides excellent coverage of the social-psychological aspects of sexuality. This is developed around the theme of "sexual scripts," learned patterns of sexual development, and expression.

Gordon, Sol, and Roger W. Libby (eds.). *Sexuality Today and Tomorrow.* North Scituate, Mass.: Duxbury, 1976.
A variety of authors have contributed to this anthology on sexual issues and behavior. This is a good source of information on variations in sexual expression.

Hite, Shere. *The Hite Report.* New York: Dell, 1976.
This nationwide best-seller is based on a survey of sexual feelings by over 3000 women. It very explicitly describes the sexual needs and frustrations of many American women.

Scoresby, A. Lynn. *The Marriage Dialogue.* Reading, Mass.: Addison-Wesley, 1977, Chapter 4.

The chapter on sexual communication in this book is very helpful in describing some of the problems couples have communicating sexually as well as some of the solutions to these problems.

Zilbergeld, Bernie. *Male Sexuality.* Boston: Little, Brown, 1978.
This is one of the first comprehensive books to explore the subject of male sexuality. Everything from sexual physiology to sexual problems is discussed.

Chapter 10

Companionship in Leisure

If there is one word that most characterizes the nature of the contemporary American family, it is probably **companionship.** The desire of men and women, husbands and wives, to spend their leisure time together is evidence of a major new priority in marital relationships today. Separate interests still remain the basis for some relationships, and most couples allow each partner to engage in independent interests also, but the expectation to share experiences has become a vital component in the majority of marriages. This emphasis on joint leisure interests is so pervasive that Burgess and Locke over thirty years ago titled their textbook on family change *The Family: From Institution to Companionship* (1945).

Today, the importance of companionship is well recognized. "The family that plays together, stays together," is a slogan that has been picked up by numerous recreation and family organizations. The majority of American men and women apparently agree with this too. One study found that both men and women ranked affection and companionship highest on a list of nine goals for marriage (Levinger, 1964). When asked what they considered to be important for a good marriage, a national sample ranked such things as liking the same kind of life and activities much higher than having children and financial security (Roper, 1974). In another study, three-fourths of the husbands and wives sampled considered the sharing of family recreation very important to them (Carlson, 1976). Data like this support the contention of researchers Blood and Wolfe (1960) that "when modern Americans think of marriage, they think of companionship more than anything else" (p. 150).

What is it about shared leisure experiences that has led to this kind of endorsement of companionship today? Is it really necessary for couples to spend some of their free moments together? What effect do separate interests and activities have on a relationship? Do our needs for companionship typically change over the family life cycle? The answers to these important questions are beginning to come in from research studies. In this chapter, we will carefully examine these issues in hopes of better understanding the roles that leisure time and activities play in the process of relational development.

THE CHANGING ROLE OF COMPANIONSHIP IN THE FAMILY

The Preindustrial Period

Companionship preferences

When we look back into American history, we find that companionship between men and women has not always been preferred or expected. Prior to industrialization, the roles of men and women were quite different. Marital partners were selected not because they shared similar interests but because each needed the skills the other could bring into the marriage. This was a time when hard work for long hours was necessary merely to stay alive.

When companionship was desired, the preference at that time was for same-sex companions. Men shared in the interests of other men; women shared in the interests of other women. Even when families came together for church or picnics or other social events, the usual custom was for the men and women to separate upon arrival into different activities. Children learned very early to participate in the activities appropriate to their own sex.

But even though these clear preferences for sex-defined activities predominated, it would be a mistake to conclude that marital and family companionship was uncommon. The isolation of rural households, the necessity for cooperation in many tasks, and the sheer proximity of family members during times when work demands had relaxed made the sharing of pleasant moments together a normal occurrence. The work was hard, but the work ethic at that time did not forbid family play as much then as it did later (Meyer and Brightbill, 1964). Doing things together, usually in work but sometimes in play, was an important source of family solidarity.

The Early Industrial Period

Family separated

With the growth of industrialization, a much clearer separation between work, leisure, and the family evolved in the United States. Not only did the roles of men and women remain different, but for the first time, family members were separated from one another for long periods of time, each and every week. Men had little time to spend with their families, let alone in leisure by themselves. The source of a man's personal identity also shifted away from the family toward the job. Men relied more on work associates for their sense of self-worth, and companionship with their wives and families declined in importance.

By the 1920s, when the Lynds reported on a study of Middletown, U.S.A., they were able to write: "In general, a high degree of companionship is not regarded as essential for marriage. There appears to be between Middletown husbands and wives of all classes when gathered together in informal leisure-time groups relatively little spontaneous community of interest" (1929, p. 118). In the 1930s, William F. Ogburn's report to the President's Research Committee on Social Trends (1934) concluded that the recreational function which the family used to provide was declining rapidly, even during the Depression when one-quarter of the labor force was unemployed.

The Recent Industrial Period

More leisure time

Ogburn's prediction that the family would lose its recreational function has not come to pass. By the 1950s and 1960s, the free time available to families had markedly increased and new values supporting leisure and marital companionship were becoming widely accepted. Part of the reason for this development was an increase in the quantity of leisure time (see Fig. 10.1). A reduction in the length of workweek to about forty hours, longer paid vacations, and more three-day weekends once again gave families time to be together. A higher standard of living and more discretionary income further enlarged the recreational opportunities of this increased time.

New leisure attitudes

Coupled with a growing availability of leisure time has been a change in our attitudes toward work and leisure. The belief that "idle hands are the devil's workshop" is waning, and society is taking a more favorable attitude toward leisure. Recently, Daniel Yankelovich (1978), a national survey researcher, reported that when work and leisure are compared as sources of personal satisfaction, only one out of five people (20 percent) states that work

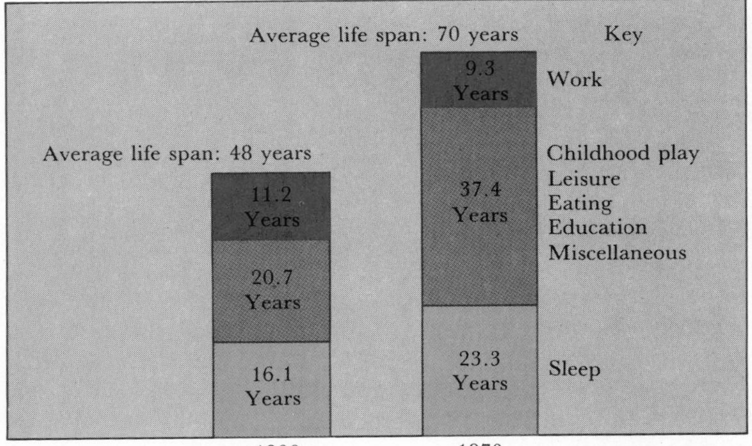

Fig. 10.1

Years Spent on Life Activities

These charts show how human life span has lengthened and how the amount of time each person spends on different activities has changed.

Source: Adapted from Best (1978), p. 124.

means more to them than leisure. A majority of Americans (60 percent) say that while they enjoy their work, it is not their major source of satisfaction.

The family has reaped many of the benefits of this reorientation toward leisure. Much more of the newly available time is spent with family members than with others (Davey and Paolucci, 1980). Husbands and wives are also more likely to prefer one another for companionship rather than their respective friends or kin, which is a change from earlier days. Since workers now spend less time on their jobs, and occupational advancement and geographical moves frequently separate friends and kin, marital partners can rarely depend on anyone besides each other to share their leisure interests consistently. Perhaps this is why among a representative sample of Detroit area wives, 60 percent picked companionship as "the most valuable aspect of marriage." Much smaller percentages picked the chance to have children (13 percent), the husband's understanding (13 percent), love and affection (11 percent), or their standard of living (3 percent) (Duncan *et al.*, 1973).

Work ethic

The potential benefits of leisure have not been realized for all families, however. Nearly one-fourth of the husbands and wives in the labor force still work over forty hours per week, and among professionals and executives, workweeks of fifty to sixty hours are not uncommon (Hedges, 1976). Another 5 percent of the labor force is employed in two jobs (Brown, 1977). For these and many others as well, a work orientation to life remains. Not only does this limit the possibilities of leisure, but available leisure often becomes worklike. Working at play has become the norm for many. Vacations are planned to the smallest detail. Weekends are an endless string of "things to do." Even sex, as Lewis and Brisset (1967) found in their study of "sex as work," can be defined in terms of schedules, "operational objectives," and techniques. According to Alexander Reid Martin:

> The complete inability to relax even for a moment is a common complaint and evidence of neurotic disturbance. The widespread and characteristic symptoms of our so-called age of anxiety stem from a fear of relaxation and leisure. This reaches its most intense expression in many individuals who are unable to take vacations, in those who are beset by severe after-work irritability, and in those who suffer from what is called the "Sunday neurosis." (In Orthner, 1975b, p. 176).

THE NATURE OF LEISURE AND COMPANIONSHIP

Leisure as resource

While the amount of leisure time available to individuals and families may be increasing, the effect of leisure on a relationship can still vary a great deal. Leisure is not the same thing as companionship although it increases the chance that companionship will occur. By itself, leisure is a *resource,* like money or a car. Whether we define leisure as free time, a set of activities, or a relaxed state of mind, it is not inherently good or bad for relationships. Some couples may spend much of their leisure time together, others may not. Some leisure activities may contribute to the cohesiveness of a relationship, others may not. Sometimes the leisure preferences of a couple are similar, for others they are not. These three leisure elements—time, activities, and preferences—greatly affect the style of companionship in a relationship.

Leisure Time

Certainly, one of the most important elements of leisure is **time.** Free time, that which is not bound by obligations, is especially crucial for personal or relational development. It takes time to relax from the rigors of the day. It takes time to open up to friends and family. It takes time to resolve conflicts that arise. It takes time for individuals or families to experience the *re-creation* that is implied in the word "recreation."

During courtship, dating couples usually try to spend as much time together as possible. This time allows them to reveal themselves to one

Shared leisure time may be reflected in a couple's understanding of each other.

Leisure and communication

another, to consider their own needs as well as those of the other person. The more time that is spent together, research studies point out, the more likely the courtship is to lead to a successful marriage.

Among husbands and wives, time shared together can also be important. In one recent study of middle-class marriages, it was found that the more leisure time that was shared, the more the husband and wife felt they understood one another (Orthner, 1976). Not only was the overall marital communication better in these marriages, but the shared leisure experiences appeared to be particularly important for communication in the early years of marriage, the period that requires the most adjustments.

Loneliness

Many husbands and wives find that work time and commitments are a major consumer of their potential leisure time. As work involvements increase, the time given to marital companionship is more likely to drop than the time given to other household or child-rearing responsibilities (Clark *et al.*, 1978). This is most often a problem for wives, as studies of the families of professional and corporate executives have discovered. In Robert Seidenburg's (1973) report titled *Corporate Wives—Corporate Casualties,* he found "loneliness" to be a common problem among the wives of executives, a situation often created by an absence of time shared with their husbands.

Employment of the wife can also reduce leisure time together (Jorgenson, 1977) but the consequences for the marriage do not appear to be as negative. Because employed wives are more likely to spend a higher proportion of their available leisure time with their husbands, overall companionship suffers very little (Orthner and Axelson, 1980). Also, husbands of employed wives are less likely to feel a need to overwork, and they are more likely to consider their wives good companions (Axelson, 1970).

Leisure Activities

Leisure-interaction patterns

While the time available to the relationship is important, equally important to companionship are the types of leisure activities in which the couple engage. Not all leisure-time activities affect relationships in the same way. In particular, it appears that it is the *interaction* that occurs during an activity that most affects the communication and relational cohesiveness of the participants. Obviously, some activities permit more interaction than others. For example, playing a game usually requires interaction while running discourages interaction. But rather than look at the relational effects of specific activities, we can identify three leisure-interaction patterns that have different potential consequences for relationships. These are joint, individual, and parallel activities.

Joint activities are the kinds of activities we most associate with companionship. These activities, such as game playing, visiting, camping, or just talking together, require interaction among the participants. While activities like these are often idealized, some families do have more joint participation than others. Lois Pratt (1976), in a study of 273 marriages, found that the

Table 10.1

Frequency of Marital Participation in Selected Joint Activities

Activity	Often (%)	Occasionally (%)	Never (%)	Total (%)
Sit around and talk	65	32	3	100
Joke together	55	40	5	100
Go for a pleasure drive in a car	45	43	12	100
Visit relatives	41	54	5	100
Visit friends	37	56	7	100
Attend church	40	34	26	100
Go to parties	9	67	24	100
Play cards	7	32	61	100
Attend sports events	5	29	66	100

Sample: Random sample of 273 couples.

Source: From *Family Structure and Effective Health Behavior: The Energized Family* by Lois Pratt.

majority of couples had a moderate amount of joint activity, a few had a large amount, and some had practically none at all. The degree to which these couples participated together in several selected joint activities is listed in Table 10.1.

Increased understanding

The primary advantage of joint activities comes from their enhancement of interpersonal communication. Being with a person in an activity which is different from the normal day-to-day routine allows new insights into that person's needs and interests. Not only does this increase understanding, but the shared leisure experience allows the release of normal pressures and tension, the opportunity to share frustrations, and the time to deal with problems that may have arisen elsewhere.

This sense of solidarity, however, is increased by more than just the experience of the shared activity. In many cases, a great deal of *planning* and preparation is done before the activity is even started. The family that plants a garden together may spend weeks deciding what will be grown, where it should be located, and what procedures need to be followed. After the activity, the process of *recollection* often reinforces the cohesiveness of the family and opens the communication of the members to new opportunities for interaction.

Marital satisfaction

There is a growing body of evidence that participation in joint activities can have positive consequences for relationships. Social-psychologist Irving Goffman (1961) concluded from his research observations that "shared spontaneous involvement in a mutual activity often brings the sharers into some kind of exclusive solidarity and permits them to express relatedness, psychic closeness, and mutual respect" (p. 40). In a study of 451 randomly selected husbands and wives, it was found that marital-satisfaction scores were significantly higher among couples who spent more time together in joint activities

(Orthner, 1975a). This was particularly true during the first few years of marriage and during the years when the children were leaving home, times when relational adjustments are often most crucial.

A second pattern of leisure activity, **individual activity,** is carried out alone. Since this requires no interaction at all, it is basically noncompanionate. But for the individuals involved, activities like reading, running, or private contemplation can have considerable benefit. They allow the individual to relax, to contemplate, to refresh, or to rebuild his or her own personal energy.

Recuperation

In moderation, individual activities do not necessarily hinder companionship. Robert M. MacIver, a noted sociologist, has observed that periods of private reflection are not unlike the creative intimacy often experienced in close relationships (see Vignette 10.1). They can also help the individual to recuperate before entering into a shared activity that will require more emotional and social investments. But sometimes, when individual activities begin

Vignette 10.1 Privacy and Intimacy

No doubt humans are social animals, but we also need times of seclusion and withdrawal. Without the sustainment of society we are lost, and long-continued solitude, whether the solitary confinement of the prisoner or the voluntary renunciation of the hermit, dehumanizes, and crazes the mind. But the lack of privacy, the inability to escape at intervals from the presence and scrutiny of one's friends, also have a pernicious effect.

Everyone needs occasions for quiet reflection, for free meditation or silent reverie, occasions for self-assessment, for the sheer detachment in which we are free from all vigilant eyes. We need times when we are not deflected by the presence of others, when we can better repossess ourselves.

There are two degrees of privacy. One is seclusion, where persons can be at one with themselves, in the "society where none intrudes." The other is intimacy, where close personal relations, confidences, the give and take of friends, the uninhibited exchange of thoughts, the ways of affection and of love, are safe from intrusion or control. Both degrees of privacy are essentially alike for the enjoyment of living and for the evocation of the qualities of humanity.

In times when life was less complicated, the privacy of solitude was easy to attain. Most everyone carried on their work, or part of their work, by themselves, not on assembly lines or in some great barrack of office workers. When individuals were so inclined they could think their own thoughts.

Nor were opportunities for intimacy lacking. The household might be narrow and congested with children and relatives. But the evenings were long and the light of the candle was dim and, without, all was darkness. Neighborly groups could meet around the hearth and lovers steal quietly into the embracing woodlands or the deserted fields.

In the far Hebridean Island where my early youth was passed, the people of the villages scattered along the bays or on the moorlands had to to dominate a relationship, interpersonal communication and role flexibility are substantially reduced. This tends to encourage each person to develop his or her own separate world with its own satisfactions.

In one study, it was found that the higher the participation in individual activities, the more likely the marriage was considered unsatisfactory (Orthner, 1975a). In another study, high individual-activity use was linked to low marital communication, and in the early years of marriage, to low marital role sharing (Orthner, 1976). Low to moderate amounts of individual activity did not affect marital satisfaction, communication, or role sharing. In both studies, however, the wives were most likely to be affected negatively by higher amounts of individual activities. This may be because they felt they needed more interaction with their husbands and were not getting it.

In between individual and joint activities is a third leisure pattern, **parallel activities.** These are shared activities that require practically no

---

depend upon themselves for entertainment. They had an institution called the *ceilidh* (pronounced, more or less, kay-lee). Congenial neighbors would foregather at nightfall in one of the thatched cottages, dropping in casually, sitting on low benches or squatting around the peat fire that occupied the center of the clay floor and sent its yellow flicker into the dim-lit room. The hum of casual gossip would gradually change into a sustained discussion. The theme might be the deeds of yore, or the strange ways of the sea, or the manifestations of the gift of second-sight, or the apparitions that haunted the lochs or the moors.

Whatever it was, it engrossed the little group, stirring their imaginations and arousing in them visions of wonder and power and pity and terror. They let their thoughts ride far beyond the everyday existence. Outside there was the beat of the surf or the quiet drop of the persistent rain. Within there was the intimacy of the give and take that unites the pleasure of being social with the pleasure of mind-free discourse . . .

The more organized we become, the more our society hems us in, the more we require preserves of privacy. We need to guard our times of leisure in order to cultivate, now and then, the mood of meditation. We need the privacy of the hearth, the privacy of our more intimate relationships. We need the openness of friendly discourse where we do not merely gossip about others but instead give free rein to our surmises about the nature of things. Then we may keep our hearts from being entangled in the tightening web of organization. Then we may find enough of our proper autonomy to make good in the business of living.

From Robert M. MacIver, *The Pursuit of Happiness* (New York: Simon and Schuster, 1955), pp. 41–43, 49. (Adapted to remove gender-specific language.)

Couples who prefer to "go their own ways" in leisure pursuits are more likely to be unsatisfied with their marriage.

interaction among the participants. In some ways they are like individual activities in a group setting. The couple spending the evening at the theater or watching television or reading in the same room are being independently affected, often with little or no conversation. In fact, should someone want to talk, this may lead to retorts like "wait until the commercial" or ". . . half-time," or ". . . the end of this chapter."

Television

Parallel activities, particularly television watching, have become a major leisure outlet in America. A recent study found that about one-half of all the free time of adult men and women is now given over to the mass media—watching television, listening to the radio, or reading newspapers and magazines. And television consumes more of this time than all of these others combined (Robinson, 1978). Like individual activities, these parallel pursuits provide personal relaxation and development, but they also provide a sense of "togetherness" with minimal responsibility for communication. Some years ago, one sociologist commented that TV was transforming the family from a "social group characterized by conversation to an audience . . . silently gazing" (McDonagh, 1950, p. 122).

In spite of the dire predictions of ill consequences to the family, there is little evidence that parallel activities like TV watching are basically harmful to relationships. The author's own research studies have found that participation in parallel activities has very little effect at all on most marriages, and in the middle years of marriage, may even be positively related to marital satisfaction and communication (Orthner, 1975a, 1976). Rosenblatt and Cunningham (1976) have found that television watching is related to lower amounts of overt family conflict. Apparently, parallel activities have the advantage of placing people in proximity to one another; at least then they are available for communication, although the opportunities may be limited. If parallel activities do cause problems, it is probably because some families may prefer a more open style of communication and activity, but instead, they become dependent on parallel pursuits that limit their relational development (Rosenblatt *et al.*, 1979).

Leisure Preferences

Favorite activities

When people are asked what they want to do with their leisure time, it is not surprising to find that their preferences often differ from their actual behavior. For example, while we noted earlier that about one-fourth of the free time of adults is spent watching television, the proportion who say that this is one of their favorite activities is quite small. In one study of over 200 marriages, very few wives picked television watching as one of their five favorite leisure activities. And while husbands were more likely to prefer to watch television, only 22 percent of them said this activity is one of their favorites (Mancini and Orthner, 1978). A listing of the most-preferred activities by these husbands and wives is found in Table 10.2.

When we compare the personal-leisure preferences of husbands and wives, we find that some of their interests are the same but most are different.

Table 10.2

The Most Frequently Cited Recreational Preferences among Husbands and Wives

Husbands	Wives
1. Attending athletic events	1. Reading books
2. Reading books	2. Sewing for pleasure
3. Golf	3. Entertaining
4. Watching television	4. Visiting friends and family
5. Fishing	5. Creative cooking
6. Just relaxing	6. Attending church
7. Playing with children	7. Attending athletic events

Sample: Random sample of 227 wives and 218 husbands.

Source: Jay A. Mancini and Dennis K. Orthner, "Recreational Sexuality Preferences among Middle-Class Husbands and Wives," *Journal of Sex Research* 14 (1978): 100.

This means that companionship often requires compromises in personal preferences. We do something because our partner wants to do it in exchange for our partner sometimes doing what we want to do. When leisure preferences are similar and this kind of negotiation is less necessary, then there tends to be more satisfaction in the marriage (Gerson, 1960). But it is quite normal in most relationships for some leisure preferences to be different.

Leisure conflicts

Conflicts over leisure interests are not uncommon in marriage. Whether to go to the mountains or the seashore is the proverbial stalemate, but these vacation disagreements are minor compared to those regularly initiated by the wife who feels "widowed" by her husband's weekend golf or the husband who feels deserted by his wife's evening bridge club. Carlson (1976) found that only one-fourth of the Washington-state families he studied could report that they never had disagreements over their leisure interests. Another one-fourth of these families experienced regular conflicts over their leisure. Only child-rearing practices were a more consistent source of marital strain for the families in his research.

Similar interests

Similarity in companionate leisure preferences is much more common in the earlier years of a relationship. In dating, couples usually submerge their respective leisure interests in favor of common interests, a situation which continues into the first few years of marriage. When couples who had been married for up to five years were asked about their leisure preferences, three-fourths of both the husbands and the wives said they most preferred being in a joint leisure activity with their spouse. Among those who had been married longer, however, the percentages who preferred joint-spouse activities were considerably lower. When those married for more than thirty-five years were queried, four out of ten of the husbands and six out of ten of the wives said they most preferred spending their leisure time in an individual or parallel activity (Mancini and Orthner).

Morning and night people

Another factor that may account for some of the similarities and differences in leisure preferences has been called **circadian rhythms.** These are daily rhythms of time that affect opportunities for and attitudes toward joint activity. Adams and Cromwell (1978) have been examining these rhythms, particularly in terms of "morning" people and "night" people. Their research is preliminary at this time, but their initial findings indicate that individuals can usually identify themselves in terms of a morning or night preference. These preferences tend to be associated with characteristics that affect the interactional qualities of a relationship. For example, morning people report that they arise early, do not like to stay up late, experience an energy peak early in the day, and prefer physical, outdoor activities. Night people say they arise with difficulty, like to stay up late, have their energy peak later in the day, and prefer an active night life to quiet activities.

Adams and Cromwell found that couples who were matched in their morningness or nightness were more likely to share common interests and experience fewer marital conflicts. The mismatched couples reported more strain, were more dissatisfied with their marriages, and were more likely to feel that their lack of togetherness was a principal problem in their marriage.

The authors of this study are careful to say, however, that sometimes couples who are having conflicts will deliberately set up their schedules to avoid one another. Thus, the poorer relational adjustment among the mismatched couples may not always be caused by their leisure preferences, but their leisure preferences may be the result of their poor adjustment. While the findings of this study should be interpreted cautiously at this time, it may be that research on circadian rhythms will be very important for understanding companionship in the future.

COMPANIONSHIP LIFE-STYLES

Stable patterns

While individuals have a variety of options for their leisure time, there is a tendency for most relationships to develop a fairly stable pattern of leisure interests. In terms of particular activities, leisure routines may include such things as Saturday golf, Sunday church, a Wednesday-evening television show, or Thursday-afternoon tennis. Yet, even broader than this is the style of companionship that characterizes a relationship. For example, in some relationships, every opportunity is taken to share time together; in others, there are few expectations for leisure time to be shared.

Joint Companionship

First of all, there are companionate relationships which tend to be dominated by jointly shared leisure interests and activities. The emphasis on interaction during leisure supports intrinsic commitments in these relationships. Separate interests may be permitted too, but only to the extent that they contribute to the vitality of the relationship, not take away from it.

Friendships

Marital friendships are often an important part of joint companionship. Among the middle-class couples studied by Babchuk (1965), half of them shared all their closest friends. These friendships especially enrich joint relationships since so many of their leisure interests do not include others. Friends introduce new ideas and new perspectives into the relationship that can be quite helpful and stimulating. This may be the reason why marital satisfaction tends to be higher among couples who visit more with close friends and relatives (Renne, 1970).

As a life-style, joint companionship is almost exclusively found in the middle class where more egalitarian role expectations and values of "togetherness" receive the most support. In the middle class, couples and nuclear families are permitted more independence, which is necessary for joint companionship. As Bott (1971) found in her research, when kin ties remain the primary bond for the individual, joint companionship is difficult to achieve.

Middle-class values

While the values of the middle class may support joint companionship, this life-style of shared leisure interests still tends to be associated with young, childless couples. Rollins and Feldman (1970) found that the number of companionate activities in marriage dropped by half after the first child was born. Other studies have found a similar drop (Orthner, 1975a). Thus, joint companionship is a rather fragile life-style and very dependent on there being few competing obligations. When responsibilities increase, time shared together declines and it is more difficult to maintain the intensity of companionship that was possible in courtship and early marriage. The couples who are most likely to continue their joint companionate life-style over time are those who are childless (Ramey, 1976) or those in dual-career marriages (Orthner and Axelson, 1980). In these marriages, there is more likelihood that the husband-wife relationship will remain more egalitarian.

Parallel Companionship

A second companionship pattern we can identify is the parallel life-style. These relationships are dominated by shared, parallel activities. Among some couples, parallel companionship is fostered by a desire to "be together," yet with few real interests in common, joint activities are minimized. Among others, companionship with the partner is not really desired but it is all that is left since the funds or friends to go out with are limited. These relationships usually experience some joint companionship, principally casual conversation, some visiting, and playing with children. But the dominant leisure activities are things like watching TV, going to the movies, or reading.

Television watching

The best example of parallel companionship is the television family. The average family TV set in America is on from six to seven hours per day (Rosenblatt and Cunningham). But in some families, the set is turned on first thing in the morning and off only before retiring at night—it is a constant companion throughout the day.

The pervasive draw of the television was recently demonstrated by a Detroit *Free Press* study (Grzech and Trost, 1978). This newspaper approached 120 families with an offer of $500 if they would agree to do without television for thirty days. The editors were surprised to find that ninety-three of these families turned down the offer without second thoughts. "My husband would never do it," one woman observed. "He comes home from work and sits down in front of the TV. He gets up twice—once to eat and once to go to bed."

The Detroit paper ultimately picked five families to participate in their "experiment." What they found was not surprising. In most of the families, conversation and sexual relations were more frequent, but conflict and tension also increased. These families were simply not used to talking and playing with one another, let alone dealing with the conflicts they had. A larger study by Rosenblatt and Cunningham confirms the anesthetizing influence of TV on family conflict. These researchers found that as family size increased, family tension also increased. But if television watching increased as well, then conflicts between family members did not rise. The tensions

In many families, television acts as a tranquilizer, minimizing communication of conflict.

remained, but they were not communicated and resolved. Commenting on the relationship between television watching and family communication, Vince Rue (1974) observes: "A simple behavioral circle might be constructed on the basis of these studies and others; the more we watch, the less we talk; the less we talk, the more we need to watch (p. 74)."

Blue-collar marriages

In the working class, parallel companionship is very common. In her study of blue-collar marriages, Komarovsky (1964) found that the primary leisure interest of both husbands and wives was watching television. Nationwide, as the level of education and income go down, television watching tends to go up (Robinson, 1978). A major reason for television addiction among these blue-collar families is that they sometimes have only a small circle of good friends and they often lack common interests (see Vignette 10.2).

Children

Still, middle-class families are not immune from the parallel life-style. As commitments to work and children increase, joint leisure interests frequently subside in favor of the passive togetherness of parallel pursuits. Children have an especially strong influence on the television habits of a family; families with children watch much more TV than families without children. In the United

Vignette *10.2* Social Life in Glenton: A Blue-Collar Community

In Glenton, joint social life with friends is far from being the important leisure-time pursuit that it is in higher socioeconomic classes. This applies to exchanges of home visits as well as to joint visits to public recreational places. . . . Even those who maintain social relations with other couples have a very small circle of friends. For one-half of them this circle consists of only one or two couples. Only 17 percent see as many as four or more different couples in the course of a year (included in this count are couples seen at least a few times a year).

When asked, the respondents attribute their meager social life to lack of money and other external obstacles. At first glance this explanation appears sufficient. In comparison with the middle classes, the poorer couples can hardly afford the cost of coffee and cake for their guests, much less a theater or a restaurant. Moreover, the working wives and their husbands often dovetail their work-shifts in such a way that they have little free time together. The cost of baby-sitters is prohibitive and, apart from the cost, strangers are not trusted in this role and relatives are not always available. Some families are newcomers to the community and attribute their lack of friends to that fact.

But there are other impediments to social life in Glenton. Opportunities of enlarging the circle of friends are limited when social life is confined to two or three couples and when the husband's job neither requires social entertaining nor serves as a source of new contacts. The friendships that these families enjoy have often been acquired in school. Because the choice of friends is made within so small a group, the chances of finding congenial persons are relatively small. A couple may lack social life simply because a husband does

---

States, preschool children watch an average of over fifty hours of TV per week (Rue). Since children often increase the potential for family conflicts, the TV is apparently used as a tension reducer and "baby sitter" in many homes. And since the children have turned the set on, the adults join in and quickly find themselves locked into this medium, too. The end result is less talking among family members (Brady *et al.*, 1980).

Segregated Companionship

Separate interests

A third leisure life-style is segregated companionship. In these relationships, individual activities and companionship with others outside the relationship predominate. Families of this type reflect the traditional, industrial family model with the husband and wife sharing few roles and little leisure time, each participating primarily with his or her own circle of friends and kin. The marriage or the family becomes little more than a meeting point for separate interests and members seem like "ships passing in the night."

not like the wife's girl friend or her husband. Occasionally the husband gives a similar explanation—his wife does not like the woman his buddy married and hence they do not meet as a foursome.

But while external obstacles may limit social life, a favorable external situation does not necessarily ensure it. A pattern of joint social participation must exist before a family avails itself of propitious circumstances. The weaker the interest in social life, the more easily will it be dissipated by even a slight hindrance. A few of our respondents appear hardly aware of the pattern of entertaining nonrelatives at home. Thus, an older woman said that such a custom may have existed in the past but must have gone out of fashion because no one she knew followed it.

Lack of common interests between men and women is another deterrent to joint social life. In the words of one woman, "Jane (her girl friend) doesn't know what to talk to men about and Jane's husband doesn't know what to talk to women about."

Where the pattern of joint social life is firmly established, marital strain does not preclude an active social life. The fiction of marital solidarity is maintained in public, and social life may even provide a welcome escape from the emptiness of marriage. But in these working-class families a reasonably satisfactory marriage appears to be a necessary condition of joint social life. Because separate social life is accepted, it takes very little to tip the scale in its favor.

From Mirra Komarovsky, *Blue-Collar Marriage* (New York: Random House, 1964), pp. 311–313.

For many individuals, segregated companionship is an accepted life-style (Rosenblatt *et al.*). Different reference groups pull at different members of the family and common friendships are rare. The husband has his friends and associates, often tied to his work; the wife has her friends and associates, usually tied to the neighborhood or kin network; and the children go their own way with their own friends.

Among the lower-educated, blue-collar families Komarovsky (1964) interviewed, she found segregated companionship quite common: "Unless the couples play cards or watch TV, men and women form separate groups. Although questions were asked about this in every interview, only one woman expressed a concern about this segregation. One of her peeves, she said, is that people leave their TV on when they have company (p. 317)."

Work involvements

Middle- and upper-class families may also experience this style of companionship. Studies of the marriages of politicians (MacPherson, 1975), ministers (Douglas, 1965), and other professionals (Gerstl, 1961) indicate that many of these husbands become so involved in their work and activities with their work associates that this forces a segregated-companionship life-style on their marriage. In the postparental years, it has been found that marriages in which the wife is not employed also tend to be more segregated (Orthner and Axelson).

The question might be asked: Is one of these styles of companionship better than the others? An honest answer would be no, since any one of these can be quite stable and satisfactory to those who wish to live that way. There are advantages and disadvantages to each of these leisure life-styles. Joint companionship can be very rewarding to a couple who share many interests in common. Yet some couples reach the point of pathogenic togetherness in which neither person is given the freedom to grow or to develop new interests (Carisse, 1975). True, joint companionship permits more communication, but it sometimes brings more conflict as well. This may be the reason why societies with the highest joint marital companionship also have the highest divorce rates (Varga, 1972).

Gender-role differences

Parallel and segregated companionship may not represent the middle-class ideal, but they do reflect well the realities of gender-role differences in families of all social classes. Parallel companionship also represents that part of our society's orientation to spectate when you cannot allocate the time to participate. As long as role definitions are well understood, and needs for communication are minimal, then parallel and segregated companionship can fulfill personal and social needs for recreation. But as Rosenblatt and Russell (1975) have suggested, if you place these same family members who are normally insulated from one another into a car on a vacation trip, where they have to communicate to get along, then you can expect trouble. The skills needed to relate to one another over an extended period of time will not have been developed well enough to make this kind of close contact comfortable.

Summary

According to current surveys, companionship in leisure has become one of the most valued elements of American marriage. This has not always been the case, however. It was not until the 1950s and 1960s that the time available and values supporting companionship in leisure became more widespread.

Three elements of leisure that have a significant impact on the extent of companionship in a relationship are leisure time, leisure activities, and leisure preferences. Different leisure activities have different effects on relationships. Joint activities tend to increase interpersonal communication and provide a sense of relational cohesiveness. Individual activities are important for personal relaxation and development, but if they become the dominant leisure pattern, communication and relational satisfaction decline. Parallel activities provide a sense of togetherness but with few interpersonal obligations. The degree of similarity in leisure preferences also can affect the nature of relationships.

While dissatisfaction with leisure patterning in a relationship is not uncommon, it is normal for most couples eventually to establish a mutually acceptable style of companionship. Joint-companionate couples place a great deal of emphasis on interacting together during much of their leisure time. Parallel companionship is associated with shared parallel activities, principally television watching. Segregated companionship is dominated by individual interests and companionship with others outside the relationship.

SUGGESTIONS FOR ADDITIONAL READING

Carlson, John. "The recreation role in the family." In F. Ivan Nye (ed.), *Role Structure and Analysis of the Family.* New York: Sage, 1976.

This article examines the degree of importance given to recreation roles in families today. Since the entire book discusses other family roles as well, the reader can see how family recreation compares in importance with these other family roles.

Iso-Ahola, Seppo E. *The Social Psychology of Leisure and Recreation.* Dubuque, Iowa: Brown, 1980.

An excellent reference work on the concept of leisure and the way in which leisure time and activities affect peoples' lives.

MacIver, Robert M. *The Pursuit of Happiness.* New York: Simon & Schuster, 1955.

Written by a sociologist interested in social change, this book examines the classic American search for personal and relational happiness. The writer was way ahead of his time in foreseeing the continuing struggle of people to use their leisure to find this elusive quality of life.

Mancini, Jay A., and Dennis K. Orthner. "Recreational sexuality preferences among middle-class husbands and wives," *The Journal of Sex Research* 14 (May 1978): 96–106.

This research article examines husbands' and wives' perceptions of sex as play, but more broadly, it also compares other recreational preferences of men and women and how these change over time.

Orthner, Dennis K., and Jay A. Mancini, "Leisure behavior and group dynamics: the case of the family." In S. Iso-Ahola (ed.), *Social Psychological Perspectives of Leisure and Recreation.* Springfield, Ill.: Charles Thomas, 1980.

This chapter reviews the major research studies on leisure and family interaction. The effects of leisure on marital cohesion and marital conflict are carefully considered.

Szalai, Alexander. *The Use of Time.* Paris: Mouton, 1972.

In this book, the results of a major multinational study of time-use are presented. This is the best study to date comparing how American families use their time compared with families from other countries around the world.

Chapter 11

Relational Economics

The expression "You can't live on love" is commonly heard. Like other such reminders, it reflects the blunt realities of survival today in our economic world. It is easy to forget in our sometimes heady discussions about relational commitments and intimacy that these commitments usually cost something, not just in terms of personal freedom, but in terms of money, too.

In the early 1970s, this point was brought home quite dramatically to a class of high-school students in Portland, Oregon. A teacher was assigned a family-relations class and, rather than following the usual format of lecture and discussion over a planned series of topics, he decided to do something quite different. He started the class by pairing off the students and then holding a mock wedding—preacher and all. Each of the "couples" was then instructed to go into the community and find out what it would cost for a married couple to live. They were to look into all the expenses that would be necessary, including housing, food, insurance, medical, automobile, and other relevant items.

The results of this exercise were startling. The students were uniformly surprised at the financial costs of marriage. They were more likely to say that they were going to wait longer to marry than they were before the class had begun. Even some of those in the class who were engaged to marry broke off their engagements. It could be argued that this was a very narrow approach to the study of marriage, but it certainly focused in on one aspect of intimate relationships that is all too often neglected in serious discussions of relational development.

In this chapter, we will see that relational stress is very closely tied to financial stability and the ability of a family to meet their financial needs. We will also examine some of the economic objectives of families, look at how those objectives are frequently met, and consider some of the means by which families manage their financial resources. Before we consider these issues, however, it is important to understand the economic environment within which relationships must cope today.

THE ECONOMIC ENVIRONMENT

A Money Economy

Two hundred years ago, 95 percent of the people in America were tied to the land. Most of them consumed what they produced and traded for the other things that they needed. Money was needed at times because the nearby town store would not always accept corn or meat for payment. But by and large, the land that was owned and the crops that were produced defined one's worth and ability to survive.

Monetary flexibility

This situation has changed dramatically. Few people any longer can live off what they alone produce. It is currently fashionable to grow a garden and eat the fruits of one's labor, but it is the rare person who considers this more than a supplement to the food bought in the grocery. Today, we receive money for our labors and then allocate this money in the marketplace for the things we need and want. This allows us flexibility in our purchases, permits us to reflect in our spending the values we hold, and gives us the freedom to move from place to place.

Yet, money is more than just a means to an end, a medium of exchange used to purchase the essentials we need for survival and the nonessentials that make life enjoyable. Money has also become a reward in and of itself. Monetary income and personal assets are often used as evidence of success and competence. In a book written for family financial counselors, Feldman (1976) warns that money "is an instrument used in our society to calibrate the individual's character and functioning while at the same time shaping the person's self-perception of adequacy and worthwhileness. These perceptions in time have an impact on the effectiveness of the individual's social and economic functioning and on the quality of family life" (p. 3).

Money and power

Money has become a source of power. "Money talks," we hear, and all around us we see the evidence that influence increases with wealth. Even in marriage this is true. Research studies point out that a husband's power increases with his income (Cromwell and Olson, 1975). Wives are also more willing to allow their husbands more control and more independence if they "earn" it with dollars contributed to the household (Clark *et al.*, 1978). Among wives, their own power increases as well when they earn money. Employed women are much more likely to have a say in family financial matters and to expect to share in all the major decisions affecting their family (McDonald, 1977).

Economic Inequality

While all families use money to some degree, it is obviously more difficult for some families to spend at the same rate as others. Economic inequality is not new, but with the rising standard of living expected by most people today, it is more disheartening in many households than ever before. One hundred years ago, 75 percent of the wealth in the United States was held by 10 percent of the families (Miller, 1978). The rest of the families learned to live on what they had and shared common values about what they could realistically expect in their lives.

Today, the dreams of the "good life" are paraded in every media to every person of every age, whatever their economic station in life. The standard for this good life, as it is packaged by Madison Avenue, usually includes such elements as a private home, a car or two, color television, and stylish clothes. For people who can afford to purchase these things, they serve as an incentive to work and produce. But for many others, the gap between what they can earn and what they want is too wide.

Poverty

In a society that pumps up economic dreams, the poor often become frustrated with their financial situation. Unfortunately, this frustration is passed on, too. Odita and Janssens (1977) note, "People who are poor for a long time develop and transmit to their children certain common characteristics. Long-term poverty has been shown to produce in people a pattern of failure where hope, faith, and initiative are replaced by resentment, despair, and apathy" (p. 254).

Inflation

Whatever people's economic station in life, **inflation** represents a consistent threat to their current financial situation. Inflation means that the cost of the same goods and services available today will be higher tomorrow. An inflation rate of 7 to 14 percent per year has become common over the last decade, and this means that a family's income has had to rise at least that much in order to maintain the same standard of living.

Throughout most of the twentieth century, the inflation rate has been topped by increases in productivity and personal income. This means that American families have come to depend upon income increases that are higher than their losses through inflation. Today, **disposable income,** that which is left after taxes are paid, is higher than ever before. And, more important, families can consume three times as many goods and services with this income today than they could at the beginning of this century, while working only about half the hours that they did then.

Inflation problems

But in the last decade, **real economic growth** for families has slowed. Income increases have just barely kept up with inflation and this has led to economic frustration for many families. In a national survey of American families in the mid-1970s, 57 percent of the husbands and wives interviewed considered inflation to be the major barrier to their future family goals (Yankelovich *et al.*, 1975). This factor was mentioned much more frequently than any other potential barrier, including age, educational background, type of job, or size of the family. Inflationary pressures are also a major factor behind the rapidly rising employment of wives. While there are many women who prefer to be employed, no matter what their family's economic situation, more women are employed today for financial reasons rather than personal commitment to a job (Perucci and Targ, 1978).

Economic Ignorance

Unwise spending

One thing that makes it difficult for many people to cope with a changing economy is their lack of understanding of economic and financial matters. Considering how basic this is to personal and family well-being, there is surprising ignorance in this area. Many people get little value out of their hard-earned dollars simply because they do not know how to spend their money wisely. This is true at all income levels, but all too often, families with lower incomes spend more than affluent families for the same food, cars, furniture, and credit. This means that the real differences in their standards of living may be greater than their income differences would suggest.

A few years ago, a national study by the Education Commission of the United States discovered how serious the amount of consumer ignorance that exists really is (Miller, 1978). They found, for example, the following:

1. Eight out of ten Americans between the ages of twenty-five and thirty-six cannot balance a checkbook; only 1 percent of the seventeen-year-olds tested could balance a checkbook.
2. Fifty percent of those between the ages of twenty-five and thirty-six are unable to fill out a simple income-tax form without making a mistake.
3. Only half the adults and the seventeen-year-olds tested could correctly pick out the most economical box of a particular product based on the unit price.
4. Only 17 percent of the seventeen-year-olds and 20 percent of the adults could calculate a taxi fare correctly.

These statistics and the lack of consumer understanding they represent mean that many families are probably as frustrated by their feelings of helplessness in the economy as by their insufficient incomes. Consumer economist Roger Miller (1978) comments: "The age of the consumer is indeed upon us. Hopefully, the age of the informed consumer is not too far away" (p. 8).

Arguments over money

It is not too difficult to transfer stress from the larger economy to stress in relationships. Many studies of personal and marital satisfaction have come to the similar conclusion that money problems are a frequent source of conflict. In the national survey taken by Yankelovich *et al.* (1975), 54 percent of the families surveyed argued frequently about money. The arguments over money often covered many topics (see Table 11.1), but the most frequent specific quarrels concerned the need to economize, the need to stop wasting money, the need to meet unpaid bills, and the failure to keep track of where money goes.

This study also found that the families most likely to argue about money are those who are least well-off economically or those whose standard of living is declining. Younger families and families with children are also more likely to experience conflicts over money. Still, families with higher incomes do not always avoid money problems (see Vignette 11.1). Among families with incomes over $20,000 per year, nearly half of them complain that they argue about money (Yankelovich *et al.*).

Conflict over money cannot always be related to squabbles over the dollars and cents themselves. Money in this society is loaded with emotional overtones, and it may serve as a vehicle for the expression of more deep-seated marital and familial issues. Hunt (1970), for instance, suggests that conflict over money may be more of a symbol than a cause of marital problems. Like sex, money issues may be only the outer manifestation of something that runs far deeper—the need for power, independence, acceptance, love, or respect.

Differences in life-styles

Nevertheless, conflicts over money are not always a symptom of underlying emotionally charged issues. Quarrels about money can be an expression

Table 11.1

Arguments about Money*

Subject	Percentage
Money in general	59
Need for family to economize	47
Wasting money	42
Unpaid bills	38
Keeping track of where money goes	33
Saving for future	25
Borrowing money	17
Bad investment	10
Lending money	8

* Based on those who say they argue about money.

Source: Yankelovich *et al.*, 1975, p. 45. Courtesy of General Mills, Inc.

Vignette *II.1* The Cory Complex

Money, education, and success don't guarantee happiness. Most of us learned in school about Edward Arlington Robinson's Richard Cory, who had everything money could buy—and went home and put a bullet through his head. But most of us grew up skeptical about that poem and believed that if we had Richard Cory's looks, social position, and money, we'd be happy.

Now comes more evidence from a national survey of Americans that supports the poem. Angus Campbell, director of the University of Michigan's Institute for Social Research, wanted to know how income and education contribute to a person's sense of well-being. His survey asked people how satisfied they felt, and also how they regarded their lives—interesting or boring, enjoyable or miserable, and so on.

At first, Campbell and his colleagues rediscovered the wheel—the sense of well-being and happiness with life increases as people earn more money and get more education. But the chart below holds a few surprises. The happiest people in the country are those who did not finish high school, but who are earning more than $12,000 a year. Their accomplishments, says Campbell, outdistanced their expectations. College graduates, on the other hand, are not especially happy, no matter how much they earn. Although they are the happiest people in the lower-income categories, they are the least happy group among those who earn the highest amounts of money. Possibly the expectations of college grads have outdistanced their accomplishments.

Campbell accounts for white-collar complaints by comparing the different values that education brings. College graduates do not value money or economic security as highly as nongraduates do, and this is not just because they have them. Grads think that having an important or exciting life is more important than having a rich or secure one, and they care more about the psychological conditions of their jobs than the material ones. It is easier to measure economic successes or failures than psychological ones, so the college

of differences in preferred life-style as well. A husband, for example, may feel that the savings accumulated should be used for an extensive vacation. His wife's goal, on the other hand, is to purchase a larger home. Such conflicts in the goals of spouses are typical and indeed understandable when one considers the often-different expectations that each spouse brings to a marriage.

ECONOMIC OBJECTIVES: OBLIGATIONS AND OPTIONS

For a relationship to be economically stable, it must meet certain economic objectives. For example, a family must have shelter, it must have means for members to be transported to work or school, it must have adequate food, and

grads may have more trouble recognizing happiness when they stumble over it.

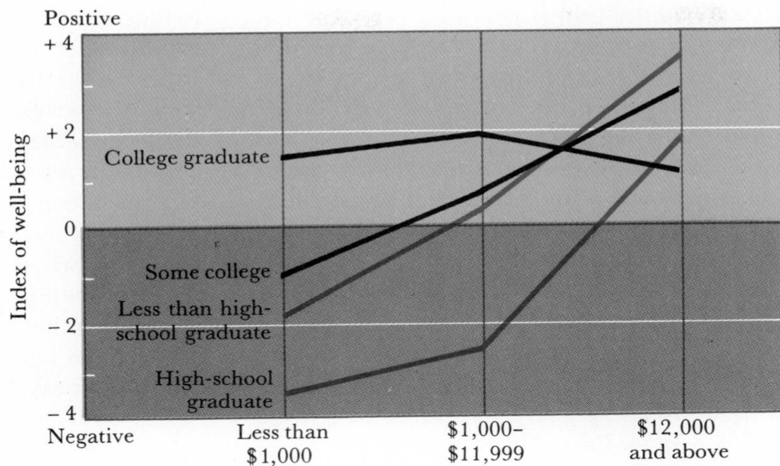

Index of Well-Being

Campbell observes that psychologists have been predicting for thirty-five years that the country would move into an era when the psychological needs of its citizens would supersede their financial needs. So it is important, he feels, to see what makes for well-being once people have the basics. If cars and microwave ovens and pots full of chicken don't make people happy, we'll have to search for the intangibles that will. Or we'll have a congeries of Corys.

it must somehow have insurance in case of the death of a member or the accidental destruction of the home. These are basic needs that have been obligations of families for a long time. Among some families, these obligations are shared with the community, but from whatever the source, it is expected that money will be allocated to meet these needs before more personal life-style expenditures are considered.

Necessities or luxuries?

The problem in many families is that the list of things considered to be economic objectives or "necessities" has grown dramatically. In a national survey of adult Americans, only one-fourth of them considered a color television, a second car, playing golf or tennis, or buying a new winter coat a "luxury" (Yankelovich *et al.*). By implication, the rest of the people surveyed must think that these things are very important, if not necessary. Yet the ability of families to acquire these and other things that have become part of the American standard of living frequently depends upon how financially astute they are when meeting the major economic objectives of their family.

Shelter

The need for shelter has always been a high priority for families. Frontier Americans built their own homes out of available materials as soon as they found a place to settle, hopefully before winter. We no longer do that. Instead, we use our money to buy or rent some type of home, whether it is an apartment, mobile home, condominium, modular home, or separate single-family house. For a middle-income family, the expense of a home will probably consume more of their take-home pay than any other single expense.

Housing costs

Nationally, housing costs amount to approximately 20 percent of a family's income after taxes—the proportion increasing with family income (McGraw, 1977). Many of these people, however, have been in their homes for some time and their housing costs have remained relatively stable while their incomes have risen. Young couples are not so fortunate and frequently must pay for the much higher costs of current housing with their lower initial incomes. For this reason, a recent study found that only 25 percent of the families in this country can now buy a home without government assistance (Gray, 1978).

While home ownership has been the preferred shelter option among most Americans, **renting** can be particularly suitable financially and socially for many. Renters have to place little of their savings into their home, they have fixed monthly payments with no surprise maintenance or repair bills, and, perhaps best of all in this mobile society, they have the flexibility to move quite easily when a new job or interest beckons.

Home as investment

Home ownership, in contrast, is more costly to begin with, but it brings to the home owner the psychological advantage of being recognized as a stable member of the community. Home owners have the freedom to remodel their house; they can deduct from their income taxes the interest on the loan and the property taxes they pay; and they can also watch their home increase in value as an investment while their mortgage payments stay the same.

It would not be a good idea to look at a home strictly from the investment point of view, however. Many studies have found that if a typical family who rents a home can put into savings the equivalent of a house down payment and monthly add the difference between renting and owning a home, they will have increased their investment *more* than if they had bought a home (Miller, 1978). Nevertheless, for those who find it difficult to save, purchasing a home can be one way to set up a forced savings plan.

Household Needs

Unlike a home, most other household expenses do not have the potential for increasing in value. But items like food, clothing, and home furnishings are necessary nonetheless. On any scale of human needs, certainly food and clothing are high-priority items. And even people in more primitive cultures provide themselves with simple furnishings that make for more comfortable sitting and sleeping.

Demand and pricing

Because of the **law of supply and demand,** prices are higher when goods are more scarce and when they are more in demand. For example, the supply of diamonds is always very low, but since they are highly desired for jewelry, their price is high. In the case of winter coats, prices are higher when the demand is high, as in October or November, but by January the demand is lower, and because stores want to sell their remaining supply of coats before spring, the prices go down. For most household goods, if the item can be bought before it is in demand or if the need for it can be delayed, then significant savings will usually be realized.

While clothing and household furnishings can often be delayed or purchased in a less expensive (and usually less reliable) form, it is more difficult for families to make similar reductions in their food expenses. Food is a daily necessity, and while it is cheaper to eat some foods than others, there are no "bargain-basement" groceries. In the mid-1800s, a German statistician, Ernst Engel, noted what is still a truism today: as income goes down, the *percent* of a family's budget allocated to food goes up. Families with lower incomes still have to buy almost as much food as wealthier families, even though it may be of lower quality.

Transportation

Car ownership

One of the necessities of our lives today is transportation. Our ancestors traveled little and the horse and wagon was adequate for their needs. But today's money economy often requires us to travel some distance to work and to purchase our necessities and pleasures away from home. Since we usually get there by car, over 88 percent of all American families own one, and one-third own two or more (Miller, 1978).

Urban families with ready access to public transportation are much less likely to purchase their own car. In New York City, for example, the costs of just parking and insurance can easily exceed $4000 per year, more than many families would want to pay. For suburban and rural families, however, there is often little choice but to own a car, and its expenses will probably be greater than anything else they own, except perhaps their homes.

Auto costs

When all of the costs are considered, including the purchase price, financing, gasoline, insurance, maintenance and repairs, and taxes, the American Automobile Association (1980) estimates that it costs between fifteen and thirty-five cents a mile or more to operate a car. The size of the car and the area in which it is driven will determine much of its expense. Also, unlike a house, a car depreciates in value. In the first year alone, the typical car loses about one-third of its original value. It then depreciates roughly another 18 percent in the second year and 14 percent in the third year. After a few years, it is worth less than half of what it cost new.

Security

An important economic objective in any continuing relationship is financial security. This means having protection against severe economic loss due to some unanticipated crisis. It also means making preparations for anticipated financial needs before they come up so that unnecessary hardships are avoided. Some of the ways security needs are met include insurances, savings, investments, and social security (see Fig. 11.1). Unfortunately, economic security is not as visible an objective as transportation or shelter—you do not drive your insurance policies or live in your savings account—but it is all too easy for a family to lose everything it has if it has not adequately planned for financial security.

Purpose of insurance

Long-term security is usually attained through various savings, investment, and retirement programs. Current security, however, is more likely to be purchased through various types of insurance. After all, illness, death, property damage, and disaster can strike any family. After years of working and saving for a house and furnishings, a family can lose everything by fire. The extended hospitalization of a family member may totally wipe out savings, possibly creating an excessive debt. Worse yet, the death of a family's primary breadwinner may cause not only personal pain, but long-term financial strain as well. Insurance is designed to protect against the financial burden of potential crises like these.

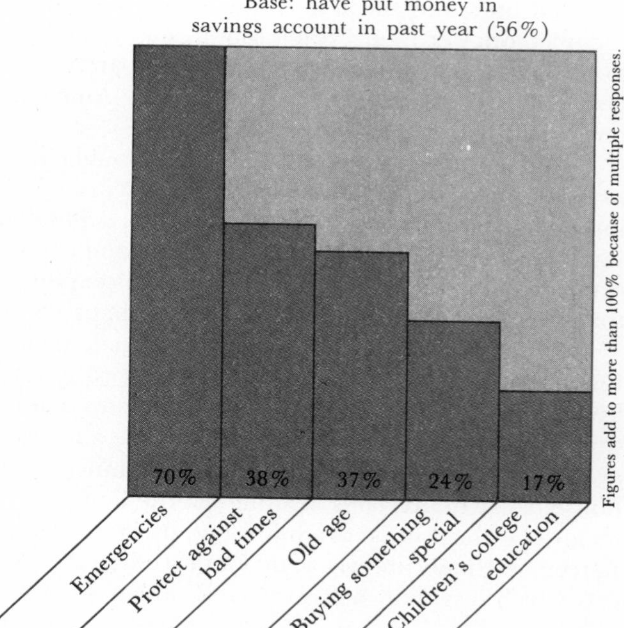

Fig. 11.1

The Reasons that Families Save Money

Source: Yankelovich *et al.* (1975), p. 95.

Health and Accident Insurance. Hospital costs and medical expenses have risen sharply over the last several years. Indeed, one day in the hospital can cost well over $400.00, and for the uninsured, the cumulative cost of medical care can be financially devastating. Many employers offer health insurance for their employees and their families, frequently paying all or part of this bill. For low-income families who qualify, government-sponsored insurance is available which provides for essential services either free or at a nominal cost. Although plans vary from state to state, American citizens age sixty-five and older, and those with serious disabilities, may qualify for Medicare and Medicaid programs. These programs furnish payment for a large portion of their hospital and doctor bills.

Disability Insurance. Disability insurance is protection that guards against loss of income due to sickness or accident. Although most employers provide some form of sick-pay insurance, for the majority of people additional coverage is required if a life-style similar to what they are used to is to be maintained under conditions of disability.

Property Insurance. Property insurance protects personal property—houses, cars, furniture, and other tangible assets—against loss from damage, accidents, or what insurance companies term **perils**—fire, vandalism, and burglary. This kind of insurance also covers liability suits or other claims by injured parties resulting from alleged negligence—for instance, dog bites, injury from broken steps, or damage caused by one's car in an accident. Adequate coverage can easily be the difference between financial disaster and the protection of assets.

Life Insurance. The primary purpose of life insurance is to provide funds for dependents upon the death of a person who provided them income or services. As such, it attempts to replace at least part of the economic value of that person. Although specific formulas are often applied to determine how much life insurance any given family should have, the amount of life insurance needed can vary a great deal depending upon particular family circumstances, life-style preferences, the income capability of the remaining members, the ages of the children, and the availability of other resources, such as social security benefits.

Types of life insurance

There are two basic types of life-insurance policies—term and whole life. **Term insurance** is both the simplest and the least expensive. This type of insurance will provide protection for a specific "term" or period of time—usually five, ten, or twenty years. At the end of each term, it must be renewed to be kept in force. The *premium* (payment) will be raised during each succeeding term reflecting the higher probability of death with advancing age.

With **whole life insurance,** also known as straight life, ordinary life, or cash-value insurance, the same premium is paid for as long as the insured is alive. The cost is normally three or four times that of term insurance in the younger age groups. Since the premium remains unchanged for the life of the policy, the company initially charges more than is necessary to help defray the cost of insuring the policyholder's life in later years. The excess amount paid goes into a reserve and is invested by the company. This reserve and the interest it earns creates the **cash value** savings of the policy. Should the policyholder decide to drop the policy, this cash value is returned. In many ways, a whole life policy resembles a forced, low-interest savings account with a life-insurance feature added.

Regular saving

Savings and Investments. Setting money aside in savings or investments can be very useful in providing for future family needs and security. Nearly three-fourths of the families in the United States have savings accounts for this purpose, but only about a quarter of all families put any money into these accounts regularly (Yankelovich *et al.*). Families who do not save tend to be living "from hand to mouth," and even though they are sometimes financially affluent, they claim to be unable to give up current satisfactions for future security.

Savings objectives

Savings not only provide protection for the unexpected, they also enable a family to accomplish planned objectives. These objectives may be either short term or long term. Long-term savings, requiring systematic savings over a period of years, may, for example, provide the funds necessary for a satisfying retirement. But whatever the reason for saving, financial experts suggest that savers begin with a predetermined purpose. Without an objective, saving provides little challenge and this is likely to result in decreased motivation.

After savings are sufficient and ample insurance has been secured, a family may consider the investment of additional funds. Although investing entails risks, sound investments can lead to additional security. The most popular investments include common stocks, preferred stocks, and bonds—collectively referred to as **securities.** Real estate represents an additional form of investment. Since there is no such thing as an absolutely sure investment, investing must be done intelligently. Half of the people who own common stocks, for example, consider this to be very risky (Yankelovich, *et al.*). Often professional consultation is wise, especially in times of economic uncertainty and with high-risk investments.

Social-security benefits

Social Security. Over nine out of ten families in the United States have joined a program that partially provides many of the economic-security benefits we have discussed to this point. The federal **social security** program was enacted in the 1930s, when society realized that families had become much more independent than had been true earlier and that the elderly no longer could count on their children or their own resources to remain economically self-sufficient after retirement. Since then, the benefits have expanded to include some degree of health insurance, disability insurance, life insurance, and retirement savings. *None* of these benefits is adequate by itself, but they are important *supplements* to the economic-security program of a family.

Long-term savings may provide funds for a satisfactory retirement.

The basic benefits of social security are as follows:

1. Medicare payments for illness in old age.
2. After death, payments to a spouse after he or she reaches old age.
3. After death, payments to dependent children until they have gone through college.
4. If totally disabled and unable to work, payments to the individual or family.
5. A retirement annuity that pays a monthly check to an individual after retirement.
6. After death, a modest lump-sum payment to the beneficiary for burial expenses.

Wills

Estate Planning. Estate planning is a necessary but often neglected part of establishing economic security. Indeed, after establishing financial goals and working to attain them, it is vital that the assets secured be properly passed on to the people who need them after the death of a spouse or parent.

Although death cannot be avoided, estate planning frequently is. In fact, 70 percent of those who die in this country fail to leave a will—they die **intestate.** If death occurs without a properly executed will, the inheritance laws of the state of residence determine who receives the person's property and money. Not only may this cause ill-feelings, substantial inconvenience, and legal problems and costs for the heirs, but the state may distribute the estate in ways that the deceased would not have wished.

For example, if a husband dies, in some states his wife and children or his wife and his parents may inherit equally; the full amount will not automatically go to the wife at all. This means she will have access to only half or less than half of the money and property that was in her husband's name. In order for her to use any of the money allocated by the state to her children, she may have to be appointed their legal guardian by a court. Thus, while it sounds incredible, the laws of some states will force a parent, usually the mother, to plead for guardianship of her own children. A properly prepared will can prevent a situation like this from happening.

FINANCIAL MANAGEMENT

Money and happiness

In order to meet their immediate and long-term economic objectives, most families have to synchronize their spending in order to meet their obligations and fulfill their realistic needs. Many families have difficulty doing this, and the issues that families usually argue about are basically financial-management issues—money is simply not being spent in the ways that best meet the requirements of the people involved (Yankelovich *et al.*). From the information we have, it appears that families often recognize this dilemma, but they frequently do nothing about it. Those that do think about it, however, are more likely to be happy with their lives. In a survey study of 52,000 readers of *Psychology Today* magazine, the researchers concluded:

> . . . happiness is in the head, not the wallet. In fact, happiness has less to do with what you have than what you want. It comes less often from absolute achievements than from relative ones. Happiness is a matter of setting personal standards, not chasing after other people's. (Shaver and Freedman, 1976)

Budgeting

Financial management

Budgeting is a means of managing money in a more or less systematic and rational way. Experts in money management suggest that preparing a well-designed budget is a first step in sound financial management. Like a blueprint, a budget or money plan is a tool that enables the family to know where their money is going, to save for the things they want, and to get the most value for the money they spend. Properly designed, it provides a means by which a family may improve upon or maintain a life-style of its selection. For couples who have difficulty with financial management, a budget may prevent financial chaos or disaster. Moreover, budgeting may be a means of keeping peace within the family by uniting them to achieve established goals.

Written budgets

According to a national survey, about half of all families practice some type of budgeting (Yankelovich *et al.*). This is true at all income levels. Only one-fourth of those who say they budget their money, however, actually have a written, formal money plan. The rest informally budget by discussing their needs and carefully spending their money. Families with children, it was found, are more likely to budget than those without children.

Just as no two people share the same fingerprint, family budgets are highly individualized. Even families at the same income level often allocate money in different ways. The United States Department of Labor regularly monitors the cost of living in the United States and projects average family budgets for people at different income levels. An example of how a median-income, urban family of four distributes its money is offered in Fig. 11.2. But data like this is of little help in family financial planning, except to indicate deviations from the norm.

There are many "rules" available to guide budget preparation, but they are beginning to come under attack. Some common rules that are frequently mentioned include:

- Keep six months' pay in the bank for emergencies.
- Don't spend over 25 percent of your salary on housing.
- Don't borrow more than 1½ times your monthly salary.

While rules such as these are still sometimes used to determine credit ratings, they are less useful in budget planning because life-style preferences vary so much today. For example, a family may consider a nice home to be their

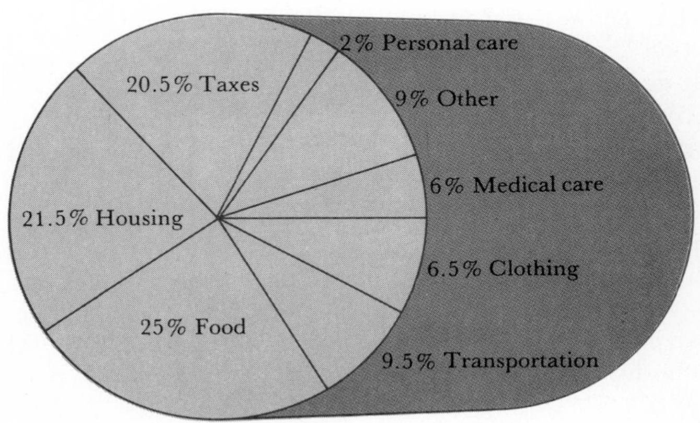

Fig. 11.2

Average American Family Budget (based on a four-person urban family at an intermediate income level)

Source: U.S. Bureau of Labor Statistics, 1980.

highest priority and be willing to skimp on other things. For them, the 25-percent "rule" is inadequate. One financial expert in discussing these rules noted: "True, they may keep more reckless spenders out of trouble, but family counselors and home economists seem to agree that universal guidelines are no substitute for tough-minded financial planning by each family to fit its own needs" (Main, 1975, p. 21).

Family involvement

Involving the entire family in the budget-making process is very important. If all members understand the financial limitations of the family, they acquire a stake in seeing that the plan is carried through. Obviously, communication about money is necessary for husbands and wives since they spend most of the family income. But children also need to be involved in this process when they are old enough to understand. This helps them know why certain decisions which affect them are being made, and it also teaches them how to manage money themselves when they are given that responsibility (see Vignette 11.2).

Budget development

In constructing a budget, it is usually recommended that a family first keep records of their actual expenditures for approximately a month or two.

Vignette 11.2 Teaching Children to Manage Money

If you like silver linings, here's one. Today's money worries certainly should make it easier for parents to teach their children that money doesn't grow on trees.

That was a hard point to make just a little while ago, when unending prosperity seemed more certain. Now, though, it's important to pay even closer attention to the dollars and cents that pass through family hands. And if family belt-tightening is going to work, it must include the kids.

That's easier said than done, of course. You can train a four-year-old to close the front door, but you can't expect him to understand the reason why—namely, that you don't want to pay for air-conditioning the whole neighborhood. A teen-ager should understand that and more. While lessons in financial responsibility must be geared to a child's age and level of maturity, there are some general guidelines you can follow.

- Give your child an allowance. Although child specialists aren't unanimous on this point, most agree that the best way for kids to learn about handling money is by having some to handle. An allowance is a teaching tool from which a child begins to learn about living within his means. How big an allowance is reasonable? When should it be started and how often should it be given? The answers depend largely on the child. For now, note this rule: every allowance should include some money the child can spend however he or she wants. If every cent is earmarked for lunches, bus fares, and the like, the child gets no experience in choosing among spending alternatives. Another rule: don't come to the rescue every time your youngster runs out of money. The amount he gets should be realistic and determined by

Such records should reveal just where actual expenditures are going, thus pointing to family spending priorities. The second step in budgeting involves making an itemized list of all income on a monthly basis. Only spendable or net income is included here, so income taxes withheld, social-security payments, and payroll deductions are subtracted. Interest on savings, dividends from stock, profits from the sale of personal property, and any other income should be included.

Since income is spent on a number of goods and services, the next step involves separating fixed from flexible expenditures (see Table 11.2). **Fixed expenditures** are those that do not change from month to month. Examples include mortgage or rent payments, life-insurance premiums, and installment repayments. Since some fixed payments are not made each month, money must be allocated to cover the bills when they come in.

Flexible expenses, on the other hand, are those that may vary from month to month. Because they are flexible, these expenses are often open to some control or management. Examples include utility payments, medical and dental fees, and food costs.

---

mutual agreement. If the child consistently spends fast and needs more, either the allowance is too small or his spending habits are sloppy. Find out the cause and act accordingly.

- Don't use money to reward or punish a child. Giving bonuses for good grades or withholding part of an allowance for misbehavior may be an effective way to teach a youngster about an economic system based on monetary rewards, but many child specialists fear it puts family relationships on the wrong footing. Such actions mix love with money, and in the minds of the young the two concepts can become confused. A better approach is to reward good behavior by showing pride and affection and to punish wrongdoing with some penalty that fits the crime. Don't give kids the idea that money can be used to buy love or to buy your way out of a jam. Paying older kids for doing extra jobs around the house is fine, as long as they realize they also have regular family responsibilities that they are not paid for performing.
- Remember that your own example is the best teacher. Your attitudes toward money, the way you handle it and discuss it make an impression on your children just as surely as your attitudes toward religion and other personal matters. If you speak longingly of the neighbor's new car or television set, if you spend impulsively, if you often quarrel about money with your spouse, the children will take note. Your behavior reveals the place of money in your life. It's unrealistic to expect your children to develop an attitude toward money more mature than your own.

From *Changing Times,* September, 1975, pp. 39–40.

The American dream of single-family home ownership has proved unreachable for many young families due to spiraling real estate prices.

Balancing the budget

At this point in the budgetary process, total income should be compared with total expenses. If expenses are less than income, money is available that may be added to savings and negotiated to meet the recreation and personal needs of family members. In other words, the difference between what is coming in and what is going out determines whether resources will be available for the establishment and fulfillment of long-term personal needs. If expenses are greater than income, it follows that there will be no money avail-

Table 11.2

An Example of a Budget

CASH FORECAST, MONTH OF ____________	ESTIMATED	ACTUAL
Cash on hand and in checking account, end of previous period	____________	____________
Savings needed for planned expenses	____________	____________
Receipts		
Net pay	____________	____________
Borrowed	____________	____________
Interest/dividends	____________	____________
Other	____________	____________
TOTAL CASH AVAILABLE DURING PERIOD	____________	____________
Fixed Payments		
Mortgage or rent	____________	____________
Life insurance	____________	____________
Fire insurance	____________	____________
Auto insurance	____________	____________
Savings	____________	____________
Local taxes	____________	____________
Loan or other debt	____________	____________
Children's allowances	____________	____________
Other	____________	____________
TOTAL FIXED PAYMENTS	____________	____________
Flexible Payments		
Water	____________	____________
Electricity	____________	____________
Fuel	____________	____________
Telephone	____________	____________
Medical	____________	____________
Household supplies	____________	____________
Car	____________	____________
Food	____________	____________
Personal expenses	____________	____________
Clothing	____________	____________
Nonrecurring large payments	____________	____________
Contributions, recreation	____________	____________
Other	____________	____________
TOTAL FLEXIBLE PAYMENTS	____________	____________
TOTAL ALL PAYMENTS	____________	____________
Recapitulation		
Total cash available	____________	____________
Total payments	____________	____________
Cash balance, end of period	____________	____________

Source: Roger LeRoy Miller, *Economic Issues for Consumers,* third edition. West Publishing Company, St. Paul, Minnesota, 1981.

able for additional goals. In fact, when a budget deficit occurs, money will usually be taken from savings for budget balancing, to the detriment of established goals (Yankelovich *et al.*). If expenses are greater than income, both flexible and discretionary expenditures need to be examined to determine where spending can be reduced.

Credit

The oft-heard phrase "Buy now—pay later" has become a symbol of modern times. In terms of financial management, credit has given many families the opportunity to live more comfortably and balance the ups and downs of their financial needs in a uniform, less chaotic manner. Few people today could afford to own a home, buy a car, or even put braces on their children's teeth without credit. And it is not just that people want more and do not know how to save; it is frequently prudent to buy major expenses on credit, rather than emptying one's savings reserve.

Bankruptcy

But not all is well in this credit-oriented economy. Some people do not manage their spending wisely and, ultimately, the bills come due. It can become too easy to overbuy on credit, to indulge every whimsical fancy, and to feel that the little plastic card in one's pocket will answer all of life's needs. One economist calls some people "credit drunks," or compulsive buyers who bit by bit get themselves deeper and deeper in debt (Miller, 1978). Every year now, nearly a quarter million Americans declare personal bankruptcy in order to remove the weight of their excessive debts. But the pain is removed only for a while—then these individuals must learn to cope in a credit economy without a good credit rating to back them up.

Credit ratings

The ability to get credit, however, depends upon a good credit rating. Before extending credit, retail firms and financial institutions attempt to evaluate the capacity of the customer to meet the terms of the loan agreement. Such an evaluation is based on information provided by the applicant and is investigated by either the agent or by a credit bureau—an agency that specializes in getting credit information. Generally, the facts for a credit report include the customer's name, address, marital history, residence and moving patterns, job data, current and past employers, earnings, court records, and history of loan repayment including credit cards and store accounts.

In the past, women have had special difficulties in establishing a good credit rating in their own names. Creditors maintained that divorced and single women in particular were bad credit risks and would even deny credit to a married woman without her husband's permission. Today, due to the Equal Credit Opportunity Act of 1975, discrimination on the basis of sex or marital status is illegal. In fact, in most cases, creditors are not even allowed to ask a credit applicant's sex. Although this law has greatly improved the rights of women in the world of credit, divorced women may still have to reveal the source and amounts of alimony and child support, if any, to obtain credit. It

The proliferation of credit cards has led many Americans deeply into debt.

must be remembered, however, that although this legislation does serve to equalize the position of men and women in the credit market, individuals of either sex still must meet basic standards to be considered a good financial risk.

Summary

It costs money to operate most relationships, at least for any length of time. To acquire the goods and services that are needed by a couple or family, money is now the necessary medium of exchange. The importance of money can be seen in its ability to give power to those who have enough of it and frustration to those who do not. Marital arguments over money are more common than those over any other subject. Often, however, these conflicts are less about money *per se* than over what it represents, such as personal needs for power, acceptance, or independence.

For a relationship to be economically stable, it must meet certain objectives. Shelter, for example, is a primary economic objective in all cultures and one of the most costly budget items in the United States. Household needs such as food, clothing, and home furnishings are also important today, as is transportation in this mobile society. An economic objective that can be easily neglected is security. Insurance programs, savings, investments, social security, and estate planning are all worthwhile elements of family economic security.

In order to meet these objectives, as well as more personal needs and wants, some form of financial management is usually necessary. Some families simply restrict their spending without any formal plan. Others use a formal or informal budget to plan their expenditures. Credit can assist in this financial planning but it can also be a problem if it is not managed wisely.

SUGGESTIONS FOR ADDITIONAL READING

Changing Times Magazine.

This monthly magazine is published by the Kiplinger Newsletter Company and each issue contains up-to-date information on a broad variety of family-finance topics. Everything from tips on how to teach children about money to the latest information on home mortgages may be covered. The magazine accepts no advertising.

Consumer Reports Magazine.

Published by the Consumers Union, this monthly magazine reports on tests of consumer products that they perform in their own laboratories. Automobiles are reported on yearly and many other major consumer products and services are tested periodically as well. This magazine also accepts no advertising.

Miller, Roger L. *Economic Issues for Consumers,* Third Edition. St. Paul, Minn.: West, 1981.

This excellent book provides detailed coverage of many consumer-related issues. Information is objectively presented on everything from budgeting and food purchasing to investing and estate planning. This is a good initial source book.

Yankelovich, Skelly, and White, Inc. *The General Mills American Family Report.* General Mills Corp., 1975.

This book is based on a national survey of American families and it documents the ways in which families use and misuse, argue about, and manage their money.

The Parental Choice Part IV

FUEL

Chapter 12

Family Planning

The birth of a child can represent many different things. If desired and planned for, a child may be welcomed as a valuable addition to a relationship. If unwanted and unplanned, the child may be met with hostility, guilt, and anger. A child can be the fruition of a couple's love and concern for one another or the result of one isolated evening when loneliness seemed to be closing in. A child may arrive into a home where the parents at least hope they are prepared for its coming and ready for their growing responsibilities. Or, its parents may consider it to be a last-ditch effort, the catalyst for saving their already shaky relationship.

Unfortunately, the child does not know what it is getting into. It does not know the reason or lack of reason that led to its birth. It only knows it has emotional, social, intellectual, and physical needs. And if these needs are not met, then it is uncomfortable, irritable, and demanding. Any child is going to disrupt its parents' previous life-style and the freedom a couple previously enjoyed. No relationship is going to be unaltered by the birth of a child. Even to think that nothing will change or that everything will get better after the child is born is probably a sign of inadequate preparation for the reality of parenthood.

Planning, especially family planning, is really a process of examining and expressing the concerns one has for the future. In the best sense of the word, planning involves the careful consideration of alternatives; it is a process in which decisions are not made spontaneously or whimsically, particularly when life-long consequences are involved. In light of this, the present chapter will focus on some of the practical decisions couples have to make regarding family planning, the means by which these decisions can best be implemented, and the outcome of those decisions that call for pregnancy and childbirth. Family planning, in this context, is more than selecting a contraceptive. It is part of the process of fulfilling mutually defined goals for a relationship.

FAMILY-PLANNING CONSIDERATIONS

If no means of controlling conception are used, about 70 to 80 percent of all couples engaging in regular sexual intercourse will be either parents or expecting by the end of a year. Many would prefer not to find themselves in this condition. Some may feel they are too old, too young, too involved in their work or school, too limited in their financial or emotional assets—or they simply may not want children, at least not now, if ever. Therefore, some means of reducing the possibility of conception is probably in the best interests of many people.

Needless to say, every couple must decide for themselves what they desire in terms of a family. Usually, this decision is based on a couple's interpretation of the examples they were provided in their respective families, an evaluation of the resources they have and want to have, the pressures placed on them by others, an analysis of their individual and shared values, and their overall concern for the future of a child and the society in which the child might live. The more carefully these and other personal concerns are weighed, the stronger will be the commitment to family planning and the more careful will be the selection of a contraceptive.

Basic decisions

For most couples, reducing unwanted pregnancies usually involves three basic decisions: (1) whether or not to have children, (2) if so, how many, and (3) when they should come in the course of the relationship. These are not decisions to be taken lightly. Once a child is born, society demands that the parent or parents take responsibility for its nurturance and support. Unfortunately, about 10 percent of the children born in the United States have parents who say they do not want them (Weller and Hobbs, 1978). But for most people, it is too late then to decide that a mistake has been made, that the child was not desired after all and that it really would be better to start all over again. A single person can more easily place an unwanted child for adoption or in foster care, but married couples will receive considerable pressure to keep their child. Unfortunately, a "mistake" in family planning is one that most couples simply have to adjust to as it is difficult to correct.

Given the relative irrevocability of family-planning decisions, it should be helpful to examine some of the major considerations individuals and couples must face in this matter.

To Have or Not Have Children

Voluntary childlessness

One of the fundamental questions facing couples today is whether children and parenthood are compatible with their personal and marital life-style. Not too long ago, most couples had little choice; if they were fertile and sexually active, a combination of social pressure and unreliable contraceptives ensured that they would become parents. Today, the situation has changed. Most voluntarily childless couples appear to be very satisfied and content with their decision not to have children. While approximately 95 percent of all married couples in the United States and Canada do want to be parents (Blake, 1979), the proportion preferring childlessness over parenthood appears to be growing, especially among younger women and men who are college educated.

The considerations that lead couples not to want children are many and will be discussed in the next chapter, but suffice it to say here, this decision requires very careful family planning. A child born to a couple expecting to be child-free is considerably more disruptive of future plans than an additional child born to parents who want children. In the latter case, parental roles are desired or already established and may have to be prolonged. But the couple not expecting children will have to make dramatic changes in their anticipated life-style. For this reason, the decision to remain childless requires the use of very effective methods of contraception and perhaps the acceptance of abortion if a pregnancy should occur. Sterilization of either person is the only sure means for effectively carrying out the decision to remain child-free.

Delaying the Birth of the First Child

Unmarried parenthood

There are two groups who are usually concerned with delaying the birth of their first child: people who are unmarried yet sexually active, and married couples who do not consider themselves ready to be parents. Admittedly, much of the concern over delaying a first pregnancy has been aimed at the unmarried, particularly adolescents. With the proportion of sexually experienced youth rising, interest in providing family-planning information to them is also being kindled. According to social demographer Harriet Presser (1974), "Motherhood is often defined as the most sacred of women's roles; but, ironically, it is the social role women are most likely to adopt unintentionally. The great majority of women do plan to be mothers at some time. . . . But little stress has been placed on the importance of planning when to begin having children" (p. 8).

This lack of planning for a possible pregnancy can have serious consequences for the adolescent. For one thing, a teenage pregnancy clearly short-circuits the educational and occupational opportunities for most of these women (Waite and Moore, 1978). Arthur Campbell (1968) of the Survey Research Center at the University of Michigan has studied the relationship between early pregnancy and eventual economic success and his conclusions are quite clear:

> In a very real real sense, it may be more important to delay the first child than to prevent the seventh. The timing of the first birth is of crucial strategic importance in the lives of young women [and men] because the need to take care of a baby limits severely their ability to take advantage of the opportunities that might have changed their lives for the better. . . . The girl who has an illegitimate child at the age of sixteen suddenly has 90 percent of her life's script written for her. (p. 238)

Delaying pregnancy in marriage

Of course, age and lack of experience or assets may also influence the family-planning decisions of married couples. The economic pressure placed on the family with small children can be very difficult for many young parents to handle. Freedman and Coombs (1966) studied a large sample of women in Detroit and reported that a delay in the birth of the first child was highly related to the parents' feelings of having spaced their child "satisfactorily." In a national sample of urban families called the "Growth of American Families Study," Charles Westoff *et al.* (1961) found that 41 percent of the women who thought they had their first child too soon considered finances to be their major problem.

Couples may also want to consider delaying the birth of their first child to better manage their relational adjustments. The early years of marriage are very important for this purpose, and the premature arrival of a child can add new, parental roles when the marriage roles are not yet well established. Again, in the "Growth of American Families Study," 45 percent of the women who felt their child had come too early considered the major interference to be in their marital adjustment and the times they enjoyed with their spouse. Even the adjustment to the child and the parental experience may be hurt by the failure to delay childbirth until a couple is ready. Several studies have found that couples who report the most stress associated with parenthood are those who have been married the fewest years (Russell, 1974).

Health risks

It is also important to recognize that the personal needs of the couple have to be weighed against the health risks involved if children are delayed too long. As people age, chromosomal abnormalities increase in egg and sperm cells and one outcome is Down's syndrome or mongolism (Holmes, 1978). This is the single highest cause of mental retardation, and it occurs in 1 out of 600 babies. But among mothers under thirty years of age, the chances of this condition are only 1 in 3000 births compared to one in 80 if she is between forty and forty-four (Apgar and Beck, 1972). Several other physical conditions that increase with age include abnormal birth position of the child, postdelivery hemorrhage in the mother, and gradually declining fertility for men and women. Both infant and maternal mortality rates also rise with age of the mother and are particularly high if she is in her forties (Siegal and Morris, 1974).

Child Spacing

Child-spacing decisions

Family planning involves not only timing the first child but also spacing subsequent children to best meet the needs of parents and children. The trend now is toward a two- to three-year interval between children, but shorter intervals are more common in the lower classes and larger intervals are more common in the middle and upper classes. It is difficult to determine whether "close" spacings between children or "wider" spacings are better for children and parents. Harold Christensen (1968) found in his studies that parents who had an interval of two or two and a half years between their children tended to be most happy with their spacing. Nevertheless, many of the couples he questioned still preferred spacings shorter or longer than this.

There is growing evidence that closer spacings, particularly two years or less, have a greater potential for producing strain than longer intervals. In the Detroit study by Freedman and Coombs (1966), women reported much more dissatisfaction with close child spacings than with wider ones, and couples who allowed wider birth intervals had accumulated more economic assets, even within the same education level. In a study of preschool children, it was found that boys from closely spaced families tended to want contact with female teachers more often. They also reported more feelings of being deprived of their mother's attention than boys from families with wider spacings between children (Waldrop and Bell, 1964). Adolescent boys who were spaced at wider intervals from their siblings are also more likely to report warmth, respect, and enjoyment from their parents compared to those spaced closer together. These children apparently had enough time alone with their parents not to feel rejected when the next child came along (Kidwell, 1978).

Potential strains

Why would close spacings be more likely to create strain? There are several factors that might be operating. With the short interval, the financial costs of childbirth and child rearing can be quite high. Also, more than one child will probably be in diapers, which can be very time-consuming. The emotional strain of having two young children may be trying for parents. True, the children may be able to share the same toys and experiences, but they are also more likely to compete for them. In short, parents who want close spacings can be successful but this will require considerable care and attention.

The factors considered most important in deciding on a birth interval will vary considerably from couple to couple. For this reason, there does not appear to be any "perfect" spacing. Some couples may be willing to accept the financial and emotional strain of having more than one young child in order to have a family in which the children can share more of their experiences or the parents can consolidate their responsibilities for young children into a smaller period of time. Other couples may want to devote more of their time and resources to each child and see each child to a particular point in development before considering another. These are highly individual decisions, but the most important concern is that the wishes of the parents are carried out and the well-being of their children considered.

Number of Children

Consequences of larger families

How many children should a family have? This is really a difficult question to answer. Nevertheless, the evidence that has been accumulating is beginning to show that there are important differences between small and large families that should be considered in family planning. Admittedly, some differences that have been related to family size are due in part to the fact that couples who have larger families are more likely to be poorer and less educated and to live in rural areas. Yet even when these factors are controlled—for example, by examining only urban, middle-class families—we still find that as the number of children *increases,* (1) the power structure of the family becomes more authoritarian, (2) husbands gain more dominance, (3) there is less sharing of tasks and responsibilities by husband and wife, (4) there is more use of physical punishment for children, (5) there is less attention given to individual parent or child concerns and more to group interests, (6) husband-wife and parent-child affection and relational satisfaction decline, and (7) there is less likelihood that a family will be able to improve its social and economic well-being (Bossard, 1956; Nye *et al.*, 1970; Hiday, 1975).

How are the children affected by being reared in a large family? According to E. James Lieberman (1970) of the Center for Studies of Child and Family Mental Health:

> One might suppose that our new technological conveniences and increasing knowledge of child development would ease the task of child rearing and make large families more practicable. Instead, new research shows that a child requires a tremendous investment on the part of his parents, one which for most of us compels a choice between quantity and quality. . . . The child may be loved just as much in a large family, but most parents, like most budgets, can be stretched only so far. (p. 4)

This "stretching" of the parent to accommodate a large number of children may not go unnoticed by the children. Ivan Nye *et al.* found that as family size increases, adolescents are more likely to feel that their parents really do not care for them as much. At the same time, the mothers of these adolescents report that they are rather pleased with their child-rearing roles. What this means is that there is an increasing emotional distance building between parents and children—and it may not even be seen by the parents. Perhaps, this is why parents of large families often prefer this family life-style, but when the children of these families are asked if they want to repeat the pattern, 70 percent indicate that they want their own families to be small (Bossard and Boll, 1960).

Only children

While small families are becoming more common, the myth that "only children are lonely children" is still widely believed (Hawke and Knox, 1978). The evidence of recent research, however, does not support the claim that these children are typically disadvantaged. Only children are more likely to feel closer to their parents and report greater respect for them (Kidwell). They are also more likely to do well in school, to go on to college, and to be financially successful later in life (Polit *et al.*, 1980). As for their parents, the marital relationship does not appear to be as strained by one child as by multiple children (Knox and Wilson, 1978). Of course, some only children feel the strain of being their parents' "only chance," but the balance of the evidence suggests that the one-child family, if desired, can be a healthy environment for child rearing.

Ecological problems

There are other concerns regarding family size that some consider even more important than personal or family interests. These involve the impact that large families have on the ecology of their community and, eventually, the world. Today, the population of this "spaceship earth" is swelling faster than ever before with about 200,000 additional (births minus deaths) persons

Recent research indicates only children are more likely to feel closer to their parents.

needing to be housed, fed, clothed, and educated each and every day. World population is now over 4 billion, and by the year 2000, it is estimated that the resources of this planet will have to accommodate over 6 billion people (Ehrlich and Ehrlich, 1979). If we are having a difficult time meeting the needs of our present world population, we should seriously question whether we can take care of all those that are likely to be coming.

The United States is not immune from these problems (Juhasz, 1980). With only 6 percent of the world's population, we use far more than our share of its resources. Other countries will not allow this to continue, and the life-style Americans have enjoyed will be more and more difficult to maintain. It is a question then of what kind of life and how crowded a life we want future generations to have. In Vignette 12.1, John Miller shares his concern, "Where will they all find good farms?" and this lament can be echoed in many different ways. Where will they all find clean water and air, uncrowded parks and recreation areas to relax and enjoy, well-rounded meals to eat, adequate housing, and the "good life" that we have come to expect?

Vignette *12.1* One Man's Family

Recently, on the eve of his ninety-fifth birthday, John Eli Miller died in a rambling farmhouse near Middlefield, Ohio, forty miles southeast of Cleveland, leaving to mourn his passing perhaps the largest number of living descendants any American has ever had. He was survived by 5 of his 7 children, 61 grandchildren, 338 great-grandchildren, and 6 great-great-grandchildren, a grand total of 410 descendants.

John Miller actually had seen with his own eyes a population explosion in his own lifetime. His data were not statistics on graph or chart, but the scores of children at every family gathering who ran up to kiss Grandpa, so many that it confused a poor old man. His confusion can be forgiven for there were among them no less than fifteen John Millers, all named in his honor. And what young man, much less an old one, could remember the names of 61 grandchildren and 338 great-grandchildren and keep straight just who their parents were?

The remarkable thing about this great clan of his was that it started with a family of just seven children. This was actually a little smaller than the typical family among the Amish, who have been found by one researcher to average 8.4 children per completed family. Two of his children died in early life: Samuel Miller, who left six children when he died at forty, and Lizzie (Mrs. Jacob Farnwald), who left four when she died at twenty-eight.

Of the sixty-three grandchildren born to John Miller's family, sixty-one lived to survive him, all but 6 now grown and married. And of 341 great-grandchildren born to the families of his fifty-five married grandchildren, only three had died, two in infancy, and one in an accident. All six of his great-great-grandchildren were born during the last year of his life and were healthy infants.

Thus, a major factor in the world-wide population crisis was vividly evident in John Miller's family: the fact that nearly all children born in the

CONTRACEPTION

Family-planning alternatives

There are a variety of means by which family-planning decisions can be implemented (see Fig.12.1). Most of them fall into the general category of **contraception,** which includes chemical, mechanical, surgical, or coital timing procedures to prevent conception or, if conception does occur, implantation of the fertilized egg. Ideally, a contraceptive method should be easy to reverse so that pregnancy can occur later if desired. Some other means of implementing family planning include **sterilization,** a special case of relatively permanent contraception; **abortion,** the disruption of a pregnancy by removing an embryo or fetus from the uterus; and **infanticide,** the killing of the newborn child. While infanticide is abhorent to contemporary standards, it was and still is practiced in many areas of the world—even in North America—by people who do not have contraception or abortion procedures.

twentieth century, who enjoy the benefits of modern medicine, are growing up to become adults and to have families of their own. A century ago, the ravages of smallpox, typhoid fever, tuberculosis, diphtheria, and the many fatalities that occurred at childbirth would have left a far different picture in a large rural family. Even though the Amish live in rural areas, they avail themselves of the benefits of medical care. Now most Amish children are born in hospital delivery rooms.

Moreover, at the end of his life, the postman was bringing John Miller word of the birth of a new descendant on the average of once every ten days. This rate, we calculated, would have accelerated to one every other day as his more than 300 great-grandchildren reached marriageable age. Only eight were married when he died and six had had children by their first wedding anniversaries.

What did John Miller think about his family? Did it worry him to see it growing so large? Indeed it did. Significantly, his concerns were the very ones that the demographers, the economists, the sociologists, and the other serious students of world population problems have been voicing. He was not an educated man, for the Amish still believe eight grades of education in a one-room country school is sufficient, but John Miller summarized it in one simple question he constantly repeated, "Where will they all find good farms?" . . .

Some day, at some point, John Miller's plaintive question, "Where will they all find farms?" will have to be answered in the bleak negative. They can continue now only by buying farms others will sell them. Some day no more farms anywhere will be for sale. A finite world is of limited size. So, ultimately, at some point, is the population it can hold.

From Glenn Everett, "One Man's Family," *Population Bulletin* 17 (1961); Courtesy of Population Reference Bureau, Inc., Washington, D.C.

Interest in family planning and reducing unwanted children is not new. Infanticide, abortion, and contraception have been selectively practiced for thousands of years. Egyptian records from as early as 1850 B.C. refer to intravaginal contraceptives. Almost all societies invented and used some means of contraception. Attention to the subject is found in the literature of the Greeks, Romans, Chinese, Indians, Islamics, and Hebrews to name a few. In general, however, these peoples did not condone birth control as a regular practice. Because the mortality rates typical of ancient times were so high, an equally high birthrate was encouraged simply to maintain population stability. Only in isolated circumstances was contraception approved.

Today, some vestiges of this opposition to birth control remain. But as population pressures continue to mount and personal and relational happiness takes precedence over parental duty and obligation, more couples are using the increasingly effective means of contraception which are available. Family planning, therefore, is becoming more than a right—indeed, it is a

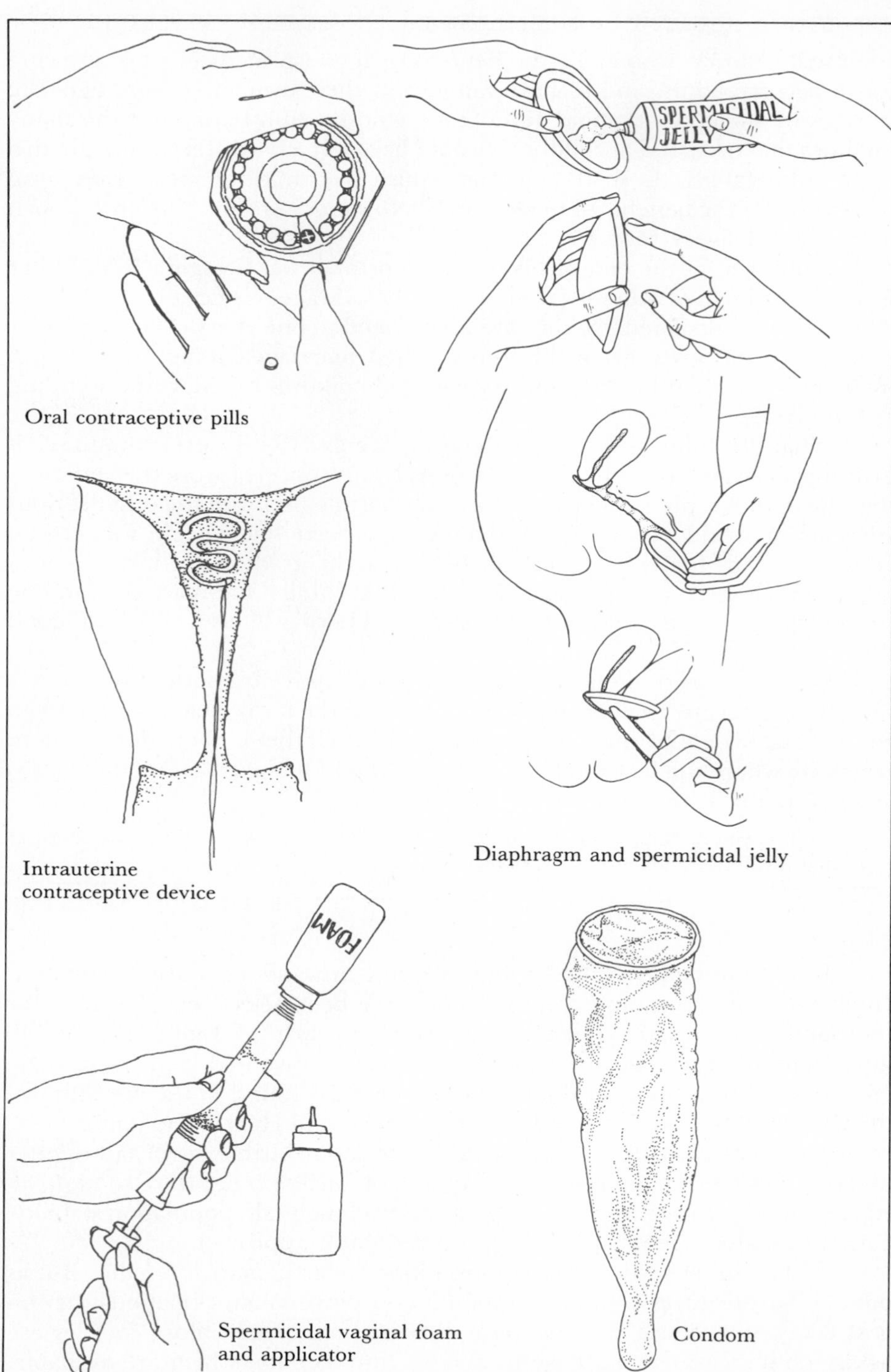

Oral contraceptive pills

Diaphragm and spermicidal jelly

Intrauterine contraceptive device

Spermicidal vaginal foam and applicator

Condom

Fig. 12.1

Major Contraceptive Measures Used Today

responsibility with important implications for the future of both the individual couple and society.

Oral Contraceptives

Oral contraceptives, often called **"the pill,"** use synthetic hormones to create artificially a condition in the woman that suppresses ovulation or implantation of an ovum. The most common oral contraceptive is the **combination pill,** which includes synthetic estrogens and progestogen. The estrogen and progestogen inhibit the development of a mature egg cell (ovum). Since the release of an egg cell (ovulation) does not occur, conception cannot take place. Progestogens also inhibit the preparation of the lining of the uterus, so if ovulation and conception should occur, for whatever reason, the fertilized ovum will not properly implant in the uterus and develop. When used correctly, this contraceptive is almost 100 percent effective.

Ill effects

Many people are concerned about the side effects and the possible long-term ill effects that may be associated with the use of oral contraceptives. The pill requires a physician's prescription because its components alter the hormonal balance in the body, and this can have unforeseen and perhaps detrimental consequences. Initial adjustments to these hormonal changes sometimes result in the following side effects: weight gain, breast tenderness, nausea, headaches, dizziness, and discoloration of the skin. Some women will experience these side effects to a greater degree than others. Also, each particular brand of pill has a different combination of hormones, and the effects vary depending on the pill and the body chemistry of the user.

The likelihood of more dangerous side effects, such as blood clotting, is small, but it remains a serious statistical risk in using oral contraceptives. If such a clot should occur, it may cause death. The risk of fatalities from blood clots is about five times higher for pill users than for nonusers (Pengally, 1978). Women with blood types A, B, and AB are more likely than those with blood type O to get blood clots when using oral contraceptives, but women with any history or tendency toward blood clotting, high blood pressure, liver problems, and kidney disorders and women over age forty should not use the pill. Women who smoke also run a higher risk of developing serious problems if they use the combination pill (Greenwood, 1979).

A second type of oral contraceptive that is presently available is called the **"minipill."** First introduced in 1973, it contains only a small amount of the synthetic progestogen. Because it has no estrogen, the uncomfortable side effects sometimes associated with combination pills are reduced or eliminated. The minipill does not suppress ovulation, but it does affect the lining of the uterus so as to make implantation very difficult. For it to be effective, women should take the minipill every day with no periodic interruptions. Even then, about 3 percent of the women who use this contraceptive will get pregnant in a year. Overall, this is a low pregnancy rate, but it is higher than with the combination type pill.

Morning-after pill

A third oral contraceptive that may be used in special circumstances is the **postcoital,** or "morning-after," pill. This contains a large dosage of a potent estrogen and is taken for a series of five days after an unprotected intercourse. This should not be considered a routine procedure because side effects such as nausea and vomiting are rather common. Treatment must begin within seventy-two hours after intercourse and, preferably, within twenty-four hours to be effective. The United States Food and Drug Administration has approved postcoital pills only for "emergency" situations.

The Intrauterine Device

An **intrauterine device (IUD)** is simply an object placed in the uterus. Most of the IUDs in use today are made of polyethylene plastic, but some also contain copper or stainless steel. The IUD is usually inserted into the uterus by a physician or other health professional. Most IUDs have short nylon threads that hang down into the vagina. The threads do not interfere with intercourse and they can be regularly checked to determine if the device has remained in place (see Fig. 12.1). If pregnancy is desired, a physician can easily remove the IUD and there will be no lingering effect on fertility.

Types of IUDs

Technically, an IUD is not a contraceptive because it does not block conception. Rather, it is a **contraimplantation** device in that it inhibits the implanting and development of a fertilized ovum. How it does this is not entirely clear, but more than likely, the cells of the uterine lining are irritated to such a degree that implantation cannot take place. **Inert IUDs** (those made only of plastic or stainless steel) depend on their mere presence for inducing sufficient irritation to be effective. **Active IUDs** contain in addition copper or even a progesterone to add a chemical or hormonal component to complement their normal function.

Complications

If properly inserted and retained, an IUD can be an effective method of birth control. There are several complications associated with the IUD, however, that may cause some concern. According to one study of 2547 IUD users, the most serious side effects are: increased menstrual flow (24.3 percent), irregular flows (26.1 percent), abdominal cramping (12.6 percent), and involuntary expulsion of the IUD (12.6 percent) (Portnoff *et al.*, 1972). These complications usually subside after the first few months of use, but they are a particular problem for women who have never been pregnant.

The greatest dangers—other than pregnancy—in the use of the IUD are infection and perforation of the uterus. Infections are unlikely if antiseptic conditions are present and if there is no history of uterine infections. Perforations of the uterus are very rare but they can occur if the physician is not exceptionally careful when inserting the IUD. Because infections can be serious and perforations fatal if undetected and untreated, a woman with a new IUD should be particularly cautious regarding side effects and have them treated quickly. There is no evidence to date that an IUD increases the risk of cancer for the user.

Condoms

The **condom,** often called "rubber," "skin," or "prophylactic," is a sheath of thin and flexible material worn over an erect penis during coitus (see Fig. 12.1). Any semen that is ejaculated is caught in the condom rather than being deposited in the vagina. To be effective, a condom should be put on only after an erection and before any intromission occurs. Because of rigid quality control, it is very unlikely that a condom will break; failure is most likely to occur when semen escapes from the base of the condom allowing sperm into the vaginal area. This can be prevented by unrolling the condom completely over the penis before intercourse and withdrawing both penis and condom shortly after ejaculation. If the condom is not held tight against the penis during withdrawal, the risk of seepage is considerable. But when properly used, the condom is a very effective contraceptive with a low risk of pregnancy.

Male responsibility

Perhaps the major advantage of this method of birth control is that the male is allowed to take some responsibility for fertility control. Some men believe it causes them to lose their sensations during intercourse but this is more myth than reality. Another consideration that should perhaps lead some men to use a condom is venereal disease. A condom cannot prevent the passing of VD, but it can significantly reduce the likelihood of the disease being passed. In more casual sexual contacts, this may be reason enough for the use of a condom.

Vaginal Diaphragm

This device is a thin rubber dome with a flexible rim that is designed to cover the cervical opening to the uterus during intercourse (see Fig. 12.1). Diaphragms are available in a variety of sizes and have to be individually prescribed by a physician. This ensures that the device can be placed properly in the vagina and fit snugly over the cervix.

While the diaphragm itself serves to block sperm from entering the cervix, usually a spermicidal (sperm-killing) jelly or cream is applied to the rim and the surface facing the cervix prior to insertion. This increases the effectiveness of the device. A properly fitted diaphragm will not be felt by either partner, and it can be left in place before or after intercourse while normal activities are carried out. When used correctly, a diaphragm can be a very effective contraceptive. The chances for pregnancy are comparable to those associated with use of the condom, but in this case control is with the woman.

Spermicidal Methods

Spermicide failure

There are a variety of substances that can be purchased without prescription and used to immobilize or kill sperm cells before they enter the uterus. Spermicidal creams and jellies are commonly used in conjunction with a diaphragm, but they can also be introduced into the vagina alone by means of a small applicator. Other methods for introducing spermicides include vaginal foam and vaginal tablets or suppositories which depend upon natural lubrication to create a melting and foaming action. Unfortunately, estimates of failure rates for spermicides used alone are very high. Approximately 20 to 40 percent of all users get pregnant in a year.

The Rhythm Method

The concept behind the rhythm method of contraception is quite simple: if a woman abstains from intercourse during her fertile period, then conception cannot occur. Nevertheless, carrying this out is considerably more difficult. For the method to be successful, a couple has to know when the period of fertility is and they must be motivated to abstain from intercourse for perhaps as many as six to twenty days.

Predetermine ovulation

Since the egg must be fertilized within twenty-four to forty-eight hours after being released, and sperm can remain active for only about seventy-two hours, the "unsafe days" are considered to be the three days before and two days after ovulation. It is often difficult, however, to predetermine exactly when ovulation is going to occur. Most rhythm methods estimate the fertile period based on the length of the menstrual cycle and hormone or temperature changes at the time of ovulation. Still, rhythm methods require a great deal of motivation, probably more than most couples have. Because of the physical and emotional strain as well as the dedication required, the pregnancy rate for couples using rhythm is rather high, comparable to the least effective spermicide. But for those couples whose moral or religious convictions allow only this method, careful following of the rhythm method can help in family planning. For most couples, however, the frustration and timing required are likely to lead to "taking chances," and this can lead to pregnancy.

Withdrawal

Faith

If the male withdraws his penis from the vagina prior to ejaculation (**coitus interruptus**), then the risks of pregnancy are reduced significantly. The method is not perfect, however, as pre-ejaculation fluids secreted from the penis can also contain sperm, and these may cause pregnancy, even if withdrawal is practiced. An even more serious limitation, however, is the psychological difficulty for the male in interrupting intercourse at the moment when the greatest pleasure is anticipated. For the female, this translates into anxiety over whether her partner will withdraw in time and also concern regarding her ability to reach an orgasm prior to his withdrawal. Nevertheless, if practiced faithfully (and from the female point of view, it may take considerable faith), coitus interruptus can be relatively effective and is certainly advisable when other methods are not being used.

Douching

It is widely believed that cleansing out the vagina (**douching**) after intercourse will serve as an effective contraceptive. However, people who depend on this method are usually called parents. The reason? It takes sperm less than two minutes after ejaculation to enter the cervix. This means that love-play must be interrupted *immediately* after the male orgasm, and there would have to be sufficient pressure in the douche to cleanse the vagina completely. This kind of pressure could actually force sperm toward and into the cervix, and it may also harm the delicate tissues of the vagina, especially if chemical agents are added to the water. For these reasons, douching is one of the least effective contraceptive procedures, probably best reserved for emergency situations only.

Sterilization

Male sterilization

Sterilization in either the man or woman is a surgical procedure blocking sperm or egg from potential conception. Since sterilization is usually irreversible, the decision to undergo this operation must be considered carefully. The important factor for most couples who decide on this procedure is its almost 100-percent effectiveness. The consent of the spouse is not usually required for sterilization, but most physicians require it as a protection against malpractice suits.

Sterilization of the male is done by means of a **vasectomy.** This involves cutting off or blocking the two vas deferens (sperm ducts) leading from the testes. The operation requires only a local anesthetic and ten to twenty minutes of time in the physician's office. The sex glands continue to function, male hormones are produced as usual, but the sperm are harmlessly reabsorbed by the body and not present in the ejaculated semen (Smith *et al.*, 1976).

Female sterilization

In the female, sterilization is usually done by a **tubal ligation,** severing the fallopian tubes to prevent the egg from traveling to the uterus. This is a more difficult procedure than a vasectomy since the fallopian tubes are not as easily reached. This operation often requires abdominal surgery, although more often it is done immediately after childbirth. Access through the uterus is easier at this time, the tubes are reached and cut with less risk of infection, and no second anesthetic may be necessary.

There are other sterilization procedures that may be more practical for many women, particularly those who have not recently had children. One is **culdoscopy,** which involves using a special instrument inserted through a small incision in the vagina to observe and then cut or fuse the fallopian tubes. **Laparoscopy** and **minilaparoscopy** are similar procedures, but access to the tubes is made by one or two small incisions in the abdomen. These procedures can often be performed in a clinic and rarely require more than an overnight stay if performed in a hospital.

Contraceptive Effectiveness and Risks

While a contraceptive may be selected for a variety of reasons, the major purpose remains to achieve with safety the family-planning goals of a couple or individual. This means that while factors such as cost, convenience, and esthetics are important, primary concern should be given to weighing the effectiveness of the method in preventing an unwanted pregnancy along with the risks that the method can create for the user.

Usually, contraceptive effectiveness is expressed in terms of a **pregnancy rate.** This is the percent of women who become pregnant during one year of normal intercourse while using a particular method. Table 12.1 summarizes the pregnancy rates for most of the methods we have considered. We can see from this data that all of the methods are considerably more effective than using no contraceptive at all, but effectiveness does vary from method to method. Also, for many contraceptives it is almost impossible to separate method and individual failures, but when the two factors are combined they usually inflate the pregnancy rate considerably.

Health risks

All couples should be concerned about the health risks involved in contraception. How safe are some of these procedures, particularly those that chemically, surgically, or mechanically interfere with bodily processes? Perhaps the best way to interpret these risks is by comparing the probability of injury or death occurring first as a consequence of using a particular contraceptive procedure, and then as a consequence of childbirth, which would normally occur if no contraceptive were used. Table 12.2 lists the mortality rates associated with childbirth, abortion, oral contraceptives, and IUDs. It is readily apparent that pregnancy and childbirth are more dangerous for women than any of these other procedures at almost every age level.

Of course, the mortality risks of other contraceptives must also be considered in light of their pregnancy risks. For example, douching and rhythm have a pregnancy rate of about 40 percent (Table 12.1), so if these methods are used by women in the 15–19 age group (Table 12.2), the mortality risk would be 40 percent of the 10.4 death rate, or approximately four deaths per 100,00 live births. This rate is more than three times the risk associated with the pill and higher than almost any other contraceptive procedure available. Other methods can be similarly compared.

Contraceptive Use and Nonuse

Contraceptive popularity

Among married couples, there has been a marked shift toward more effective means of family planning. This is very evident when the results of the fertility surveys taken in the United States in 1965 and 1976 are compared (Ford, 1978). The most frequently used contraceptive now is the pill, and the IUD and foam are also growing in popularity. Among those over age thirty-five sterilization is the most frequently used method of contraception, with almost half of the couples reporting that either the husband or the wife had been

Table 12.1

Pregnancy Risks* for Selected Contraceptives

Method	Failure of Method Only	Method and Patient Failures Combined
Combination pill	0.1	0.7
Minipill	—	2.54
IUD—large Lippes loop (pregnancy rate with device in place)	1.9	2.7
Diaphragm (with spermicidal jelly or cream)	2.6	14.4
Condom	2.6	13.8
Withdrawal	—	16.8
Vaginal foam	—	28.3
Vaginal jelly or cream alone	—	36.8
Rhythm	—	38.5
Douche	—	40.8
Laparoscopy sterilization	0.6	—

* Number of pregnancies per 100 women per year.

Source: B. Goldstein, *Human Sexuality* (New York: McGraw-Hill, 1976).

Table 12.2

Morality Risks of Pregnancy and Childbirth, Abortion, Oral Contraception, and IUDs

Age (years)	Pregnancy and Childbirth[a]	Legal Abortion[b]	Oral Contraceptives[c]		IUDs[c]
			Nonsmokers	Smokers	
15–19	10.4	1.0	0.6	2.1	0.8
20–24	9.5	1.4	1.1	4.2	0.8
25–29	12.1	1.8	1.6	6.1	1.0
30–34	22.8	1.8	3.0	11.8	1.0
35–39	43.7	2.7	9.1	31.3	1.4
40–44	68.2	2.7	17.7	60.9	1.4

[a] Per 100,000 live births (excluding abortion).
[b] Per 100,000 first trimester abortions.
[c] Per 100,000 users per year.

Source: C. Tietze and S. Lewit, *International Journal of Gynaecology and Obstetrics,* 1979. Reprinted by permission.

sterilized. The diaphragm, condom, rhythm, and douche methods have been declining in popularity (Westoff and McCarthy, 1979).

Contraceptive use among youth

The use or nonuse of contraceptives among the unmarried, particularly adolescents, is of considerable concern to many people, such as parents, schoolteachers, youth workers, and religious leaders. Today, they are all having to recognize that sexual activity among youth has increased, yet they are uncertain whether contraceptive knowledge will further increase or decrease this activity (Fox, 1980). The result is what Frank Furstenberg (1971) calls "the conspiracy of silence." His research on birth-control use among pregnant adolescent girls concludes:

> Mothers, fearing that advice about contraception will encourage their daughters to become sexually active, prefer to maintain a protective silence. Their daughters, to avoid upsetting or disappointing their mothers conceal their sexual activity. . . . Our findings indicate as long as girls are forced to depend on their parents for information and their boyfriends for protection, we can continue to expect a high prevalence of premarital pregnancy. (p. 202)

This scenario is apparently all too common. In a national sample of United States teenagers. Zelnick *et al.* (1979) found that by nineteen years of age, nearly two-thirds of the women had experienced sexual intercourse and by sixteen years of age one-fifth had already had sexual intercourse. The use of contraceptives among these adolescents was quite irregular. While most used a contraceptive at least some of the time, less than two-thirds had used one the last time they had intercourse. Also, when we examine the methods that these women most recently used (Table 12.3), we find that only about half of them relied on effective methods. Thus, while contraceptive usage among youth is improving, the number of women who are still unprotected is high and the premarital pregnancy rate is not declining (Zabin *et al.*, 1979). Not surprisingly, what this means is that many parents who withhold information about contraception are increasingly being faced with a second choice—whether to recommend an abortion or not.

Table 12.3

Contraceptives Used by Sexually Experienced Unmarried Women, Aged 15–19

Method Used at Last Intercourse	Black (%)	White (%)
Pill	40.4	40.5
Condom	5.7	12.1
Withdrawal	2.1	8.1
IUD	4.1	4.0
Douche	5.7	0.6
Other*	3.1	7.5
None	38.9	27.2

* Foam, jelly, cream, diaphragm, and rhythm.

Source: M. Zelnick and J. Kantner. Reprinted with permission from *Family Planning Perspectives*, Vol. 9, Number 2, 1977.

ABORTION

In medical terms, any termination of a pregnancy before the twentieth week of embryo or fetus development is termed an abortion. This may result from natural causes or it may be medically induced. If occurring naturally, it is termed a **spontaneous abortion** or **miscarriage.** When a pregnancy is terminated by artificial means, this is **induced abortion.** It has been known for thousands of years that introducing some object or chemical into the uterus during pregnancy will cause contractions and subsequent abortion. Following this line of thinking, women or their "helpers" have used everything from sticks and rocks to knitting needles, coat hangers, kerosene, or household cleaners as **abortificients.** Sometimes these efforts succeed, but very often they also cause hemorrhage, infection, permanent damage to reproductive organs, or death.

Abortion risks

Medical techniques to induce abortions have progressed to the point where they are relatively safe (see Table 12.2 for comparison of risks). This is particularly true if performed in the first trimester (three months) when mechanical means for removing the uterine contents through the cervix is possible. After the twelfth week, abortion is considerably more difficult and the risks of hemorrhage and death increase dramatically.

Court decisions

The controversy over whether a woman should have the right to make a decision about the product of an unwanted conception is still the subject of emotionally charged debates. Some suggest that the unborn child also has rights and that abortion should be illegal or permitted only when the mother's life is threatened. Others take the position that the inability of the fetus to maintain life independent of the mother gives the woman the authority to make this decision. In 1973, the United States Supreme Court supported the latter position and struck down all state laws forbidding abortion during the first two trimesters of pregnancy. In the case *Roe* v. *Wade* the Court ruled: (1) that the unborn have never been recognized in the law as persons in the whole sense; (2) that the rights extended to the unborn depend on a live birth; and therefore, (3) a state's interest in protecting fetal life cannot override a woman's right to privacy (Sarvis and Rodman, 1974). The Court further judged that only during the last trimester could a state regulate the abortion decision "because the fetus then presumably has the capability of meaningful life outside the mother's womb." In 1979, the United States Supreme Court also ruled that parental consent for abortion is not necessary for a "mature" minor.

Of course, these statements have not ended the debate. While 80 percent of Americans favor having therapeutic abortion available during at least the first trimester of pregnancy, 17 percent feel abortion should be legally forbidden at all times (Gallup, 1979b). In terms of the physical well-being of the woman, the new laws have provided safer alternatives to the maternal death and misery associated with self-inflicted or illegal abortions. But concerns over the moral, social, and psychological effects of abortion remain.

A woman's right to abortion is still the subject of emotionally charged debate.

In summarizing their report on the after effects of abortion, Sarvis and Rodman conclude:

> For a woman at one of the two polar ends of the controversy, there is little problem. If she strongly believes that abortion is wrong and that she ought to bear the child, or if she strongly believes in her right to have an abortion, then her course of action may be clear and unconflicted. But if she falls somewhere between, then regardless of whether she decides to have an abortion or to bear the child, she will experience conflict (p. 106).

PREGNANCY

It is difficult to imagine a more exacting test of personal strength or a couple's resolve than pregnancy. In its simplest terms, pregnancy is a physiological process that begins with a fertilized egg implanting in the uterus and ends with childbirth. But it is also a relational process initiated by sexual intercourse that culminates in parenthood. It is not a process to be considered lightly, either physically or relationally.

Relational process

How the process of pregnancy actually unfolds has been the subject of speculation for centuries. In fact, the link between sexual intercourse and pregnancy, although it had been assumed in much of the world, was not understood until the nineteenth century when biologists had developed the techniques and equipment necessary to observe cell fertilization. And even then, it took the discovery of chromosomes and genes in human cells in the twentieth century to explain the means by which the gametes (sperm and egg) carry the information to generate and specify the characteristics of a new human being.

Conception

Fertilization

The event that triggers the onset of pregnancy is conception. In order for conception to take place, there must be (1) a viable ovum from the female, (2) viable sperm from the male, and (3) a uniting of the two shortly after ovulation. Fertilization occurs when the nucleii of the egg and sperm cells are joined, and the product is called a **zygote.**

When ovum and sperm do meet, only one sperm can enter the ovum; all others are subsequently denied access. At this time, the twenty-three chromosomes in the nucleus of each gamete combine to make the full complement of forty-six chromosomes (twenty-three pairs) required for cell maturation and human development. The **genes** contained in these chromosomes include all the hereditary information necessary to determine the color of hair or eyes, physical build, and the other myriad characteristics that will make the developing child unique. A special pair of chromosomes, called X and Y, also determine the sex of the offspring. Sperm carry either an X or a Y chromosome while ova carry only the X chromosome. If an X-carrying sperm fertilizes the ovum (X + X), the result is a girl. If a Y-carrying sperm fertilizes the ovum (X + Y), the result is a boy.

Signs of Pregnancy

Pregnancy test

One of the first signs that a pregnancy has begun is a missed menstrual period. This is not, however, a positive indication of pregnancy since it can occur for a variety of reasons, including worry over being pregnant. Other symptoms that may indicate pregnancy include breast enlargement and tenderness, frequent urination, and nausea or morning sickness.

If a more reliable determination of pregnancy is desired, then a urine analysis for the hormone human chorionic gonadotropin (HCG) can be done. This hormone is produced by the implanted zygote, and by the third or fourth week of pregnancy, enough of it will usually be present in a urine sample to cause a reaction in a simple agglutination test. Other procedures for determining the presence of HCG using animals or frogs are rarely required any longer. In addition to the hormone tests, pregnancy can be verified after the fourth month by fetal movements, fetal heartbeat, or scanning the uterus by means of ultrasonic sound. X-ray can also be used, but this is usually avoided because it may be dangerous to the fetus.

Infertility

While many couples seem to have little problem demonstrating their fertility, whether intended or unintended, approximately one out of six couples report considerable difficulty in becoming pregnant (Mazor, 1979). There are many reasons for this infertility, but often the causes are linked to problems with the male sperm, female ovulation, some condition that blocks the meeting of egg and sperm, or difficulties in implantation.

Sperm count

In about 40 percent of infertile relationships, the man is sterile or his sperm count may be too low to cause conception normally. When there are less than 150 million sperm in the ejaculated seminal fluid, fertilization is almost impossible. Hormonal treatments will remedy the problem in some cases, but in others, low sperm counts can be handled through **artificial insemination.** In this procedure, the sperm from several ejaculations over a period of weeks are stored, frozen, concentrated, then injected through the cervix by a physician. If the husband's sperm are simply insufficient, then this concentration will usually lead to a pregnancy.

Infertility resulting from female disorders can be more difficult to pinpoint. Ovulation inconsistency or failure can be determined by body-temperature charts and often corrected through hormonal treatments. But this is a very delicate procedure, and sometimes "fertility drugs" can cause blood clotting or multiple births. Other fertility problems related to the female include the production of antibodies that kill sperm cells, obstructions in the cervix or fallopian tubes, and uterine problems that prohibit implantation.

Sex Choice of Child

Amniocentesis

A new dimension to family planning may be realized in the near future—the ability to preselect with some accuracy the sex of offspring. This means that if a couple wants two children, perhaps a girl and a boy, they can plan to have exactly what they want. Vignette 2.2 examines some of the issues involved in this aspect of family planning. Preselection may be a significant addition to those methods already available for determining the number and spacing of children.

At the present time, the only sure means for sex preselection would require amniocentesis and abortion. After conception and pregnancy are verified, a sample of the amniotic fluid surrounding the fetus is taken and the cells sloughed off from the fetus are examined to determine whether they have XX chromosomes (girl) or XY chromosomes (boy). If the couple are not

Vignette 12.2

Sex Control: Bane or Blessing?

It is getting easier every year to choose the sex of a baby, and many scientists agree that today's experimental techniques of sex control could become cheap, easy, and reliable within a decade or two. Widespread use may be years away, but forward-looking scholars have already begun to guess how it may affect our society and the world. Their scenarios range from near-utopias to horrors. Clearly sex control could shake up the human race to its roots. The only strange thing is that no one *really* knows how much this extraordinary technological step will change our lives. And that's worth thinking about.

Now we have both a new technology and its justification. Supporters say that sex control will please parents, lead to smaller families, defuse the population bomb, relieve mothers of their burdens, lower the incidence of sex-linked hereditary diseases, and perhaps even "facilitate the marriage market," in the words of Charles E. Westoff, a sociologist at Princeton.

Conversely, others charge that the new technology may inundate the world with boys. It may lead to quarrels over the relative values of the sexes, lock society into a pattern of firstborn boys and secondborn girls, and, in the view of Amitai Etzioni, a sociologist at Columbia, encourage homosexuality, frustration, and chaos.

Various arguments have since appeared that dispute Etzioni's pessimism, yet no one has suggested that parents would prefer girls. In the industrialized nations of the West the preference for boys is relatively mild, but it's still a preference. In many other countries it is pronounced, and there is good reason to believe that if the blue pill cost no more than a condom, the world's male population would be boiling upward within nine months.

Several sociologists at Princeton, however, feel that an increase in males would eventually, and perhaps very soon, lead to a baby boom in females. Charles Westoff, for example, has based a scenario of eventual balance on two considerations: first, Americans and Europeans seem to want balanced families, and second, since a shortage of any commodity raises its value, a shortage of girls would lead to a rising demand for them and presumably an increase in production.

Proponents of sex control foresee a growing satisfaction with the composition of families. Parents who do not want two boys or three girls will not have to have them. More people will probably have a girl and a boy. Others will have a single child of the sex they want. The anthropologist Margaret Mead has gone so far as to suggest that any females that are born will at last be wanted, since they will have been chosen.

True, but far fewer females are likely to be born, and the proponents of sex control have, in general, exaggerated the satisfactions of conscious choice. Couples might also quarrel and separate over whether to have boys or girls, and some otherwise agreeable pairs might not marry in the first place. Some parents will regret their choice of a boy or girl, while others will regret their failure to choose.

satisfied with the sex, an abortion would be performed and they may try again.

Intercourse timing

A more promising procedure, however, takes advantage of the knowledge that sperm carry either X or Y chromosomes and that X-bearing sperm are larger and may respond differently than Y-bearing sperm. Landrum Shettles (1972) has suggested that if couples can time intercourse according to ovulation and use an appropriate acid or alkaline douche, four out of five will get the child of the sex they want. Despite wide publicity, the Shettles procedure is highly controversial. A study of intercourse timing alone in 1318 pregnancies (Guerrero, 1974) reports that when artificial insemination is used, insemination on the day of ovulation leads to a boy in 62 percent of the cases while insemination three or more days earlier leads to a girl in 62 percent of the cases. This follows from Shettles' theory. Among couples using sexual intercourse, however, the results were not this predictable. Another study found that intercourse two days after ovulation led to conception of a boy 65 percent of the time. The chances of a girl increased when intercourse occurred at the time of or before ovulation (Harlap, 1979). These results do not clearly refute or support Shettles' claims, but at the present time this method should be used only with the understanding that the chances for sex preselection are slim.

Nevertheless, there are procedures being developed that may provide reliable sex control. Selective spermicides that affect only X or Y sperm are one possibility. Of course, as the day of the blue and pink pill comes closer, a serious question must be considered: *should* we have the ability to choose the sex of offspring? We noted in the beginning of this book (Chapter 2) that one of the basic reasons for pairing is the approximately equal ratio of males to females in the population. What will happen to this ratio if sex preselection becomes possible? According to recent surveys, adults in America would have two boys for every one girl (Simpson, 1979). This could have serious effects on mate selection. This is one new "development" in family planning that we may want to be somewhat cautious about.

CHILDBIRTH

After nine months of pregnancy, most women are physically and emotionally ready for childbirth. The "due date" suggested by the physician stands out like the symbolic light at the end of a tunnel but, unfortunately, it is the rare baby who is born on this hypothetical date. Some women produce healthy, full-term babies at 8½ months while others require 9½ months, so predicting the exact date of birth is almost impossible. In any case, childbirth is inevitable, and we call the events surrounding the birth process "labor," a term which respects the work that is involved.

Approaches to Childbirth

There is little question that we have come a long way in our childbirth procedures. Modern hospitals, trained medical assistance, pain-relieving drugs, prenatal care, and other such improvements have had important benefits. The maternal mortality rate, for instance, has declined from fifty-eight deaths per 10,000 live births in 1935 to about 1.2 deaths per 10,000 today (National Center for Health Statistics, 1978). Infant mortality has experienced a similar decline. In general, any complications in pregnancy, childbirth, and postpartum (after birth) are much more likely to be diagnosed and effectively treated today.

Maternal mortality

But in some areas of medical intervention, there are indications that more care must be taken. This is particularly true in the case of routine drug use in labor and delivery. While few question the motive of reducing discomfort for the mother, the effects of pain-relieving drugs on the fetus are now becoming a serious concern.

Medication

Any drug the mother receives also affects the unborn child and, in some cases, the results can be dangerous. Newborns can survive only if they breathe properly and can maintain their body temperature. Yet, most pain-relieving drugs have the effect of depressing these important functions, particularly if taken in large doses (Brackbill, 1978). This is why many babies whose mothers have been "knocked out" with a general anesthetic have to be slapped after birth. The slap is done to shock the baby into breathing. But even the mildest tranquilizers have been found to depress infant respiration and psychological reactions (Broman and Brackbill, 1979).

Certainly, only qualified medical personnel can properly weigh the immediate needs of the mother against the potential risks to the child, and in the case of birth complications, pain-relieving medications may be absolutely necessary. But parents also have to recognize this issue of relative benefits, particularly in the majority of normal deliveries. It is often their demand, in combination with the physician's philosophy and training, that determines the extent of drug use in labor. The parents, however, may be influenced longer by the decision since the initial parent-child relationship can be affected for some time after birth. In studies of medication and newborn behavior, it has been found that all drugs, general anesthetics, narcotics, tranquilizers, barbiturates, and muscle relaxants affect the child's behavior, reduce his or her ability to be consoled, and increase general irritability. The drugs continue to have these effects for as long as a month after birth (Aleksandrowicz, 1974).

Childbirth preparation

Concerns such as these have led to a minor revolution in obstetrics. There is now considerable interest in better preparing both women *and* men for childbirth, encouraging healthier psychological attitudes to reduce fear and pain, and improving the husband-wife and parent-child relationship before and after birth. Classes in childbirth preparation are quite common in many communities in the United States and Canada, and most of these classes stress the importance of knowing what is going to happen and how best to maximize natural processes to make childbirth less stressful.

The term "natural childbirth" was coined by an English physician, Grantley Dick-Read. He believed that pain was most often psychologically exaggerated through fear, tension, and generations of misunderstanding. His method for reducing these sources of pain calls for eliminating fear through understanding the birth process, learning how to relax tension, physical preparation for birth, breathing exercises, and having the husband present to provide a continual support. Dick-Read was one of the early proponents of having husbands in the delivery room as well as replacing the term "labor pain" with "uterine contraction."

Lamaze method

Following the conditioning principles of Pavlov, Russian physicians in the 1940s began to develop what was called a "psychoprophylactic method" of childbirth. In this method, the woman is conditioned to concentrate on selected sensations in order to reduce the brain's ability to perceive other sensation, such as pain. A French obstetrician, Ferdinand Lamaze, added to the Russian techniques a conditioning sequence of breathing exercises, a course of childbirth instruction, and many of the ideas on relaxation earlier proposed by Dick-Read. The resulting Lamaze method has become the most popular approach to childbirth preparation in North America.

Some obstetricians, particularly those more inclined toward traditional approaches to delivery, have questioned the real value of these exercises. But in a recent study comparing matched samples of Lamaze-prepared and nonprepared births delivered by the same physicians, it was found that the prepared women tolerated labor and delivery with significantly less medication, that they were more likely to have normal spontaneous deliveries without forcep seizure of the child, and that the mother was helped, not harmed, by the breathing techniques used (Scott and Rose, 1976).

In the early 1970s, another approach to childbirth was proposed by a Denver, Colorado, physician, Robert Bradley. His method is based on the natural techniques observed in animals during their labor and delivery. Bradley advocates the use of no medication, only deep abdominal breathing during labor, total relaxation, nursing the baby shortly after birth, and most important, husband coaching throughout labor and delivery. No artificial conditioning schedules are encouraged by Bradley. In many areas of North America this more "natural" approach combined with a predelivery preparation is becoming very popular.

Partners in Childbirth

Until comparatively recently, fathers were completely ignored in the pregnancy and childbirth process. They contributed to conception, but the responsibility for nine months of pregnancy was not considered theirs—it was the wife's and her physician's. Fathers were supposed to be concerned, but not involved. This scenario usually ended with the man pacing the hospital corridor waiting for word that his wife and baby were "progressing satisfactorily."

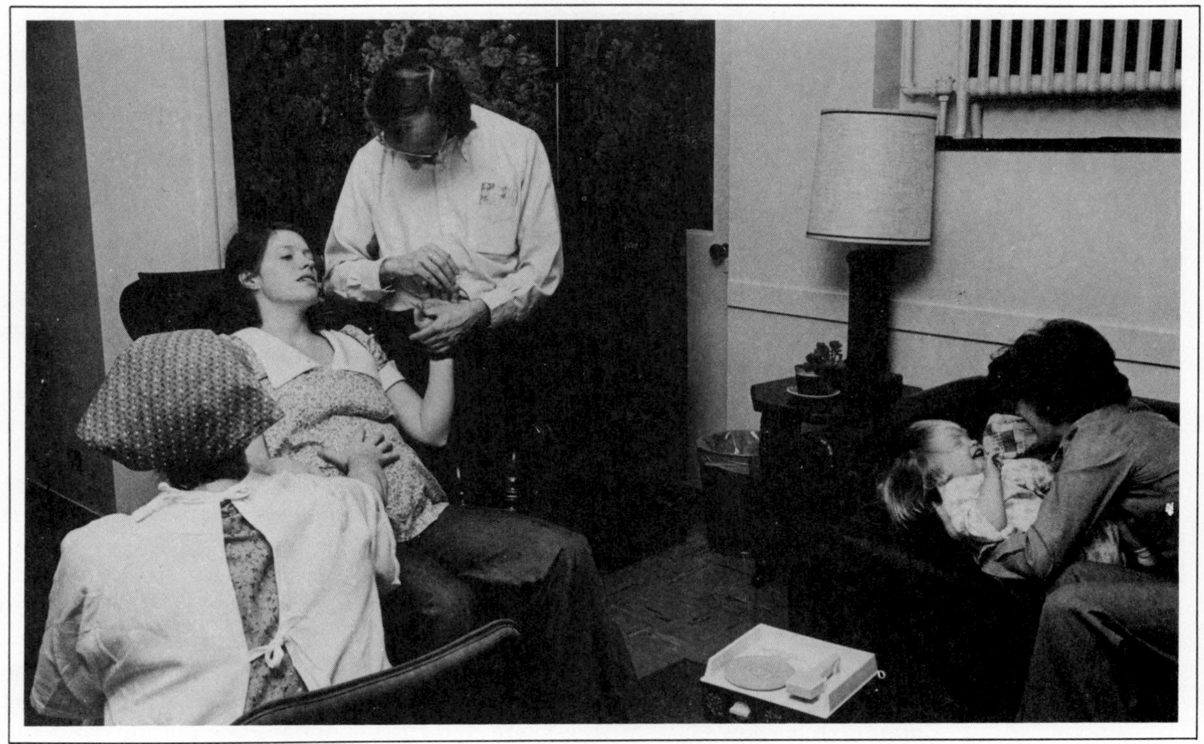

Husband "coaching" throughout labor and delivery and the presence of children and friends in the "birthing room" are part of a revolution in obstetrical practices.

Father participation

Nevertheless, these perspectives are changing, especially as intrinsic relational commitments and expressive fatherhood roles are becoming more acceptable. Fathers who choose to be involved can now be with their wives throughout labor and birth in most hospitals. While some men feel very uncomfortable sharing this new, very physical experience, other men are equally committed to being a partner throughout pregnancy, labor, and delivery. Childbirth-preparation classes, in fact, have created a new role for the husband to make him an important part of the team in the process of labor (see Vignette 12.3). In the Read, Lamaze, and Bradley approaches, men are taught to time and prepare the woman for contractions, look for signs of tension, ease relaxation, provide support, give backrubs, and generally provide a positive atmosphere.

The initial reactions from medical personnel were unfavorable to fathers' participation in labor and delivery. It was not until the 1950s that husbands were considered suitable companions in the labor room and some

Vignette 12.3
A Father's View of Childbirth

When Jeff and Liz were born eleven and nine years ago, I really acted as an outsider. Also, no other fathers seemed to be involved with pregnancy and birth that many years ago. We really weren't expected to participate, so why would we even think of being in the delivery room?

Actually, I never saw Jeff for 1 to 1½ hours after he was born, and then it was through glass nursery walls in an incubator. It was the same way with our second child, except that lack of sleep due to a bout of false labor made us very tired at the second birth so that we just wanted it to be over.

By the time we were expecting Rebecca, five years ago, I wanted a different experience—one that would involve me and let me experience this birth. A couple in our church had their baby using Lamaze techniques with the husband present and told us what a terrific experience it was for them. So Karen and I talked it over and decided to attend Lamaze classes to prepare for a shared birth.

The total experience was tremendous. Preparation was the key thing for me, and without all the preliminaries and involvement ahead of time, I probably wouldn't have gone through the birth experience because to me, the preliminary preparation for birth was part of the birth experience. All the learning and sharing we did made me part of the experience—not just an observer.

This time when we went to the hospital, we were excited and ready to go as a team. What made the experience so fantastic was knowing quite a bit about what takes place during labor, and thus being able to help my wife and the doctor. I remember saying, "Push, push, now hold it," and seeing the baby's black hair appear, and then ten minutes later, holding her, all wrapped up and warm.

---

hospitals still do not permit this. The presence of fathers in the delivery room is even more controversial, but current research does not support the notion that they impede the process of childbirth (Phillips and Anzalone, 1978). Nevertheless, policies on husbands being allowed in the delivery room vary as widely as the desires of men and women to have them there.

The benefits that have been claimed for coparticipation in labor and childbirth are also beginning to be supported in research. In one study (Manion, 1977), couples who had participated in Lamaze courses were compared to those who had not had any childbirth preparation. The prepared parents were found to share more positive attitudes toward pregnancy, and after delivery, the husbands who were present at the births were considered by their wives to be stronger and more helpful than the husbands who had not been present.

Consequences for marriage

In a second study, fathers' attitudes toward their wives and children were evaluated according to their degree of childbirth preparation and presence in the delivery room (Cronenwett and Newmark, 1974). This research found that fathers who attended the birth of their child, whether prepared or

Karen and I were crying because we were so happy. I remember counting all the baby's fingers and toes and asking, "Does she have them all?" As soon as I knew she was all right, I relaxed. The aura of newness, awakening, and joy was so strong that I don't remember all the little details about the experience; however, I do remember the feeling of completeness that I experienced. I felt complete as a father. Because I was there at the birth and was active in preparing for it, there was a sense of fulfillment for me as a father and as a husband. The experience gave me great joy. The neat thing about Rebecca's birth was that I saw her so closely, from only a few feet away, for her birth and aftercare. Then when I came back to see her the next day, I recognized her, which was a different experience than I had with the first two babies. To get acquainted with them, I had to look them over closely on the day after they were born. With Rebecca I felt that I knew her.

Several years after Rebecca's birth we shared a similar feeling after we had worked very hard planting, tending, and then harvesting grapes. On our way home from unloading a gondola of grapes, we experienced a fantastic sunset together, and felt elation and joy. After all the work we had done together, it was like an applause, a final acknowledgment, a "well done." We compared our feeling to that unique experience we had when Rebecca was born. It was valuable, rewarding, everlasting joy.

From Celeste Phillips and Joseph Anzalone, *Fathering: Participation in Labor and Birth* (St. Louis: Mosby, 1978), pp. 40–44.

not, were more appreciative of their wives' efforts and evidenced greater feelings of affection for their wives compared to fathers who had not been present in delivery. The men who accompanied the entire process of labor and delivery tended to feel that they, not the medical staff, provided the primary support for their wives. However, this study did not find that the fathers' presence in delivery affected their attitudes toward the child or toward parenthood, so the primary benefit of father participation may be for the marital relationship.

It should not be too surprising that the husband's involvement in labor and delivery is more likely initially to affect the marital rather than the parent-child relationship. After all, marital-adjustment studies have found that it is the adult pair relationship rather than the parent-child relationship that usually suffers when children enter the family. Nevertheless, the husband who shares this important time with his wife may sow the seeds for future coinvolvement in parenting. And if the sharing of pregnancy and childbirth can serve to strengthen the marital bond, then the environment for child rearing in the long run may be bolstered as well.

In this chapter we have examined some of the decisions couples have to make regarding their families. These include whether to have children or not, reasons for delaying the birth of the first child, considerations in the spacing of subsequent births, and the various consequences of family size. Contraception has been viewed as one means for implementing family-planning decisions. Generally, the most effective methods of contraception are sterilization, the pill, and the IUD. The least effective methods are withdrawal, rhythm, douching, and the spermicides. Abortion is an increasingly frequent backup to contraception, although it is controversial in many circles.

Pregnancy, planned or unplanned, results from conception and implantation of a fertilized ovum in the uterus. Some couples who desire children, however, are relatively infertile or sterile. Many of them can become pregnant after medically determining the problem. Also, a procedure which may be added to the list of family-planning options in the near future is sex predetermination.

Normally, pregnancy culminates in childbirth after a period of nine months. A major change that has occurred over the past decades is the less frequent use of medication in labor. This is partially because of the danger drugs pose for the fetus and newborn and partially because of the popularity of more "natural" approaches to childbirth. In general, pregnancy and childbirth programs are becoming more family-centered, emphasizing careful planning, preparation, and coparticipation.

SUGGESTIONS FOR ADDITIONAL READING

Family Planning Perspectives.

A bimonthly magazine that has up-to-date articles on research and issues that are related to family planning, contraception, pregnancy, and childbirth.

Pengally, Eric T. *Sex and Human Life,* Second Edition. Reading, Mass.: Addison-Wesley, 1978.

Detailed, yet easy-to-understand coverage of the fundamentals of reproduction, contraception, and childbirth.

Phillips, Celeste, and Joseph Anzalone. *Fathering: Participation in Labor and Childbirth.* St. Louis, Mo.: Mosby, 1978.

This book discusses the father's role in childbirth from a medical and interpersonal support perspective. The feelings of mothers and fathers who have shared childbirth together are expressed as well.

Sarvis, Betty, and Hyman Rodman, *The Abortion Controversy,* Second Edition. New York: Columbia University Press, 1974.

Examines the sociological, psychological, medical, and moral controversies involved in the abortion issue. Good summary of the 1973 United States Supreme Court decision on abortion.

Scales, Peter, and Sol Gordon. *The Sexual Adolescent.* North Scituate, Mass.: Duxbury, 1979.

Good overview of the sexual needs and behavior of adolescents. Sensitively written.

Zelnick, Melvin, and John F. Kantner. "Sexual and contraceptive experience of young unmarried women in the United States, 1976 and 1977," *Family Planning Perspectives* (March 1977): 55–72.

Based on a national sample of young women, the authors describe the way in which contemporary youth obtain information about and use and misuse contraceptives.

Chapter 13

Parenthood: Challenge and Choice

After a relationship has become established, especially after marriage, a new set of pressures begin to emerge—this time, to parent. So clear is this mandate that over 95 percent of all young married women and men in the United States say they want to be parents. Only about 1 percent consider the childless family "ideal" (Silka and Kiesler, 1977). One woman who had a particularly difficult time deciding whether she and her husband should have children wrote a book about their quandary titled *A Baby? . . . Maybe!* A few years later, Elizabeth Whelen (1977) announced the birth of their daughter with the statement: "We didn't want to miss the experience of having at least one child."

Ellen Peck (1971) argues that people rarely ask *if* a couple is planning to have children; they ask *when.* Most newlyweds begin fielding questions regarding the "blessed event" even before the wedding reception is over. In about one out of four marriages in North America, the wedding party will not have long to wait because the bride is already pregnant. But if a married couple delays their announcement of future parenthood for several years, subtle queries about their health, their marriage, and tales about the joys of children strongly hint that the time has come to join the ranks of parenthood.

Despite these pressures, attitudes about parenthood and parental responsibilities are changing. We are beginning to admit that parenthood contains a demanding set of roles and that a realistic view must take into account the potential costs as well as the rewards of the experience. Also, unlike most roles we acquire, parenthood is uniquely irrevocable. For example, some college students may feel uncomfortable or unsuccessful in their student role but they can drop out for a time or permanently if they want. Even marriage and work roles are somewhat optional or interchangeable today. But as Alice Rossi (1968) suggests, "We have ex-spouses and ex-jobs but not ex-children."

Desired or not, once children are born there are strong social and legal obligations to rear them, and to do it well.

The present chapter explores some of the challenges parents face in defining and fulfilling their new responsibilities. The changing societal context of parenting is to be examined, particularly as it affects the differing role expectations of mothers and fathers. Attention will also be given to some contemporary options, such as adoption and remaining childless.

THE SOCIAL CONTEXT OF PARENTHOOD

Parental anxiety

In many ways, the stability and clarity of parental roles reflects the general social stability of a society. The more social change a society experiences, the more unclear or idiosyncractic will be its parental norms. This link is a vital one since parents are the primary socializers of the next generation, and parents can develop common roles only if they have common expectations about the future. When there is rapid social change, the future is unclear and parents have to grope independently for the security that the child demands. This leads to more anxiety, more debates over what is right or wrong, and more inconsistency in parental roles.

Does this sound familiar? It should because this is the confusion expressed by many parents. We see it in conflicts between parents over appropriate discipline, arguments with neighbors over whether Susan is old enough to cross the street alone, debates between the "experts" on the use of spanking, and terms like the "generation gap." But these are only surface signs of an underlying change in the social context of parenthood.

Parental Folklore

Folk beliefs

According to the sociologist E. E. LeMasters (1977), whenever a society has an important function that must be performed, it creates a set of **folk beliefs** to encourage support of that function. Parenthood, in particular, has a rather large body of romantic, widely held beliefs that sometimes have very little basis in fact or, at best, are half-truths. LeMasters has identified the following as some of the rather common folk beliefs in North America:

> Rearing children is fun.
>
> Children turn out well if they have "good" parents.
>
> Today's parents are not as good as those of yesterday.
>
> Child rearing today is easier.
>
> There are no bad children—only bad parents.
>
> All married couples should have children.
>
> Children improve a marriage.
>
> Childless couples are frustrated and unhappy. (pp.19–29)

Statements such as these gloss over much of the reality of parenting. They oversimplify to the point that some people are encouraged prematurely to become parents and others are made to feel unnecessarily guilty over their parental performance. For example, few parents who are going through the experience would describe their feeling as "fun." The day-to-day demands are simply too great to make it a continually pleasurable experience. While parenthood may be rewarding and the highlights fondly remembered, "fun" is not an accurate general description.

The Parental Mandate

Traditional demands for parenthood were largely based on the need for farm labor. An agricultural economy with little machinery placed a premium on the number of hands a family could muster for help with the crops. The childless couple had considerable difficulty in farming so being "barren" was considered very unfortunate.

Labor value of children

With the advent of mechanized agriculture and urbanization, the labor value of children declined, but proparental attitudes were retained. After all, according to most commercial advertising, parenthood is easy. If we simply use paper diapers and throw-away baby bottles and set up a savings plan for future college expenses, we will not have any problems. Then there are the more subtle governmental supports—tax deductions for families with children and, in Canada, monetary allowances to parents with dependent children. While it is true that many parents need all the support they can get, the underlying point is that society provides a value system in which couples have to justify their reasons *not* to be parents since it is parenthood that is viewed as normal.

The Parental-Support Network

Authorities on children

Not only are parents culturally supported in their role, they receive personal support as well. Fathers and mothers who want help and counsel can call on a host of informal or formally designated personnel. The advice of kin is still valued, but it is often weighed against that of pediatricians, school counselors, social workers, child psychiatrists, teachers, youth ministers, recreation directors, and the multitude of "authorities" who write books and articles on child rearing. Skolnick (1978) suggests that this results in a rising "standard" for parents, who in effect become amateurs and increasingly dependent on the cadre of specialists assigned to help them in their roles.

Parental responsibility

While this increased sharing of parental responsibilities relieves parents of some of the burden, it has also resulted in a new set of stresses. Parents now must ensure that the child benefits from all the "opportunities" that are available. This means that it becomes the parents' *responsibility* to see that their children are appropriately linked to the many medical, recreational, academic, religious, psychological, and social specialists and organizations in their community. And the child who is not maximally involved is considered "deprived," and the parents are labeled as "failures." No longer are crooked teeth, an inability to play tennis, a failure to get a booster shot, a weakness in algebra, or a lack of preparation for school permissible. The *authority* over these matters may be shared with the appropriate specialists, but the *responsibility* for placing the child into their hands remains with the parents.

This decline in parental authority is also furthered by a decreasing amount of time exclusively shared by parents and children. With more mothers entering the labor force, more television viewing, earlier entrance into schooling of some type, and greater control being given to peer groups, parents have lost some of their control over the ideas and behavior of their children. James Coleman (1961) summarized his research on the youth culture this way: "The adolescent lives more and more in a society of his own; he finds the family a less and less satisfying psychological home. As a consequence, the home has less and less ability to mold him" (p. 312).

Parental options

At first glance, this may appear to be a rather dismal picture of contemporary parenthood. But for many parents, the costs involved can be outweighed by the new possibilities offered. As the number of child rearing experts increases, for example, so do the options for parents. No longer is a particular parental role culturally mandated. Parents have more freedom to select the style of parenting with which they feel most comfortable. Richard Clayton (1975) reacts to the present situation this way:

> Because each child is entirely different from all others, the lack of explicit norms and guidelines provides a justification for making parental role enactments something that varies to some extent with each child. It encourages a craftsman's approach to the parental role as opposed to the impersonal and monotonous track that emerges with the efficient industrial approach to life. I, for one, hope that we never get so self-assured that we think parental behavior can be programmed. (p. 397)

From the perspective of the child, there are advantages to these new parental roles. For one, children can have more input into the course of their own development, more freedom to help determine their academic and occupational future. Smaller families and more respect for the needs of the individual can also enhance the creative potential of each child. And this can be further supported by the variety of services, agencies, and social groups available to maximize the child's interests and potential.

PARENTHOOD: THE REWARDS

When we consider the conflicts and insecurity inherent in changing parental roles, it is somewhat surprising to find that parenthood remains so popular. Not long ago, this could have been explained by the nature of sexual outcomes; that is, committed heterosexual pair relationships usually led to sexual intercourse and thus to pregnancy and childbirth. Today, however, more effective contraceptives and the widespread use of therapeutic abortion have made the connection between affection and parenthood less necessary. Nevertheless, there often remains an almost natural progression from pairing to parenting since most women and men still *desire* to have children.

Anticipated rewards and costs

Fundamentally, this desire for parenthood can be explained in terms of anticipated rewards and costs. In simple terms, people tend to be motivated toward those goals that offer more rewards than costs. Likewise, it is apparent that couples expect a better costs/rewards ratio from being parents than from remaining childless.

It is important to understand at the outset, however, that these expectations do not necessarily have to conform to reality. The fact that parenthood is in such demand can be because the actual rewards strongly overshadow the actual costs or, alternatively, because the actual rewards are inflated or romanticized while communication about the real costs involved is minimized. This last interpretation is very possible, particularly when we consider that there is very little realistic preparation for parenthood and that parents tend to shield the problems they experience from their children. It might be argued that this situation is quite common in North America and, to the extent that this is true, some couples may find that parenthood is not exactly what they had expected. Others, however, may be very satisfied with their new roles.

With the above in mind, let us examine some of the rewards that attract couples into parenthood.

Feelings of Pleasure

Gratifications

While it is quite difficult to measure accurately general impressions of parenthood, there is little question that the majority of parents report their experience as pleasurable. In a large study of first-time parents in Minnesota, Candyce Russell (1974) found that both fathers and mothers were much more likely to report their feelings of enjoyment than their problems. When they were presented checklists of possible "gratifications" and "problems" of parenthood, they indicated having felt more of the positive items than the negative ones, even though the list of potential problems was larger. Many of the parents were even quite "indignant" over what they considered a bias toward more problems than satisfactions (Russell, 1975).

Overall, the gratifications most often checked by both men and women in the Minnesota study tended to provide more personal pleasure than benefits for the husband-wife relationship. But the mothers and fathers who indicated the greatest parental pleasure were still those who were happily married and those who felt comfortable with their identity of "mother" or "father." In addition, the men who prepared for parenthood by attending classes, reading books, or taking care of other children were more likely to report pleasure.

Lower-class satisfactions

It is also important to note that men and women with lower education or occupational status tend to express the most pleasure in parenthood. For example, a recent national survey of American parents found that the fathers and mothers who were more traditional and had less education were more likely to find their children "fun" and "stimulating" (Hoffman *et al.*, 1978). Among parents from the lowest social classes, the satisfaction of being needed by a dependent child and seeing that child develop under their care may be their most consistent source of pleasure. Bernard Berelson (1972) put it this way: "Life cannot make the poor man prosperous in material goods and services but it can easily make him rich with children."

Social Compliance

Symbols of approval

One of the most observable rewards of parenthood comes from the satisfaction of having complied with the expectations of parents, friends, and the larger society (Blake, 1979). New parents send out birth announcements to let everyone know that they have "joined the ranks." Fathers pass out cigars in order to solicit congratulations from peers. The gifts and well-wishes from friends and parents are welcomed symbols of approval for this new role. For some couples, there is a feeling that the admonition to "Be fruitful and multiply" has been met. The pressure is finally off from the couple's own parents who have wanted to be grandparents. And once again, channels of communication are open to the many friends and associates who had previously become parents. For, like it or not, a principal topic of conversation among adults who are parents is children, and this often causes childless couples to feel left out, even out of place.

Sign of maturity

Parenthood yields a sense of having completed the social order of things. In the national study of parents mentioned earlier (Hoffman *et al.*), one of the most frequent reasons cited for having children was "to have a complete family." In a subtle way, this reflects the social pressure placed on couples to have children. Otherwise, it is implied, they will feel "incomplete." Along with this, couples become increasingly aware of the support they will receive after parenthood. One study of the social value of children came to the conclusion that there are a number of ways in which people signify their maturity, such as by getting a college education, having successful work experience, or by marrying, but that parenthood, even more than these, "establishes a person as a truly mature, stable, and acceptable member of the community" (Hoffman and Hoffman, 1973).

Social Reincarnation

Vicarious pleasures

There is a sense in which parents have a unique opportunity to turn the clock back and start all over again. Obviously, no one can go "back to the womb," but parents can relive many of their early experiences vicariously through their children. Even better, they have the opportunity to take advantage of what they have learned so their children can be or have what the parents had

Seeing the world anew through the eyes of their child is one of the great satisfactions of parenthood for many people.

really wished for themselves. This means that parents can have the reward of seeing their world afresh through the eyes of their children. They can feel once again the sense of excitement at each new discovery. And parents can take pride in the accomplishments of their children throughout their lives.

Of course, this identification with the child can have negative effects as well. Insecure parents may project their anxieties onto their children and push them into activities out of their own interest, not those of the children. As one example of this, studies of Little League baseball have found that many children experience a considerable amount of tension from carrying the responsibility for their parents' displaced need of achievement in athletics (Watson, 1974). In a similar way, parents can project onto their children their need for achievement in other sports, or in school grades, music, beauty contests, even dating.

Immortality

The family name

Closely allied to the notion of reliving one's childhood through parenthood is the reward of generational immortality. In Eastern cultures, particularly India, preindustrial China, and Japan, this was very important as children were seen as the means by which one's "name" and influence lived on after death. Ancestors were revered, worshipped, and consulted in a variety of matters, usually related to their expertise during life. In this same sense, some people today seek parenthood in order to have their contributions remembered and their family name continued. This interest is more likely to be expressed by men than women (Hoffman *et al.*.), and by people in the upper classes who hope to hold their family wealth intact for future generations (Coles, 1977). In many ways, the upper-class custom of hanging portraits of influential family members over the mantel is not unlike the ancient shrines for ancestors in Eastern societies. For less wealthy people, however, the feeling of continued influence may come more from the satisfaction of rearing children who are competent and successful in their own right than from the legacy of property passed down.

Power

For some individuals, parenthood might also provide an outlet for their need for power or mastery over another. Most of us have this need, whether we recognize it or not, yet there are some segments of society in which the opportunity directly to influence or control the actions of another is rare. This general feeling of powerlessness is quite common among the economically or socially disadvantaged and it may also be found in some women in traditional households. Among these people, parenthood leads to a unique feeling of importance because someone is now dependent on their directions. The mother who has little control over her husband can still tell her child, "Go clean up your room!" The father who is on the bottom of the totem pole on the job feels that he can still order his son to mow the lawn or do his homework.

Instrumental vs. intrinsic benefits

Nevertheless, there are limits to the power reward for parents today. Demonstrating one's power through the biological fact of paternity or maternity will result in very little public acclaim if the more demanding responsibilities of parenthood are not carried out. No longer do parents have life and death control over their children, and as more parental roles are shared with others, the opportunity for parents to exert exclusive control declines even further. The rewards that accompany parenthood, therefore, are becoming less dependent on the instrumental benefits children have for parents and more dependent on the intrinsic satisfaction parents can receive from sharing experiences with their children.

PARENTHOOD: THE COSTS

In a very insightful way, Thomas Murray (1976) calls our attention to the increased number of warnings that now confront us in our daily lives. While often inconspicuous, they are carried on cigarette ads, food and drug packages, clothing labels, and many other products we regularly purchase and use. Likewise, he suggests, pictures of babies might carry a warning something like:

> This baby will quickly grow into a full-size girl or boy, requiring constant attention, love, understanding, encouragement, guidance, and discipline. He should be given priority in most major decisions you make in the next twenty-five years. He can be expected to often be uncooperative, unloving, and unappreciative of your time, energy, money, and sleepless nights. He may at times defy and disappoint you, lie to you, and even spit at you. He will also do a great deal of damage to your house, your yard, your car, and to the quiet hours you had planned to squander on yourself.

Murray's "warning" is offered tongue-in-cheek, but his point is quite valid: most parents-to-be know very little about the totality of parenthood, including the personal, relational, and financial costs that are incurred. The potential rewards of being a parent are well acknowledged in our folklore but the costs are often hidden.

Weaknesses in parental preparation

Alice Rossi considers this lack of adequate preparation to be one of the most critical problems couples face in their transition to parenthood. In her analysis, she focuses on four weaknesses in parental preparation. First, unlike most areas of training, there is little supervised practice for parental roles. The knowledge most people have about child rearing is limited to their experiences in baby sitting, some care of younger siblings, or perhaps a course in child psychology. Second, pregnancy provides little parental readiness other than a "minor nesting phase" in which a place for the baby is prepared, a book may be read, and some discussions entered into with the spouse and friends about parenthood. There is little opportunity at this point to develop the skills or emotional supports that will be necessary later. Third, the birth of the child signals the beginning of a twenty-four-hours-a-day, seven-days-per week responsibility, with no breaks for coffee, weekends, or holidays. There is no opportunity for gradually acquiring this kind of responsibility. Fourth, Rossi suggests that there are few clear guidelines for successful parenthood. "How-to-parent" books provide information on the medical, nutritional, environmental, and, to some degree, emotional and social needs of preschoolers. But when it comes to guiding this child into adulthood, parents are left to their own devices.

Financial Costs

Most people who hope to become parents have come to believe that children are "priceless." This may be a healthy concept since, as with most priceless possessions, their financial costs can be quite high. Unfortunately, in the case of child rearing, few parents-to-be really understand the monetary commitment they are about to make. Also, their new financial obligation is often coupled with a temporary or long-term loss of the wife's income and this

Table 13.1

The Cost of Raising a Child

These costs are based on raising a child to age 18 at 1980 prices and a moderate budget level. Add at least $25,000 for college expenses.	Food—at home	$16,429
	Food—away from home	1,755
	Clothing	6,129
	Housing	22,502
	Medical care	3,749
	Education	1,067
	Transportation	10,719
	Miscellaneous	8,354
		$70,703

Source: Roger L. Miller, *Economic Issues for Consumers*, second edition, West Publishing Co., St. Paul, Minn., 1981, p. 106.

situation of rising costs with declining income is especially unsettling in many marriages (Bartz, 1978).

Direct child-rearing expenses

Parents are required to spend larger sums then nonparents for food, clothing, travel, medical and dental care, entertainment, toys, and education; plus they need larger and more expensive homes and automobiles. Many of these costs rise considerably when children reach adolescence. Based on data from the United States Bureau of Labor Statistics, it is estimated that the *direct costs* of rearing a child from infancy through high school come to over $70,000 per child in a middle-income family (Miller, 1981). This figure assumes that inflation will continue to escalate child-rearing costs in the future (see Table 13.1).

Indirect expenses

There are also *indirect costs* involved in parenthood that should be considered in an objective analysis of child-rearing expenses. For example, if a couple does not have children, they have the opportunity to invest and earn interest on the money that would have gone into child-rearing expenses. Also, the mother who is not employed is "costing" the relationship her lost wages and even if she is employed, her net contribution is often reduced by expenses for child care or extra household help. It is estimated that the indirect costs in terms of lost interest from child-rearing expenses and lost income from the wife-mother amount to over $100,000 for the average family (Miller, 1981).

Personal Costs

While the specter of increasing financial costs may seem forbidding, parenthood more immediately affronts the personal needs for free time, energy, and identity. The seemingly innocent saying that parenting is a "twenty-four-hour responsibility" becomes all too true within days after the first child arrives home, and subsequent children require even more of their parents' personal resources. In a practical sense, few people are adequately prepared for the amount of additional time it takes to do the extra laundry, feed and comfort the baby, prepare food and formula, clean the house, and pick up toys.

Household work

In a study of time devoted to household work, Walker and Woods (1975) confirm the impact children can have on their parents' home responsibilities. As the family size increases, they found, so does the total amount of household work. Most of the increased time and energy, however, is contributed by the wife-mother, and this is true whether she is employed or not. For example, the employed wife with no children spends less than four hours per day in household work compared to over six hours per day after the first child is added to the family, an increase in effort of over 50 percent. Husbands, they found, not only spend much less time than their wives in these tasks, but they also are less inclined to increase their time contribution as children come into the family, and this makes the strain on the mother even greater.

In Russell's (1974) study of 271 couples, she found several personal "crises" associated with becoming a parent. While not all of the parents experienced severe problems, a majority admitted to being bothered at least "somewhat" in a number of areas. In general, Russell found that the concerns of the wives centered around their emotional and physical adjustments while the husbands tended to worry about the baby's influence on their life-style. The five problems most frequently mentioned by husbands and wives are listed in Table 13.2.

Career commitments

Another pressure that often accompanies parenthood is associated with changes in occupational-career commitments. For the woman, there is still a tendency to give up her career for a time in favor of full-time motherhood. We can see this in the fact that nearly six out of ten wives without children

Table 13.2

Most Frequently Indicated Parental-Adjustment Problems

Problem	Percent Who Indicated This Problem
Husbands:	
Interrupted sleep and rest	61%
Suggestions from in-laws about baby	54
Changing of future plans	54
Increased money problems	53
Additional amount of work required	53
Wives:	
Physical tiredness and fatigue	78%
Interrupted sleep and rest	76
Worry about personal appearance	74
Feeling "edgy" or emotionally upset	68
Worry about "loss of figure"	61

Source: Data from Candyce Russell, "Transition to Parenthood: Problems and Gratifications," *Journal of Marriage and the Family* 36 (1974): 294–302.

were employed in 1976 compared to only one-third of the wives with preschool children (Bednarzik and Klein, 1977). Jessie Bernard (1974) notes that this loss is not only costly to the family in terms of lost income, but it is also costly to the woman because of her loss in career seniority and skill. She comments:

> There has been not only an attrition of her skills but also a degrading of her professional knowledge, for a very fast pace is necessary to keep up with any occupation these days. An absence of even a few years can render one's knowledge obsolete. Vacant spaces appear in the woman's work history when she applies for a position. All these intangibles militate against her when she looks for employment after several years' absence. (p. 290)

The personal costs for the husband often result from the pressure to maintain the family's standard of living after a loss of the wife's income and a considerable rise in expenses. This leads many men to work longer hours at their jobs to earn extra pay or to try to enhance their possibilities for advancement. This is particularly true of men in professional or managerial positions (Hedges, 1976). Other men feel they have to take a second job to handle the additional financial load. In the United States, about 6 percent of these men hold multiple jobs, but it is the married men in the child-rearing years who are the most likely to be in this situation (Rosenfeld, 1979).

Relational Costs

Marital satisfaction

The strain that parenthood can have on the husband-wife relationship is perhaps the least anticipated cost. Nevertheless, when marriages are studied over time or when couples at different points in their marriages are compared, there is a very strong tendency for marital satisfaction to decline during the parenting years (Cowan *et al.*, 1979). So strong is this tendency that when the child-rearing years are over, the overall marital satisfaction scores of husbands and wives rise once again. This pattern can be seen clearly in the findings of one investigation charted in Fig. 13.1. Some researchers (Rollins and Cannon, 1974) have cautioned that not all couples experience this decline, and that for those who do, the actual change in marital satisfaction may not be very great. But the consistency with which studies find some decline in marital satisfaction after parenthood begins still serves notice of the potential strain involved.

Mother-child coalitions

What kinds of conditions tend to increase marital stress after parenthood? For one, there is a decrease in the amount of time available to the married couple for maintaining their own special relationship. As we noted in Chapter 2, the pair-dyad relationship is a fundamental social unit, and there is a tendency for three-person and other larger relationships to form coalitions of pairs so that one pair relationship becomes stronger at the expense of the others (Simmel, 1950; Caplow, 1968). Usually, the relationship that receives the most time and effort becomes the stronger. Because of the

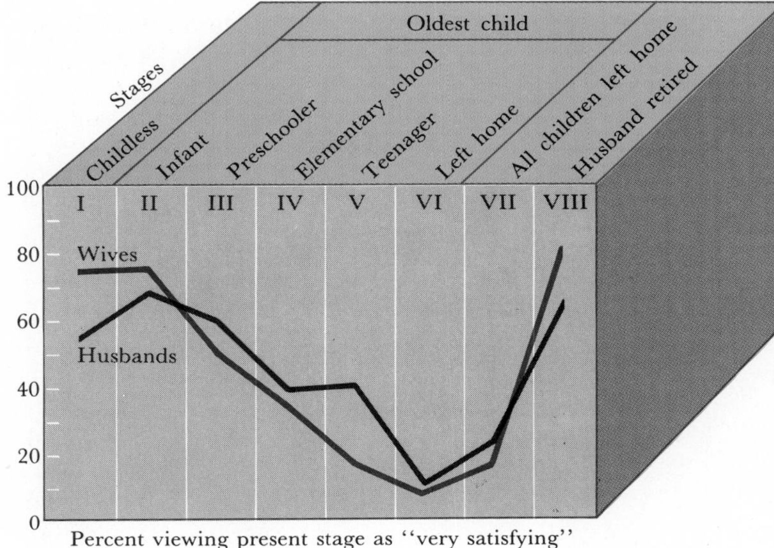

Fig. 13.1

Life Cycle Changes in Marital Satisfaction

Source: Boyd C. Rollins and Harold Feldman, *Journal of Marriage and the Family*. Copyrighted 1970 by the National Council on Family Relations. Reprinted by permission.

physical tie of the mother and child before birth which is often difficult to share with the husband, and because of the social obligation and perhaps physical link through nursing between mother and child after birth, there is often a tendency for the mother-child relationship to grow at the expense of the husband-wife relationship.

In support of this, Helena Lopata (1971) reports that many of the mothers in her large interview study came to be more afraid of "neglecting" their children than their husbands. The demands of the child and a growing feeling of personal parental competence led to "a tendency of young mothers to feel that the baby is theirs, a possessiveness that excludes male ownership" (p. 198).

When these new coalition strains are added to the other personal and financial costs noted earlier, then a tendency emerges for the roles of husbands and wives to become more separate and distinct. Fathers focus more of their attention on occupational and other outside interests while mothers become the child-care specialists. Neeley and Orthner (1978) found that although neither engaged men nor women particularly desired this outcome, almost every couple with young children had already established this pattern, whether the wife was employed or not.

Added to this role strain is the sexual frustration that may accompany parenthood. In addition to the period shortly before and after childbirth when sexual intercourse is often abstained from for medical or comfort reasons, many couples report being too fatigued to reinitiate the sexual relationship they once enjoyed. Most intimate relationships require some physical contact to maintain intensive commitments, but some mothers are overly exposed to body contact and this may lessen their interest or under-

The close bond between mother and infant leaves some fathers feeling "excluded."

standing of their husband's needs for physical reassurance (Phillips and Anzalone). Since the husband is not receiving this kind of contact comfort, he may interpret this as rejection of him.

Differences in parental experiences

How can we reconcile this tendency for marriage to be strained by parenthood with the oft-conceived notion that "parenthood brings a couple closer together"? One explanation is offered by Lopata based on her interviews with over 1000 women in the Chicago area. In her study, she found two quite distinct marital reactions to the parental experience. Among most of the lower-class and many of the middle-class parents, the husbands and wives lived in traditional, sex-segregated worlds, even in early marriage. For these couples, Lopata (1971) discovered, "parenthood roles add an important and meaningful bond in a relatively limited relation, bringing the husband and wife 'closer together' through the creation of a common interest" (p. 199). In contrast to this, however, most of the middle-class women, particularly those who were college educated, had based their marriage on companionship and intrinsic commitments and they were more likely to speak of strain and "express a feeling of increased social distance between themselves and their mates" (1971, p. 199). Since traditional, sex-segregated values were dominant not long ago, it is not hard to see how the belief that children bring about parental closeness has been carried forward to the present day when it is less likely to be true for many couples.

CHANGING PARENTAL ROLES

Parental roles are not and have never been particularly easy roles to learn or successfully carry out. They are very complex since the **role-set** encompasses a wide variety of expectations and obligations that change as the child matures, the number of children increases, and the social norms and values surrounding the family evolve. The transition into parenting, in fact, may be considerably more demanding than the transitions involved in pairing. According to the research by Lopata (1971), "Many of the women interviewed explained that the greatest change in their lives was created not by marriage but by the birth of their first child" (p. 33). A rather large proportion of parents do not adapt well to these new roles; the costs become overwhelming to the point that few rewards are ever realized. This is evident in the rising divorce rate among parents, parental desertion, child abuse, and the increases in juvenile delinquency in all social classes. Other parents, however, control their potential costs more effectively, allowing the rewards rather than the costs to be the driving force behind their role performance.

Reducing parental costs

The research by Russell (1974), Lopata (1971), and others suggests that the middle-class parents who consider themselves successful in adapting to their new roles reduce their potential costs by strengthening *all* of the relationships in the expanded family. This involves giving continued attention to the marital relationship while maintaining a high level of parental commitment on the part of *both* parents. Admittedly, this is difficult to do because it is more efficient and traditional to strengthen the mother-child relationship at the expense of all others. But through more involvement of the husband, the husband-wife and father-child relationships can relieve some of the growing strain on the mother. In turn, this reduces the mother's rising personal costs, lessens the father's sense of isolation, strengthens the marriage as a foundation for parenting, and creates a more efficient system for parenting.

To make this new system work, however, men and women must have a different set of role definitions. Indeed, this is beginning to happen, and these new parental roles are now challenging traditional concepts of motherhood and fatherhood.

Motherhood

Maternal myth

Not too long ago, motherhood was regarded as the ultimate fulfillment for all women. Marriage was the means by which this was achieved, but motherhood was the real goal. Myth even had it that women were "natural" mothers, that they had exclusive maternal instincts to guide them internally toward successful parenthood. But as with other myths, social scientists soon exposed the fact that not all women felt comfortable as mothers, and from the evidence of child neglect and abuse by mothers, it is unlikely that women are biologically endowed to be perfect parents either.

Part of the problem women inherit, however, is that cultural definitions of the motherhood role place almost the entire responsibility for child-rearing

Vignette 13.1
Child-Rearer = Mother

Of all the social "roles" associated with the female sex, the one most firmly bolstered by references to nature, biology, and anatomy is undoubtedly that of mother. Assumptions that all women are possessed of a maternal instinct, that they innately want to raise children and have the ability to care for them, that children need to be "mothered" by a mother or at least a "mother substitute," or they will suffer from "maternal deprivation," are at the core of both popular and scientific thinking about child rearing.

The use of terms derived from "mother" to denote caring for children is far too commonplace to require documentation. The activity called "mothering" involves tending children, servicing their needs, and supplying the tender concern vital to healthy personality development. There is no effort to separate these functions semantically from the female person who typically performs them. These things constitute "maternal care," and the implication is that, *ipso facto,* they can only be provided by a female.

Consider the different meanings brought to mind by the following statements: The child was mothered by X; The child was fathered by Y. The first sentence suggests tender loving care, while the second implies mere physical paternity.

So far I have been speaking as if this were all a matter of semantics. But sociologists don't just happen to *say* "mother" for "child-rearer," they *mean* it. Identity in word reflects identity in thought.

The linguistic/conceptual equation of child-rearer and female parent is most pernicious, from a feminist perspective, when it appears in statements about the needs of children. Experts on child development ought to tell us simply that a child needs loving care, but what they proclaim instead is "a child needs a mother."

on their shoulders. As Margaret Polatnick (1974) carefully points out (Vignette 13.1), the language of parenthood implies that "mothering" and "maternal" are distinctly more personal to the child than "fathering" and "paternal." Therefore, as the standards for parenting rise and as the support networks for child rearing decline, mothers, not fathers, take on the increased load. In addition to this, mothers have acquired a whole host of additional responsibilities, which include companion to the husband, family manager, community liaison, and often, cobreadwinner. The result is the role overload mothers often experience.

It is this kind of pressure that has left many women anxious and guilty about their own personal interests outside of being a mother. The desire to continue a career, to have moments of peace to oneself, to take up the hobbies that once were enjoyed, even to share in an uninterrupted adult conversation, are coupled with the feeling, "What will happen to the children?" or "What are they doing right now?" As this exaggeration of the motherhood role increases, identification with the child plus identification with the husband leads to the woman becoming "somebody's" mother and "somebody else's" wife—in effect, to becoming a nonperson in her own right.

Let one example suffice: Anna Freud and Dorothy Burlingham, in their study of war-time children's relocation centers, state that a growing child's basic requirements include "intimate interchange of affection with a maternal figure." Are we to conclude that men are incapable of providing this affection? Is their affection biologically not the right sort? Must we refer to those men who do exchange intimate affection with growing children by an exclusively female term?

The term and concept "maternal deprivation" presents similar difficulties. Can a child receive loving care only from a woman? Is it possible for a man to be a "mother substitute"? Are males constitutionally impotent when it comes to "maternal love"?

It might be argued that all these female-specific words for intensive "parenting" are merely *descriptive,* since in the societies familiar to us, women *are* almost exclusively the providers of "maternal care." Nonetheless, there exist a few societies and some individual men in our society that do not conform to this pattern. And the constant use of female terms for the rearing of children becomes obviously *prescriptive.* With messages like this omnipresent—. . . when deprived of maternal care, the child's development is almost always retarded—physically, intellectually, and socially. . .—few mothers will reject the primary parenting role (and few fathers will give them the opportunity to do so).

Reprinted with permission from Margaret Polatnick, "Why Men Don't Rear Children," *Berkeley Journal of Sociology,* 1974.

Loss of identity

This loss of personal identity is not a universal problem. For many women, the satisfactions of full-time motherhood and devotion to the accomplishments of husband and children are clearly sought and preferred. But the trend today is away from this kind of identification and toward finding personal fulfillment in other roles as well. After examining the research on mother-child interaction, Janet Chafetz (1978) concludes:

> Motherhood cannot be an all-encompassing activity, for the sake of both mothers and the offspring. Quantity of attention (past some absolute minimum) is simply not an important consideration in how children "turn out." A few hours a day of intensive, loving, high "quality" attention to a child by a mother who is happily growing and fulfilling herself the rest of the time is worth infinitely more than the never-ending hours of incessant bickering that passes for child rearing in so many homes today. (p. 196)

Alternatives for mothers

How can a woman relieve this potential strain between motherhood and selfhood? There are several alternatives: (1) by not becoming a parent (to be discussed later in this chapter), (2) by denying her own personal needs (the usual pattern but one which is increasingly becoming unacceptable), (3) by purchasing the help needed to free her from some of her role obligations (this takes money that may not be available to all families), or (4) by sharing her responsibilities with her husband who must then adjust some of his own role expectations. The last two alternatives, in particular, require greater acceptance of mothers entering the labor force and/or fathers becoming more active in child-rearing roles. In both cases, unless men change their own traditional expectations of male-female roles, women may find their satisfaction with motherhood waning.

Fatherhood

Traditional concepts of fatherhood

In the sense that we usually use the term, "fatherhood" rarely carries the same notion of parental role commitments that "motherhood" does. The roles are culturally defined almost as opposites: fathers are "hard," instrumental, competitive, exacting; mothers are "soft," expressive, accommodating, loving. A "good" father is one who "brings home the bacon"; a "good" mother is one who gives up everything she has for her children. While these are certainly traditional images, the characterizations are all too real today in many families. Witness, for example, the following two "stories about my parents" written by an eight-year-old boy in a Wisconsin elementary school (Boss, 1974):

> My dad is a businessman.
> He is gone during the week.
> But he is home on weekends.
> He watches football every weekend.

> My mom does not work.
> She buys me lots of toys for Christmas.
> My mom takes me lots of places.
> We do lots of things together.

There are definite forces operating to keep fathers from straying too far from this perspective. Perhaps the most important is the early socialization toward what Leonard Benson (1968) calls the "survival" dimension of the fatherhood role. Males are taught that it is their responsibility to ensure the basic existence of the family unit. This includes being physically capable of causing reproduction, protecting the family from outside harm, ensuring order within the home, and materially supporting the family through outside labor. This need to ensure survival means that if the mother is employed, the father still sees himself as the "primary" breadwinner. Also his feeling of fatherhood is more closely linked to his biological *paternity* than to his close, interpersonal father-child relationship. When we hear, "Do as I say, I am your father!" this usually refers to a biological fact, not an earned quality.

Survival role of fatherhood

A second problem faced by fathers is the lack of clear guidelines on how to be a nurturing parent. Benson (1968) indicates that fathers have traditionally had an "expressive" dimension to their role but that this has been clearly secondary to their survival responsibilities. Men have never been expected to be totally aloof from the rest of the family, but information designed to help fathers better understand the parent-child relationship has, until recently, been exceptionally scarce (McLaughlin, 1978). Even more scarce are models that can guide men toward accepting new views of nurturing parenthood. According to Polatnick, "Boys undergo a significant learning process about parenthood: they learn they *don't* have to take care of children. . . . Nurturance, they discover, is not regarded as a suitable ingredient of masculinity or male identity (p. 211).

Father expressiveness

Nevertheless, despite these strong cultural pressures, fatherhood roles are beginning to change. While a 1980 Gallup poll found only one-third of the younger fathers participating regularly in the duties of infant care, this is still twice the participation rate of fathers a generation ago (Hunt and Hunt, 1980). Indeed, the primary force behind this change has come from women, who themselves seek to share more of their expressive roles and accept more survival responsibilities. As mothers have increased their participation in the labor force, by choice or necessity, and in general experienced an expansion of roles, fathers have begun to feel guilty about their lack of household and child-care participation. No longer is the image of the father coming home from the office to sit in "his" chair and read the evening paper while mother prepares the meal, fends off hungry children, and mixes his drink considered very positive. The privileges he used to enjoy were earned by outdated notions of father-work being outside the home and mother-work being inside the home—concepts fostered by an early industrial economy in which men labored ten to twelve hours per day, six days a week. But now, fathers have more free time, they return home in the midst of family routines, and it is difficult for them or their wives to justify their sense of isolation from the rest of the family.

Pressures to change

For many fathers, these new opportunities for total family involvement are also quite attractive (see Vignette 13.2). As their exclusive hold on the survival roles declines and their work environment becomes increasingly impersonal, fathers are opting for more emotional fulfillment in their parental and marital relationships. Based on his observations of fathers and children, James A. Levine (1976) offers this hypothesis:

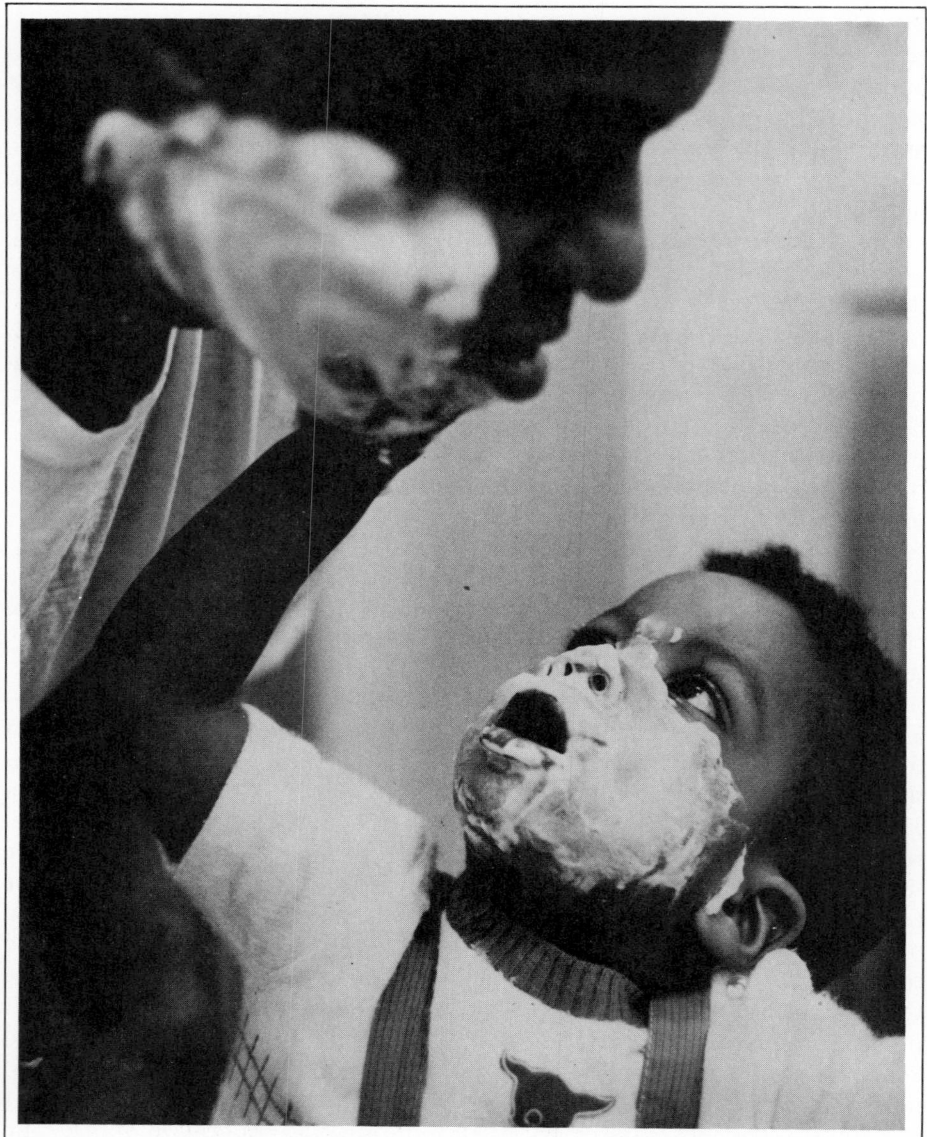

Fatherhood roles are changing to include men as nurturers of children, too.

If men are encouraged from childhood through adolescence and adulthood to feel that their own sense of personal identity can be built on direct caring, and not just on providing, they will feel less of a need to invest everything in breadwinning and career. . . . This is not to say they shouldn't be providers or take pride in their success. But a broadened sense of manhood will relieve men of some of the burdens attached to providing, and will allow some to experience more fully the achievement of helping their children grow (p. 169).

Vignette 13.2

Men and Young Children

Noontime in busy Boston. A tall, suited man walks down Beacon Street holding hands with a small girl. She stops and insistently pulls on his sleeve. Bending, he listens attentively to her ear-aimed whisper. And with a whoosh and a giggle, she is whisked onto his shoulders. They continue down the street together, his hands firmly gripping her knees, her face showing delight at being "bigger than the big people."

A classroom in a day-care center in Salt Lake City, Utah. In the middle of the tousled room, a bushy-eyed, rumply-looking young man sits reading to the little boy and girl nestled in his lap. Around him an ethnic salad-bowl of four-year-olds are engaged in block-playing, crayoning, book-looking, and truck-riding. Each child seems aware of the man's quiet presence: it is as if he is the hub of their activity. A small, teary boy comes over for comfort, his feelings hurt in a spill. The teacher soothes him gently with a hug, then sends him back to his play.

A small town in rural Colorado. A spare, middle-aged man with weathered western features is making his weekly visits to families in the Parent-Child Center Program. He worked for twenty-five years on the railroad, then retired at the age of fifty to take a job working with children and families because, "I figured there was more to do than juggling numbers in an office." Three small children spot him heading toward their house and, shouting excitedly, run to his open arms. He will take them on an "outing" to show them the trees on a nearby farm, then spend an hour talking with their mother about the nutrition and health care of her infant.

An administrator tells of lunching twice a week with his five-year-old son. "I blocked out Tuesdays and Thursdays on my calendar and simply said I was having lunch with Michael. The first two weeks I got some funny looks from people who dropped in to see me as I was on my way out and some 'Who's Michael?' comments. Pretty soon, though, people realized that they could see me just as well at other times."

An expectant father who works in a metal-parts factory tells of his conversations at work. "Two other guys are also expecting children, so we talk a fair amount about kids, our wives, and fatherhood. You know, in the last few years, even the traveling salesmen have started talking about their children. It's almost like a guy seems more alive when he talks about children."

Nurturant moments . . . each with a gracefulness that gives it a life of its own. Men with young children. Relationships long ignored and abused by the media, social scientists, politicians, teachers, clinicians . . . and mothers and fathers. Relationships being rediscovered today, often with a richness born of exile, by men who are coming home, to themselves and to their loved ones.

From Robert A. Fein, Program Director, McLean-Bridgewater Program Instructor, Harvard Medical School. "Men with Young Children." In Joseph Fleck and Jack Sawyer, *Men and Masculinity* (Englewood Cliffs, N.J.: Prentice-Hall, 1974), pp. 54–55.

ADOPTIVE PARENTHOOD

The transition into parenthood for many couples begins with adoption rather than pregnancy and childbirth. The reasons for wanting to adopt children vary widely, but among nonparents, it is most often because a couple's chances for parenthood are hindered by infertility or other medical problems. Not all couples who want to adopt children, however, are able to do so. Unlike natural parenthood, which has few qualifications and ample opportunity to overproduce babies, prospective adoptive parents are faced with standards they must meet and a diminishing supply of adoptable children.

Drop in adoption

Approximately 2 percent of the children in America have adoptive parents, but in two-thirds of these cases, the children were adopted by a relative, such as a step-parent or another relative after the death of the natural parents (Bonham, 1977). Of the nonrelative adoptions, four-fifths are handled by adoption agencies and one-fifth by private arrangements. Nevertheless, since 1970, the number of children available to unrelated persons has dropped significantly. Nearly nine out of ten children adopted by nonrelatives are born to unmarried women, but many of these women are now terminating their pregnancies by abortion or keeping their babies rather than putting them up for adoption. In the late 1960s, 90 percent of the children born out of wedlock were placed for adoption compared to only 10 percent today (Scales and Gordon, 1979).

Adoption failures

After the child is in the home, adoptive parents appear to adjust to their new roles in much the same way natural parents do. Adoptive parents have the advantage of being able to choose their child, within limits, and they have a probationary period of six months to a year in which they can decide to return the child, if they are displeased (LeMasters). Nevertheless, only about one out of ten children placed in homes are removed before final adoption. This "failure rate" is lowest when the child is under two years of age and highest when the child is over six years of age. In the mid-1970s, 60 percent of the children placed for adoption were under two years of age (Touliatos and Lindholm, 1976), but the overall failure rates in some areas have begun to rise as the percentage of infants available for adoption has declined. In Los Angeles County, for example, the adoption failure rate rose from 2 percent in 1970 to 13 percent in 1978 (Rooney, 1979).

In general, the majority of adopted children and their parents view their relationships very positively. Benson Jaffee (1974) conducted a study of previous adoptions for the Child Welfare League of America and found that 85 percent of the young adults who had been adopted as children felt they had encountered little or no adoption-related problems; 91 percent of their parents felt the same way. In another study of one hundred adoptees and their parents, seventy-six of the ninety adoptees who responded to the questions felt they were "very close" or "somewhat close" to their parents (Jaffee and Fanshel, 1970). The adoption of older children is somewhat more likely to lead to stress, but when ninety-one parents who adopted older children were

In the aftermath of United States' withdrawal from Vietnam, some Americans adopted mixed-race children fathered by servicemen during the war.

questioned, the investigator still found that the majority reported being "extremely" satisfied with their experience (Kadushin, 1967). Results such as these suggest that adoptive parenthood can be a very meaningful and rewarding way of fulfilling parental desires.

SINGLE PARENTHOOD

Parenthood today does not always involve a two-parent home. A growing number of children are being reared in single-parent families. Currently, about one out of five children are living with only one parent, either their mother or their father (United States Bureau of the Census, 1980). The cause for this may be the death of one parent, separation or divorce of both parents, an unmarried pregnancy, or adoption by a single person. Except for death, each of these conditions is becoming more common, increasing the odds that a man or woman might at some time be a single parent.

Routes to single parenthood

Nine out of ten single parents are women. Traditionally, the higher mortality rates of men left many women as widows to rear their children. Now, divorce and unwed pregnancy are also principal routes to single parenthood, which means that single parents and their children are usually younger than was true earlier. At the present time, divorce alone is creating nearly 600,000 new single-parent families each year. One-fourth of the children in these families are under six years of age (Johnson, 1978). If present trends continue, over one-third of all U.S. children in the United States will spend part of their childhood in a single-parent home as a result of disrupted marriage (Bumpass and Rindfuss, 1979).

While there is a tendency to categorize all single parents together, we are now finding important differences in the life-styles of single parents depending upon how this family pattern was started. For instance, the single parents who usually experience the most difficulty are unwed mothers. The majority of these are teenage mothers who are handicapped by a lack of education and job skills. This makes it almost impossible for them to be financially independent so they typically remain at home dependent on their own parents. The household then becomes three generational with the older parents controlling the child rearing and the young mother finding herself caught between the demands of her child and her parents. Older unmarried parents are usually more independent, but they too face the social disapproval that society still metes out to unwed mothers (Stinnett and Birdsong, 1978).

Adoptive single parents are comparatively rare but growing in number (Ewing, 1980). At one time, adoption agencies forbade single persons from adopting a child, especially since the number of children available to intact families was declining. But there are still a large number of hard-to-place children who need love yet are not usually wanted by married couples. Those children who are older, mixed racially, or handicapped are more likely candidates for adoption by single persons. Not surprisingly, if these women and men are motivated enough to want a child, they tend to be quite successful parents (Kadushin).

Widowhood is often unanticipated, but it is the second most common cause of single parenthood among women. Widowed mothers and fathers are the most likely to receive community and kin support, but they are also more likely to feel a greater shock in the transition to single parenthood (Mendes, 1976). There is a finality to death that does not linger on, like divorce. Yet the sharp reorganization of the family, frequently without warning, usually requires a longer period of adjustment than other forms of single parenthood.

Tender-years doctrine

Marital separation and divorce are now the most common causes of single parenthood. Nine out of ten times, child custody is awarded by the court to the mother, often because of parental preferences but also because of the "tender-years doctrine" in American law which had assumed the mother to be the logical parent of choice for young children (Orthner and Lewis, 1979). Single parenthood after divorce usually requires considerable adjustment since community support is minimal, the desire to establish independence is great, and the new relationship to the "ex-spouse" and other parent of the child must be negotiated.

Children of divorce

Still, both divorced mothers and fathers have been found to be capable as parents. Children of divorce do not usually grow up forever harmed by the experience; they adjust to their circumstances along with their parents, but not without a good deal of pain and not without loving assistance (Wallerstein and Kelly, 1980). For the divorced single-parent mother, economic strains often accompany the adjustment, and she usually must seek employment, all too frequently at low pay. When this is accompanied by the rising costs of child care and household upkeep, it is not surprising to find that one-third of these mothers are living below the poverty level (Johnson) and that the majority find it hard to readjust their lives to lower incomes (Brandwein *et al.*, 1974).

For those divorced fathers who are able to surmount the legal obstacles to child custody, the adjustment to primary parenthood is usually more difficult than managing the economic needs of the household. But those fathers who get custody appear to become capable in their parenting roles. In a recent study prepared for lawyers and judges, it was reported that single fathers tend to seek custody because of their sincere interest in the children, not to hurt their former wives; that single fathers do not experience great difficulty in rearing daughters; and that most single fathers receive a good deal of support from friends and kin for their parenting responsibilities (Orthner and Lewis).

Adjustment to single parenthood

As trying as early adjustments usually are for both single mothers and single fathers, the single parents who adapt to their roles most easily have several characteristics in common. For one thing, those men and women who have previously been both employed and involved parents find it easier to achieve a balance in these roles after they become single parents. Mothers and fathers who are thrust into employment or parenthood without much experience suffer the most strain.

Other factors which usually ease the adjustment into single parenthood include the support of relatives and friends, participation in support groups such as Parents Without Partners, continuing contacts between the other parent and the children, and acceptance by the children and the single parent of their situation. The inability of the parent to make the break into the new life-style with a new sense of independence and energy translates to the children a feeling of loneliness and hopelessness that hampers their adjustment as well (Smith, 1980). But children also react differently, and each requires a different kind of support to which the single parent must be sensitive. One divorced mother found:

> The first week or so my daughter cried herself to sleep about every night. She didn't want to go to school because it would be written all over her face. I made her go to school. I made her face it immediately. And I told her teachers so they were aware of it. And then she got over it, when she knew that everything was going to stay the same basically . . .

My son is older, in high school. Now my son is quite different from my daughter. My daughter was able to vent her feelings. My son is very cool. You could see tears in his eyes, but he wouldn't let it out. Even though I said it was good to cry if you feel that way, he didn't. So he was the one I worried about.

We had one heck of a year. (Weiss, 1975, p. 205)

VOLUNTARY CHILDLESSNESS

While most of this chapter has dealt with the transition involved in becoming parents, there are a growing number of persons who are seriously questioning if parenthood is really compatible with their adult life-style plans. In the past, such people did not marry, or if they did, these thoughts were quickly squashed by social pressure and the lack of effective contraceptives. But today, rising concerns over the effects parenthood can have on some personal and relational goals are making the decision to be "child-free" a more reasonable option for married couples.

Child-free preferences

Estimates vary as to the proportion of couples who prefer to be childless, but the fact remains that they are in the minority. Most surveys in Canada and the United States have found fewer than 5 percent of the respondents do not want to be parents (Blake). Even smaller is the actual rate of voluntary childlessness, generally regarded to be about 2 to 3 percent in North America. Preferences for childlessness, nevertheless, are rising, particularly among the college educated, and this may be partially reflected in the current decline in the birthrate. In the mid-1970s, one-quarter of the childless wives aged twenty-five to twenty-nine expected to remain childless over their entire lifetimes (United States Bureau of the Census, 1976).

The problem with predicting trends based on "planning," however, is that the best plans often go awry. Many of those who plan to be childless later change their minds and become parents. Others, who were not at first serious about being child-free, almost "stumble" into it. Jean Veevers (1973) found that only one-third of the childless wives she interviewed had seriously decided not to have children before they were married. Most of these women, in fact, had made this decision early in adolescence. The remaining two-thirds of the women became childless only after repeatedly postponing their decision to become parents.

Decision-making stages

Veevers explains that this unfolding decision to remain childless usually passes through four stages: first, an ambivalent period when parenthood is only casually considered; second, a period of postponement during which the couple becomes indefinite about when they will begin parenting, even though their friends are often already parents; third, a period of admitting that they might prefer childlessness; and fourth, an open recognition of the fact that they will not have children. At this time, the women in the study did not feel

Some women elect to remain childless to better pursue their careers.

that it was "too late" to have children; they had simply become more aware of the relative advantages and disadvantages of opting for parenthood and decided that they preferred their present life-style.

Career preferences

Whether the decision to be childless is made early or later, there appear to be three factors involved in selecting the life-style. The first factor, and perhaps most important, is a strong desire to take advantage of career opportunities and to fulfill other personal and relational goals (see Vignette 13.3). The higher incidence of childlessness among the college educated is evidence of this since this group is likely to be career rather than job-oriented. But more than this, some women and men may not feel that, overall, children are worth sacrificing their other commitments. They usually prefer to devote more of their energies to their careers. Childless women in particular tend to be more successful in their careers than women with children. Even the

Vignette 13.3 The Decision To Be Child-Free

In the six years we've been married, we have gone not only to different countries but to different parts of our own country and city, because we want to glimpse a little of the world, to see some of the forces that have shaped it, are shaping it.

It is part, I think, of a kind of unspoken theory of marriage that we have. Marriage is not to resign from living, but to begin to live. Marriage should not signal a "settling down," but a waking up. Marriage is rather like a growing plant that should be enriched, fed, with stimulating experiences from outside sources; if it is not, it will shrivel into boredom and routine. We have not been bored . . .

And we do not have children.

We do not want children.

I think that many couples do not want children. They want *something*; perhaps they define that "something" as a child. But that may not be what is wanted at all. And this fact may become obvious only some time after the decision to have children is made, after the unparalleled complexities of child raising (truly, *no* other task is so difficult to do well, in this society at least) begin to make their demands on a couple, to take their toll from a marriage. Many children become "unwanted" long after birth, as their parents begin to resent the requirements of parenthood, to regret lost opportunities for freedom and for time alone. There are wives who live for the summer weeks when the children visit relatives or go to summer camp. There are husbands who seek to escape the realities of fatherhood by avoiding their homes, or who long for the time when their children will be grown. There are motels that advertise "The family that plays apart stays together" and provide separate activities and even separate residences for children and parents. And these motels are usually booked weeks and months in advance.

What most couples really want is to live life as fully and deeply as possible. That is what we want, anyway. And we do not feel that we can do this and still raise a family. A family would provide its own kind of change and experience, true—but not the kind we want. It would be, when you get right down to it, a repetition of experience—a repetition of the childhood experience.

I could never justify it.

I'm grown up, and I want my life now, thank you. My adult life. And I want to live that adult life—directly. I don't care to live a second childhood—vicariously.

From Ellen Peck, *The Baby Trap* (New York: Bernard Geis, 1971).

husbands in these marriages are quite ambitious and more likely to believe that they will achieve their financial goals in life (Silka and Kiesler).

A second factor in deciding to be childless is cost avoidance—the fear that parenthood might have potential harmful effects. There are concerns over the ability to rear children competently and worries about the world in which the children would grow up. Some couples question the worth of changes in their personal freedom and fear the possible health consequences involved. Another concern is related to the feeling that the world already has a population problem and that more children are simply not needed. According to one study (Gustavus and Henly, 1971), this concern was a primary justification, but not necessarily the real reason, for the decision of many childless couples to be sterilized.

Marital equality

Another concern often expressed by childless couples is related to the fear that children will harm their marital relationship. Veevers (1975) found that several themes dominated the child-free life-style, two of which were idealization of the husband-wife relationship and a quest for pair equality. Comments such as "A child would come between us" or fears that through parenthood they would have "lost something" in their marriage were common. In part, the women Veevers interviewed tied this potential loss to the sense of equality they felt they had in their marriage; they viewed parenthood as leading to sex-role separation and as threatening the shared authority and competence they contributed to the relationship. They also feared a loss in marital affection, which many of them reported having seen in their own parents and in the marriages of friends. This is a realistic concern since large-scale studies by Karen Renne (1970) and Harold Feldman (1968) indicate that childless marriages are on the average more likely to be happier than marriages with children. On the other side, divorce is also more common among childless couples, perhaps because children provide some stability and their absence makes it emotionally easier to divorce. But for those childless couples who remain together, there is a good chance they will have a satisfactory marriage.

Couple independence

The third factor in choosing to be child-free is an ability to cope with the continued pressure to be parents. This comes from all sides and increases the longer a couple is married. Childless couples seem to counter this pressure by adopting several defense mechanisms. They become less involved in religious activities; they gravitate toward the anonymity of the larger cities; they selectively observe conflicts in parent-child relations; they avoid associating with persons or groups, even parents, who will make their decision more difficult; they view the negative opinions of others as jealousy or envy; and they may even "borrow" a friend's baby to justify their feelings about not being parents (Veevers, 1975). In general, childless couples become more independent of others and more dependent on each other for support (Houseknecht, 1977). This enhances their interpersonal relationship, but as we noted earlier in our discussion of pair commitments (Chapter 2), it is sometimes difficult for couples to "put all their eggs in one basket" and maintain an exclusive pair relationship over a long period of time. However, if the couple can do this successfully or if they can find a supportive network of other childless couples (such as in the National Organization for Non-Parents), there is every reason to believe that the child-free life-style can be very rewarding.

Summary

For the majority of married couples, parenthood is a normal extension of their relational commitment. The transition into parental roles, however, is not always easy, especially since there are conflicting expectations for parents today. Nevertheless, the desire to be parents and the satisfactions that are ultimately derived from the experience are closely linked to the rewards and costs that are expected and encountered.

As a result of the social changes in sex-role definitions and the greater realization of potential parental costs, the roles of motherhood and fatherhood have been changing. The role of mother, in particular, has expanded to such a point that many women experience considerable strain. Fathers are beginning to change some of their expectations and are contributing more to parental responsibilities, but these changes are coming more slowly.

Not all couples follow the same route to parenthood. Among some couples, the transition into parenthood begins with adoption. There are also single parents who have a different set of adjustments to make depending upon whether their single-parent status is a consequence of widowhood, marital separation, divorce, adoption, or unwed pregnancy. In addition, some couples prefer to remain child-free.

SUGGESTIONS FOR ADDITIONAL READING

Bernard, Jessie. *The Future of Motherhood.* New York: Penguin, 1974.

A carefully documented examination of the motherhood role—past, present, and future. The emphasis is on the way this role is changing in light of the larger sex-role changes in society.

Bronfenbrenner, Urie. *The Ecology of Human Development.* Cambridge: Harvard University Press, 1979.

Understanding children, their needs, and developmental processes is what this book is all about. Written in a scholarly but sensitive manner.

LeMasters, E. E. *Parents in Modern America,* Third Edition. Homewood, Ill.: Dorsey, 1977.

A general overview of parenthood in its variety of sociological aspects.

Rossi, Alice. "Transition to parenthood," *Journal of Marriage and the Family* 30 (1968): 26–39.

Almost a modern classic in its treatment of how parenthood can change a marriage and why parental roles require more adjustment today.

Veevers, Jean. "The life style of voluntarily childless couples." In Lyle Larson (ed.), *The Canadian Fanily in Comparative Perspective.* Toronto: Prentice-Hall, 1974.

Describes the process childless couples went through in deciding not to have children and their attitudes toward being child-free in a proparental society.

Walters, James (ed.). *Fatherhood.* Special issue of *The Family Coordinator* (October 1976). Series of articles on various dimensions of the changing fatherhood role.

Breakups and New Beginnings in Marriage Part V

Chapter 14

Marital Separation: Divorce and Remarriage

". . . 'till death do us part."
". . . as long as we both shall live."

Marital pledges such as these, whether spoken or assumed, are frequently broken today. According to current divorce statistics, over one-third of all married couples are parted before death. Obviously, marriage, despite its strong social and legal support, has become a relatively fragile interpersonal relationship.

Recent increases in the rate of marital separation have not gone unnoticed. Changing divorce statistics are now considered "news" and are the subject of frequent commentaries. In 1975, when the number of divorces per year in the United States first exceeded the 1-million mark, headlines in major newspapers recorded the event. New specialists have emerged, including "matrimonial" lawyers to handle the legal aspects of marital separation and divorce counselors to ease the personal transition from being married to being single again. Supportive organizations for single parents, divorced people, step-parents, and step-children have also been founded in many communities.

All marriages eventually end. Marriage is a social and legal arrangement between only two people, and the dyad, as Georg Simmel (1950) has noted, is inherently the most fragile form of social group. If either person leaves or dies, the dyad no longer exists. Thus, marriage, by its very nature, must end at some point, either in death or in separation and divorce.

Why are a growing number of marriages ending in separation and divorce? In this chapter we will explore this question as well as various dimensions of marital separation and postseparation adjustment, including remarriage. The dissolution of marriage, we will see, is rarely a simple matter.

INCIDENCE OF MARITAL SEPARATION

Marital separation—in the broadest sense of the word—is not uncommon. Husbands and wives are often separated for brief periods during business trips, childbirth, or separate visits to family and friends. Our interest here, however, is not with temporary separations but with those separations that result in a relatively permanent dissolution of the marriage. Thus, most of our attention will be given to divorce since this is most frequent and it refers to the legal dissolution of a previously valid marriage. Other forms of marital dissolution, such as annulment, legal separation, and desertion will be examined in brief.

Annulment

Invalid marriage

An **annulment** is the legal termination of what the state considers to be an invalid marriage. From the point of view of the state, the marriage was not legally contracted in the first place since conditions *prior* to the marriage—such as fraud, bigamy, insanity, or duress—violated the implied marriage agreement assumed by the state. From the couple's point of view, however, their interpersonal (as opposed to legal) marriage did exist for a time and it ended with their eventual separation.

Less than 2 percent of all marriages in the United States are now terminated by annulments. This percentage is similar to that which existed in the early 1900s when marital separations occurred considerably less frequently than today. From the 1940s to the 1960s the number of annulments increased rapidly, peaking in 1950 when 4 percent of all marriages were terminated by annulments (Reinstein, 1972). This rise in annulments sought and granted was largely caused by an increased demand for legal terminations of marriage at a time when severe restrictions were placed on getting a legal divorce. As states relaxed their divorce laws, annulments were reserved once again for those special circumstances for which they had originally been intended.

Desertion

Illegal separation

Desertion occurs when a marital separation is not legally sanctioned and when it is contrary to the will of one spouse. The marriage in this case continues legally but not interpersonally. Desertion can be a serious legal offense if the deserter withholds obligations for family support since this often leads the family to seek community and state financial aid. For this reason, many states are now making serious attempts to locate and prosecute people who have deserted their marriages.

Compared to information we have on other forms of marital separation, we know very little about desertion. Desertions are not usually reported unless support is requested or the illegal separation is used as grounds for divorce. Divorce records indicate that men are more likely to be the ones who desert, although recent evidence from studies of single parents suggests that the number of women who desert their families may be on the rise (Orthner *et al.*, 1976).

Social class and desertion

It is generally thought that desertion rates vary according to social class. In fact, desertion is sometimes called the "poor man's divorce." Because statistics on desertion are necessarily incomplete, it is difficult to prove that lower-class people are more likely to desert their marriages. We do know that legal separations tend to be of short duration, usually not more than a year or two. Therefore, people who remain separated for longer periods of time are more likely to be involved in a desertion than in a legal separation. Since United States Census Bureau data indicate that longer separations include a "disproportionately larger number of men with a relatively small amount of education and income" (Glick and Norton, 1977), we can tentatively conclude that desertions are more frequent among the lower classes.

Legal Separations

A **legal separation** differs from desertion in that it is agreed upon by both marital partners and it provides for the support of dependents. Usually, separations like these are of short duration and serve as an intermediate step

Not all legal separations are of short duration. Some, like that of Canadian Prime Minister Pierre Trudeau and his wife Margaret, go on for years.

to divorce or as a test of the couple's commitment to the marriage. But whatever the reason, this type of separation represents the temporary or permanent dissolution of the interpersonal marriage, not the legal marriage. Therefore, the couple may live apart but they may not marry or have sexual contact with anyone else and the husband remains responsible for financial support of the family.

Provisions of separation

Sometimes, a legal separation will be guided by the formal principles of a **separation agreement.** This is a document recognized by a court that specifies the conditions of the separation. These conditions are similar to those of divorce but they stop short of terminating the legal marriage. Commonly included are such provisions as custody arrangements for children, visitation rights, level of support payments required, and limited freedom from interference by the other spouse. These provisions can be altered in divorce if the couple desires, but until then, they represent a limited divorce pact.

Quite often, couples who separate do so by mutual consent without any legal document at all. As long as both agree to the separation and adequate financial support is provided, this arrangement is legally permissible.

Vignette 14.1 Historical Perspectives on Divorce

Ancient Hebrews

When a man hath taken a wife, and married her, and it comes to pass that she find no favour in his eyes, because he hath found some uncleanness in her: then let him write her a bill of divorcement, and give it in her hand, and send her out of his house.

And when she is departed out of his house, she may go and be another man's wife.

(Deuteronomy 21:1–2)

Ancient Romans

As among the early Hebrews, it was only men who could take the initiative to terminate an unsatisfactory marriage. However, in contrast to a Hebrew husband, a Roman was restricted in a number of ways. If the marriage had been celebrated with the formal ceremony called *confarreatio,* it could be dissolved only with considerable difficulty and a corresponding ceremony of *difarreatio.* If a man were contemplating the dismissal of his wife, he was required by law to assemble a council of his own and her male relatives, unless he caught her in adultery, in which case his hands were free and he might punish her even with death. The grounds for divorce were, in addition to adultery, making poison, drinking wine, and possessing counterfeit house keys.

Divorce

Divorce-rate comparison

Divorce involves the legal and social termination of a previously valid marriage. In any society, some marriages eventually deteriorate, so all known cultures have permitted divorce under certain circumstances (see Vignette 14.1). Currently, the United States has the highest divorce rate in the world, but other societies in times past, including Japan, Israel, the Soviet Union, and Egypt, have had higher divorce rates than this. In 1976, when the divorce rate in the United States reached a record (at that time) 5.0 divorces for every 1000 persons in the population, other countries with relatively high divorce rates included Australia (4.3), the Soviet Union (3.4), Sweden (2.7), Denmark (2.5), Canada (2.2), Finland (2.1), and Egypt (2.0) (Glick and Norton).

Over the years, the United States divorce rate has fluctuated widely, but the overall rate has clearly increased. In sheer numbers, the frequency of divorce has risen from about 12,000 per year in the 1870s to 60,000 in 1900, 246,000 in 1940, 708,000 in 1970, and 1,200,000 in 1980. When we examine *the number of divorces per 1000 persons in the population,* this helps us interpret

---

Early Christians

And unto the married I command, yet not I, but the Lord, let not the wife depart from her husband: but and if she depart, let her remain unmarried, or be reconciled to her husband: and let not the husband put away his wife. But to the rest speak I, not the Lord: If any brother hath a wife that believeth not, and she be pleased to dwell with him, let him not put her away. And the woman which hath an husband that believeth not, and if he be pleased to dwell with her, let her not leave him.

(I Corinthians 7:10–13)

Anglo-Saxons, Seventh Century

If any layman dismiss his own wife and take the wife of another, let him do penance eight years . . . Whoever dismisses his own wife and takes another woman in marriage, not however the wife of another man, but a single woman or virgin, let him do penance seven years.

A man and woman being joined in matrimony, if he wishes to dismiss her and she objects, or if she wishes to dismiss him, if he is infirm, or if she is infirm, let them not be separated, except with the consent of both . . .

If a woman separate from her husband, despising him and being unwilling to return and be reconciled to him; after five years and with the consent of the bishop he may take another wife.

(Nineteenth *Paenitenticle* of Archbishop Theodore)

From Stuart A. Queen and Robert W. Habenstein, *The Family in Various Cultures,* 4th ed. (Philadelphia: Lippincott, 1974), pp. 169, 185, 215, 238.

---

change in the frequency of divorce in light of population changes. Or even better, we can examine *the number of divorces per 1000 married women,* since many people in the total population, notably children and other unmarried people, cannot possibly be subject to divorce themselves. These rates are illustrated in Fig. 14.1.

Divorce-rate changes

The data reported in Fig. 14.1 indicate that the United States has experienced two major peaks in its divorce rate since the 1920s. The first peak occurred shortly after World War II, following a period of comparatively low divorce rates in the 1930s. This postwar peak in the divorce rate has been generally attributed to several factors, including the tendency for many wartime courtships to be hasty and often ill-considered, the long periods of separation when the husbands were overseas, the growing independence of women who worked in war industries, and the higher wages which made divorce more affordable. Many husbands returned to their hometowns only to find that they and their bride had changed considerably since their marriage, that a severe housing shortage limited their independence, and that neither of them had a strong enough commitment to the marriage to handle the necessary postwar adjustments successfully.

After a downturn and a period of some stability in the divorce rate during the 1950s, it began to increase again during the 1960s. This time the reasons for the rising incidence of divorce were more general, not linked to any particular event. Changing gender and marital roles had begun to create more confusion in marriage; increasing employment among women gave wives more independence from their husbands; access to birth control permitted couples to delay having children (who might have complicated their decision to separate); legal restrictions on divorce were eased; and religious sanctions on divorce were liberalized. Taken together, these changes created

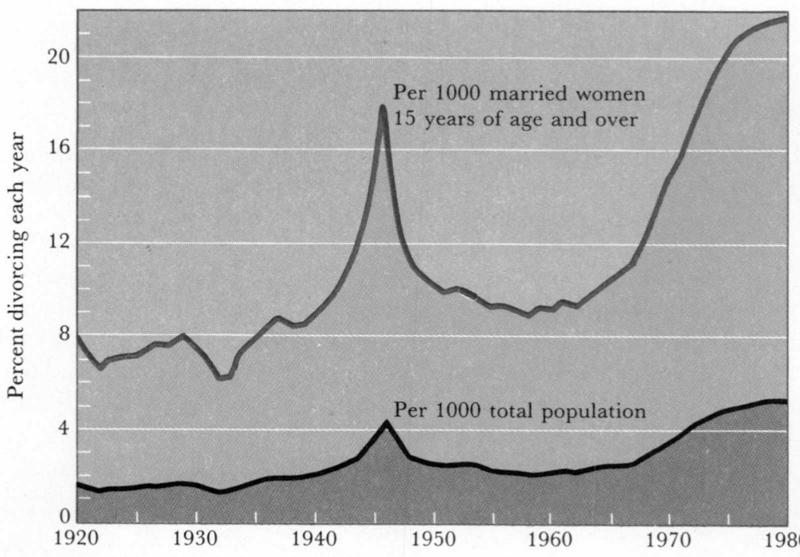

Fig. 14.1

United States Divorce Rates, 1920–1979

Source: U.S. Department of Health, Education, and Welfare, Selected Public Health Service Publications and Vital Statistics Reports.

an atmosphere of decreasing tolerance for marital stress and increasing tolerance for divorce. The result has been a divorce rate that was steadily increasing into the 1970s with some evidence of leveling off in the latter part of the decade.

Divorce-probability estimates

What do today's high divorce rates indicate about the possibility that a particular marriage will end in divorce? Actually, not very much, although this does not lessen the impact of statements like "one-third . . ." or "one-half of all marriages now end in divorce." Estimates such as these raise anxieties; in people's minds they become more than statistical summaries, they become *odds* against which couples wager their chances for success or failure in marriage. This is unfortunate. People should understand that divorce-probability estimates are based on data for all marriages—they cannot account for individual marriage variations—and some of the methods of determining divorce probabilities are clearly misleading (Crosby, 1980).

One of the most-often-quoted and least reliable measures of divorce probability is the **current-marriage to current-divorce ratio.** For example, in 1978 there were 2,240,000 marriages and 1,120,000 divorces in the United States, figures which might suggest that one out of every two marriages failed. This interpretation would *not* be correct, however. The divorces in any particular year were granted to couples who probably had married in earlier years, usually several years earlier in fact. The logical absurdity of the marriage-divorce ratio can also be illustrated by comparing it to the other major cause of marital dissolution—death. In 1978, 1,924,000 individuals died and 4,480,000 individuals were married. Can we conclude, therefore, that 43 percent of all marriages end in death? Obviously not, since the majority of those who are marrying now are not those most subject to dying.

Current estimates

A much better way of predicting divorce probabilities is by **demographic projection.** Based on the assumptions that divorces in the future will be caused by many of the same factors that cause divorces today and that the divorce probability for newly marrieds is similar to that for people who have been married for several years, this method uses mathematical formulas to project the chances for future divorce experience. Current projections by demographers Paul Glick and Arthur Norton estimate that about 38 percent of the first marriages of women now in their late twenties will end in divorce. Then, of the three-quarters who later remarry, about 44 percent may redivorce. Of course, these projections assume that the conditions surrounding marriage will not change—an unlikely possibility—but they do provide a better *estimate* of current divorce probabilities than other methods.

FACTORS INFLUENCING THE PROBABILITY OF DIVORCE

The probability that any one marriage will end in divorce can vary considerably from the national average. Some marriages are quite prone to divorce, others more immune depending upon the characteristics of the couple involved.

Age at Marriage

Teen marriages

Perhaps the most predictive factor in divorce is the age at which the husband and wife marry. The lower the age at marriage, the higher the probability of divorce. Using 1970 United States Census Bureau data, Glick and Norton report that couples who marry in their teens are twice as likely to divorce as those who marry in their twenties. For example, among women who married for the first time six to ten years before the 1970 census, 18 percent of the marriages that had taken place when the women were in their teenage years had failed compared to 9 percent of the marriages that had taken place when the women were in their twenties. Using more specific data for California (where the divorce rate is only slightly higher than in the United States as a whole), Robert Schoen (1975) determined the risks of divorce over thirty-five years of marriage for males marrying between the ages of eighteen and twenty-nine and for females marrying between the ages of sixteen and twenty-seven (see Table 14.1). These data indicate that all first marriages in that state have a probability of divorce of about 42.5 percent. But among females who marry at age sixteen, 64 percent will likely divorce compared to only 27 percent of those who marry at age twenty-seven. The percentages for the men are very similar.

Table 14.1

First Marriages Remaining Intact over Time Out of 1000 Original Marriages for Selected Marriage Ages (California females, no mortality assumed)

Completed Years of Marriage	Age at First Marriage 16	19	22	27
	(Number of marriages left at the end of year, assuming no deaths)			
1	991	992	996	997
2	975	979	987	987
3	938	952	970	965
4	869	911	951	955
5	804	881	925	930
6	748	844	906	913
8	658	782	868	877
10	587	743	837	851
15	470	660	782	802
20	407	599	737	770
25	372	563	702	749
30	348	537	679	737
35	338	523	668	726

Source: Data from Robert Schoen, "California Divorce Rates by Age at First Marriage and Duration of First Marriage," *Journal of Marriage and the Family* 37: 554.

Why are early marriages more likely to fail? One reason is the relatively high number of these marriages that are "forced" by an unplanned pregnancy. Since nearly one-third of the women marrying in their teen years are pregnant at the time of marriage (Ventura, 1977), many of these marriages begin simply to legitimize the child, without careful consideration of the consequences to the would-be parents. Other reasons for the high divorce rate among the young include their emotional immaturity, poorer financial resources, lower educational background, and lack of preparation for marital roles.

Later marriages

What about the chances of divorce among people who marry later than normal? Recent statistics indicate that men and women who marry for the first time after age thirty "were close to half again as likely to end their first marriage" as those who married in their twenties (Glick and Norton). This may be attributed to the problem some people have in giving up the habits of independent living that singlehood had fostered.

Length of Marriage

Divorces can occur at any time over the family life cycle. Some couples separate within days, others after decades of marriage. Over half of the divorces, however, are granted in the first seven years of marriage with the highest frequencies occurring in the second to fourth years. Since most couples separate some months or years before finally divorcing, the highest periods of marital separation occur even earlier. One study of United States marriages found more couples separating in the first year than in any subsequent year (Plateris, 1973).

As Fig. 14.2 illustrates, there is a steadily declining probability of divorce after the fourth year of marriage. The divorce risk in a teenage marriage peaks in the fourth year, with a higher than normal divorce rate over the entire length of marriage. Marriages in the mid-twenties experience their greatest divorce risk in the third year and have a lower than normal divorce rate over the length of marriage. We should also note that, contrary to popular belief, there is no evidence of a "seven-year itch" or "twenty-year itch," periods commonly thought to be more critical and to have a higher divorce rate. Rather, divorce rates continue to fall as the investments in the relationship continue over the years.

Level of Education

College-educated rates rising

The relationship between years of education and the likelihood of divorce is less clear than it used to be. In the early 1960s, the highest divorce rates were generally found among the least educated and the lowest divorce rates among the most educated. But during the 1960s and 1970s, the divorce rate for college-educated men and women rose faster than for those without college

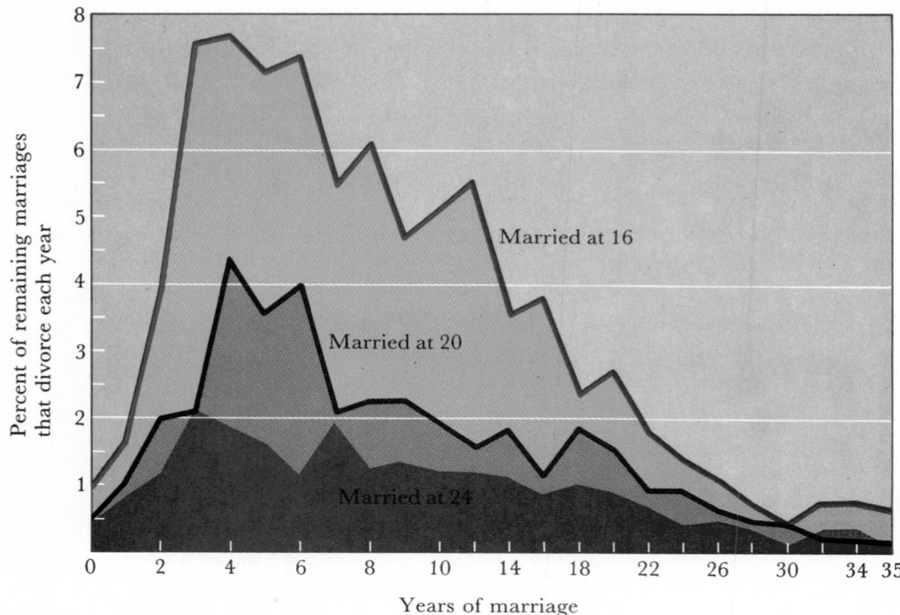

Fig. 14.2

Percent of Remaining Marriages that End in Divorce over Time for Selected Marriage Ages (California females)

Source: Shoen (1975), p. 552.

experience. Today, the lowest rates of divorce still occur among men and women with bachelor's degrees. Very high rates of divorce are found among those men and women who have some college experience (but not a degree), and even higher rates exist among women with postgraduate education (Glick and Norton). Apparently, the inability to go on and complete the college degree is an indication of a willingness to give up on other commitments as well, such as marriage. The very high divorce rates among postgraduate women are probably due to increased conflicts between their career and marital roles.

Social Class

Economic security

Prior to the twentieth century, divorce was considered a privilege reserved for the elite. The poor, even though often disenchanted with their marriages, had neither the influence nor the money to get a divorce. At the turn of the century, this began to change, and now the rates of marital separation and divorce are highest in the lower classes and lowest in the upper classes. The financial factor, recent studies suggest, may be very crucial to marital stability. Certainly, money does not "make" a marriage, but it does provide the resources to reduce the frustration of trying to meet the mounting and conflicting needs of family members. Also, in some marriages economic security may replace marital satisfaction as the reason for staying together. Scanzoni (1965) adds that higher incomes also encourage independence from kin relations. Among the lower classes, conflicts often stem from parental interference and the polarization of the husband and wife, each holding on to his or her own family-of-orientation allegiances and neither giving their complete support to the marriage.

Family Stability

Divorce as remedy

Do divorces run in families? Apparently they do to some extent, since parental divorce is more likely to be found in the background of individuals who become divorced themselves. Nevertheless, when we allow for the effect of social class, the relationship is not so strong as to lead us to interpret parental divorce as a major cause of marital instability. Nevertheless, it is a factor, and there is evidence to suggest that it may be a more important factor in the background of women than of men (Mueller and Pope, 1977). Since women are often required to make the critical role adjustments in marriage, and since they are often the ones pushed into filing for divorce, those women whose parents did not successfully make marital adjustments may view divorce as a more viable remedy for the adjustment problems they are experiencing in their own marriages. Also, there is evidence that individuals whose parents were divorced are less careful in their mate-selection. They tend to marry younger and to have less education than individuals from intact families of their same social class (Mueller and Pope). Perhaps the feelings of insecurity experienced by many children of divorced parents encourage certain susceptible individuals to seek a premature marriage. Clearly, all the factors that may be involved here are not adequately understood as yet.

THE PROCESSES OF DIVORCE

There is a popular tendency to think of divorce as an *event*—something that happens at one point in time, radically changing the lives of the people involved. Along these lines, divorce is often considered the end of one relationship, a correction for a past error in judgment, and the beginning of "a new life" for all concerned. This image is quite different from reality.

More properly, divorce should be understood as a process. Indeed, we shall see that it is a very complex series of processes. Westman and Cline (1973) describe it as an "*adjustment of a relationship* that does not erase the past nor create an unrelated future. . . . Divorce legally dissolves the marriage, but it only realigns the material and intangible bonds between the affected parties" (p. 465). Paul Bohannan (1971), an anthropologist who has written extensively on the subject of divorce, carefully notes:

> Divorce severs the legal contract between the husband and wife—but leaves a moral and emotional "contract" between ex-husband and ex-wife.

It shatters the household that was based on the marriage. But it definitely does *not* break the kinship network that the children of the marriage create merely by their existence. (p. 283)

Disentangling marriage

Because of the complexity of marital commitments, the disentangling of a marriage often takes years, not simply the months required to obtain a legal divorce decree. As Bohannan describes it, divorce includes emotional, legal, economic, parental, community, and psychic adjustments, all of which require time before they can be successfully resolved. While it is possible to examine each of these elements of the divorce process separately in some detail, they are very interrelated in practice. Nevertheless, we can isolate three primary divorce processes based on the breaking of the major contractual obligations of marriage. These include the interpersonal divorce, the legal divorce, and the coparental divorce.

The Interpersonal Divorce Process

Factors in marital bonds

Just as we saw that interpersonal commitments to marry precede legal commitments to marry (Chapter 4), the breakdown of these interpersonal commitments precedes the legal termination of the marriage. Interpersonal divorce, then, involves the gradual deterioration of the marriage relationship and the **bonds** that have held the couple together. George Levinger (1976) has found that the strength of these marital bonds and the likelihood of divorce are determined by three factors: (1) attractions to the marriage, (2) barriers to divorce, and (3) attractions to other relationships.

Barriers to divorce

Some of the things that have been shown to be important **attractions** in marital bonding include companionship, sexual enjoyment, home ownership, similarity in values, moderate level of income demand, and, in general, those factors that enhance husband-wife communication (Peters, 1978). **Barriers** to divorce include those factors that create marital obligations and serve to shield the couple from entertaining the idea of divorce. Several conditions that can serve as such barriers include the presence of children, marital support from friends and kin, a strong religious orientation, a feeling of personal insecurity away from the marital partner, and a strong sense of obligation toward the marital bond (Turner, 1970; Peters). When these attractions within and barriers around the marriage are present and highly regarded, then the couple is unlikely to consider divorce (Levinger).

But if these attractions and barriers weaken or if alternative attractions increase, then the marital bonds will probably become more fragile. **Alternative attractions** that are likely to increase the possibility of divorce include a satisfactory extramarital sexual relationship, an increased sense of independence and self-assurance, and more contacts with people of the opposite sex. Ordinarily, the obligations of marriage restrict people from considering others as a replacement for their present spouse. But when men and women associate with one another more as equals on the job or increase their level of self-confidence, they are more likely to see others as attractive and themselves

Table 14.2
Factors Affecting the Likelihood of Divorce

Marital Bond Factors	The Likelihood of Divorce			
	Poor	Slight	Good	Excellent
Attractions to the Marriage	High	Moderate	Moderate	Low
Barriers to Divorce	High	High	High	Low
Attractions to Others	Low	Moderate	Moderate	High

as more attractive to others too, conditions which may lower their marital commitment (see Table 14.2).

Awareness of unfulfillment

Disillusionment. Practically no couple is fail-safe from divorce. Any person can be affected by a change in the relative attractiveness of their marriage or by a relaxation of their barriers to divorce. Usually, the interpersonal divorce process begins with **disillusionment,** a gradual awareness that the marriage is not personally fulfilling. J. Louis Despert (1953) characterizes this first stage as "emotional divorce," and Riva Wiseman (1975) characterizes it as a period of "denial." The husband, wife, or both of them recognize that the marriage is not working, conflicts arise over even minor issues, but neither may openly admit to the possibility of divorce.

Some married people are disillusioned almost indefinitely. The barriers to divorce are maintained, but the attractions of the marriage are weak to nonexistent. The spouses may admit to unhappiness, but like the "devitalized" couples that Cuber and Harroff (1966) studied, they rationalize their marriage as normal or for the sake of the children. These marriages can continue to drift along until some stress which cannot be accommodated enters in. It might be the birth of a child; it might be a change of job or residence. But the reaction is a severe crisis since the marital system is not flexible enough to adjust.

Testing. When the disillusionment becomes acute or surfaces after enough conflict, then a period of marital **testing** usually emerges. Divorce is suggested by one or both spouses and is sometimes mentioned as a possibility to friends as well. One or the other may temporarily leave the household, but more out of anger and a desire to shock the spouse into realizing his or her real frustration. These are signals that the couple is "testing the waters," deciding whether to continue the marriage or not.

Reaction of friends

During this testing phase of the interpersonal-divorce process, outside counsel is frequently sought. Friends are talked with first, and their reaction may take one of several forms. Most common is the **rehabilitative reaction,** in which the friends try to convince the couple, or each of them separately, that things are not as bad as they seem (Weiss, 1975). Statements such as "Your marriage doesn't really sound all *that* bad" might be voiced. A **supportive**

reaction might come from other friends, particularly those with divorce histories themselves. Miller (1971) found that divorce can become "contagious" in some friendship groups when the group as a whole comes to view divorce as an acceptable solution to marital stress. Opposite-sex friends who see the divorcing person as "available" for their sexual advances may display an **opportunity reaction.** Sometimes this is veiled in a supportive context (checking to "see if everything is all right"); at other times sexual overtures are less hidden. The **withdrawal reaction** comes from those friends who "do not want to get involved," perhaps because they are afraid of having their own conflicts aroused or perhaps because they do not want to have to choose sides should a separation occur.

Marital testing might also involve seeking advice from lawyers and marital therapists. From legal counsel, people considering divorce can learn their rights and obligations under the laws of a particular state as well as what they can look forward to in terms of financial costs and the time required for a divorce decree. Marriage counseling is sometimes considered and may lead to a readjustment of the relationship if initiated early and jointly.

Many troubled couples benefit from marriage counseling.

Separation. Unless reconciliation occurs, **marital separation** follows the testing period. Like the previous periods, separation takes time and requires its own adjustments. The physical fact of separation between spouses does not end the relationship entirely. It takes time for habits developed over the years, no matter how annoying at times, to be given up and replaced by new role expectations. But clearly, as important a step as legal divorce is, far more personal and relational adjustments are required during the initial period of separation (Weiss).

Reaction of parents

For one thing, kin are more likely to be informed of the divorce possibility at this time. Surprise is a common reaction, given the emotional distance that frequently separates married people from their parents, but in one study, 60 percent of the parents approved and only 20 percent disapproved of their child's divorce (Goode, 1956). Dependency on parents, however, is not a likely reaction after separation. Contacts with parents do not appear to increase markedly for either men or women (Spicer and Hempe, 1975): and the amount of financial and moral support given by parents does not affect the overall adjustment to marital separation (Hansen and Spanier, 1978). If anything, parental encouragement is desired, but too much parental involvement is often related to poor separation adjustment. Robert Weiss observes:

> Kin, much more than friends, believe that their commitment to one another confers on them the right to evaluate one another's behavior. Parents, especially, assume the right to comment on the separation, to criticize it, to disapprove or approve it, perhaps going on until the separated individual is driven to exasperation. (p. 132)

In-laws

Relationships with former in-laws and friends divide according to where their loyalties lie. He has his friends, she has hers. And contacts with the parents of the former partner decline markedly, particularly for men. One-half of the men in one study never saw their former in-laws again, compared to only one-seventh of the women (Spicer and Hempe). A major factor in this difference appears to be the desire of the husband's parents to maintain a relationship with their grandchildren. Another reason may be the greater affectional bond that apparently develops between a wife and her husband's parents than between a husband and his wife's parents.

Reconciliations

Reconciliations after separation do occur. Weiss estimates that "almost certainly not more than half of all separations go on to divorce" (p. 11). Nevertheless, many of these reconciliations are between couples who have not yet taken the step of filing for divorce. Once this formal step is taken, the chances of reconciliation drop substantially. In recent Florida statistics, for example, only 28 percent of the divorce petitions were withdrawn (Gunter, 1977). When reconciliations do occur, they are more likely when the husband has filed for divorce, the family income level is higher, the number of children is low, and the grounds for divorce are few (Kitson *et al.*, 1977).

For those marriages that end after separation, few do so without some rancor. There are instances of "friendly" or "amicable" divorces (Framo, 1978), and these may increase in the future if expectations for marital permanence decline. But at present, "It is extremely difficult for a couple who have shared for many years a house, a life, children, and friends to end a relationship, however painful, without some major focus of anger to facilitate the break" (Wiseman, p. 208).

Resolution of anger

Identity Reorientation. The last stage of the interpersonal-divorce process involves the development of a separate, nonmarried identity. This includes accepting the fact of the divorce, creating a self-image of being single again, and resolving the anger that encourages one to look backward instead of focusing on the present and the future.

Paul Bohannan calls this stage the **psychic divorce,** the separation of self from the personality and influence of the ex-spouse. He explains:

> The psychic divorce involves becoming a whole, complete, and autonomous individual again—learning to live without someone to lean on—but also without somebody to support. There is nobody on whom to blame one's difficulties (except oneself), nobody to shortstop one's growth, nobody to grow with. (pp. 60–61)

The major task in creating a new identity is to acquire a set of roles and responsibilities that do not use the previous marriage as their reference points (Goode, 1956). Since our image of ourself is closely tied to our significant relationships, developing new friendships, activities, surroundings, and possessions helps to create a new self-image. When old life-style patterns persist—and they may persist for years in some cases—the "psychic marriage" continues and the divorce process is extended.

The first year

Most research studies indicate that the first year after separation is the most difficult. This is the period of "coming out," when the newly divorced person experiments with new experiences. A study of divorced men and women found what the researchers called a "hip, Honda, and hirsute syndrome" among many of the men as they traded in their old activities, dress, hair-styles, and four-door sedans for a new "swinging single" life-style (Hetherington *et al.*, 1977). Divorced women were less likely to experiment with such a radical change, but they were also more likely to consider this period stressful than the men were. By the end of the first year, nearly half of the men and women thought that the divorce was a mistake and that they should have tried to resolve their differences.

Factors in stress resolution

After this initial transition phase, a period of recovery gradually resolves many of these identity conflicts. Radical attempts to change their life-style diminish among the divorced, and by the end of the second year in the above study, only one out of eight men and one out of six women felt that the divorce had been a mistake. Helen Raschke (1976), in her study of separation stress among 277 divorced men and women, discovered several factors that are related to the resolution of stress and the development of a new single identity. One factor is social participation, getting out and meeting with other people. This was found to be most important after the first few months of separation. Sexual permissiveness was also related to lower degrees of stress for both men and women, and among women only those more tolerant of change in their roles and values experienced less separation stress. For men, higher occupational level meant lower stress, but for women, it meant higher stress, probably because the demands of the job competed with their child-rearing responsibilities.

How long does it take to achieve identity reorientation? According to Robert Weiss:

> My impression, corroborated by the observations of others, is from two to four years, with the average being closer to four than to two. Overwhelming upset may disappear after the first anniversary of the separation, but achievement of a firmly established new identity and new way of life appear to take much longer. Full recovery from separation requires more time than most people think. (p. 236)

The Legal Divorce Process

In 1923, Lester and Margaret Anderton were married in Cambridge, Massachusetts. From the beginning, they quarreled constantly and separated frequently. The couple never had children and Lester finally left for good in 1931, but he continued to send weekly checks to Margaret for living expenses. After forty-two years of separation, Lester filed for divorce in 1973. He was old but he wanted to marry a woman he had met in his nursing home. He based his divorce plea on the ground of "cruel and abusive treatment" since a few years earlier, when he was recovering from a stroke, Margaret had insulted him and charged him with "criminal nonsupport." This charge was dismissed, but Margaret contested the divorce now based on the fact that her rights to Lester's social-security payments would be terminated. The trial judge ruled against Lester's petition. Even though the couple had been separated for more than four decades, he denied the divorce because Margaret's misconduct was not sufficiently cruel and abusive to be adequate grounds for divorce (Wheeler, 1974).

The rights of courts

In this actual case, the Andertons remained legally married even though their interpersonal marriage had ended decades earlier. The decision illustrates the fact that once the state has recognized a marriage, it retains the right through its courts to decide whether and how that marriage can be terminated. In this way, states have made it more difficult for couples to divorce than to marry, a situation that has been amply criticized (see Vignette 14.2). Even if the Andertons had mutually agreed to the divorce, which would not have been possible in Massachusetts at the time, a court would still have had to meet to approve this decision. Since divorce laws are created by state legislatures and interpreted by judges, provisions for divorce vary considerably from state to state and from court to court. Perhaps if Lester Anderton had brought his case to a different state or had come before a different judge, he would have been permitted his divorce.

The fault system

From Fault to No-Fault. Divorce laws in North America have traditionally been based on the assumption that marital failure is caused by a fault in either the

Vignette 14.2

Suggestions for Marriage and Divorce Reform

I'd kept our marriage certificate carefully tucked away inside the cover of my wedding book. I didn't take it out until the day I went downtown to get divorced.

It was an impressive parchment sheet decorated with gold scrolling and signatures of the wedding party and my minister. I read them once more before handing it to the hearing officer.

"That's it," he said at the end of the proceedings, slapping the open folder of legal papers supplied by my lawyer and my husband's lawyer. Then he raised the slender metal shafts of the binder and impaled my certificate.

Cringing, I wished he had waited until I'd left. But the defacement did provoke thoughts about the difference between a wedding and a divorce. People get carried away with the emotion and festivities surrounding a wedding, and they pay a lot of attention to proper form. There's not much etiquette to getting divorced. For me, it was mostly months of confronting facts about myself, my partner, our marriage, and our finances. Maybe, I decided, marriages would work out better if the situation were reversed.

To start with, a couple would have to spend a reasonable amount of time getting to know each other before they could become engaged, let alone married. That would correspond to the period a married couple spends trying to work out life together before they give up and separate.

In the District of Columbia, where I live, divorce proceedings can't start until one year after the separation date. And you can't file for divorce until you've been a resident one year. Under the new system, betrothal would correspond to the date of separation. A couple couldn't file for a marriage license until a year later. The residency requirement would add some stability to the whole thing.

During the year, the couple would be required to evaluate their lifestyles, finances, and aspirations to make sure the final marital arrangements

husband or the wife, but not both. Therefore, divorces in all states before 1970 and in many states still today follow an **adversary** procedure in which the "innocent" person (the *plaintiff*) proves the "guilty" person (the *defendant*) at fault. This adversary or fault system requires specific **grounds,** such as adultery, cruelty, desertion, or nonsupport, which can be demonstrated to have deliberately hurt the innocent party.

The major problem with the fault system of divorce is its premise that one can identify a single cause of the marital failure and that this cause can be blamed on only one person. In some cases this may be true, but most often both people share much of the blame. Yet if this is admitted in court, a fault divorce will not be granted since the parties are considered to be adversaries and cannot be acting "in concert." To do so would be **collusion,** grounds for dismissing the case. To get around this, most couples used to agree to some acceptable fault, like "mental cruelty," and further agree on the evidence that would suit both parties. Because we're talking about a lifetime contract with lots of vital interests to protect, each one would hire a lawyer to assist in the arduous negotiations. All the terms would have to be expressed in writing in notarized, legal documents.

When it finally came time to get the license, the individual most committed to the proposed union would file for it. To help impress both parties with the seriousness of the legal and moral commitments, an officer of the court would serve the papers on the other party, who would then have to file a separate answer. This takes even more time, so society is assured the couple can't rush into wedlock.

After the papers are recorded, the court would write both the man and woman, explicitly stressing the gravity of their decision to marry. To parallel the reconciliation services offered to divorcing couples, the letters would recommend "singles" counselors. They would remind each one of the joys of single life and the realities of marital responsibilities.

At my hearing for an uncontested divorce, one of the participants was my required witness. She swore she knew me well and saw no possibility the marriage could be saved. The party who files for a marriage license would have to get a similar witness who could testify he or she saw no reason the marriage couldn't succeed.

When the hearing concluded, the couple would not yet be married. There could be no honeymoon, no setting up housekeeping until the end of a thirty-day appeal period. That day would be a good time to hold the traditional wedding. Then perhaps the bride, the groom, the maid of honor, the best man, and the preacher could believe their signatures would long be preserved in a wedding book, not on a courthouse spindle.

would be used before the court to demonstrate their case. The fact that nearly 90 percent of all adversary divorces in the 1960s were uncontested suggests that this scenario was quite common before no-fault divorces were permitted (Eisler, 1977).

No-fault divorce

In 1970, California became the first state to permit no-fault divorce. Other states soon followed, and nearly all states now provide some type of no-fault divorce for those who want it. Basically, these divorces permit either or both parties together to initiate the divorce, eliminate the "contest" in which specific grounds are presented, allow both parties to accept partial blame for the divorce, and limit the testimony of others to supporting the claims of marital breakdown.

There are two basic forms of no-fault divorce now available. The first permits a period of voluntary separation to be used as grounds for divorce. Standard fault grounds are usually retained in these states too. But if the

While "no-fault" divorces are increasingly popular, protracted, bitter divorces, such as that of Bianca and Mick Jagger, continue to make headlines.

couple can demonstrate that they have lived apart willingly for the specified period of time, then they will be assumed to be irreconcilable and the divorce will be granted on that basis.

The second type of no-fault divorce is permitted based on the claim of "irreconcilable differences," "incompatibility," or "breakdown of the marriage." If this is mutually agreed upon and observed by the court, then the marriage is dissolved. Some states permit either a contested divorce based on traditional grounds or a mutual decision of marital breakdown. The couple has the choice over which type of proceeding they prefer. In other states, such as California, fault grounds are not permitted at all, and adverse testimony can be introduced only when custody of the children is contested.

Steps in Legal Divorce. Usually, the first step in obtaining a divorce is **legal consultation** with an attorney or someone informed about the divorce laws of the state. Representation by a lawyer is rarely required in divorce cases, but it is usually advisable since divorce changes each person's legal status in terms of taxes, inheritance, retirement, property, and parental obligations. These points should be clearly understood before proceeding; competent legal assistance can ease the surprises and paperwork that frequently strain the divorce process.

Change in legal status

The second step is for one of the parties to file a complaint or **petition for divorce.** In most states and in all adversary divorces, one person, the **plaintiff,** files a complaint against the other, the **defendant,** and the specific grounds are listed. In some no-fault states, these harsh labels are replaced with **petitioner** (who files a petition for divorce) and **respondent** (who receives this petition). Traditionally, women have been more likely to file for divorce, even though research indicates that men are the first to desire it (Goode, 1956). This filing behavior is changing, however, since in no-fault states, men are now more likely to be the ones who file or petition for divorce (Gunter).

Divorce filing

After the complaint or petition is filed, the court issues a **summons** to the other spouse who is ordered to appear in court at a specified time and date. The summons and the complaint or petition are usually delivered (served) in person by a representative of the court. The next major step in a legal divorce is the **interlocutory hearing.** At this time, the divorce-settlement agreement is examined and approved, or if the divorce is contested or no settlement is agreed upon, the case is tried and the settlement determined by the court. In some cases, the interlocutory hearing is preceded by one or more other preliminary hearings, often to compel one spouse or the other to provide some evidence or answer questions which will affect the divorce settlement. The outcome of these hearings, if the divorce is approved, is an **interlocutory decree,** which for all intents and purposes legally ends the marriage.

The **final divorce decree** is made a prescribed period of time after the interlocutory decree, usually six months to a year. This waiting period is prescribed to give couples one last chance to reconcile their marriage before it is officially terminated. From the data available, it is apparent that few such reconciliations take place at this late stage of marital dissolution.

The Divorce Settlement. In some divorce cases, like that of the Andertons mentioned earlier, the divorce itself will be contested. But most often, the marriage will have deteriorated by this time to such an extent that the fact of divorce is less of an issue than the **terms** of the divorce settlement. These terms usually center around several basic concerns: the distribution of property, support for the dependent spouse, and, if there are children, child support and child custody.

The **property settlement** is concerned with fair distribution of the assets that have accumulated over the course of the marriage. Some assets are considered separate property and not open to distribution, such as personal

Property laws

gifts or property contributed from a previous marriage. But other property is family property and states differ widely in their assumptions regarding how this should be divided. States that have "community-property" laws assume that all earnings and accumulations are jointly owned, irrespective of the name on the title or deed, or the person who purchased it. Other states follow "common law" in which ownership is defined by whoever earned the money to pay for it. In the latter states, a nonemployed wife has legal rights only to assets that have been put in her name or to which she has been granted joint title.

While common law places the wife at a legal disadvantage in property settlements, most states still require judges to ensure that an equal and fair distribution takes place. This is determined on a case-by-case basis, but Bohannan estimates that wives typically receive from one-third to one-half of the value of the marital property.

Provisions for the financial support of the spouse after the marriage, or **alimony,** are sometimes part of the divorce-settlement package. When included, alimony is almost always paid to the wife because it is assumed that she has been financially dependent on her husband, thus requiring continuing support until she can find a new husband to care for her. While alimony provisions were once common in divorce, they are rare today. Short periods of support, such as one to three years, are somewhat common, but for most wives, an outright financial settlement at the time of divorce is the most likely monetary benefit they can expect from the marriage.

Determining amount of support

Compared to alimony, **child support** is a much more common provision in divorce settlements. The obligation of fathers, and in some cases mothers, to continue to fulfill their parental-support responsibilities remains strong today. The amount of child support is determined by the court, supposedly based on the needs of the child and the resources of the parent. But as attorney Riane Eisler observes:

> . . . the problem is really more a practical one than a legal one. The manner in which support is actually awarded has always been guided more by mathematics than by guilt or equity. First, the judge takes a look at what the man earns and makes sure he has enough to live on. Whatever is left, he gives to the wife and children. If, as in the majority of cases, there is not much of a surplus, the wife and children simply do not get very much. (p. 47)

Because child support is a continuing obligation, either the father or the mother can later petition the court to change the amount of the payments or force payments if none are coming. The latter problem occurs particularly often. One study found that within one year after divorce, 42 percent of the fathers were making no child-support payments and another 20 percent made only partial payments. By the tenth year, only 13 percent of the fathers continued to pay their required support and 79 percent payed nothing at all (Nagel and Weitzman, 1971). Since this situation forces many parents and children to seek public help, the United States Congress has recently passed legislation permitting states to get federal assistance, including the IRS, in locating and forcing delinquent parents to pay their required child support.

Contested custody

A related part of the divorce settlement is **child custody.** Legally, when there is a divorce, the decision of custody is not up to the parents but up to the court. The state retains the right to protect the child and decide whether to place the child with either parent or with neither parent—whatever it feels is "in the best interests of the child" (Orthner and Lewis, 1979). Usually, the court will go along with any decision the parents agree upon. But if the parents cannot agree and decide to contest custody, even in a no-fault divorce, then the court will hear arguments from the parents and make the decision based on the evidence presented. Once this decision is made, custody can be altered only if it is shown that the custodial parent is clearly unfit as a parent, something courts are very reluctant to reconsider (Eisler). The custody decision will also indicate the rights of the noncustodial parent to visit with the children.

The Coparental Divorce Process

Divorce alters the bond between a husband and wife both legally and interpersonally. Yet in 60 percent of all divorces, children under eighteen years of age are involved too, and their bond to both parents often remains. The parent-child relationship may change, particularly with the noncustodial parent, but as Paul Bohannan explains, the notion of a "coparental divorce" is "useful because it indicates that the child's parents are divorced from each other—not from the child."

Guilt over children

The coparental divorce is often the most difficult adjustment couples must make. Parents frequently feel more guilt over disappointing and hurting their children than over the concerns of their spouse, friends, or kin (Weiss). Children are reminders of better days, of a past when love and sexual intimacy once united the couple. They also remain a vestigial link between the divorced couple for years to come, even after a new marital bond has been established for one or both parents.

In some marriages, the parent-child bond serves as an effective barrier to divorce, but this influence is declining. The number of children involved in divorce has been rising, and recent statistics indicate that the presence of children deters separation and divorce only when the children are in their preschool years. Once all the children are in school, they no longer seem to influence the probability of divorce (Cherlin, 1977).

Presumptions of competence

The coparental divorce in most families coincides with the interpersonal divorce. As the marriage is disillusioned, usually the children become gradually aware of parental tension and, while often hoping for reconciliation, become more closely allied to one parent or the other. In most families, the relationship between mother and children remains stronger than that between father and children, so nine times out of ten, the children remain with their mother when parents separate (Orthner and Lewis). Since social and legal presumptions of motherhood competence support this arrangement, the divorce court usually agrees to legally continue the child custody of the mother (Roth, 1977). Nevertheless, there are growing indications that this custody situation is beginning to change. Many fathers are now participating more in child rearing, and some of these fathers are actively seeking a continuing, more meaningful role in the lives of their children.

Changing Patterns of Child Custody. Until a little over a century ago, the father's rights to his children were not questioned in American law. In fact, for centuries common law had said that paternal authority was supreme in the family. By the mid-1800s, however, American courts began to follow the British example of determining custody for children in the "tender years"—under seven years of age. Gradually, this **tender-years doctrine** became associated with almost automatically granting mothers custody of preadolescent children based on an assumption that they are naturally better parents. In 1938, this assumption had become so entrenched that the Missouri Supreme Court could say: "There is but a twilight zone between a mother's love and the atmosphere of heaven, and all things being equal, no child should be deprived of that maternal influence unless it can be shown there are special or extraordinary reasons for doing so" (Orthner and Lewis).

Father-custody discouraged

By the 1960s, these legal presumptions of maternal competence meant that very few fathers had any chance of getting custody of their children. The divorce rate was rising, but lawyers patently discouraged fathers from trying to hold on to their children (Roth). Psychologists were even beginning to recommend that fathers' rights to visitation with their children be limited (Goldstein *et al.*, 1973). In an analysis of the legal and social restrictions placed on fathers in divorce, the author and a colleague wrote the following:

> Admittedly, not all fathers want custody of their children upon divorce; but for those who do, the biases in the legal system tend to frustrate even those cases where there is extraordinary evidence in favor of the father's competence as a child rearer. In fact, these biases suggest a presumption of guilt before the father has even been tried, the antithesis of American law. Many fathers who would be excellent custodial parents are discouraged from seeking custody while many mothers are implicitly encouraged by present societal norms to accept custody when in fact this may not be their primary desire or interest. (1979, p. 28)

"Best-interests" doctrine

Today, nearly every state has formally eliminated from its laws the biases of the tender-years doctrine. Although the legacy of this bias remains, there is a growing movement for courts to consider carefully "the best interests of the child," whether that means custody for the mother or for the father. Fathers are now finding it easier to have **visitation rights** to their children enlarged and protected, especially since no-fault divorces have reduced the family's hostility toward the father. Some couples are even experimenting with **joint custody,** an arrangement in which the children move back and forth from parent to parent over a set period of time. While these arrangements do not

Divorce leaves many men the role of "weekend father."
© Ellis Herwig, 1980.

always work successfully (Weiss), the fact that they are being tried more often today indicates that some parents are attempting to break the traditional pattern of coparental divorce. If parents truly work at maintaining joint custody arrangements, studies suggest that the children will be better off as a result (Luepnitz, 1980).

Effects of Divorce on Children. How do the children of divorce fare? Are they permanently harmed by the experience, or do they adjust to their new family situation with little psychological consequence? These questions have plagued many divorcing parents, and the answers are beginning to come in from research studies.

Initial responses

The initial response of most children is apparently distress. Wallerstein and Kelly (1980) studied 131 psychologically normal children from the time of their parents' separation through the months and years of postdivorce adjustment. They found that almost all of the children were intensely upset at the time of separation. Most of the children wanted their parents to get back together again and tried in various ways to reconcile their parents. The predolescent children were most upset by the separation and often fantasized that their absent parent was still around. Young children frequently regressed, acted even younger than they were, and played with toys long-since neglected. Complaints of sleeplessness and cramps were also common, as were feelings among preschool children that they were somehow to blame for the separation.

Adolescent anger

Older children appear to be more stoic in their response to divorce. Most were obviously upset, but they tried to maintain more distance from the painful situation. Anger was a more obvious response among adolescents—anger at parents for letting them down, anger for the shame they felt around their friends, anger for what one parent was doing to the other, and anger for having their adolescence made so much more difficult for them.

After the first year of parental separation, the researchers found that most of the children had adjusted to the divorce. After five years, one-third of the children had returned to their previous levels of self-confidence and had made normal developmental progress. These children remembered their earlier pain but were now free of the guilt and anger they had felt. About one-third of the children were experiencing some school or home difficulties, but they were doing reasonably well. Another one-third, however, had actually become more troubled over the years of separation. Among these children, some personal guilt remained, their self-esteem continued to drop, and they had difficulty relating to others (Wallerstein and Kelly).

Factors in adjustment

There are a number of factors that seem to help children adjust in the first year of coparental divorce. Most important for young children was consistent, loving care from the parent with whom they lived. The children whose parents were so preoccupied with their own lives that they had little time or energy for them fared quite poorly. Older children and adolescents adjusted better to divorce if they had siblings or friends they could count on for support. Isolated, immature adolescents experienced more trauma after divorce. For all the children in the Wallerstein and Kelly study, continued contacts with the father also played an important role in their adjustment. Apparently, an ongoing relationship with both parents helps children resolve their distress, guilt, and anger—things they must do if they are going to develop normally.

Research on the long-term consequences of divorce for children is particularly useful in revealing the remarkable personal resilience of children to the separation of their parents. Studies comparing children and adults from divorced and intact families most often find no significant differences in their personalities or ability to relate to others (Burchinal, 1964; Raschke and Raschke, 1979). In comparative studies of children from divorced families with children from nondivorced but unhappy families, it has been found that

Vignette 14.3

The Bill of Rights of Children in Divorce Actions

I. The right to be treated as an interested and affected person and not as a pawn, possession, or chattel of either or both parents.

II. The right to grow to maturity in that home environment which will best guarantee an opportunity for the child to grow to mature and responsible citizenship.

III. The right to the day-by-day love, care, discipline, and protection of the parent having custody of the child.

IV. The right to know the noncustodial parent and to have the benefit of such parent's love and guidance through adequate visitations.

V. The right to a positive and constructive relationship with both parents, with neither parent to be permitted to degrade or downgrade the other in the mind of the child.

VI. The right to have moral and ethical values developed by precept and practices and to have limits set for behavior so that the child early in life may develop self-discipline and self-control.

VII. The right to the most adequate level of economic support that can be provided by the best efforts of both parents.

VIII. The right to the same opportunities for education that the child would have had if the family unit had not been broken.

IX. The right to periodic review of custodial arrangements and child-support orders as the circumstances of the parents and the benefit of the child may require.

X. The right to recognition that children involved in a divorce are always disadvantaged parties and that the law must take affirmative steps to protect their welfare, including, where indicated, a social investigation to determine, and the appointment of a guardian *ad litem* to protect their interests.

Adapted from recent decisions of the Wisconsin Supreme Court
The Family Court of Milwaukee County

From Harry D. Kraus, *Family Law* (St. Paul, Minn.: West, 1976), p. 1033.

---

the latter children suffered the most psychosomatic illness and parent-child adjustment problems and were the most likely to commit delinquent acts (Nye, 1957; Berg and Kelly, 1979).

Long-term consequences

The notion that childhood stress inevitably leads to adult trauma was also tested in a long-term longitudinal study at the University of California. Approximately 200 people were studied from the time of infancy to age thirty. It was hypothesized that children from troubled homes would be troubled adults while children from happy homes would be happy adults. The researchers were wrong in two-thirds of their predictions. What they found was that most of the children from stressful families had adjusted quite well as adults, and even more surprising, that some of the children who grew up in the best of circumstances had become unhappy, insecure adults (Skolnick, 1978).

These studies suggest that divorce may not be the ultimate, adverse factor in child development that we once thought it was. True, divorce is stressful for children, but most children bounce back quite readily *if* they are given the love and support of at least one parent. Childhood is full of potential stresses for children, and any number of incidents or conditions can affect their personal competence. Thus, we can agree with the conclusion of Robert Weiss (1975) that, for children, "while parental separation will be critically important in their autobiographies, in the long run it will be only one of the many determinants of their well-being and is likely to be outweighed by the others taken together" (p. 223).

REMARRIAGE

American law forbids polygamy, being simultaneously married to more than one person. Yet, as one sociologist has observed, "it is likely that a greater number, as well as proportion, of people in America experience a multiple number of spouses than in many, if not most, countries recognized as polygamous" (Eshleman, 1978, p. 651). The rapid rise in the divorce rate has been accompanied by an equally rapid rise in remarriage, so that marriages between formerly divorced persons are no longer uncommon. This has led to what some have called an emerging pattern of **serial polygamy,** the acceptance of multiple spouses as long as they come one after the other, not all at once.

Incidence of Remarriage

At the turn of the twentieth century, the incidence of remarriage was low. Over 90 percent of all marriages were first marriages and, with a lower divorce rate and higher mortality rate, most remarriages involved widowed, not divorced, people. By 1960, the situation had dramatically changed: only about eight out of ten marriages were first marriages, and most of the remarriages included divorced instead of widowed people. With the rise in the divorce rate during the 1960s and 1970s, the trend in remarriage increased even more sharply. By the mid-1970s, only seven out of ten brides and grooms had never been married before, and remarriages after divorce accounted for nearly one-fourth of men's marriages compared to less than one-seventh in 1960 (Glick and Norton).

Remarriage rates

Eventually, four out of five divorced people remarry. On the average, these remarriages occur approximately three years after the divorce was granted. Younger people and childless people are the most likely to remarry, and they do so more quickly. For example, divorced childless women under age thirty remarry after an average of only 2.6 years since their divorce while women of the same age but with three or more children usually take over five years to remarry (Glick and Norton). Perhaps the responsibility of children delays the courtship of these women or makes them more selective. And perhaps the prospect of marrying into a family already complete with children causes men to consider this arrangement more carefully as well.

Marriage in Remarriage

Is love better the second time around? From the responses of remarried husbands and wives, we might think so. William Goode (1956) found that 95 percent of the remarried divorced mothers he interviewed felt that their present marriage was "better" than their former marriage. Other studies have found similar results, indicating that remarried people believe very strongly that *this* marriage is different from the former one—and that its chances of success are better as well.

Success probabilities

When we examine divorce statistics, however, we find that the chances of success in second marriages are not quite as good as they were the first time around, but they are not that much worse either. While it has been projected that about 38 percent of all first marriages end in divorce, we can likewise expect that 44 percent of these remarriages will end in divorce (see Fig. 14.3). This may seem to be a high likelihood of redivorce, but from the other side, the chances for success in remarriage are not that much less than the chances for success in first marriages today.

Potential adjustment problems

Given the fact that remarried people have had at least two chances to succeed in marriage, we might wonder why the divorce probabilities are still so high. Some of the reasons for this were identified by Benjamin Schlesinger (1977) in his study of "reconstituted families" in Toronto, Canada. After intensively interviewing ninety-six remarried couples, he reported that these

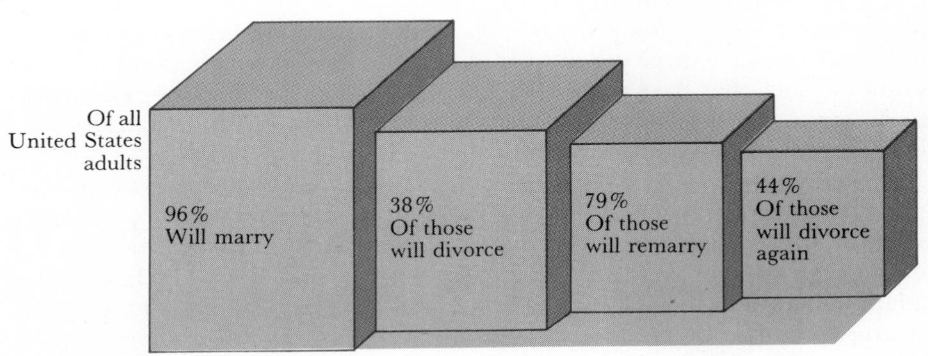

Fig. 14.3

The Marriage Odds

Source: Data from Glick and Norton (1977).

husbands and wives faced practically the same adjustment problems that confronted couples in first marriages, with the addition of several new ones as well. One new problem was that of **developing a new couple identity** after having gone through the pain of giving up an old one. Since they had already "loved and lost," the remarried had come to depend more on their own resources and were somewhat reluctant to trust and yield themselves to someone else. A second problem was the **fear of marital failure,** a fear that is coupled with anything that links their present and former marriages, including the fear of disagreements, of making comparisons, of behaving according to old patterns, or of seeing faults in the new relationship. These fears made it difficult to learn from previous mistakes and to communicate in "sensitive" areas of the relationship. Another new problem was that of the **former spouse,** the "invisible third party" to the remarriage. Ex-spouses sometimes interfere and often cause resentment, particularly when there are children involved (Goetting, 1979).

Marital happiness

Despite these potential problems, the majority of remarriages are successful and, apparently, satisfying as well. When the marital happiness of previously divorced and never-divorced married persons was compared in a recent series of national surveys, the remarried husbands and wives reported their marriages to be almost as happy as the first-married husbands and wives (Glenn and Weaver, 1977). Remarriage may be somewhat more difficult for wives, since their marital-happiness scores were lower than the scores of their husbands or the scores of the wives in first marriages, but "so far," the researchers concluded, "divorce and remarriage seem to have been rather effective mechanisms for replacing poor marriages with good ones" (p. 336).

Children in Remarriage

Blended families

A large number of remarriages include children from former marriages. In the United States, it is estimated that about one child in ten is living with a step-parent (Rallings, 1976). These "blended" families are often complex, sometimes including children from the previous marriages of both husband and wife as well as children from the new marriage—the "his, hers, and ours" phenomenon. This complexity is even further increased because children of divorce often have three parents instead of two; they have at least three sets of grandparents; they have more uncles, aunts, and cousins than they know what to do with; and they have new terms like "step-mother" and "half-brother" that they must add to their vocabulary.

Research studies indicate that some situations in remarriage can be more difficult than others. For example, younger children and older adolescents seem to adjust more easily to remarriage than children caught in the quandary of the pre- and early teen years (Bowerman and Irish, 1962). Children adapt somewhat more easily to step-fathers than to step-mothers, probably because of the closer contact and, therefore, possible friction between mothers and children (Duberman, 1975). Disciplinary issues are often unresolved since decisions over behavioral guidelines take time to develop (Kompara, 1980). Also, there is a growing concern among some family professionals over the lack of appropriate incest taboos between nonblood kin relations in remarried families (Cohen, 1978).

Child adjustments

Nevertheless, despite these potential problems, children remain remarkably adaptable to the family relationships in which they find themselves. In a study of 1500 Iowa high-school students, there were found to be no significant personality differences between students from "unbroken," "broken," and "reconstituted" families (Burchinal). From a random sample of remarried parents in an Ohio county, Lucile Duberman obtained Parent-Child Relationship Scores which indicated an "excellent" adjustment in 64 percent, a "good" adjustment in 18 percent, and a "poor" adjustment in only 18 percent of the families.

Even more convincing evidence of children's adaptability to remarriage comes from national surveys that have made possible comparisons between individuals from step-parent families and individuals from natural-parent families. In such an analysis (Wilson *et al.*, 1975), it was found that among the adults surveyed there were very few differences in social and social-psychological characteristics between those reared in step-parent and natural-parent families. When the youths were similarly compared, there were *no differences* found on these characteristics. After examining the overall picture, the researchers concluded that children's experiences in a family, whether formed by remarriage or first marriage, can lead to a predominantly positive, negative, or mixed response, but that the differences between children from step-parent and natural-parent backgrounds may be less today than earlier. Apparently, they go on to say, the step-parent family is "not inevitably inferior to the natural-parent family for the well-being of the child" (Wilson *et al.*, p. 535).

Summary

Historically, marital separations have not been unusual. Most cultures have permitted some means by which unsatisfactory marriages can be terminated. But while annulments, desertion, and legal separations have been declining in recent history, divorce rates have been rising rapidly and have become the major means for marital termination today.

Some marriages are more prone to divorce than others. Most important is the age at marriage, with marriages between teenagers much more likely to end in divorce. The peak period of divorce occurs in the third and fourth year of marriage and, in general, the higher the education and social class of the couple, the lower their chances of divorce. Divorce in one's family background can also increase one's own divorce probability.

Interpersonally, divorce is a process that involves the gradual deterioration of the marital bond. This process begins in disillusionment with the marriage and is finalized in the formation of separate, nonmarried identities. Legally, the divorce process is more clearly defined, even though the provisions for divorce vary considerably from state to state. A legal divorce usually begins with legal consultation and proceeds with the the filing of a divorce complaint or petition, the issuing of a court summons, an interlocutory hearing and decree, and the judgment of a final divorce decree.

In 60 percent of all divorces, children are involved. In these situations, marital separation leads to coparental divorce as well. After divorce, children appear to be quite distressed during the first year but most settle into a more normal developmental pattern after this initial period of adjustment.

Four out of five divorced people eventually remarry. The majority of those remarriages are successful. Children in remarriages often experience some initial strains, but over the long term, they adapt quite well to their new family environments.

SUGGESTIONS FOR ADDITIONAL READING

Duberman, Lucile. *The Reconstituted Family: A Study of Remarried Couples and Their Children.* Chicago: Nelson-Hall, 1975.

This is an easily understood analysis of the relationships among members of eighty-eight remarried families. The importance of parent-child adjustments is particularly noted.

Eisler, Riane T. *Dissolution: No-Fault Divorce, Marriage, and the Future of Women.* New York: McGraw-Hill, 1977.

Written by an attorney who specializes in divorce, this is an excellent guidebook to the economic and legal elements of the divorce process. The author is particularly sensitive to the role of women in divorce.

Framo, James L. "The friendly divorce," *Psychology Today* (February 1978): 77–79, 100–102.

This article is written by a pioneer in family therapy and attempts to demonstrate to couples how divorce can be accomplished with a minimum of pain to everyone involved.

Levinger, George. "A social psychological perspective on divorce," *Journal of Social Issues* 32 (Winter, 1976): 21–47.

A well-documented examination of the forces that create and break down marital bonds today. Excellent theoretical rationale for interpersonal divorce.

Wallerstein, Judith, and Joan Kelly. *Surviving the Break-up: How Children Actually Cope with Divorce.* New York, Basic Books, 1980.

Based on a five-year study of divorced families, this sensitive and perceptive book examines the many factors involved in the adjustment of children to the divorce of their parents.

Weiss, Robert. *Marital Separation.* New York: Basic Books, 1975.
This is an outstanding resource book on coping with the end of a marriage and the transition to being single again. Examples from actual cases are included throughout.

The Middle Years and Beyond Part VI

Chapter 15

Marriage and Family in the Middle Years

There is an old saying that "life begins at forty." However, not many men and women really believe that. The United States is a youth-oriented culture, and most people find the inevitable process of aging very difficult to accept. When we consider the prospect of middle age, most of us experience ambivalent feelings. On the one hand, perhaps middle age will bring a relaxation of the pressure to achieve that is so urgent among young adults. But on the other hand, most people fear new pressures, new physical limitations, and new career and family adjustments. A sampling of these possibilities and fears is offered in the following birthday invitation sent to the friends of Maia Craig and Roberto Almazon:

> Growing older means getting wiser. Growing older means thinking about exercising regularly and quitting smoking. Getting older means remembering all the people who have meant something to you and all the different freaky things you've done. Getting older means looking forward to even more because you're starting to learn to get it on, even when you're scared to death. Getting older means learning to appreciate yourself. (Kalish, 1975, p. vii)

In terms of the family life cycle, the middle years are usually considered the years between the time the children leave home and retirement from work begins. Not all middle-aged couples have children, but for those who do, the middle years often start when they are in their mid- to late forties and end when they are in their mid-sixties. These years are usually marked by a decline in parental responsibilities, a peaking of careeer involvements, the reestablishment of the nonparental-couple relationship, the onset of grandparenthood, and a decline in physical health and well-being.

Historically, this period now identified as the middle years is rather new. A century ago, very few couples experienced a long postparental period together since marriages tended to occur later, parenthood continued longer, and death took one of the marital partners earlier. Today, it is likely that married couples can expect to have one-third of their married years still to look forward to after their children, if any, leave home (Glick, 1977).

In this chapter, we will explore some of the transitions, adjustments, and relationships that are commonly experienced in these middle years of the family. This period of life represents new challenges to individuals and families, challenges which have only recently begun to be examined and understood.

TRANSITIONS IN THE MIDDLE YEARS

For most couples, the middle years involve a series of important transitions. Parenthood, once so dominant a role for many women and men, begins to take a new, less central position in their lives. Work careers reach their peak of

Vignette 15.1 Middle Age and a Sense of Future

Is the normal developmental phase of middle age always a crisis? For some, surely, there will be a realization that at least some of the promises of youth have been realized. Some will be at the height of their creative productivity, some will be wise rather than merely smart, humane instead of egocentric, the mentor rather than the student. Yet when we think about middle age we tend to ignore the constructive aspects and concentrate on the negatives. Middle age seems to be a period when people mourn for the things they have not done, for the roles they have not participated in, for the experience they have not had. I think that is because for most Americans middle age is the first intimation in the experientially real sense that they will die, and it is reasonable that experiencing your mortality, acknowledging your restricted alternatives, and understanding the permanence of decisions you make now, provokes psychological crises. In other cultures where death is less feared and age and experience are venerated and life's rhythms are repeated, flowing from one generation to the next, then one could imagine that someone's fortieth birthday would be as full of promise as the twenty-first is for us. In a culture of rapid social change that is much less likely.

It may be useful to conceptualize adult phases as periods when one attempts to create new existential anchors. Existential anchors are roles or commitments such as work, marriage, and parenthood that literally anchor you to your present reality because they force you to cope with real tasks and people. Existential anchors have the inherent capacity to focus effort and provide feelings of growth as the nature of the tasks change. Anchors are central organizers in one's present time . . .

Sadly, technological societies threaten members by dint of the very rate of change within the society. Individuals within rapidly changing societies are influence and earnings. Marital roles, freed from the obligations of parenthood, become more flexible and companionate. Taken together, these changes often lead to what has been called the "prime of life," a description that fits the majority of middle-aged men and women who report their highest levels of life satisfaction in these years (Mancini and Griffin, 1979).

Life satisfaction

This picture darkens, however, when we look at the numerous complaints about the so-called mid-life crisis (Bardwick, 1978). Not everyone is able to meet the goals that he or she has set out to accomplish in life. For some people, the loss of parental responsibilities creates a void in their central life identity. For others, their push to "get ahead" in business or their profession finally runs head-long into realization that they are not going to go much further. Menopause, gray hair, baldness, and altering physiques are also reminders that there may be fewer years left to live than years left behind.

Generativity or stagnation

Whether mid-life transitions will lead to crises or not depends in large part on whether individuals or couples can transfer their interests to new opportunities that become available to them (see Vignette 15.1). Some years

---

those most in need of anchors. If one's world is in a vortex of change at least one's own identity ought to remain stable, like the eye of a storm. Yet that is exactly what cannot happen because the definitions of what constitute anchors are themselves being changed. A decade ago, for example, the existential anchor for women was to be found in the family relationship. Today, in the radical ideal, that anchor is rejected in favor of anchoring within the self and there is the specific rejection of finding one's existential anchor or identity within relationships. For women the anchor of parenthood is rejected, in the radical ideal, for the anchor of work. For men, the anchor of competitive success is rejected in favor of family or individual self-sufficiency.

The people who will emerge more mature and stronger from the crisis that is the awareness of their aging, will be those who have been able to create a sense of future. It seems necessary for people to be involved in a commitment which is real. It seems necessary to believe that it will be a good, that is a moral, thing for you to achieve what you do. It seems necessary to experience yourself as initiating and controlling change, for then change for its own sake is perceived as exhilarating. It seems necessary to experience yourself as coping and as becoming as you work toward your future which is also your present. Those who experience the crisis of middle age as a developmental or growth phase are those who are able to create an existential anchor which fills their present time and creates a reality which extends endlessly forward and thereby creates a future.

From Judith M. Bardwick, "Middle Age and a Sense of Future" (1978). Reprinted with permission from the *Merrill-Palmer Quarterly of Behavior and Development.*

ago, Erik Erikson (1964) described the central issue of the adult years as the pull between **generativity** and **stagnation.** According to Erikson, those who hold on to their past roles and fail to shift gears creatively toward new ways of energizing themselves and others eventually fall prey to a negative self-image and an inability to relate to others.

In a more popular version of this theme, Gail Sheehy writes in her book, *Passages* (1976):

> The chief virtue traditionally associated with middle age is experience, but that cuts two ways. The person who arrives at fifty having ignored the opportunities for reassessment in midlife passage may take the familiar, mulish stance of protector of the status quo. It is no mistake that such people are called "die-hards" . . .
>
> On the other hand, people who have seen, felt, and incorporated their private truths during mid-life passage no longer expect the impossible dream, nor do they have to protect an inflexible position. Having experimented with many techniques for facing problems and change, they will have modified many of the assumptions and illusions of youth. They are practiced. They know what works. They can make decisions with a welcomed economy of action. (pp. 496–497)

The "Passage" of Parenthood

"Empty-Nest"?

Certainly, one of the major "passages" of the middle years occurs when the children finally leave home. This leads to what is sometimes called the "post-parental" or "empty-nest" phase of the family life cycle. Actually, however, these terms do not reflect the experience of most parents at this time. Parental identity and concern do not end when adult children develop more independence. Parenthood changes with less direct involvement in child rearing, but for most mothers and fathers, it is not over. Also, contrary to the bland, sterile image suggested by the term "empty-nest," this is not a period when most parents mourn the loss of children around the house. Rather, parents more commonly adjust quite well to their new independence and the opportunities this offers them.

In a study that followed a group of women from adolescence into middle age, it was recently reported that nearly all the women had emerged from their child-rearing years contented and "psychologically healthy" (Livson, 1977). Not all of them, however, took the same path to contentment. Some of these women, the "traditionals," had particularly welcomed parenthood, but as their children grew older, they gradually developed new satisfying relationships with their children, husbands, and friends. The "independents," however, tended to be less pleased with domestic roles. Parenthood made them more depressed and irritable, "out of touch with their intellectual and creative potential" (Livson, p. 91). These women revived their earlier interests when their children left home and their satisfaction with life increased as well.

Departure of children

The reason that this mid-life change in parental responsibilities does not create the crisis we often expect is that it is gradual and anticipated. The majority of couples in one study told the researcher that they considered the departure of their children to be a "natural and expected process" (Petranek, 1975). Today, it is considered unhealthy for parents to hold on to their children too dearly and most parents do not. Parents are also eased more gently and satisfactorily into the middle years when their children leave one at a time, when they have experienced temporary separations from their children in the past (as in sending them to camp or other places), and when they have had a closer relationship with their partner, a relationship that will continue. The importance of preparation for parental change and an understanding of its benefits to parents and children alike is offered in the statement by a father:

> I think there is a parental anxiousness as children embark on their own; but one must realize that the ordinary progressions of life bring departures from joys of the past to new joys of the future. Our children have prepared for their new life as we have prepared for ours. (Petranek, p. 4)

Parent–older-child relationships

Relationships with older children rarely end after their departure from home. Compared to the days of active child rearing, however, middle-years parents shift their parental roles toward support and availability and away from direction and coercion (Benson, 1971). Continued contact and mutual aid between parents and children is the norm rather than the exception. Even in these days of high residential mobility, the majority of adult children continue to live relatively close to their parents and visit with them quite often.

Help patterns

Although marriage is traditionally associated with independence for grown children, research studies suggest that parental assistance in the form of financial aid, advice, and services like child care and shopping continue (Hill, 1970). Adult children also provide some services to their parents, largely in the form of care when sick, assistance with home repairs, and emotional support, but the parent generation tends to give disproportionately to their children. Most parents, however, do not feel they should provide aid or services on anything but a temporary or emergency basis. On this, adult children tend to agree (Adams, 1964). Clearly, the relationships between parents and adult children that are most satisfactory are those that have the fewest financial and service ties and the most emotional-support ties (Kelley, 1979).

In general, there is no reason why contact and exchange cannot continue between middle-years parents and their children. However, the quality and mutuality of this relationship depends on the type of relationship that has been developed over the years. If the parents played a highly controlling and directive role with their young children, the transition to a less active, more egalitarian relationship with adult children may be difficult. When the parents have been able to phase out their parental responsibilities more slowly and develop relationships with their children not only as parents, but as adults as well, the middle-years parent-child relationship is more likely to be comfortable for all concerned.

The marriage of their children marks a release from parental responsibilities for some people.

Mid-Life Career Changes

For many men and women, the middle years bring the reorganization of their career roles as well. Job changes, new occupational ventures, re-education, and a careful analysis of career preferences have become a growing part of the mid-life transition for men and women. Psychologist Daniel Levinson, in his recent book, *The Seasons of a Man's Life* (1978), notes that the mid-life period brings on a tumultuous struggle within the individual who up until then has been primarily career oriented but now begins to find that he or she has other personal needs as well. It is a time of moderate or severe reappraisal. Levinson finds that for many people: "Every aspect of their lives comes into question, and they are horrified by much that is revealed. They are full of recriminations against themselves and others. They cannot go on as before, but need time to choose a new path or modify the old one" (p. 199).

Work commitments

The effects of career restlessness have been widely noted. A study of corporation managers, for example, found that those who were in their early forties expressed the lowest commitment to work as part of their central life interest (Goldman, 1973). Other surveys have found that this is the period of life most associated with occupational stress and poor reactions to this stress (Harry, 1976).

Women's employment

Women represent a large percentage of those who experience mid-career realignments. Some of these women are entering the labor force after full-time devotion to marriage and parenthood. (This number is now rather small since 60 percent of the mothers with school-age children are already employed.) Other women shift at this time from primarily part-time to full-time employment, and still others change to jobs that they find more personally meaningful. A recent national study found that the women who had completed their child rearing were the most likely to be free to take jobs that matched their interests and skills (Waite, 1977). For many of these women, this is the first time in many years that they have been able to work in jobs that require travel, irregular hours, weekend responsibilities, or re-education.

To some degree, there is a growing pressure on women to perform well in the job market, especially after their children are grown and gone. While representatives of the women's movement have stressed that women should be free to make their own decisions, this frequently carries the implication that if a woman is not employed, she is not accomplishing much with her life (Heddescheimer, 1977). Consequently, many middle-aged women report that they feel pressure from both the media and peers to move into the labor force or to upgrade their occupational position. In a study of people who had made mid-life career changes, one woman put her feelings this way:

> I feel among my contemporaries that there is social pressure to go to work at the present time. This is completely different from the way it used to be. I think that this is what got me thinking along the way. I found myself explaining at parties why I didn't work, and feeling inadequate because I didn't. (Ziegler, 1978, p. 12)

Among some employed women and men, the mid-life period is a time of learning to face the truth about their accomplishments. The dreams and aspirations of their youth stand in stark contrast to the current realities of life. If success is less than they had originally anticipated, a sense of sadness or frustration may envelop them, and they may feel that they have attempted too little, not expanded themselves, and not seized upon opportunities (Schlossberg, 1977).

New risks

Other employed people are drawn to career changes by the attractions of starting over at a time in their lives when it is again possible to take new risks. The man or woman with dependent children may not feel that he or she can attempt to start a new career or go back to school once the family has become accustomed to a certain standard of living. Once these responsibilities are lifted, however, the individual may once again feel free to train for a new skill, to take a cut in income, if necessary, and to seize a career opportunity that offers new satisfactions. According to Levinson's research, this "breaking out" of the old career path is becoming more common.

Mid-life seminars

Some business organizations, sensing this restlessness in their employees, offer mid-life seminars to help employees redefine their life goals, hoping that in doing so they can help them to remain effective and productive at work. In the program developed by the Menninger Foundation, one of the typical tasks of their seminars is to help people in mid-life link their families more closely to their overall goals in life. To do this, participants are advised to reconsider the "psychological contracts, the unwritten and often unconscious expectations, assumptions, and understandings that exist between husbands and wives, parents and children." They are told, "these contracts need to be periodically renegotiated, based on changing mutual needs. If they're not, you end up with conflicts at home, or ulcers at work" (Rice, 1979, p. 74).

Physical Changes in Mid-life

Much of our concern about the middle years centers around the physical aging of the body. Both men and women often become concerned about the fatigue they experience and the flabbiness of their muscles. They also become more concerned about heart attacks and other physically debilitating diseases (Friedman and Rosenman, 1975). In hopes of reducing the effects of aging, the middle-aged are increasingly taking up such things as dieting, running, and health foods.

Menopause

Certainly, one of the unavoidable changes of the middle years occurs in the production of hormones. In both women and men there occurs a change in the hormones produced in the body, and this is usually associated with **menopause.** In women, this change is more pronounced. Menopause follows a gradual drop in the hormone **estrogen,** which leads to a slight hormonal imbalance in the body and the eventual halt to menstruation and ovulation. Sometimes, these changes are accompanied by hot flashes, nervous disturbances, and weight gain. After a period of time, this imbalance is corrected and the body restores its internal chemical order (Kennedy, 1978).

Men also experience a hormonal imbalance in the middle years. It is caused by a gradual drop in the hormone **testosterone,** which is produced in the testes. The effects of this are similar to the effects experienced by women: fatigue, nervousness, and problems with blood circulation. But since the drop in testosterone in men is more gradual than the drop in estrogen in women, the changes experienced by men are less pronounced than the changes experienced by women.

Sexuality

According to folklore, the tribulations of menopause bring a woman's sexual life to an end. This has little basis in fact. Menopause may bring to an end the possibility of pregnancy, but it has little physical effect on a woman's capabilities for sexual stimulation or orgasm. Reported decreases in sexual desire can usually be attributed to psychological or relational difficulties rather than to physical changes in the woman's body (Mancini and Orthner, 1978). Indeed, a woman who continues to remain sexually active should retain the capacity for sexual pleasure throughout her life span. In fact, Masters and Johnson (1966) found that many women experience a rise in sexual activity when menstruation and the chances of pregnancy are eliminated.

Among men also, there is little physical basis for reported declines in sexual activity in the middle years. After age fifty, the incidence of impotence and orgasmic difficulty in men rises sharply, but this is often coupled with personal and relational frustrations. Men can expect slower physical reactions to sexual stimulation as they age but this should not cause serious problems. The man who maintains a high level of regular sexual activity will usually be capable of continued sexual expression well into his seventies or eighties (Masters and Johnson, 1970). The general advice of sex researchers is "use it or lose it." This suggestion can be applied to other aspects of physical health as well.

MARRIAGE IN MID-LIFE

Several years ago, there was a television commercial that vividly portrayed a couple in transition to their middle years of marriage. The scene took place at a breakfast table with the husband and wife calmly reading their respective sections of the morning paper. Almost unexpectedly they looked at one another, and the husband asked something like, "When did you get those glasses you're wearing?" to which his wife replied, "When did you go bald?"

Obviously, the questions asked by this Madison Avenue husband and wife are less important than the rediscovery of one another they symbolize. The din created by children at the table is gone and perhaps, for the first time in many years, couples like these have the opportunity to see one another again in roles other than that of coparents. Scenes like this are replayed daily in real homes as some couples attempt to reopen their communication with one another. Sometimes, this results in a stronger, more intimate relationship. Sometimes, it does not.

Marital Adjustments

Marital satisfaction

Research on marital satisfaction in the middle years has yielded mixed results (Schram, 1979). Married couples who have not had children appear to maintain fairly high levels of relational satisfaction and little change is noted when they move into middle age (Renne, 1970). Couples who have reared children, however, have often experienced some decline in their marital satisfaction, separation of their marital responsibilities, and diminished openness in their marital communication during their parenting years (Orthner, 1975a). These latter couples may find themselves at a mid-life crossroads in which they must now redirect their marriage, let it continue as is, or give it up.

Most recent studies have found that the majority of husbands and wives report some improvement in their marital relationship after the children have left (Glenn, 1975a). This is usually interpreted to mean that some of the time and energy that they had been investing in their parenting and job careers can now be transferred to the marriage, thereby restrengthening this relationship. Indeed, many couples take advantage of marriage-enrichment programs at this time in order to help them improve their marriages (Kerckhoff, 1976).

"Devitalized" couples

Many other married couples do not experience much change in their marital relationships in middle age. Some of these husbands and wives report that they are "happily married" because their children and spouse do not bother them anymore. Cuber and Harroff (1966) characterized most of the middle-years, middle-class couples they interviewed as outwardly happy and contented but relationally "devitalized" and "passive-congenial." Richard Kerckhoff comments: "Middle-aged marriages may be considered 'good' then when they are to a great extent unpainful and unexamined rather than when they are stimulating and challenging. They may be comfortable when they are easy to endure *and* easy to ignore" (p. 9).

Sometimes, it is difficult to ignore a relationship that is not fulfilling, particularly at a time of life in which so many personal reexaminations are being made. In Robert Anderson's play *Double Solitare,* one of the characters, George, thinks about marriage in much the same way that many other middle-aged men or women do. He ponders: "I have friends who wrangled along in the city, always with the illusion that if they could get away from the clutter of their lives and be alone in the country, things would be better for them. . . . When their kids left home, they took to the woods, and looked at each other across the uncluttered space and promptly got a divorce."

Divorce

For a growing number of middle-years couples, divorce is an option they are choosing. This does not mean that divorce rates rise in the middle years. They do not. But divorce rates have been rising for all age groups and the middle years are no exception. Couples today are less likely to "wait until their children are grown" before getting out of an unsatisfactory marriage, but they are also less likely to remain obligated to a marriage that is considered stagnant and boring. No longer are the middle years, even the late middle years, "safe" from divorce. Marriages that do not meet the needs of the individuals involved might be candidates for dissolution at any time.

Togetherness and Separateness in Mid-life

Among married couples in their middle years, two contrasting tendencies have been noted in research studies. One is a shift toward more sharing of their time together; the other is a shift toward more independence and separation in activities. To some extent, these tendencies reflect differences in the marital preferences of middle-aged people. Some men and women wish to maintain or redevelop their intrinsic commitments to their marriage, and they do this by sharing more with their partner. Others prefer to retain more of their independence and do not want to depend as much on their marital partner for companionship. It is also possible in some middle-aged marriages for both increased separation *and* increased togetherness to occur at once. Since the children have departed, husbands and wives may have more time to devote to one another and to their own interests as well.

Many middle-aged couples find they have more time to share together.

Companionship

Overall, studies of couples in their middle years tend to find that those who experience more sharing of their lives express more satisfaction with their marriages (Schram). Relationships in which the husband has increased his participation in housework and other family responsibilities are more often viewed as satisfactory by both husbands and wives (Lowenthal and Chiraboga, 1972). This is also true of relationships in which husbands and wives share their leisure-time activities. Couples who report that they share more of their leisure time together, particularly right after the children have grown and left home, are more likely to feel that their marriage is satisfactory (Orthner, 1975a).

Some degree of mid-life independence, however, is normal and frequently welcomed. Wives who are employed in their middle years more often feel self-confident and worthwhile (Barnett and Baruch, 1980). They are also more likely to be the ones who share leisure interests with their husbands (Deutscher, 1964; Orthner and Axelson, 1980). For many of these women, their new sense of self-respect makes it easier for them to share ideas, time, and activities with their husbands. Some studies have even reported that a new sense of relational equality once again appears in many middle-aged couples; an equality that results from an increase in passive and family interests on the part of husbands and an increase in active and work interests on the part of wives (Neugarten, 1968). For many of them, this reversal of their earlier roles and interests helps them to understand one another better and increases their commitment to their marriage.

Interiority

Somewhat complicating this picture, however, is the tendency toward what Bernice Neugarten (1975) calls the "interiority" of middle age. In her psychological studies of mid-life men and women, she finds that the majority of them experience "measurable increases in inward orientation and measurable decreases in cathexes for outer-world events beginning in the late forties and fifties (p. 321). This increase in self-examination and self-interest is then coupled with a withdrawal from social and family interests. Indeed, preferences for personal hobbies and private recreational activities are much more common among middle-aged husbands and wives (Mancini and Orthner).

Withdrawal

For some of these men and women, the satisfactions of a self-directed and self-focused life make it difficult for them to emerge once again from their growing shell of interpersonal isolation. They continue to withdraw into their own private world of work and hobbies for their primary source of gratification. For most others, Neugarten notes, this period of withdrawal is temporary. After having considered more carefully their goals in life, they emerge to reengage themselves to their family and friends, often renewed by the reexamination.

The "Caught Generation"

One of the labels that is increasingly being applied to the middle-aged is the "caught generation." During this period of life, individuals are involved not only in occupational, marital, and personal reconsiderations, but also must cope with the demands of their children on the one hand and their parents on the other. Their children, the younger generation, often ask for the mid-life couple's help with college expenses, their own children, and the personal support they need to get ahead in life. Meanwhile, their parents, the older generation, may be demanding help with their adjustments to retirement, old age, and death. Clark Vincent (1972) describes the dilemma for middle-aged people in this way:

> The respect you were taught to give your parents may have been denied you by your children. . . . The threat of "love withdrawal" used by your parents to keep you in line as a child, may now be used by your children to keep you in line as a parent. As a child, you were to be seen and not heard; now as a parent you may feel you are to be neither seen nor heard. (p. 143)

Financial pulls

This feeling of being caught in the middle can put a great deal of strain on middle-aged people and their marriages. The financial strain of simultaneously helping to support a child in college and a parent in retirement can severely burden the resources of many couples. Likewise, the psychological strain of dealing with two generations that are supposed to be independent and want to be independent, but may not be able to be independent can be exhausting. These pressures can certainly tax mid-life marriages.

Pleasures

On the positive side, the obligations of the middle-aged can be satisfying as well. There is comfort to be derived from being needed by one's parents. The pleasure of seeing the accomplishments of one's children and grandchildren can be more than adequate reward for the investments in time, money, and energy. Richard Kerckhoff reminds us:

> Middle-aged people are not to be accurately characterized as *just* squeezed, pressured, disappointed, exploited, and exhausted. They are often that, but they are also, according to our studies, comparatively well-off, and they know it. . . . Middle-aged people may feel squeezed by being in the middle, but they may, in addition, feel their own importance. They often know that they are the nation's decision-makers; they set the tone for life in this society. Society depends on middle-aged people's leadership and productivity. (p. 7)

GRANDPARENTHOOD

Contrary to many of our popular images, "grandparenting has become a middle-age rather than an old-age phenomenon" (Troll, 1971, p. 278). Given the trends in this century toward earlier marriage, earlier and more closely spaced childbearing, and increased life expectancy, many parents are now acquiring grandparent status in their forties and early fifties. Not only are these grandparents today more likely to be middle-aged, they are also more likely to consider themselves still youthful (Troll, 1975). This allows many grandparents to be more active and energetic in their relationships with grandchildren, if they want to be.

Grandparenting styles

In a study which included in-depth interviews with seventy grandparent couples, it was found that grandparents' involvement with their grandchildren varied a great deal (Neugarten and Weinstein, 1964). Nevertheless, five different styles of grandparenting were identified. **Formal grandparents** followed very proper and prescribed roles. Although they occasionally provided baby-sitting services or special treats for the grandchildren, they were careful to leave parenting to the mother or father and to avoid offering unsolicited advice. **Fun-seeking grandparents,** in contrast, regarded their grandchildren primarily as a source of enjoyment, and the relationship was centered on mutual satisfaction. These grandparents felt comfortable playing with their grandchildren, taking care of them, and offering advice on child rearing to the parents.

Surrogate parents were found among grandmothers who assumed responsibility for their grandchildren while the children's mother worked. **Reservoirs of family wisdom** were typically grandfathers who tried to maintain rather strong, authoritarian positions over the entire family, including adult parents and grandchildren. **Distant figures** were grandparents who emerged largely on special occasions, such as holidays or birthdays. These grandparents were somewhat removed from the daily lives of their grandchildren.

Involvements with grandchildren

While older grandparents tended to be more formal in their relationships with grandchildren, younger grandparents—those under sixty-five years of age—were more likely to be either fun-seekers or distant figures. About one-fourth of these grandparents felt little attachment to their grandchildren, even though they may have basically liked the children. Distant grandparents were much more deeply involved in their own social world of work and friends so they had little time for being a grandparent and even found it difficult to identify themselves as grandparents. One middle-aged woman summarized her situation this way: "It's great to be a grandmother, of course—but I don't have much time" (Neugarten and Weinstein, p. 203).

The majority of grandparents, however, expressed only comfort, satisfaction, and pleasure with their grandparent role (see Vignette 15.2). For these men and women, grandparenthood was linked to such feelings as biological continuity to the future, emotional fulfillment, being a resource person for a child, and vicarious achievement through the accomplishments of their grandchildren. In a recent study limited to grandmothers, 80 percent of these women reported that they were actively enjoying their grandparent role (Robertson, 1977). In fact, one-third said that they enjoyed this role more than being a parent. It seemed that these grandmothers particularly liked the pleasures and satisfactions of parenthood without many of the associated responsibilities of day-to-day child rearing.

From the perspective of grandchildren, grandparents almost always carry a very favorable image (Kahana and Kahana, 1971). Preschool children eagerly seek the indulgence and treats that grandparents often bring. Young,

Vignette 15.2

On Being a Grandmother

I did think how delightful it would be, if it happened, to see my daughter with a child. . . . When the news came that Sevanne Margaret was born, I suddenly realized that through no act of my own I had become biologically related to a new human being. This was one thing that had never come up in discussions of grandparenthood and had never before occurred to me. In many primitive societies grandparents and grandchildren are aligned together. A child who has to treat his father with extreme respect may joke with his grandfather and playfully call his grandmother "wife." The tag that grandparents and grandchildren get along so well because they have a common enemy is explicitly faced in many societies. In our own society the point most often made is that grandparents can enjoy their grandchildren because they have no responsibility for them, they do not have to discipline them, and they lack the guilt and anxiety of parenthood. All these things were familiar. But I had never thought how strange it was to be involved at a distance in the birth of a biological descendant.

I always have been acutely aware of the way one life touches another—of the ties between myself and those whom I have never met, but who read *Coming of Age in Samoa* and decided to become anthropologists. From the time of my childhood I was able to conceive of my relationship to all my forebears, some of whose genes I carry, both those I did not know even by name and those who helped to bring me up, particularly my paternal grandmother. But the idea that as a grandparent one was dealing with action at a distance—that somewhere, miles away, a series of events occurred that changed one's own status forever—I had not thought of that and found it very odd.

school-age children especially like to go places and do things with their grandparents. Only teenage grandchildren tend to feel too busy or too involved in other activities to want to spend much time with their grandparents. This progression of decreased involvement over time works both ways, however. As grandparents age, many of them report that it is more difficult to communicate with older children. Instead, they prefer to interact with younger, more malleable grandchildren. Sometimes, older grandparents prefer not to be bothered with the noise and activity of children and youth at all (Aldous, 1978).

Grandparent responsibilities

Relationships between grandparents and grandchildren are often determined by the degree of interdependence expected between the generations. Among lower social-class families, grandparents are more likely to have clearly defined responsibilities for taking care of children; their roles in the family are considered very important by parents and grandparents alike (Clavan, 1978). In the middle class, however, the grandparent role is not very well defined and there is much anxiety concerning how much grandparents should do without "interfering" in child rearing. Many middle-class grandparents echo the frustration of Margaret Mead (1974) who complained about the contemporary "obligation we lay on grandparents to keep themselves out

---

Early this year I spent a month living in my sister's hospitable home so that I could be a resource, but not a burden, in the nearby Kassarjian household while Catherine and Barkev were preparing for a two-year work period in Iran. This crowded month, during which I could be a full-time grandmother to Vanni, has rounded out my understanding of something for which I have pleaded all my life—that everyone needs to have access both to grandparents and grandchildren in order to be a full human being.

In the presence of grandparent and grandchild, past and future merge in the present. Looking at a loved child, one cannot say, "We must sacrifice this generation for the next. Many must die now so that later others may live." This is the argument that generations of old men, cut off from children, have used in sending young men out to die in war. Nor can one say, "I want this child to live well no matter how we despoil the earth for later generations." For seeing a child as one's grandchild, one can visualize that same child as a grandparent, and with the eyes of another generation one can see other children, just as light-footed and vivid, as eager to learn and know and embrace the world, who must be taken into account—now. My friend Ralph Blum has defined the human unit of time as the space between a grandfather's memory of his own childhood and a grandson's knowledge of those memories as he heard about them. We speak a great deal about a human scale; we need also a human unit in which to think about time.

From Margaret Mead, *Blackberry Winter* (New York: William Morrow, 1972).

Grandparents can enjoy the pleasures and satisfactions of parenthood without the associated responsibilities.

of the picture—not to interfere, not to spoil, not to insist, not to intrude . . . to say they are happy when, once in a great while, their children bring their grandchildren to them" (p. 80).

Still, with men and women living longer today, more children now know their grandparents better than ever before. Since more of these grandparents are middle-aged, there are also greater opportunities for them to make a lasting contribution to their grandchildren, if they desire. Grandparents can serve as resources of love, knowledge, wisdom, and understanding and can affect the self-esteem of the youngest generation as never before.

Generations

Whether this will happen or not, however, depends on the strength of the trend toward greater independence between the generations. If grandparents become less involved with grandchildren, this not only severs some of the children's links to the past but it also sets the tone for further noninvolvement with the family in the next generation. If grandparents interact with their grandchildren, the children have a broader base of experience upon which to build their self-esteem and the grandparents have more opportunities to lend their experience to the future development of society. As Mead (1974) suggests, "In the presence of grandparent and grandchild, past and future merge in the present" (p. 84).

Summary

The middle years are a rather new stage in family life. Until recently, not many husbands and wives experienced a period of years together when they were finished with child rearing yet not ready to retire. Today, the middle years can easily last a decade or two. This is often a time when couples and families experience some dramatic changes in their lives.

Descriptions of the middle years vary from calling this the "prime of life" to calling it a time of mid-life crises. Adjustments do not appear to be a major problem for most parents. Mid-life career shifts and reexaminations are common for both men and women, although women are more likely to make changes in the job and career commitments at this time. Physical changes in aging become more evident in the middle years with both sexes experiencing some of the hormone shifts associated with menopause.

Marital relationships often go through some change in mid-life as well. While most couples report an increase in marital satisfaction after their children have left, other couples do not adjust well to having only one another around and they may remain psychologically distant.

Grandparenthood is increasingly a middle-age phenomenon and it too represents new adjustments for husbands and wives in mid-life.

SUGGESTIONS FOR ADDITIONAL READING

Levinson, Daniel. *The Seasons of a Man's Life.* New York: Alfred Knopf, 1978.
Based on studies on middle-age men, this book examines the mid-life career and psychological changes many men experience. This is a very timely and challenging book to read.

Neugarten, Bernice (Ed.). *Middle-Age and Aging.* Chicago: University of Chicago Press, 1968.
This very important collection of studies and writings on middle age has prompted much of the current professional interest in the middle years of life. Most of the articles are clear and easy to understand.

Sheehy, Gail. *Passages.* New York: E. P. Dutton, 1976.
This well-written, best-selling book summarizes much of the research on mid-life changes and adds the insights and observations of a skilled journalist. It is well worth reading.

Troll, Lillian, Joan Israel, and Kenneth Israel (Eds.). *Looking Ahead: A Woman's Guide to the Problems and Joys of Growing Older.* Englewood Cliffs, N.J.: Prentice-Hall, 1977.
Articles included in this book explore many aspects of life for women who are approaching their middle years. Issues such as sexuality, menopause, marriage, friendships, and jobs are discussed.

Chapter 16

Marriage and Family in the Later Years

Erich Fromm (1947) has thoughtfully written, "Birth is only one particular step in a continuum which begins with conception and ends with death. All that is between these two poles is a process of giving birth to one's potentialities, of bringing to life all that is potentially given to us in two cells" (p. 91). Today, as more men and women remain healthier longer, our chances to remain active, involved, and capable of realizing our potential in life have increased. Fewer old people see themselves as "over the hill," waiting to die. More are seeking some of the opportunities and pleasures that were deferred during their young and middle-adult years.

The French have an interesting term for the later years. They call this period *"le troisième age"*—The Third Age. Coming on the heels of the childhood and adult "ages," the Third Age suggests a new plateau in life, a new period of discovery, a time when new contributions can be made to oneself and to others. True, there are death, loneliness, illness, and pain in these years, but there are also beauty and novelty to be sought and shared with others.

Opportunities to share the later years with family and friends have increased the influence and decreased the loneliness of the aged. With both men and women living longer, children are more likely to know their grandparents and great-grandparents than was true earlier. Contacts between older people and their own adult children are often quite frequent despite the distances that sometimes separate them. Half of all marriages now survive into the retirement years, and one out of five married couples can expect to share their "golden," fiftieth anniversary together (Glick and Norton, 1977). Because the elderly now have better health and vitality, they are better able to make and retain friendships than was possible a few decades ago.

If this image of the later years sounds more positive than the one we usually receive, it should. A more healthy concept of old age is certainly warranted today. Unfortunately, there are many old people tucked away in dreary rooms with few visitors and little hope, but they are vastly outnumbered by those who are still active and involved with others. While it is difficult to rid ourselves of the stereotype of the doting, dependent elderly, it is important for people of all ages to better understand the strengths, weaknesses, and adjustments of older men and women. In this chapter, we will examine this last stage of life and the prospects it holds for individuals and families.

Being "old"

For purposes of simplicity, the discussion in this chapter will focus on persons sixty-five years of age and older. Gerontologists who study older people most often use this age to distinguish the "later years" from the "middle years" of life. We should realize, however, that people age at different rates, and while one person may be "old" in feelings and behavior at fifty-five, another person may not yet feel "old" at seventy-five (Shanas, 1980). Even old people do not usually like to think of themselves as being old, despite the number of birthdays they have accumulated. A study at Duke University found over half of the men and women between sixty-five and sixty-nine years of age classifying themselves as "middle-aged" rather than "elderly" (Busse *et al.*, 1970). It is apparently not easy for most people to accept themselves as being in the later years of life.

ADAPTING TO THE LATER YEARS OF LIFE

Elderly population

Today, over 1000 Americans celebrate their sixty-fifth birthday every day. Ten percent of the population is now sixty-five years of age or older, and we can expect that nearly 16 percent of the population will be in that age group in another forty years. In 1900, 39 percent of those who were born that year could expect to survive to their sixty-fifth birthday. Today, nearly 75 percent can expect to reach that age (Siegal, 1978). The increased population of the elderly, however, does not always mean that their adjustments to being older have eased.

"Getting old," a retired friend once said, "takes some getting used to." This is not surprising since the later stages of life are accompanied by many social, physical, psychological, and work-role changes to which older men and women typically must adjust. Some of these changes occur gradually and are adapted to quite easily. Other changes are more difficult to accept and may cause problems in adjustment.

Disengagement

Until as recently as two decades ago, it was widely believed that a proper adjustment to the later years involved "disengagement" from previous activities and relationships (Cumming and Henry, 1961). This approach to aging emphasized "letting go," a graceful acceptance of mortality, and a separation of the elderly from the mainstream of society. More recently, however, we

Activity

have observed that disengagement is not preferred by most older people (Atchley, 1977). In fact, they feel quite the opposite; they want to remain active and engaged in the activities and relationships they feel are important. Personal adjustment for many of these elderly people means accepting some changes in their lives but not readily accepting the downhill slide toward dependence and death.

"Young-old" or "Old-old

Bernice Neugarten (1975), a noted gerontologist, suggests that the speed and style of adjustments in old age depends upon whether a person is "young-old" or "old-old." The young-old, she says, are relatively healthy, involved with others, and usually retired from their jobs but not from life. While age is not the major factor, these elderly are typically under seventy-five years of age and have not yet faced a debilitating physical problem. The old-old, in contrast, are usually over seventy-five, less healthy, without a spouse, and more dependent on others. For them, adjustments to the limitations of old age come much faster and with a greater sense of finality. The death of a spouse or a serious stroke can quickly accelerate a person from young-old to old-old status, but for either group there are certain conditions of old age that must be faced.

Stereotypes and Images of the Elderly

One of the major difficulties for the elderly comes from adapting to society's definitions of what elderly people are supposed to be like. Just as men and women are often ascribed certain characteristics because of their sex, people in their later years have to deal with the images and roles that we all too often associate with old age. In a culture that still extols youthfulness, the elderly can find it difficult to locate a comfortable niche.

Stereotypes of the elderly abound. Once people reach their sixties, they are supposed to graciously give up their jobs, their sex life, their sporty cars, their in-style clothing, and their time in favor of sitting, watching television, and rocking on their porch eagerly waiting for someone to visit them (see Vignette 16.1). The popular image of the elderly in the media, including children's books and programs, portrays them as being sickly, passive, incompetent, and less self-reliant than other adults (Barnum, 1978).

Negative images

Unfortunately, the images the elderly hold of themselves frequently conform to these stereotypes. In a national study of attitudes toward aging, it was found that both older and younger people share a rather negative image of "most people over sixty-five" (see Table 16.1). The elderly are assumed to be not very bright or alert, not very good at getting things done, and not very active physically and sexually. However, when those over sixty-five years of age were asked about themselves, a quite different picture emerged. Compared to the views of others, the elderly are much more likely to *see themselves* as bright, alert, open-minded, adaptable, able to get things done, and physically and sexually active. Apparently, the negative images of the elderly that

Vignette 16.1 Stereotypes of Old Age

Let us look at the stereotype of the ideal aged American as past folklore presents it. He or she is a white-haired, inactive, unemployed person, making no demands on anyone, least of all the family, docile in putting up with the loneliness, rip-offs of every kind, and boredom, and able to live on a pittance. He or she, although not demented, which would be a nuisance to other people, is slightly deficient in intellect and tiresome to talk to because folklore says that old people are weak in the head, and asexual because old people are incapable of sexual activity, and it is unseemly if they are not. He or she is unemployable, because old age is second childhood and everyone knows that the old make a mess of simple work. Some credit points can be gained by visiting or by being nice to a few of these subhuman individuals, but most of them prefer their own company and the company of other aged unfortunates. Their main occupations are religion, grumbling, reminiscing, and attending the funerals of friends. If sick, they need not, and should not, be actively treated, and are best stored in unsupervised institutions run by racketeers who fleece them and hasten their demise. A few, who are amusing or active, are kept by society as pets. The rest are displaying unpardonable bad manners by continuing to live, and even on occasion by complaining of their treatment, when society has declared them unpeople and their patriotic duty is to lie down and die.

If this picture of aging offends you, visit a few of the places where old people are kept. If you dislike what you see, recognize that you have a few years to change it before the stereotype hits you. If it has hit you already, you will know it better than anyone and you will want any help available to fight back.

The odd thing about this unlovely stereotype, apart from the fact that it is wholly untrue, is that it is relatively recent. Throughout history and in most cultures the old person is a figure of recourse. There is the fisherman, now retired from fishing, whom the village nevertheless consults if the fishing goes sour, because he is the only one who saw this happen before. There is the women who has ten children and has delivered hundreds, who knows what to do with a difficult labor. Any infirmity such people have is considered a misfortune to the community, because it limits their contribution.

In not-so-distant America, even in pioneering towns where youth for obvious reasons predominated, the old-timer was the bearded figure, less agile than he had been, who was still a crack shot, or the apple-faced lady who in an emergency could drive a team like a devil out of hell. These were romanticized stereotypes and they were false, too. Every age has those to whom aging brings some degree of personal crumbling and disaster, but at least the romantic stereotype neither demeans persons of long life nor lays on them our own fears and false imaginings.

From Alex Comfort, *A Good Age* (New York: Crown, 1976), pp. 23–27.

Table 16.1

Personal Qualities of Older People

Personal Quality	"Most People over 65" as Seen by Persons 18 to 65 (%)	Self-Image of People 65 and over (%)
Very friendly and warm	82	72
Very wise from experience	66	69
Very bright and alert	29	68
Very open-minded and adaptable	19	63
Very good at getting things done	35	55
Very physically active	41	48
Very sexually active	5	11

Source: Adapted from Louis Harris and Associates, 1975.

are shared by young and old alike are not often warranted for most elderly persons.

Morale

Not only are the images of the elderly not often warranted, individuals who conform to these stereotypes are usually less satisfied in their old age. Higher morale among old people is closely tied to whether they are able to remain active, maintain their friendships, and stay involved in their work or leisure interests (Harris and Associates, 1975). Just as many older people as younger people say they are satisfied with their lives, and those who become apathetic, passive, and dependent are much more likely to have low morale—at any age. The ability to remain independent is a much more significant influence on life satisfaction than age (Kennedy, 1978).

Physical Health and Sexuality

The ability of older people to remain active and independent is often determined by their physical condition. With aging comes normal deterioration of our bodies, changes in our appearance, and increasing risks of serious medical problems. Everyone does not physically age at the same rate—diet and exercise can improve the physical health of individuals at any age. But for most older people, their physical health is a major factor determining their sense of personal well-being (Mancini, 1978).

Physical capacities

Biological changes in the later years are reflected in the saying that "the spirit is willing but the flesh is weak." Physical capacities decline even though individuals may feel the same desires as when they were younger. It is common for older men and women to lose some clarity in their vision, to experience a loss of muscle tone and control, to have a drop in their blood pressure, and to have more difficulty hearing and tasting foods (Atchley, 1977). These conditions may affect some individuals more than others. For the young-old, this can be quite irritating—but for the old-old, control over their bodily functions can be reduced to a crippling degree.

Sexual intimacy

Changes in sexual functioning also accompany old age but not nearly to the extent that was earlier believed. Frequencies of sexual intercourse typically decline over time but capacities for sexual feelings and behavior continue throughout life. Both men and women can experience orgasms in their later years, and while their sexual responses are somewhat slower, their physical ability to maintain a sexual relationship is hindered very little (Masters and Johnson, 1966). One seventy-two-year-old man commented that "Now it takes my wife and me all night to do what we used to do all night" (Huyck, 1974, p. 25).

Social attitudes toward sexuality among older people still remain a major problem. Even though it has been found that satisfactory sexual expression is an important contributor to health and well-being among the elderly (Butler and Lewis, 1976), it is still often assumed that older adults are without sexual needs. Somehow, our stereotypes of the later years make it easier to picture older couples rocking on the front porch than sexually stimulating one another. Indeed, sexual expressiveness is somewhat infrequent in many couples. But among those who have continued to be sexually active, sexual intimacy remains an important source of personal and relational satisfaction. Butler and Lewis, in their study of "sex after sixty," found many men and women who reported that their most gratifying sexual experiences occurred later in life. The researchers concluded:

> Perhaps only in the later years can life with its various possibilities have the chance to shape itself into something approximating a human work of art. And perhaps only in later life, when personality reaches its final stages of development, can love-making and sex achieve the fullest possible growth. Sex does not merely exist after sixty; it holds the possibility of becoming greater than it ever was. (p. 144)

Psychological Adjustments in Aging

Personalities

Aging is a subtle process. Gradually, we accumulate years of experience, and the choices we have made over the decades affect our maturity and personality. Radical shifts in personality or self-concept are rare, even in the later years of life. Much more common is the gradual changing awareness of our strengths and limitations and the adjustments we must make to our declining health, the death of our loved ones, and the realization of our own mortality. While sometimes these adjustments are observable to others, older people are much more likely to view themselves as having maintained their same personality over the years. For example, Wilma Donahue (1971), a retired gerontologist, talked about her own experience of seeing people again whom she had not seen since her youth:

> I have never thought of them as older people and suddenly I see them as old and I gather a sense of their being different. . . . To them, just like I

> am to myself, there is a consistent personality. I don't recognize that I was twenty, thirty, forty, fifty, sixty, and so forth. I just seem to be a consistent personality that's lived a whole life.

Integrity or despair

Erik Erikson, a developmental psychologist, notes that life unfolds in a series of choices or crises. In late adulthood, the choice that influences adjustment centers about whether a person feels *integrity or despair* over his or her life. Those with integrity feel that their lives have been good, right, and meaningful. Those who feel integrity share Donahue's sentiment above of having "lived a whole life." Studies of older people who report high morale consistently find that this is associated with the feeling of having had a purpose in living and having contributed to others. These people are more likely to feel they have a place in the scheme of things and usually they remain active and involved with others as long as they can (Kalish, 1975).

Not all older people, however, are able to achieve or hold onto this sense of integrity. Suicide rates are higher among those over sixty-five than any other age group (Bock, 1972), and this is only one indication of the despair that can accompany the later years. Those unable to assure themselves that they have done "the best they can" in life may find it easy to slip into discouragement and experience a major drop in their self-esteem. Depression in old age can also be caused by accumulated grief over the deaths of friends and family or by an unwanted new dependency on others.

Retirement

One adjustment in the later years that is becoming less difficult for many is retirement from full-time work. With the number of employed women increasing, they too are now joining the ranks of the retired. A century ago, retirement was unusual before health made further work difficult. In 1900, a man at sixty-five still worked an average of 6.5 more years, followed by 2.8 years of retirement. Today at sixty-five, 80 percent of all men and 90 percent of all women are retired and they have an average of ten to fifteen more years of living before them (Puner, 1974; Rones, 1978).

Retirement ages

Some people at sixty-five want to keep working, and recent court decisions have begun to require employers to relax their compulsory-retirement rules. The majority of Americans, however, now wish to retire *before* they reach sixty-five. Social security retirement is permitted at sixty-two years of age and some unions have negotiated an option for retirement as early as fifty-five. By 1977, only 63 percent of the men aged sixty to sixty-four were still employed (Rones).

Contrary to some popular folklore, retirement is not usually accompanied by frustrations and physical decline. Few people actually "waste away" their lives in postretirement depression; retired people are no more likely to be sick or depressed than people of the same age who are still on the job. Of course, there are some who are so wedded to their jobs that they cannot reorient their lives, but most men and women adjust quite well to voluntary

Depression in old age can be caused by accumulated grief from the deaths of friends and family.

retirement, and studies consistently report that personal-life satisfactions are fairly high among the majority of retirees (Atchley, 1977).

Retirement problems

When a feeling of personal loss does occur after retirement, this is more likely to be linked to at least one of three factors: (1) inadequate income, (2) poor preparation for retirement, or (3) unmet occupational goals. Today, most retirees are able to live comfortably, if not extravagantly, although a visible minority does not have sufficient money to maintain a satisfactory life-style or even to get the food and health care they need. For these people, many of whom had been poor earlier in their lives as well, life continues to be a struggle and age has merely compounded their difficulties.

Some individuals find it hard to retire because they are inadequately prepared for it. Surprisingly, studies point out that this is more a problem for women than for men (Streib and Schneider, 1971). One reason that planning for retirement is difficult is the word itself—"retirement" connotes as much a withdrawal from life as from an occupation. Many people do not find the idea of growing old pleasant, and they associate with retirement a sort of bland, uninvolved prelude to death. If, however, new activities have been planned, money has been set aside, leisure interests have been developed, and friendships have been cultivated, retirement is less likely to be a problem.

Another group that finds retirement difficult is those who did not achieve their job goals. Atchley (1975) found that retirement is relatively easy for those who gave their job a low priority in their lives. This is often true of blue-collar men who see their work primarily as a source of income. People who have found fulfillment in their work yet are able to turn over the reins to others can also retire more easily. The people who have a problem retiring are often those who see themselves as uniquely capable in their jobs—irreplaceable—and who are concerned about finishing the work they have begun. These persons find it difficult to disengage from work and are usually frustrated with retirement.

Homemakers

Wives too can sometimes find their husband's retirement difficult, especially if they have been full-time homemakers. One study found that 55 percent of the wives of retired men (and 67 percent of the wives of early retirees) were distressed by the change (Palmore, 1970). As one wife put it: "I have twice as much husband on half as much income!" Couples with higher incomes are more likely to be mutually happy about retirement, but among couples with lower incomes the wife is likely to experience much more retirement stress. This stress is particularly high when the husband has not been involved very much in household affairs and then begins to interfere with the roles in which the wife has developed some competence (Kerckhoff, 1966). In marriages characterized by companionship and shared roles, the adjustment to retirement is much less of a problem.

RELATIONSHIPS IN THE LATER YEARS

One of the common images of the later years is that these are lonely years. Among the very old and widowed, this is sometimes true, but for the majority of the elderly, this is a period when life is still shared intensely with others. Marital partners, family, and friends remain important to adults in their later years. Those who have had active family and social relationships usually want to continue them—in fact, the roles of husband, wife, parent, grandparent, sibling, and friend often take on new importance as the time that can be given to them expands.

Husbands and Wives

With the increase in life expectancies for men and women, more marriages are now surviving into the later years. Today, over half of the women and over three-fourths of the men in their sixties are married and living with their spouses. It is no longer unusual for first marriages to last thirty, forty, or even fifty years (see Table 16.2). More elderly men than women are still married because women tend to be younger than their husbands and they live six to seven years longer than men.

The unmarried

A marital relationship has some important benefits for the elderly. For one thing, morale is usually higher among those who are married than those who are single or widowed. This is true even when the ages of the married and nonmarried people are the same (Lee, 1978). Marriage also increases the independence of the elderly since older couples are able to assist each other when one is ill and they can shift some of their tasks to one another when physical limitations are a problem (Kivett, 1980). Unmarried people are more likely to become dependent on others when difficulties arise, and this is associated with a decline in morale.

Separateness and togetherness

Styles of marriage in the later years can vary almost as much as in the younger years. Some couples are very close and share most of their time and activities together. Other couples remain distant, interested in activities with others more than with their spouse (Darnley, 1975). Either of these types of

Table 16.2

Estimated Likelihood of Celebrating Selected Wedding Anniversaries

Wedding Anniversary	Proportion Who Celebrate the Anniversary after—	
	First Marriage	Remarriage
5th	5 of every 6	4 of every 5
10th	4 of every 5	3 of every 4
20th	3 of every 4	1 of every 2
30th	2 of every 3	1 of every 3
35th	1 of every 2	1 of every 5
40th	2 of every 5	1 of every 8
45th	1 of every 3	1 of every 15
50th	1 of every 5	1 of every 20
55th	1 of every 10	1 of every 50
60th	1 of every 20	1 of every 100
65th	1 of every 50	very rare
70th	1 of every 100	very rare

Source: Paul Glick and Arthur Norton, Marrying, Divorcing, and Living Together in the U.S. Today, 1977, p. 14. Courtesy of the Population Reference Bureau, Inc., Washington, D.C.

Happily married older couples usually feel increasingly comfortable sharing their lives together.

couples may consider their marriage to be meeting their needs but the couples who share few interests together are more likely to become disenchanted with their marriages over time. Unless these couples have the resources to maintain their separate interests, they will find themselves increasingly in one another's presence. Illness can also cause a dependency that is difficult for either spouse to accept and this can further strain the marriage (Clark and Anderson, 1967). Evidence of these strains comes from the rising divorce rate among people over sixty (Kalish, 1975): every year, over 10,000 older people get divorced.

Happily married older couples, in contrast, usually feel increasingly comfortable sharing their lives together. There is more equality in these marriages, and over time, gender roles become less and less defined. Summarizing his research, Atchley (1977) comments:

> For the happily married older couple, marriage is a blessing. It is a source of great comfort and support as well as the focal point of everyday life. . . . In addition, there is often a high degree of interdependence in

> these couples, particularly in terms of caring for each other in times of illness. The older husbands in this happily married category are particularly likely to view their wives as indispensable pillars of strength. (p. 292)

The major problem that affectionate, happily married couples face is loss of their partner in death. This can be a traumatic blow from which recovery is difficult. People from more emotionally distant marriages, however, find it easier to adapt to a life of independence after the death of their spouse. They may be lonely, but their eventual recovery is more likely (Darnley).

Remarrying Couples

A growing number of widowed people are remarrying. Older women are less likely to remarry since there are fewer older men available, but by the late 1970s, over 35,000 marriages per year took place among people age sixty-five and older (Vinick, 1978). The majority of these marriages are considered very satisfactory by the couples. Usually, the individuals involved have known one another for a number of years, often before their former spouses died (McKain, 1972).

Remarriage reasons

The main reason for remarriage given by both men and women is companionship. Having shared most of their life with someone else, they now found it difficult to live alone. Some other couples mentioned financial security, love, and a desire to be cared for as motivations for their remarriage. Sexual satisfaction was also mentioned as a reason for remarriage but in indirect terms. One study concluded:

> The role of sex in the lives of these older people extended far beyond love making and coitus; a woman's gentle touch, the perfume of her hair, a word of endearment—all these and many more reminders that he is married help to satisfy a man's urge for the opposite sex. The same is true for the older wife. One woman had this comment on her remarriage. "I like the little things; the smell of his pipe, the sound of steps on the back porch, his shaving mug—even his muddy shoes." (McKain, 1969, p. 36)

Success

Older marriages are most likely to be successful if they have the approval of friends and children, if the couple has adequate financial resources, if the couple enjoys sharing activities together, and if each of them is personally well adjusted and satisfied with life. Problems in older marriages are more likely to occur if the couple maintains separate financial accounts, does not pool their resources, and continues to live in the house that one of them had shared with a former spouse (McKain, 1972; Vinick). These latter conditions can indicate a lack of mutual trust and an inability to give their new marriage the priority it needs to be successful.

Interference

Children can be a major interference in later marriages and probably prevent many of them from ever taking place. Half or more of these older married couples initially encounter the objections or hostility of their children. One woman who was having a particularly frustrating experience said, "His children are against it. They do not dislike me but they don't want me to inherit any part of their father's estate. . . . I'd be happy to sign a premarital agreement leaving everything to his children. (I will leave what I have to my daughter.) All I want is his love and companionship" (Puner, p. 160).

Eventually most children are pleased with the remarriage of their older parents but their first reactions are often quite selfish. They fear that the memory of their deceased parent will be tarnished; they wonder why older people really want to be married anyway; they are concerned that their inheritance will be diluted. Nevertheless, when these objections can be overcome or when a mature, accepting reaction is received from others, then the older couple can more comfortably integrate their new marriage into the network of friends and family.

Family Relationships

To most older people, their family roles remain quite important. Being a parent, grandparent, or sibling is still a vital part of their identity and a potential source of satisfaction. Four out of five older Americans have at least one living child. Of these, three-fourths have children living less than one-half hour's distance away and four out of five see at least one of their children every week (Shanas, 1979). Eighty percent of older people also have living brothers and sisters, 70 percent have grandchildren, and about 40 percent have great-grandchildren. Only 8 percent of these older men and women share a household with a relative but contacts within these family relationships are quite frequent and often mutually supportive.

Contact and morale

Most older Americans want to be independent of their children but available in case they need one another. Studies of the elderly have repeatedly found that contacts with children are *not very important* to the morale of elderly parents (Mancini, 1979) even though the independent elderly seem to want at least some periodic contact. This is a case in which the *quality* of contact may be more important than the *quantity* of contact. As a rule, elderly parents do not want to become dependents and they do want the right to live their own lives. This right is also reciprocated since older people often express the belief that they too should not interfere in the lives of their children (Hess and Waring, 1978).

Help exchanges

The exchange of help between elderly parents and their children is quite important to both generations. The help older people receive most often takes the form of financial aid, help in shopping and transportation, cleaning their house, and personal support in times of crisis. Even in these areas, however, most of the elderly are not that dependent on their children and prefer to rely on friends or their own resources (Seelbach, 1978). In contrast, the aid from older parents to their adult children is quite substantial, particularly in the form of services they perform for their children (see Table 16.3). Young adults, most often sons, frequently look to their parents for financial

Table 16.3

Family Services Received from Elderly Parents or Grandparents

	Total Public (%)	Public 18–24 (%)	Public 25–39 (%)	Public 40–45 (%)	Public 55–64 (%)
Give you gifts	85	94	85	80	73
Give general advice on how to deal with some of life's problems	58	62	61	57	34
Help out when someone is ill	57	74	57	49	28
Take care of small children	42	53	46	35	16
Give advice on running a home	42	50	41	40	25
Give advice on bringing up children	40	45	40	39	23
Help out with money	35	52	34	24	20
Give advice on job or business matters	31	44	33	19	17
Shop or run errands	30	42	31	22	17
Fix things around your house or keep house for you	22	31	20	18	9
Take grandchildren, nieces, or nephews into their home to live with them	21	25	23	15	10

Source: Louis Harris and Associates, 1975, p. 81. Conducted for the National Council on the Aging. Used by permission.

help and young parents may rely heavily on the babysitting and advice of their older, more experienced parents. The economic advantages of these help patterns have been noted:

> In economic terms, the contributions that older people make to younger members of their family is substantial. . . . As resources for the ill, as babysitters for small children, as shoppers and errand runners, as home repairers and housekeepers, even as surrogate parents, the public sixty-five and over offer assistance to their children and grandchildren that would cost them dearly otherwise. (Harris *et al.*, p. 78)

Grandparenthood

Being a grandparent is a family role in which many older people take special if infrequent pleasure. Most elderly men and women attribute a great deal of significance to their grandparent role, even though the majority of them spend only a few days per year with their grandchildren (Wood and Robertson, 1978). For many of these grandparents, there is a new sense of immortality that comes from grandchildren; others derive satisfaction from seeing the accomplishments of these children and serving as a resource or teacher to them (Kalish, 1975).

The quality of the grandparent-grandchild relationship can be influenced by several factors. First of all, the distance between them and the attitude of the child's parents toward the grandparent will affect the relationship. Also, some grandparents are more accepting of children than others, and this will influence their interaction. Older grandparents are less likely to be involved in the activities of their grandchildren and more likely to take a "formal" role of providing them treats and services (Neugarten and Weinstein, 1964). The age of the grandchildren can also make a difference. Young children are more likely to enjoy being with their grandparents, and this feeling is reported to be mutual (Kahana and Coe, 1969). The following perspective on grandmothers was written by a third-grader in a class assignment:

What is a Grandma?

A Grandma is a lady who has no children of her own, so she likes other people's little boys and girls.

A Grandfather is a man Grandmother. He goes for walks with the boys and they talk about fishing and things like that.

Grandmas don't have to do anything except be there. They're so old they shouldn't play hard. It is enough if they drive us to the supermarket where the pretend horse is and have lots of dimes ready.

Or if they take us for walks, they should slow down past things like pretty leaves or caterpillars. And they should never say, "Hurry up!"

Usually they are fat, but not too fat. They wear glasses and funny underwear. They can take their teeth and gums off.

They don't have to be smart, only answer questions like why dogs hate cats, and how come God isn't married.

They don't talk baby talk like visitors do because it is hard to understand.

When they read to us they don't skip words and they don't mind if it is the same story.

Grandmas are the only grownups who have got time—so everybody should have a Grandmother especially if you don't have television.

(Huyck, p. 77).

Friendships

In reviewing the research on adjustments to old age, one study noted that "an older person with a single good friend is more able to cope in old age than one with a dozen grandchildren but no peer-group friends" (Wood and Robertson, p. 367). This should not be taken to mean that children and grandchildren are not important to the elderly; they certainly are. But on a day-to-day, week-to-week basis, good friends are much more likely to provide the support and intimacy needed by older persons than anyone else except a spouse.

Similarity in generations

Friendships among the elderly tend to occur among individuals of similar age, race, ethnic background, and social class. It is unusual for older people to have close friendships with those who are somewhat younger than themselves. Kalish (1975) remarks, "perhaps they feel more at home with people who have shared their life spans, memories, and—probably more

The friendships of older men tend to be homogeneous and long-standing.

important—period of early socialization. They share recollections of the same ballplayers, movie actors, automobiles, and politicians; they remember the same dances, using the same slang, fighting in the same wars, wearing the same clothing styles" (p. 87).

Friends of men and women

One of the stereotypes of the later years portrays older women as being much more active socially than older men. This image, however, may not be correct. Older men actually report that they have more friends and they visit with them more often than older women do. Nevertheless, these friendships are more likely to be "acquaintances" and not as likely to be as close as the friendships of women. The close friendships of older men tend to have been long-standing, were often formed in the middle years of life, and are not as easily replaced when these friends die or move away. In contrast, the friendships of older women are more likely to be close, more recently formed, and replaced after death or separation (Powers and Bultena, 1976). It is this capability of making new friendships that seems to serve women so well in the adjustments many of them must make to widowhood.

DEATH AND DYING

As most of us grow older, we come to recognize in a more personal way the inevitability of death. Among those over age sixty-five death is more likely, and it takes approximately 6 percent of this age group every year. The cause of death for most of these older people is usually listed as one of several chronic illnesses such as heart disease, cancer, stroke, influenza, or pneumonia. But usually in these cases, the real cause of death is tied to a wearing out of the body. Eventually, the bodily system collapses when one of its organs fails to function in its prescribed manner.

Death fears

Until recently, the topic of death has been carefully avoided in American society. We have gone to great lengths to shield ourselves from its inevitability. Discussions of death and planning for its coming are considered in poor taste and often neglected. Exceptionally old and ill people are typically removed from their homes and placed in some type of institution where they are isolated from family and friends. Young children are usually barred from visiting the dying person. While every effort is made to protect the family members, relatively little consideration is given to the person who is dying. Unfortunately, these efforts have accomplished little more than to reinforce our already strong fears of the death process and death itself.

Phases of dying

One recent attempt to reduce fear of the death process for both the dying person and the family has been made by Elizabeth Kübler-Ross (1969). After interviewing some 500 people who were dying, she identified five phases in the process of dying. Some of these phases may be skipped, and for some people, the phases overlap, but some combination of them usually occurs in most death experiences.

Normally, the first phase in coping with death takes the form of **denial and isolation.** The sense of shock is buffered by the feeling that "It cannot be me!" and the individual seeks reassurance that the diagnosis is wrong. When no reassurance occurs, the phase of **anger and resentment** develops. This can be just as painful to family and friends since they are often the recipients of this displaced frustration. The third phase involves **bargaining** and **attempting to postpone** the death. When anger does not work, then the person may try a more positive approach. A typical feeling is, "If God has not responded to my angry pleas, He may be more favorable if I ask nicely" (Kübler-Ross).

The fourth phase of dying takes the form of **depression.** By this stage, death is no longer denied and the discomfort one feels cannot be ignored. Depression comes from having to redefine oneself as mortal and letting go of the roles and responsibilities that once dominated nearly every thought and action. Reconciling oneself to the end of one's work, parental, friend, and other roles is not easy, but once this is done, then the final **acceptance** of death is allowed to develop. This phase is eased if each of the previous phases has been resolved and if the dying person can achieve a sense of satisfaction with his or her accomplishments in life (Kalish, 1976).

Family involvement

Kübler-Ross and others have noted that it is important for the family as well as the dying person to go through these phases (see Vignette 16.2). By

Vignette 16.2

On the Quality of Life and Death

Like many people today, I had as a youngster, little direct personal experience with death—the loss of one grandparent when I was six, and another at eighteen while I was away at college. My first truly impactful encounter with death was at the loss of my father, some fifteen years ago. As an intellectually oriented student and a product of my culture, I had few handles to deal with my loss. I could relate his death to little.

My thoughts were quite different that Friday afternoon following my brother's call. Driving home my mind was racing. We had had some preparation for the event. My mother had a weakening heart—yet at seventy-three she seemed much younger, much more active and vital, somehow not old. Just three weeks before, ironically, for the first time that any of us could recall, all of the family—her three sons, their wives, and her nine grandchildren—were together on the occasion of my niece's college graduation.

Speeding down the expressway I thought, momentarily, how strange I must have appeared to the drivers in the cars which passed me as I became aware of the fact that I was crying (though now I doubt that they even noticed). It dawned on me that I was an orphan. Somehow, that seemed absurd for the middle-aged father of four to consider himself an orphan, but indeed it was not absurd. Some links to the past had been severed. A repository of knowledge and experience was lost. No longer was there a way of checking whether I had ever had the mumps or chicken pox or how old I was when cousin Bert was married. Never another taste of the magnificent pastry that she had learned to make only by watching her mother—the recipe for which (for some reason) never was translated into cups and teaspoonsful. Little things and large—memories bombarded me. I became supersensitive to the past, and who I was in relationship to her and the rest of my family. It was now I who was the older generation. It was this kind of thinking that was the harbinger of a week of such thoughts, islands of which even now still occur.

recognizing their own denial, anger, bargaining, and depression, the family can also prepare itself for the inevitable death and learn to function as it will have to when the death finally occurs. Sorrow over the death of a loved one is normal, but the sometimes harsh pragmatics of funeral arrangements, property disposal, and the meeting of last requests are eased when the death is accepted, even though reluctantly.

Reactions to the prospect of dying can vary. Some older people maintain a strong fear of death, but the more common view is one of only minimal fear (Kalish, 1976). Most older people have known others who have died and have already begun to deal with some of their own feelings about death. Their major difficulty, however, usually comes in communicating their feelings about death to those they love. The greatest fear of dying people is *not* death, it is the fear of being abandoned, humiliated, and lonely at the end of their

---

We had prepared the children for this eventuality. Yet, as anticipated, each seemed shocked and each reacted in her or his own personal way. While we discussed the subject as openly as we could, no preparation could have been adequate for the funeral in Cleveland that they would have to experience. I was concerned over their reactions to my grief—the possibility of seeing me, their father, in an emotionally overwhelmed state. My wife and I talked of it. We momentarily discussed the desirability of leaving the children at home, and realized that we were being seduced into the dilemma of the modern parent—how to protect ones' children from the realities of life. . . .

For me, the next day was the most difficult. There was the business of closing my mother's apartment. In many respects it was the internment through dissemination of the bits and pieces of her life. The three pairs of us were there deciding which of the tangible anchor points to our memories we wanted; there was little of great extrinsic value. There were not "fights" as I understand are common in such instances. But the situation was extremely difficult, nonetheless. And as the chaos slowly disappeared into boxes, pair by pair we left. First one brother who drove my mother's car back to New York for my nephew, then the other whom we drove to the connection for their plane. In between we talked, about the past and of the future. As we dropped them off, my sister-in-law commented with great intensity, "we must make the effort to keep in touch." And I realized that, indeed, my mother had been a kind of mortar that cemented the bond between my brothers' families and mine over distance and time, a kind of clearing-house of information and affection about relatives seldom seen anymore. And I mourned again, this time for myself.

---

lives (Weisman, 1972). For this reason, Kalish (1976) recommends that the subject of death be permitted in conversations with the dying. Only then can these relationships remain open and mutually supporting and only then can each person resolve the question of death in the company of those they love.

BEREAVEMENT AND WIDOWHOOD

Sometimes death comes suddenly, without warning. On other occasions, it is a lingering process. But no matter how long one has to prepare for it, the **finality** of death for the living is usually most difficult to accept. Death comes as a shock to most loved ones, even when it has been expected, even when it is the death of an older person. Bereaved spouses offer complaints like: "Why did nobody warn me that I would feel so sick . . . or tired . . . or exhausted? Nobody ever told me that grief felt so like fear" (Pincus, 1974, p. 113).

Dealing with death

Bereavement is the process of adjusting to another person's death. This process may take a short time for some, but for others, it may never be finished. Nearly half of the widows in one study said they had got over their husbands' death within a year while another 20 percent said they had not got over it and did not expect to (Lopata, 1973). In general, the women and men who adjust more quickly in bereavement are those who were aware of the impending death. This allowed them to begin the grief process before the death and also to prepare for a life without their partner (Peterson and Briley, 1977). Adjustment is more difficult, however, when the couple have been very emotionally close and companionate. A death in these relationships can leave a void very difficult to replace (Glick *et al.*, 1974).

Individual responses to bereavement usually take several forms (Atchley, 1977). **Physical** reactions to grief usually occur immediately after the death and continue for a short time. The shock of the death and personal loss commonly cause uncontrollable crying, tightness in the chest, shortness of breath, loss of energy, and stomach upset (Kalish, 1976). These reactions encourage many widowed people to seek medical help but it is only the rare person who actually dies of grief after the death of his or her spouse.

Loneliness

Emotional reactions to bereavement often take the form of anger, guilt, depression, and feelings of loneliness. "What could I have done to prevent this?" "If only I had . . . ;" or "Why did he leave me like this?" are common reactions at this time. Although these responses usually subside, feelings of loneliness can remain for some time. Older widows are more likely to complain of loneliness than anything else (Kivett, 1979). The more socially isolated they are, the less likely the bereaved will be to climb out of their depression successfully.

Idealization

The **intellectual** aspect of bereavement involves developing a new image of oneself and of the deceased. Over time, the memory of the person who died is usually cleansed of faults, leaving a more idealized image that is free to be remembered and less apt to interfere in the adjustment of the widow or widower. This idealization of the dead is useful because it permits the living to see that the dead person's life had meaning which in time allows them to seek new meaning in their own lives (Atchley, 1977). Too much idealization, however, can hinder the development of new relationships since no one else can compete with an unreal image.

Social reorganization during bereavement is also a necessary part of adjustment since there are often new roles and obligations that need to be accepted. At first, family and friends frequently take over many of these responsibilities and decisions. But within a few weeks, the widowed are usually expected to begin taking control over their own lives again. For many widowed people, particularly women, this means reorganizing their financial situation and learning to adjust to having less income. For most of the widowed, their social relationships also change since they are no longer part of a couple and now must seek new sources of intimacy and personal support.

ALTERNATIVE LIVING ARRANGEMENTS AMONG THE ELDERLY

When the elderly in America are queried about where and how they want to live, their responses are generally consistent. Most want to continue to live with their spouse if they have one, in the home and community in which they have been living, near their children and other relatives, and to remain relatively independent in their day-to-day activities (Shanas, 1980). Indeed, these preferences reflect the living arrangements of about half of all the elderly, even though for some of them, other alternatives are preferred or necessary (Puner).

Medical dependence

Living in a **nursing home** is not preferred by most elderly men and women and fewer than 4 percent of those over age sixty-five live in one. This small proportion of dependent elderly is largely made up of those who need regular medical attention and who are not able to get the assistance they need from friends and relatives. Unfortunately, there are some elderly who are institutionalized for no medical reason at all—obviously, this is a demoralizing experience for them (Bouvier *et al.*, 1975).

Family dependence

Another living arrangement that is not preferred by the elderly is **moving in** with one of their children or another relative. Fewer than one-fourth of the elderly live with one of their children, and this usually occurs after widowhood. From the evidence we have, however, most families report being uncomfortable with the arrangement and feel unprepared to provide for the ongoing needs of elderly parents. In turn, the elderly are not usually provided with meaningful roles and are placed in a difficult position of dependence (Ward, 1978). This often hinders the affectional ties between parents and children.

One alternative to dependence on children for those elderly who need help but still want to maintain their own residence is **home care.** Through the

Elderly persons with adequate means often find retirement communities appealing.

use of government- and private-sponsored programs which supply housekeeping assistance, Meals-on-Wheels, visiting nurses, therapists, transportation services, and home repairs, it is often possible for some elderly people to continue to live relatively autonomous lives. These programs are expensive but they have enabled many elderly to avoid becoming prematurely dependent on others.

"Sun-city"

For those elderly who are independent and who have substantial resources, **retirement communities** represent another potential living arrangement. The southern "Sunbelt" of the United States has attracted many of these older couples and individuals into a type of age-segregated subculture with activities and programs primarily designed for them, particularly the "young-old." Studies indicate that residents of these communities are usually very satisfied with the life-style (Jacobs, 1974), but we must realize that only about 2 percent of those over age sixty-five move across state lines toward this alternative.

Retirement hotels represent another type of living arrangement for some elderly. These hotels usually provide basic services for a fee and are often satisfactory for the younger, active, and independent elderly (Streib, 1978). However, for those whose mental and physical capacities have deteriorated, retirement hotels cannot usually provide the services they need. This type of living arrangement is also not likely to be satisfactory if it attracts only the poor elderly who cannot pay for many services. These elderly become little more than tenants and the hotel often deteriorates.

"Share-A-Home"

The **cooperative household** is a relatively new type of living arrangement that attempts to resolve some of the problems the elderly face in matters of economic security, dependence, and loneliness. These households are made up of unrelated individuals and couples who live together in a house and share in the responsibility for its upkeep (Hilker and Streib, 1979). In some of these arrangements, each elderly resident helps out in housekeeping, cooking, and household management. In some of the more successful households, however, the residents pay a fee to have someone else do the chores. This permits those who cannot regularly help out in performing these tasks to remain members of the household. Also, the familylike atmosphere of these homes personally benefits the residents. James Gillis, founder of the Share-A-Home in Florida, writes:

> These elderly people live together as a family. They eat together, work together, and play together, thereby eliminating loneliness. They have formed an association together for their economic and social benefit. All members share birthdays, outings, expenses, fun, and joys that only a loving family can know. These are the necessary ingredients to retain their self-respect and to live a life with dignity. (Streib, p. 416)

Each of these alternative living arrangements, as well as numerous others, attempts to meet the special needs of the elderly. Streib reminds us, however, "that there is no one desirable form of retirement environment that is endorsed by *all* older persons, or that can be recommended for *all* elderly people" (p. 414). Thus, the elderly are similar to other age groups in our society: there is no one form of living arrangement, household, or family pattern that can or should be prescribed for everyone. Intimate relationships and personal needs are infinitely variable. Only through knowledge of oneself and others and careful consideration of our alternatives can we make decisions that will prove to be satisfactory to ourselves and those for whom we care.

Summary

Growing old is a normal process. As the health of Americans has improved, so has the likelihood of reaching old age increased. In this period of life there are adjustments to be made and problems to be faced. These include negative stereotypes of the elderly, physical health problems, psychological adjustments, and retirement.

For the majority of the elderly, relationships with marital partners, family, and friends remain very important. Marriages today often continue into retirement and those who are married are the most likely to retain high morale. Most older people live near their children, but friends are more likely than kin to contribute to the day-to-day satisfaction of the elderly.

One of the inevitable components of old age is death and dying. Death regularly takes its toll among older people and the real possibility of dying becomes ever so much more real to older men and women. After death, the widowed partner goes through a period of bereavement usually lasting for some months and years.

A fact that is easing the adjustment of the elderly is that their life-style alternatives are becoming more varied. Still, most older people prefer to remain as independent as possible.

SUGGESTIONS FOR ADDITIONAL READING

Atchley, Robert. *The Social Forces in Later Life,* Second Edition. Belmont, Calif.: Wadsworth, 1977.

An excellent overview and introduction to the subject of human aging and life among older people in America.

Brubaker, Timothy, and Lawrence Sneden (Eds.). *Aging in a Changing Family Context.* Special Issue of *The Family Coordinator,* Vol. 27, October, 1978.

This volume contains numerous articles written by a variety of professionals who have studied and provided services for the elderly and their families.

Glick, Ira, Robert S. Weiss, and C. Murray Parker. *The First Year of Bereavement.* New York: Wiley, 1974.

This book is the result of a study of widows and widowers. The authors use many case studies to illustrate the adjustments that occur during bereavement.

Kübler-Ross, Elizabeth. *On Death and Dying.* New York: Macmillan, 1969.

This is a very important study and a book that has revolutionalized the way Americans have looked at the process of dying.

Peterson, James A., and Barbara Payne. *Love in the Later Years.* New York: Association Press, 1975.

Myths abound about marriage and sexuality in later life. The authors attempt to look realistically at the experiences of older people to determine the factors that contribute to relational adjustment in this period of life.

Troll, Lillian, Stephen Miller, and Robert Atchley. *Families in Later Life.* Belmont, Calif.: Wadsworth, 1979.

This book summarizes much of the literature on the family relationships of older people as well as providing fresh insights from the authors' own studies.

References

Adams, Bert (1964). Structural factors affecting parental aid to married children. *Journal of Marriage and the Family* 26:327–331.

Adams, Bert, and Ronald Cromwell (1978). Morning and night people in the family: a preliminary statement. *The Family Coordinator* 27:5–13.

Albro, Joyce C., and Carol Tully (1979). A study of lesbian lifestyles in the homosexual micro-culture and the heterosexual macro-culture. *Journal of Homosexuality* 4:331–344.

Aldous, Joan (1978). *Family Careers: Developmental Change in Families.* New York: Wiley.

Aleksandrowicz, Malca K. (1974). The effect of pain relieving drugs administered during labor and delivery on the behavior of the newborn: a review. *Merrill-Palmer Quarterly* 20:121–141.

Alston, Jon P., William A. McIntosh, and Louise M. Wright (1976). Extent of interfaith marriage among white Americans. *Sociological Analysis* 37:261–264.

American Council of Life Insurance (1978). Home no longer woman's place. *Greensboro Daily News.*

Ammons, Paul, and Nick Stinnett (1980). The vital marriage: a closer look. *Family Relations* 29:37–42.

Anderson, Robert (1972). *Solitaire and Double Solitaire.* New York: Random House.

Apgar, Virginia, and Joan Beck (1972). *Is My Baby All Right?* New York: Trident.

Applebaum, Ronald L., E. M. Bodaken, K. K. Sereno, and K. W. E. Anatol (1974). *The Process of Group Communication.* Palo Alto, Calif.: Science Research Associates.

Argyle, M., V. Salter, H. Nicholson, M. Williams, and P. Burgess (1970). The communications of inferior and superior attitudes by verbal and nonverbal signals. *British Journal of Social and Clinical Psychology* 9:222–231.

Aron, A. *et al.* (1974). Relationships with opposite-sex parents and mate choice. *Human Relations* 27:17–24.

Atchley, Robert C. (1975). Adjustment to loss of job at retirement. *International Journal of Aging and Human Development* 6:17–27.

——— (1977). *The Social Forces in Later Life.* Belmont, Calif.: Wadsworth.

Athansiou, Robert, Phillip Shaver, and Carol Tavris (1970). Sex. *Psychology Today* 4:37–52.

Axelson, Leland (1970). Some differences in the perception of the working wife by husbands and wives. Paper presented at the meeting of the Southern Sociological Society.

Babchuk, Nicholas (1965). Primary friends and kin: a study of the associations of middle-class couples. *Social Forces* 43:483–493.

Bach, George R., and Ronald M. Deutsch (1970). *Pairing.* New York: Avon.

Bach, George R., and Peter Wyden (1969). *The Intimate Enemy.* New York: Avon.

Bachman, Jerald, and Lloyd Johnson (1979). The freshman, 1979. *Psychology Today* (September):79–87.

Bachofen, J. J. (1861). *Das Mutterrecht.* Stuttgart: Krais and Hoffman.

Bahr, Stephen, and Randal Day (1978). Sex role attitudes, female employment, and marital satisfaction. *Journal of Comparative Family Studies* 9:53–67.

Balswick, Jack O., and Charles W. Peek (1971). The inexpressive male: a tragedy of American society. *Family Coordinator* 20:363–368.

Bane, Mary Jo (1976). *Here to Stay: American Families in the Twentieth Century.* New York: Basic Books.

Bardwick, Judith (1978). Middle age and a sense of future. *Merrill-Palmer Quarterly* 24:129–138.

Barnett, Rosalind, and Grace K. Baruch (1980). How to be happy though middle aged. *Psychology Today* 14 (June): 30, 98.

Barnum, Phyllis (1978). Aging in children's books. *Human Nature* 1:13.

——— (1971). *The Family Bond.* New York: Random House.

Bartz, Karen W. (1978). Selected childrearing tasks and problems of mothers and fathers. *The Family Coordinator* 27:209–214.

Bateson, Gregory (1972). *Steps to an Ecology of Mind.* New York: Ballantine Books.

Baumrind, Diana (1978). Parental disciplinary patterns and social competence in children. *Youth and Society* 9:239–276.

Beck, Dorothy, and Mary Ann Jones (1973). *Progress on Family Problems.* New York: Family Service Association.

Bednarzik, Robert W., and Deborah Klein (1977). Labor force trends: a synthesis and analysis. *Monthly Labor Review* (October):3–15.

Bell, Alan P., and Martin S. Weinberg (1979). *Homosexualities.* Bloomington, Ind.: Institute for Sex Research.

Bell, Robert R. (1976). Changing aspects of marital sexuality. In S. Gordon and R. Libby (eds.), *Sexuality Today—And Tomorrow.* North Scituate, Mass.: Duxbury.

——— (1979). *Marriage and Family Interaction.* Homewood, Ill.: Dorsey.

Bell, Robert R., and Norman Lobsenz (1977). Marital sex. In John Gagnon (ed.), *Human Sexuality in Today's World.* Boston: Little, Brown.

Bem, Sandra L. (1975). Androgeny vs. fluffy women and chesty men. *Psychology Today* (September):58–62.

——— (1977). Beyond androgeny: some presumptive prescriptions for a liberated sexual identity. In Arlene Skolnick and Jerome Skolnick (eds.), *Family in Transition,* 2d ed. Boston: Little, Brown.

Benson, Leonard (1968). *Fatherhood: A Sociological Perspective.* New York: Random House.

Berelson, Bernard (1972). The value of children: a taxonomical essay. *Population Council Annual Report, 1972.* New York: The Population Council.

Berg, Berthold, and Robert Kelly (1979). The measured self-esteem of children from broken, rejected and accepted families. *Journal of Divorce* 2:363–369.

Bernard, Jessie (1972). *The Future of Marriage.* New York: Bantam.

——— (1974). *The Future of Motherhood.* New York: Penguin.

——— (1975). *Women, Wives, and Mothers.* Chicago: Aldine.

Berscheid, Ellen, and Elaine Walster (1974). A little bit about love. In Ted Huston (ed.), *Foundations of Interpersonal Attraction.* New York: Academic Press.

Best, Fred (1978). Recycling people: work sharing through flexible life scheduling. In *1999: The World of Tomorrow.* New York: The World Future Society.

Biblarz, Arturo, and Biblarz, Delores (1976). The sociology of fantasy. (Unpublished manuscript.)

Bienvenu, Millard (1970). Measurement of marital communication. *The Family Coordinator* 19:26–31.

Blake, Judith (1979). Is zero preferred? American attitudes toward childlessness in the 1970's. *Journal of Marriage and the Family* 41:245–257.

Blau, Peter M. (1964). *Exchange and Power in Social Life.* New York: Wiley.

Blood, Robert O. (1974). Resolving family conflicts. In Ruth Cavan (ed.), *Marriage and Family in the Modern World.* New York: Crowell.

Blood, Robert O., and Donald Wolfe (1960). *Husbands and Wives.* New York: Free Press.

Bock, E. Wilber (1972). Aging and suicide. *The Family Coordinator* 21:71–80.

Bohannan, Paul (1971). *Divorce and After.* New York: Anchor Books.

Bonham, Gordon Scott (1977). Who adopts: the relationship of adoption and social-demographic characteristics of women. *Journal of Marriage and the Family* 39:295–308.

Boss, Pauline (1974). Psychological absence in the intact family: a systems approach to fathering. Paper presented at the National Council on Family Relations Meeting, St. Louis, Missouri.

Bossard, James H. S. (1956). *The Large Family System.* University of Pennsylvania Press.

Bossard, James H. S., and Eleanore Boll (1960). *The Sociology of Child Development.* New York: Harper.

Boston Women's Health Book Collective (1973). *Our Bodies, Ourselves.* New York: Simon & Schuster.

Bott, Elizabeth (1971). *Family and Social Network.* New York: The Free Press.

Bouvier, Leon, Elinore Atleegand, and Frank McVeigh (1975). The elderly in America. *Population Bulletin* 30.

Bower, Donald, and Victor Christopherson (1977). University student cohabitation: a regional comparison of selected attitudes and behavior. *Journal of Marriage and the Family* 39:447–453.

Bowerman, Charles, and Donald Irish (1962). Some relationships of stepchildren to their parents. *Marriage and Family Living* 24:113–128.

Bowlby, J. (1980). *Attachment and Loss.* Vol. 3, Loss. New York: Basic Books.

Brackbill, Yvonne (1978). Long term effects of obstetrical anesthesia on infant autonomic function. *Developmental Psychobiology* 11.

Bradburn, Norman M. (1969). *The Structure of Psychological Well-Being.* Chicago: Aldine.

Brandwein, Ruth, Carol Brown, and Elizabeth Fox (1974). Women and children last: the social situation of divorced mothers and their children. *Journal of Marriage and the Family* 36:498–514.

Brannon, Robert (1978). Androgeny: unstereotyping human roles. *Current Life-styles* 1:3–12.

Briffault, Robert, and Bronislaw Malinowski (1956). *Marriage: Past and Present.* Boston: Porter Sargent.

Broderick, Carlfred (1965). Social heterosexual development among urban negroes and whites. *Journal of Marriage and the Family* 27:200–203.

——— (1971). Beyond the five conceptual frameworks: a decade of research and action. *Journal of Marriage and the Family* 33:139–160.

Broderick, Carlfred, and George Rowe (1968). A scale of preadolescent heterosexual development. *Journal of Marriage and the Family* 30:97–101.

Brody, Gene, Z. Stoneman, and Alice Sanders (1980). Effects of television viewing on family interaction: an observational study. *Family Relations* 29:216–220.

Broman, Sarah, and Yvonne Brackbill (1979). Obstetric reassessment. *Behavior Today* (February):4.

Bronfenbrenner, Urie (1979). *The Ecology of Human Development.* Cambridge: Harvard University Press.

Broverman, I. K., D. M. Broverman, F. E. Clarkson, P. S. Rosenkrantz, and S. R. Vogel (1970). Sex role stereotypes and clinical judgements of mental health. *Journal of Consulting and Clinical Psychology* 34:1–7.

Brown, Jerri J., and Darrell H. Hart (1978). Feminine fantasies. *Human Behavior* 7:50.

Brown, Scott C. (1977). Multiple jobholders in May 1977. *Special Labor Force Report* 211. Washington, D.C.: U.S. Department of Labor.

Brubaker, Timothy, and Lawrence Sneden (eds.) (1978). Aging in a changing family context. *The Family Coordinator* 27 (October).

Bullough, Vern L. (1978). Variant life styles: homosexuality. In Bernard Murstein (ed.), *Exploring Intimate Life Styles.* New York: Springer.

Bumpass, L., and R. Rindfuss (1979). Children's experiences of marital disruption. *Family Planning Perspectives* 11:115–119.

Burch, Thomas K. (1967). The size and structure of families. *American Sociological Review* 32:358.

Burchinal, Lee G. (1964). Characteristics of adolescents in unbroken, broken, and reconstituted families. *Journal of Marriage and the Family* 26:46–47.

Burgess, Ernest W. (1926). The family as a unity of interacting personalities. *The Family* 7:3–9.

Burgess, Ernest W., and Harvey Locke (1945). *The Family: From Institution to Companionship.* New York: American Book Company.

Burgess, Ernest W., and Paul Wallin (1953). *Engagement and Marriage.* Philadelphia: Lippincott.

Burr, Wesley (1976). *Successful Marriage.* Homewood, Ill.: Dorsey.

Burr, Wesley, G. K. Leigh, R. Day, and J. Constantine (1979). Symbolic interaction/role theory and the family. In W. Burr, R. Hill, I. F. Nye, and I. Reiss (eds.), *Contemporary Theories about the Family.* New York: Free Press.

Busse, Ewald, Frances Jeffers, and Walter D. Christ (1970). Factors in age awareness. In Erdman Palmore (ed.), *Normal Aging.* Durham, N.C.: Duke University Press.

Butler, Robert N., and M. I. Lewis (1976). *Sex after Sixty.* New York: Harper & Row.

Campbell, Angus (1975). The American way of mating. *Psychology Today* (May):37–43.

Campbell, Arthur A. (1968). The role of family planning in the reduction of poverty. *Journal of Marriage and the Family* 30:236–245.

Campbell, Colin (1976). What happens when we get the manchild pill? *Psychology Today* 10:86–91.

Caplow, Theodore (1968). *Two Against One: Coalitions in Triads.* Englewood Cliffs, N.J.: Prentice-Hall.

Carisse, Colette (1975). Family and leisure: A set of contradictions. *The Family Coordinator,* 24:191–198.

Carlson, John (1976). The recreational role. In F. Ivan Nye (ed.), *Role Structure and Analysis of the Family.* New York: Sage.

Carter, Hugh, and Paul Glick (1970). *Marriage and Divorce: A Social and Economic Study.* Cambridge, Mass.: Harvard University Press.

Casler, Lawrence (1973). Toward a re-evaluation of love. In Mary Ellen Curtin, *Symposium on Love.* New York: Behavioral Publications.

Casserly, Patricia Lund (1978). Study finds girls are diverted from careers in math and science. *ETS Developments* 25 (Fall):4–5.

Centers, Richard (1975). *Sexual Attraction and Love.* Springfield, Ill.: Thomas.

Centers, Richard, Bertram Ravens, and Aroldo Rodrigues (1971). Conjugal power structure: A re-examination. *American Sociological Review* 36:264–278.

Chafetz, Janet S. (1978). *Masculine/Feminine or Human?* Itasca, Ill.: Peacock.

Chafetz, Janet, P. Sampson, P. Beck, and J. West (1974). A study of homosexual women. *Social Work* 19:714–723.

Changing Times (1975). Teaching your kids to manage money (September):39–41.

Cherlin, Andrew (1977). The effect of children on marital dissolution. *Demography* 14:265–272.

Chesser, Barbara Jo (1980). Analysis of wedding rituals: an attempt to make weddings more meaningful. *Family Relations* 29:204–209.

Christensen, Harold T. (1968). Children in the family: Relationship of number and spacing to marital success. *Journal of Marriage and the Family* 30:283–289.

Clark, Margaret, and Barbara Anderson (1967). *Culture and Aging.* Springfield, Ill.: Thomas.

Clark, Robert A., F. Ivan Nye, and Viktor Gecas (1978). Husband's work involvement and marital role preference. *Journal of Marriage and the Family* 40:9–21.

Clavan, Sylvia (1978). The impact of social class and social trends on the role of grandparent. *The Family Coordinator* 27:351–356.

Clayton, Richard (1975). *The Family, Marriage, and Social Change.* Lexington, Mass.: D. C. Heath.

Clinebell, Charlotte H., and Howard J. Clinebell (1970). *The Intimate Marriage.* New York: Harper & Row.

Cohen, Yehudi (1978). The disappearance of the incest taboo. *Human Nature* 1:72–78.

Colbert, S. A. (1968). *The Interpersonal Process of Self-Disclosure: It Takes Two To See One.* New York: Renaissance Editions.

Cole, Charles L. (1977). Cohabitation in social context. In R. Libby and R. Whitehurst (eds.), *Marriage and Alternatives.* Glenview, Ill.: Scott-Foresman.

Coleman, James S. (1961). *The Adolescent Society.* New York: Free Press.

Coles, Robert (1977). The children of affluence. *Atlantic Monthly* (September):52–66.

Comfort, Alex (1976). *A Good Age.* New York: Crown.

Constantine, Larry (1978). Multilateral relations revisited: Group marriages in extended perspective. In Bernard I. Murstein (ed.), *Exploring Intimate Life Styles.* New York: Springer.

Constantine, Larry, and Joan Constantine (1972). The group marriage. In M. Gordon (ed.), *The Nuclear Family in Crisis: The Search for an Alternative.* New York: Harper & Row.

——— (1973). *Group Marriage: A Study of Contemporary Multilateral Relations.* New York: Macmillan.

Cooper, David (1970). *The Death of the Family.* New York: Vintage.

Cowan, Carolyn, P. Cowan, Lynne Coie, and John Coie (1979). Becoming a family: the impact of a first child's birth on the couple's relationship. In L. Coie and J. Coie, *The First Child and Family Formation.* Chapel Hill, N.C.: Carolina Population Center.

Cowan, John (1880). *The Science of a New Life.* New York: Cowan and Company.

Cozby, P. W. (1973). Self-disclosure: a literature review. *Psychological Bulletin* 79:73–91.

Critelli, Joseph (1977). Romantic attraction as a function of sex role traditionality. Paper presented at the meeting of the American Psychological Association.

Cromwell, Ronald, and David Olson (1975). *Power in Families.* New York: Wiley.

Cronenwett, Linda R., and Lucy L. Newmark (1974). Fathers' responses to childbirth. *Nursing Research* 23:210–217.

Crosby, John F. (1975). The death of the family revisited. *The Humanist* 35:12–14.

——— (1980). A critique of divorce statistics and their interpretation. *Family Relations* 29:51–58.

Cuber, John, and Peggy Harroff (1966). *Sex and the Significant Americans.* New York: Appleton-Century.

Cumming, Elaine, and William Henry (1961). *Growing Old: The Process of Disengagement.* New York: Basic Books.

Curtin, Mary Ellen (ed.) (1973). *Symposium on Love.* New York: Behavioral Publications.

Dailey, Dennis M. (1979). Adjustment of heterosexual and homosexual couples in pairing relationships: an exploratory study. *Journal of Sex Research* 15:143–157.

Danziger, Carl, and Matthew Greenwald (1977). *Alternatives.* New York: Institute of Life Insurance.

Darling, J. (1976). An interactionist interpretation of bachelorhood and late marriage. Unpublished Doctoral Dissertation, University of Connecticut.

Darnley, Fred (1975). Adjustment to retirement: integrity or despair. *The Family Coordinator* 24:217–226.

Darrow, William W. (1976). Social and behavioral aspects of the sexually transmitted diseases. In S. Gordon and R. Libby (eds.), *Sexuality Today—And Tomorrow.* North Scituate, Mass.: Duxbury.

Davey, Alice J., and Beatrice Paolucci (1980). Family interaction: a study of shared time and activities. *Family Relations* 29:43–49.

David (1978). The commune movement in the middle 1970s. In Bernard Murstein (ed.), *Exploring Intimate Life Styles.* New York: Springer.

David, Deborah, and Robert Brannon (1976). *The Forty-Nine Percent Majority: The Male Sex Role.* Reading, Mass.: Addison-Wesley.

Davis, Murray S. (1973). *Intimate Relations.* New York: Free Press.

Dean, Dwight, Edward Powers, Rita Braite, and Brent Bruton (1975). Cultural conditions and sex roles revisited: a replication and reassessment. *Sociological Quarterly* 16:207–215.

Dean, Dwight, and Graham Spanier (1974). Commitment: an overlooked variable in marital adjustment. *Sociological Focus* 7:113–118.

Delora, Joann S., and Carol Warren (1977). *Understanding Sexual Interaction.* Boston: Houghton Mifflin.

Denfield, Duane, and M. Gordon (1970). The sociology of mate swapping: or the family that swings together clings together. *Journal of Sex Research* 6:85–100.

Derlega, Valerian, and Alan Chaiken (1975). *Sharing Intimacy.* Englewood Cliffs, N.J.: Prentice-Hall.

de Rougemont, Denis (1949). The crisis of the modern couple. In Ruth Anshen (ed.), *The Family: Its Function and Destiny.* New York: Harper & Row.

Despert, J. Louis (1953). *Children of Divorce.* New York: Doubleday.

Deutsch, Morton (1973). *The Resolutions of Conflict.* New Haven, Conn.: Yale University Press.

Deutscher, Irwin (1964). The quality of postparental life: definitions of the situation. *Journal of Marriage and the Family* 26:52–59.

Diamond, Milton, and Arno Karlen (1980). *Sexual Decisions.* Boston: Little, Brown.

Dinnage, Rosemary (1980). Understanding loss: the Bowlby canon. *Psychology Today* 13 (May):56–60.

Diepold, John, and Richard D. Young (1979). Empirical studies of adolescent sexual behavior: a critical review. *Adolescence* 14:45–64.

Dies, D. R., and L. Cohen (1973). Content consideration in group therapist self-disclosure. Paper presented at the American Psychological Association Convention.

Dobrin, Arthur, and Kenneth Briggs (1974). *Getting Married the Way You Want.* Englewood Cliffs, N.J.: Prentice-Hall.

Donahue, Wilma T. (1971). *46 National Leaders Speak Out on Options for Older Americans.* Washington, D.C.: National Retired Teachers Association and American Association for Retired Persons.

Douglas, W. (1965). *Ministers' Wives.* New York: Harper & Row.

Duberman, Lucille (1975). *The Reconstituted Family.* Chicago: Nelson-Hall.

Duncan, Otis Dudley, Howard Schuman, and Beverly Duncan (1973). *Social Change in Metropolitan Detroit: The 1950's to 1971.* New York: Russell Sage.

Durkheim, Emile (1897). *Le Suicide.* Paris: Felix Alcan.

——— (1933). *The Division of Labor in Society.* Translated by George Simpson. New York: Macmillan.

Duvall, Evelyn (1957). *Family Development.* Philadelphia: Lippincott.

Edmiston, Susan (1972). How to write your own marriage contract. *MS* (Spring).

Edmonds, Vernon (1967). Marital conventionalization: definition and measurement. *Journal of Marriage and the Family* 29:681–688.

Edwards, John N. (1967). The future of the family revisited. *Journal of Marriage and the Family* 29:505–511.

Ehrlick, Paul, and Anne H. Ehrlick (1979). *Population, Resources, and Environment,* 4th ed. San Francisco: Freeman.

Eisenberger, Katherine (1978). News roundup. *Behavior Today* (May 1):7.

Eisler, Riane T. (1977). *Dissolution: No-Fault Divorce, Marriage, and the Future of Women.* New York: McGraw-Hill.

Elkin, Meyer (1977). Premarital counseling for minors: the Los Angeles experience. *The Family Coordinator* 26:429–443.

Erickson, Julia, William Yancey, and Eugene Erickson (1979). The division of family roles. *Journal of Marriage and the Family* 41:301–313.

Erikson, Erik (1964). *Insight and Responsibility.* New York: Norton.

——— (1968). *Identity, Youth, and Crisis.* New York: Norton.

Eshleman, J. Ross (1978). *The Family: An Introduction,* 2d ed. Boston: Allyn and Bacon.

Eshleman, J. Ross, and Chester L. Hunt (1965). *Social Class Factors in the College Adjustment of Married Students.* Kalamazoo: Western Michigan University.

Everett, Glenn D. (1961). One man's family. *Population Bulletin* 17.

Ewing, Elizabeth (1980). Singles becoming adoptive parents. *Marriage and Divorce Today* 5 (January 21):1–2.

Fanning, Patricia (1975). Marriage and Divorce. *The National Observer* (August 23):12.

Farber, Bernard (1964). *Family: Organization and Interaction.* San Francisco: Chandler.

Farrell, Warren T. (1975). Beyond masculinity: liberating men in their relationships with women. In Lucile Duberman, *Gender and Sex in Society.* New York: Praeger, 1975.

Fein, Robert (1974). Men with young children. In Joseph Pleck and Jack Sawyer, *Men and Masculinity.* Englewood Cliffs, N.J.: Prentice-Hall.

Feldman, Francis (1976). *The Family in Today's Money World.* New York: Family Service Association.

Feldman, Harold (1968). The effects of children on the family. In Andrée Michel (ed.), *Family Issues of Employed Women in Europe and America.* Leiden, Netherlands: Brill.

Feldman, Margaret, and Harold Feldman (1975). The family life-cycle: some suggestions for recycling. *Journal of Marriage and the Family* 37:277–286.

Fink, Paul J. (1974). Causes and effects of nonorgasmic coitus in women. In L. Gross (ed.), *Sexual Behavior.* New York: Spectrum.

Foote, Nelson, and Leonard Cottrell (1955). *Identity and Interpersonal Competence.* Chicago: University of Chicago Press.

Ford, Kathleen (1978). Contraceptive use in the United States. *Family Planning Perspectives* 8:264–269.

Forisha, Barbara Lusk (1978). *Sex Roles and Personal Awareness.* Morristown, N.J.: General Learning Press.

Fox, Greer Litton (1980). The mother-adolescent daughter relationship as a sex socialization structure. *Family Relations* 29:21–28.

Framo, James L. (1978). The friendly divorce. *Psychology Today* 11 (February):77–79, 100–102.

Francoeur, Robert, and Anna Francoeur (1973). Hot and cool sex: fidelity in marriage. In R. Libby and R. N. Whitehurst, *Renovating Marriage.* Danville, Calif.: Consensus Publishers.

Frank, Ellen, Carol Anderson, and Debra Rubenstein (1978). Frequency of sexual dysfunction in "normal" couples. *New England Journal of Medicine* 299:111–115.

Freedman, Jonathan (1979). *Happy People.* New York: Harcourt, Brace, Jovanovich.

Freedman, Ronald, and Lolagene Coombs (1966). Childspacing and family economic position. *American Sociological Review* 31:631–648.

Freud, Sigmund (1922). *Group Psychology and the Analysis of Ego.* New York: International Psychoanalytic Press.

——— (1927). Some psychological consequences of anatomical distinction between the sexes. *International Journal of Psychological Analysis* 8:133–142.

Friedd, Ernestine (1978). Society and sex roles. *Human Nature* 1:68–75.

Friedman, M., and R. H. Rosenman (1975). *Type A Behavior and Your Heart.* Greenwich, Conn.: Fawcett Crest.

Fromm, Erich (1947). *Man for Himself.* New York: Rinehart.

——— (1956). *The Art of Loving.* New York: Bantam.

Fullerton, Gail Putney (1972). *Survival in Marriage.* New York: Holt, Rinehart and Winston.

Furstenberg, Frank F. (1971). Birth control experience among pregnant adolescents: the process of unplanned parenthood. *Social Problems* 19:192–203.

Gagnon, John (1977). *Human Sexuality.* Glenview, Ill.: Scott, Foresman.

Gallup, George (1978a). Youth survey. *Behavior Today* 9 (October 23):7.

——— (1978b). More than half say it is wrong. *Greensboro Daily News* (August 7).

——— (1979a). Contraceptive information favored by teenagers. *Family Planning Perspectives* 11:255–259.

——— (1979b). Eighty percent of Americans believe abortion should be legal. *Family Planning Perspectives* 11:189–190.

——— (1980). Family life has deteriorated. *Marriage and Divorce Today* 5 (June 16):3.

Garai, J. E., and A. Scheinfeld (1968). Sex differences in mental and behavioral traits. *Genetic Psychology Monographs* 77:169–299.

Gawin, Frank (1978). Pharmacologic enhancement of the erotic: implications of an expanded definition of aphrodisiacs. *Journal of Sex Research* 14:107–117.

Gaylin, Ned (1975). On the quality of life and death. *The Family Coordinator* 24:250–255.

Gecas, Viktor, F. Ivan Nye, and Don Dillman (1977). The Equal Rights Amendment and family patterns. Paper presented at the Meeting of the National Council on Family Relations, San Diego.

Gelles, Richard (1979). *Family Violence.* Beverly Hills, Calif.: Sage.

Gerson, Walter M. (1960). Leisure and marital satisfaction of college married couples. *Marriage and Family Living* 22:360–361.

Gerstl, J. (1961). Leisure, taste, and the occupational milieu. *Social Problems* 9:56–68.

Gilbert, Lucia, and Carole Holahan (1978). Dual working couples. *Behavior Today* (April 10):7.

Gilbert, Shirley J. (1976). Self-disclosure, intimacy and communication in families. *The Family Coordinator* 25 (July):221–232.

Gilmartin, Brian (1977). Swinging: who gets involved and how. In R. Libby and R. Whitehurst (eds.), *Marriage and Alternatives.* North Scituate, Mass.: Duxbury.

Glass, Shirley P., and Thomas L. Wright (1977). The relationship of extramarital sex, length of marriage, and sex differences on marital satisfaction and romanticism. *Journal of Marriage and the Family* 39:691–704.

Glenn, Norval D. (1975a). Psychological well-being in the post-parental stage. *Journal of Marriage and the Family* 37:105–110.

——— (1975b). The contribution of marriage to the psychological well-being of males and females. *Journal of Marriage and the Family* 37:594–600.

Glenn, Norval D., and Charles N. Weaver (1977). The marital happiness of remarried divorced persons. *Journal of Marriage and the Family* 39:331–338.

——— (1979). Attitudes toward premarital, extramarital and homosexual relations in the U. S. in the 1970's. *Journal of Sex Research* 15:108–118.

Glick, Ira, Robert S. Weiss, and C. Murray Parkes (1974). *The First Year of Bereavement.* New York: Wiley.

Glick, Paul (1977). Marrying, divorcing, and living together in the U.S. today. *Population Bulletin* 32 (October).

——— (1979). Changing adult population: implications of family composition. Address before the Southeastern Conference on Family Relations, April.

Glick, Paul, and Arthur Norton (1977). Marrying, divorcing, and living together in the U. S. today. *Population Bulletin* 32 (October).

Glick, Paul, and Graham Spanier (1980). Married and unmarried cohabitation in the United States. *Journal of Marriage and the Family* 42:19–30.

Goetting, Ann (1979). The normative integration of the former spouse relationship. *Journal of Divorce* 2:395–414.

Goffman, Irving (1961). *Encounters: Two Studies in the Sociology of Interaction.* Indianapolis: Bobbs-Merrill.

Goldman, Daniel R. (1973). Managerial mobility motivations and central life interests. *American Sociological Review* 38 (February):119–126.

Goldstein, Bernard (1976). *Human Sexuality.* New York: McGraw-Hill.

Goldstein, Joseph, Anna Freud, and A. Solnit (1973). *Beyond the Best Interests of the Child.* New York: Free Press.

Goode, William (1956). *After Divorce.* Chicago: Free Press.

——— (1959). The theoretical importance of love. *American Sociological Review* 24:38–47.

——— (1963). *World Revolution and Family Patterns.* New York: Free Press.

——— (1971). *The Contemporary American Family.* Chicago: Quadrangle.

Goodman, Ellen (1978). We're still mum about sex. *Greensboro Daily News* (December 16).

Gordon, Michael (1978). *The American Family: Past, Present and Future.* New York: Random House.

Gordon, Sol (1976). Freedom for sex education and sexual expression. In S. Gordon and R. Libby (eds.), *Sexuality Today—And Tomorrow.* North Scituate, Mass.: Duxbury.

Gordon, Sol, and Roger Libby (eds.) (1976). *Sexuality Today and Tomorrow.* North Scituate, Mass.: Duxbury.

Gray, Rick (1978). Housing costs. *Greensboro Daily News* (June 18).

Greenwood, Sadja G. (1979). Warning: cigarette smoking is dangerous to reproductive health. *Family Planning Perspectives* 11:168–172.

Greven, Philip J., Jr. (1973). Family structure in seventeenth century Andover, Massachusetts. In Michael Gordon (ed.), *The American Family in Social-Historical Perspective.* New York: St. Martins Press.

Gross, Arnold E. (1978). The male role and heterosexual behavior. *Journal of Social Issues* 34:87–107.

Grzech, Ellen, and Cathy Troot (1978). The success of a series. *Behavior Today* 8 (January 9):6–7.

Guerrero, R. (1974). Association of the type and time of insemination within the menstrual cycle with the human sex ratio at birth. *New England Journal of Medicine* 291:1056–1060.

Gunter, B. G. (1977). Notes on divorce filing as role behavior. *Journal of Marriage and the Family* 39:95–98.

Gurman, Alan S., and David P. Kniskern (1978). Deterioration in marital and family therapy: empirical, clinical and conceptual issues. *Family Process* 17:3–20.

Gustavus, Susan O., and James R. Henly, Jr. (1971). Correlates of voluntary childlessness in a select population. *Social Biology* 18:277–284.

Hacker, Helen (1975). Gender roles from a cross-cultural perspective. In Lucille Duberman (ed.), *Gender and Sex in Society.* New York: Praeger.

Hall, Francine, and Douglas Hall (1979). *The Two-Career Couple.* Reading, Mass.: Addison-Wesley.

Hansen, James C., and Barbara Putnam (1978). Feminine role concepts of young women. *Sex Roles* 4 (February).

Hansen, Sandra, and Graham Spanier (1978). The role of extended kin in the adjustment to marital separation. Paper presented at the meeting of the Southern Sociological Society.

Harlap, S. (1979). Gender of infants conceived on different days of the menstrual cycle. *New England Journal of Medicine* 300:1445–1448.

Harlow, H. F., and M. K. Harlow (1966). Learning to love. *American Scientist* 54:244–272.

Harris, Louis, and Associates (1975). *The Myth and Reality of Aging in America.* New York: National Council on Aging.

Harry, Joseph (1976). Evolving sources of happiness for men over the life cycle. *Journal of Marriage and the Family* 38:289–296.

Hatkoff, Terry Smith, and Thomas E. Casswell (1976). Male/female similarities and differences in conceptualizing love. Paper presented at the National Council on Family Relations Meeting, October.

Hawke, Sharryl, and David Knox (1978). The one child family: A new life style. *The Family Coordinator* 27:215–220.

Heckman, Norma, Rebecca Bryson, and Jeff Bryson (1977). Problems of professional couples: A content analysis. *Journal of Marriage and the Family* 39:323–330.

Heddescheimer, J. C. (1977). Multiple motivations for mid-career changes. *The Personal and Guidance Journal* 55:109–111.

Hedges, Janice (1976). Long workweeks and premium pay. *Monthly Labor Review* (April):7–12.

Heer, David M. (1963). The measurement and bases of family power: an overview. *Journal of Marriage and the Family* 25:133–139.

——— (1966). Negro-white marriages in the United States. *Journal of Marriage and the Family* 28:262–273.

——— (1974). The prevalence of black-white marriage in the United States, 1960 and 1970. *Journal of Marriage and the Family* 36:246–259.

Heiman, J., L. LoPiccolo, and J. LoPiccolo (1976). *Becoming Orgasmic: A Sexual Growth Program for Women.* Englewood Cliffs, N.J.: Prentice-Hall.

Henley, Lynda (ed.) (1977). The family and the law. Special Issue of *The Family Coordinator* (October).

Henly, Nancy, and Barrie Thorne (1977). Womanspeak and manspeak: sex differences and sexism in communication. In Alice Sargent (ed.), *Beyond Sex Roles.* St. Paul, Minn.: West.

Henry, Jules (1964). *Jungle People: The Kaingang People of the Highlands of Brazil.* New York: Vintage.

Henze, Laura, and John W. Hudson (1974). Personal and family characteristics of cohabiting and noncohabiting college students. *Journal of Marriage and the Family* 36:722–727.

Herold, Edward S. (1974). Stages of date selection: a reconciliation of divergent findings on campus values in dating. *Adolescence* 9:113–120.

——— (1979). Variables influencing the dating adjustment of university students. *Journal of Youth and Adolescence* 8:73–79.

Hess, Beth B. (1979). Family myths. *Behavior Today* 10 (January 22):8.

Hess, Beth B., and Joan M. Waring (1978). Changing patterns of aging and family bonds in later life. *The Family Coordinator* 27:303–314.

Hetherington, E. Mavis, Martha Cox, and Roger Cox (1977). Divorced fathers. *Psychology Today* 10 (April):42–46.

Hiday, Virginia (1975). Parity and well-being among low income urban families. *Journal of Marriage and the Family* 37:787–797.

Hilker, Mary Anne, and Gordon Streib (1979). A variant family form for the elderly: some preliminary findings. Paper presented at the Southern Sociological Society Meeting.

Hill, Charles T., Zick Rubin, and Letitia Peplace (1976). Breakups before marriage: the end of 103 affairs. *Journal of Social Issues* 32:147–168.

Hill, Reuben (1970). *Family Development in Three Generations.* Cambridge, Mass.: Schenkman.

Hilpert, F., C. Cramer, and R. A. Clark (1975). Participants' perceptions of self and partner in mixed sex dyads. *Central States Speech Journal* 26:52–56.

Hirsch, Barbara (1976). *Living Together.* Boston: Houghton Mifflin.

Hirschman, L. (1974). Analysis of supportive and assertive behavior in conversations. Paper presented at the Linguistic Society of America Meeting.

Hite, Shere (1976). *The Hite Report.* New York: Dell.

Hobart, Charles W. (1963). Commitment, value conflict, and the future of the American family. *Marriage and Family Living* 25:405–412.

Hochschild, Arlie R. (1973). *The Unexpected Community.* Englewood Cliffs, N.J.: Prentice-Hall.

Hodgson, James W., and Judith L. Fisher (1979). Sex differences in identity and intimacy development in college youth. *Journal of Youth and Adolescence* 8:37–50.

Hoffman, Lois W., and Martin L. Hoffman (1973). The value of children to parents. In James T. Fawcett (ed.), *Psychological Perspectives on Population.* New York: Basic Books.

Hoffman, Lois W., and F. Ivan Nye (1974). *Working Mothers.* San Francisco: Jossey-Bass.

Hoffman, Lois W., A. Thornton, and J. D. Manis (1978). The value of children to parents in the U. S. *Journal of Population* 1:91–131.

Holmes, Lewis (1978). How fathers can cause the Down's syndrome. *Human Nature* 1:70–72.

Holstrom, Linda (1972). *The Two-Career Family.* Cambridge, Mass.: Schenkman.

Houseknecht, Susan K. (1977). Reference group support for voluntary childlessness: evidence for conformity. *Journal of Marriage and the Family* 39:285–294.

Hunt, Bernice, and Morton Hunt (1980). Your father/yourself. *Ladies Home Journal* 97 (May):101, 169–180.

Hunt, Morton (1970). Money and sex: two marital problems or one? *Redbook* (January).

——— (1974). *Sexual Behavior in the 1970's.* New York: Dell.

Huston, Ted L. (1974). *Foundations of Interpersonal Attraction.* New York: Academic Press.

Huyck, Margaret H. (1974). *Growing Old.* Englewood Cliffs, N.J.: Prentice-Hall.

Ickes, William, and Richard Barnes (1978). When men and women meet. *Psychology Today* 12 (October):44.

Jacobs, J. (1974). *Fun City: An Ethnographic Study of a Retirement Community.* New York: Holt.

Jacques, Jeffrey M., and Karen J. Chason (1979). Cohabitation: its impact on marital success. *Family Coordinator* 28:35–39.

Jaffee, Benson (1974). Adoption outcome: a two-generation view. *Child Welfare* 53:211–224.

Jaffee, Benson and David Fanshel (1970). *How They Fared in Adoption: A Follow-Up Study.* New York: Columbia University Press.

James, Muriel (1979). *Marriage Is for Loving.* Reading, Mass.: Addison-Wesley.

James, Muriel, and Dorothy Jongeward (1971). *Born to Win: Transactional Analysis with Gestalt Experiments.* Reading, Mass.: Addison-Wesley.

Johnson, Beverly L. (1978). Women who head families, 1970–1977. *Monthly Labor Review* (February):32–37.

Johnson, Ralph E. (1970). Some correlates of extramarital coitus. *Journal of Marriage and the Family* 32:449–455.

Jorgenson, David E. (1977). The effect of social position and wife/mother employment on family leisure time: a study of fathers. *International Journal of Sociology and the Family* 7:197–208.

Jourard, Sidney M. (1968). *Disclosing Man to Himself.* New York: Van Nostrand.

——— (1971). *The Transparent Self.* New York: D. Van Nostrand.

Juhasz, Anne M. (1980). Adolescent attitudes toward childbearing and family size. *Family Relations* 29:29–34.

Jurich, Anthony, and Julie A. Jurich (1975). Alternative family forms: preferences of nonparticipants. *Home Economics Research Journal* 3:260–265.

Kacerguis, Mary Ann, and Gerald Adams (1979). Implications of sex typed child rearing practices, toys and mass media materials. *The Family Coordinator* 28:369–375.

Kadushin, Alfred (1967). *Child Welfare Services.* New York: Macmillan.

Kadushin, Alfred, and Frederick Seidl (1971). Adoption failure: A social work post-mortem. *Social Work* 16.

Kahana, Eva, and R. M. Coe (1969). Perceptions of grandparenthood by community and institutionalized aged. *Proceedings,* American Psychological Association, 735–736.

Kahana, Eva, and Boaz Kahana (1971). Theoretical and research perspectives on grandparenthood. *Aging and Human Development* 2:261–268.

Kalish, Richard (1975). *Late Adulthood: Perspectives on Human Development.* Monterey, Calif.: Brooks-Cole.

——— (1976). Death and dying in social context. In Robert Binstock and Ethel Shanas (eds.), *Handbook of Aging and Social Sciences.* New York: Van Nostrand.

Kanin, Eugene J., Karen Davidson, and Sonia Scheck (1970). A research note on male-female differentials in the experience of heterosexual love. *Journal of Sex Research* 6:64–72.

Kanter, Rosabeth Moss (1973). *Communes: Creating and Managing the Collective Life.* New York: Harper & Row.

Kanter, Rosabeth M., D. Jaffe, and D. K. Weisberg (1975). Coupling, parenting, and the presence of others: intimate relationships in communal households. *The Family Coordinator* 24:433–452.

Kantor, David, and William Lehr (1975). *Inside the Family.* San Francisco: Jossey-Bass.

Kaplan, Helen Singer (1975). *The Illustrated Manual of Sex Therapy.* New York: Quadrangle.

Katz, Barbara (1976). Saying goodbye to superman. In Deborah David and Robert Brannon (eds.), *The Forty-Nine Percent Majority: The Male Sex Role.* Reading, Mass.: Addison-Wesley.

Kelley, Robert (1979). *Courtship, Marriage and the Family.* New York: Harcourt, Brace, Jovanovich.

Kelly, Charles (1977). Empathic Listening. In John Steward (ed.), *Bridges, Not Walls.* Reading, Mass.: Addison-Wesley.

Keniston, Kenneth (1968). *Young Radicals.* New York: Harcourt, Brace, and World.

Kennedy, Carol E. (1978). *Human Development: The Adult Years and Aging.* New York: Macmillan.

Kephart, William (1973). Evaluation of romantic love. *Medical Aspects of Human Sexuality,* 92–112.

——— (1977). *The Family, Society, and the Individual.* Boston: Houghton-Mifflin.

Kerkhoff, Alan C. (1966). Family patterns and morale in retirement. In Ida Simpson and John McKinney (eds.), *Social Aspects of Aging.* Durham, N.C.: Duke University Press.

Kerckoff, Richard (1976). Marriage and middle age. *Family Coordinator* 25:5–12.

Kidwell, Jeannie S. (1978). Adolescents' perceptions of parental affect: an investigation of only children or firstborns and the effect of spacing. *Journal of Population* 1:148–166.

Kieffer, Carolyn (1977). New depths in intimacy. In Roger Libby and Robert Whitehurst (eds.), *Marriage and Alternatives: Exploring Intimate Relationships.* Glenview, Ill.: Scott, Foresman.

Kinsey, Alfred, W. B. Pomeroy, and C. E. Martin (1948). *Sexual Behavior in the Human Male.* Philadelphia: Saunders.

Kinsey, A. C., W. B. Pomeroy, C. E. Martin, and P. H. Gebhard (1953). *Sexual Behavior in the Human Female.* Philadelphia: Saunders.

Kitson, Gay C., William Holmes, and Marvin Sussman (1977). Predicting reconciliation: a test of the exchange model of divorce. Paper presented at the Meeting of the American Sociological Association.

Kivett, Vira (1979). Discriminators of loneliness among the rural elderly. *The Gerontologist* 19:108–115.

——— (1980). The kinship network. In James Walters (ed.), *Aging: A Home Economics Guide to Independent Living.* Washington, D.C.: American Home Economics Association.

Knapp, Jacquelyn (1976). An exploratory study of sexually open marriages. *Journal of Sex Research* 12:206–219.

Knapp, Jacquelyn, and Robert N. Whitehurst (1978). Sexually open marriage and relationships: issues and prospects. In Bernard Murstein (ed.), *Exploring Intimate Life Styles.* New York: Springer.

Knox, David, and Michael Sporakowski (1968). Attitudes of college students toward love. *Journal of Marriage and the Family* 30:638–642.

Knox, David, and Kenneth Wilson (1978). The differences between having one and two children. *The Family Coordinator* 27:23–26.

Koch, J., and L. Koch (1976). A consumer's guide to therapy for couples. *Psychology Today* 9 (October):33–36.

Koller, Marvin (1974). *Families: A Multigenerational Approach.* New York: McGraw-Hill.

Komarovsky, Mirra (1964). *Blue-Collar Marriage.* New York: Random House.

——— (1976). *Dilemmas of Masculinity.* New York: Norton.

Kompara, Diane R. (1980). Difficulties in the socialization process of stepparenting. *Family Relations* 29:69–73.

Kraus, Harry D. (1976). *Family Law.* St. Paul, Minn.: West.

Kübler-Ross, Elizabeth (1969). *On Death and Dying.* New York: Macmillan.

Landis, Judson T., and Mary Landis (1973). *Building a Successful Marriage.* Englewood Cliffs, N.J.: Prentice-Hall.

Larson, Lyle (1974). System and subsystem perception of family roles. *Journal of Marriage and the Family* 36:123–138.

Lederer, William, and Donald Jackson (1968). *Mirages of Marriage.* New York: Norton.

Lee, Gary (1978). Marriage and morale in later life. *Journal of Marriage and the Family* 40:131–142.

Lee, John A. (1973). *The Colours of Love.* Toronto, Canada: New Press.

——— (1974). Styles of loving. *Psychology Today* 8:44–51.

——— (1976). Forbidden colors of love, patterns of gay love and gay liberation. *Journal of Homosexuality* 4:401–418.

LeMasters, E. E. (1977). *Parents in Modern America,* 3d ed. Homewood, Ill.: Dorsey.

Lester, Julius (1973). Being a boy. *MS* 1 (July):112–113.

Levine, James A. (1976). *Who Will Raise the Children?* New York: Bantam.

Levinger, George (1964). Task and social behavior in marriage. *Sociometry* 27:433–448.

——— (1976). A social psychological perspective on divorce. *Journal of Social Issues* 32:21–47.

Levinson, Daniel (1978). *The Seasons of a Man's Life.* New York: Alfred Knopf.

Lewis, Lionel S., and Dennis Brissett (1967). Sex as work: a study of avocational counseling. *Social Problems* 15:8–18.

Lewis, Michael (1972). Culture and gender roles: there's no unisex in the nursery. *Psychology Today* (May):54–57.

Lewis, Robert A. (1973). A longitudinal test of a developmental framework for premarital dyadic formation. *Journal of Marriage and the Family* 35:16–25.

——— (1973). Social reaction and the formation of dyads. *Sociometry* 36:409–418.

Lewis, Robert, and Wesley R. Burr (1975). Premarital coitus and commitment among college students. *Archives of Sexual Behavior* 4:73–79.

Lewis, Robert A., G. B. Spanier, V. L. Atkinson, and C. F. Lettecka (1977). Commitment in married and unmarried cohabitation. *Sociological Focus* 10:367–374.

Lewis, Susan H. (1977). Directions of change on family law. Paper presented at the Institute on Family Law (January).

Libby, Roger W. (1977). Creative singlehood as a sexual lifestyle. In Roger Libby and Robert Whitehurst (eds.), *Marriage and Alternatives: Exploring Intimate Relationships.* Glenview, Ill.: Scott, Foresman.

Libby, Roger, Louis Gray, and Mervin White (1978). A test and reformulation of reference group and role correlates of premarital sexual permissiveness theory. *Journal of Marriage and the Family* 40:79–89.

Libby, Roger, and Gilbert Nass (1971). Parental views on teenage sexual behavior. *Journal of Sex Research* 7:226–237.

Lieberman, E. James (1970). The case for small families. *The Family Planner* 3 (June):4–5, 8.

Lindsey, Ben B. (1926). The companionate marriage. *Redbook* (October).

Lindsey, J. (1972). On the number in a group. *Human Relations* 25:47–64.

Livson, Florine B. (1977). *Looking Ahead: A Woman's Guide to the Problems and Joys of Growing Old.* Englewood Cliffs, N.J.: Prentice-Hall.

Lockheed, Marlaine (1978). Fifth grade study finds boys view girls as smart but not as leaders: girls agree. *ETS Developments* 25:4–5.

Lopata, Helena Z. (1971). *Occupation: Housewife.* New York: Oxford University Press.

——— (1973). *Widowhood in an American City.* Cambridge, Mass.: Schenkman.

Lowell, Amy (1972). *Love Is Now: The Moods of Love Today.* Jane Morgan (ed.), Kansas City, Mo.: Hallmark Cards.

Lowenthal, M. F., and D. Chiriboga (1972). Transition to the empty nest: crisis, change, or relief? *Archives of General Psychiatry* 26:8–14.

Luepnitz, Deborah (1980). Effects of custody patterns on family members. *Marriage and Divorce Today* 5 (June 30):2.

Luepton, Lloyd (1980). Social structure, social change, and parental influence in adolescent sex-role socialization. *Journal of Marriage and the Family* 42:93–103.

Lynd, Robert J., and Helen M. Lynd (1929). *Middletown.* New York: Harcourt.

McCary, James L. (1978). *Human Sexuality,* 3d ed. New York: Van Nostrand.

McClelland, David C., Carol Constantian, David Regalado, and Carolyn Stone (1978). Making it to maturity. *Psychology Today* 12 (June):42–53, 114.

Maccoby, Eleanor, and Carol Jacklin (1974). *Psychology of Sex Differences.* Stanford, Calif.: Stanford University Press.

McCubbin, Hamilton (1979). Integrating coping behavior in family stress theory. *Journal of Marriage and the Family* 41:237–244.

McDonagh, E. (1950). TV and the family. *Sociology and Social Research* 35:113–122.

McDonald, Gerald (1977). Family power: reflection and direction. *Pacific Sociological Review* 20:607–621.

McGraw, Louise (1977). Family budgets. *Monthly Labor Review* 100 (July):35–39.

McGuinness, Diane (1979). How schools discriminate against boys. *Human Nature* 2:82–88.

MacIver, Robert M. (1955). *The Pursuit of Happiness.* New York: Simon & Schuster.

McKain, Walter C. (1969). *Retirement Marriage.* Storrs, Conn.: University of Connecticut Agricultural Experiment Station.

McKain, Walter C. (1972). A new look at older marriages. *The Family Coordinator* 21:61–69.

McLaughlin, Barry (1978). The mother tongue. *Human Nature* 1 (December):89.

MacPherson, M. (1975). *The Power Lovers: An Intimate Look at Politicians and Their Marriages.* New York: Putnam.

Mace, David (1979). Marriage and family enrichment—a new field? *The Family Coordinator* 28:409–419.

Mace, David, and Vera Mace (1960). *Marriage East and West.* Garden City, N.J.: Doubleday.

Macke, Ann Statham, George Bohrnstedt, and Ilene Bernstein (1979). Housewives' self-esteem and their husbands' success: the myth of vicarious involvements. *Journal of Marriage and the Family* 41:51–57.

Macklin, Eleanor (1974). Cohabitation in college: going very steady. *Psychology Today* 7:53–59.

——— (1978). Nonmarital heterosexual cohabitation. *Marriage and Family Review* 1:1–12.

Main, Jeremy (1975). Bringing your budget back to earth. In Denis Raihall (ed.), *Money Management for the Consumer.* Boston: Little, Brown.

Malinowski, Bronislaw (1929). *The Sexual Life of the Savages in Northwest Melanesia.* New York: Eugenics Publishing.

Mancini, Jay A. (1978). Leisure satisfaction and psychological well-being in old age: effects of health and income. *Journal of the American Geriatrics Society* 26:550–552.

——— (1979). Family relationships and morale among people 65 years of age and older. *American Journal of Orthopsychiatry* 49:292–300.

Mancini, Jay A., and William Griffin (1979). Life satisfaction across stages of adulthood. Paper presented at the Southeastern Council on Family Relations Meeting.

Mancini, Jay A., and Dennis K. Orthner (1978). Recreational sexuality preferences among middle-class husbands and wives. *Journal of Sex Research* 14:96–106.

Manion, Jo (1977). A study of fathers and infant caretaking. *Birth and the Family Journal* 4:174–179.

Mariano, William R. (1978). State marriage regulations. *The World Almanac and Book of Facts.* New York: Newspaper Enterprise Associates, Inc.

Markowski, E. M., J. W. Croake, and J. F. Keller (1978). Sexual history and present sexual behavior of cohabiting and married couples. *Journal of Sex Research* 14:27–39.

Maslow, Abraham (1943). A theory of human motivation. *Psychological Review* 50:370–396.

Masters, William, and Virginia Johnson (1966). *Human Sexual Response.* Boston: Little, Brown.

——— (1970). *Human Sexual Inadequacy.* Boston: Little, Brown.

——— (1975). *The Pleasure Bond.* Boston: Little, Brown.

——— (1979). *Homosexuality in Perspective.* Boston: Little, Brown.

Mathes, Eugene W. (1975). Effects of physical attractiveness and anxiety on heterosexual attraction over a series of five encounters. *Journal of Marriage and the Family* 37:769–773.

Mazor, Miriam D. (1979). Barren couples. *Psychology Today* 13 (May):101–112.

Mead, Margaret (1966). Marriage in two steps. *Redbook* 127 (July):48–49.

Mead, Margaret (1968). A continuing dialogue on marriage. *Redbook* 130 (April):44.

——— (1972). *Blackberry Winter.* New York: William Morrow.

——— (1974). On being a grandmother. In M. H. Huyck (ed.), *Growing Older.* Englewood Cliffs, N.J.: Prentice-Hall.

Mendes, Helen (1976). Single fathers. *The Family Coordinator* 25:439–444.

Meyer, Harold, and Charles Brightbill (1964). *Community Recreation.* Englewood Cliffs, N.J.: Prentice-Hall.

Miller, Arthur A. (1971). Reactions of friends to divorce. Chapter 3 in Paul Bohannan (ed.), *Divorce and After.* New York: Doubleday.

Miller, Daniel R., and Guy Swanson (1958). *The Changing American Parent.* New York: Wiley.

Miller, Michael V. (1977). Intimate terrorism. *Psychology Today* 11:79–82.

Miller, Roger (1981). *Economic Issues for Consumers.* 3d ed. St. Paul, Minn.: West.

Miller, Sherod, Elam Nunnally, and Daniel Wackman (1975). *Alive and Aware: Improving Communication in Relationships.* Minneapolis, Minn.: Interpersonal Communication Programs.

Mitchelson, Marvin (1977). Quoted in "Non-nuptial contracts are legal." *Greensboro Daily News* (December 25):10.

Monahan, Thomas P. (1971). The extent of interdenominational marriage in the United States. *Journal for the Scientific Study of Religion* 10:85–92.

Money, John, and Anke Ehrhart (1972). *Man and Woman, Boy and Girl.* Baltimore: Johns Hopkins University Press.

Morgan, Marabel (1973). *The Total Woman.* Old Tappan, N.J.: Revell.

Mueller, Charles, and Hallowell Pope (1977). Marital instability: a study of its transmissions between generations. *Journal of Marriage and the Family* 39:83–92.

Munro, Brenda, and Gerald Adams (1978). Love American style: A test of role structure theory on changes in attitudes toward love. *Human Relations* 31:215–228.

Murdock, George P. (1949). *Social Structure.* New York: Macmillan.

Murray, Linda (1977). Sexual boredom. *Family Health/Today's Health* (June):13–17.

Murray, Thomas (1976). *A Child to Change Your Life.* Hudson, Ohio: Alan Bailey Press.

Murstein, Bernard (1970). Stimulus-value-role: a theory of mate choice. *Journal of Marriage and the Family* 29:689–696.

——— (1978). *Exploring Intimate Life Styles.* New York: Springer.

Murstein, Bernard, M. Cerreto, and M. G. McDonald (1977). A theory and investigation of the effect of exchange orientation on marriage and friendship. *Journal of Marriage and the Family* 39:543–548.

Myricks, Noel (1980). Palimony: The impact of *Marvin* vs. *Marvin. Family Relations* 29:210–215.

Nagel, Stuart, and Lenore Weitzman (1971). Women as litigants. *Hastings Law Journal* 23:189–191.

National Organization for Women (1972). *Dick and Jane as Victims: Sex Stereotyping in Images.*

Natural Center for Health Statistics (1978). *Vital Statistics in the United States.* Public Health Service.

Navron, Leslie (1969). Communication and adjustment in marriage. *Family Process* 6:173–184.

Neely, Rebecca, and Dennis K. Orthner (1978). The institutionalization of marital roles: a reexamination and racial comparison. Paper presented at the Southern Sociological Society Meeting, New Orleans.

Neugarten, Bernice L. (1968). *Middle Age and Aging.* Chicago: University of Chicago Press.

——— (1975). The future and the young-old. *Gerontologist* 15:4–9.

Neugarten, Bernice, and Carol Weinstein (1964). The changing American grandparent. *Journal of Marriage and the Family* 26:199–204.

Neulinger, John (1974). *The Psychology of Leisure.* Springfield, Ill.: Charles Thomas.

Newcomb, Paul R. (1979). Cohabitation in America: an assessment of consequences. *Journal of Marriage and the Family* 41:597–604.

Nias, David K. B. (1977). Husband-wife similarities. *Social Science* 52:206–211.

Nye, F. Ivan (1957). Child adjustment in broken and unhappy homes. *Marriage and Family Living* 19:356–361.

——— (1976). *Role Structure and Analysis of the Family.* Beverly Hills: Sage.

Nye, F. Ivan, John Carlson, and Gerald Garrett (1970). Family size, interaction, affect and stress. *Journal of Marriage and the Family* 32:216–226.

Odita, Florence C., and Mary Ann Janssens (1977). Family stability in the context of economic deprivation. *The Family Coordinator* 26:252–258.

Ogburn, William F. (1934). The family and its functions. *Recent Social Trends, Report to the President's Research Committee on Social Trends.* New York: McGraw-Hill.

——— (1938). The changing family. *The Family* 19:139–143.

Olson, David (1980). Using a premarital inventory to strengthen marriage. *Marriage and Divorce Today* 5 (May 25):2.

O'Neill, Nena, and George O'Neill (1972). *Open Marriage.* New York: Avon.

——— (1974). *Shifting Gears.* New York: Avon.

Orden, Susan, and Norman Bradburn (1969). Working wives and marriage happiness. *American Journal of Sociology* 74:352–407.

Orthner, Dennis K. (1975a). Leisure activity patterns and marital satisfaction over the marital career. *Journal of Marriage and the Family* 37:91–102.

——— (1975b). Familia ludens: reinforcing the leisure component in family life. *The Family Coordinator* 24:175–183.

——— (1976). Patterns of leisure and marital interaction. *Journal of Leisure Research* 8:98–111.

Orthner, Dennis K., and Leland Axelson (1980). Effects of wife employment on marital sociability. *Journal of Comparative Family Studies,* 11.

Orthner, Dennis K., Terry Brown, and Dennis Ferguson (1976). Single parent fatherhood: an emerging family life style. *Family Coordinator* 25:429–437.

Orthner, Dennis K., and Ken Lewis (1979). Evidence of single father competence in childrearing. *Family Law Quarterly* 13:27–49.

Orthner, Dennis K., and Jay A. Mancini (1980). Leisure behavior and group dynamics: the case of the family. In S. Iso-Aloha (ed.), *Social Psychological Perspectives of Leisure and Recreation.* Springfield, Ill.: Charles Thomas.

Osborne, Candice, and Robert Pollack (1977). The effects of two types of erotic literature on physiological and verbal measures of female sexual arousal. *Journal of Sex Research* 13:250–256.

Palmore, Erdman (1970). *Normal Aging.* Durham, N.C.: Duke University Press.

Palson, Charles, and Rebecca Palson (1972). Swinging in wedlock. *Society* 9:43–48.

Parlee, Mary Brown (1979). Conversational politics. *Psychology Today* (May):48–54.

Parsons, Jacquelynne, and Diane Ruble (1978). Is anatomy destiny? Biology and sex differences. In Irene Frieze *et al.* (eds.), *Women and Sex Roles.* New York: Norton.

Parsons, Talcott, and Robert F. Bales (1955). *Family, Socialization and Interaction Process.* Glencoe, Ill.: Free Press of Glencoe.

Patterson, K., R. Helmreich, and J. Stapp (1975). Likeability, sex-role congruence of interest, and competence. *Journal of Applied Psychology* 2:95–109.

Pearlin, Leonard, and Joyce Johnson (1977). Marital status, life-strains and depression. *American Sociological Review* 42:704–715.

Peck, Ellen (1971). *The Baby Trap.* New York: Bernard Gris.

Pengalley, Erik T. (1978). *Sex and Human Life,* 2d ed. Reading, Mass.: Addison-Wesley.

Perlman, Daniel (1974). Self-esteem and sexual permissiveness. *Journal of Marriage and the Family* 36:470–474.

Perucci, Carolyn, and Dena Targ (1978). Early work orientation and later situational factors as elements of work commitment among married women college graduates. *Sociological Quarterly* 19:266–280.

Peterman, Dan J., Carl A. Ridley, and Scott Anderson (1974). A comparison of cohabiting and non-cohabiting college students. *Journal of Marriage and the Family* 36:344–354.

Peters, John F. (1978). Factors associated with divorce. In J. Ross Eshleman and Juanne Clarke (eds.), *Intimacy, Commitments, and Marriage.* Boston: Allyn and Bacon.

Peterson, James A., and Michael Briley (1977). *Widows and Widowhood.* New York: Association Press.

Peterson, James A., and Barbara Payne (1975). *Love in the Later Years.* New York: Association Press.

Petranek, Charles F. (1975). Postparental period: an opportunity for redefinition. Paper presented at the National Council on Family Relations Meeting.

Petroni, Frank A. (1973). Teenage interracial dating. In Helena Z. Lopata (ed.), *Marriages and Families.* New York: Van Nostrand.

Phillips, Celeste, and Joseph Angalone (1978). *Fathering: Participation in Labor and Birth.* St. Louis: Mosby.

Pincus, Lilly (1974). *Death and the Family.* New York: Pantheon.

Pitsiou, Helen N. (1977). Multilateral relationships: Early family experiences and present involvement in unconventional family forms. Paper presented at the meeting of the National Council on Family Relations, San Diego, California.

Plateris, A. A. (1973). Divorces: analysis and changes, U.S., 1969. *Vital and Health Statistics,* Publication (HSM) 73-1900.

Pleck, Joseph (1976). My male sex-role—and ours. In Deborah David and Robert Brannon, *The Forty-Nine Percent Majority: The Male Sex Role.* Reading, Mass.: Addison-Wesley.

Polatnick, Margaret (1974). Why men don't rear children: a power analysis. *Berkeley Journal of Sociology* 18:45–86.

Polit, Denise, Ronald Nuttall, and Ena V. Nuttall (1980). The only child grows up. *Family Relations* 29:99–106.

Poloma, Margaret, and Neal T. Garland (1971). The married professional woman: a study in the tolerance of domestication. *Journal of Marriage and the Family* 33:531–540.

Portner, Joyce (1978). *Inpacts of Work on the Family.* Minneapolis: Minnesota Council on Family Relations.

Portnoff, J. C., *et al.* (1972). The intrauterine contraceptive device. *American Journal of Obstetrics and Gynecology* 114:934–937.

Powers, Edward, and Gordon L. Bultena (1976). Sex differences in intimate friendships in old age. *Journal of Marriage and the Family* 38:739–748.

Powers, William G., and Kevin Hutchinson (1979). The measurement of communication apprehension in the marriage relationship. *Journal of Marriage and the Family* 41:89–95.

Prather, Hugh (1977). Quoted in John Stewart, *Bridges, Not Walls.* Reading, Mass.: Addison-Wesley.

Pratt, Lois (1976). *Family Structure and Effective Health Behavior: The Energized Family.* Boston: Houghton Mifflin.

Presser, Harriet B. (1974). Early motherhood: Ignorance or bliss? *Family Planning Perspectives* 6:8–15.

Pringle, Bruce M. (1974). Family clusters as a means of reducing isolation among urbanites. *The Family Coordinator* 23:175–180.

Puner, Morton (1974). *To the Good Long Life.* New York: Universe.

Queen, Stuart A., and Robert W. Habenstein (1974). *The Family in Various Cultures,* 4th ed. Philadelphia: Lippincott.

Rallings, E. M. (1976). The special role of stepfather. *The Family Coordinator* 25:445–450.

Ramey, James W. (1972). Emerging patterns of innovative behavior in marriage. *Family Coordinator* 21:435–456.

——— (1975). Intimate groups and networks: frequent consequences of sexually open marriage. *The Family Coordinator* 24:515–530.

——— (1976). *Intimate Friendships.* Englewood Cliffs, N.J.: Prentice-Hall.

——— (1978). Lifestyles of the future. In Bernard Murstein (ed.), *Exploring Intimate Life Styles.* New York: Springer.

Rapoport, Rhona, and Robert Rapoport (1976). *Dual-Career Families Re-Examined.* New York: Harper & Row.

Raschke, Helen (1976). Sex differences in voluntary post marital dissolution adjustment. Paper presented at the Meeting of the American Sociological Association.

Raschke, Helen, and Vernon Raschke (1979). Family conflict and children's self-concepts: a comparison of intact and single-parent families. *Journal of Marriage and the Family* 41:367–374.

Raven, Bertram, Richard Centers, and Aroldo Rodrigues (1975). Bases of conjugal power. In R. Cromwell and D. Olson (eds.), *Power in Families.* New York: Wiley.

Reinstein, Max (1972). *Marriage Stability, Divorce, and the Law.* Chicago: University of Chicago Press.

Reiss, Ira (1965). The universality of the family: a conceptual analysis. *Journal of Marriage and the Family* 27:443–453.

——— (1973). *Heterosexual Relationships: Inside and Outside of Marriage.* Morristown, N.J.: General Learning Press.

——— (1976). *Family Systems in America,* 2d ed. Hinsdale, Ill.: Dryden.

Renne, Karen (1970). Correlates of dissatisfaction in marriage. *Journal of Marriage and the Family* 32:54–67.

Rheingold, H. L., and K. V. Cook (1975). The content of boys' and girls' rooms on an index of parents' behavior. *Child Development* 46:459–463.

Rice, Berkeley (1975). Midlife encounters: the Menninger seminars for businessmen. *Psychology Today* 12:66–74, 95.

Roache, Joel (1972). Confessions of a househusband. *Ms.* 1:25–27.

Roberts, Elizabeth (1979). *Family Life and Sexual Learning.* Cambridge, Mass.: Project on Human Sexual Development.

Robertson, Joan F. (1977). Grandmotherhood: a study of role conceptions. *Journal of Marriage and the Family* 39:165–174.

Robinson, John (1977). *How Americans Use Time.* New York: Praeger.

——— (1978). Women still shoulder home jobs. Associated Press Release in *Greensboro Daily News.*

Robinson, John, Janet Yerby, Margaret Fieweger, and Nancy Somerick (1977). Sex role differences in time use. *Sex Roles* 3:443–458.

Rollins, Boyd, and Kenneth L. Cannon (1974). Marital satisfaction over the family life cycle: a reevaluation. *Journal of Marriage and the Family* 36:271–282.

Rollins, Boyd, and Harold Feldman (1970). Marital satisfaction over the family life cycle. *Journal of Marriage and the Family* 32:20–27.

Rones, Phillip L. (1978). Older men: the choice between work and retirement. *Monthly Labor Review* (December):3–10.

Rooney, Rita (1979). When adoption doesn't work. *Parade Magazine* (March 4):23–25.

Roper Organization (1974). *The Virginia Slims American Women's Opinion Poll.* New York: The Roper Organization.

Rosen, Benson, Thomas Jerdee, and Thomas Prestwich (1975). Dual-career marital adjustment: potential effects of discriminatory managerial attitudes. *Journal of Marriage and the Family* 37:565–572.

Rosenberg, R. G., and Brian Sutton-Smith (1972). *Sex and Identity.* New York: Holt, Rinehart and Winston.

Rosenblatt, Paul (1974). Cross-cultural perspective on attractions. In Ted Huston (ed.), *Foundations of Interpersonal Attraction.* New York: Academic Press.

Rosenblatt, Paul, and Michael Cunningham (1976). Television watching and family tension. *Journal of Marriage and the Family* 38:103–111.

Rosenblatt, Paul, and Martha Russell (1975). The social psychology of potential problems in family vacation travel. *The Family Coordinator* 24:209–216.

Rosenblatt, Paul, Sandra Titus, and Michael Cunningham (1979). Disrespect, tension, and togetherness-apartness in marriage. *Journal of Marital and Family Therapy* 5:47–54.

Rosenfeld, Carl (1979). Multiple jobholding. *Monthly Labor Review* (February):59–61.

Rossi, Alice (1968). Transition to parenthood. *Journal of Marriage and the Family* 30:26–39.

——— (1978). The biosocial side of parenthood. *Human Nature* 1 (August):72–79.

Roth, Allan (1977). The tender years presumption in child custody disputes. *Journal of Family Law* 15:423–462.

Rubin, Lillian B. (1976). *Worlds of Pain.* New York: Harper & Row.

Rubin, Zick (1970). Measurement of romantic love. *Journal of Personality and Social Psychology* 16:265–273.

——— (1973). *Liking and Loving: An Invitation to Social Psychology.* New York: Holt, Rinehart and Winston.

Rue, Vince (1974). Television and the family: the question of control. *The Family Coordinator* 23:73–81.

Russell, Bertrand (1929). *Marriage and Morals.* New York: Liveright.

Russell, Candyce (1974). Transition to parenthood: problems and gratifications. *Journal of Marriage and the Family* 36:294–302.

——— (1975). The transition to parenthood and beyond. Paper given at the Meeting of the National Council on Family Relations.

Ryder, Robert G., John Kalka, and David Olson (1971). Separating and joining differences in early marriage. *American Journal of Orthopsychiatry* 41:450–464.

Safilios-Rothschild, Constantina (1977). *Love, Sex, and Sex Roles.* Englewood Cliffs, N.J.: Prentice-Hall.

Sarvis, Betty, and Hyman Rodman (1974). *The Abortion Controversy,* 2d ed. New York: Columbia University Press.

Satir, Virginia (1970). Marriage as a human-actualizing contract. In Herbert Otto (ed.), *The Family in Search of a Future.* New York: Appleton-Century-Crofts.

——— (1972). *Peoplemaking.* Palo Alto, Calif.: Science and Behavior Books.

Sawin, Margaret M. (1977). Theoretical foundations of the family cluster model. (Mimeograph.) Rochester: Family Clusters, Inc.

Saxton, Lloyd (1977). *The Individual, Marriage and the Family,* 3d ed. Belmont, Calif.: Wadsworth.

Scales, Peter, and Sol Gordon (1979). *The Sexual Adolescent.* North Scituate, Mass.: Duxbury.

Scanzoni, John (1965). A reinquiry into marital disorganization. *Journal of Marriage and the Family* 27:483–491.

——— (1972). *Sexual Bargaining.* Englewood Cliffs, N.J.: Prentice-Hall.

——— (1975). *Sex Roles, Life Styles, and Childbearing.* New York: Free Press.

——— (1978). *Sex Roles, Women's Work, and Marital Conflict.* Lexington, Mass.: D. C. Heath.

——— (1979). Social exchange and behavioral interdependence. In Robert Burgess and Ted Huston (eds.), *Social Exchange in Developing Relationships.* New York: Academic Press.

——— (1979). Social processes and power in families. In W. Burr, R. Hill, F. I. Nye, and I. Reiss (ed.), *Contemporary Theories about Families.* New York: Free Press.

Schachter, Stanley (1959). *The Psychology of Affiliation.* Stanford, Calif.: Stanford University Press.

Schauble, Paul G., and Clara Hill (1976). A laboratory approach to treatment in marriage counseling: Training in communication skills. *The Family Coordinator* 25 (July):277–284.

Scheff, Ted (1967). Toward a sociological model of consensus. *American Sociological Review* 32:32–46.

Schlesinger, Benjamin (1977). Husband-wife relationships in reconstituted families. *Social Science* 52:152–157.

Schlossberg, N. K. (1977). Breaking out of the box: organized options for adults. *The Vocational Guidance Quarterly* 25:313–319.

Schoen, Robert (1975). California divorce rates by age at first marriage and duration of first marriage. *Journal of Marriage and the Family* 37:548–555.

Schram, Rosalyn W. (1979). Marital satisfaction over the family life cycle: a critique and proposal. *Journal of Marriage and the Family* 41:7–14.

Schulman, Marion L. (1974). Idealization in engaged couples. *Journal of Marriage and the Family* 36:139–147.

Scoresby, A. Lynn (1977). *The Marriage Dialogue.* Reading, Mass.: Addison-Wesley.

Scott, James R., and Nancy Rose (1976). Effects of psychoprophylexis (lamaze preparation) in labor and delivery in primaparas. *New England Journal of Medicine* 294:1205–1207.

Seelbach, Wayne C. (1978). Correlates of aged parents' filial responsibility, expectations and realizations. *The Family Coordinator* 27:341–349.

Seelinger, Wes (1977). Bug spray #5. In Edward Powers and Mary W. Lee (eds.), *Encounter with Family Realities.* St. Paul, Minn.: West.

Seidenburg, Robert (1973). *Corporate Wives—Corporate Casualties.* New York: Doubleday.

Seligson, Marcia (1974). *The Eternal Bliss Machine: America's Way of Wedding.* New York: Bantam.

Seward, Rudy Ray (1978). *The American Family: A Demographic History.* Beverly Hills, Calif.: Sage.

Shanas, Ethel (1979). Social myth or hypothesis: the case of the family relations of older people. *The Gerontologist* 19:3–9.

——— (1980). Older people and their families: The new pioneers. *Journal of Marriage and the Family* 42:9–15.

Shanor, Karen (1978). *The Shanor Study: Sexual Sensitivity of the American Male.* New York: Dial.

Shaver, Phillip, and Jonathan Freedman (1976). Your pursuit of happiness. *Psychology Today* (August).

Sheehy, Gail (1976). *Passages.* New York: Bantam.

Sheresky, Norman, and Marya Mannes (1972). A radical guide to wedlock. *Saturday Review/World* (July 29).

Shettles, Landrum (1972). Predetermining children's sex. *Medical Aspects of Human Sexuality* (June):172.

Shorter, Edward (1977). *The Making of the Modern Family.* New York: Basic Books.

Shulman, Alix (1971). A marriage agreement. *Redbook* (August).

Shuttlesworth, Gary, and George Thorman (1973). Living together unmarried relationships. University of Texas, Austin, Texas. Unpublished paper.

Siegal, Earl, and Naomi M. Morris (1974). Family planning: its health rationale. *American Journal of Obstetrics and Gynecology* 118:995–1004.

Siegal, Jacob S. (1978). Testimony before the House Select Committees on Aging and Population. *Behavior Today* (June 26).

Silka, Linda, and Sara Kiesler (1977). Couples who choose to remain childless. *Family Planning Perspectives* 9:16–24.

Simmel, Georg (1902). The number of members as determining the sociological form of the group. *The American Journal of Sociology* 8:1–46.

——— (1950). *The Sociology of Georg Simmel.* Translated by Kurt H. Wolff. Glencoe, Ill.: Free Press.

Simpson, Joe L. (1979). Sex preselection. *New England Journal of Medicine* 300:1483–1484.

Singh, B. K. (1980). Trends in attitudes toward marital sex relations. *Journal of Marriage and the Family* 42:387–394.

Skolnick, Arlene (1978). The myth of the vulnerable child. *Psychology Today* 12 (February):56–60.

Smith, Daniel Scott (1973). Parental power and marriage patterns: an analysis of historical trends in Hingham, Massachusetts. *Journal of Marriage and the Family* 35:419–428.

Smith, Daniel Scott, and Michael Hindus (1975). Premarital pregnancy in America, 1640–1971. *Journal of Interdisciplinary History* 4:537–570.

Smith, James R., and Lynn Smith (1975). *Consenting Adults.* Baltimore: Johns Hopkins University Press.

Smith, K. D., R. K. Tcholakian, M. Chowdhurn, and E. Steinberger (1976). An investigation of plasma hormone levels before and after vasectomy. *Fertility and Sterility* 27:145–150.

Smith, Michael J. (1980). The social consequences of single parenthood. *Family Relations* 29:75–82.

Sorokin, Pitirim (1937). *Social and Cultural Dynamics.* New York: Harper & Row.

Spanier, Graham (1972). Romanticism and marital adjustment. *Journal of Marriage and the Family* 34:481–487.

——— (1977). Sources of sex information and premarital sexual behavior. *Journal of Sex Research* 13:73–88.

Spicer, Jerry W., and Gary Hempe (1975). Kinship interaction after divorce. *Journal of Marriage and the Family* 37:113–120.

Sprague, W. D. (1972). *Case Histories from the Communes.* New York: Lancer.

Spreitzer, E., and L. E. Riley (1974). Factors associated with singlehood. *Journal of Marriage and the Family* 36:533–542.

Sprenkle, Douglas, and David Olson (1978). Circumplex model of family systems: an empirical study of clinic and non-clinic couples. *Journal of Marriage and Family Counseling* (April):59–74.

Sroufe, L. Alan (1978). Attachment and the roots of competence. *Human Nature* 1 (October):50–57.

Steel, B. F., and D. Pollack (1968). A psychiatric study of parents who abuse infants and small children. In R. E. Helfer and C. H. Kempe (eds.), *The Battered Child.* Chicago: University of Chicago Press.

Stein, Peter (1976). *Single.* Englewood Cliffs, N.J.: Prentice-Hall.

——— (1978). The lifestyles and life chances of the never-married. *Marriage and Family Review* 1 (July):1–11.

Steinmetz, Suzanne (1977). *The Cycle of Violence.* New York: Praeger.

——— (1978). Violence between family members. *Marriage and Family Review* 1 (May):1–16.

Stephens, William (1963). *Cultural Perspective.* New York: Holt, Rinehart and Winston.

Stinnett, Nick, and Craig W. Birdsong (1978). *The Family and Alternative Life Styles.* Chicago: Nelson-Hall.

Stockard, Jean, and Miriam Johnson (1980). *Sex Roles: Sex Inequality and Sex Role Development.* Englewood Cliffs, N.J.: Prentice-Hall.

Stoll, Clarice (1974). *Female and Male.* Dubuque, Iowa: William C. Brown.

Stone, Gregory (1965). The play of little children. *Quest* 4:23–31.

Straus, Murray (1974). Leveling, civility and violence in the family. *Journal of Marriage and the Family* 36:13–19.

Straus, Murray, Richard Gelles, and Suzanne Steinmetz (1980). *Behind Closed Doors.* New York: Doubleday.

Streib, Gordon (1978). An alternative family form for older persons. *The Family Coordinator* 27:413–420.

Streib, Gordon, and Clement Schneider (1971). *Retirement in American Society.* Ithaca, N.Y.: Cornell University Press.

Strong, Bryan, S. Wilson, L. M. Clarke, and T. Johns (1978). *Human Sexuality: Essentials.* St. Paul, Minn.: Mosby.

Strong, Leslie (1978). Alternative marital and family forms: their related attractiveness to college students. *Journal of Marriage and the Family* 40:493–504.

Sullivan, Harry Stack (1953). *Conceptions of Modern Psychiatry,* 2d ed. New York: Norton.

——— (1953). *The Interpersonal Theory of Psychiatry.* New York: Norton.

Sussman, Marvin (1975). Marriage contracts: social and legal consequences. Paper presented at the International Workshop on Changing Sex Roles in Family and Society.

Szalai, Alexander (1972). *The Use of Time.* Paris, Mouton.

Tavris, Carol (1976). The Cory complex. *Psychology Today* (August).

——— (1977). Men and women report their views on masculinity. *Psychology Today* 10 (January):35.

Tavris, Carol, and Susan Sadd (1977). *The Redbook Report on Female Sexuality.* New York: Delacourte.

Thibaut, John W., and Harold H. Kelley (1959). *The Social Psychology of Groups.* New York: Wiley.

Thomas, Edwin J. (1977). *Marital Conmunication and Decision Making.* New York: Free Press.

Thurber, James, and E. B. White (1929). *Is Sex Necessary?* New York: Harper & Row.

Tietze, Christopher, and Sarah Lowit (1979). Life risks associated with reversible methods of fertility regulation. *International Journal of Gynecology and Obstetrics* 16:456–459.

Toffler, Alvin (1970). *Future Shock.* New York: Random House.

Touhey, John C. (1979). Sex role stereotyping and individual differences in liking for the physically attractive. *Social Psychology Quarterly* 42:285–289.

Touliatos, John, and Byron W. Lindholm (1976). Recent trends in adoptions. Paper presented at the National Council on Family Relations Meeting, New York City.

Troll, Lillian E. (1971). The family of later life: a decade review. *Journal of Marriage and the Family* 33:263–290.

——— (1975). *Early and Middle Adulthood.* Monterey, Calif.: Brooks-Cole.

Troll, Lillian, Stephen Miller, and Robert Atchley (1979). *Families in Later Life.* Belmont, Calif.: Wadsworth.

Turner, Ralph (1970). *Family Interaction.* New York: Wiley.

Udry, J. Richard (1974). *The Social Context of Marriage.* Philadelphia: Lippincott.

U. S. Bureau of the Census (1972). *Census of Population, 1970, PC(2)-4C.* Washington, D.C.: U.S. Government Printing Office.

U. S. Bureau of the Census (1976). Fertility history and prospects of American women: June, 1975. *Current Population Reports, Series P-20, No. 288.* Washington, D.C.: U. S. Government Printing Office.

U. S. Bureau of the Census (1979). Perspectives on American husbands and wives. *Current Population Reports, Series P-23, No. 77.* Washington, D.C.: U.S. Government Printing Office.

U.S. Bureau of the Census (1980). *Current Population Reports, Series P-20,* Marital status and living arrangements: March, 1979. Washington, D.C.: U. S. Government Printing Office.

U.S. Bureau of the Census (1980). A statistical portrait of women in the United States. *Current Population Reports, Series P-23, No. 100.* Washington, D.C.: U.S. Government Printing Office.

U.S. Bureau of Labor Statistics. News release, March 8, 1977.

U. S. Bureau of Labor Statistics (1980). Family budgets. *Monthly Labor Review* (July).

U. S. Department of Health, Education and Welfare (1979). *Monthly Vital Statistics Reports, (PHS) 79-1120.*

U. S. Department of Labor (1980). Marital and family characteristics of the labor force. U. S. Department of Labor: Bureau of Labor Statistics.

Van Deusen, Edmond L. (1975). *Contract Cohabitation: An Alternative to Marriage.* New York: Avon.

Vanek, Joan (1974). Time spent in housework. *Scientific American* (November).

Varga, Karolyn (1972). Marital cohesion as reflected in time budgets. In Alexander Szalai (ed.), *The Use of Time.* Paris: Mouton.

Veevers, Jean (1973). The child-free alternative: rejection of the motherhood myth. In Maryles Stephenson (ed.), *Women in Canada.* Toronto: Free Press.

Veevers, Jean (1975). The moral careers of voluntarily childless wives. *Family Coordinator* 24:473–487.

Ventura, Stephanie J. (1977). Teenage childbearing: United States, 1966–1975. *Monthly Vital Statistics Report 26* (September 8).

Veroff, Joseph (1979). News roundup—Institute of Social Research Newsletter. *Behavior Today* (February 12):7–8.

Veroff, Joseph, and Shiela Feld (1970). *Marriage and Work in America.* New York: Van Nostrand Reinhold.

Vincent, Clark (1966). Familia spongia: the adaptive function. *Journal of Marriage and the Family* 28:29–36.

——— (1972). An open letter to the "caught generation." *The Family Coordinator* 21:143–150.

Vinick, Barbara H. (1978). Remarriage in old age. *The Family Coordinator* 27:359–364.

Voydanoff, Patricia, and Hyman Rodman (1978). Marital careers in Trinidad. *Journal of Marriage and the Family* 40 (February):157–164.

Waite, Linda J. (1977). Social and economic determinants of employment of wives over the family life cycle. Paper presented at the American Sociological Association Meeting.

Waite, L. J., and K. A. Moore (1978). Early childbearing and educational attainment. *Family Planning Perspectives* 9:220–225.

Waldrop, M. F., and R. Q. Bell (1964). Relation of preschool dependency behavior to family size and density. *Child Development* 35:1187–1195.

Walker, Kathryn, and Margaret Woods (1975). *Time Use as a Measure of Household Production of Family Goods and Services.* The Center for the Family, American Home Economics Association.

Wallerstein, Judith, and Joan Kelly (1980). *Surviving the Break-Up: How Children Actually Cope With Divorce.* New York: Basic Books.

Walster, Elaine, Vera Aronson, Darcy Abrahams, and Leon Rottman (1966). Importance of physical attractiveness in dating behavior. *Journal of Personality and Social Psychology* 4:508–516.

Walster, Elaine, J. Traupman, and G. W. Walster (1978). Equity and extramarital sexuality. *Archives of Sexual Behavior* 7:127–142.

Walster, Elaine, and G. William Walster (1978). *A New Look at Love.* Reading, Mass.: Addison-Wesley.

Walters, James (ed.) (1976). Fatherhood. Special Issue of *The Family Coordinator* (October).

Walters, James, Patrick McHenry, and Lynda Henly Walters (1979). Adolescents' knowledge of childbearing. *The Family Coordinator* 28:163–172.

Walum, Laurel R. (1977). *The Dynamics of Sex and Gender.* Chicago: Rand McNally.

Walzer, Stuart (1977). Quoted in "Non-nuptial contracts are legal." *Greensboro Daily News* (December 25):10.

Ward, Russell A. (1978). Limitations of the family as a supportive institution in the lives of the aged. *The Family Coordinator* 27:365–374.

Wasserman, Harry, Gerald Bubis, and Alan Lert (1979). The concept of Havarah. *Journal of Reform Judaism* 26:35–49.

Watson, Geoffrey (1974). Family organization and little league baseball. Paper presented at the meeting of the Pacific Sociological Association.

Watzlawick, P., J. Beavin, and D. Jackson (1967). *Pragmatics of Human Communication.* New York: Norton.

Weis, Charles B., and Robert N. Dain (1979). Ego development and sex attitudes in heterosexual and homosexual men and women. *Archives of Sexual Behavior* 8:341–356.

Weisberg, D. Kelly (1975). Alternative family structures and the law. *The Family Coordinator* 24:549–559.

——— (1977). The Cinderella children. *Psychology Today* (April):84–86, 103.

Weisman, Avery D. (1972). *On Dying and Denying.* New York: Behavioral Publications.

Weiss, Robert (1975). *Marital Separation.* New York: Basic Books.

Weitz, Shirley (1977). *Sex Roles.* New York: Oxford University Press.

Weitzman, Lenore (1974). Legal regulation of marriage: tradition and change. *California Law Review* 62:1169–1288.

——— (1975). To love, honor, and obey? Traditional legal marriage and alternative family forms. *The Family Coordinator* 24:531–547.

Weller, Robert H., and Frank Hobbs (1978). Unwanted and mistimed births in the United States. *Family Planning Perspectives* 8:168–172.

Wells, J. Gibson (1976). A critical look at personal marriage contracts. *The Family Coordinator* 25:33–37.

Wendy and Burt (1978). Our open marriage. In Bernard Murstein (ed.), *Exploring Intimate Life Styles.* New York: Springer.

West, D. J. (1977). *Homosexuality Re-Examined.* Minneapolis: University of Minnesota Press.

Westman, Jack, and David Cline (1973). Divorce is a family affair. In Marcia Lasswell and Thomas Lasswell (eds.), *Love, Marriage, Family: A Developmental Approach.* Glenview, Ill.: Scott, Foresman.

Westoff, Charles, and J. McCarthy (1979). Sterilization in the United States. *Family Planning Perspectives* 11:145–149.

Westoff, Charles, Robert Potter, Philip Sagi, and Elliot Mishler (1961). Family Growth in Metropolitan America. Princeton, N.J.: Princeton University Press.

Westoff, Leslie A. (1979). Women in search of equality. *ETS Focus,* #6.

Wheeler, Michael (1974). *No-Fault Divorce.* Boston: Beacon.

Whelen, Elizabeth (1977). To have or not to have a baby. *Greensboro Daily News* (July 31):1.

Williamson, N. E. (1978). Boys or girls: parents' preferences and sex control. *Population Bulletin* 33:1–35.

Wilmot, William W. (1975). *Dyadic Communication: A Transactional Perspective.* Reading, Mass.: Addison-Wesley.

Wilson, K., L. A. Zurcher, D. C. McAdams, and R. L. Curtis (1975). Stepfathers and stepchildren: An exploratory analysis from two national surveys. *Journal of Marriage and the Family* 37:526–535.

Wilson, Sam, Bryan Strong, Leah Clarke, and Thomas Johns (1978). *Human Sexuality.* St. Paul: West.

Winch, Robert F. (1958). *Mate Selection: A Study of Complementary Needs.* New York: Harper and Brothers.

——— (1963). *The Modern Family,* rev. ed. New York: Holt, Rinehart and Winston.

Wiseman, Riva (1975). Crisis theory and the process of divorce. *Social Casework* 56:205–212.

Wolfenstein, Martha (1957). The emergence of fun morality. In Eric Larrabee and Rolf Meyersohn (eds.), *Mass Leisure.* New York: Free Press.

Wood, Vivian, and Joan F. Robertson (1978). Friendship and kinship interaction: differential effect on the morale of the elderly. *Journal of Marriage and the Family* 40:367–376.

Yankelovich, Daniel (1978). The new psychological contracts at work. *Psychology Today* 11 (May):46–50.

Yankelovich, Skelly, and White, Inc. (1975). *The General Mills American Family Report, 1974–75.* Minneapolis, Minn.: General Mills.

Zabin, Laurie S., John F. Kantner, and Melvin Zelnik (1979). The risk of adolescent pregnancy in the first six months of intercourse. *Family Planning Perspectives* 11:215–222.

Zablocki, Benjamin, and Rosabeth Moss Kanter (1976). The differentiation of life styles. *Annual Review of Sociology* 2:269–298.

Zelnick, Melvin, and John Kantner (1977). Sexual and contraceptive experience of young unmarried women in the United States. *Family Planning Perspectives* 9:55–65.

Zelnick, Melvin, Kim Young, and John Kantner (1979). Probabilities of intercourse and conception among U. S. teenage women, 1971 and 1976. *Family Planning Perspectives* 11:177–183.

Ziegler, Herbert (1978). Role re-negotiation during mid-life career change. Paper presented at the Southern Sociological Society Meeting.

Zilbergeld, Bernie (1978). *Male Sexuality.* Boston: Little, Brown.

Zimmerman, D. H., and C. West (1975). Sex roles, interruptions and silences in conversation. In B. Thorne and N. Henly (eds.), *Language and Sex: Differences and Dominance.* Rowley, Mass.: Newbury House.

Photo Credits

2, Charles Campbell, Taurus Photos
9, Charles Gatewood, Stock, Boston
13, Jean-Claude Lejeune, Stock, Boston
18, Cary Wolinsky, Stock, Boston
26, Florence Sharp
31, Rick Smolan
36, Struan Robertson, Magnum Photos
42, Owen Franken, Stock, Boston
46, Donald Dietz, Stock, Boston
50, Charles Gatewood, Magnum Photos
56, Jean-Claude Lejeune, Stock, Boston
62, David Burnett, Stock, Boston
66, Rick Smolan
74, Bohdan Hrynewych
80, United Press International
86, Arthur Grace, Stock, Boston
90, Cary Wolinsky, Stock, Boston
98, Shirley Zeiberg, Taurus Photos
104, Hiroji Kubota, Magnum Photos
109, Bob Adelman, Magnum Photos
114, United Press International
120, Jeff Albertson, Stock, Boston
128, Dennis Stock, Magnum Photos
134, Henri Cartier-Bresson, Magnum Photos
139, United Press International Photo
144, Sergio Larrain, Magnum Photos
150, David Austen, Stock, Boston
154, Peter Simon, Stock, Boston
159, Costa Manos, Magnum Photos
164, Florence Sharp
171, Ellis Herwig, Stock, Boston
175, Anna Kaufman Moon, Stock, Boston
180, Joan Menschenfreund, Taurus Photos
184, Abigail Heyman, Magnum Photos
191, United Press International
194, Laimute E. Druskis, Taurus Photos
199, Jerry Berndt, Stock, Boston
206, Abigail Heyman, Magnum Photos
210, Rick Smolan
215, Paul Fortin, Stock, Boston
219, United Press International
224, Ellis Herwig, Stock, Boston
229, Brown Brothers
235, Owen Franken, Stock, Boston
244, Bohdan Hrynewych
250, United Press International
258, Martin M. Rotker, Taurus Photos
263, Eric Kroll, Taurus Photos
268, Rick Smolan
273, Marc Riboud, Magnum
278, Eric Kroll, Taurus Photos
291, Fredrik D. Bodin, Stock, Boston
296, Eric Kroll, Taurus Photos
299, Mike Mazzachi, Stock, Boston
304, George W. Gardner, Stock, Boston
311, Bohdan Hrynewych
324, Erich Hartmann, Magnum Photos
331, Abigail Heyman, Magnum Photos
336, Burk Uzzle, Magnum Photos
343, Rick Smolan
350, Florence Sharp
356, Burk Uzzle, Magnum
359, Arthur Grace, Stock, Boston
363, R. D. Ullmann, Taurus Photos
370, John Running, Stock, Boston
373, United Press International
384, Wayne Miller, Magnum Photos
390, United Press International
406, Mike Habicht, Taurus Photos
412, Peter Simon, Stock, Boston
417, Peter Menzel, Stock, Boston
422, Florence Sharp
424, Burt Glinn, Magnum Photos
432, Charles Gatewood, Magnum Photos
435, Elizabeth Crews, Stock, Boston
440, Paul Seder, Taurus Photos
446, Eric Kroll, Taurus Photos

Author Index

Subject Index